A Rhetoric of the Unreal

A Rhetoric of the Unreal

Studies in narrative and structure,
especially of the fantastic

CHRISTINE BROOKE-ROSE

CAMBRIDGE UNIVERSITY PRESS

Cambridge
London   New York   New Rochelle
Melbourne   Sydney

28528

Published by the Press Syndicate of the University of Cambridge
The Pitt Building, Trumpington Street, Cambridge CB2 1RP
32 East 57th Street, New York, NY 10022, USA
296 Beaconsfield Parade, Middle Park, Melbourne 3206, Australia

First published 1981
First paperback edition 1983

Printed in Great Britain at the
University Press, Cambridge

British Library Cataloguing in Publication Data

Brooke-Rose, Christine
A rhetoric of the unreal.
1. Fantastic fiction, European – History
and criticism
2. European fiction – 20th century – History
and criticism
I. Title
809.3′9′15   PN3435   80–41720

ISBN 0 521 22561 2   hard covers
ISBN 0 521 27656 X   paperback

Contents

Acknowledgements

The following chapters are revised versions of essays originally published in various reviews.

Part of chapter 2 was originally published under the title, 'Round and round the Jakobson diagram: a survey' in *The Hebrew University Studies in Literature*, vol. 8, no. 2 (1980).

Chapter 3 was originally published under the title 'Historical genres/theoretical genres: a discussion of Todorov on the fantastic' in *New Literary History*, vol. 8, no. 1 (1976).

Chapter 5 was originally published under the title 'The readerhood of man' in *The Reader in the Text*, edited by Susan Suleiman and Inge Crosman, and is reprinted by permission of Princeton University Press, 1980.

Chapter 6 was originally published under the title 'The squirm of the true – an essay in non-methodology' in *Poetics and Theory of Literature*, vol. 1, no. 2 (1976).

Chapter 7 was originally published under the title 'The long glasses – a structural analysis' in *Poetics and Theory of Literature*, vol. 1, no. 3 (1976).

Chapter 8 was originally published under the title 'Surface structures in narrative' in *Poetics and Theory of Literature*, vol. 2, no. 3 (1977).

Chapter 9 was originally published under the title 'The evil ring: realism and the marvellous' in *Poetics Today*, vol. 1, no. 4 (1980).

Chapter 11 was originally published under the title 'Baroque imagination of Robbe-Grillet' in *Modern Fiction Studies*, vol. 11, no. 4 (1965/6).

Chapter 12 was originally published under the title 'Transgressions: an essay – say on the novel novel novel' in *Contemporary Literature*, vol. 19, no. 3 (1978).

Chapter 14 was originally published under the title 'Where do we go from here?' in *Granta 3* (1980).

PART I

The real, the unreal and the rhetoric

1

The real and the unreal

That this century is undergoing a reality crisis has become a banality, easily and pragmatically shrugged off. Perhaps it is in fact undergoing a crisis of the imagination; a fatigue, a decadence. And rhetoricians usually appear in times of decadence, that is, when stable values disappear, when forms break down and new ones appear, co-existing with all the old ones. Their task is then to try to make sense of what is happening by working out reasoned typologies of structures and trying to account for 'deviations from the norm' (the norm being what they, and people generally, have been used to). But since they have to start, humbly, with simple structures, their attempts never wholly account for the explosions of forms taking place around them, they become more and more complex, more cumbersome, themselves more 'deviating' from their own original principles, more and more self-questioning. Today the rhetoricians, of innumerable kinds, are more voluble than they have been for centuries, and since the literary work of art is itself a rhetorical system, superimposing, on the first arbitrary system of natural languages, yet another system of representation, the complications of modern rhetoric have become both fascinating and discouraging. Fascinating for itself, in a self-reflexing way that itself reflects what is happening in the work of art, but discouraging and confusing for others. The defence of the reader, the journalist and the teacher is usually to reject all this as nonsense and, in effect, to stay with or propagate whatever notions they were brought up on.

There is a similar split in attitudes to 'reality'. For professional philosophers, the commonsense division that defines the real as the physical and empirical, and the unreal as the metaphysical has ever been contested, from Plato who regarded our familiar reality as mere shadows of perfect ideas (truer, so more 'real'), to modern

3

post-Hegelians such as Derrida, for whom 'truth' is for ever post-poned (see p. 46), and modern philosophy generally, which has long come to recognise that the brute ontological fact is inaccessible to us, since man can only re-present it through his many arbitrary systems, including language and the languages of science.

The difference here is that, whereas the various rhetorics are simply dismissed or ignored by the average reader, the sense that empirical reality is not as secure as it used to be is now pervasive at all levels of society. Certainly what used to be called empirical reality, or the world, seems to have become more and more unreal, and what has long been regarded as unreal is more and more turned to or studied as the only 'true' or 'another and equally valid' reality. Witness, for example, Foucault on madness (1961), Laing on schizo-phrenia as a breakthrough (1967), and since then what Shoshanna Felman (1978) calls 'cette inflation discursive *pour* la folie' as well as psychic research on paranormal phenomena or, on a more general level, the return of religious belief, the vast rise of occultism, mystical sects, drugs, and the renewed waves of ideological and religious fanaticisms.

This apparent and for the moment still partial (and perhaps transient) inversion of real/unreal is perfectly logical: if the 'real' has come to seem unreal, it is natural to turn to the 'unreal' as real: the two propositions are interrelated. This 'naturalness' however is due to man's need to impose significance on the empirical reality around him, which in itself is without significance. But of course, the very statement that the ontological fact is itself without significance is a signifying statement, imposing a view of reality as non-significant, imposing, that is, the significance of non-significance; a contradic-tion which seems to escape Clément Rosset who, in a brief but remarkable book (*Le réel – traité de l'idiotie*, 1977), first demonstrates that all reality is both necessarily determined (in virtue of the identity principle that $A = A$) and necessarily fortuitous in the sense that it is not necessarily this or that, but cannot escape the necessity of being something (i.e. anything). This property inherent to all reality of being both fortuitous and determined he calls 'the in-significance of the real', and what makes reality tip over into non-sense is precisely the necessity we impose on it of always being significant (pp. 13–14).

The only enigma then, for Rosset, is the ontological fact, that is, the necessity of being something (anything) is valid for all reality excepting only the fact of its existence. Similarly, all significance given to the real is illusory, excepting only the fact that it is (p. 40).

But, he says, we perceive reality as either necessary or fortuitous. When an occurrence or object seems to us *both* necessary *and* non-necessary, this is an isolated perception, at once sanctioned by laughter (as in certain types of humour) or by irritation (as when losing a game of chess, the moves of which are both necessary and fortuitous, pp. 29–30). Or again, there are four main means of access to the real in its necessary/fortuitous non-significance, its mere being itself (its 'idiocy' in the original sense of singular, unique): that of the drunk, whose seeing double is a superficial optical phenomenon (it is we who see double), and who in fact sees things in their prodigious ontological singularity; that of a person suddenly bereft of love, who sees things divested of all emotional investment (wash-basins exist, coffee exists); that of the work of art; and that of philosophy, which sums up the other three in the sense that the philosophical state, in Plato's words, is a state of being perpetually drunk, in love, and an artist.

All other perceptions of the real pass through the double, the mirror-image, the 'value added' of significance (pp. 34–5, 41–6). And the double has three main functions: (1) practical – to displace somehow a reality that must at all cost be evacuated (A is A, but also equal to all its doubles); (2) metaphysical – to make reality less 'idiotic' by endowing it with another meaning; (3) fantasmatic – to produce an object lacking in an incomplete world and thus account for desire. All these betray a refusal to apprehend the real in its singularity (pp. 46–51).

However, the direct access to the real which Rosset generously attributes to art and philosophy is surely highly ambiguous, for on his own showing (he deals with many literary texts, as well as with what he calls the philosophies of (a) the 'illusionist', which stems from Hegel, and (b) the 'incurable', which stems from Kant), both are largely and deeply involved in this doubled vision, and philosophy not the least, since the notion of the incomplete world and indeed all idealism goes back to Plato (see also Rosset 1979).

This question of responsibility apart, there may seem to be an apparent contradiction in the very fact that Rosset is constantly 'interpreting' or giving significance to the many literary works he mentions (from Sophocles to a comic strip by Hergé), and to the philosophies he discusses, even if it is only *his* significance that reality has no significance. The contradiction is only apparent, at least as far as the works are concerned, for it is at two removes from the contradiction I mentioned above when I said that his view of *reality* as non-significant is itself a signifying *statement*. Any statement in language must signify, but literary works form yet another signifying system. The *texts* he is looking at and interpreting are not 'reality' but man-made 'artefacts' (Frye 1957), 'secondary modelling systems' (Lotman 1970), or meaning-making machines, just like philosophies, ideologies or any other meaning-making machines, which he interprets as such, and quite legitimately within his postulates. The difference between philosophical systems and art-systems is that philosophical systems are wholly and avowed meaning-making machines, while the art-systems display a graduating scale from works that are avowed meaning-making machines or claim to be, and works that come as close as communication systems can to mere ontological existence ('pure' poetry, 'concrete' poetry, abstract art, music); but of course even these have at least the structural significance of similarity and difference, on which all communication systems (and ultimately all criticism) are based.

If significance is necessity, as opposed to fortuitousness which seems to us meaningless, it is certainly true that, on a much more popular level than that of philosophers, this century seems to us more and more fortuitous despite all our attempts at rational planning, scientific analysis and system-building (including rhetoric). Never before have the meaning-making means at our disposal (linguistic, economic, political, scientific) appeared so inadequate, not only to cope with the enormity of the problems we continue to create (since every apparent solution creates new problems), but simply to explain the world. This seems to be the century which, despite or because of the pace of technological advance, has taken the longest, relative to that pace, to emerge from the mental habits of the previous century. We know that all the old secure values have gone, that a radical change is occurring which man must undergo or perish, yet we somehow go on *as if*, ensconced still in relics of nineteenth-century ideologies, in a way which other times in parallel situations apparently did not. Apparently, because it seems so in the midst of it and retrospectively. But this too is probably an illusion of culture, of history books which impose their neatly significant patterns of periods calmly succeeding each other as we turn to the next chapter, whatever the anguish and turmoil we have just read about.

In one of his most important books (1966, esp. p. 95), Frank Kermode argues persuasively against this illusion of culture, and shows that although 'there is a powerful eschatological element in modern thought' (the modern apocalypse), it is commonplace but wrong 'to talk about our historical situation as uniquely terrible and in a way privileged, a cardinal point of time'. Eschatological anxiety has always existed, it was even a feature of Mesopotamian culture, he tells us, but since 'it attaches itself to the eschatological means available, it is associated with changing images'. The book is important for the links it establishes with philosophical and art systems, and, more particularly, with narrative literature, which most clearly fulfils our need for 'a beginning, a middle and an end'. On that high level, I agree with Kermode, but since I am here trying to account for the return of the fantastic in all its forms, some of ..ch were until not so long ago ignored or despised by intellectuals as crude, I shall stay with this pervasive 'sense of an ending' as it is understood (in my view) more popularly.

There are, we feel, some essential differences between this century's crisis and those undergone by others. One, obvious even to the layman, is that the very notion of progress is now untenable in its secure nineteenth-century sense of man's perfectibility – indeed in the moral sphere we seem on the contrary to be capable of regressing several centuries, or rather, of making 'progresses' in iniquity unimaginable before.

Another is that man is now wholly decentralised, having been partially so by the Copernican revolution, after which man placed his centre in human consciousness. But now this too has been dethroned, after, on the one hand, Freud's 'Copernican revolution' and its sequels and, on the other, the advances in modern physics, which questioned the very possibility of totalisation, of postulating an ordered, systemisable universe. After Einstein's equivalence of matter and energy, after de Broglie's dual nature of particle and light wave, after Planck's demonstration that energy is emitted in discontinuous quanta, and Heisenberg's uncertainty principle which replaced the determinism of classical physics with a state of probability and randomness, and showed that observable phenomena are affected by the instrument observing them, a certain tolerance of ambiguity was introduced into science, and man is now faced with a philosophy of indeterminacy and a multivalent logic. As Zavarzadeh (1976:16) points out, the prevalent cultural metaphor, now more or less banalised, is no longer that of order, or 'organic unity', but that of entropy.

Thirdly, and equally banalised, man has learnt that he is mortal;

not of course in the sense that he as an individual must die, for he has always known that, and has coped with it in various signifying ways. Even within that knowledge of individual death, there is a vast difference between knowing that I (or X, whom I love) must die, and being aware that when I die my whole world of cognition and all that I have loved and invested with significance must also disappear with my cognition of it. This too, however, man has coped with by simply denying it, through various fictions which in some way enable this very love, in some purified form or other, to conquer death. These fictions are the fruit of desire, and are 'true' in re-presenting the undeniable fact that desire, though by definition of an absent object, is channelled towards specific and present objects and thereby appears to conquer individual death – in works of man that remain after him, and more usually in progeny, not just as repetition of self but as creation of another signifying complex.

Never before, it is felt, has man been so squarely faced with the possible annihilation of mankind and all his works, his planet and perhaps more. Certainly the end of the world has always been present in his fictions, and surges especially at a millenium, but this notion was itself part of his survival fictions: he as individual could be saved. We have no such generally accepted fictions today, unless of course we wish individually to retain one of those.

These essential differences, and no doubt others, are deeply linked to the sense we have that the real has become unreal. If significance is necessity and fortuitousness meaningless, how has the situation become necessary? In the popular view, it is the result of rational science, based on necessary connections, science on which we had based all our hopes, and which has 'let us down', with what seems to the layman wholly fortuitous discoveries. In his mania for significance, man looks for moral meanings; his own guilt, or, displaced, the myth of the mad scientist. Or he looks for mystical meanings: man, not content with the created light, has discovered the un-created light, the secret of the universe (in some versions, long known but undivulged by the wise men of ancient occult traditions); man-Prometheus, or man-Lucifer. These can take optimistic forms: man will be wise, will control this force, and merely manipulate its existence to prevent its use; or this force will be the solution to the death of the planet by other means – these means however being also the result of unwisdom – greed, sloth, power-games, so that the force will enable us to go on being greedy, polluting, powerful.

Such myths have always existed, but never before have they been so dangerously, yet so obviously (for any man to see) ambiguous, self-cancelling, 'meaningless', perched so visibly, at one and the same time, on the necessary and the fortuitous – popularly exemplified, on the one hand, in the vast and rational scientific apparatus, even with built-in failsafe, and, on the other, in the famous pressing of the button.

The burden of this meaningless situation being unbearable, we naturally escape, and easily, into our more familiar reality, endowed with significance by our desire, whatever it might be, and displace the meaningless situation into a mere backdrop, apocalyptic no doubt, but a backdrop we cease to see. This displacement also partly explains the banalisation of the scientific 'marvellous': since the excitement of the moon landing, nobody cares much about Russians circling the earth for six months or a Pioneer photographing Saturn. It is 'meaningless'. Inversely, nature films have rendered 'marvellous' what is perfectly natural and happening all the time, everywhere around us, unperceived by us before the telescopic lens and accelerated filming. Then this too becomes banalised, from repetition. But the meaningless pursues us daily even in that more familiar reality, in the all too visible contradictions of our discourse; for example in the way in which all discourse manipulates us and doesn't even bother to hide the fact; in the purposeful inflation of an item by the media, followed by down-toning or inexplicable silence; in daily catastrophes that we cease to react to, guiltily of course, so that we do react, and hysterically, as soon as we are in some way involved, personally, or by proxy of friends or fortuitous presence, or nationally, by proxy of close geographical or political connection, that is, through vested interests, through investment of significance. And this significance, if not itself obvious at once, is given to us by the media who can whip up or tone down or obliterate at will; just as a bestseller can be created wholesale, or the death of a film star become a world event juxtaposed with a local genocide, or an alliance with a dictator presented as necessary, and quietly dropped when inconvenient.

I say 'all discourse' because it is fashionable to pick on the obvious ones, like the media above, or publicity, but no discourse is innocent, from the supposedly neutral administrative discourse to the pseudo-scientific occult, from the authoritarian dogmatic discourse of theology or political ideology to the personally neurotic discourse of desire, from the elitist jargon of supposedly revolutionary groups to that of supposedly pedagogic ones, or even in the obvious contradictions of our educational systems. It is perhaps one of the saddest aspects of all the verbiage that the, very intellectuals who show most relish in analysing such manipulative discourse themselves fall easy victims to at least one type.

Fudge: this is the term for a 'rule' invented by a group of linguists who analysed the way certain rules of transformational grammar were somehow not as logical or explicit as they seemed (*Where the rules fail: a student's guide*, edited by Ann Borkin 1972). Somewhere the fudge-rule occurs. As in all system-building. However, all human discourse is fudged, not only, as is natural, in personal and spontaneous situations, not only, as is right and proper, in poetry, with its black holes of density, its great gaps of non-significance through the veil of significance (for poetry is very close to the real), gaps which we can fill in with all and any significance; but also and more dangerously in carefully planned ideological discourse. Dogma by definition must fudge. And insofar as a basic premiss is at any time shown or declared to be untrue, or only partly true, or not true in the sense earlier accepted, a whole edifice collapses, an abyss remains: the real, which must quickly be filled with new idols, readjusted significance. The differences between the collapse of earlier systems and today would seem to lie in the pace, and hence in our increased and inescapable awareness of successive changes.

Our very capacity for being thus manipulated, either into ignorance or into sincere convictions and (equally sincere) indifference – each producing the other in turn – also helps to create, in the long run, this new consciousness we have of the real having become unreal, because brutally endowed with significance and then as brutally deprived of it. With the death of the planet in the conveniently displaced background, the feeling that not only can no one be trusted but that we ourselves cannot, and contribute constantly, makes us unavoidably aware of the real's meaningless. Not its absurdity, which is itself a significance, through which we saw reality earlier in the century, but its non-significance. As Robbe-Grillet put it (1962; 1965, p. 53), 'the world is neither meaningful nor absurd. It quite simply *is*.'

This awareness, as a generalised phenomenon, seems new. Until now, only a few philosophers, madmen or cranks would maintain the thesis of the non-signifying real. And if, as Rosset maintains, we do have access to the 'idiocy' of the real, half consciously, in sudden moments – a certain type of humour, irritation in certain specific situations, drunkenness, loss of love, or through (some) art and (some) philosophy, then it could be argued that the present time has peculiarly increased those moments, with its apocalyptic backdrop, its freedom of mores, its visibly nonsensical discourse, forever increasing in volume as a kind of ghastly western parallel to the birthrate on the rest of the planet, and its inheritance of two main philosophical currents (Hegel/Kant) which both manage in different ways to duplicate the ontological fact with a significance somehow absent. We are peculiarly privileged in our access to that meaningless ontological fact: we have become irritated clowns, drunk or drugged, perpetually bereft of love, artists and philosophers of the meaningless. Hence our voluble and frenzied attempts to find meaning, to build new systems. Hence the emergence of semantics, semiology, and later semiotics, which study meaning and how it functions; and psychoanalysis, sociology, the philosophy of history, linguistic philosophy, phenomenology, hermeneutics, modern rhetoric, generative grammar, psycholinguistics, sociolinguistics, anthropology, etc., all of which accept as given the arbitrariness of language systems, all of which try desperately to establish the mental structures underlying human discourse, rather than merely to note and expound upon the discourse. But either way the discourse upon discourse that man has always needed since writing began has now expanded to a vast industry of unprecedented proportions.

2

The rhetoric

The word *rhetoric* is as ambiguous as the word reality, both in denotation and in connotation. In denotation it can mean the verbal art used by the poet and apprehended by us; and it can also mean the critic's method of discerning and analysing that verbal art. It shares that denotative ambiguity with other names of disciplines, notably history, which is both the events and the discourse about the events, or anatomy. Indeed most of the old disciplines have that ambiguity, and it is only in relatively recent times that the distinction has become clear; for instance grammar is both 'the mechanism we have in our brain even if we cannot read and write', and the discipline that studies these mechanisms (Paolo Valesio 1978: 16).[1] Valesio suggests that the same applies to semiotics (the science of meaning), which he opposes to semiotic (the occurrence of meaning), on the analogy with rhetorics and rhetoric, but in practice 'rhetorics' is rarely used, nor is the distinction possible in all languages, so the ambiguity remains.

In connotation, rhetoric can mean the verbal art as skill or, in older terms, the art that charms, that 'instructs and delights'; and it can also mean grandiloquence, 'mere' rhetoric, a meaning which no doubt comes from the fact that the late classical and mediaeval rhetoric was prescriptive as well as descriptive; it claimed to tell the poet all the 'felicities' he could use, a claim gently mocked by Chaucer and Shakespeare. But the meaning of 'mere' rhetoric may also go back further to the original sense of rhetoric as the art of persuasion, the means used to persuade an audience of the 'truth' of one's statements, even if they are false, for rhetoric was born in the law-courts of Syracuse, out of disputes over property, from which it is but a small step to political or mercantile rhetoric.

Today rhetoric has chiefly acquired the second denotative meaning of critical method, as applied to the verbal art, but it retains its denotative ambiguity; Wayne C. Booth's *The rhetoric of fiction* (1961)

for example, deals with narrative techniques, but also implies
Booth's way of dealing with them. The rhetoric of the verbal art
has, on the whole, the first (non-pejorative) connotation, but in
critical method it is also used for pejorative evaluation, particularly
in analysing and exposing the contradictions of manipulative techniques (the rhetoric) of publicity or political discourse; or to analyse
and expose the critical methods of others, for rhetoric is rarely
innocent, and rarely turns its floodlights upon itself.

I am well aware of these difficulties and the pitfalls of language.
Critical discourse on written works is particularly vulnerable since it
is discourse, which is re-presentation, about a discourse which is a
re-presentation of 'reality'. Since the chapters which follow all
analyse in one way or another the 'rhetoric' of the text, I shall here
speak only of critical methods – and I use the plural because I shall
use many, for reasons that will become apparent. I do not believe in
one method, infallible for every text. On the contrary I shall pick,
here and there, concepts of modern theory (or rhetoric) that are
useful to me, but will eschew pure theory in the sense of a closed,
self-contained 'system', in favour of intuitive criticism.

The quarrel between theory and criticism (as two types of
'rhetoric') is in fact a false one. They are indeed two different
procedures, but each is weak without the other. In chapter 6 I shall
show, with reference to one text, the weakness of the worst type of
traditional criticism, and in chapter 3 I shall analyse the differences
in detail, with reference to the fantastic. But here I shall outline the
problems and brief history of both more generally, for readers who
are not yet familiar with modern theory, and also, since some of *its*
rhetoric may be obscure to newcomers, by way of introduction to
some of the terms I shall be using.

1. Theory and criticism

Traditionally, criticism judges (evaluates), interprets and describes.[2]
It proceeds, on the whole, empirically, finding in texts whatever it
finds (or wants to find), and any theory it may evolve emerges from
these findings. Theory (in theory) works the other way round,
proposing, like science, a hypothesis, a model, and testing it against
the facts.[3] Science does not simply collect phenomena and hope that
some generalisation will emerge; it has to have a viewpoint, a
model, to know what it is looking for.

To give two simple examples. Plato, as Todorov (1970b) points out, divided narrative into three types: (a) where only the narrator speaks; (b) where only the characters speak; (c) mixed. This does not, strictly speaking, represent the facts at his time since the first type then existed only in historical narrative, and drama had at least a narrator-like chorus. The theory is based on one hypothesis, that the act of speaking is central to narrative, and according to that criterion it covers all the theoretical possibilities (cp. here, ch. 3, p. 58). However a theory, especially when it does not deal with empirical reality but with artefacts, can also be a model which no concrete object wholly exemplifies; that is, the concrete examples show a *predominant* characteristic that place it in this or that category of the hypothesised model. Aristotle (*Rhetoric* I. cc. 4. 15) divided styles into (a) epidectic (for praise or blame), which uses the present tense; (b) deliberative (political), which uses the future tense; (c) forensic (the facts), which uses the past. Obviously he was not implying that one cannot praise or blame in the past tense or that a political speech must be entirely composed in the future. It is a question here of predominance, or even mere likelihood: one praises or blames someone present to receive the compliment or reproach; one makes election promises or reassuring statements about the future.

It must be stressed here that a theory may be wrong, yet 'work' for a time, or for a limited purpose: e.g., the Ptolemaic theory of the universe, though wrong, 'worked' for many centuries, in the sense that the movements of the stars could be accurately predicted and so on. A theory can also be a 'strong' hypothesis, which accounts for all the known facts, or a 'weak' hypothesis, which accounts for only some. By the same token a theory may be criticised in some aspects but accepted as a working hypothesis. Science in other words is always questioning itself.

In literary practice the distinction is by no means so clear-cut. Criticism shares with science the impossibility of looking at any object without some preconceived notion of what we are looking at and for, and of its significance in relation to other similar objects. In literature, we know that what we are reading is a poem (or even a sonnet, an ode, an epic), a play, a novel, and we will not 'judge' or even appreciate a sonnet as if it were a novel. And as we gather more of these preconceived notions together, we automatically evolve some kind of viewpoint, which is a (very elementary) theory. And if this 'viewpoint' in the more empirical, traditional criticism is sometimes vague, inconsistent, subjective, and rarely and only very slowly requestioned, it does not have to be so, that is merely a mark of weak criticism.

Theory however, when its object is not empirical reality but a literary artefact, is rarely as 'scientific' as it purports to be, and when it is, it can become a rigid system, like some versions of structuralism, that can remain purely theoretical only by not quite daring to test itself against the contradictory richness of the texts, or, if it does, finding only what fits the theory, thus rejoining, but in a dryer, more difficult way, the worst kind of subjective criticism.

Criticism and theory, at their best, are complementary, and should work together. Personally I do not believe in the pure 'science' of literature many have dreamt of, a totalising 'system' or 'universal' theory of literature called poetics, and now generally admitted to be an impossible illusion. Theory cannot be a science because it deals with cultural, not natural products. (Hence the adoption of the term 'human' science, versus 'pure' science, for disciplines like sociology, psychoanalysis etc., which literary theory wants to join.) It has been important to reverse the traditional non-scientific procedure of accumulating facts and hoping that some general principle will emerge, and to adopt (or try to adopt) the scientific method of first postulating a hypothesis through which to look at the phenomena so as to test it against them. It has been important to develop a metalanguage distinct from the language of the object examined, thus getting away from subjective paraphrase or the mere retelling of the text in one's own words, even if technical jargon is often abused and varies too much from one school to another. And if the difficulty lies in the fact that, important though the model may be, there must always remain in our minds the sheer flexibility of the cultural, as opposed to natural, phenomena, this flexibility should not, conversely, confuse our recognition of the abstract nature of the model. The position of many structuralists is to postulate and defend their model as model, each historical work then representing a manifested ('impure') version of this model, with individual divergences that could be called mixtures of categories, a question of predominances (Todorov 1968).

The task of elaborating these models belongs to the theoretician. That of interpreting the divergences and predominances belongs to the critic. The fact that they are sometimes, like Todorov, like Frye, like Barthes, Genette and many others, one and the same person, makes the task difficult but not impossible to disentangle, and is in any case most hopeful for both theory and criticism. The opposite fact that theoreticians and critics are often different people (rather like philologists and literary critics in the old days), the critic refusing (or being bad at) theory and the theoretician refusing (or being bad at) intuitive criticism, is far more serious.

Theory, at the moment, is in any case in a state of utter confusion as we shall see, with different and individual 'systems', some based on symbolic logic, some on the modal logics, some on linguistics, some on psychoanalysis (etc.), some purely private, each with its different metalanguage and notation. In physics, whatever the disagreements, everyone uses the same notation. Similarly in linguistics and logic. But as long as literary theory continues to borrow, here one concept, there another, it cannot hope to be scientific – nor, probably, should it.[4]

2. A few examples of muddled thinking

In his pioneering *The morphology of the folk-tale* (1928, trans. 1968), which I shall briefly describe in a moment, Vladimir Propp complained that earlier and contemporary attempts to deal with the folk-tale were simply *ad hoc* lists of motifs found, lists which inevitably overlap and are inevitably open-ended. To give only two of his several examples (Wundt and Volkov), Wundt divided folk-tales into: (1) mythological tale-fables, (2) pure fairy-tales, (3) biological tales and fables, (4) pure animal fables, (5) 'genealogical' tales, (6) joke-tales and fables, (7) moral fables.

As Propp points out, the term *fable* (which describes a formal category) occurs five times in seven classes. The term *joke-tale* is unacceptable since the same tale might be treated heroically or comically. Nor is the difference between *pure animal fable, pure fairy-tale* and *moral fables* clear: 'In what way are the "pure fables" not "moral" and vice-versa?' (1968: 7).

Volkov finds fifteen 'themes' (Propp in exasperation gives only ten of them). For clarity I shall put the criterion for each category to the right, to show there is no principle at all in Volkov's division.

Tales about	Determined by
(1) those unjustly persecuted	the action
(2) the hero-fool	the character of a hero
(3) the three brothers	the number of heroes
(4) dragon-fighters	one moment of the action
(5) finding a bride	another moment of the action
(6) the wise maiden	the character of a heroine
(7) those placed under a spell	another moment in the action

(8) the possessor of a talisman   ⎫ a type of character (same) + a moment
(9) the possessor of magic objects ⎭ in the action
(10) an unfaithful wife   the character of a wife and/or a mo-
                                        ment in the action.

It would in fact be possible to compose a folk-tale containing all
these elements. As Propp says:

The result is actually chaos. Do not tales exist in which three brothers (third
category) procure brides for themselves (fifth category)? Does not the
possessor of a talisman, with the aid of this talisman, punish the unfaithful
wife? Thus, the given classification is not a scientific classification in the
precise sense of the word. It is nothing more than a conventional index, the
value of which is extremely dubious. (1968: 8)

And Propp goes on to mention Aarne's *Index of Folk-themes*,
recognising its usefulness as index, but criticising it on similar
grounds.

In *Les mots et les choses* (1966), Foucault traces the long history of
the relationship between language and reality, and shows how this
confused way of thinking underwent a radical change at the
Renaissance, especially in the seventeenth century, which made
modern science possible (but which was only very slowly followed
by the humanities, with constant relapses). He quotes a story by
Borges, of a Chinese encyclopaedia that gives the following categories for animals: (a) those that belong to the Emperor, (b)
embalmed ones, (c) those that are trained, (d) suckling pigs, (e)
mermaids, (f) fabulous ones, (g) stray dogs, (h) those that are
included in this classification, (i) those that tremble as if they were
mad, (j) innumerable ones, (k) those drawn with a very fine camel's
hair brush, (l) others, (m) those that have just broken a flower vase,
(n) those that resemble flies from a distance. This of course is
comical exaggeration, but the mental confusion it exemplifies continued for a long time, and still exists, even in literary criticism;
especially in literary criticism.

For example, and more to my purpose in this book, Propp's
complaint in 1928 is exactly the same as that made by Tzvetan
Todorov in his book on the fantastic (1970b, trans. 1975), which I
shall examine in more detail in chapter 3. He too gives earlier lists of
themes (1975: 100–1): Dorothy Scarborough (modern ghosts, the
devil and his allies, supernatural-life); Penzoldt (ghosts, phantoms,
vampires, werewolves, witches and witchcraft, invisible beings, animal spectres); Vax (vampires, parts of the human body, the pa-

thology of the human personality, the interplay of invisible and visible, alterations of causality, space and time, and finally regression); Caillois (the pact with the devil, the anguished soul that requires a certain action to find peace, the spectre doomed to an incoherent and endless journey [= a specific instance of the former], death personified appearing among the living, the indefinable invisible 'thing' that haunts, vampires, the statue/figure/suit of armour/automaton that suddenly comes to life, the phantom woman seductive and deadly, the room, house, or street erased from space, the cessation or repetition of time).

These are much more modern critics than those cited by Propp, yet they exhibit the same mental habits. Many categories overlap, and there is a confusion in levels of abstraction: supernatural life includes 'modern ghosts' and the devil and his allies (Scarborough); a vampire can be a ghost (or a phantom, whatever the difference is supposed to be), a werewolf is at least half an animal spectre, invisible beings can include ghosts and phantoms (Penzoldt); parts of the human body can include blood, i.e. vampires (Vax), just as the phantom woman seductive and deadly can be a vampire (Caillois, whose list is perhaps the most empirical and unsystematic). And in Vax there is, as Todorov points out, a curious shift from images to their causes in the human personality. And of course all such lists are open-ended, that is, one could add more motifs as one finds them. An empirical list of specific features cannot be sufficiently abstract to cover all the possibilities (each possibility being then exemplified by specific examples). It does not construct a theory. Todorov himself, in his chapter on themes of the fantastic, divides them much more simply into two groups: themes of the self (*thèmes du 'je'*) and themes of the other (*thèmes du 'tu'*), each then linked *analogically* with psychoanalysis; the themes of the self with psychosis, the themes of the other with neurosis. This may not be psychoanalytically valid, indeed some would say that this linking is much too arbitrary. But it is only suggested later, as an analogy from another discipline, *after* the two groups have been analysed from a literary point of view. And my point here is that the grouping exhausts the theoretical possibilities: linguistically because I/you are the only two pronouns caught up in an interpersonal relationship (the third person being the topic of discourse, see p. 23); and psychoanalytically because psychic disturbances belong either to psychosis or to neurosis. I shall be discussing the more formal (i.e. non-thematic) part of Todorov's theory in chapter 3.

3. A brief account of modern theory and criticism

Naturally I cannot here give a detailed history, or include everyone, but will simply give an outline, concentrating on those critics whose terms and concepts I shall be using.

3.1. The Russian Formalists and their influence

The first modern literary theorists were the Russian Formalists.[5] They were all still empirical enough (in the good sense) to work closely with literary texts and not just to theorise. It was Chklovski (1919) for instance who first expounded the now familiar notion (already found embryonically in Novalis and others) of distancing (*ostranenie*) or estrangement from the familiar, analysing an example from Tolstoy, who describes a theatre as if it were an unknown object. This distancing, to which I shall refer with regard to science fiction (chapter 4), is a main structure in the eighteenth-century *roman philosophique* (our familiar world viewed by other beings as in *Gulliver's Travels*, or foreign visitors as in Montesquieu, Voltaire, Goldsmith).

Another key-concept is the difference the Russian Formalists established between the *fabula* (the basic story) and the *sjužet* (its treatment, organisation or *agencement*, through manipulations of time, viewpoint, types of discourse etc.). Except in simple tales, we rarely get the story 'straight', but have to reconstruct it through the discourse. This distinction has been more recently exploited and analysed by Genette (1972), under the categories of *histoire/discours* (see pp. 35–8, and chapter 12 below for detail).

The only other Formalist concept I shall occasionally use is that of *function*, a term invented for narrative by Propp (1928). Propp's method was first to determine the constants and the variables, and secondly to find the minimal unit among the constants (just as, in linguistics, the phoneme is the minimal, i.e. distinctive, unit at the sound level, the morpheme is the minimal unit at the level of significance).

In the folk-tale, the variables are the characters, the constants are their actions or *functions*. Thus a king, a father, an old man, a sorcerer, may perform the identical action of giving to the hero an eagle, a boat, a magic ring, which in turn perform the identical action of transporting the hero elsewhere. The function (*type* of action) is therefore the minimal unit to be analysed.

In the Russian folk-tales he examined, Propp found thirty-one functions, always in the same order if not always all present, and certain groups always go together: e.g. *injunction* (not to go into the forest for instance) is inevitably followed by *transgression* (otherwise there is no story), which leads, through the giving away of information (*interrogation/information*) and the falling into a trap (*fraud/complicity*), to the villain's *misdeed*, which institutes a *lack* (harvest stolen, princess kidnapped, etc.), at which point the real story can start; *mediation* (misdeed made known and help called for), hero's *acceptance, departure, test* by donor, hero's *reaction* (successful this time), *receipt of magical auxiliary, transport* to place of object sought, *struggle, marking* of hero, *victory, return, pursuit, rescue, arrival incognito, false hero's claim, task, solution, recognition of hero, exposure* of villain, *transfiguration* of hero (new clothes, or through the task he builds a magic palace, or is a prince, etc.), *punishment* of villain, *wedding* (or other reward).

This was a tremendous step forward in the analysis of basic structure, although Propp is still partly empirical: his work is based on one hundred Russian folk-tales, and the details inside his categories naturally often apply only to these. Moreover he adds a last function called Y, for anything as yet unknown, not fitting into his system, which reminds us a little of Borges's *etcetera* category. Nor do his thirty-one functions form a very 'scientific', i.e. symmetrical and systematic, model. However it represents, long before modern linguistics, a primitive generative model, in the sense that given this system or simple 'grammar', it can generate all the types of folktale that use these functions, as a grammar, however simple, can generate all the types of sentences modelled on the phrase-structure rules given in that grammar. For instance, noun phrase + verb phrase at basic structure, NP then rewritten as ($\rightarrow$), for instance, (determiner) + (adjective) + noun; and VP$\rightarrow$verb + noun phrase. This, with the bracketed terms as optional, will generate quite a few types of sentences, from *John eats cheese* to *the beautiful girl saw a handsome man*, but it will not generate *the beautiful girl went to the beach*, because no rule has been introduced to say that a prepositional phrase can follow the verb in the verb phrase. So the phrase-structure rules must be modified, and a more complex grammar constructed. A generative grammar should generate all the grammatical (acceptable) sentences of a language and none of the ungrammatical (unacceptable) sentences. Propp's later work developed this generative aspect of his theory, but in a historical sense (one type of structure evolving into others).

Propp's system was later criticised by the French Structuralists, notably Bremond (1964, 1966), for its finalistic postulate or mechanical causality which makes it impossible to open an alternative (e.g. the possibility of failing). Alternatives do exist in Propp's corpus but have only a delaying role, so that he assimilates them to the triplication phenomenon (three heroes, only one of whom succeeds, or three tasks, etc.). Another of Bremond's reproaches is the lack of freedom within groups of functions: if ABD or LMN *always* go together, the minimal unit is no longer the function but the sequence of actions. Bremond develops his own much more abstract theory (1966, 1973) based on amelioration and worsening of a situation (and all their variants and interlocking possibilities) but without corroborating texts, and in my view remaining at such a level of generalisation that its very universality limits its particular use to the obvious; a form of reductionism that has led pure structuralism to an *impasse*. Greimas (1966:174–203) brilliantly reduces Propp's thirty-one functions to four couples: contract/acceptance, confrontation/success, presence/absence of hero, communication (positive/negative, e.g. the loss of information, heroic vigour and object at the beginning of a tale through interrogation, fraud and misdeed, are followed during the story by re-acquisition). Later (1970: 249–69) he produces his famous 'actantial' model; the actant being the abstract role, such as addresser (e.g. of quest, task, message), and addressee (the hero), the opposant and the adjuvant (helper); the actor being the specific semantic investment (king, woodcutter's son, etc.). His three-level narrative 'grammar' (1970: 135–83), which though in principle generative and considerably more sophisticated than Propp's, is not (any more than Propp's, which did not claim to be) a grammar in any accepted modern sense since no explicit rules are given to pass from one level to another.[6]

The Russian Formalists were long unknown in the West, but their work was later continued by the Prague School of Structuralists, of which Roman Jakobson and Jan Mukařovsky are perhaps the best-known exponents, as well as René Wellek who, however, later moved away from pure structuralism to general literary theory. Their ideas reached the West, partly through the exile of Jakobson, Wellek and others, partly via American and Scandinavian structural linguistics which had advanced independently, in the work of the French Structuralists. In Russia, after the Formalists, some work continued more or less surreptitiously (and very differently) during the thirties, notably with Bakhtin and Voloshinov (see later). Meanwhile structuralist linguistics had given way to generative models (Chomsky 1957), the principles of which in turn influenced

French and other Structuralists (e.g. Todorov 1970c, 1975, Zumthor 1971, 1972). These linguistic models themselves soon had to incorporate transformational rules and became known as transformational grammar (Chomsky 1957 *et seq.*). The purely grammatical, abstract and universalist assumptions of Chomsky were later challenged (or rather widened) by generative semantics, psycholinguistics, and sociolinguistics, while structuralism itself developed into semiotics, with such a profusion of models, based sometimes on linguistics, sometimes on types of logic or other disciplines, that it would be fastidious, and confusing for the beginner, to go into further detail here. Meanwhile again, the purely literary movements of the new criticism had developed in England and America between the twenties and forties, with the reaction against it by the Chicago school of rhetoric, counter-reactions and refinements. The situation today is thus extremely complex.

3.2. *An attempt to clarify the situation*

It may be useful here to recall Roman Jakobson's diagram of communication (1960). All communication, he tells us, has six essential aspects: the addresser, the addressee, the message, a context (or what the message refers to), a physical contact (parchment, stone, paper, sound-waves, and of course the signs used, in their phonetic or graphic form), and a code. All systems of communication, including language, consist of six functions (f) which correspond to these six aspects.

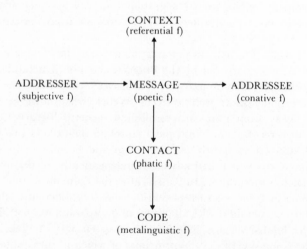

CONTEXT
(referential f)

ADDRESSER ⟶ MESSAGE ⟶ ADDRESSEE
(subjective f)   (poetic f)   (conative f)

CONTACT
(phatic f)

CODE
(metalinguistic f)

Thus, in language, the subjective function includes the first-person pronouns, modals expressing doubt, certainty, feeling (*may, must, feel,* etc. the performative (e.g. I promise) and other illocutionary speech acts (Austin 1962), and certain 'shifters', that is, certain adverbials and tenses that change when one passes from one's own present instance of discourse to historical, impersonal narrative (e.g. *today, last week, next year, here, in this room, I am,* etc. become *that day, the previous week, a year later, there, in that room, he was,* etc.); indeed the historian cannot use 'I' or the present tense without passing into his present instance of discourse (Benveniste 1966). The conative function includes the second-person pronouns, modals, the imperative, the vocative, forms of address, and the same shifters. In fact this I/you relation is what is now called 'interpersonal features', I/you being inextricably involved with one another (the *I* becoming *you* when this *you* speaks to his *I*) in a personal relationship which excludes the third person (he/she/it/they), which may not even be present, but a mere topic of discourse, and in this sense a non-person (Benveniste 1966, chapters 18–19). The referential function includes the third person pronouns, and all declarative sentences. The phatic function includes all the things we say simply to reinforce the contact (e.g. *hello* on the telephone, and the many polite or friendly exchanges such as *lovely day* etc.). The metalinguistic function includes anything we say when we use words about words, as for instance in criticism, or in linguistics, but also daily when we explain in other terms or query what has been meant. And, last but not least, the poetic function includes everything that draws attention to the form of the message itself, such as word-play, alliteration, rhyme, rhythm, repetition, figures of syntax, etc., as in poetry, but also in ordinary speech and in slogans (Jakobson's example is the election slogan *I like Ike*). This is often now called the *literarity* of the message.

The poetic function had already been defined more precisely in Jakobson's famous division between the syntagmatic and the paradigmatic axes of language (1956). Language is structured either on *combination* of elements in presence (sequence of sounds, of words, of sentences), that is to say, contiguity (the syntagmatic axis); or on the *selection* of elements from the system (selection of sounds, words, sentences), that is to say, substitution (the paradigmatic axis). This theory is the result of research on types of aphasia, which fall into two main groups: aphasics with paradigmatic disturbance will stress only the link words, or associate only by contiguity (*lamp* would give *table* or *ceiling*), while aphasics with syntagmatic disturbance will lose the link words and produce a sort of telegraphese, and associate only by substitution (*lamp* would give *moon*). These two axes are manifest, at the rhetorical level, in metonymy or synecdoche (contiguity, i.e. part for whole, material for object etc.) and metaphor (substitution). Naturally both axes are always present, since it is impossible to substitute without a context of contiguity (e.g. *lamp* cannot mean *moon* without some sort of syntax), while even the most syntagmatic forms will contain at least dead metaphors and substitutions of variation, expansion, etc. There is also a very close link between this linguistic theory and the language of the unconscious as formulated by Freud, dreams and fantasmatic discourse functioning either by displacement (metonymy) or by substitution (metaphor, or the famous Freudian ('symbols'). This theory has had enormous influence, and I shall return to it in chapter 13, but here I only want to recall Jakobson's definition of the poetic function as projecting the principle of equivalence from the paradigmatic axis on to the syntagmatic axis.

Jakobson's six-function model has been criticised, notably by Halliday (1970, 1973) who proposes three functions only. More important for me, he insists that his three functions are simultaneously operative, whereas Jakobson, although his theory allows for simultaneity and although he specifically concedes an overlap, in critical practice regards them as alternatives. In a poem, only the poetic function is operative, and *that* is what he analyses (see also Fowler 1979). A text is either poetic or referential. A novel for instance would for him be referential, that is, it refers to a described world.

We may in fact say that different schools of literary criticism have gone round and round that diagram. Traditional (pre-twenties) criticism concentrated on the addresser (the *subjective function*) that is, on the author (his life, his view of the world, his readings, his intentions) and on the context or *referential function*, that is, the world represented (characters, themes, realistic achievement etc.).

The New criticism, and parallel to it, the European criticism emanating from the Prague school and ultimately from the Formalists, rejected both these and concentrated wholly on the poetic function, the text: 'structure' and 'texture' for the new critics, including irony, ambiguity, paradox, metaphor, etc.; stylistics for the continental school. This to the explicit exclusion of all references to 'the outside world' or to the 'real author'. I. A. Richards (1924) was perhaps the prime mover with his distinction between 'emotive' language (poetry) and 'scientific' language (the rest), the purpose of poetry not being to tell the 'truth' about the world. Poetry had its own truth. 'A poem should not mean/But be', said Macleish later. It may be noted that this kind of 'two truths' argument is exactly the same as that used by religion, especially in its nineteenth-century crisis when Darwinism and other scientific discoveries revealed that creation had not taken place in four thousand odd B.C. and that Adam and Eve were not 'literally' the first humans on earth, and other things. Religion has its own truth. No doubt, but it is a little odd to find champions of poetry adopt this concessionary argument, thus in a sense weakening poetry, just as religion was 'weakened' in relation to the absolute belief that had prevailed. But here we touch inevitably on the long dispute about poetry as 'lies', which goes all the way back to Plato, and rather than digress, I prefer to remain with the new criticism's firm exclusion of both the author and his 'intentions' and of all 'truthful' or valid reference to the world. However the new criticism also rejected the addressee, or reader. Richards had at first included him in his *Practical criticism* (1929) with classroom reactions to poems, but this was a didactic experiment, the implication being that certain reactions were aberrant. By the late forties (1946, 1949) Wimsatt and Beardsley had published their notorious pronouncements against (1) the 'intentional fallacy' (the author's intentions) and (2) the 'affective fallacy' (the reader's reaction), in two essays with those titles (in *The Verbal Icon*, Wimsatt 1954). Criticism has taken a long time to recover.

The Prague school, and later the Structuralists, also concentrated on the poetic function, or what it called the literarity of the text, what makes it literary and not ordinary language, to the exclusion of subjective and referential functions. They also brought in the phatic function, not explicitly as such, but through the constant distinction they make (which derives from Saussure's linguistics (1915); third edition 1969) between the *signifiant* (signifier) and the *signifié* (signified). The signifier is the sign in its physical (phonetic or graphic) shape, and the signified is, not the object it represents (which is the referent) but the concept evoked in our mind by the word (or sentence, or text). A text that plays with typography, for instance (italics, capitals, titles, shaped poems like those of Herbert or Dylan Thomas or Apollinaire's *calligrams* or Carroll's mouse-tail), is particularly susceptible to analysis of the signifier, as are comic strips, with their drawings, huge exclamation marks, bubbles, capitalised sound-words and other conventions, or publicity images.

Structuralism however, later began to bring back the subjective and conative functions (author and reader), but only indirectly, as they are inscribed in the text through the interpersonal features described above, in the form of the distinction between *énoncé* (the assertive sentence or 'objective' statement, e.g. *the coffee-pot is on the table*) and *énonciation* the subjectively marked utterance, e.g. *I thought/I supposed/I felt/I was almost sure* the coffee-pot was on the table/the coffee-pot *seemed* to be/*may* be on the table, etc.). I shall return to this distinction in chapter 8.

Modern linguists, notably some transformational grammarians who turn their attention to poetry (Fowler, Ruwet, Guéron and others) could moreover be said to take the metalinguistic function of a text into account (as opposed to the metalanguage we use in talking about the text), in the sense that the various violations of grammar they analyse in poems may be regarded as poetry's metalinguistic function or the way a poem is *also* about grammar and its potential (just as the 'self-reflexive' novel is also about narrative technique). However this is rarely stated explicitly, and tends in any case to be treated exclusively, in isolation from other functions. Since Structuralism, and in a parallel but distinct movement in America and elsewhere, modern theory has been catching up on these various exclusive concentrations.

Interestingly, this happened mostly in America, where literary theory, as Shoshanna Felman points out (1978), is more closely related to logic and philosophy than it has been in Europe, whose modern rhetoric came out of formalism and structuralist linguistics as a subcategory of semiology. In America, and only to a certain extent in Europe (e.g. Kristeva, and, in a different way, Eco), the linguistic tradition emerged out of the work of Charles S. Peirce, whose definition of the sign is as follows: 'The sign or *representamen* is what replaces, for someone, something in a certain aspect or position. It is addressed to someone, that is, it creates in the mind of that person an *equivalent* sign, or perhaps a barely developed sign' (1955: 99).

Pierce alters the Saussurean definition of the sign (referent, signifier and signified). The referent he calls its object, the signifier (elsewhere) its iconicity, and the signified he splits into two, meaning and interpretant: 'That for which [the sign] stands is called its *object*; that which it conveys, its *meaning*; and the idea to which it gives rise, its *interpretant*' (*Collected Papers* 1, 1960, p. 171). The sign must be interpreted in order to exist, and the interpretation is not a meaning but another sign, which is in turn interpreted into another sign and so on. This concept will have important consequences.

At any rate the exclusive concentrations on one function only were soon questioned. That on the poetic function only has in its turn been denounced (e.g. Miner, 'The objective fallacy', 1976, but also others), just as the 'intentional' and 'affective' fallacies were, and these themselves have now been brought back as not fallacies at all (Hirsch 1967, Searle 1975 and others for the author's intentions, and Fish 1970 and since, most trenchantly for 'affective stylistics'). As Roger Fowler (1979) puts it:

Although repeatedly discredited by aestheticians and critics, these fallacious fallacies are still rehearsed in the dominant text-books used in England and America. They are fallacious because all discourse emanates from a person, and any discourse received by a person has some effect on that individual's behaviour or state. All languages are provided with 'interpersonal' structures which effect these particular links between text and life. To deny these links seems to me to dehumanize the very texts which the critics claim have a special significance for humanity. (p. 9)

This is of course true, but it does not take into account the distinctions made by literary critics since Booth (1961) between actual author and implied author (Booth, see p. 29 here), or, within a narrative, between narrator and narratee, i.e. the fictional entities ostensibly emitting and receiving the message (see p. 35). Here I will only say that the best-known attempt to bring the actual author back is in *The Princeton Encyclopaedia of Poetry and Poetics* (Preminger 1975), and, more ambiguously, E. D. Hirsch (1967), who merely harks back to the author's intentions, not quite admitting it but talking of the author's 'will' (see Suleiman 1976b: 16–17 for a discussion of Hirsch's position). Another (incidental) attack on the intentional fallacy is that of J. R. Searle (1975), on the illocutionary act of writing fiction:

There used to be a school of literary critics who thought one should not consider the intentions of the author when examining a work of fiction. Perhaps there is some level of intention at which this extraordinary view is plausible; perhaps one should not consider an author's ulterior motives when analyzing his work, but at the most basic level it is absurd to suppose a critic can completely ignore the intentions of the author, since even so much as to identify a text as a novel, a poem, or even as a text is already to make a claim about the author's intention. (p. 325)

The level is indeed very basic, and this kind of intention, like the illocutionary act of writing fiction that Searle analyses, is obviously encoded in the text, as are many other intentions. The 'fallacious' part of the intentional fallacy surely concerns unwarranted critical appeals to extratextually expressed author's intentions, or unsubstantiated appeals to intentions supposedly in the text but really in the critic's mind (see ch. 6, p. 133). For Wimsatt wrote in 1968: 'As Mr. Beardsley and I were careful to point out ... interpretation based on the author's intention often in fact refers to an intention as it is found in, or inferred from, the work itself.' And he explicitly states that his argument was not directed at such cases.

Fowler also vigorously challenges the exclusion of the referential function, particularly for the novel, and the habit of discussing narrative, or the practice of writing it, in terms only of the absolute and arbitrary nature of fiction:

> reference to, or reflection of, the real world gives way to the absolute shaping power of the novelist (Kermode, 1967; Fowles, 1969). But, in fact, to claim that the imaginative writer creates through language a new world distinct from the real world referred to by history-books, newspapers, etc, is not to justify separating imaginative writing absolutely from 'referential' discourse. A series of propositions about non-existent people or events has, for the reader, the same status as a series of propositions about real historical circumstances of which the reader was previously unaware. In both cases, the reader has to make sense of the content by reconstructing it as a world which is plausible in terms of the world he knows. (Or, in the case of the fantastic, related to 'our' world by systematic transformations). In both cases, the writer's arrangements of words and sentences impose an artificial order upon the events real or non-real referred to ... And in both cases – indeed, in all examples of linguistic performance – the writer's choice of words and sentences may be explained in terms of the social and historical circumstances in which the writer and his readers communicate; so that words which refer to fictional entities may be interpreted in the light of real material and social situations. (Fowler 1979: 9)

It is true that the twentieth-century reaction against realism has in many ways been strong, varied and continued. It is also true that the exclusive concentration on the literarity of the text (the poetic function) led to extreme and elitist positions, such as the notion that each text has its own complex, ambiguous, paradoxical (etc.) language, which it is the critic's equally complex task to decode, and that the ideology lurking behind this attitude is, as Fowler points out, fairly sinister. Much the same could be said of many Structuralists and post-Structuralists today, despite their claims to subversion, revolution, *éclatement*, and other fashionable concepts. All exclusion has its dangers. But we shall be looking at some aspects of realism, and of the 'self-reflexive' movement back to literariness, in more detail later in this book. Curiously, Fowler does not attack those who exclude, say, the poetic function in favour of *only* the referential and the subjective, such as traditional nineteenth-century criticism and its modern equivalents, the sociological, or the ideological interpretation of literature (e.g. the writer as *bourgeois*, imprisoned by his class concepts etc.), or psycho-analytical investigations of the author through his texts (or even of non-existent characters, see ch. 6). But that is probably a chance omission, or due to his sociolinguistic 'functionalism' (Fowler 1979: 14), for he is explicitly against all *a priori* exclusion of any linguistic aspects of a text.

Modern criticism has moved towards a much greater plurality, and tries, not always successfully, to integrate all the six aspects of communication in Jakobson's diagram. It is difficult, since one cannot do all things at once, and some texts do exploit one more than another. The most controversial, because until about ten years ago the most neglected, is the problem of the addressee. Is he a 'real' reader (you, me, aunt Lucy), or an 'ideal' reader, or a reader inscribed, encoded in the text? And is the addressor the 'real' author (who has toothache, marital troubles, a stamp-collection), or an 'ideal' author as reflected in the text, or is he simply the narrator?

3.2.1. Real and unreal tale-bearers and hearers. Wayne C. Booth's pioneer work, *The rhetoric of fiction* (1961) was the first to set forth the notions of implied author and implied reader. The real author is extratextual, but projects, through his work, an 'ideal' image of himself, more controlled, or more amusing (or whatever). This image of the implied author should not be confused with the narrator, who may be an anonymous voice very close to the implied author, but may also be dramatised as someone quite different (e.g. an idiot, in Faulkner, or a governess in James, etc.). And the implied reader is also projected in the text, not as a specific reader or even an addressed 'Dear Reader', but in the very rhetoric through which he is required to 'make sense of the content' or reconstruct it 'as a world', in Fowler's terms; the rhetoric, that is to say, not only of the words and sentences he reads, but of the organisation (*agencement* or *sjužet*), such as viewpoint changes, temporal changes, dialogue, irony and so forth. Irony in particular, as a collusion between narrator and reader, a sort of indirect comment on the characters, assumes and therefore constructs a reader capable of catching it, in other words an ideal interpreter or ideal reader. This implied and ideal reader therefore parallels the ideal image of the author.

Booth's book contains a good deal more than that, notably the first clear analysis of types of narrator and a severe critique of certain fashions of post-Jamesian criticism such as the insistence on the elimination of the narrator's voice (in James's and, later, Lubbock's terms, one must 'show', not 'tell', see also ch. 12 below). But for my present purpose I shall only make two points.

First, the very fact that the implied reader is 'implied' through the irony, the organisation, the rhetoric generally (and indeed how else can he be implied?), tends to bring us back to the ambiguity of the word rhetoric as (a) the techniques of 'persuasion', which 'implies' someone to persuade, and (b) the study of these techniques. For a long time Booth's work was regarded more as a study of techniques, and in a sense that ambiguity remains in much subsequent work, even in Genette, and in Booth's later *Rhetoric of irony* (1974). Perhaps it is inherent to critical discourse in general.

Second, Booth's notion of implied author, and indirectly that of implied reader, is distinctly linked to a moral judgment. For although the narrator may be a criminal or an idiot, the image of the implied author is not that of a criminal or an idiot, a certain 'distance' is established (by various means); or, if that distance is not sufficiently clear between the unpleasant values of a character (or a narrator-character) and those of the implied author, Booth wants to know where the author stands. Distance is thus a criterion, hence the importance of irony. As we shall see, irony is rejected by Barthes (perhaps influenced by Nietzsche for whom this was a symptom of decadence) as a mark of the 'classic' novel, and is said to have disappeared from modern writing. For Booth, however, the author 'makes his reader as he makes his second self [the implied author], and the most successful reading is one in which the created selves, author and reader, can find complete agreement' (1961: 138). Thus the implied reader and the implied author are caught up in that moral judgment, albeit a liberal one, since the implied reader identifies with the values of the implied author, at least for the reading-time, subordinating his own beliefs, However, this identification may fail, not just in insufficiently distanced works which

Booth would regard as inferior, but, precisely, in certain modern works of what he calls 'infinitely unstable irony', such as those of Beckett, who 'refuses to declare himself, however subtly, *for* any stable proposition, even the opposite of whatever proposition his irony vigorously denies' (Booth 1974: 240).

In a fascinating book, *The reader in the text* (1980), edited by Susan Suleiman (to whose introductory survey I am indebted for half of the above paragraph and for some of what follows), Suleiman points out that the notions of implied author and implied reader are relevant today, not because they are linked to ethical judgments, but because they are *interpretive constructs*, a fact not sufficiently emphasised and perhaps not fully recognised by Booth himself. And as interpretive constructs they 'participate in the circularity of all interpretation. I construct the image of the implied author and implied reader gradually as I read a work, and then use the images I have constructed to validate my reading. The full recognition of this circularity does not render the notion of implied author and implied reader superfluous, but it does relativize them' (Suleiman 1980: 11).

The notion of implied reader as ideal interpreter of the implied author gave way, in America and particularly for poetry, to that of ideal reader in the sense of an amalgam of actual but thoroughly informed readers. In Riffaterre's structuralist stylistics (1966, 1971a) the reader is a 'super-reader' who, in the case of Baudelaire's *Les chats* (1966) is composed of everyone from Baudelaire, his translators and critics, including Jakobson, to Riffaterre himself; for Fish (1970), the 'informed reader', for Culler (1975), the 'qualified' reader. But the new 'subjectivist' critics like Norman Holland and David Bleich, no doubt reacting against the 'objectivist fallacy' and other exclusions, have made a return to the classroom Richards of *Practical criticism* (1929), though in a more sophisticated and psychoanalytically oriented way, by analysing the fantasies of actual students responding to poems (see especially Holland 1968, Bleich 1976 vs. Holland 1976). As I shall not be using their specific notions in this book, I shall say no more about them here, but they could be borne in mind when I analyse certain traditional critics' reaction to *The Turn of the Screw*, and the way these unconsciously 'act out' the governess's 'symptoms' (chapter 6).

The 'actual' reader has also been dealt with sociologically and historically, not only in simple research on the reading public, but in analyses of how sociological changes:

in the composition (and consequently in the ideology and taste) of a national reading public have contributed to the emergence of new literary forms. Ian Watt's classic study, *The Rise of the Novel* (1957), attempted to answer this question by examining the works of Defoë, Richardson and Fielding in light of the changing social conditions and ideology of the eighteenth-century English middle class reading public. (Suleiman 1980: 33)

Georg Lukács is perhaps the best-known figure in a more Marxist theory of the novel, and his disciple Lucien Goldmann in *Le dieu caché* (1955), 'went further than Watt, however, for he sought to give an explicit (essentially Marxist) theoretical account of this relationship... According to Goldmann's model, all great works of literature express the 'vision of the world' of a specific social class – a class to which the writer himself belongs, and which constitutes, therefore, both the source and the destination of his works' (Suleiman 1980: 33). But as Suleiman points out (and Jacques Leenhardt in his essay within Suleiman's book), the model does not sufficiently take into account 'the situation of rupture that has characterized the relationship between "serious" writers and the bourgeois reading public (which is the only real public they have had) in France since the mid-nineteenth century. This rupture and its consequences were analysed by Sartre in *Qu'est-ce que la littérature?* (1947), and by Barthes in *Le degré zéro de l'écriture* (1953)' (1980: 34). Other research on 'real' readers are the attempts by Teun Van Dijk (1972, 1975b, 1976) to evolve a generative grammar of types of texts according to experiments with the reactions of real readers to certain texts given to them: 'at least some groups of speakers of a language can produce and interpret a potentially infinite number of different literary texts [as they do sentences]' (Van Dijk 1972: 184). And Culler himself suggests (in a brilliant paper in Suleiman's volume) a transformational grammar of actual readings, without, however, proposing to do it himself.

Meanwhile, in Europe, the phenomenological movement had produced Roman Ingarden and various followers. Ingarden's theory of the work of art (1931; trans. 1960, 1973) is a purely philosophical one, that is to say, it is an inquiry into the ontological status of the work of art, but thereby also an inquiry into our apprehension of it. The work of art is an 'intentional' object, that is, a product of acts of consciousness, an object different from 'ideal' objects in that it is subject to contingencies, and not eternal in the sense that, say, a triangle is eternal. It is also different from 'real' objects in that it transcends itself by designating something other than itself, as does a

word or a sentence. Analysis must therefore eschew both psycho-
logism and empiricism, to be replaced by what he calls 'eidetic'
reduction (*eidos*: essence, i.e. reduced to its essences).

This in practice seems to mean considering the different 'strata' of
the work: the sound-strata (Ingarden: ch. 4), the units of meaning
which combine into sequences and sentence patterns (chs. 5 and 6),
the stratum of the objects represented, i.e. the world of the novelist
(ch. 7), and the stratum of schematised objects, e.g. the implied or
stated viewpoints from which this 'world' is seen (chs. 8 and 9). In
their account of Ingarden, Wellek and Warren (1949) and Miner
(1976) after them add a fifth stratum, that of 'represented objectivities', including the (not indispensable) 'metaphysical' qualities
(the holy, the tragic, the sublime, etc.) that art enables us to
apprehend (ch. 10). But this is a misunderstanding of Ingarden, for
whom these 'represented objectivities' are manifest in all strata, or
perhaps more particularly as a function of the object stratum.[7] In
this pyramid, reminiscent of the 'levels' of analysis insisted on by
Roman Jakobson in particular and the Prague School in general
(phonological, morphological, syntactical, rhetorical), each stratum
needs its subordinate in order to exist.

For Ingarden the 'sound-stratum' (the physical means of expression, or what Structuralists call the signifier) is not to be
confused with 'the actual sounding of words', which belong to
performance. In chapter 14 Ingarden admits that readers may alter
pronunciation in silent reading, and thus 'read the work in such a
manner that they intentionally think of the word sounds [theirs] as
belonging to the work itself, and in this way *change* the work itself'
(1973: 368). But of course this applies even more to all the other
strata. Yet Ingarden insists that 'the founding of the stratum of units
of meaning in ideal concepts both protects the work ontically from
subjectivization and makes it possible, at least in principle, to
change it back to its original form', and that therefore, 'despite the
indisputable fact of its "life", the literary work cannot be psycholo-
gized' (1973: 368).

As Earl Miner puts it in 'The objective fallacy' (1976), discussing
Ingarden, we should

postulate four entities: an original creator of aesthetic knowledge about the
world, a physical means of expression, and via the physical means of
expression a re-knowing of the created knowledge by those who are capable
of reading the expression. We must recognize what literary history shows us
with irrefutable fact: that we readers are incapable of knowing *Hamlet*

exactly as Shakespeare knew it or exactly as other readers have known and will know it in another time. These differences are real but do not destroy the integrity of the work. (p. 27)

Earlier Miner had insisted: 'no scientist would consider his knowledge of an object to be itself an object' (p. 25). That is unclear (his knowledge of an object may not be *the* object, but *is* an object, e.g. a model), and perhaps a little naive. A scientist's knowledge of an object consists *also* of knowing what other scientists have said. Moreover his interpretation of the object (e.g. the behaviour of molecules) is what he regards the object as being, until disproved. In other words, the text of nature also changes through these different knowledges. However, it is true that we literary people find it very difficult not to confuse 'our' reading, enriched by those of others, with the text. Moreover, 'eidetic' reduction is itself a critical human activity, imposing a system, and Ingarden's attempts to define an ontological existence for the literary work of art seem to Miner to reduce it to the same status as the 'real' world.[8]

Despite his insistence on the theoretical possibility of changing a work 'back to its original form', Ingarden does however also insist on its 'life' through readings and aesthetic perceptions, which he calls *realisations* (*Konkretization* in the German translation, *konkretyzacja* in the original Polish), and which transform the text. He was the first to formulate the notion of gaps of indeterminacy (found however, already in James, see 'the glory of the gap' chapter 8, p. 227), which the reader fills in as the 'realizes' the work. Nevertheless there seem to be, for Ingarden, true and false realizations of a literary work, a notion that has been criticised by one of his disciples, Wolfgang Iser (*The implied reader* 1974: 14n) as essentially classical (Suleiman).

Iser's conception, however, turns out, as Suleiman shows, to be not very different in practice, as opposed to his theory, which insists that 'the work is more than the text' (Iser 1974: 274), for the realisations impose a pattern on it through selection, anticipations and their retrospective modifications and other similar reader-activities (see Genette, below). Later he goes further and says that 'the potential text is infinitely richer than any of its individual realizations' (1974: 280), suggesting that all individual realisations are acceptable and enrich the text through the reader's creative role, 'thus allowing for a high degree of "free" variation' (Suleiman 1980: 23), which enables him to distinguish between a contemporary and a later Implied Reader, who is 'transhistorical', the later one filling in 'gaps' unperceived by the earlier one.

On the other hand, he suggests that it is ultimately the text itself that directs the reader's realization of it. Iser does not treat the question of idiosyncratic readings directly, but his discussion clearly implies that only a limited number of patterns are realizable for a given text (in which case some readings must be considered idiosyncratic), and more importantly his own readings of specific works ... leave no doubt that he considers some realizations more correct, more true to the intentions of the text, than others. (Suleiman 1980: 23–4)

Suleiman's analysis is masterly, and points indirectly to the same contradiction noted in Ingarden, and more directly to Iser's link with Booth, in the fact that, for Iser, certain judgments (e.g. as to the sham values in *Vanity Fair*),

'have to be inferred. They are the blanks which the reader is supposed to fill in, thus bringing his own criticism to bear' (1974: 113). This notion of inference, as well as the clear formulation of the conclusion that the inference 'is supposed' to lead to, render problematic the subsequent statement that texts are infinitely richer than any individual realization. The notion of reading implicit in Iser's analysis is here very close to Booth's notion; though one certainly need not object to this, it is important to realize that Iser's theoretical description of the reading process allows for a great deal more latitude in individual realization than does his actual critical practice. (Suleiman 1980: 24).

That, of course, and as we shall see in later chapters, is one of the plagues (or perhaps a saving grace) of literary theory: the 'system' never quite gells with the practice. It is also inherent in the ambiguity of the word rhetoric I have noted before (pp. 12, 30). This ambiguity is more obvious, because less contorted, in the work of the European Structuralists and Semioticians (cp. p. 96).

For them, there is no question of an implied reader as 'ideal' interpreter (since they do not 'interpret' or evaluate), but rather an analysis of how meaning functions in a text, and of what are the codes (cultural conventions) that enable the 'inscribed' reader (inscribed in the codes which the author has inscribed in the text) to make 'sense' of the text.

This is where the *narrataire* (narratee) of Genette (1972) and Prince (1973) replaces Booth's implied reader. For the implied reader paralleled the implied author and was, as we saw, his ideal interpreter. The *narrataire* however parallels the *narrateur*, as analogy to *destinateur/destinataire* (addresser/addressee), and the narrator is the one who speaks the narrative, and therefore implicitly speaks to someone. Narratees in fact can be analysed in exactly the same way as Booth analysed narrators. They can be intrusive or (more usually) effaced; they can be dramatised inside a story (e.g. when a story within a story is told by someone to someone in the outside or frame story, or even, for that matter, when a character in an unframed story tells another character something that has just happened to him, or explains it in his own terms, or tells his background, etc.); they can be one or several, and they could, I suppose, even be 'unreliable', corresponding to Booth's 'unreliable narrator' (e.g. in James, some of Douglas's listeners in the prologue to *The Turn of the Screw*, see chapter 7, p. 173).

But Genette does not really exploit this notion, though it is implicit in his whole analysis of a narrative's 'discourse' (*sjužet* or organisation), as opposed to 'story' or *fabula* (1972). I shall be dealing in detail with Genette's categories of discourse in chapter 12. Here I will only mention certain aspects in their relation to the implicit narratee (and also by way of explanation of certain terms I shall be using before chapter 12). The three main categories are time, mood and voice.

Under time, Genette deals with order, duration and frequence. His treatment of duration (pace, i.e. pause, scene, summary, ellipsis) is fairly traditional, merely tidying up what the post-Jamesian critics have said about 'telling' and 'showing', but his analysis of order and frequence is very revealing. Order is divided broadly into *analepsis* (flashback) and *prolepsis* (flash-forward). Each can be external or internal, e.g. an analepsis can go back to a time before the beginning of the story (external) and this usually happens early on, to explain the past of a character or given situation, or later on, as recalls (repetitive internal analepses) or to fill in a previous ellipsis (completive internal analepsis). Or it can be mixed, that is, going back in *range* to a time before the beginning of the story, but rejoining a point inside the story in its *amplitude*. For instance (my example), Herrera's explanation of his past (as Vautrin) to Lucien de Rubempré in Balzac's *Splendeurs et misères des courtisanes* tells the story up to the point (inside the story) when he came upon Lucien about to shoot himself by the river. Genette's examples are from Homer: the famous analepsis about Odysseus' wound goes back in *range* several decades but has an *amplitude* of two or three days (the hunt), then leaps back to the nurse washing Odysseus' feet (external analepsis). But when Odysseus arrives on the shores of Phaeacia and tells his previous adventures (untold by the omniscient narrator before) up to the point of his arrival, this is a mixed analepsis, filling in a huge ellipsis, but also explaining the arrival; the reason for the analepsis being 'this is why I am here'. An analepsis can also be partial (giving only part of the information) or complete.

Prolepses work in the same way, although they are rarer since they destroy suspense. They are not to be confused with *amorces* or hints about the future, for they are definite statements by the narrator, giving information, earlier in the narrative, about a later point in the story (or after the story), the canonic formula being 'to anticipate', or 'we shall see later that' (inside the story) or 'X eventually married Y'/'today the house is deserted' etc. (outside the story), e.g. in Proust, the allusion to the death of Charlus, or to the marriage of Mlle de Saint-Loup, which *were to occur* after the end of the story. The completive prolepsis fills in advance a later ellipsis, the repetitive prolepsis tells in advance something that will be retold later.

Under frequence, Genette points out that one can tell once what happens once (singulative); or n times what happens n times (also singulative since several same events are each time told singly); or n times what happens once (repetitive, e.g. from different viewpoints, or to represent obsession, etc.); or once what happens n times. This last he calls the *iterative*. It is used chiefly to set a scene, a society, to introduce a character or his family, their habits and customs (every day he would go and buy his paper), and it has its own tense in French (the imperfect), while English, having established the iterative nature with *would*, *used to*, or locutions like *often*, *daily*, etc. can rarely keep this up without clumsiness, and slides into its only past (*went* . . .). The moment of the action is always clearly marked however, with the *passé simple* in French, and locutions at least in English (one day, that morning, etc.). Genette shows how Proust made a particularly full and original use of the iterative, each *soirée* or *dîner des Guermantes*, though particular, coming to represent all *soirées*, all dinners.

Obviously the reader is very much involved in all the reconstruction of the 'real' order and the singulative nature of the events; analepses tend to explain things to him, while prolepses arouse his expectations, as does the iterative (since something singulative must occur for a story to exist). It must be said, however, that Genette rather loses sight of his narratee, and tends to describe these techniques objectively as techniques. This is perhaps most evident under *mood*, where he has nothing very original to say. He divides mood into distance and perspective. But he considerably reduces Booth's complex notion of ironic distance by merely analysing types of discourse (direct, indirect, free indirect) according to traditional French stylistics (the notion of 'free indirect style' goes back to Bally, 1912, or even further, as *verschleierte Rede*, to Kalepsky, 1899, and has been much studied since).[9] Although his account of these is subtle (see chapter 12 here), the reader's 'creative role' is quite forgotten. Similarly for perspective, he simply falls back on Pouillon (1946, see chapter 12 here). It is only with *voice* that the narratee returns, obviously since voice deals with the narrator's narrative instance (not of course to be confused with the writer's writing instance), before, during or after the events told, and with narrative levels (stories within stories), and with person (a narrator telling his own story or that of someone else, i.e. in Booth's terms, 'dramatised' to a greater or lesser degree). And where there is a voice speaking there must be an ear hearing. Yet even here, the narratee is very much implicit, and we tend to read Genette as a technical account, fascinating, often revealing, but 'objective' and scientific.

Roland Barthes's *S/Z* (1970, trans. 1974) is the first sign of his shift away from the more rigid structural analysis of his earlier period (e.g. *Analyse structurale des récits*, 1966). It is a remarkable study, line by line or passage by passage (*lexia*), of *Sarrasine*, a long short story by Balzac. And it is a much closer analysis of the reader's creative (or, at times, uncreative) role than Genette's. Barthes proposes that in every narrative we may find five 'codes' or voices, conventions that function as exits from the text, or signals that exercise our minds in a specific way. The first two are (my additions and examples in square brackets):

(1) *The code of actions* (the empirical voice) – which he unfortunately calls 'proaieretic', but I will stick to action code. This signals, not just the 'functions' in Propp's sense, and not just the plot, but sequences, great and small, that start and end (departure, journey, arrival; an orgy, its segments, its end; to laugh, to stop laughing; to stand on the threshold, to enter, etc.), not necessarily in one consecutive bit of text but also scattered, at a distance, over the text. [For example, *refusal to work*, in Melville's *Bartleby*, occurs many times in varied forms, but always with the same formula 'I would prefer not to', and of course it structures the text; or, less structural, Bartleby stands, first on the threshold, later staring out of the window, etc.] The action code is said to be the voice of experience, of the *déjà-écrit, déjà-fait*, rousing our expectations on the line of least

resistance since we know (for instance) that a door opening will lead to an entrance or exit, and of course transgressions of this expectation cause a 'scandal', or at least a surprise, on which suspense is based. [Frequently by a simple shift of viewpoint at a crucial moment, for instance when Dmitri Karamazov looks in through the window at his father, and there we leave him, so that the whole novel can play on the suspense as to who killed old Karamazov – a technique much abused in film thrillers, by simple camera-shift, e.g. the famous shower-scene in Hitchcock's *Psycho*. And of course the fantastic plays on this 'scandal': a door opens and no one visible comes in.]

(2) *The hermeneutic code* (the voice of truth), whereby a mystery or enigma is either quickly resolved or thoroughly postponed by means of partial answers, delayed answers, lying answers, false clues, implicit but false syllogisms. In a sense there can be an enigma in every line, especially at the beginning, and certainly the title (who is *Bartleby*? Who or what is *Sarrasine*?), but most minor enigmas are resolved as we read, and are what make us read. [Narratives which depend on mystery will exploit the hermeneutic code more than narratives which depend on irony. (Booth's distinction: with irony we watch a character making mistakes because we know something he doesn't know; with mystery we share his mistakes because we don't know more than he does.) The classic detective story for instance is one long exploitation of the hermeneutic code, more than others, as is the fantastic, and as is, in a weaker way, much romantic fiction or what the French realistic school called the *romanesque*, which it rejected (see chapter 4); whereas realistic fiction prefers to explain all to the reader, reducing suspense to simple narrative suspense (what happens next) and avoiding mystery, or clearing it up quickly if introduced.]

These two codes are both linear (sequential) and irreversible: obviously one must not depart before one journeys (except in analepsis, clearly marked), and the solution of a mystery must not be given to the reader before it is delayed. The reader knows this, and reacts accordingly. The other three codes are non-sequential and reversible, that is, they can occur anywhere and in any order. They are:

(3) *The semic code* (the voice of the person), which is simply the way a character is built up, through identical 'semes' (femininity, grace, beauty, wealth, poverty, miserliness, hardness, cruelty etc.) that converge upon a proper name. These can be grouped, as in a

static 'portrait', or scattered throughout the text, gradually constructing the character, or of course both. And here too the reader
follows the code, constructing his own vision of the character,
different from anyone else's vision, since the character does not exist
except through these 'semes' [and, it must be said, through his
actions, which also construct him; see also ch. 4, p. 95, and ch. 7,
for the fantasmatic aspect of this procedure].

(4) *The referential code* (the voice of science, or 'the big voice of
small science'), through which the author (and here it *is* the author)
gives us information about the world (chronological, geographical,
moral, cultural), often directly in authorial comment, but also in
allusions, to art, medicine, law, life in the provinces etc. These
function like expanded maxims. 'Life, in the classic text, becomes in
fact a nauseating mixture of common opinions, a smooth layer of
received ideas' (Barthes 1974: 206). The referential code, although
derived from books, establishes 'reality', turns culture into nature,
appealing to our general knowledge, to another text, *déjà-connu*, and
Balzac's novels are said to be clotted with it (*empoissé*). Barthes adds
that the only way the text can 'criticize [its own] stereotype', 'vomit
it up', is through irony, but that irony is merely another stereotype,
part of the referential code since it appeals, in collusion, to the
reader's cultural knowledge. 'In fact the cultural code occupies the
same position as stupidity: how can stupidity be pinned down
without declaring oneself intelligent? How can one code be superior
to another without abusively closing off the plurality of codes?'
(1974: 206). His answer is, only in *écriture* (writing, in the modern
sense, as opposed to *littérature*, see below for *readerly/writerly* texts).
Elsewhere (1974: 98) he says that the function of *écriture* is 'to make
ridiculous, to annul the power (the intimidation) of one language
over another, to dissolve any metalanguage as soon as it is constituted'. [We are a long way from Booth, and this curt dismissal of
irony will seem unsatisfactory to Anglo-American critics who have
done so much complex work on it, from the new criticism onwards.
There is after all a sense in which everything in a text appeals to the
reader's knowledge and recognition of it, at varying levels.
However, Barthes's comments are very relevant to modern writing,
and I shall briefly return to the question of irony in my last
chapter.]

(5) *The symbolic code* (the voice of the symbol – which seems
curiously circular). This is perhaps Barthes's most weirdly idiosyncratic code, for he reduces it, in effect, to three 'entries' or 'routes'

into it, without ever quite explaining what he means by symbol: *the economic route*, which discovers the disappearance of all fake currency; *the route of castration* (as a symbolic psychic structure), which discovers the pandemic void of desire and the collapse of the creative chain (bodies and works); and *the rhetorical route*, which discovers the transgression of antithesis (inner/outer, feminine/masculine, etc.), 'the passage through the wall of opposites, the abolition of difference' (1974: 215). These 'routes' seem to apply specifically to *Sarrasine*, which is unique in representing both the symbolic structure of castration and a physical castration (a soprano-castrato), together with the success and riches brought by the latter. Barthes also makes an interesting distinction between 'character' (semic code), and 'figure', which is:

not a concentration of semes concentrated in a legal Name, nor can biography, psychology, or time encompass it: it is an illegal, impersonal, anachronistic configuration of symbolic relationships ...: the symbolic figure is completely reversible; it can be read in any direction. Thus, the child–woman and the narrator–father, momentarily effaced, can return, can overtake the queen–woman and the narrator–slave. As a symbolic ideality, the character has no chronological or biographical standing; he has no Name; he is nothing but a site for the passage (and return) of the figure. (1974: 68).

Whatever we may think of Barthes's codes as a theory, (which it is only partly, for he explicitly refuses to structure his codes into a system), his book is an exciting experience in reading, or rather in *writing*, for it exemplifies throughout his now well-known distinction between the 'readable' (*lisible*) text, which one reads passively, and the 'writable' (*scriptible*) modern text, which makes the reader not a consumer but a producer of the text. Richard Miller (1974) has translated these terms as *readerly* and *writerly*, which brilliantly avoids the more common distinction readable/unreadable. Thus the reader's creative role is ever present, even though reduced, as he shows, in the 'classic' text (readerly), as compared with the modern writerly text. But all texts have this creative role inscribed in them, it has simply been developed to a finer art in modern writing. Hence of course, the sudden critical interest in it, even if, alas, mostly analysed in classic readerly texts.

S/Z also shows how several codes can be present in one sentence (plurality of voices), or only one in a whole paragraph. And like Frye's five modes (see ch. 3 below), they can be useful to generic typology: certain types of narratives will exploit one code more than another (the referential code in realism for instance, or the hermeneutic in the detective story), or less skilfully (the referential code falls to pieces in science fiction and romance, see ch. 4, p. 101, and ch. 9, pp. 243–5, on 'the parallel story' or megatext). Similarly Frye shows that some of Shakespeare's comedies belong both to the high mimetic and the romance modes, or that it is possible to read *Antony and Cleopatra* not only as tragedy (high mimetic), but also, if weakeningly, as romance (a love story) or as myth. So Barthes's codes are also a question of predominance in any one text, but above all of plurality. I shall be making some use of them in chapter 5, on the encoded reader, with reference to several fantastic texts.

Another approach to the reader is that of Hans-Robert Jauss's aesthetics of reception, though others, notably Iser and Harald Weinrich (whose study of time in the novel, 1964, trans. 1973, is as interesting as Genette's) also form part of the group. Jauss's central notion, (as expounded in his article 'Literary history as a challenge to literary theory', 1970), is that of 'horizons of expectations', which we have already seen functioning in Genette (e.g. in prolepses) and in Barthes (e.g. the action and hermeneutic codes). But for Jauss the notion includes all codes, cultural, ethical, as well as specifically literary, and literary expectations can be roused not only by style, theme, and presumably by most of the techniques examined by Genette (pause, scene, analepsis etc. are all recognised as such by the reader, who then expects, say a description, or information about the past as soon as the 'marking' occurs, such as the pluperfect for analepsis), but also by *genre* (generic expectation), an aspect I have not yet properly touched on but will deal with in chapter 3, and others.

These horizons change, that is, a modern reading of a past work will be different from a contemporary one, and the task of *Rezeptionsgeschichte* (history of reception) is to reconstruct the horizons of expectations at the time of the work's publication, and thus to clarify the differences between the past and the present reception of a work. The reconstruction can use both extrinsic and intrinsic information. I must admit that I can see very little difference, except in theoretical rigour, between this aspect of Jauss and the very traditional historical criticism I was taught at Oxford: first find out the author's 'intentions', his historical and social situation, his relationship to other works, to current knowledge, etc. etc., and only then give your own judgment ('personal effusions' would probably have been my tutor's words).

However, the rigour is important, and the notion allows Jauss to examine the changes in understanding (of reader *and* author) arising from cultural, political and social changes, as well as the relationship between works appearing in the same period but received differently (or not received at all), which is always a fascinating and mysterious phenomenon. More dubious perhaps is his evaluative use of the notion, in the sense that it is the distance between the horizon of expectations and the work which determines the artistic nature of the work. A small distance means that little demand is made on the reader to change his horizons, a great distance applies to the masterpiece recognised only years or decades later. But as we all know, things are not so simple (or critics of contemporary works would never make mistakes); to put it crudely, a bestseller or a book that 'everyone talks about', is not *ipso facto* 'bad' and to be forgotten, nor is a non-seller, or a book no one talks about, *ipso facto* a misunderstood masterpiece to be integrated later into the corpus of 'literature'. As Suleiman (who also comments on this essay) points out: 'It seems especially difficult to make such a claim without considering the possibility of *different* horizons of expectations co-existing among different publics in a given society' (1980: 37) and later she suggests even different 'publics' within one 'audience'. Her example is the audience of courtly love poems being different from the audience of the *Chanson de Roland*, 'although it may also have been the audience of some of the same works'. I am not sure that it was different, but be that as it may, it is easier to see the question in modern terms: we may read Joyce (which audience Y will not), but also detective stories (which audience Y will), and comic strips (audience Z), etc., and although we may read comic strips quite differently from the way audience Z reads them, we do as it were 'join' Z to a certain extent. We belong, in fact, in Stanley Fish's felicitous term, to different 'interpretative communities' (1976a), which fluctuate and overlap.

Closely connected with this notion (in effect, not in influence, for it came long before), is the theory of Mikhail Bakhtin (1929a, trans. 1973), who makes a distinction between the 'dialogical' (or polyphonic) novel (Dostoevsky) and the 'monological' (Tolstoy). This does not of course mean a novel in dialogue as opposed to a novel with no dialogue. In the dialogical novel (which he traces back, historically, to the carnival and to the Menippean satire), the author refuses to 'delimit' his characters, to have the last word on them, or for that matter to delimit himself (to make it clear 'where he stands', as Booth would say) – hence the strong influence of

Dostoevsky on modern writing (Faulkner, Sarraute, and others). No man is ever exactly what others think him, or even what he thinks himself to be at any one moment, no man ever 'coincides with himself', let alone with another's 'word' on him. And this doesn't apply merely to the author but to the characters. The character seems constantly in revolt against his own author's tendency to delimit him, and is having a constant metatextual dialogue (implicit, between the lines, in parody or many other means, analysed in Bakhtin's ch. 5, 'The word', and including the 'interpersonal features' I mentioned earlier as a present concern of linguists), with the author, with himself, with an imagined other, over and above any conventional dialogue he may have with other characters. The dialogical text is essentially an ambiguous text, leaving characters and their ideologies open-ended. The monological novel, on the other hand, however complex, and however many different viewpoints may be set against each other, is essentially delimited by the author's controlling power. Thus, although it seems, with its frequent faithful portrait of society on a large canvas, closer to 'reality' than the dialogical novel, it is ultimately more of an artefact, at the same time giving the reader a finalised picture, letting him absorb it passively.

Bakhtin was one of the Russian post- (and anti-) Formalists, who had to 'disappear' for many years (by administrative exile to a small university in Mordovia). But his influence has been immense, and eventually gave rise to the present Tartu school of semiotics, of which Yuri Lotman is the best-known exponent in the West (e.g. *The structure of the artistic text* and many articles), as well as Boris Uspensky (*Poetics of composition* 1970, trans. 1974).

Other Western semioticians have studied readability in a more linguistic perspective, notably elements such as redundancies, in the sense used by information theory; that is, repetitions for the clear reception of a message despite 'noise' or disturbance; or, in linguistics, the repetition of gender in a sentence (The girl ... she ... her) or of the plural marking (*les petites filles sont jolies*), a notion clearly transposable to the repetition of information in narrative; or the interpersonal features I mentioned on p. 23; or the function of presupposition as analysed in the 'possible worlds' or presuppositional logic of Grice (1975), or Keenan (1971). Umberto Eco, for instance, has analysed a weird brief story by Alphonse Allais, in which Raoul and Marguerite, a happily but quarrelling married couple, each gets an anonymous note saying that the other will appear at a masked ball, the wife disguised as a 'pirogue congolaise' and the husband as a 'templier fin de siècle'. Each makes up an excuse for absence and, at the ball, the 'pirogue congolaise' and the 'templier fin de siècle' meet.

The reader's presuppositions have of course been played upon to lead him to expect the obvious confrontation. But when each tears off the other's disguise, 'Lui, ce n'était pas Raoul./Elle, ce n'était pas Marguerite'. Any conceivable explanation the reader may work out for this situation is then contradicted by the statement that they both learnt their lesson from it and never quarrelled again (Eco 1978).

But here we are in what Barthes calls the undecidable. And I shall end this survey of reader-oriented criticism with a brief consideration of the 'new' hermeneutics, whose debate agitated the pages of *Critical Inquiry* a few years ago ('The Limits of Pluralism', 3/3 Spring 1977, and subsequent numbers). Traditional hermeneutics goes back to the nineteenth century (Schleiermacher, Dilthey, Heidegger, Gadamer, see R. D. Palmer 1969), and its aim was to get away from subjectivist interpretation and to establish universally valid interpretation. Modern hermeneutics, whose chief spokesman is Paul de Man (e.g. 1971, 1973), is just the opposite, in fact Geoffrey Hartman (1976) has explained it as 'negative' hermeneutics, since its basic assumption is that the notion of universally valid interpretation is untenable. I should have thought that was obvious, but the violence of the debate has shown that many more things were at stake than the determinacy of meaning.

3.2.2 The explosion of the Jakobson diagram. The movement in fact parallels the Derridean deconstructionism in France but has its own source in American and English logic, notably Pierce and his *interpretant* as a sign (see p. 26) that generates a new sign, and Austin's theory of the performative. Paul de Man (1973), following Pierce's notion that rhetoric and grammar are heterogeneous modes (rhetoric studying the infinite process of interpretant-signs, grammar the formal conditions necessary for signs to have meaning, logic the formal conditions of the truth of signs), also questions the Structuralist assumption that they are on a par. He assumes an absolute discontinuity between them, in fact replacing grammar with Austin's notion of the performative, but passed through, as it were, a Nietzschean conception of rhetoric as aporia, that deconstructs its own performance: its figures are to be read not as forms but as dynamic and interacting forms, rather like Derrida's constant differing/deferring of meaning (*différance*, spelt with *a*). As Shoshanna Felman (1978) points out in her (sympathetic) account of Paul de Man, the whole notion of a science of literature is impossible in such a theory, which by definition cannot predict or account for the functioning of figures nor control the rigour of its own rhetoric. But what seems to have frightened some of the participants most in the debate is the loss of textual authority.

It is true that Nietzsche and Derrida are important influences, and Nietzsche means 'nihilism', a bogey-word. Derrida is one of the post-Hegelians whom Rosset (1977, discussed in chapter 1), puts in what he calls 'philosophical illusionism', which consists in announcing the meaning without showing it. At its origin is Hegel,

> who discovers in each thing the manifestation of Reason, of the Idea, of the Mind, but omits to describe the nature of this Mind, this Idea, this Reason. With extraordinary speculative power ... he develops the circumstances, the mediations, the ruses ... through which meaning is realised as the becoming takes shape. But we learn nothing as to the nature of meaning itself, unless we admit, with Hegel, that Idea, Reason and Mind are sufficiently clear notions to need no definition or comment. (Rosset 1977: 54–5, my translation.)

And Rosset claims that the modern Hegelians, from Mallarmé via Bataille to Lacan and Derrida, use the same 'illusionism' except that now the meaning is no longer announced as there, *hic et nunc*, a sort of gift in the reconciliation with the present after laborious mediations, but for ever 'postponed' in an unfinalised dialectic of perpetual difference and deferring (Derrida's *différance*) which both fissures and retards presence. The meaning, as in James's *The Figure in the Carpet*, runs away, contained wholly in its evocation (pp. 55–9).

But isn't that precisely, what is happening today? It is certainly what is reflected in some of the texts I shall be analysing. There is, I feel, a certain 'fudge', as I called it earlier, in Rosset's dismissal of both Derrida and Lacan as post-Hegelian 'illusionists', when each in his own way has done most to demonstrate, however complexly, the same position as his own, namely that meaning is an illusion, absolutely necessary to us but an illusion. For Lacan, as for Freud before him but ignored by most Freudians, the unconscious is not simply a text to be read and interpreted (i.e. limited, by exclusion, to one significance or set of significances), it is *also* a faculty of reading. It was by listening to hysterical discourse that Freud discovered, not only that there was an unconscious, but that he was deeply implicated, through reading that unconscious, in reading his own, in other words that this other discourse was itself an active reading of his own unconscious. *L'inconscient, c'est le discours de l'Autre*, says Lacan (1966: 16 – 'l'Autre' with a capital letter being not just a specifically invested other or *autre* but a very structure of the unconscious), or again, in the preface: '*dans le langage, notre message nous vient de l'Autre, et pour l'énoncer jusqu'au bout, sous forme inversée* (p. 9, 'in language our message comes from the Other, and, to be precise: in inverted form'). Above all, everything is left open in an infinite displacement, or, in Lacan's terms, an infinite 'rehandling of signifiers' (retelling, redreaming, re-interpreting, in different terms), an infinite game of mirrors, an infinite taking flight: 'If analytical discourse [my translation] shows that meaning as such is sexual, this is only a way of accounting for its *limits*. There is nowhere a last word.' And a little later: 'Meaning indicates only the direction, only the sense towards which it fails' (1973a: 66). We can't help being reminded here of Bakhtin's theory of fiction. The psychoanalytical situation, which is based on transfer, that is, love, or 'the acting out of the reality of the unconscious' (which here apparently *does* have a 'reality'; Lacan 1973a: 158) is a situation in which this constant reading, this constant re-interpreting, is done by love, by an interpreter caught up in the love-relationship that constitutes the transfer. It is done by love, but through language (speech, dreams, omissions, silences, resistance, forgetting to turn up, etc.). Similarly sexuality, so atrociously simplified by well-bred and half-baked Freudians, is not just a literal physical fact but a multiplicity of conflicting elements, just as neurosis, for Freud, is not 'simply' due to the 'repression' of sexuality but to 'a conflict between two forces' (1910: 223), the second (i.e. repression) negating and subverting the first, which 'returns' with equal (strength) in other symptoms. The meaning of sexuality, in other words, is its own obstruction. Sexuality is not something that is disguised or hidden by discourse, by rhetoric, it is itself a rhetoric because essentially ambiguous (the two opposing elements of an antithesis in Barthes's symbolic code).

The same basic link with Rosset's position can be found in Derrida's theory of textual deconstruction, in his infinite regressions through *la trace* and *l'écriture*. For both Derrida and Lacan, reality is a *béance*, an emptiness, filled in by man and his manic systems of meaning, and if they can justly be called post-Hegelian, they are also post-Nietzschean. Suleiman (1980: 17), in her account of modern hermeneutics, gives a passage from Nietzsche's *On the genealogy of morals*, quoted by this 'new Yale School': 'Whatever exists ... is again and again reinterpreted to new ends, taken over, transformed, and all events in the organic world are a subduing, a becoming master, and all subduing and becoming master involves fresh interpretation, an adaptation through which any previous 'meaning' and 'purpose' are necessarily obscured and even obliterated' (Nietzsche, trans. 1969: 77–8). And she also quotes a brief sentence by Hartman (1976) which defines the project of hermeneutics: 'On its older function of saving the text, of tying it once again to the life of the mind, is superimposed the new one of doubting, by a parodistic or playful movement, master theories that claim to have overcome the past, the dead, the false.' But the sentence goes on: 'There is no Divine or Dialectical Science which can help us purify history absolutely, to pass in our lifetime a last judgment on it.' And that, surely, is the point, the 'crisis' of criticism (same Greek root).[10]

The debate in *Critical Inquiry* (1977, 'The limits of pluralism', 3/3) was both high flown and ultimately negative (exactly like Hartman's description of modern hermeneutics, which, though high-flying, is proudly a negative hermeneutics). The very title gave leave to doubt whether (strictly) *pluralism* can be 'limited', and indeed the debate continued over several numbers with Morse Peckham's 'The infinitude of pluralism' (3/4, Peckham being against), and Meyer Abrams's response in 4/1, and J. R. Kincaid's 'Coherent readers, incoherent texts' (3/4). The debate moreover, had arisen out of Booth's review of Abrams's *The Natural Supernaturalism*, a fact that Abrams did not fail to recall, so that there was a slightly unedifying aspect of *côterie*-quibbling. However, the main issue was the elimination of 'valid' meaning in deconstructive interpretation which 'goes beyond the limits of pluralism, by making impossible anything that we would account as literary and cultural history' (Abrams, himself a pluralist'). And, concomitantly with this main issue, the equality of interpretation (are all interpretations equally valid?), and therefore the 'authority' of the text. Both Booth and Abrams argued against the elimination of textual authority (the 'supporting medium' for Booth), and with it the unicity of the writing subject, which however, Hillis Miller declared to be an illusion:

The poem, like all texts, is 'unreadable' if by 'readable' one means open to a single, definitive, univocal interpretation. In fact, neither the 'obvious' reading nor the 'deconstructionist' reading is 'univocal'. Each contains, necessarily, its enemy within itself, is itself both host and parasite. The deconstructionist reading contains the obvious one and vice versa. Nihilism is an inalienable presence within Occidental metaphysics, both in poems and in the criticism of poems. (1977: 447)

The Jakobson diagram, in fact, has been exploded: no addresser, no addressee, no reference, no message, only (perhaps), a contact and a vast metalanguage, which is declared by Lacan not to be one: 'Il n'y a pas de métalangage, plus aphoristiquement, il n'y a pas d'Autre de l'Autre' (1966: 313). Or as Abrams vividly put it (blaming Derrida):

What Derrida's conclusion comes to is that no sign or chain of signs can have a determinate meaning. But it seems to me that Derrida reaches this conclusion by a process which, in its own way, is no less dependent on an origin, ground, and end, and which is no less remorselessly 'teleological' than the most rigorous of the metaphysical systems that he uses his conclusions to deconstruct. His origin and ground are his graphocentric premises, the closed chamber of texts for which he invites us to abandon our ordinary realm of experience in speaking, hearing, reading and understanding language. And from such a beginning we move to a foregone conclusion. For Derrida's chamber of texts is a sealed echo-chamber in which meanings are reduced to a ceaseless echolalia, a vertical and lateral reverberation from sign to sign of ghostly non-presences emanating from no voice, intended by no one referring to nothing, bombinating in a void. (1977a: 431)

In the next number of *Critical Inquiry* Morse Peckham attacks Barthes, Derrida and Kermode for not accepting 'the perfectly obvious consequences of their notions' [that any interpretation is as good as another], and compares deconstructionism to the 'banana' phenomenon: if you repeat 'banana' or any other word often enough it becomes pure sound without a signified. Deconstructionism is merely a logical result of structuralism. Peckham urges us rather to concentrate on 'semiotic transformation' of context for our response to any given sign (since 'the meaning of a sign is the response to that sign, or, to be a touch more precise, is the determination of the appropriate response', 1977: 805). From this he derives three corollaries: '(1) Theoretically any sign can elicit all responses . . . ; all interpretations are equally valid. (2) Theoretically all signs can, in any individual organism, elicit but a single response. Indeed, in instances of extreme psychosis, that is exactly what can and does happen. Yet behaviour that can be subsumed by these two corollaries is extremely rare. (3) Sign response is controlled, and ultimately can be controlled only by force ... (pp. 805–6). And he argues for a finite pluralism, 'since presumably the number of semiotic patterns in Abrams's Romantic texts [in that instance, but meaning any texts] is not infinite' (p. 807).

Well of course there can be no 'last word'. The debate, like all quarrels, seemed to me to over-dramatise. Derrida is not the Nietzschean monster he is represented to be (and nor was Nietzsche). Deconstructive criticism simply accepts the void, but only in the sense that it refuses definitive meanings, and 'plays' with the endlessness of signification as already present in the text itself. The very contradiction of endlessly using the meaning-making machine of language to demonstrate the endless flight of meaning is inherent to our self-conscious and self-reflexive stage of culture. Perhaps it is the very playfulness (Derrida's and Lacan's puns and fun with language) with which authorial authority and textual textuality is deconstructed that so exacerbates.

And it is exacerbating: the terror of a textual void. And yet, and yet: is not this also a philosophical reflection of what occurs at a much more popular level? Is not 'Derrida's conclusion', so colourfully described by Abrams as 'a sealed echo chamber ... a ceaseless echolalia ... bombinating in a void', also a truthful representation of the unease we all feel, without admitting it (for it's not done), in our now 'global village', itself a ceaseless echolalia of ideologies, dialogues of the deaf, repeated 'banana' slogans, 'banana' economics, 'banana' politics, and daily news of massacres, political murders, revolutions, genocides and famines that become 'banana' to us unless and until we feel personally threatened. And if the 'real' really is meaningless, if we can only perceive its utter singularity, its 'idiocy', to use Rosset's term, in a drunken void or a love void (*or* through the language 'double' of art and philosophy), we are condemned either to play or to pretend (which is to play) at significance(s). To be or not to be? To be perpetually drunk or bereft of love (of investment)? Rosset says earlier in his book that materialism, not the Marxist kind but that of Lucretius and Epicurus, is the only antidote to the madness of meaning (1977: 37). But later he specifies (or alters?) this antidote to what he calls *allégresse*: the real, though insupportable in its non-significance, and insofar as we have access to it in privileged but painful moments, exists for us in those moments, even if we and all the works that celebrate it disappear. Death has no dominion over that real, and it is that real we must learn to know and celebrate, with *allégresse* (pp. 78–80).

4. And what of this text, and my texts?

Ah yes. I shall not be 'nihilistic' or 'deconstructive', but neither shall I impose a system, or use one theory. I shall be eclectic, plural ltd, for no reader or critic can see all aspects at the same time, and some texts respond better to some methods (that is indeed the difficulty, the great 'cheat' of the 'scientific' dream). I shall not be dealing with the 'real' in its 'idiocy', but with texts or secondary modelling systems, and with the apparent inversion of real and unreal as reflected in them. Nor is this a history of such texts. I have chosen these few simply because they interest me in relation to this problem: the instability of genre-theory (chapters 3 and 4), the treatment of what used to be called the unreal as real (first apparent in Gogol's *Nose* and Kafka's *Metamorphosis*), here approached through a type of science fiction (chapter 10); or the totally ambiguous (the old 'pure' fantastic, chapter 3, and chapters 5–8), the marvellous weighed down with realism (chapter 9), and the treatment of what used to be called the real as unreal (the *nouveau* and *nouveau nouveau roman* and, to some extent, contemporary 'metafiction', chapters 11–14). These are the aspects of the novel that I shall try to bring out in these selected texts, I hope with *allégresse*.

PART II

Method and non-method in genre analysis

PART II

3

Historical genres/theoretical genres: Todorov on the fantastic

In his book on the fantastic (1970b), Tzvetan Todorov poses the question of theoretical genres, as opposed to historical ones. He poses it first as a particular case through a critique of Frye's modes and then more generally as part of the larger dichotomy between theory (or poetics) and the more empirical tradition of criticism. I shall deal with these two aspects in turn, and then with other more particular but less important aspects of Todorov's practice as theoretician.

1. Frye's modes

Northrop Frye is generally considered, and presumably considers himself as a theoretician. Certainly his *Anatomy of criticism* (1957) broke new ground and was one of the first studies in English to insist, first on the literality of text (also sometimes called 'literarity' to avoid confusion with the other sense of 'literal'), or what Jakobson calls the poetic function as opposed to the referential (see chapter 2, p. 22 above); and secondly, on a type of analysis that describes, and explains, without evaluating or judging, which is the job of criticism.

Nevertheless, Frye thinks more as a critic, and a brilliant one, than as a theoretician. Todorov cites several examples, two of which I shall discuss here more fully than he does, in order to show, more precisely than in chapter 2, where the difference lies.

The first comes in Frye's fourth essay, 'Theory of genres', where he is discussing the difference between 'novel' and 'romance', and decides that although both are *personal*, the novel is an *extroverted* genre, the romance an *introverted* genre. This perhaps seems arbitrary, since he has just demonstrated that the characters of romance are archetypes (and therefore general) and not individuals. Arbitrary decisions of this kind, however, are part of the theoretical way of thinking: one postulates a hypothesis and then sees how it works out. If we suppose that by archetypes Frye means here the fundamental psychic movements (collective as well as individual), we can so far accept, with reservations, the hypothesis that romance is personal and introvert, the novel personal and extrovert.

Frye then discusses the 'confession', or autobiography (St Augustine, Rousseau), and comes to the conclusion, empirically, that this genre 'nearly always' has a predominantly theoretical and intellectual interest. He therefore labels it *intellectual*.

He has thus arrived, in a discursive manner, at four categories: *personal, extroverted, introverted, intellectual*. But the first three belong to the novel and romance (both personal, one extroverted, the other introverted), the last only to the confession. And it is here that we watch Frye use a truly theoretical way of thinking; if there are four categories, there must be a fourth genre. And he finds it, in the Menippean satire, which he prefers to call the 'anatomy'. The confession and the anatomy are thus both intellectual, but the former is introverted, the latter extroverted, thus perfectly balancing the levels of categories for novel and romance.

Todorov does not in fact criticise this passage; he simply gives a summary and adds a diagram without commentary. But the diagram reveals the lack of logic and the discursive trap Frye has fallen into:

	Personal	*Intellectual*
Introverted	romance	confession
Extroverted	novel	anatomy

Introvert/extrovert is a logical opposition; *personal/intellectual* is not. The opposite of personal is *non-personal* or *impersonal* (contradictory or contrary; and according to the semic axis, the contrary could be *universal, general, mass*, etc.). The opposite of *intellectual* is, for the contradictory, *nonintellectual*, and for the contrary and according to the semic axis chosen, *corporal, emotive, psychic, practical*, etc.[1]

The result is that the only genre unambiguously placed is the last, the 'anatomy', at which Frye arrived theoretically, even though on shaky premises; inversely, the confession is by definition 'personal' even if, in the historical cases cited (and perhaps in all historical cases), it happens also to be ideological, intellectual. Theoretically, given that odd opposition, the confession should be personal; historically, given the examples chosen, it goes against the theoretical genre and is intellectual, though no doubt other examples could be found that are purely personal. In fact, the logic of the scheme is faulty.

Another example, more to my purpose here, is the criticism Todorov makes of Frye's 'theory of modes'. This theory postulates as its criterion the hero's power of action, which can be superior, inferior, or equal in kind and/or degree to that of man and/or nature. Already from all these categories we can surmise a certain complexity, but Frye does not in fact state them in this way. He presents five modes, one after the other, selecting categories for each, discursively and of course very persuasively.

Todorov first points out that one unit, the hero (never defined), is being compared with two others: nature and the reader (in a text, 'man' can only be us). We thus have two unequal polarities: hero (i.e., man, superman, or god) versus nature, and hero versus reader. Secondly, the superior/inferior relation is divided into two: qualitative (kind) and quantitative (degree). This complexity wouldn't matter if it were correctly used from a theoretical viewpoint.

For Todorov's most pertinent criticism concerns, precisely, the notion of historical and theoretical genres. Having postulated these categories, Frye does not in fact pursue all the possibilities. The category 'kind' is applied only once, as is the category 'inferior'. On the given premises, there are in fact thirteen possibilities instead of five. Todorov does not give them, but for the sake of the present argument it is easy to reconstitute them in tabular form ('man' is not permutable since the reader is always present, and 'equal' can be eliminated since it is equivalent to 'neither superior nor inferior', where Frye places low mimetic). See table 3.1.

Seven on each side, of which two are equivalent, which makes thirteen. The table incidentally reveals the intrinsic links between high mimetic and ironic, the latter being the only genre on the 'inferior' side, but with the same subcategories. More to my purpose here, it shows that all the permutations in parentheses are theoretically possible genres based on these chosen criteria. For example, in science fiction the hero's power (if the hero is not earthly man) could be superior in kind only to that of man but not to that of nature, or superior (or inferior) in kind and in degree to that of man but not to that of nature (e.g. although they are not heroes, the Gollum, the orks and dwarves of Tolkien, but not the elves and wizards, who belong properly to romance). At least it is possible to conceive of such a hero. The hero of McElroy's *Plus*, for instance (analysed in chapter 10 below), is a human brain in orbit, which

Table 3.1

	Superior				Inferior				
	in		to		in		to		
	kind	degree	man	nature	kind	degree	man	nature	
Myth	+	+	+	+	(+	+	+	+	∅)
Romance	−	+	+	+	(−	+	+	+	∅)
High mimetic	−	+	+	−	−	+	+	−	Ironic
Low mimetic	−	−	+	− =	−	−	+	−	Mimetic
(∅	+	+	+	−)	(+	+	+	−	∅)
(∅	+	−	+	+)	(+	−	+	+	∅)
(∅	+	−	+	−)	(+	−	+	−	∅)

starts growing limbs, but is eventually brought down by Ground and dies. We could regard him (it) as inferior, not in kind, but in degree, to man and to nature, which would situate *Plus* in the (non-existent) category opposite to 'romance' under 'inferior'. And all the other combinations are theoretically possible, given Frye's criteria.

To exemplify the notion of theoretical criteria, Todorov cites Plato, who divides narrative into three types: (a) where the narrator speaks, (b) where the characters speak, (c) mixed. Plato's division is not really based on historically existing genres (see chapter 2, p. 4), but on the theoretical supposition that the act of speaking is central to narrative, just as Frye's theory is based on the theoretical supposition that the hero's power of action is central to fiction.

Todorov's reproach to Frye is that he bases his theory on criteria which he then does not apply correctly. It is as if he had on the contrary started with five existent modes, empirically arrived at, and then applied the criteria, also empirically arrived at, empirically.

In a sense it is absurd to reproach Frye, whose learning and range are immense, for not considering examples that are non-existent. Nor is this really a reproach, but rather an observation about theoretical as opposed to critical thinking. Frye's theory of modes is a theory of historical modes, not of theoretical modes. Inasmuch as Frye tells us explicitly that it is historical (and even cyclical), Todorov's criticism is unjustified. Inasmuch as Frye calls his critical work theoretical, Todorov is, in a rigorous sense, right. Frye is a critic with brilliant theories, but not the pure theoretecian he is often thought to be, and we can surely be glad of it, for it in no way detracts from his impressive contribution in leading criticism towards theory in the sense defined in chapter 2 and at the beginning of this chapter. The breakthrough was immensely important, but perhaps not consistent enough. His different theories are impossible to coordinate because based on different kinds of premises, behind which, Todorov insists, is another postulate, namely that:

the *structures* formed by literary phenomena *manifest themselves at the level of these phenomena* – i.e., these structures are directly observable. Lévi-Strauss writes, on the contrary: 'The fundamental principle is that the notion of social structure is not related to empirical reality but the model constructed according to that reality.' To simplify, we might say that in Frye's view, the forest and the sea form an elementary structure; for a structuralist, on the contrary, these two phenomena manifest an abstract structure which is a mental construction and which sets in opposition, let us say, the static and the dynamic . . . the forest and the sea *can* often be found in opposition, thus forming a 'structure'; but they do not *have to*; while the static and the dynamic necessarily form an opposition, which can be manifested in that of the forest and sea.[2]

This kind of confusion leads Frye into other categories, such as the four seasons, the four times of day, the four elements, etc., the manipulation of which (what texts represent what season) seems subjective and impressionistic.

Another inconsistency of application, not noted by Todorov, is that of the opposition between 'naive' and 'sophisticated'. Frye's laudable insistence on a break from evaluation leads him to make this distinction for romance, without, however, defining the terms. 'Naive' romance in fact reveals the structures more clearly. This notion is at the basis of the Russian Formalist movement (e.g., Propp on Russian folk-tales) and of the Structuralist movement (e.g., Eco or Barthes on James Bond stories, etc.). But Frye abandons the principle for modes other than romance, presumably because there happened to be naive romances in his corpus, but not naive tragedies. His later book (see below) is in fact a full development of this opposition. In both books we have historical theories of what actually happened. This one is a cyclical theory, and as a cyclical historical theory it 'works'. Frye says, for instance, that after the ironic mode there is inevitably (for existential reasons he explains) a return to the mythic mode (Joyce, Pound, etc.), and the cycle starts again. And today we are indeed witnessing a return to the mode of romance, not in the sense that it stopped existing, but in the sense that 'serious' writers turn to it and critics give it their 'serious' attention, exactly as Frye describes in *The secular scripture* (1976). Here he makes another division between the mythical and the legendary or fabulous, the mythical representing 'the most important group of stories in the middle of a society's verbal culture', and the fabulous ('it is difficult to make an adjective out of the word folk-tale') representing 'the more peripheral group, regarded by its own society, if not necessarily by us, as less important'. Epic and tragedy and the Bible for instance make up 'the central mythical areas' for Greek or Judeo-Christian civilisation, whereas folk-tale, legends and romance, while not constituting a totalising central pattern in this way, create a more peripheral tradition of interconnected stories that reproduce, though in original and varied ways, a limited number of patterns representing the core of fiction. This he calls 'secular' literature, and he distinguishes it from the central group with a simple (perhaps over-simple) formula: romance uses 'and then' narrative, while the central (mythic) tradition (tragedy, epic and its avatar the novel) uses a 'hence' narrative, that is, it tries to disguise its archetypal nature by presenting an action as a complex of cause and effect.

Whenever the conventions developed by the central, sophisticated, elitist literature become exhausted, there is a return to the simpler forms and themes of popular literature, with its sentimental plots and adventure stories. 'This happened with Greek literature after New Comedy, when Greek romance emerged; it happened at the end of the eighteenth century in Britain, when the Gothic romances emerged, and it is beginning to happen now after the decline of realistic fiction.' Frye is a little modest here, for it has been 'beginning to happen' earlier than his 'now', and his earlier theory was already implicitly on to it. His explanation is not here a cycle but a pendulum.

I might add that this theory expresses a diametrically opposite view to that of certain writers, for instance Nathalie Sarraute (1956a), for whom the true realists are the so-called formalists, who try hard to look at reality in a new way and to evolve new forms that will capture that new, unfamiliar reality. While the so-called realists are in fact formalists in the sense that they are essentially reporters, however acute, who look fairly hard but see whatever any intelligent person would see, and who for ready intelligibility pour that surface reality into the now familiar forms evolved by the previous generation's experimenters; indeed one might say that their very seeing is conditioned by those now diluted and stereotyped forms. Certainly one can see this very clearly (because faster) in film and television, where the 'pretentious tricks' of the so-called experimenters soon get diluted into clichés. Thus the 'exhausted' forms, for Sarraute, are regalvanised by experimental writers, not by 'popular' forms. However, Sarraute's theory is itself within Frye's 'central, mythic, elitist' tradition, which is undeniably 'exhausted', so that we are witnessing a return of serious attention to romance: science fiction, which is a form of romance, Tolkien's more naive attempt to revive romance, Lovecraft, and others, as well as comic strips, a return to the Gothic in the mass media etc.

Whether this will have the galvanising effect Frye says remains to be seen. According to his earlier theory this romance phase should be followed by a return to high mimetic, despite 'the death of tragedy'.

2. Criticism of theoretical genres as a notion

Stanislaw Lem (himself a science fiction writer) takes up Todorov's criticism to criticise it in turn from a traditional standpoint, holding that the examination of theoretically possible genres would constitute an *a priori* history of humanity, unverifiable empirically.[3] Lem points out that Todorov ignores the distinction between natural and cultural taxonomies. The classifications of nature, he says, call for no reaction on the part of the objects (animals, plants) classified, whereas cultural classifications are projected onto the phenomena classified, acting as catalysts so that, for example, a finite list of genres will incite rebellion and hence an alteration of genres or the creation of new ones. It is thus a self-destructive prognostication, and the author of such a list can be (unconsciously perhaps) a co-author of creative mutations.

This empirical argument against the postulation of theoretical genres is a little odd, and perhaps even self-contradictory. Odd because it implies that a list of all theoretical possibilities on given criteria might *stop* or discourage creation, and that creation of new genres can only happen through rebellion against existing genres (and indirectly through the publication of a finite list); self-contradictory because the very mention of the new genres to be created in rebellion admits the theoretical possibilities. And these, though apparently impossible to foresee, according to Lem and no doubt other traditional critics (and hence, indeed, usually rejected or misunderstood when they occur), can nevertheless be *theoretically* envisaged on any given criteria.

In fact, Lem fails on a more general level, as Frye fails, to make

the very distinction Todorov so emphasised, between abstract structure and manifestation, a distinction fundamental in linguistics
between system and speech (*langue/parole*).

Indeed, Lem's other criticisms lead one to wonder whether he has
understood theoretical principles at all: for example, he pronounces
himself against Todorov's mutually exclusive binary categories such
as *natural/supernatural, rational/irrational,* and [*sic*] *poetic reading/allegori-
cal reading.* Leaving aside the more general question of binary
oppositions and their validity, this attribution to Todorov of *poetic
reading/allegorical reading* as mutually exclusive shows Lem's own
misreading. Todorov does not oppose them (as a structuralist he
could not), but unites them as both killing the 'pure fantastic' in his
definition (see below). The oppositions he gives are: poetic vs.
fictional (which includes the fantastic) and allegorical vs. literal
(which includes the fantastic).

3. The fantastic as theoretical genre: the three requirements

I now want to make my own critique of Todorov's position, or
rather, since 'critique' is too strong a word for an author I admire,
to expound some of the problems this work has posed for me, if only
in the form of questions. The first is unimportant, but as it is related
to other problems I shall discuss, I state it at the outset.

Lem, who has argued against theoretical genres, is naturally silent
on this slight contradiction in Todorov, who, having postulated
theoretical possibilities as a concept, in practice relies wholly on
historical genres to elaborate his own theory of the fantastic. And
the fantastic turns out, in his narrow definition, to have occurred in
a relatively narrow historical period, that of the Gothic novel and its
brief aftermath, for reasons Todorov explains (a) in sociological terms
(nineteenth-century taboos) and (b) in historical terms (the themes
of the fantastic having been largely taken over by psychoanalysis).
Lem's only objection here is not to the reliance on historical genres
but to the narrowness of the period; he cites Sade, who, despite the
direct expression of sexual perversion admitted in the eighteenth
century, nevertheless uses the detour of the fantastic (though not, it
must be said, in the sense defined by Todorov, a fact apparently
ignored by Lem).

I shall return to this question of the narrow period later, and now
turn to the fantastic as defined by Todorov (1970b, trans. 1975). He

postulates three requirements for what he calls the 'pure' fantastic. (1) The reader's hesitation (produced of course by the ambiguity of the text) between natural and supernatural explanations of apparently supernatural events must be sustained to the end. (2) This hesitation may also be shared by the leading character, i.e., it may be 'represented', become one of the themes; the reader, at least the naive reader, then identifies with the leading character. (3) The reader must adopt a certain attitude toward the text; he must reject a poetic reading and an allegorical reading, both of which destroy the pure fantastic (i.e., the hesitation). These three requirements do not have equal value, as Todorov says: the first and third constitute the genre, while the second may not be fulfilled, but 'most examples' satisfy all three conditions.

In fact both (2) and (3) depend on (1), and are therefore not on the same level of abstraction. The basis of the fantastic is thus the ambiguity as to whether the weird event is supernatural or not. The mere fact of the supernatural is not sufficient. As Todorov points out, it can occur in epic and tragedy, but provokes no hesitation.

This hesitation for the reader, as encoded in the text, may be resolved by a natural explanation (a dream, drugs, trickery, etc.) in which case we are no longer in the pure fantastic but in the uncanny (*l'étrange*). Alternatively, we may have to accept a supernatural explanation, or the supernatural may be accepted from the start and throughout as supernatural (magic powers and auxiliaries), in which case we are not in the fantastic but in the marvellous (e.g., elements of accepted supernaturalism in epic and tragedy would pertain to the marvellous).

Todorov himself raises the possible objection against the notion that a mere last-minute explanation of the type 'he woke up' can alter the genre of a text, but answers it with a grammatical analogy: the fantastic is an evanescent genre, like the present tense, while the uncanny (which returns us to the familiar) is like the past, and the marvellous (which presents unknown phenomena) is like the future.

It is true that even when the marvellous seems to be telling us a tale of the distant past there is often a visionary (even a moralistic) element in it, a tone which implies a truth lost but to come again (e.g., Lovecraft, Tolkien). I am not sure, however, that this analogy takes us very far as a theoretical postulate, I mean, whether it is usable, a 'strong hypothesis' as the generative grammarians say.

What it means in effect is that the pure fantastic is not so much an evanescent *genre* as an evanescent *element*; the hesitation as to the

supernatural can last a short or a long moment and disappear with
an explanation. And although Todorov says it would be wrong to
claim that the fantastic can exist only in part of a work, because
there *are* some texts which sustain the ambiguity to the very end
(i.e., beyond the narrative), he supplies in fact only two examples:
James's *The Turn of the Screw* and Mérimée's 'La Vénus d'Ille'.
Personally I do not feel that the possible natural explanation in the
latter has equal weight with the supernatural one, as it does in *The
Turn of the Screw*, but if we admit the ambiguity this leaves us with
two (or one and a half) clear examples. (See later for Poe's 'The
Black Cat'.)

Of course giving a few examples is a fortuitous result of actual
work on a particular corpus and does not preclude the existence of
other historical examples. I shall return to the theoretical aspect of
this in a moment. But the dearth of examples seems to bother
Todorov, for he *also* argues that 'if we decide to proceed by
examining certain parts of the work in isolation, we discover that by
temporarily omitting the end of the narrative we are able to include
a much larger number of texts within the genre of the fantastic',
such as Potocki's *Saragossa Manuscript*, which resolves the hesitation
only at the very end, and Nodier's *Ines de las Sierras*, the first part of
which ends in perplexity, the narrator actually hesitating between
two procedures: to break off the narrative (and remain in the
fantastic) or to continue (and abandon the fantastic). Todorov later
makes the point that the explanations given are often (as in these
two texts) so implausible that a supernatural one would have
seemed more convincing, so that we remain, retrospectively as it
were, in the fantastic. However, I do find the procedure of 'temporarily omitting the end' a little dubious, more dubious, at any
rate, than that of taking a phrase like 'I woke up' (or an expanded
equivalent) as altering the genre.

Todorov then produces two transitory categories, or subgenres,
according to the explanation received, or rather, according to *when*
the explanation is received, i.e., the length of the hesitation. Here is
his schema:

Uncanny | fantastic–uncanny | fantastic–marvellous | marvellous

The 'pure' fantastic is represented by the central line – a frontier
between two adjacent realms. If the supernatural *eventually* receives a
natural explanation, we are in the fantastic–uncanny; if the events
are not supernatural but strange, horrific, incredible, we are in the

uncanny (with the accent on the reader's fear, not on his hesitation). On the other side of the line, if the supernatural has to be *eventually* accepted as supernatural, we are in the fantastic–marvellous; if it is accepted as supernatural at once, we are in the marvellous (with the accent on wonder). Presumably, then, on the left of the line, in the fantastic–uncanny, not only is the reader's hesitation resolved but his fear is purged; whereas on the right of the line, in the fantastic–marvellous, this fear is turned to wonder.

Nevertheless, there is something basically unsatisfactory, from a practical and not from a theoretical point of view, about this narrow line, this evanescent genre, or in fact *element*. Todorov, for instance, seems very uncertain about where to place Poe's 'The Black Cat', which he mentions under the fantastic–uncanny as a possible exception ('perhaps') to his statement that Poe's tales belong to the uncanny and not to the fantastic. It is in fact thoroughly ambiguous (see chapter 5 below). And the same applies to Hoffmann's 'The Sandman'.

There is another aspect of the pure fantastic that Todorov does not point out, which is that if its main constituent feature is total ambiguity between two interpretations, this is a feature it shares with non-fantastic texts. James himself wrote other ambiguous texts besides *The Turn of the Screw*, texts, that is, in which the ambiguity of interpretation is not between supernatural and natural explanation (*The Lesson of the Master*, *The Figure in the Carpet*, and, possibly, *The Sacred Fount*, where the 'supernatural' interpretation concerns not ghosts but a psychic transfer of energy, i.e. not necessarily supernatural but, according to some, psychically possible; see Rimmon 1977, for analysis of these, and chapter 8 here for account of Rimmon). And modern fiction also exploits total ambiguity: in the novels of Robbe-Grillet for instance it is usually impossible to decide between several interpretations (see chapter 11).

If the only feature that distinguishes the pure fantastic from the uncanny and the marvellous is ambiguity, which in turn is shared with some non-fantastic fiction, we must either emphasise (as Todorov does) that this ambiguity concerns only the supernatural (thus in effect falling back on the supernatural as basic element), or treat such other non-'fantastic' texts as a displaced form of the fantastic, which is what I shall be doing in this book.

To return to the question of the 'few' examples of this pure fantastic, this evanescent element on the central line, there is of course no theoretical reason why even a *historical* genre should not be historically validated by only a single text. Where did one place Rabelais, or Swift, before the term 'Menippean satire' was rediscovered? Or Cervantes, before the term 'anti-novel' (which actually dates from the seventeenth century) came into fashion in the 1950s? Such questions would support Todorov's argument for theoretical genres, for a *theoretical* genre need need be exemplified by no existing text. Inversely, if a text fits into no previously existing categories, it must logically constitute a genre that did not exist, and thus a genre which would have been 'theoretical' if someone had made Todorov's distinction before, say, Mérimée or James (or Poe) wrote. Since, however, Mérimée, Poe, and James wrote their texts first, the historical situation is more like that described by Lem (or any other historical critic), though the theoretical situation today (for future texts) is on Todorov's side.

In other words, there seem to me to be two reasons for postulating theoretical genres. First to mark a distinction, in any one genre, between the 'pure' type and others (on the basis of any stated criteria), the 'pure' type perhaps not existing but representing an abstract model, more or less predominant in the others; in the case of the fantastic, the distinction here would be between a text (existent or not) in which the hesitation is maintained to the end, and the others. Secondly to predict, on those criteria, all possible developments (future or existent, but unknown), much as a grammar, however simple, can predict all possible sentences it can generate.

It is in this second function that Todorov's theory seems to me to be flawed. This can be seen in his treatment of Kafka's *Metamorphosis* (1970b; 1975: 171–5) and indirectly, of Gogol's *Nose* (1970b; 1975: 171–3), which he places in a world apart, as it were, proposing in the end a new category. We are in the marvellous, since a supernatural event is introduced at the start, yet is accepted at once and provokes no hesitation. The event is nevertheless shocking, impossible, yet becomes paradoxically possible, so that in this sense we are in the uncanny. And Todorov simply concludes that Kafka's narratives 'relate both to the marvelous and to the uncanny; they are the coincidence of two apparently incompatible genres'.

Now this is very different from the case of *The Turn of the Screw*, which could have been postulated on Todorov's theory. Here again we have a work which does not fit into earlier genre-theory and which therefore, in principle, would have been a 'theoretical

possible' genre before it occurred, had it been postulated. The difference here is that Todorov's theory, had it existed before Kafka (or
Gogol), could not have postulated it, for it would have been
logically impossible in the given schema. It is as if his 'grammar'
(though he would not make such a claim for his theory) were
inadequate.

It is in his treatment of Kafka that we understand why Todorov
in fact relies on historical genres, despite his theoretical plea and
apparently theoretical procedure. In the fantastic, he tells us, the
supernatural or strange event was perceived against a natural,
normal background, but in Kafka it provokes no hesitation since
everything is abnormal and bizarre. Even if a hesitation remains
within the reader, it does not affect the character, and identification
is no longer possible; the second condition of the fantastic has been
abandoned (this second condition, however, was an optional requirement and identification as part of it was attributed only to the
naive reader). In other words his theory no longer holds, and is
bound therefore to apply only to the nineteenth-century texts
examined, a particular genre with a short life (for the social and
historical reasons he gives).

In all fairness, this is all he presumably set out to examine: his
title in English is *The fantastic – a structural approach to a literary genre*
(the French title – *Introduction à la littérature fantastique* – seems to
make a larger claim until we come to his narrow definition). But in
view of his strictures on Frye and his strong stand on theory, it is
strange that his own theory should in the end be unable to predict
theoretically possible developments. The theory does not *logically*
account for Kafka (except by saying that the fantastic stops before
Kafka), nor could it *logically* postulate a work in which (for instance)
the area on which the pure uncanny opens out (i.e., all slightly
strange but realistic novels) might 'coincide' with the pure marvellous. Yet much of the 'new' science fiction, notably Vonnegut's *The
Sirens of Titan*, and, less visibly, *Slaughterhouse Five*, or McElroy's *Plus*,
as well as, though differently, certain *nouveaux romans*, could be said
to be just that (see chapters 10–14 below).

Although his model is in a sense a generative model, Todorov
might not agree that the function of a theory is to predict *historically*,
i.e., with my second reason for postulating theoretical genres.
Nevertheless, I would defend his notion of theoretical genres for
both reasons, and would go so far as to say that if they are not both
there, the first reason alone is insufficient. For the notion of theore-

tical genres then becomes *only* a method of determining (and even of evaluating) historical texts, important though that is. In a discussion with Todorov on this point, he has told me that this is in fact his position now, which was only slightly perceptible in his book. In other words he has moved back towards historical as opposed to theoretical genres. I told him this was a pity.[4] After all, Frye's theory of modes, however weak 'theoretically', does, as a historical theory, fulfil both functions: it enables us to determine predominances in any one historical text *and* it predicts, so far correctly.

4. The third requirement

The third requirement for the fantastic as defined by Todorov (the rejection of both a poetic and an allegorical reading, see 1975: 58–74) poses a problem of a different order, at least as regards the constraint on an allegorical reading, which seems to me a little too rigorous, although I think this is a question of nuance.

I agree as to the 'poetic' reading, in the sense clearly defined by Todorov: a fantastic text must be read as a fiction (whatever its rhetorical devices, either in figurative language or in structural parallels, inversions, and repetitions), and if we read it as a poem, that is, as a text that can only be read as poem (that exploits the poetic function to a maximum and the referential function not at all), then we cannot read it as a fiction, and obviously we destroy the pure fantastic contained in the fiction.[5]

I am less happy, however, about the constraint on an 'allegorical' reading. Todorov's contention is that an allegorical reading kills the 'truth' of the story as story. By allegorical reading he does not mean a subjective allegorical reading, such as anyone can make of any text, but an allegory we may find encoded in the text. The (fictional) 'truth' of the story would then be the 'literal' level in allegory ('literal' here in its older sense of the story as opposed to its allegorical meaning, not in the sense of literality or literarity as defined at the beginning of this chapter), and this literal level tends to be destroyed by the allegorical meaning. He gives the example of the fable, in which the 'fantastic' element such as animals' talking is obliterated by the moral.

So far so good. Todorov would, however, on his own principle, presumably argue also that Dante's fictional journey is not a proper fiction, being in the service of allegory. And yet, strictly speaking, Dante's 'I' nowhere says that he is dreaming (as does Langland's

'Will' in *The Vision Concerning Piers Plowman*), nor does he tell us how he returned to write his poem; he remains at the end nailed to the circle of light, and we are left to infer, with the required hesitation, either that it was all a dream (the medieval dream-vision, a genre in itself, with in this case the 'ending' or awakening truncated precisely as Todorov proposed for certain types of fantastic–uncanny), or that it all occurred as a supernatural event, 'Dante' being privileged in much the same way as James's governess or any other character in the fantastic is privileged with special visionary powers, here dramatised as a guided journey.

Todorov would no doubt reply that I am reversing his constraint and making a referential reading of a text which can only be read as allegory (and as poem, of course, the circle of light being a poetic image), and he would of course be right. But the very fact that I can make such a reading at all must also surely mean that his fantastic genre (evanescent element) exists as an element outside the narrow historical period to which he assigns it.

Inversely, on Todorov's own ground, if his first condition (the sustained hesitation of the reader) is truly fulfilled, does not this automatically produce a text with two meanings (at least), two levels, both present at every moment? In the case of *The Turn of the Screw*, both interpretations are constantly possible; there is no clue that is not wholly ambiguous. Thus the natural explanation (hallucinations) could be equivalent to the 'literal' level in allegory, with a touch also of the 'moral' level, and the supernatural explanation (ghosts) would be equivalent to the 'allegorical', the 'moral', and the 'anagogic' levels, according to the richness of the reading (Todorov considerably simplifies his definition of allegory into two levels only, the literal and the allegorical, fusing in fact, for the fable, allegorical and moral).

The significant differences would be: first, the lack of hierarchy, the constantly equal weight of the two interpretations in the pure fantastic (although the supernatural could, subjectively in the mind of any reader, be felt as 'higher' because supernatural or, on the contrary 'lower' because pertaining to superstition or, on the literal level, to the ghost story, an 'inferior' genre); and second, the fact that the two levels are mutually exclusive yet, in the pure fantastic, unresolvable, constantly held in the tension of the paradox.

On this second difference, however, it must be said that this paradoxical element is very much part of medieval allegory in its more sophisticated form, as it is of the 'pure' (i.e., sophisticated)

fantastic. In *Piers Plowman*, for example, the levels (long ago analysed by Nevill Coghill 1974) are:

Sensus literalis	*S. allegoricus*	*S. moralis*	*S. anagogicus*
Piers the farmer	the laity	Do-Well	God the Father
Piers the teacher, healer, sufferer	the clergy	Do-Bet	God the Son
Piers the builder of the Barn	the episcopacy	Do-Best	God the Holy Ghost

It is only on a purely abstract level (and in a perfectionist sense)
that we can equate the three elements of the *sensus allegoricus* with
those of the *sensus anagogicus*; on the referential and fictional levels
Langland fulminates against the sins of the laity, the clergy, and the
episcopacy, so that the tension of the paradox is held. A similar
schema could be applied to Dante. The second column could be
more political, the fourth could be *Inferno, Purgatorio, Paradiso*, the
third would be 'man who does well, better, best', rather than
fictional characters, though each would be represented by the
various people he meets on his journey. Only the first column (the
story) would be radically changed: Dante the traveller (and Virgil
as co-traveller, Beatrice as instigator of the journey); Dante who sees
suffering and suffers, consoles, informs, and learns (and Virgil as
guide and instructor, Beatrice as encourager); Dante the poet who
builds his poem of love and beauty and who saves his soul (and
Beatrice as redemptress, vision of perfection). The paradoxical
tension of the equations is even stronger in Dante, since they appear
not only in the apparent contradictions of the second and fourth
columns (as in Langland), but also in those of the first and fourth
columns: Dante as 'autobiographical' protagonist = *Inferno* (etc.);
whereas in Langland the 'dreamer' is 'Will' (William Langland),
though the *sensus literalis* applies to Piers Plowman as a 'good' and
mysterious character within the fiction.

In other words, is not the fantastic as defined by Todorov a
modern development (non-hierarchised levels, stronger paradox) of
medieval allegory – two among various ways of writing metaphorically, or on several levels, or paradigmatically – just as the
marvellous is a version of Frye's romance mode? I say 'as defined by
Todorov' because clearly his constraint applies only to the 'pure'
fantastic: the marvellous, including *le merveilleux scientifique* (science
fiction) can easily tend towards encoded allegory, just as the uncanny and indeed all 'strange' fiction onto which the uncanny opens
out can easily tend towards at least a moral meaning.

Or, to put it more generally: is not the pure fantastic, with its absolute ambiguity, a (historical) prefiguring of many modern (non-fantastic) texts which can be read on several and often paradoxically contradictory levels, and which would thus all be modern developments of medieval allegory?

Is not the very condition that defines the pure genre (or evanescent element) merely a particular (historical) manifestation of a more general feature (at least two contradictory readings) which can and perhaps should be found in all sophisticated (complex) narrative, at any time, with varying degrees of predominance and various types of manifestation according to the period?

This question is, as I say, a nuance on Todorov's constraint rather than a disagreement: I am never happy with a definition of a genre, however 'theoretical', which appears to exclude all notion of contamination or, to use a less pejorative word, flexibility. But here I feel that Todorov would broadly agree, especially since there is no such apparent exclusion in his basic definition of the genre; his pure fantastic is a theoretical model found, with more or less predominance, in a given set of historical texts.

At any rate, despite my criticisms of some aspects of his theory, I shall in this book accept his basic division (uncanny/pure fantastic/marvellous) and his criteria for it, as an extremely useful working hypothesis.

4

Science fiction and realistic fiction

1. Science fiction as genre

Todorov as we saw treats science fiction very briefly as one particular subtype of the marvellous, of which he gives four: the hyperbolic (e.g. Sinbad's huge serpents), the exotic (strange lands), the
instrumental (gadgets such as magic lamps), the scientific (science
fiction). On his own premises there is no objection, since the marvels
of science fiction, though impossible according to the empirical laws
known to the author's and reader's period, are at once accepted, just
like magical impossibilities. However, since I shall be discussing two
modern science fiction texts later (chapter 10), I should like to step
out of Todorov's narrow premiss (hesitation/non-hesitation) and
place science fiction in a wider perspective.

Certainly science fiction has its roots in the marvellous. As
Kingsley Amis (1960) and Robert Conquest (1963) both pointed
out long ago, books and essays on science fiction customarily trace it
back to Lucian or even Plato's *Timaeus*, sometimes even taking in
Beowulf and the Arthurian romances, and tracing its development
via Kepler's *Somnium*, Bishop Godwin's *Man in the Moone*, Cyrano de
Bergerac, Swift and so forth. But if demons, or dreams, or evaporating dew or a raft drawn by wild geese, are the means 'of locomotion
we are still in the realm of the marvellous. Not that the 'science'
part of science fiction is necessarily all that scientific. Amis defines
science fiction as 'that class of prose narrative treating of a situation
that could not arise in the world we know, but which is hypothesised
on the basis of some innovation in science or technology, or pseudo-
science or pseudo-technology, whether human or extra-terrestrial in
origin', and the 'pseudo' is particularly important for, as Amis also
points out, the very real scientific impossibilities (such as several
hundred years to reach other galaxies) are simply got around by
means of now conventional devices like the 'space-warp' or the
'hyper-drive' etc.

Many critics in fact, have recently reaffirmed the links between science fiction and the marvellous, and with very valid arguments. I shall return to these later. For the moment I would like to consider the only 'theorist' of the genre, Darko Suvin (*Metamorphosis of science fiction*, 1979).

Suvin does not deal with narrative technique in any detail, but on his own ideological premises would certainly object to Todorov's quasi-dismissal of science fiction as a subcategory of the marvellous; indeed, perhaps fortunately for him, he shows no sign of having read him, and himself dismisses what *he* calls the fantastic ('fantasy' in the English version), as 'ghosts, horror, gothic weird'. His premises, sociologically and even politically axed around the idea of utopia and satire, are so different from Todorov's formal ones that the two books can hardly be compared, but he makes some interesting preliminary distinctions that are well worth considering, for they lead him to place science fiction at an opposite pole to that of the marvellous. These distinctions are as follows:

Science fiction is opposed to the fairy-tale, which contests the author's empirical laws, simply in order to escape them. The flying carpet counters the law of gravity but only because the author refuses to take this law into account; he does not wish to imply that carpets could fly but to postulate another world in which 'some carpets do, magically, fly, and some paupers do, magically, become princes' (p. 8). Any science fiction, such as space-opera, 'retrogressing into fairy-tale ... is committing creative suicide'. Frye, as we have seen, would not call a return to popular forms 'retrogressive' but an attempt to refresh exhausted conventions, and, as we shall see, science fiction, though itself a popular form, has its own exhausted conventions.

Science fiction is also opposed to the fantastic ('fantasy', ghosts, horror, etc.), which interposes anti-cognitive laws into a supposed empirical world (whereas the fairy-tale ignores them).

The thesis could be defended that the fantasy is significant insofar as it is impure and fails to establish a superordinated maleficent world of its own, causing a grotesque tension between arbitrary supernatural phenomena and the empirical norms they infiltrate. Gogol's Nose is significant because it is walking down the Nevski Prospect, with a certain rank in the civil service, and so on; if the Nose were in a completely fantastic world – say H. P. Lovecraft's – it would be just another ghoulish thrill. When fantasy does not make for such a tension between its norms and the author's empirical environment, its monotonous reduction of all possible horizons to Death makes of it just a sub-literature of mystification. (Suvin 1972:8–9)

We are a long way from Todorov, who regards unresolved tension as the mark of the 'pure' fantastic, whereas Suvin regards the tension as 'grotesque' and a mark of the only 'significant' because 'impure' fantastic, *his* 'pure' fantastic or fantasy being the marvellous (e.g. Lovecraft). Suvin adds that the 'commercial [in French: the capitalist book industry] lumping of it into the same category as Science Fiction is thus a grave disservice and rampantly socio-pathological phenomenon' (p. 9).

He exonerates the pastoral from this condemnation (obviously since the socio-pathological confusion of the capitalist book industry did not exist), for pastoral is closer to science fiction in that it postulates a world without money economy, state apparatus, and depersonalising urbanisation, and can thus 'isolate, as in a laboratory, two human motivations: erotics and power-hunger ... SF has much to learn from the pastoral tradition, primarily from its directly sensual relationships which do not manifest class alienation ... at least when pastoral escapes precocity its hope can fertilize the SF field as an antidote to pragmatism, commercialism, other-directedness and technocracy' (p. 10). I confess I don't quite follow Suvin here. Since one of the main attractions of science fiction is its structuring paradox in that it both beautifies and neutralises our fears of science's dehumanisation and displays the inexorable 'necessity' of science with the 'freedom' of fiction (see Sontag 1966; Huntington, cited here p. 80), science fiction would surely also commit generic suicide if it really learnt much from the pastoral.

Science fiction is also opposed to myth in that it treats the norms of its period as 'unique, changeable, and therefore subject to a *cognitive* view', whereas myth 'conceives human relations as fixed, and supernaturally determined'. Myth 'absolutizes and even personifies apparently constant motifs from the sluggish societies', while science fiction, which focuses on 'the variable and future-bearing elements from the empirical environment, is found predominantly in the great whirlpool periods of history ... It does not ask about Man or The World, but which man?: in which kind of world?: and why such a man in such a kind of world?' (Suvin 1979:7).

Suvin also deals with estrangement (distancing or defamiliarisation) in the sense defined by the Russian Formalists (see chapter 2, p. 19) and later taken up by Brecht, that is, a way of treating fiction as if it were an empirical fact but in a perspective that implies a new set of norms. Estrangement he regards as the chief formal frame of the genre, but it is shared also by myth and the marvellous, which are thus, together with science fiction, opposed to 'realistic' fiction (in the French version), 'naturalistic' fiction in the 1979 English version.

A further distinction however, re-separates them: that between a 'dialectical, and cognitive epistemé' (p.20), said to be the approach of the natural sciences and materialist philosophy, and shared by naturalistic fiction and science fiction; and the 'non-cognitive', mystical or metaphysical approach, in which physical laws are determined magically or religiously by ethics. In 'cognitive' literature for instance nature is neutral, environmental circumstances are not in any way oriented favourably or unfavourably towards the protagonists (p. 11). There is no 'pathetic fallacy', an earthquake does not announce an assassination or a mist the heroine's melancholy (p. 18). Any such 'predetermination as to its outcome is felt as an ideological imposition and genological impurity' (p. 11). Whereas in the fairy-tale and other 'estranged' but 'metaphysical' genres there is such metaphysically determined orientation. In fact science fiction is rarely so pure; the hero, and heroine if there is one, do survive incredibly or quasi-fantastically against all natural and scientific odds, where lesser characters often do not; and many monsters or even ghosts have infiltrated it, 'scientifically' disguised as psychic creations of men affected by the features of the planets they visit. This occurs even in *Solaris*, by Stanislaw Lem, an author Suvin much admires for his 'open-ended parables' (see his Afterword to the novel): presumably he considers such apparitions as held in suitable 'tension', and not as 'ghoulish thrills' like Lovecraft's, but he nowhere discusses in what way Lovecraft fails to create such a tension or in what way others succeed. In another vein, Lem's delightful stories in *The Cyberiad* (1967; 1974) are more like cybernetic, comic-strip versions of *The Arabian Nights* than true *romans philosophiques*. Be that as it may, Suvin (p. 20) gives us the following diagram:

	Naturalistic	Estranged
Cognitive	'realistic' literature	SF (& pastoral)
Non-cognitive	subliterature of realism	*metaphysical*: myth, folk-tale, fantasy

Finally 'to test the above taxonomy' Suvin introduces 'a new basic parameter of time' (strictly speaking it doesn't 'test' it but simply expands it). Naturalistic literature extends over all empirical times, particularly exploring the present but also able to explore the past and to prospect the future in the form of hopes, fears, premonitions and dreams, as in the psychological novel after Stendhal and Dostoevsky (p. 20). Whereas indifference to time, or the unidimensional consciousness of the present – which are both ways of not questioning human behaviour – are the mark of current subliterature from Renaissance ballads to contemporary *kitsch*. Metaphysical genres ignore historical time: myth is above it, the marvellous is non-temporal despite a grammatically conventional past, and the fantastic is situated in the hero's abnormally perturbed present, a temporal void or extra-historical time.

In fact the fantastic also uses hopes, fears, premonitions and dreams, and in both realism and the fantastic their primary and surface function is to arouse expectation. The difference is in the underlying function. In realist literature it is to assure the general coherence (readability) of the narrative by constant reference to its past and future (see Hamon 1973 and p. 86 here). In fantastic literature it is to arouse fear and horror, but replacing fortuitousness with an imaginary causality that suggests, or states, the intervention of supernatural forces (cp. Todorov on pan-determinism, 1975: 109–14). Moreover this replacement of fortuitousness by an imagined causality is not as alien to realistic fiction as is often supposed, but the imagined causality there, instead of being supernatural, is social, psychological (dreams, a warning by a 'knowledgeable' character etc. see p. 86). Still Suvin's basic distinction is valid. Science fiction thus shares the pluritemporality of realist fiction (p. 21):

	Historical	Estranged
Pluritemporal	'realistic' literature	SF
Unitemporal	subliterature of realism	myth, folk-tale, fantasy

Myth, the marvellous, and the fantastic are clearly devalued, not of course by their position beneath SF in the diagram (under Estranged), but by their horizontal equivalence with what Suvin calls the 'subliterature of realism', as well as by his previous definitions and terminology.

Science fiction itself Suvin divides into two broad categories (pp. 27–30): the *extrapolating model*, in which certain cognitive notions or premises (biological, cosmological, technological etc.), usually reduced in number, are temporally extrapolated and oriented towards a sociological problem (utopian or anti-utopian); the cognitive significance of these premises establishing the value of the fable, together with the coherence with which they are developed in the narrative.[1] And the *analogical model*, which invents new visions of the world, satirically or otherwise applicable to ours, like parables. The extrapolating model would include London's *Iron Heel*, Wells's *The Sleeper Awakes, Men Like Gods, The Time-Machine*, Zamyatin's *We*, Yefremov's *Andromeda* and others, including the 'new maps of hell' of post-war science fiction. The analogical model would include, in its most 'primitive' form, analogies with the earth's past (geological, ethnological, historical etc.); adventure-stories furbished with a super-science supposedly transforming them into science fiction (space-operas); and in its 'highest' form, the eighteenth-century philosophical tales of Swift, Voltaire, Diderot, or mathematical models as in Abbott's *Flatland*, or ontological models found in condensed form in Borges and Stanislaw Lem, or, with a suffering protagonist, in Capek's *Krakatit*, Ursula Le Guin's *The Left Hand of Darkness*, Lem's *Solaris*, Kafka's *Metamorphosis* and *In the Penal Colony*.

I have spent some time on Suvin's hypotheses in order to show how two very differently orientated theoretical methods can arrive at such opposite conclusions about a genre. In Todorov's theory science fiction is a development of the marvellous, i.e., to the right of his diagram, while, to the far left, the uncanny opens out onto all unusual stories and hence onto realistic fiction (off-diagram). In Suvin's theory, science fiction is opposed, horizontally to realistic fiction on the distancing criterion, and, vertically, to the marvellous, the fantastic, and myth, on the cognition and pluritemporality criteria, which *unite* it to realist fiction. I have already discussed (chapter 3) the fact that Todorov's theory does not account for Kafka (and perhaps Gogol), but has to 'consider this type as a mixture of the opposite ends of his diagram (realist←marvellous + uncanny). The link which Suvin clearly establishes between science fiction and realism would then, if science fiction is *also* the marvellous in Todorov's sense, express a different form of this 'mixture'. Another basic difference is that Todorov's fantastic is 'pure', Suvin's 'impure'.

Todorov's theory is based on two formal premises: hesitation (as encoded in the text), and the impossibility of a poetic or an allegorical reading (because non-encoded in the text). Suvin's theory is based on ideological content and how it is organised. And the ideological content is sociologically and politically oriented in a manner explicitly derived from Marxist critics like Lukács and Goldmann. If the structuralist method excludes all evaluation of texts, distinguishing them only by formal characteristics irrespective of 'goodness' or 'badness' (a feature of structuralism which was much attacked by non-structuralist critics), the danger of the sociopolitical method, even when rigorously applied, would be on the contrary to tend towards arbitrary and/or biased judgments; any type of text that does not fall into the category which is considered as the 'highest' form being dismissed as 'lowest' form, or 'primitive', or 'bourgeois', or an 'ideological imposture', a 'genological impurity', 'subliterature' etc., terms which all inevitably imply that there is only one acceptable standard and, of course, only one acceptable ideology. This I find more disturbingly subjective than the supposedly objective lack of evaluation of the rigid Structuralists, which at least leaves the reader to make his own evaluation from the analysis given. But clearly a middle course between this Scylla and that Charybdis is preferable.

One feature, however, that Todorov and Suvin have in common is that both ultimately refer their definition to empirical laws, to what is generally considered as the 'reality' of the author's environment. Todorov's 'natural explanation', for instance, places a narrative in the uncanny, a 'supernatural' explanation in the marvellous. (In science fiction the 'supernatural' is supernatural or impossible in the norms known to author and reader, but assumed as 'natural' in the sense that it is 'scientific' or 'pseudo-scientific'.) And when discussing science fiction as an aspect of the marvellous Todorov makes an interesting distinction between instruments, however primitive, and magical objects (1975:56): a flying carpet, a far-seeing pipe, a curing apple, are primitive imaginative versions of later technology unrealised then but quite possible (the helicopter, binoculars, antibiotics) products of human skill; but a magic lamp that calls a genie, or an invisibility ring, are magical objects serving to communicate with other (supernatural) worlds.

Both Todorov and Suvin then stress (as does Rabkin, cp. n. 1) the 'impossibility' in relation to the author's norms. For Suvin, as we saw, magic carpets belong only to the marvellous, but he does insist that it is absurd to treat the extrapolating model of science fiction as a servant to technology or as a prophet, blaming it if it's wrong and glorifying it if it's right (1978:28).[2] He points out that Wells's narrator in *The Time-Machine* does not explain the exact working of the machine (French version, p. 146, simplified in English to 'technical motivations' p. 211), and manages to convince his friends by establishing its plausibility rather than through gadgetry or the 'crumby' theory of the fourth dimension. And Suvin blames Jules Verne as *bon bourgeois libéral* for too much concentration on the mere mechanics of locomotion within a safely homogeneous space (p. 209). Jules Verne, he tells us, accused Wells of 'inventing' objective counter-truths, but for an evolutionist like Wells it was Verne who 'invented' mere vulgar gadgetry (p. 210).

It is certainly true that traditional science fiction has not worried much about scientific plausibility: Cyrano's travellers try to reach the moon first by dew-evaporation (which fails), and then by firework-like rockets, and Mary Shelley's Frankenstein created a living man from a corpse. Science then catches up (or may catch up), but by other means (e.g. if it ever creates life it will not be from death but presumably from synthetic molecules). The scientific trappings of modern science fiction now seem to us far more sophisticated, but there is very little difference, as Amis pointed out, between bottles of dew and a 'space warp'. Nevertheless, the scientific trappings are not the real point, and many writers continue to ignore them (e.g. Vonnegut) or, like McElroy in *Plus*, to treat them as the stuff of poetry (see chapter 10 below).

What we have then is a theory which places science fiction in the marvellous and another which places it with realistic fiction as against the marvellous. Most critics from C. S. Lewis on have in fact linked science fiction with the marvellous and pointed out that early magazine titles were *Amazing Stories, Thrilling Wonder Stories, Astounding Science Fiction, The Magazine of Fantasy and Science Fiction*, etc. Suvin stands almost alone.

Mark Rose (1976) in his Introduction reiterates that science fiction is a romance form, which calls its magic a 'space warp' or a 'matter transformer' and its giants and dragons 'extraterrestrials', (or, as Lem points out in the same book, p. 81, the 'closed millenia' to which only tempocrats have access in Asimov's *The End of Eternity* is remarkably similar to the closed-room enigma in fairy-tales and detective-stories). Like romance, science fiction is a generalising mode, using representative rather than individual characters (good or 'enlightened', for the quest, bad or 'ignorant', against it), and many others including Conquest and Lewis have pointed out the type characters as a feature of romance. For Rose the hero is the new environment:

In *The Fairie Queene* for instance, the most memorable and often the most dramatic parts of the poem tend to be the descriptions of such crucial locales as Lucifera's palace in Book I or the Garden of Adonis in Book II.

The phenomenon of *landscape as hero* is particularly common in science fiction, where the story is frequently neither character nor plot but the world the writer creates. (Rose 1976:4)

Whereas in realistic fiction the setting 'tends to be primarily a context for the portrayal of character'. We may compare Amis's concept of *idea as hero* in science fiction, which would bring him closer to Suvin. The chief difference, according to Rose, is in the kind of rhetoric science fiction evokes to justify its marvels ('scientific patter' as Wells called it). More disparagingly Huntington (1975, in Rose 1976) suggests that science fiction 'answers a craving, not for a new and plausible technology, but for a science which will mediate between a conviction of the necessity of events – that is, a strict determinism – and a belief in creative freedom.' Science thus functions rather like religion, 'a "law of physics" is every bit as absolute as a "law of God", and both laws promise security and perhaps even transcendence to those who understand and obey', except that the final catastrophe is no longer God's to initiate and forestall, but man's.

Paradoxically, SF is one of the least scientific of fictions because it owes hardly anything to the facts of experience . . . SF closely resembles pure fantasy in that it escapes nature's rules and makes its own. SF addicts, however, insist that there is an important difference between SF and fantasy. What seems to pacify the SF addict is the bow to science, even if it is a mere gesture, that SF makes, and what disturbs him about fantasy is that it acknowledges no law that prevents the freedom of imagination from seeming arbitrary. The SF addict wants to feel the tension of the paradox of freedom within a structured imperative. (Rose 1976: 160)

Ketterer (1974) also links science fiction with romance but suggests that most of its features, such as apocalyptic imagination, or the slighting of character in favour of the expression of ideas and metaphysical abstractions, are already to be found in American fiction, which, since Richard Chase, *The American novel and its tradition*, New York, 1957, is generally recognised to have the romance as its basic form.

Robert Scholes goes further in *Structural fabulation: an essay on fiction of the future* (1975), and pleads for science fiction as 'a special case of romance'. Both exploit radical dislocation (estrangement), but romance does so by suspending the laws of nature:

to give more power to the laws of narrative, which are themselves pro-jections of the human psyche in the form of enacted wishes and fears. These pure enactments are at the root of all narrative structures . . . whether found in 'realist' or 'fantastic' matrices. But there is another way to exploit radical dislocation between the narrative world of romance and that of experience, and this way emphasizes cognition ... When romance returns deliberately to confront reality it produces various forms of didactic romance, or fabulations that we usually call allegory, satire, fable, parable and so on. (Scholes 1975:28–9)

Fabulation is fiction 'that offers us a world clearly and radically discontinuous from the one we know, yet returns to confront that known world in some cognitive way' (p. 29). It has always been a favourite vehicle for religious thinkers, since religions teach that the commonsense view of reality is incomplete and therefore false. 'Thus it is not surprising that what we call "science" fiction should employ the same narrative vehicle as the religious fictions of the past' (p. 29). But there are two varieties of didactic romance, romances of religion and romances of science, or 'dogmatic' and 'speculative fabulation' (as a tendency of course). *The Divine Comedy* would be dogmatic fabulation, More's *Utopia* speculative fabulation. What Scholes calls 'structural' fabulation is simply 'a new mutation in the tradition of speculative fiction. It is the tradition of More, Bacon and Swift, as modified by new input from the physical and human sciences' (p. 39).

Scholes's book is the clearest statement, which may help us to reconcile the contradictory theses: science fiction as marvellous/ science fiction as realism. For clearly it is both. On Todorov's and others' criteria it belongs to the marvellous and romance, on Suvin's cognitive and pluritemporal criteria it is akin to realism. In Ketterer's sense that much American realistic fiction is basically romance, concerned with the expression of ideas rather than with character, the two are loosely united. And in Scholes's sense that science fiction is 'structural fabulation', a new form of speculative fabulation, which uses the radically discontinuous world it invents to confront the known world in a cognitive way, it must be *also* realistic.

But in what way? Obviously there is a realistic basis in all fantastic narrative, and even a fairy-tale will have some point of anchorage in the real, since the unreal can only seem so as against the real. But the realism of science fiction is considerably more pervasive than is required by this contrastive and persuasive function. Critics have occasionally remarked on a minimum need for plausibility, and many have complained of stereotypes killing the genre (see Stanislaw Lem's remarkable essay on 'The time-travel story' in *Science Fiction Studies* I (1974, reprinted in Rose 1976)), but these remarks refer only to ideas. Scholes says that 'since fiction is a cognitive art it cannot be considered adequately in purely formal terms. Formal changes, to be understood, must be seen in the light of other changes in the human situation.' True, but that is no reason to ignore the formal elements. Huntington (1975) does mention the odd fact that science fiction, 'which one might expect to explore the possibilities of fictional styles and forms, has traditionally conformed closely to a clear and powerful set of stylistic narrative conventions', but he does not tell us what these are, beyond attributing them to the narrow views of editors of early pulp magazines. Later he says that stimulating contact with new ideas did gradually develop, in some writers, 'increasingly accurate and subtle modes of depicting realities', again not telling us what modes, and then adds, mysteriously, that 'the conventions anchor Science Fiction, give it a form of believability, though the dependable aspect that the Science Fiction addict recognizes and trusts is not a semblance to a known physical reality, *as in ordinary fiction*, but a set of purely literary mannerisms' (my italics). This seems meaningless since 'ordinary fiction' or realistic fiction is also 'a set of purely literary mannerisms' (see section 2, below), unless, as so often, we have slid from the *modes* of depicting reality to the reality depicted.

Personally I agree with Suvin on the close link between science fiction and realistic fiction, not only because they are both 'cognitive' and 'pluritemporal' but, *pace* Scholes, for more formal reasons. One of the most striking features of much science fiction until fairly recently has been its lack of imagination with regard to narrative technique, as opposed to its imagination with regard to ideas. It took over wholesale the techniques of the realistic novel. And this Suvin does not deal with at all.

It is in fact quite remarkable how often theorists abandon their own theories as soon as they analyse texts. Suvin, for example, having established his cognitive/pluritemporal criteria and his distinction between extrapolative and analogical models, forgets them in his subsequent chapters which discuss utopias, Wells, Verne, Russian SF and Capek, without in any way linking his analyses to his typology. Nor *a fortiori* does he link this typology with language or questions of narration.

2. The discourse of the fantastic

Todorov (1970b; 1975) does deal with 'the discourse of the fantastic', in a special chapter (5), but here too the 'fantastic' suddenly becomes the fantastic in the more generally accepted sense, that is, all that he says of its discourse seems to apply arbitrarily to the uncanny, the pure fantastic and the marvellous. Or rather, on further analysis of what he says, some applies to some, unequally though he doesn't say so. He deals first with the *verbal aspect* under *énoncé* and *énonciation* (see above, ch. 2, pp. 23, 26).[3] Under *énoncé*, he merely mentions the tendency of the fantastic to use figurative language literally (e.g. in Beckford's *Vathek*, the Indian 'huddled into a ball' which becomes a whole episode, or in Villiers de l'Isle-Adam's *Vera*, the story takes literally the expression 'love as strong as death'). All his examples are from the pure fantastic ('La Vénus d'Ille') and the marvellous. Under *énonciation*, he merely emphasises the frequent use of first person narrative, more appropriate to ambiguity (since a narrator cannot lie or be in error but a character can). His examples however come from the pure fantastic and the fantastic–uncanny. For the *syntactic aspect* (narrative syntax) he mentions only irreversibility (we cannot have the 'explanation' first), and his examples apply to all (uncanny, fantastic and marvellous); besides, on a more general level this applies to all narrative. Later (in chapter 10), he returns to narrative syntax to say that a fantastic tale starts with an initial equilibrium, which is broken in a median disequilibrium to provoke the long quest for the second (and, for the tale, or the episode, final (equilibrium. A fixed law immobilises narrative, and 'for a transgression of the law to provoke a rapid modification, supernatural forces must intervene' (1975: 165). Todorov's only examples are from the marvellous, but of course this applies to all fantastic, and in a more general way (as he says) to all narrative (*something* must alter the equilibrium), the only differences being that in the fantastic the supernatural alters it more 'effectively'.

To resume schematically:

(1) *Verbal aspect*	*Examples*
éoncé (figurative→literal)	pure fantastic and marvellous
énonciation (I – narrative)	pure fantastic and fantastic–uncanny
(2) *Syntactic aspect*	
irreversibility	all (and on another level, all narrative)
alteration of equilibrium	marvellous (but in fact all, and on a more general level all narrative)

Similarly when Todorov deals with the semantic aspect, i.e., the themes of the fantastic (chapter 7, themes of the self, chapter 8, themes of the other), he makes no use of his typology, obviously, since thematics usually cuts across formal categories. Nevertheless it would have been interesting to have some kind of link made, to know for instance whether the themes of the self (the perception and consciousness system – linked analogically with psychosis), or the themes of the other (desire, sexuality – linked analogically with neurosis) are more, or less, predominant in the marvellous or the uncanny or the pure fantastic. We can't even glean this indirectly from his examples since these are from all sub-types (and he says so explicitly), but this could be fortuitous, and we are left with two completely different theoretical groupings, one formal, one thematic, each immensely stimulating, but unlinked (rather like Frye's different theories). The formal one (apart from the verbal and the syntactic aspects), is much more rigorous than the thematic. Suvin is less rigorous, but has the merit of bringing out the close link between realism and science fiction, which Todorov places in the marvellous. Could science fiction then be another but more extreme version (marvellous & realism) of a 'mixed' genre, in which the opposite ends of Todorov's diagram somehow join up, impossibly in his theory, which supposes alternative movements along the diagram, as I suggested earlier (p. 67)? We can of course join up the extremes by making Todorov's linear model into a circle. This resolves the SF aspect (marvellous + realism) but not the Kafka problem (uncanny + marvellous) if Todorov's model supposes a linear movement on the hesitation criterion. (See the diagram on p. 64.)

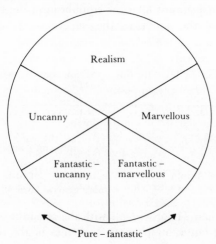

As for Suvin, he does not examine the technical features of realism in science fiction. Let us now try and see what these are.

3. The features of realistic discourse

3.1. Hamon's fifteen procedures

The mechanisms of realism have been much studied recently, but I shall use the provisional findings of Philippe Hamon (1973), who derives much from Barthes, especially S/Z (1970), but who, despite a certain amount of confusion, is more convenient for my purpose here in that he lists fifteen specific procedures.[4]

Hamon first distinguishes two types of realism that do *not* account for realistic discourse, though they can come into it:

Realism I (textual), which holds that language can only imitate itself. Within one text, its typical figures would be anaphora, tautology, repetition; and, intertextually, metalanguage (language on language), quotation retranscription, parody, pastiche.[5]

Realism II (symbolic), which holds that elements of the real (noise, movement, shape, lines) are iconifiable through writing. Its typical figures are onomatopoeia, diagrammatic and calligrammatic effects.

Hamon then shows that the presuppositions of realism go far beyond these: namely, that the world is rich, diverse, discrete, that one can transmit information about it, that language can copy the real, that language is secondary in relation to the real (is exterior to it, expresses but does not create it), that the textual support of this transmission must be effaced to a maximum (be 'transparent', a window on the world), as must be the producing gesture, and that the reader must believe in the truth of that information on the world. From these presuppositions two main features emerge: readability and description (1973:422).

Readability, in particular (in the Barthesian sense of 'readerly', see above, ch. 2, p. 41), implies respect of all the rules, of grammar of course, of selection restrictions (Chomsky 1965: 95, e.g. to avoid generating *sincerity admires John*), of anaphorisation (a repetition must clearly refer back to what it repeats, e.g. a pronoun must have a clear coreferent), and of substitution (same principle of clear linking); non-perturbance of discursive and narrative habits; absense of ellipsis; typographic stability; respect of cultural subcodes such as conformity to the genre (or plausibility).[6] The realistic project is identified with the pedagogic desire to transmit information, and must avoid all disturbance or 'noise' (such as narrator interference), although (contradiction), it will indirectly compensate for this by a pedagogic authority in the utterance of the author who is theoretically expelled in the name of the text's autonomy and transparence. Its procedures include a hypertrophy of redundancy and of disambiguation processes (Hamon 1973:422–3). As Barthes says, 'the realistic text is "replete", with multiple, discontinuous, accumulated meanings, and yet burnished, smoothed by the "natural" movement of its sentences; it is an egg-text' (Barthes 1970: 200).

Hamon then finds fifteen procedures that arise out of these preconceptions of realism (I summarise, and give them in his terms, explaining them, and in his order, which we shall see is itself somewhat redundant and illogical):

(1) *The appeal to memory*, to assure general coherence (readability). In practice this necessitates a constant circulation of information (about ancestry, tradition, a childhood traumatism etc.). The text, via flashback, summary, returning obsessions of the character and other means, refers to its *déjà-dit*, or, inversely, to its own future with flash-forwards (prolepses, i.e. by the narrator, see above, chapter 2, p. 37), or through characters via prediction, presentiment, project, contract, injunction, warning, desire, a lack to be remedied. There is usually a character who knows the antecedents, and who warns and infers, such as the family doctor, the childhood friend (1973: 424).

(2) *The psychological motivation of characters*, particularly emphasised in realistic narrative. In fact it functions as an *a posteriori* justification for the narrative sequences, the *post hoc ergo propter hoc* of narrative.[7]

(3) *The parallel story (history)*. For Hamon, realistic narrative is hitched to a megastory which doubles and illuminates it, creating expectations on the line of least resistance through a text already known, usually as close as possible to the reader's experience (and if it is not it has of course to be extensively *described*). Exoticism is reduced to the familiar.[8] Historical and geographical names (Rouen, Notre Dame de Paris ...) are stable semantic entities, functioning like quotations in a pedagogic discourse, as landmarks that link the text to an extra- or mega-text, itself valorised. This allows an economy of description and ensures a general effect of the real that transcends any actual decoding since the references are not so much 'understood' as simply recognised as proper names (pp. 425–6).[9]

(4) *The systematic motivation of proper names* (names that signify, or suggest a signification such as class, origin, character, etc.). Not a specific feature of realism. See discussion below.

(5) *Semiological compensation*, or redundancy and over-coding: if the reader has no access to cultural code A of the setting he will have access to complementary code B, even, in extreme cases, to illustrations (Jules Verne, regarded as a science-fiction writer solidly based in realism), photographs, drawings, diagrams, genealogical trees. This is clearly related to his Realism II (iconic). Hamon includes Flaubert's 'mimetic' sentence, and, indirectly, references to the visual arts in Balzac and Stendhal, or to photography in the *nouveau roman* (p. 427).[10] And one could certainly add, as a modern relic, short-cut descriptions via film-star names (like the well-known names in the megatext of history) or similar allusions to other media in the twentieth-century realistic novel.

(6) *The author's knowledge circulated through substitutes.* (This is really the same as (1), except for the type of knowledge circulated.) The realistic author is in possession of slices of knowledge, index-cards as it were, which are distributed through the text as descriptions (a mine, a workshop, an interior). And since the pedagogic act disguises its utterance in the name of 'objectivity', this information is often given to a specialist character (guide, engineer, doctor, painter ...), who informs a non-specialist. The real is thus a linguistic mosaic (learned, worldly, soldier's slang ...).[11] The index-card creates the character, as well as regressive chains: to tell presupposes a wish to tell (character A, voluble, benevolent, pedantic ...); and a question or questioning look presupposes a wish to learn (character B, curious, suspicious, a spy, a voyeur ...); and a capacity to see and learn (windows, high points, light, scenes of demonstration or explanation). We thus get three pretext–functions: the attentive look, the explanation, the technical act. They are pretext–functions in that they rarely play a role in the logical correlation of sequences, they are not part of a vital quest for knowledge, as in the fantastic (or for that matter the detective-story). Their role is simply to convey information about the world (pp. 428–38). A good example is of course the description (which Hamon gives as a separate tenet, see procedure (15)).

(7) *Redundancy and foreseeability of content*, that is, description of the character's social sphere and daily activities. Someone is, say, a butcher, or an office clerk, or a business magnate. His place of activity (shop, office) is inevitably described, followed or conjoined

with the activity itself. This merely 'conjugates a virtual paradigm' (pp. 432—4). 'Realism cannot avoid the description of programmed acts, and the effect of the real is an euphoric recognition of a certain lexic' (p. 433). Thus the inventory is a typical figure, as are scenes of ritualised activities (meals, banquets, religious or civic ceremonies, fixed timetables).

(8) *The narrative alibi* (delegation of author's task to a narrator, not specific to realistic discourse. See discussion below.)

(9) *Demodalisation*, that is, a strongly detonalised, merely assertive discourse, to achieve the realistic author's ideal of 'transparent' writing: no 'subjective' locutions like *seems, as it were, perhaps* etc., no emphases, italics, quotations, which are the privileged marks of narrator-utterance in the fantastic. It is a 'serious' discourse. This also leads to a refusal of euphoric or dysphoric themes such as idyllic places, passionate love-scenes, ecstasies, miseries, tear-jerker scenes, spectacular deaths, as for instance in Dickens. These belong to the *romanesque* [novelistic] whose euphoric and dysphoric scenes, in addition, depend considerably on 'realistically' unlikely and visibly organised coincidences (e.g. in *David Copperfield*). The *romanesque* is refused by realism, though it can appear in ironic contexts such as Emma Bovary's reading-matter (pp. 434–5).

(10) *The defocalisation of the hero*. This is perhaps the most interesting of Hamon's tenets, deriving in fact from the demodalisation of tone, which must not be so neutral as to blur the *identity of the hero*, who is an important element of readability and disambiguation, and emphasised as hero by several procedures: quantitative (he is the one who appears most often); and functional (he is the one who receives adjuvants – helpers – who liquidates the initial lack, who acts as actant-subject). He thus grids and organises the moral space of the narrative and hitches it to the cultural extratext common to author and reader (pp. 435–6).

But, Hamon goes on, if the author over-differentiates the hero in this way, he risks a deflation of the realistic illusion, thus reintroducing the heroic, the marvellous, the *romanesque*. He therefore uses several *counter-procedures* to level down the text, the chief of which is defocalisation by constant variation of viewpoint (hero abandoned for other characters), or by not giving the actantial position and the valued qualities to the same character. Unlike the hero of the marvellous, that of realistic narrative will not cumulate the roles of subject and beneficiary. He may become an object, or a virtual subject, never acceding to the status of real (and glorified) subject, or a beneficiary of negative values (illness, false information, bad luck). Hence the nineteenth-century *roman de l'échec*, the anti-hero, or even, sometimes, the difficulty of deciding who the hero is.[12] He can even be 'forgotten' (or can 'forget himself', lost in thought) while the narrator gives a description, and this feature may also be extended to other characters, who can then function as mere openers of description. Hence also the discontinuity of their emotional lives, made up of euphoric and dysphoric moments, often scattered (pp. 436–7).

(11) *Reduction of ambiguity*

(12) *Reduction of the being/seeing opposition*

(13) *Accelerated semantisation* (rapid explanation of mystery)

I bracket these three together as they are mere aspects of one process, the reduction of ambiguity, or disambiguation. No word or scene will be allowed to suggest several possibilities (they will be *monosemic*), any play with the being/seeing opposition will be effaced as much as possible and, as necessary corollary, there will be no false clues, no mysteries, or as few as is compatible with the retention of narrative suspense, and they will be swiftly cleared up. Hamon calls this 'the text in a hurry', and these three features are all aspects of the need for clarity, but the last creates a tension between the slowness and fullness of the information circulation, and the swift explaining away of any mystery (pp. 437–41).

(14) *A cyclothymic narrative rhythm*. This arises out of the realistic (i.e. procedure (7), redundancy and foreseeability) desire for exhaustiveness which provokes a need to review each term of any logical opposition, and this in turn produces the cyclothymic rhythm, each 'bad' phase succeeded by a 'good' phase (p. 441).

(15) *Exhaustiveness of description*. In realistic discourse, the world is describable, accessible to denomination, whereas in the fantastic it is unnamable, indescribable. This tenet of realism generates a desire for exhaustiveness, while the assumption of the world's discreteness leads to an aesthetic of the discontinuous, a composition in *tableaux*, slices of life, scenes, descriptions, details, a synecdochic fragmentation, an impression of mosaic.

Description is obviously not specific to realistic discourse, but its length, its distribution and its function are, and Hamon analyses the framing of description (which slows down or stops the narrative) in the light of the readability requirement (which must pretend that the description is part of the narrative). Thus certain characters and narrative syntagmas (sequences) function as description-openers and continuers. For instance a *narrative* sequence 'night had fallen' unfolds into a *descriptive* sequence (night, stars, breeze, etc.), but also leads to another *narrative* sequence. 'Peter closed the shutters', which unfolds into more narrative sequences (lighting up, lighting the fire, cooking, eating), and also leads to a descriptive sequence (the kitchen was cosy, etc.), which unfolds into a description (p. 443, see also Hamon 1972, on description).

From these fifteen tenets, certain contradictions inherent to realism emerge, which Hamon summarises at the end of his article:

technical denomination	vs	problem of readability
immediate explanation of mystery	vs	descriptive retardations
the knowledge of the author	vs	knowledge of character to be made plausible
multiplication of characters to guarantee slices of knowledge	vs	danger of psychological fragmentation and disappearance of character
redundancy, foreseeability, semantic saturation, readability, anaphoras	vs	how to place the non-functional detail which produces the effect of the real
style as element of cohesion, of continuity, of author's *savoir-faire*	vs	text as linguistic mosaic of jargons, demodalisation of author's style
linguistic knowledge (the unfolding of stereotyped paradigms) common to author and reader	vs	ontological knowledge (the real, intimate being of the world) not common to author and reader (pedagogic relation)
discontinuity of selection denomination	vs	loss of overall coherence claimed by pedagogic assumption

3.2. *Reservations*

I have quite a few reservations about Hamon's analysis, not only because it is disorderly and therefore unclear, but because the list is thrown down in any order (as he admits), rather like the lists of features by traditional critics examined by Propp for the folk-tale and by Todorov for the fantastic (see above, chapter 2). The tenets thus overlap, nor are they exhaustive; one could add more and more as one finds them. Moreover, some of his tenets are not specific only to realistic discourse (he happens to have found the features there), while others on the contrary seem over-specific (to one school only, the one he is studying). Finally, there is the question of evaluative criteria, which is as it were 'fudged'.

3.2.1. Disorder in general

His couplings are sometimes unclear: are the two main emerging presuppositions, readability and description, in opposition or complementary? If in opposition, one would expect his final list of contradictions to fall under these two heads, but they don't. If complementary, one would expect the fifteen tenets to be grouped under these two heads, but they are not: 'exhaustiveness of description' is merely one of his tenets (15), while 'readability' applies to several, and could therefore be said to summarise them. In fact of course description is merely part of the more general notion of excessive information. Description and readability are in fact in opposition, but the first is part of a larger concept, and the fifteen tenets could be more clearly redistributed in two main groups: the (pedagogic) plethora of information to be circulated, and the (pedagogic) need for clarity or readability, and *this* is the basic contradiction of realistic discourse, although each group interacts with the other all the time in any one text.

Or again, in his summary of contradictions, the exact nature of the contradiction in the fifth is unclear. On the left is redundancy (which of course *includes* the other items such as foreseeability, semantic saturation and anaphora, especially the latter since redundancy *means* repetition).[13] But why should this create a contradiction with 'how to place the non-functional detail which produces the effect of the real'? One would have thought that in a highly redundant system the non-functional detail could (and usually does) go anywhere.

3.2.2. The empirical list

3.2.2.1. *Overlapping.* I have already pointed out in my summary that (11), (12) and (13) are all part of one process, that of disambiguation (under readability in my division, p. 99), and that (1) (memory) and (6) (knowledge of author) are really the same (circulation of information) except for the type of knowledge circulated: in the first it is within the fiction (the hero's past etc.), in the second it is outside but brought in (what a mine, workshop, type of interior, etc. look like, and how they function). The difference is purely theoretical since (for instance) the hero's past can equally be made up of 'slices of knowledge' outside the fiction (schools, families, jobs), and Hamon is right to separate them, but he should have grouped them together (i.e. in my division, under plethora of information), just as he should have put (7) (redundancy and foreseeability) and (14) (cyclothymic rhythm) together since he says that (14) is a result of (7).

The haphazardness of the list in fact prevents him from seeing another inherent contradiction of realism: the cyclothymic rhythm of 'good' and 'bad' phases, insofar as it is not, at a general level, a feature of all narrativity, is surely a feature of the *romanesque* (euphoric/dysphoric scenes), which realism is said, under *demodalisation* (9) and *defocalisation* (10) to refuse. In other words realism 'tones down' a *romanesque* feature which it can't help keeping, for reasons of readability (foreseeability), and this feature is itself a result of saturation (plethora of information).

3.2.2.2. Non-exhaustiveness of the tenets. This is not a criticism of Hamon's work in finding the fifteen procedures, only of his *ad hoc* system of presentation. Obviously there are and must be many other features, and a more abstract and logical model would have exhausted the possibilities, so that specific types and subtypes later discovered would then merely be further examples. I shall mention a few at the end of this section.

3.2.2.3. Non-specificity. As I pointed out, (4) and (8) are not specific to realistic discourse. Hamon in fact admits that *the systematic motivation of proper names* (4) is not specific to realism and occurs also in the marvellous, but says that realism plays more on social content (aristocratic or tradesmen's names, etc.) than on character traits. In fact this is a feature of so many different genres, from tragedy to comedy, from epic to romance or allegory, and from the eighteenth-century novel onwards, that it seems valueless as a specific feature. The same applies to the *narrative alibi* (8), which includes 'the alibi of narrative performance' whereby an author delegates his task to a narrator, and the importance of plausible-making prefaces (e.g. the narrator telling the origin of his story), or even of chapter headings. All these devices are said to provide what is most lacking in realistic discourse and present in the fantastic: mediation by appeal to the genre (p. 434). But since all these elements can occur in other genres (the picaresque, the *romanesque*, the fantastic) and do not always occur in realism, I do not see the usefulness of this category. Nor for that matter does Hamon point out that (if it is as he thinks a mark of realism) both the preface and the chapter headings would be part of realism's inherent contradiction, since realism also effaces narrator interference (including the use of italics, capitals, and hence presumably chapter headings).

One could also add here the whole question of redundancy and foreseeability (7), which in the slightly different sense of over-determination of other types of information (the action, the mystery) applies also to the marvellous (see chapter 5 below).

3.2.2.4. Over-specificity. Hamon is dealing with an ultra-realistic school, that of naturalism (and Zola in particular), so that some of his formulations seem too specific to be generalised. This school for instance rejected the heroic and the mythic (which however reappear surreptitiously),[14] but also the *romanesque*. Yet this *romanesque* is surely *also* realistic in most of the senses he describes (e.g. Dickens's descriptions of prisons, legal offices, etc.), unless he means something else by *romanesque*, which he does not define, except implicitly (the euphoric/dysphoric scenes; Emma Bovary's reading). But Balzac has euphoric/dysphoric scenes (or is he not a 'realist'?), as does James (the sober, ironical, and yet extremely 'moving' death of Milly in *The Wings of the Dove*). This raises the subsidiary question: does irony absolve a realistic author of *romanesque*? (E.g. the surely 'spectacular' death of Emma Bovary, which is not part of her 'reading', though perhaps a result of it.) But I shall return to this vexed question of irony, in chapter 14.

Some of his tenets, too, seem to me exacerbated forms of what must be present in any narrative. Thus *the psychological motivation of characters* on the *post hoc ergo propter hoc* principle (2) is a question of degree, of how much 'masking' there is of the real function (i.e. motivation in Genette's sense, see note 7 above) by psychological analysis and build-up. Similarly the cyclothymic rhythm (14) must form part of any narrative to create the necessary disequilibrium of any previous equilibrium (since the latter stops narrativity). Or, again, *redundancy and foreseeability* (of social description, 'programmed acts', etc.) which merely 'conjugates a virtual paradigm', is more a question of relative length and relative foreseeability than of mere presence, since characters can hardly exist (fictionally) without their surroundings. In both *knowledge of the author* (6), filtered through knowledgeable characters, and *description* (15), Hamon is referring to a particularly saturated form of what any narrative will do: a scene, a gesture, a fact of knowledge, must be perceived by someone, and the narrator must either describe it directly (15) or filter it through the perception or dialogues of characters (6). And there is also a general sense in which 'the real is nothing but a linguistic mosaic' in *any* text. The problem of too much information for readability would therefore seem to be one of (a) relevance: whether the information is functional or gratuitously present *only* for the effect of the real; (b) degree: for how long does it interrupt or clog the action; (c) distribution: in chunks or in small bits inserted here and there (the technique of twentieth-century realism); (d) repetition: how often are the same devices used; and concomitantly (e) foreseeability: how visible are they (e.g. the description-openers etc.).

Barthes had discussed the problem of gratuitousness in 'L'effet du réel' (1968), and seemed to answer it himself (at least for the replete text, the 'readerly' text) in *S/Z: Tout signifie*.

3.2.3. A few other possibilities

Robbe-Grillet (1962; 1965: 63) states that the past tense (by which he means the French *passé simple*) is the mark of the traditional novel, and seems in the context to mean the realistic novel. If he does, he is not strictly right since all narratives have used the past tense until relatively recently, and the present tense (favoured by Robbe-Grillet) only for purposes of describing a scene vividly in the mind of the narrator, in George Eliot for instance (*Scenes from Clerical Life*), or in *David Copperfield* when he is remembering a scene with intensity (see chapter 12 for tense in modern narrative).

But there is a sense in which realism *must* use the past tense, since it has to convince us that the events told 'really' occurred, that the characters and places 'really' existed, and that the author has full and retrospective knowledge of them.

I would also add explanatory flashback in the pluperfect or equivalent as a (now exasperating, at least to me, because stereotyped) mark of realistic discourse, as well as the (relatively recent, i.e. early nineteenth-century) development, the over-exploitation of free indirect discourse, where the narrator slips into the mind of the character, giving his thoughts, in his style, terms and more colloquial language, while nevertheless retaining his 'authority', his own voice, by leaving that discourse in the past (or equivalent) and in the third person, so that we do not get the words that would have been actually used by the character: e.g. *I will* becomes *he would*, *I didn't* becomes *he hadn't* etc. It is a mixed discourse, also for the effect of the real (what the character is thinking, in his own words), but also typical of the inherent contradictions of realism (the effacement of the narrator, nevertheless inescapably there, in the tenses and the pronoun). I shall be discussing this in more detail in chapter 12, and return to it in chapter 14 ('metafiction').

Hamon does not deal with tenses or time-shifts or types of discourse but only with the broad techniques of information-circulation and readability (though his title is 'Un discours con-traint'). My point is that his lack of system does not really allow him to bring in these categories, unless he had chanced upon them.

He does deal with character, but by no means fully, and here it is on the contrary his semi-system which limits him. Since he happens to have a category about circulating information, and another about psychological motivation, character is merely, under the first, a construct of index-cards (slices of knowledge) and a pretext-function (the knowledgeable person), and, under the second, an *a posteriori* justification for the narrative sequences. Yet character is the pride of realism, its greatest achievement for many critics and still part of blurb or reviewing jargon ('beautifully realised' etc.), and the way that this illusion is created surely deserves closer analysis, especially if it can be shown to be also part of the *discours contraint*, and, moreover, from a psychoanalytic viewpoint, a wholly fantasmatic procedure, characters being verbal structures, more and more swollen with words, as it were stray phalluses wandering our minds, cut off from the body of the text (hence the endless character-analysis of traditional criticism) which is why we are inevitably disappointed when we see them incarnated by real actors on stage or screen.

Barthes led the way (a little summarily) with the semic code (see above, chapter 2, p. 39). But a great deal more work could be done (and has been suggested by Olga Scherer, see n. 15 below) on semic contradictions alone, on the way for instance contradictory aspects can diverge, character A becoming A_1 and A_2 (so that $A - A_1 = A_2$ and $A - A_2 = A_1$); or converge $(A_1 + A_2 = A)$, which would be the formula of social realism as well as *kitsch* (which Suvin calls the 'subliterature of realism'), benevolent realism (*Uncle Tom's Cabin*), and collective realism (e.g. Chernychevsky's *What is To Be Done About It?* 1862, publ. 1905). All of which could go under the more general term of synthetising realism; or, on the contrary, A_1 and A_2 can have a quasi-independent evolution (themes of the double).[15]

4. Categorial criteria and literary evaluation

The two theoreticians examined here, Suvin and Hamon, are obviously not 'scientific' semioticians in the sense described in chapter 2 – which is why they are more 'useful' to me. However, beyond the questions of illogical order raised with reference to Hamon, there are the questions of categorial criteria and of evaluation (theoretically expelled but surreptitiously very much there).

Categorial criteria are not touched on by Hamon. For example, since characters love, die, rest, are happy or unhappy in realistic novels, at what point does a scene relating this become 'idyllic', 'spectacular', 'ecstatic', 'tender'? Or how long must a description be to be called 'hypertrophied' (i.e. realistic)? Or how neutral or 'transparent' is a 'demodalised' style? Clearly these are subjective terms, which in turn involve the whole problem of the implied reader.

Much the same applies to Suvin: at what point does a writer's approach to the empirical world, said to be 'dialectical and cognitive', like that of natural sciences and materialist philosophy, become 'non-cognitive', mystical and metaphysical? At what point is a form 'high', 'low', 'primitive', 'bourgeois' etc.? There must, surely, be a sliding scale.

The more general problem of literary evaluation is obviously related to categorial criteria. Theory claims not to evaluate. Nevertheless by describing processes (and especially in France, after the shift from purely abstract analysis of action-structures to more surface features), it cannot help evaluating if it implicitly or explicitly takes up firm positions in favour of, for instance, the *scriptible* as against the *lisible*, which is specifically stated by Barthes to be the 'negative, reactive value of the scriptible' (1970; 1974: 4), and even if negative is used here as equal simply to 'opposite'. Barthes's stand throughout is clear, in favour of plural significance as against univocity, the cognitive and pluritemporal as against non-cognitive and unitemporal (Suvin), or economy as against expansion (etc.). Hamon's terms are by no means neutral (hypertrophy, foreseeability, saturation – the latter from Barthes), indeed they are loaded, and he seems throughout to be condemning realism, under the guise of descriptive cataloguing. I do not mind the condemnation, I mind the guise of objectivity. And, since evaluation creeps in, isn't there one good thing to be said for the genre he works on? Why are these novels still widely read, and with pleasure?

He never asks the question. Readability, I suppose, but even that is a negative value. Suvin at least likes and defends the genre he writes about, even if it is at the cost of arbitrary and total exclusion of all others outside science fiction as he defines it (cognitive/pluritemporal). Moreover he makes his ideological premises clear, even if it is at the cost of not even pretending to objectivity, with terms like 'subliterature' which, ironically, Marxist scholars are now studying with great interest, under the name of 'infraliterature', as what the popular masses actually read. Curiously enough, it would seem that the journalistic practice of literary massacre, now that newspapers have so reduced the space devoted to fiction that only 'praiseworthy' books get a look in, has surreptitiously passed to the scholars, but in scholarly disguise, without the frank relish and witty swashbuckling that journalism demands.

But it is not only a question of tone, terminology or disguised/undisguised prejudice. Many of the features described by Hamon, notably over-determination (redundancy, repetition), but also discontinuity and fragmentation, contrast (cyclothymic rhythm), parallel structures (here only implicitly present in the 'parallel story' of history), are not as such specific to realistic discourse, nor are they as such negative values; indeed redundancy is a necessary feature not only of any text but of language (cp. chapter 2 above, p. 44). On the contrary, these features are all the privileged marks of poetry, where they are particularly concentrated, and they must structure any literary text.

What then is the criterion that transforms these 'positive' features into 'negative' ones, the 'writerly' text into a 'readerly' text which, moreover, can become 'unreadable' in the more current sense, precisely because of those features? Clearly they must be ideological and therefore (in the usually unneutral misuse of that term) biased. But even if that particular misuse is ostensibly refused (as it explicitly is not by Suvin), it creeps back in the terms and, at times, in the lack of rigour. In part 4 of his article, Hamon (1973: 433) enumerates four main procedures (which he then further splits into his fifteen tenets):

(a) hypertrophy of redundancy
(b) hypertrophy of anaphoric procedures [= redundancy]
(c) hypertrophy of phatic (see chapter 2, p. 23) and disambiguation procedures
(d) indirect compensation or re-establishment of authority in the authorial utterance theoretically expelled from the text.

The word 'hypertrophy' occurs three times, and the fourth procedure should really appear (and does) among his contradictions
(see p. 90 above). But two main notions indirectly emerge:

(1)   that of, precisely, hypertrophy (though a criterion of what con-
      stitutes 'hyper' must surely be evolved, empirically, for any one
      text) in the techniques of realism, but as we shall see it also occurs
      in the marvellous, in another form (reduplication)

(2)   that of transparency, not in the neutrality of the textual support
      which is the aim of realism, but transparency of both technical
      motivations and significance, particular and overall. In this latter
      sense, transparency is *also* a feature of the marvellous.

Even these two notions however, are not *in themselves* 'negative',
for if they were they would not account for the many works in which
both hypertrophy and transparency of technical motivations are
used to structure the text by laying bare and exaggerating its
devices, as happens in every 'anti-form' to regenerate exhausted
genres (*Don Quixote, Le Roman bourgeois, Jacques le fataliste, Tristram
Shandy, Tom Jones*, and many others, including many 'postmoderns', see chapter 14). Moreover, they do not account either for
'hypertrophied' or technically 'transparent' works that do not turn
devices upside down, that use them seriously, and nevertheless
'succeed' – and I do not mean commercially but aesthetically, giving
lasting pleasure (Proust for instance being an example of at least
hypertrophy).

It is not my purpose to resolve this problem in this book, only to
produce analyses of various kinds that may indirectly contribute
towards its resolution. Clearly more work needs to be done on the
theoretical problem of why the very same features that are considered the privileged marks of the poetic function (features that
structure the text), should also, when hypertrophied and rendered
transparent, become (but not always) the very same features of, let
us say, the unpoetic function, or the way the poetic function
collapses (as for instance happens in Tolkien, see chapter 9 below).
Is it only a question of close organisation? In lyric poetry it seems to
be, but in narrative, and even in narrative poetry, 'hypertrophied'
and apparently chaotic works can be works of art. And if all the
complex procedures of theory are put to work merely to arrive at
the conclusion that the poetic function consists of a maximum of
plurality achieved with a minimum of means (or a maximum of
economy), well, intuitive criticism knew that all along, and theory
must also account for such a conclusion, if indeed it is correct.

5. Realistic discourse in science fiction

For the moment I shall simply summarise Hamon's tenets, but in my own regrouping (and omitting (4) and (8) which are not specific), under 1: the (pedagogic) plethora of information to be circulated; and 2: the (pedagogic) need for clarity and readability. Opposite, I shall give a general indication as to which are probably, in my opinion, shared by realistic fiction (RF) and SF.[16] Hamon's number is given in brackets.

RF	SF
1 PLETHORA OF INFORMATION	
(1) *The appeal to memory* (1): assuring the coherence and readability of the text by constant circulation of information about the fiction's past and future, often through a character specific to that purpose.	Yes for past of characters (career etc.). Yes for past of the world as seen from the future, and for future of the undertaking (warnings, orders, scientific predictions).
(2) *Knowledge of the author circulated through substitutes* (6): slices of knowledge, pretext characters and pretext-functions.	Yes where scientific aspect is detailed (in early magazines, with footnotes even) and for socio-politico-economic descriptions of new societies, or the history of their discovery. Sometimes lengthy explanations (Clarke's *Childhood's End*, Asimov's *The End of Eternity*), Heinlein's *Stranger in a Strange Land* or crude preaching (Bradbury's *Fahrenheit 451*).
(3) *Description* (15): exhaustiveness in re-presenting the real within the fiction, pretext syntagmas and characters as description-openers.	Yes in most traditional SF, even in the so-called 'New Wave' SF (Aldiss, Ballard, Disch, Delany, Heinlein and on).
(4) *Redundancy and foreseeability* (7): the programmed acts (a character's social sphere and ritualised activities).	Yes for scientific activities and the activities of unfamiliar societies, which often rely on recognition through repetition.
(5) *Cyclothymic rhythm of good/bad* (14): a result of 3 (15) and 4 (7), the realistic desire for exhaustiveness producing a need to review each term of an opposition.	Yes, but in normal sense that any adventure story will vary success/failure, danger/overcoming, adventure/rest etc.

(6) *Defocalisation of hero* (10): hero important element of readability, but defocalized to avoid *le romanesque* so partakes in plethora of information (several heroes, description-openers, discontinuity so redescription etc).

Yes on whole: often a whole spaceship team, who may get separated, or different elements of new society or scientific team.

2 READABILITY

(1) *Semiological compensation* (5): extra codes (illustrations, genealogical trees etc.)

No (except in pulp and early SF, and in Verne). SF does not require that amount of technical understanding. Some exceptions (Crichton's *Andromeda Strain*, graphic print-outs etc.).

(2) *Psychological motivation of characters* (2): the justification for a narrative sequence.

Yes, but more transparent, less densely masked. The psychology is superficial, sufficient only for the types necessary to the plot.

(3) *Demodalisation* (9): the neutral, 'transparent' style, window on the world, detonalised and simply assertive. Avoidance of subjective locutions, italics, quotations.

In general yes, but insofar as SF tilts into pure marvellous, no. Also strong influence of highly colloquial 'thriller' idiom, as in modern realism.

(4) *Disambiguation* (11, 12, 13 regrouped): reduction of ambiguity (11), effacement of being/seeming opposition (12), refusal of false clues or text in a hurry (13).

Yes in general, especially the quick learning of false clues (cp. early editor Campbell's advice to writers: 'must solve the problems directly raised in the story – and do it succinctly. Quick and sharp', quoted in Huntington).

(5) *The parallel story* (3): reference to names and events familiar in history, geography etc. insuring effect of real while allowing economy of description.

No, since the SF world is *un*familiar, but known places may be used for contrast (return) or inverted effect (San Francisco destroyed etc). The unfamiliar world can only be made familiar through description, explanation, repetition etc.

As we can see, most of the features of realistic discourse as described by Hamon seem to be shared by science fiction, the only exceptions being *the parallel story* and *semiological compensation* (of which there are in any case important examples). The interesting exception is therefore the parallel story: an 'ungrammatical' sentence such as those given in note 8 above is unconceivable in SF since the world described is denuded of these signposts. The unfamiliar world must either be left poetically blurred or fall back on realistic means of circulating the information. And although these are usually slightly more economical than in the nineteenth-century realistic novel dealt with by Hamon, the circulation of information about the invented world seems to be a real and unsolved problem in SF. We tend to get long chunks of narrator explanation (Heinlein's *Stranger in a Strange Land*), or explanations by knowledgeable characters, so that we get scientists explaining basics to each other, with impatient interruptions such as 'Skip all that' (Asimov), or, more contrived, characters *thinking* the information, political or historical or scientific, even in italics (Poul Anderson), or documents. The hero of Lem's *Solaris*, for instance, a man thoroughly trained in and familiar with the problems of Solaris, consults book after book in the Station library, each duly summarised by the narrator for the reader, on the history of all the theories; this chapter admittedly has another function as (rather facile) satire on scientific scholarship, but earlier instances seem a transparent device to inform the reader, as when, shortly after arrival, the hero quite unnecessarily brushes up his history of the discovery of Solaris and the theories that followed. The referential code is often unskilfully used in SF (cp. p. 42). I shall return to this parallel story in chapter 9 (with regard to Tolkien) and in chapter 10 will examine one SF narrative by Vonnegut, who uses all these techniques but turns them as it were inside out, with irony, and above all uses them with extreme and comic brevity, poking fun at SF conventions in the process (as does Lem in *The Cyberiad*, more exuberantly but less skilfully). But this too is a natural development out of SF itself, which, even in the 'information' tenets it shares with RF, is rarely 'hypertrophied', except by a few writers (some Asimov, Delaney, Heinlein). The element of adventure-story in it could not stand it. I must add here that this is in itself another link with the *modern* realistic novel, which also reduced the 'hypertrophy' of the earlier type examined by Hamon. In fact the best SF is frequently in the form of short stories, and some of the novels are stories padded out with 'information', moral, psychological or political analysis and such, in the sometimes sad attempt SF makes to be 'serious' or 'great' fiction.

As for the other features of realistic discourse I briefly suggested as not explored by Hamon, or indeed by anyone to my knowledge as specific to realism, it is clear that traditional SF at least does take over wholesale and unmodified most of the techniques of RF: the post-dated narrative in the past tense, the explanatory flashback and the abuse of free indirect discourse for a character's thoughts. Unlike the ultra-realism of the late nineteenth century and early twentieth, it tends to go back to Balzacian narrator – comment and omniscience, i.e. not to eliminate the narrative voice in favour of substitute transmitters, but this varies a good deal, and certainly the demodalised assertive style is the ideal, which tones down the narrative voice, even if this style is pepped up with colloquialism for the characters. But dialogues tend to be abysmally banal. Susan Sontag has commented on this feature for SF films ('The Imagination of Disaster', in Sontag 1966), showing how lines like ' "Come quickly, there's a monster in my bathtub", "We must do something about this", "Wait! Professor. There's someone on the telephone", "But that's incredible", and the old American standby "I hope it works!" are hilarious in the context of picturesque and deafening holocaust' (pp. 223–4). Films are of course a special case, but SF novels are not immune to this naive tempering of 'otherness, of alien-ness, with the grossly familiar' (p. 224).

The other main feature of RF not systematically analysed by theorists (no doubt in reaction to over-exploitation by traditional criticism) was character, but clearly this is the one feature that SF does not share with RF, as all its defenders proudly proclaim. The disappearance of character (in the traditional sense) from contemporary ('postmodern') fiction is one of the ways in which SF and the more 'serious', experimental fiction have come close together, and it is interesting in this respect to note that a modern critic of 'postmodernism', Mas'ud Zavarzadeh (1976) makes a broad division of postmodern of what he prefers to call 'supramodernism' into 'transfiction' and the non-fiction novel (the real simply reported, but more unreal than the familiar real); and transfiction he further divides into metafiction, surfiction, and science fiction (by which he means the 'new science fiction'). I shall return to postmodernism in my last chapter, and mention it here only to show that in this 'merging' of a certain type of SF with 'serious fiction', which includes the non-fiction novel, SF reveals its close connections with the mainstream realistic novel in the 'good' sense of the great tradition, undergoing similarly painful and revolutionary transformations.

PART III

The pure fantastic: types of analysis

The pure landscape: aspect analyses

5

The encoded reader

1. Hypocrite lecteur, mon semblable, mon frère

After a long period when the actual (flesh and blood) author had
been enthroned by criticism, his every 'laundry-list' (as Pound
called biography) scrutinized, he was, in true carnivalesque fashion,
unthroned, the wild and happy crowd of actual readers taking over
– but, as is the way with carnival, only for a time. Extremes bring
natural reactions, and the two polarities, called at the time the
intentional and the affective fallacies, seem to have compromised on
a safe buffer state called the text as object, an apparently
autonomous unit that encodes not only its author (implied), and its
reader (implied), but also (or) its narrator and its narratee.

Buffer states, however, rarely remain safe or buffer, and wars (or
carnivals) continue, as we have seen in chapter 2. To simplify I shall
restrict myself here to the reader as encoded in the text, although
this again is bound to be 'my' reading of the reader as so encoded;
nor do I claim to escape professional deformation any more than
others have, though many try.

First, I shall retain the more neutral term, the 'encoded reader',
which makes my option for the textual buffer state clear. Second, I
shall stick to very simple problems in simple narratives, on the
grounds that these reveal encoded structures more easily than do
complex poems or even complex narratives. Finally, I shall divide
my material into three broad categories: texts in which a code is
over-determined, texts in which it is under-determined, and texts in
which it is non-determined or so haphazardly determined as to be in
effect non-determined.[1] These are operational terms: the contrast
needed to reveal the first category will automatically touch on the
second (so that the first section will be longer); and the last may
turn out to be a transient category.

2. A code over-determined: hypocrite lecteur

A code is over-determined when its information (narrative, ironic, hermeneutic, symbolic, etc.) is too clear, over-encoded, recurring beyond purely informational need. The reader is then in one sense also over-encoded, and does in fact sometimes appear in the text, dramatised, like an extra character: the 'Dear Reader'. But in another sense he is treated as a kind of fool who has to be told everything, a subcritical (*hypo-crite*) reader.

2.1. A folk-tale: over-determination of action and mystery codes

I shall start, not with the pure fantastic but with an ultra-simple example from an American short story very like a folk-tale, in which narrative information, both proaieretic (the action) and hermeneutic (the mystery), is over-determined.[2]

In Washington Irving's *Rip Van Winkle*, Rip wakes up from his adventure on the mountain, and the reader naturally supposes that this happens the next morning. No indices suggest otherwise, or rather, the time indices are carefully unspecified, under-determined, although this could escape a first reading (my italics):[3]

On waking, he found himself on the green knoll whence he had first seen the old man of the glen [reader assumes he was transported there after drinking from the flagon]. He rubbed his eyes – *it was a bright sunny morning* ... 'Surely', thought Rip, 'I have not slept here *all night*.' [counter-index 1, = one night, but in character's view-point]. He recalled the occurrences *before he fell asleep*.

And he gives (like the reader), a 'natural' explanation: 'Oh, that flagon! That wicked flagon!' From narrator to reader, Rip's 'all night' is a false clue (Barthes's *leurre*) but, on second reading, a character-error.

There follows a long series of thirty indices, all partaking of both the action and hermeneutic codes, and upon any one of which any actual reader may guess the truth, long before Rip.

In the mountains

Index 1:	his gun is rusty	⎫	
Index 2:	his dog Wolf is gone	⎬	could all receive natural explanation (one night)
Index 3:	he is stiff in joints	⎭	

Index 4:	he can't find amphitheatre	s.t.s.p. 1 (suggestion of time supernaturally passed, no. 1), but could still have natural explanation
Indes 5:	the landscape has changed (stream where none before,) etc.)	

In the village

Index 6:	he meets people he does not know	s.t.s.p. 2
Index 7:	they stare at him in surprise and stroke their chins	s.t.s.p. 3
Index 8:	stroking his chin, he finds his beard is a foot long	s.t.s.p. 4
Index 9:	(change to external viewpoint) strange children hoot at him and point to his gray beard	s.t.s.p. 5 } see later for implausibility
Index 10:	the dogs are unfamiliar	s.t.s.p. 6
Index 11:	the village is altered (more populous, old haunts gone, new houses built)	s.t.s.p. 7
Counter-Index 2:	the mountains and river are unaltered	provokes both natural explanation (flagon) and supernatural (bewitched)
Index 12:	his own house is decayed	s.t.s.p. 8
Index 13:	'A half-starved dog, that looked like Wolf', shows his teeth. Rip feels his very dog has forgotten him.	clearly presented as other dog, hence character-error. As such no s.t.s.p., only in context: s.t.s.p. 9
Index 14:	the village inn (his refuge) is different	s.t.s.p. 10
Index 15:	it has a different name and owner: 'The Union Hotel, by Jonathan Doolittle'	s.t.s.p. 11. Here a *specific time code* (s.t.c.) is added (post Revolutionary War): s.t.c. 1
Index 16:	it has a different flag (description)	s.t.s.p. 12 + s.t.c. 2
Index 17:	the sign has changed, from King George in red coat and	

	sceptre to same face but in buff and blue coat with sword (etc.), legend: George Washington	s.t.s.p. 13 + s.t.c. 3
Index 18:	the drowsy tranquillity has become bustling disputation	as such no s.t.s.p. or s.t.c., only in context: s.t.s.p. 14 + s.t.c. 4
Index 19:	his old friends (named) gone	s.t.s.p. 15
Index 20:	people speak in a 'Babylonish jargon'	s.t.s.p. 16 (later revealed as election talk but no s.t.c. here)
Index 21:	'The appearance of Rip, with his long grizzled beard, his rusty fowling-piece, his uncouth dress. . .'	repeat of Indices 8 and 9 (also with external viewpoint) and of Index 1
Index 22:	questions about how he voted, Federal or Democrat, and why he brings a gun to an election	s.t.s.p. 17 + s.t.c. 5
Index 23:	accused of being a spy and threatened	as such no s.t.s.p., only in context: s.t.s.p. 18 + s.t.c. 6
Index 24:	Rip protests, only looking for neighbours, names them and himself asks questions: where are they?	
	(a) Nicholas Vedder (dead eighteen years)	s.t.s.p. 19
	(b) Brom Dutcher (killed at war)	s.t.s.p. 20 + s.t.c. 7
	(c) Van Brummel (now in Congress)	s.t.s.p. 21 + s.t.c. 8
Index 25:	'Does nobody here know Rip Van Winkle?' They point to a counterpart of himself (identity crisis for Rip, who still clings to his one night supposition)	s.t.s.p. 22
Index 26:	young woman appears with child in her arms, whom she calls Rip	s.t.s.p. 23
Index 27:	Rip's memories aroused, asks her name (Judith Gardenier), then her father's name (Rip Van Winkle, who left home twenty years ago)	s.t.s.p. 24

Index 28:	Rip has tumbled to the truth, and only asks: 'Where is your mother?' (dead, though recently)	s.t.s.p. 25
Index 29:	Rip embraces his daughter and reveals himself as her father, much to general amazement	s.t.s.p. 26
Index 30:	an old woman recognises him: 'Why, where have you been all these twenty long years?'	s.t.s.p. 27

Then comes the 'explanation', by an old inhabitant who turns up and tells the legend of Hendrick Hudson in the Kaatskill Mountains. The explanation is supernatural.

Clearly any actual reader, first identifying with Rip in his puzzlement, must quickly unidentify (probably at index 8, and possibly before); without knowing the exact explanation, he knows that time has mysteriously elapsed and starts watching Rip's puzzlement instead of sharing it. The encoded reader, however, is encoded throughout the thirty indices, in an over-determined way, at least as regards hermeneutic information (the aesthetic pleasure derived from the details of the changed village is another question).

Interestingly, it is at index 8 that the narrator 'cheats', as it were, in the *vraisemblable* necessary to the supernatural, with the implausibly late realisation by Rip about the length of his beard (one must surely *see* one's own beard if it is a foot long, especially if one is picking up a gun from the ground, looking for a dog, a path, etc., but I am ready to be corrected by any long-bearded man). And at index 9 the narrator switches to an external view of the beard for its colour, repeating the procedure at index 21. Such a change of viewpoint (the only examples), justified only by the need to delay Rip's recognition, is like an extra encoded wink which increases the distance between hero and encoded reader. And of course the specific time codes (s.t.c.) about the Revolutionary War, belong to Barthes's referential code, which appeals to our general knowledge.

This over-determination of the hermeneutic and action codes is of course specific to the fairy-tale, as when an adult, telling a story to a child who knows it but wants to hear it again, may overplay a known formula, giving the equivalent of a heavy wink. But *Rip Van Winkle* is more than a children's story, and if we want to account for this, the over-determination of the action and hermeneutic codes inevitably shifts the actual reader's interpretation powers onto other codes: the semic, slightly (the build-up of Rip's character through semes, good nature, laziness, etc.), the referential (historical, general, such as indirect reference to the virago wife as a type), and the symbolic.

I realise that this sounds like the desperate teacher or critic who, unable to excuse the 'bad' (or here, naive) aspects of a classic, takes refuge in the symbolic, a sin also besetting critics of contemporary fiction in those innumerable studies of the symbolism, allegory and thematics of otherwise mediocre works (see 5, *Codes non-determined*). But that is only the abuse of a theoretically valid procedure. As Barthes (and Frye) have shown, a work, genre or period can exploit one code (or mode) more than others, but can be read in each or all of them, the dominance of any one or more becoming highly relevant to generic expectation. Realistic fiction tends to over-determine the referential and the semic codes, and could, but might not, under-determine the proaieretic and/or the hermeneutic and/or the symbolic. A folk-tale will over-determine the proaieretic and sometimes (as here), the hermeneutic, but under-determine (or not code at all) the referential, the semic, the symbolic.

Rip Van Winkle is a relatively sophisticated folk-tale, for all its over-determination, and it appeals to us as a folk-tale with sophisticated variants. Without using any complex (Greimasian or other) analysis, we can recognise most of Propp's functions (see above, chapter 2, p. 19), occasionally displaced (*e.g. pursuit* and *rescue* shifted to the beginning as Rip's wife chases him from home and then from his refuge, the inn; *interrogation* shifted to the end and fused with *task*; *victory* shifted to the end); or if not displaced, transmuted.

There is first an exposition of the initial situation, in the iterative mode, made up in fact of all the elements that turn up later (reversed) as indices. The *transgression* is transmuted as not serious, a charming transgression of an implicit (social) injunction to work. Dame Van Winkle is a wicked-stepmother figure indirectly responsible for Rip's escape into the mountains. Rip's 'transgression' does not cause an explicit *misdeed* by a villain, nor a *lack*, but his indolent nature does create a lack of marital happiness. The *mediation* (call for help) is not the king's but is assumed by the hero and motivated by his own reaction to that unhappiness. The hero *departs*, is *tested* by a 'donor' (call for help by the old man of the glen), *reacts*, indirectly receives a *magic auxiliary* (the drink, albeit taken sub-reptitously), which *translocates* him, it seems only in space (back to the knoll), but actually in time. The *struggle* is shifted to a more metaphysical level, but is first presented as a physical struggle with the situation, and only later becomes a struggle with his own identity. There is naturally no immediate *victory*, as in Propp, but there is a physical *marking* (of age), and there is an *arrival incognito*, a *false hero's claim* (society threatening him, in his identity), a *task*, assimilated to the struggle with identity in time (he solves the task and wins the struggle by asking questions himself), a *solution*, first for himself then for others (though the encoded reader knows the answer, as in the folk-tale), followed by *recognition*, through his daughter in the role of the princess whose 'marking' of the hero (identity through name and blood) leads to the identification and is the more metaphysical counterpart to the physical marking of age.

Above all there is an (ironic) *transfiguration*; Rip is no longer the reckless young fellow but a respected patriarch, and as an (ironic) *reward* (Propp's 'wedding' function) he goes to live with his daughter, and as a respected patriarch is not required to work. This is also his victory; he has all the peace and comfort of marriage (albeit incestuous) without the responsibility and the nagging. He has paid a heavy price for it, that of his youth and lived experience, but he is evidently happy to pay it.

Even if the actual reader has not read Propp he will, from a general as opposed to a skilled literary competence (and this general competence is the closest analogy to linguistic competence), be familiar with and recognise these folklore elements. But they are under-determined, they have as it were shifted into the symbolic code. The 'villain' (and, ambiguously, the 'hero') is in fact really time, itself ambiguous (an antithesis transgressed): (a) working time (society versus laziness), and (b) free time (society and Rip's good relations with it – he helps everyone except himself). His wife, often thought to be the villain, is merely a specific manifestation of the real villain, society in its bad aspect. She is punished by death (time). He is rewarded by the free time of old age, but is also punished by the loss of youth (time). Good society (for him) has won, even if bad society (for others) goes on (wars, elections, disputations). What we have is not, as some critics have argued, an attack on the American Woman, but a typical American story of the hero opting out of society. And all this, including the carefully balanced rhetorical structure, belongs to the symbolic code, which is under-determined.

I have spent some time on a simple narrative in order to over-determine my point about over-determination. With or without a Proppian (or any other) analysis, and even if this reading can be disputed, it is clear that over-determination in one area does not alter our feeling of something else being there, less immediately accessible, which gives the story its charm and quality (to use evaluative words, or (to avoid them) its underlying structure and coherence.

If this is true, we can only conclude that whatever over-determination may occur in any one work or genre, some under-determination is necessary for it to retain its hold over us, its peculiar mixture of recognition–pleasure and mystery.

In other words, the function of the over-determined part of a text is to make things clear to the Dear Reader who is encoded as hypo-critical, while the function of the under-determined part is to blur, to keep something back (and it may be much more in a complex text), so as not to insult the Dear Reader's intelligence enough to alienate him.

So I shall turn to a very different kind of text, Flann O'Brien's *At Swim-Two-Birds* (1939), which uses a very sophisticated form of over-determination, in the best Sterne tradition.[4]

2.2. *The playful text: over-determination of the symbolic code*

The novel opens with the I–narrator's reflections on narrative openings:

Having placed in my mouth sufficient bread for three minutes' chewing, I withdrew my powers of sensual perception and retired into the privacy of my mind, my eyes and face assuming a vacant and preoccupied expression. I reflected on the subject of my spare-time literary activities. One beginning and one ending for a book was a thing I did not agree with. A good book may have three openings entirely dissimilar and interrelated only in the prescience of the author, or for that matter one hundred times as many endings.

Examples of three separate openings – the first: The Pooka MacPhelliney, a member of the devil class, sat in his hut in the middle of a firwood meditating on the nature of the numerals and segregating in his mind the odd ones from the even. He was seated at his diptych or ancient two-leaved hinged writing-table with inner sides waxed. His rough long-nailed fingers toyed with a snuff-box of perfect rotundity and through a gap in his teeth he whistled a civil cavatina. He was a courtly man and received honour by reason of the generous treatment he gave his wife, one of the Corrigans of Carlow.

The second opening: There was nothing unusual in the appearance of Mr John Furriskey but actually he had one distinction that is rarely encountered – he was born at the age of twenty-five and entered the world with a memory but without a personal experience to account for it. His teeth were well-formed but stained by tobacco, with two molars filled and a cavity threatened in the left canine. His knowledge of physics was moderate and extended to Boyle's Law and the Parallelogram of Forces.

The third opening: Finn MacCool was a legendary hero of old Ireland. Though not mentally robust he was a man of superb physique and development. Each of his thighs was as thick as a horse's belly, narrowing to a calf as thick as the belly of a foal. Three fifties of fosterlings could engage with handball against the wideness of his backside, which was large enough to halt the march of men through a mountain-pass. (p. 9)

The symbolic code is gloriously evident throughout, in the transgression of narrative levels (see chapter 2, p. 38, and chapter 12, pp. 333–5 here): the narrative inside a narrative but both from the same narrator, with the passage from one to the other emphasised by titles in italics. Within this transgression there is a rhetorical stylisation in the parody of literary models, all 'realistic': the initial 'portrait', the non-functional detail (*'a firwood meditating on the nature of numerals . . . His rough long-nailed fingers toyed with a snuff-box of perfect rotundity*, etc.; *two molars filled . . . Boyle's Law . . .*'), and explanatory description (*'his diptych or ancient two-leaved hinged writing-table with inner sides waxed'* – also perfectly pointless, parodying the effect of the real).

This parody of realism, however, is about 'unreal' characters: a member of the devil class, a man born at twenty-five, a legendary hero of old Ireland. Two models (legendary/realistic) are thus juxtaposed and interparodied; another antithesis transgressed. And within the legendary model, the relative measurements of the giant Finn MacCool (a relativity about which Swift was so meticulous), are wrong (if his thigh is as thick as a horse's belly his backside can hardly stop an army), recalling Rabelais rather than Swift.

Thus the symbolic code contains or is made up of a referential code, that is itself rhetorical, that is, it refers to our knowledge of opposing literary conventions, transgresses the oppositions. This symbolic code is highly determined (assuming our knowledge of the rhetoric or cultural conventions), except perhaps for Mr John Furriskey, the significance of whose adult birth and memory 'without a personal experience to account for it' is only implicit, but will be over-determined later; for that, of course, describes fictional characters though realistic fiction gives them a past in pluperfect analepsis. This is the only functional 'detail', none of the others playing any part in the 'story' (what there is of it) or recurring later.

It may be noted that since it is technically impossible to have more than one beginning to a narrative, owing to the linear sequential nature of language, the three 'examples' have to be given consecutively, so that the second and the third are not textually 'beginnings' (except under each subtitle), and none of them is the beginning of the I–narrator's narrative. Further transgression: a beginning is not a beginning.

The I–narrator then takes over again in an extremely episodic narrative about himself (a lazy student), his uncle, his friends, his uncle's friends: a non-narrative, in fact, that is frequently broken into by, and frequently breaks back into, other narratives produced by the student while he pretends to work in his room; these narratives are often discussed with his friends, and concern, among others, the above three personages.

The first of the narratives, however, is about a Mr Dermot Trellis, author, who lives at the Red Swan Hotel with the characters he creates, and who locks them up at night so that they won't be up to any mischief while he sleeps. Mr Trellis, like the narrator, writes in bed, and creates characters fully grown (such as Mr Furriskey, and as does any novelist), which amazing scientific feat calls for extracts from the press, including a medical correspondent, who claims however that some of the research was done by a Mr William Tracy, another author. This is where the implicit element of the opening rhetoric becomes over-determined. It turns out that most of the characters in the book (except those at the student–narrator's level) have been created by Mr Trellis (himself created by the narrator), and that some of them also remember episodes experienced in Mr Tracy's books. The narrator had earlier expressed certain views of the novel according to which: 'Characters should be interchangeable as between one book and another ... The modern novel should be largely a work of reference. Most authors spend their time saying what has been said before – usually said much better' (p. 25). Characters are not only said to be 'used' or 'employed' by an author, but 'hired'.

Mr Dermot Trellis creates the Pooka MacPhelliney, Finn MacCool, Mr Furriskey and his friends, some of whom tell stories about other characters or quote poets who then appear in the 'story' (such as it is). Finn tells ambling and incoherent legends, mostly about Sweeney, a travelling outcast bird-creature who utters poems.

At one point Finn appears to be Mr Trellis, half asleep in the same room. Mr Trellis also makes an indecent assault on one of his own characters (to protect whose virtue he had created her brother), the result of which is Orlick Trellis, to whose birth at the Red Swan all the other characters travel, coming across each other on the way. Orlick Trellis is of course also born adult, and Furriskey and his friends, perceiving that their author Dermot Trellis is becoming immune to the drugs they give him to keep him asleep while they act independently, induce Orlick to write a narrative against his father. After various false starts this narrative gets going and poor Dermot is beaten about, tortured and finally tried by all the other characters, including twelve judges acting also as witnesses and jury, the evidence against him being produced from their past 'employment' in other books.

What we have then is constant and deliberate transgression of narrative levels, a procedure not in itself new (see chapter 12), but so complicated, with so many levels (stories within stories and transgressions of narrators from one level to another), that it would be almost impossible to follow if the procedure itself, as part of a symbolic code super-encoded, were not thoroughly over-determined.

Thus we are given, at the mere level of the student–narrator's narrative, constant rhetorical headings followed by colons, such as:

'*Description of my uncle*: Red-faced, bead-eyed, ball bellied. Fleshy about the shoulders . . .'; '*Quality of rasher in use in the household*: Inferior, one and two the pound.'; '*The two senses referred to*: Vision and Smell'; '*Nature of chuckle*: quiet, private, averted'; '*Name of figure of speech*: Anaphora (or Epibole)'; '*The texts referred to, being an excerpt from "A Conspectus of the Arts and Natural Sciences", volume the thirty-first*' (etc.).

There are, as well, marked transitions to other levels: '*Extract from my typescript descriptive of Finn MacCool and his people, being a humorous or quasi-humorous incursion into ancient mythology*' (this notwithstanding the fact that Trellis is later said, in a synopsis for the late-coming reader, to have created Finn); '*Further extract from MS, Oratio Recta*'; or, for returning to the student–narrator level: '*Biographical Reminiscence, Part the First*'; '*. . . the Second*'; '*. . . the final*'; '*Conclusion of the book antepenultimate*'; '*. . . penultimate*'; '*. . . ultimate*'. (Nor of course are these three 'conclusions' real endings in any traditional sense.) And all the interruptions at all the levels end with a similar marking, such as '*End of foregoing*'.

The book is funny in much the same way that *Tristram Shandy* is funny, each being in different ways concerned with the difficulty and absurdity of writing fiction. A 'real' reader (Dylan Thomas) recommended it to a 'fictionally real' reader in these terms: 'Just the book to give to your sister, if she's a loud, dirty, boozy girl.' But for the loud, dirty, boozy girl to follow, there is a heavy over-coding on the rhetorical level, which does not detract from the book (as the over-determination of the hermeneutic code in *Rip* does not) but is necessary to its comprehension (unlike *Rip*). More important, it also constitutes one of its chief delights. It is an integral part of the delight in the constant transgressions, transgressions being delightful only if the rules are both clear and firm. Once again, but in a very different way, over-determination is counterbalanced by under-determination, but here it is the proaieretic (action) code which is under-determined, not only by the carnivalesque structure (society turned upside down, insertion of other genres, see chapter 2, p. 43 above, and p. 370 for Bakhtin) and by the constant transgression of levels, but also by its ambling, non-proaieretic nature at every level, including the narrator's. The transgression of narrative levels, calling attention to narrative procedure, is then itself thoroughly over-determined rhetorically, in the symbolic code (which is about the practice of *écriture*), and by the same token 'unconfuses' the pro-aieretic code, so as not to alienate the Dear Reader (the very much encoded reader), with the result that he is flattered by his own understanding. Without the under-determined area, the over-determined one would alienate him as an insult to his intelligence.

3. A code under-determined: hypercrite lecteur

In order to emphasise the balance needed by over-coding, I have necessarily and unhermeneutically encroached on this second category (though as we shall see the two are inversely linked), and so will analyse only one example (pure fantastic) and give more space to theoretical discussion.

Just as the function of over-determination is to make clear, so the function of under-determination is to blur. The encoded reader is then required to cooperate actively, to be hyper-critical. This indeed was one of the avowed purposes of the *nouveau roman*. A more popular and obvious example is the detective-story, in which the whole art is to give all the clues but in such a way that the important ones pass unnoticed. Here too there must be a careful balance between over-determination and under-determination, but the under-determination is stronger, either remaining so throughout or remaining so till the last few pages. And of course when a narrator cheats, as in the much cited instance of Agatha Christie's *The Murder of Roger Ackroyd*, where the reader is allowed inside the detective's thoughts throughout and then finds that the detective 'dunit', he feels this not only as a transgression of the implicit contract to keep the fair balance: the hermeneutic code is over-determined for wrong clues (through the wrong viewpoint), but under-determined (through the hidden fact that the viewpoint is wrong) for the 'truth'.

The clearest type is the truly ambiguous text, such as, among others, the *nouveau roman*. There seems, however, to be an important difference: the detective-story in general blurs by simply over-determining false clues and under-determining right ones (a code within the hermeneutic code, which the adept soon learns to look for); the ambiguous text, on the contrary, *seems* to over-determine one code, usually the hermeneutic, and even to over-encode the reader, but in fact the over-determination consists of repetitions and variations that give us little or no further information. The over-determination functions, paradoxically, as under-determination, provided there is also a strong element of under-determination within the same code.

The classic example is James's *The Turn of the Screw* (1898), in which the over-determination of the enigma (ghosts vs. hallucinations) is constant yet unresolved and can be read both ways each time (see chapters 6, 7 and 8 below). Here I shall use a shorter text, Poe's 'The Black Cat' (1843),[5] which Todorov places 'perhaps' in the generic category of the pure fantastic (wholly undecidable as to whether the supernatural is indeed supernatural or can receive a natural explanation), even though he places Poe's tales as a whole in the category of the uncanny (natural explanation). I shall look only at the hermeneutic code, since the ambiguity depends on this code alone, the others being clear and relatively unexploited.

There are, throughout most of the text, only three enigmas (E) introduced from the start, but three more are introduced at the end. Here is the first paragraph (p. 390):

Title: THE BLACK CAT
For the most wild, yet most
homely narrative which I am
about to pen,
	(E1: What – later which – black
	      cat?)
	E2: is it wild or homely?
	      (supernatural/natural)

I neither expect nor solicit belief.	E2^a: wild (+ reader encoded)
Mad indeed would I be to expect it,	E2^b: (2^a reversed): is *he* wild (mad)? = natural explanation (+ reader encoded)
in a case where my very senses reject their own evidence.	E2^a: reversed: supernatural
Yet, mad I am not – and very surely I do not dream.	E2^a: still reversed: madness denied, so supernatural
But to-morrow I die,	E3: why?
and to-day I would unburthen my soul.	E2^{ab}: from madness? (natural explanation) or from supernatural?
	(reader encoded)
My immediate purpose is to place before the world, plainly, succinctly, and without comment,	
a series of mere household events.	E2^b: homely
In their consequences, these events have terrified – have tortured – have destroyed me.	E2^a: homely→wild; E2^b: mad? E3: how destroyed?
Yet I will not attempt to expound them.	(reader encoded)
To me, they have presented little but Horror –	E2^{ab}: homely→wild; E2^b (supernatural) or mad? (natural explanation)
to many they will seem less terrible than *barroques* [Poe's italics]	E2^b: homely (+ reader encoded)
Hereafter, perhaps, some intellect may be found which will reduce my phantasm to the commonplace –	E2^b: his fantasy (natural explanation) + E2^b: homely (+ reader encoded)
some intellect more calm, more logical and far less excitable than my own,	E2^{ba}: E2^b mad; or E2^a: events are wild (supernatural) and have merely horrified him (+ reader encoded)
which will perceive, in the circumstances I detail with awe,	E2^a: wild (+ reader encoded)
nothing more than an ordinary succession of very natural causes and effects.	E2^b: homely; therefore E2^b; mad (+ reader encoded)

Enigma 1 (what cat?) is *apparently* solved at the beginning with the introduction of *a cat* (in italics), called Pluto, and does not recur till after the murder of Pluto and the appearance of the second cat.

E2^a and E2^b are not two separate enigmas but merely the narrative/narrator aspects of the same enigma: are the events supernatural (wild) or has the narrator (mad) imagined natural events as supernatural? This and what enigma 1 becomes (which black cat? Are there two or one?) will not be resolved. Enigma 3 will be reposed only twice, once clearly ('even in this felon's cell'), and once soon after a contextually clear premonition, the white splotch on Cat 2 that grows to the shape of the gallows.

Enigma 2 is very much over-determined, as we can see here, since it is the basis of the pure fantastic. In seminar work[6] we have discovered that, in general, the short story uses few semes of any one code (and of the semic and hermeneutic in particular), but that they recur often, a form of semantic over-determination also found in poetry (see note 1 above). But over-determination also seems to apply to the pure fantastic text, whether long or short (and most tend to be short, in order to sustain the ambiguity to the end). Obviously a pure fantastic short story will be particularly marked in this way.

The reader, too, is over-encoded. But contrary to the example of *Rip Van Winkle*, he is over-encoded not for over-clarity, but for further confusion. Far from being ahead of the protagonist, he lags behind, the main enigmas being merely repeated, reversed and re-reversed. Nevertheless he is flattered ('some intellect ... etc.'), and has to be thus flattered, rather grossly, since he is not allowed, as in *Rip*, to feel more clever than the protagonist.

The story will continue to repeat enigma 2, from the wife's superstition that all black cats are witches in disguise (supernatural) to the narrator–protagonist's 'wild' and dual behaviour (mad, i.e. natural explanation) and his constant comment upon it in terms of split personality ('the Fiend Intemperance'; 'the fury of a demon seized me'; 'the spirit of PERVERSENESS'; 'half horror, half remorse', etc.). This natural explanation (mad) is more emphasised than the supernatural one. The first clear suggestion of the supernatural does not occur until after the hanging of Pluto, with the image of a gigantic cat, a rope around its neck, impressed on the wall after the (fortuitous?) fire; but a 'natural' explanation, wholly implausible, is immediately given, to be followed by ambiguous phrases about 'fancy', 'the phantasm of the cat', and so on.

It is with the appearance of the second cat, its splotch of white on the breast (unlike Pluto) gradually growing to the shape of the gallows (E1, E2, and E3) and like Pluto after the narrator's first cruelty, deprived of one eye, that the element of the supernatural makes itself felt. Here it is worth noting that the narrator cheats a little (as in *Rip*, with the beard), in not giving us the highly visible detail of the cat's missing eye either at the moment when he sees, strokes and describes the cat in the 'den of more than infamy' (though this is justified *a posteriori*, in analepsis, and the den appears to be dark), or in his account of their later relationship; rather, it is after these two passages that he states: 'What added, no doubt, to my hatred of the beast, was the discovery, on the morning after I brought it home (justification), that, like Pluto, it also had been deprived of one of its eyes.' The ellipsis (under-determination) functions as a *leurre* (false clue: two cats) for the reader, but the subsequent analepsis draws his attention (over-determination) to the possibility of the second cat (who is never named) being the ghost of Pluto. It is, however, the only example of over-determination for E1, and only as a possibility.

E3 (why must he die?) is solved towards the end, the moment the narrator, tripped by Cat 2 in the cellar and prevented by his wife from venting his rage on the beast, buries his axe in her brain. And, because E3 is introduced at the outset, we also know, *un*hermeneutic-ally, that he will be caught, but not how. A sick calm invades him as he entombs the body in the wall. Enigma 4 is then introduced: where is the cat? It has disappeared, and the narrator expresses his profound relief. Four days later the police arrive, 'very unexpec-tedly' (E5 – why? Inquiries and a search had already satisfied them.) This is never answered: it can be regarded either as hermeneutically obvious, from unstated continued inquiries (ellipsis) or as hint of the supernatural action by the cat, a hint reinforced by the ellipsis, by the now uncanny atmosphere and by one ambiguous phrase at the end, the cat's 'informing voice', which ostensibly refers to its action after the wall-tapping, but could *also* suggest action before. They search the house. In the cellar the narrator is hideously calm ($E2^b$) and he praises the solid walls, tapping on them, whereupon:

But may God shield and deliver me from the fangs of the Arch-fiend!	$E2^b$: E1:	split personality THE CAT (connoted)
No sooner had the reverberation of my blows sunk into the silence, than I was answered by a voice from within the tomb!	E6:	whose voice? dead wife's? or cat's?

– by a cry, at first muffled and broken, like the sobbing of a child,	$E2^a$:	wild
and then finally swelling into one long, loud and continuous scream,	$E2^a$:	wild
utterly anomalous and inhuman	E6:	inhuman = ghost, dead human? or animal?
– a howl – a wailing shriek, half of horror and half of triumph,	E6:	cat's or wife's triumph? + $E2^a$: wild (horror)
such as might have arisen only out of hell, conjointly from the throats of the damned in their agony and of the demons that exult in the damnation.	$E2^b$: E1:	mad? $E2^a$: wild (hell) IF CAT (E6): = ghost of Pluto?
Of my own thoughts it is folly to speak [...]	$E2^b$:	mad (+ encoded reader)
a dozen stout arms were toiling at the wall. It fell bodily. The corpse, already greatly decayed and clotted with gore, stood before the eyes of the spectators.	$E2^a$:	wild
Upon its head, with red extended mouth and solitary eye of fire,	$E2^a$:	wild
sat the hideous beast whose craft had seduced me into murder,	E4: $E2^b$:	(where is the cat?) resolved split (mad)
and whose informing voice had consigned me to the hangman.	E3: E6: E5:	solution repeated; E6 (whose (voice?) E5 (why?) resolved supernatural reinforced but ambiguous
I had walled the monster up within the tomb!	E4: $E2^{ab}$:	explained wild, mad.

What we get ostensibly is a 'natural' explanation: Cat 2 (fortuitous) hated by the narrator out of guilt for (madly) murdering Cat 1, got walled up by mistake in the further madness of the murder and entombment of his wife. It remained half alive and screamed when the wall was (madly) tapped. E2 (madness or objective horror) is continuously encoded, E4 (where is the cat?) and E6 (whose voice?) are simultaneously solved, E3 (why does he have to die?) having been solved at the moment of the murder and being merely repeated here in the final chord. E5 (why do the police arrive?) remains ambiguous. It is: either resolved realistically by obviousness (ellipsis); or a momentary hint of the supernatural (through the same ellipsis, which is thus ambiguous, and through an ambiguous phrase).

There remains E1: which black cat? And E1, unlike E2, has been under-determined, with mere suggestions that Cat 2 is the ghost of Cat 1 (the noosed impression of the wall after the hanging of Cat 1, the weird appearance of Cat 2 in the den, the gallows mark, the one eye, his oppressively haunting behaviour). All these elements of course could receive natural explanations, and also belong to E2 (madness), which is over-determined but is itself in the end unresolved: either the narrator is mad and the events are 'natural'; or he is not mad, merely unbalanced and cruel, the latter traits being exacerbated by 'supernatural' events.

In other words, the balance of over-determination and under-determination is once again essential. But whereas in the folk-tale the balance was between two or more codes (hermeneutic and proaieretic over-determined, symbolic under-determined), as it was in Flann O'Brien's playful text (proiaeretic under-determined, symbolic over-determined), here the balance operates within one code (the hermeneutic), but between enigmas: the first two are essential to the pure fantastic and remain unresolved, E1 (which cat?) being under-determined, E2 (supernatural/natural) over-determined; the others are incidental and resolved: the third, introduced with the first two, is under-determined but is clearly resolved toward the end; the fourth and sixth, under-determined, are introduced only at the very end, and are immediately resolved; the fifth (a minor enigma), introduced just before the last paragraph, is under-determined and unresolved (or half-resolved: natural explanation obvious but elided/supernatural explanation hinted).

Beginning	E1	under-determined			unresolved
	E2	over-determined			unresolved
	E3	under-determined	resolved		
End	E4	under-determined	resolved		
	E5	under-determined	resolved	+	unresolved
	E6	under-determined	resolved		

4. The balance of determination and the dialogical text

This difference in the balance of over and under-determination (between codes for the first, ostensibly over-determined category, between enigmas of one code for the second ostensibly under-determined category of ambiguous texts) may be a fortuitous and empirical result of the texts analysed, and only further research can show whether the hypothesis is correct. The main difference is, as I have said, one of relative dominance in the final result: for the over-determined code of the first type of text, the under-determined area lies *in the reader's interpretation* (if he wishes); for the under-determined code of the second type of text (ambiguous), an area seems to be over-determined but in fact remains under-determined *within the text* (unless, as in the detective-story, it is neatly over-determined right at the end).

The ambiguous text is essentially 'dialogical': in the dialogical novel (e.g., Dostoevsky, according to Bakhtin, as opposed to Tolstoy), the author has a constant metatextual dialogue with his characters, and characters with each other; above all, the character has a dialogue with himself as against an imagined other.[7] The author in practice refuses to 'delimit' his character, to have the last word on him (as in the monological novel), and for that matter he refuses to delimit himself. The character revolts, as it were, against his own author's tendency to delimit him, and Flann O'Brien's comic treatment of this in *At Swim-Two-Birds* is a dramatised (explicit, over-determined) version of what is done more metatextually (or with an over-determined enigma unresolved, as here) in the dialogical novel.

I shall analyse types of metatext in detail in chapter 8 on *The Turn of the Screw*, and will say no more about it here. But in the case of the ambiguity that must remain unresolved in the pure fantastic, this dialogical metatext is clearly generated by the underlying balance of the over-determined and under-determined unresolved enigmas, whereas the marvellous (supernatural accepted, as in *Rip*), in which this particular ambiguity does not exist, will contain only a minor (and over-determined) hermeneutic code, which can generate only a monological and minor metatext, although the under-determined other codes, often symbolic, can generate other metatexts. In this respect the marvellous is often more akin (*apart* from the element of the accepted supernatural) to realistic fiction: witness the heavy over-determination of the referential and symbolic codes in Tolkien's trilogy, which has all the trappings of the realistic novel, and encourages symbolic, thematic, historical, etymological criticism of a traditional kind (cp. ch. 9). Here again we find yet another link (over-determination) between the marvellous (to the right of Todorov's schema, see p. 64 above) and the realistic novel (to the extreme left, off-diagram, i.e. upon which opens out the uncanny).

The kind of over-determination examined in *Rip* is surely the counterpart, in the marvellous, of the 'redundancy and foreseeability' which Hamon regards as specific to realism. There the over-determination occurs chiefly in the referential code (e.g. 'conjugating the virtual paradigm' of a character's status, cultural conventions, or literary conventions, seen in 'description-openers' etc.). In the marvellous it occurs in the action and hermeneutic codes.

The 'pure fantastic' is not, of course, the only type of ambiguous text, as I pointed out in chapter 3 (p. 65), with reference to James, and to Robbe-Grillet. The novels of Robbe-Grillet function, though differently from those of James, on a similar balance of apparent over-determination and under-determination, as do other types of *nouveau* and *nouveau nouveau roman*. Or again, in Alphonse Allais's *Un drame bien parisien* (see chapter 2, p. 44 above), for instance, the joke-ambiguity does not depend on a supernatural/natural enigma but on an over-determination, followed by a sudden under-determination (based on non-coreference, as Eco has shown) within the ultra-simple action code. And no doubt other codes are similarly exploitable.

The monological narrative, which delimits its characters and its ideological position, is the only type which, by over-determining a stance, say 'unpleasant' to an actual reader, produces the questions: 'where does the author stand?' This question simply cannot be asked of a dialogical text. In the case of Poe's 'unpleasantness', the fact that the question cannot (or should not) be asked is often attributed to his 'irony'. No doubt. But few critics seem to take Bakhtin's theory into account when discussing irony, and some dismiss it.[8] I think, however, that it is essential to any consideration, not only of the encoded reader, but of the ways in which the reader is encoded as I have tried to examine them here.[9]

5. Codes non-determined: hypnocrite lecteur

I really do not have a great deal to say about this category, nor do I propose to analyse examples. It not only must exist theoretically, once the two previous categories have been posed, but does exist, in the effects we know: namely that the reader, not being properly encoded, is or feels free to read everything, anything, and therefore also nothing, into the text.

Theoretically this type of reading should only occur with texts in which the balance of over-determination and under-determination is apparently (but see below) not respected or structured, some codes being over-determined here, under-determined there, with no other reason than the author's whim.[10] In other words, it is not necessarily a *non*-determination of codes which makes this kind of text; on the contrary, *all* the codes may be over-determined (or under), therefore producing no structured metatextual tension for an encoded reader, hence no encoded reader. It is haphazard .determination rather than a total absence of determination that results in non-determination, so that the actual reader then takes over, with his feelings and ideology, his period-bound enthusiasms and limitations, his fashionable prejudices and his moral alienation, which as it were hypnotise him, turn him into a *hypno-crite lecteur*.

I know that this is a thorny topic, many critics having in various ways, from damnation to reticence, condemned an author for his 'views', not sufficiently 'distanced' from those of the hero, for 'not making it clear where he stands' or on the contrary for making it too clear. I should like briefly to digress on this actual reader in the light of my analysis of the encoded reader and previous remarks. This is in response to a particularly interesting essay by Susan Suleiman,[11] devoted to Drieu la Rochelle's novel *Gilles*, in which she analyses specific manipulating devices that negate certain values such as foreignness, Jewishness, psychoanalysis, Marxism, and portray them as decadent and sinister. She frankly (and honestly) analyses her *own* process of 'dissent' from the values posited by the text and comes to the conclusion that

(1) Ideological dissent from works of fiction is a reading experience involving the 'perception' of certain formal devices as masks for the novelist in his role as manipulator of values.

(2) A formal device of this type (i.e. identifiable ... as a mask ...) is a device of ideological manipulation. (Suleiman 1976a:173)

She at once puts forward the objection that a reader might share those values *and* be aware of the manipulating devices, but counter-objects that since the 'perception' of a device 'is a quasi-wilful *act of non-cooperation with the text* on the part of the reader', a reader who shared the values embodied in *Gilles*, though aware of the devices, 'would not find it difficult to cooperate with the text' and to 'act as if' he were unaware of them, 'as if' he did not perceive them.

This may well be true, since political manipulation is so easy, but the circularity of the argument makes that ease even more depressing (perception of device = non-cooperation; cooperation can occur despite perception of device). And what bothers me is that it seems to be true only of certain texts (i.e., those belonging to this third category), this is in two ways:

> (1) It is perfectly possible to disagree totally with a *past* author's ideology (say Dante's religious and political beliefs, or Langland's or Milton's, or even Shakespeare's violence) *and* to perceive the devices of over-determination, and *yet* not to 'dissent' in the way described. After all we may perceive the devices of all literary works. Can a Catholic really not read Du Bartas or a Methodist Donne? This could be due to the passage of time since the Guelfs and the Ghibellines, the Papal Schism or the Religious Wars; but (2) the same is mysteriously (though more complexly) true of, say, Pound's political views, or Eliot's or Wyndham Lewis's, or for that matter Neruda's, or Lawrence's or Henry Miller's extravagant (over-determined) treatment of sex, or Burroughs's similar treatment of drugs. Pound's over-determination is at times extremely unpleasant, and we perceive it, yet we do not have that same easy reaction as the one Susan Suleiman describes with *Gilles*. Why?

I should like to suggest that it is after all a question of the balance of encoding I have described, and of the metatextual (dialogical) tension produced for the encoded reader by this balance. The text over-determines certain codes, but must compensate either by under-determining others (as I have shown, in easier terms, with *Rip Van Winkle* and *At Swim-Two-Birds*), or by over and under-determining within the same code but in such a way that the final result is under-determined ('The Black Cat'). Drieu's devices, which amount to an over-determination of the semic code and of the referential code, are not only 'patent' (Suleiman), they are also un-counter-balanced by non-determination in any other codes that would open up areas of mystery and above all dialogise the characters. The referential code which backs the semic code is, if anything, both over-determined, and under-determined in the sense that it is simply taken for granted, and hence cannot allow for ideological dissent or evolution of ideas. I would suggest that Susan Suleiman reacted as she did, not, or not only, from ideological dissent, but also, or even chiefly, from intelligence: the actual reader could not coincide with the encoded reader, who is either over-encoded as hypocrite, or haphazardly encoded, if at all, as hypnocrite (which in a sense is what she means by his not perceiving the devices he does perceive). In fact the encoded reader, insulted in his intelligence, is so alienated that he withdraws, becomes passive, and leaves a great gap for the actual reader to take over – from the contemporary reader whom the author takes for granted as sharing his prejudices to the adverse or later reader who will dissent because of these prejudices, or who on the contrary will blindly reverse them, like the critic Suleiman quotes who regards Drieu's portrait of *Gilles* as 'one of the most damning documents about French fascism of our time'. The implied or encoded author, by the same token, tends to be eliminated and leave a gap for the actual author of traditional criticism.

Contemporary hypnosis, however, leads me to close this digression on the actual reader and return to my non-determined category. I said above that in this case the balance of over-determination and under-determination is 'apparently' not respected or structured. It is clear, however (as Jauss states in other terms, see chapter 2, p. 43 above) that an 'apparent' non-determination of codes (i.e. an apparent unbalance, producing no metatextual tension) may in some instances turn out to be a mere contemporary blindness to an unfamiliar form of this necessary balance, the encoded reader being as it were invisible, for a while, to the actual reader, until later actual readers discover him; whence a lack of comprehension, a lack of reaction, or on the contrary, sometimes, over-reaction, but for the wrong reasons.

The category of the non-determined code is, in other words, a transient category: either the text, after a fashionable success, dissolves into limbo because of its unstructured or non-existent balance between over-and under-determination; or the apparent non-existent balance turns out to be a structured balance, in which case the text will rejoin one of the first two categories, and keep critics happy for generations.

6

'The Turn of the Screw' and its critics: an essay in non-methodology

The Turn of the Screw (1898), by Henry James, is one of the rare texts which more than perfectly illustrates the narrow definition of the pure fantastic given by Todorov: the hesitation of the reader must be sustained to the end. It must not be resolved, either by a natural explanation of the supernatural events (the uncanny, which includes certain types of detective-stories), or by the simple acceptance of these events as supernatural 'the marvellous), see chapter 3 above.

And it is precisely because of the perfect ambiguity (undecid- ability) of the text that, paradoxically, I must here adopt the position of 'limited pluralism' (see chapter 2, p. 48 above) and say that no, all interpretations are *not* equally valid, and yes, there *are* aberrant (or partly aberrant) readings. Some are due, simply, to weak criticism, and to a certain extent some of the critics examined here are easy Aunt Sallies. But the 'case' of *The Turn of the Screw* is also particular in that, (a) the very undecidability was for a long time unperceived, or, when perceived, seems to have exacerbated critics into taking up positions for or against one of the interpre- tations; and, not unrelated, (b) the text invites the critics uncon- sciously to 'act out' the governess's dilemma. But 'acting out' a text is a tribute to its 'life' (in Ingarden's terms), and I also have to say that 'aberrant' readings are necessary, are part of this life, and that it is also thanks to them that the text lives and gives rise to greater understanding; Bacon is necessary to Shakespeare. And, of course, the current interpretation of absolute ambiguity, which I accept, may one day turn out to be itself aberrant, though naturally I hope to show this is unlikely.

As to the hesitation of the experiencing character, Todorov poses it as a non-obligatory constituent element of the genre. In *The Turn of the Screw* it is rapidly resolved on the side of the supernatural. The hesitation of the reader, however, is encoded in the ambiguity of the text, and so efficiently that it has continued for three quarters of a century, building itself up into a literary 'case'. It is with this 'case' and the innumerable interpretations of the text arising out of that hesitation that I propose to deal here, partly as a study of non-methodology (how not to read), and partly to release the text from the entanglements of traditional criticism, before proceeding to a more objective type of analysis.

A preliminary distinction must be rigorously made between the reader encoded in a text (see chapter 5 above) or what Genette (1972) has called *le narrataire*', and the specific individual reader or – more easily available – the specific readings that have been made of a text. This chapter will deal exclusively with the latter, and not with the encoded reader except in so far as he gets woven into the specific readings.[1]

Until very recently the readings of TS have been those of traditional criticism, that is to say, discussions about:

(1) the author's intentions (in the sense defined below)
(2) 'psychoanalysis' of the author
(3) the characters in the text, the events in the text
(4) the significance (moral, theological, allegorical, poetic) of the text.

These of course constantly overlap, and are separated here for operational purposes: I shall in fact further separate (1) and (2) from the others, since the errors of reading I shall be analysing occur chiefly in (3), contributing to the confusion which inevitably affects (4). And cutting across (3) and (4) (and occasionally (1) and (2) as well) is the psychoanalysis of the central character, the governess, who is also the narrator.

I shall not dwell on the first two, which do not concern textual analysis, except for a brief clarification.

1. The author's intentions

Edna Kenton (1924) was the first to suggest that TS was not a simple ghost-story but an author's joke at his reader's expense ('an *amusette* to catch those not easily caught' as James describes it in the Preface). Although her essay is a declaration of the author's intentions rather than a demonstration, it is still one of the best in that it insists on the importance James attached to the reader's attention and participation.

Edmund Wilson (1934) then took up the idea but vulgarised it considerably, concentrating however (at least for TS) on the text itself. I shall return to him later and mention him here because he really launched the whole 'case', not only setting the tone but leaning heavily on the side of one interpretation (the psychological or natural explanation), despite his insistence on 'The Ambiguity of Henry James', which is also the title of his essay, and thus destroying the ambiguity essential to the pure fantastic.

Since then, the discussions have continued to opt for or against the supernatural.[2] Among the arguments on both sides are found declarations of supposed intention, with the same quotations from the Preface, the *Notebooks*, the Letters, and sometimes from other prefaces and other writings. We are constantly plunged into the 'intentional fallacy' as fallacy, by which I mean, either (a): critical appeals to author's intentions expressed extra-textually (which I shall ignore, for the reasons given below); or (b) unwarranted, unsubstantiated or even erroneous appeals to the author's intentions as supposedly clear in the text; for example, the narrator being confused with the author:

There are times when the governess herself questions her sanity, but in every case she is faced with *what James considered* [= what *she* considers] irrefutable proof that she is on the right track. (Reed 1949: W 196, italics mine.)[3]

As to (a), extratextual intentions, each critic quotes what suits him. The objections for this particular text, however, are evident:

1.1. The idea jotted down by James (12 Jan. 1895) in his *Notebooks* (1947), with its source or supposed source (for even this has been questioned, by Wolff (1941, and again by Cargill 1956) antedates the execution by over two years, and James does not even keep to his intention, explicitly stated, of having a narrator exterior to the action – a change which of course largely constitutes the compositional principle mentioned by Perry and Steinberg (see note 2 above): this principle being the inability to decide between the two interpretations.

Moreover, and this has not been remarked upon, there is no other note on this idea or its execution, despite James's habit of enthusiastic expansion on his ideas and the problems they produce. Further, the *Notebooks* are interrupted from October 1896 to December 1898 (before the writing and after the publication of TS); between January 1895 (the original jotting) and October 1896 (the interruption) he expands considerably on his other ideas and works in progress.

The *Notebooks* therefore are eloquent only by their silence.

1.2. The Preface was published, like the other Prefaces, in 1908, that is (for TS) ten years later, and belongs to the author's post-factum reflections and not to the preliminary 'intentions'. *A fortiori* it also belongs to the joke, if joke there is. In practice the Preface is as ambiguous as the text, as already noted by Edna Kenton ('its exquisitely ironical Preface') and thus sustains the hesitation of the reader(s).

1.3. Obviously the same applies to the few letters which James wrote about TS.

2. The 'psychoanalysis' of the author

Wilson mentions the fact that an Austrian novelist (Franz Höllering), to whom he had given the tale, had read it as a ghost-story but had remarked that the author was a *Kinderschänder* (child-profaner). And when discussing *The Wings of the Dove* he quotes a study of James (in general) by a Dr Saul Rosenzweig, who discusses the 'partly neurotic' origin of the author's backache, his guilt and the theme of impotence in his work. Wilson comments:

One can agree with Dr Rosenzweig that a castration theme appears here ['An Extraordinary Case', 1868] – one recognizes it as the same that figures through the whole of James's work; but that work does not bear out the contention put forward by Dr Rosenzweig that James was to suffer all his life from unallayed feelings of guilt for not having taken part in the war . . . etc. (1934: W151).

Since then, poor James as author of TS has been put through the lot, except, oddly enough, the castration theme, peculiarly relevant to this text (as part of *textual* analysis, not author analysis), but taken up again, after this one hint, only by Katan (1962: 334ff) and very naively. We even get, in Katan, 'little Henry's' primal scene traumatism ('little Henry' being identified with the child in the ghost-story reportedly told by Griffith, at the beginning of the prologue, a story which leads to the other story, of *two* children, read to his listeners by Douglas, i.e. the untold story of TS. Thus the author is identified with a character in an untold story which merely frames the frame of TS.) This primal scene traumatism is then read into the text in such a confusing way that 'little Henry' is barely distinguishable from little Miles. I shall leave all this aside as irrelevant to textual analysis, though I shall return to the 'Freudian' interpretation later.

3. The characters and events

Here there occurs a phenomenon almost as 'hallucinating' as the narrated events themselves, and worth studying in some detail: the state of the governess is contagious.

The critics reproduce the very tendencies they so often note in the governess: omission; assertion; elaboration; lying even (or, when the critics do so, let us call it error). Since there are many critics (as opposed to one narrator) these tendencies have caused much flowing of ink. Some errors and omissions are never noticed, some are picked up and corrected by others later, but so many years after the publication of the story, that the author (if joke there was) must be laughing in his beyond (if beyond there is), or maybe lamenting at these many examples of the reader's inattention.

These errors of reading can be divided into four methodological categories:

- the rehandling of the signifier
- the fallacious argument
- the extratextual argument
- the tone or uttering act (*énonciation*).[4]

In practice this last occurs throughout the other three. I shall therefore not deal with it separately but give two examples here, then print at least the adverbial type of 'shifter' in bold-face without further comment in subsequent quotations.

Several critics for instance have pounced on the governess's 'clearly' in the scene in which she looks out from a room inside the tower and sees Miles:

looking up to where I had appeared, looking – that is, not so much straight at me as at something that was **apparently** above me. There was **clearly** another person above me – there was a person on the tower. (James 1966: 45)

The narrator's habit of sliding from supposition (**apparently**) to assertion, precisely for what ought to be supposition, deserves (and will get) an analysis in itself. But as I have said, the governess's state is contagious, and the critics constantly do the same thing, using **somehow**, **in some manner or other**, **in a manner of speaking**, etc., where precision is required, and **evidently**, **clearly**, etc. (not to mention simple assertion, as we shall see) for what is only supposition. Sometimes this is combined with psychoanalysis of the author (see Katan 1962: 334), or with the 'intentional fallacy' as defined above:

Clearly, James did not intend to portray the governess as a sex-starved spinster, a hysterical personality subject to hallucinations, a deliberate liar . . . [nothing is less clear than this]. (Jones 1959: W 317)

I shall now deal with the other three methodological categories, with reference to the characters and events.

3.1. The rehandling of the signifier

The above phrase is translated from Lacan ['*le remaniement du signifiant*'] (1966: 577), and I am using it in the subtitle only to stress the fact that it is itself a neurotic process, that is, a specific version of our general propensity to use the meaning-making machine of language to alter one meaning with a new meaning, another 'version' (in neurosis, a ' more 'acceptable' version). In critical practice it means paraphrase, retelling in one's way, which is usually loaded with subjective interpretation.

3.1.1. The characters. The distinction between actant and action is of course crucial in purely structural analysis. Characters and events, however, at a more surface level, and as textual creations, are easily fused, since characters are not only 'supports of actions' in the Proppian sense, but are constructed partly out of their own actions, which on this level function in much the same way as Barthes's semic code.[5] And traditional criticism fuses them easily, not in theory but in the practice of a certain logorrhoea when 'analysing' characters, their faults and qualities, their physical features and their psychic states as well as their actions. Since I am quoting such critics I shall be forced to consider characters chiefly under events, and will cite here only a few examples of 'critical' description, one for each character. All show how inextricable subjective interpretation is from this kind of description (bold-face for 'shifters' and italics for other types of subjective interpretation are mine throughout, unless otherwise stated):

THE GOVERNESS: '"One of the thoughts," wrote the *little* governess in her desperate diary [sic] ... So the *little* governess says ...' (Kenton 1924: W109, 111; which does not prevent Muriel West 1964, from arguing later that the governess is big and strong and killed Miles with the physical strength of her last embrace.)

QUINT: 'who has red hair and red whiskers, the conventional guise of the *Devil*' (Fagin 1941: W157; repeated by Porter, in Porter, Tate and Van Doren

1942: 163 who add 'strange pointed eyebrows' and '*the evil eye*'.) Compare Van Doren in the same symposium: 'I am also interested in the fact that he is pale – that he has a pale face with light hair. If he is the devil, at least he *is a very special sort of devil*; he's not swarthy or grimacing; his face is rigid. He has a thin face and light curly red hair.' (1942: W164)

FLORA: 'And little Flora *is another Beatrice Rappaccini*, outwardly marvelously beautiful, but *inwardly corrupted by the poison of evil*.' (Fagin 1941: W158)

MILES: 'And **somehow** the "rose flush of his innocence" is never so intense as when he is most actively engaged in *positive evil*.' (Evans 1949: W211 – no demonstration.)

THE CHILDREN TOGETHER: 'How *completely innocent and natural* the children **really** were through all these earlier passages of the drama anyone will see who will divest himself of the suggestion that the governess has planted in his mind.' (Goddard 1957: W260)

MRS GROSE: 'If she is the incarnation of practical household sense and homely affection she is **utterly** *devoid of* worldly experience and *imagination*.' (Goddard 1957: W258; cf. Cargill 1956: W229: 'it is Mrs Grose ... who embroiders ...' quoted below, and the text: 'She couldn't have stayed. Fancy it here – for a governess! And afterwards I imagined – and I still imagine. And what I imagine is dreadful' James 1966: 33.)

MRS GROSE AND THE UNCLE: 'Mrs Grose, a simple, illiterate, *undiscerning* person ... The rôles of the uncle and Mrs Grose have less significance; primarily they help the physical story; secondarily, they represent *lack of vigilance, nay, indifference* (especially the uncle) to the possibilities of evil.' (Fagin 1941: W157, 158)

THE UNCLE: 'Having provided Bly and its staff, *a new Eden*, he *withdraws* to his worldly pursuits *as completely as the Old Testament God withdraws to heaven*, leaving behind him a state of being which seems to him satisfactory for anyone in *a condition of innocence*, and rules which make him inaccessible to any attention but the most distant and *awestricken worship*. He does not provide for the fact that *probable change in the state of innocence* will require his assistance, yet *he does provide the agents* – Quint and Miss Jessel – *even as the Old Testament God provided the snake – which will assure the fall from innocence. That fall occurs, and when it does, he turns his back, providing*, not a new moral code based upon the assumption of knowledge, but the governess, *a priestess of an old moral code*, based on an assumption of innocence and its desirability, in a state where innocence no longer exists ... *Unlike many of his priests, God recognized the inadequacy of Eden to a state of knowledge*, but the Harley Street uncle does not. He employs as governess a woman *competent only to preserve an innocence that no longer exists*, just as many priests who have served in the name of God have sought to preserve an innocence which could survive only in an Eden without a serpent:' (Firebaugh 1957: W293)

This last quotation shows how inextricable analysis is from that of events, and thus serves as a useful transition. The critic is so enthralled by his biblical analogy that he misrepresents the events: the uncle had not 'withdrawn' when he appointed Quint and Miss Jessel; on the contrary, the text specifically states that he was often there with them (and that Quint stole his waistcoats). It also presupposes that he was aware of all that Mrs Grose tells the governess about the goings on at that time, an awareness which the text leaves wholly ambiguous. Apart from this it is both theologically and theoretically weak (God does not 'recognize the inadequacy of Eden to a state of knowledge', he simply forbids knowledge of good and evil, a type of command which, as Propp has shown in his analysis of the folk-tale, 1928, must be transgressed for a tale to begin). I pass over the subjective anti-clericalism which is part of the American Puritan and anti-Puritan tradition.

3.1.2. The events. The rehandling of the events by the critics is truly amazing. On both sides of the critical controversy (ghosts versus hallucination), the story is retold, not only less well but in order to prove what the author leaves unproven. The paraphrases are not only loaded but frequently erroneous. The most flagrant example is that of Wilson (1934: W115ff). Extracts from the first two pages of his article (quoted below), set not only the tone but the method of error, beginning with a gross misrepresentation of Edna Kenton (1924):

'I believe that Miss Edna Kenton ... was the first to write about it ... The theory is, then, that the governess who is made to tell the story is *a neurotic case of sex repression*, and that the ghosts are not real ghosts but hallucinations of the governess.' (Wilson 1934: W115)

[Edna Kenton certainly does not express herself in these terms, rather: 'exquisite dramatizations of her little personal mystery' (1924: W113.]

'The boy, she finds, has been sent home from school for reasons into which she does not inquire but which she colors, *on no evidence at all*, with a significance **somehow** ominous.' (Wilson 1934: W116)

[True, but Wilson ignores the cultural code: a boy is not expelled, without explanation, for no reason.]

'As she wanders about the estate, she thinks often how delightful it would be if one should come suddenly round the corner and *see the master just arrived from London*: there he would stand, handsome, smiling, approving.' (Wilson 1934: W116)

[The text (James 1966: 15) is much more subtle: the immediate subject of 'would appear' is 'some one'; the less immediate subject – a whole paragraph away – is 'he ... the person to whose pressure I had responded'. In other words a fantasy, presented as such – 'the person', 'some one' – would simply 'appear' (like a ghost), and certainly not have 'just arrived from London', an interpolated detail that suggests transport, baggage, timetables, wholly incompatible with a fantasy.]

'She is never to meet her employer again, but what she does meet are the apparitions. *One day when* his face has been vividly in her mind ...' (Wilson 1934: W116)

[The narrator, more honestly, does not separate her rambling fantasies from the day in question, the day occurs – 'It was plump, one afternoon ...' (James 1966: 15) – then the fantasies are told in the iterative, which expresses habit, the often, the usual, the sometimes, then she takes up the singulative event.]

'she *comes out* in sight of the house'. Wilson 1934: W116)

['I stopped short on emerging from one of the plantations and *coming into view* of the house' (James 1966: 15).]

'and, looking up, sees the figure of a man on a tower, a figure which is not the master's. Not long afterwards, *the figure appears again* ...' (Wilson 1934: W116)

[an independent subject, not as object of 'sees', and therefore contradicting Wilson's own theory.]

'She sees him at closer range and more clearly: *he is wearing smart clothes but is obviously not a gentleman.*' (Wilson 1934: W116)

[This is revealed only later, in conversation with Mrs Grose, a technique which will be crucial.]

'The governess tells her [Mrs Grose] about the apparition and *learns that it answers the description of one of the master's valets*, who had stayed down there and who had sometimes stolen his clothes.' (Wilson 1934: W116)

[the identification of Quint by Mrs Grose being the greatest obstacle to the hallucination theory, as Wilson admits later and from which he extricates himself clumsily, this paraphrase of a complex and subtle scene is wholly inadequate.]

'*The valet had been* a bad character, *had used* "to play with the boy ... to spoil him*"; *he had finally been* found dead, having apparently slipped on the ice coming out of a public house – though one couldn't say he hadn't been murdered.' (Wilson 1934: W116)

[These details appear from the paraphrase to be given at once, and all by Mrs Grose, but in fact they are not given till the following chapter, and the details of the valet's death are given by the narrator herself, in free indirect discourse, an important point which I shall comment on later.]

'The governess *cannot help believing* that he has come back to haunt the children.' (Wilson 1934: W116)

[Another wrong impression of order: she had the impression already before the identification that the apparition 'had come for someone else'; the elaboration of the children's danger comes before the identification and partly provokes it.]

'Not long afterwards, she and the little girl are out on the shore of a lake, the child playing, the governess sewing. The latter becomes aware of a third person on the opposite side of the lake. But she looks first at little Flora, who is turning her back in that direction and who, she notes, has "picked up a small flat piece of wood, which happened to have in it a little hole" [. . . Flora's game].' 'This **somehow** "sustains" the governess so that she is able to raise her eyes: *she sees a woman "in black, pale and dreadful"*.' (Wilson 1934: W116–17)

[Then I again shifted my eyes – I faced what I had to face' (James 1966: 30). End of chapter. The elaboration comes as always in conversation with Mrs Grose. (The same misrepresentation occurs in Cargill 1956: W228.)]

The paraphrase continues in this way after a reminder that only the governess sees the apparitions: 'The housekeeper insists that she does not see them; it is **apparently** the governess who frightens her. The children too, *become hysterical*, but this is **evidently** the governess' doing' (Wilson 1934: 117). This is followed by an explanation of the sexual character of Flora's game and a crude interpretation of the identification obstacle (later withdrawn). I shall not continue the analysis but will simply quote two typical phrases: '*she is now, it seems*, in love with the boy' and '(*He has*, in spite of the governess's efforts, succeeded in seeing his sister and *has heard from her of the incident of the lake.)*' The parentheses in no way excuse this interpolation, into a certitude, of a possibility which is only very subtly suggested in the text.

This urge for transforming possibility into certainty is of course what the governess is most blamed for, but the critics are rarely free of it themselves. Here is a selection, presented in the order of events:

According to the introduction, little Henry suffered from nightmares when he shared the bedroom with his mother. (Katan 1962: W334)

A total confusion of fiction and 'biography' (extrapolated from the fiction): the introduction starts with a report (by the I–narrator) of another ghost-story just told by one of the party. It is the boy in this (untold) ghost-story who has nightmares and sleeps with his mother (Cp. pp. 144–5 below).

But to add to the intensity of the situation the young woman falls instantly and *passionately* in love with the man who has inserted the advertisement. *She scarcely admits it even to herself*, for in *her heart she knows that her love is hopeless, the object of her affection being one socially out of her sphere.* (Goddard 1957: W249)

The 'passionate' love is an interpolation of the guests (represented as silly) and Douglas is very ambiguous as to whom she was in love with. Nor does she 'scarcely admit it', she admits it easily, as many critics have remarked, to Mrs Grose, in non-passionate terms ('I'm easily carried away, I was carried away in London'), and in the fantasy already quoted. In itself 'easily carried away' is ambiguous since it could merely mean 'easily persuaded to take the job'. But the context (the way Mrs Grose understands it and the governess does not contradict her) tend to lift that ambiguity. Never for one moment does she elaborate it in terms of hopelessness or social impossibility. In this connection it is interesting to note that James carefully places his narrative (written in 1897) fifty years back, 1847 being the date of *Jane Eyre*, in which a governess does marry her employer.[6]

But even this is not all. *In her overwrought condition, the unexplained death of the former governess, her predecessor, was enough to suggest some mysterious danger connected with the position offered, especially in view of the master's strange stipulation ... Something extraordinary, she was convinced, lurked in the background. She would never have accepted the place if it had not been for her newborn passion; she could not bring herself to disappoint him when he seemed to beg compliance of her as a favor* ['of her as a favor' is italicised by Goddard] – *to say nothing of severing her only link with the man who had so powerfully attracted her.* (Goddard 1957: W249)

This introductory part of the story (James 1966: 5–6) is filtered through the I–narrator reporting Douglas's words, partly in free indirect discourse (see chapters 2, and 4, p. 94 above), partly in dialogue. The danger is suggested by *him*, in a question, and Douglas's reply is ambiguous: 'Necessary danger to life? ... "She did wish to learn, and she did learn. You shall hear tomorrow what

she learnt. Meanwhile ..."' The conversations between the governess and Douglas being extratextual we cannot know the exact
process of her hesitation, which is told in quite other terms:
'Meanwhile of course the prospect struck her as slightly grim. She
was young, untried, nervous: it was a vision of serious duties and
little company, of really great loneliness.' She asks for two days to
consider and accepts for purely financial reasons. It is only at the
second interview that he tells her that other applicants had found
the conditions prohibitive, were 'somehow, simply afraid. It sounded dull – it sounded strange; and all the more so because of his
main condition', which is given only now (at least by Douglas, but
he is all we have), and which she accepts without hesitation, feeling
'already rewarded' when he thanks her for her sacrifice, holding her
hand. Goddard's version is highly coloured.

[she] takes seriously *an accusation made against the little boy* by the head-master
of the school when he is sent home with *a note saying that he had been an
immoral influence* (Porter *et al.* 1942: W164).

The note says nothing, there is no accusation. This is the governess's
later interpretation (rectified by Hoffmann 1953: W216).

an inadvertent hint *about Peter Quint* dropped by the housekeeper, Mrs
Grose, is just the seed that that soil requires ...' (Goddard 1957: W250)

The hint that the housekeeper dropped of *an unnamed man in the neighborhood*
has done its work. (Goddard 1957: W252)

has already dropped an unintentional hint of *someone in the neighborhood* who
preys on *young and pretty governesses*. This man, to be sure, is dead, but the new
governess, who did not pay strict enough attention to Mrs Grose's tenses,
does not know it. (Goddard 1957: W253)

Goddard mixes viewpoints: Mrs Grose's hint *about Peter Quint*
(unnamed then) is from *her* viewpoint, i.e., about Quint before his
death, therefore he cannot be 'in the neighborhood'. From the
governess's viewpoint the second quotation is correct, but then it
cannot (at that moment) be Peter Quint, nor a dead man. Goddard
is obliged to repeat the whole argument a page later with an
explanation that could have been avoided (but he has already 'sown
the seed' himself, and wrongly, in his reader's mind). Nor does he
pay attention to his own tenses: from Mrs Grose's viewpoint it
cannot be *preys*, only from the governess's viewpoint. Mrs Grose
anyway says 'liked', or rather (with the famous confusion of pro-

nouns), she is thinking of Quint and the governess of her employer: 'Oh he *did*' to the governess's 'He seems to like us young and pretty' (p. 12) and adds 'it was the way he liked everyone' (i.e. not just governesses).

Mrs Grose is still far from convinced [about Miss Jessel]. This seems a trifle odd in view of *the fact* that Peter Quint *is known to be haunting the place* ... (Goddard 1957: W253)

Known by whom? It is the governess who asserts it. Mrs Grose appears to believe her (according to the governess–narrator, previous chapter, 8 [James 1966: 34]), but the impersonal passive here, together with *the fact*, are misleading (and against Goddard's own hallucination thesis).

But when she tells Mrs Grose *about Quint* [= about apparition]. (Porter *et al.* 1942: W163)

When we learn later that Bly *is really haunted* ... (Lydenberg 1957: W278)

It is Mrs Grose, out of the petty jealousy common to domestic servants [only?], who at the prompting of the governess, *embroiders* the tale about a relation between the pair; *it is the governess who gobbles every morsel* of this and *invents* the theme of their evil designs upon the children. (Cargill 1956: W229)

This notion, expressed with a highly coloured word, that Mrs Grose is a liar, has given rise to an interpretation by Knight Aldrich (1967) according to which Mrs Grose is the villain of the piece (see my remarks in section 3.3., pp. 147ff, on extratextual arguments).

When she [Mrs Grose] balks, as she does on several occasions, the governess faces her, and us, with *one undeniable fact*: '... I had only to ask her how, if I had "made it up," I came to be able to give, of each of the persons appearing to me, a picture disclosing, to the last detail, their special marks – a portrait on the exhibition of which she had instantly recognized and named them'. (Reed 1949: W196; James 1966: 34)

The identification of Quint (the main obstacle for the hallucination theory) has been explained in various ways, but here Reed takes upon himself the governess's patent lie as to Miss Jessel (she has done the identification herself and certainly does not describe her 'special marks' and 'to the last detail', but in conventional ghostly terms). This lie has been picked up by several critics.

but with the *realization* by the governess that the ghosts of Peter Quint and Miss Jessel have come for the children ... (Hoffmann 1953: W219)

Once she realizes that she does not know enough to teach the boy, it occurs to her to seek out a school for him. But she does not do so. This would be to put him 'on his own' – *it would thwart her determination to return him to a state of innocence* – or, as she puts it, *to 'save' him from knowledge superior to her own.* (Firebaugh 1957: W295)

Pure interpretation. The word 'save' is used in a much more imprecise way (James 1966: 65) even if the school was ostensibly in question in the preceding conversation.

Why do the children *deny seeing the ghosts? Such denial,* according to the governess, shows the extent to which the children have been corrupted. (Reed 1949: W197)

When, in the tension of the final scene, Miles utters the corrupting servant's name, *which he has so long withheld* ... (Reed 1949: W198)

Both Miles and Flora *have denied seeing the ghosts,* but the governess is convinced they *are lying.* (Hoffmann 1953: W220)

The children have never had the slightest occasion either to 'deny seeing' except once, in the governess's imagination ('They're here ... I would have cried, "and you can't deny it now!" The little wretches denied it with all the added volume of their sociability and their tenderness' p. 52), or to 'withhold the name' of the previous servants (or ghosts), since the governess restrains herself from ever mentioning them directly to either, and her indirect efforts are so ambiguous (narrator) or so clumsy (character), that it is perfectly possible for them, if they are innocent, to understand them differently (the nocturnal pranks or the business of the school).

The horror of the situation is heightened, moreover, by *the fact that* the boy has been corrupted by the male servant; the girl, by the female. Peter Quint's abnormality is hinted at ('There had been matters in his life ... secret disorders, vices more than half suspected'), and *Mrs Grose says in so many words* that he had been 'much too free' with little Miles [...] Then there is the *unambiguous* dialogue between the governess and Mrs Grose. (Evans 1949: W209–10)

All these 'facts', so 'unambiguous' here, are filtered not only through Mrs Grose but through the governess as narrator, and could in themselves be innocent (the children had no one else to talk to, Miss Jessel was after all Flora's governess, and Miles, not wanting to spend all his time with his young sister, could have struck up a perfectly natural friendship with the valet. Of course the interpretation of corruptness is also possible and indeed *could* have

come from another source, the (interpolated, extratextual) witnessing of the primal scene (Katan 1962) rather than homosexuality; or
both. It is the language of the critic I am objecting to, for it reduces
James's filtering subtlety to zero.

Cut off from all information, Miles will seek any means of getting it [. . .]
Subject to a teacher who has *no knowledge to give*, and who would cut them
off from other sources of knowledge, the children are trapped. They seek
ways of asserting the independence they have been denied. *Failing* [?], they
find imposed on them the governess's visions of sin – Quint and Miss Jessel.
(Firebaugh 1957: W296).

Highly coloured and based on the same presuppositions as the
previous quotation. The children do not 'fail', they assert their
independence continually. The governess's 'visions of sin' are never
overtly 'imposed on them', witness the shock at the end, which *could*
be due (certainly for Flora) simply to the sudden mention of the
dead governess's name, death alone being a shock for so young a
child, and soon repressed. The final scene with Miles is also much
more complex, intertwined as it is with the pressure for a confession,
ostensibly about what happened at school.

under the *enforced* [?] demonstrations of a *conventional* [?] love *smolders a
resentment and hatred* that will burst out all the more violently because *so long
suppressed*. (Lydenberg 1957: W283)

Totally unwarranted by the text. Same remarks as above.

With the governess as narrator, *the children can never speak for themselves*:
according to her they at first appear cherubic, later fiendish. Indicatively,
the one positive trait which makes them lower than angels *depends upon their
aping vocabulary*. Mrs Grose condemns Flora: 'On my honour, Miss, she says
things – !' Miles, likewise, pleads guilty to his obscure behavior at school;
'Well – I said things.' (Enck 1966: K265)

A nonsensical argument since *everything* is told by the governess,
including all that Mrs Grose tells her (who also 'says things', and
that's the trouble). Through the governess as narrator the children
also and elsewhere have a complete autonomy of expression which
surprises her each time.

And 'as if to blight his confession and stay his answer,' Peter Quint *appears*.
Miles *acknowledges his presence*: the governess has triumphed; *Miles is saved,
Peter Quint has lost*. But the experience – the fright, the horror, the
recognition of evil – is too much for Miles. He utters an anguished cry of
horror and dies in the governess's arms. (Hoffmann 1953: W221)

Hoffmann has just declared (previous paragraph) that 'Miles's death is caused by the governess' insistence on his confession; the confession is wrested from him, but he dies from the shock.' Peter Quint 'appears' only to the governess. Miles does not 'acknowledge his presence' but answers a question. The whole scene is highly charged with ambiguity and the theological implications are the governess's interpretation.

The climax of his *disease* [?], the binding together of all the strands we have been tracing, is his malevolent cry *to the governess* – 'you devil!' (Heilman 1948: W183)

The recipient of that cry is wholly ambiguous in the text: 'Whom do you mean by "he?"'' 'Peter Quint – you devil!' (James 1966: 88). The same error occurs in Cargill (1956, see below). In any case, this so-called confession or 'proof' ends with a question: '"Peter Quint – you devil!" His face gave again, round the room, its convulsed supplication. "Where?"'' (p. 88). As for the notion of Miles's illness, it arises (as Heilman has just demonstrated) from the metaphors and comparisons of the governess–narrator, but Heilman at once takes them over in a literal sense, as does Evans, more correctly: 'it is suggested to the reader (always through the medium of the governess, to whom the impressions occur in appropriate images) that little Miles is *sick*, spiritually sick' (Evans 1949: 209, italics author's own). The 'suggestion' however, only too easily generates 'fact':

Along with precocious sexuality, they [the Freudians] ignore the clear signs of extreme repression in Miles's *illness*. (Spilka 1963: K248)

Such constant rehandling of the signifier through subjective paraphrase induces not only errors of interpretation (or at least biased interpretation which destroys the ambiguity), but also errors of reading, such as, for instance, Lydenberg's assertion that a long quotation he has just given (1957: W277) comes after Quint's *first* appearance (in fact the second), or Edna Kenton's mention of the governess's narrative as a *diary* (1924: W109), or her quotation out of context ('There were states of the air') to imply that the governess 'came to know the moods that brought them [the apparitions] which moods would in fact bring them' (1924: W112). In fact that quotation is followed by 'But they remained unaccompanied and empty' (James 1966: 52), and comes in the middle of a long period when she does not see the ghosts. And from errors of reading to misquotation there is but one step. For example Katan, whose argument is based on the primal scene between Quint and Miss Jessel, supposedly witnessed by the children:

Mrs Grose also supplies further corroboration: 'the children *saw more things*, terrible and unguessable, that *came* from *passively watching intercourse* in the past. 'I think James's choice of words speaks for itself.' (Katan 1962: W325)

Unfortunately not, and for three reasons. First, these words do not come from Mrs Grose but from the governess in free indirect discourse, without any allusion to Mrs Grose. She is thinking of what the children are *now* seeing (i.e., more than *she* sees), referring to the contact she supposes them to be having with Quint and Miss Jessel), a contact allegedly prolonging the one they had when the servants were alive. Second, Katan misquotes (errors in italics). Here is the text:

What it was least possible[7] to get rid of was the cruel idea that, whatever I had seen, Miles and Flora saw *more* – things terrible and unguessable and that sprang from dreadful passages of intercourse in the past. (James 1966: 53 – James's italics on *more*.)

There is not only no 'more things' but no 'passively watching', and 'sprang' is more to the point than 'came'. And the 'intercourse' refers to the children's contact, albeit 'corrupt', with Quint and Miss Jessel when they were alive.

Third, the word 'intercourse' is never used in the modern sense by James, either here or elsewhere (e.g. in the first few pages of *Daisy Miller*), but always for contact, conversation, social intercourse (a sense still valid in Virginia Woolf). For example communication with the ghosts:

He appeared thus again ... with a nearness that represented a forward stride in our intercourse and made me, as I met him, catch my breath and turn cold. (James 1966: 20)

'Surely you don't accuse *him* – '
'Of carrying on an intercourse that he conceals from me? Ah remember that, until further evidence, I now accuse nobody'. (p. 37)

... if ... I were the first to introduce into our perfect intercourse [with Miles] an element so dire? (p. 47)

The stress in the second quotation for instance is not on 'intercourse' but on the fact that Miles keeps such contacts secret. Of course the 'Freudian' interpreters would argue that contact with the ghosts does 'symbolise' sexual intercourse, as would contact with Miles. But it is only in the twentieth century that the legal term 'sexual intercourse' loses its adjective and becomes sufficient on its own for this meaning, so much so that today it is the adjective 'social' which has to be added. And even if the sexual connotation existed in colloquial language at the time, James would surely not use it in print, let alone lend it to the governess, in this sense; at most there would be ambiguity. But nothing justifies the *changes* made by Katan.

Clearly the rehandling of the signifiers directly influences interpretation (and vice versa) as well as readings. I shall return to the question of 'significance' later and pass straight on to the fallacious argument.

3.2. The fallacious argument

There are fewer of these, and I shall drop the subdivision into characters and events, which as we have seen is not rigorous enough in this type of criticism. The point here is again that what the governess is accused of is contagious:

It seems to me that the story would shrink a great deal in power and significance if it were merely a story which *psychoanalyzed an old maid.* (Porter *et al.* 1942: W162)

The premises are false: the narrative does not 'psychoanalyse' anyone; the governess is twenty and pretty at the time of the events (which is the time Van Doren in Porter *et al.* refers to, rather than the time of her narration ten years later). Wilson had thrown out this notion but it has been frequently rejected.

In a manner of speaking Mrs Grose is the testing ground for just how far the reader may be expected to go in accepting the tenuous evidence of the governess. *To the degree that Mrs Grose accepts the evidence, so are we as readers to accept it.* (Reed 1949: W196)

Why? (This is followed by the 'one undeniable fact', quoted from Reed previously.) The notion that the reader must identify with the good but foolish (or, in Knight Aldrich's 1967 interpretation, wicked and cunning) Mrs Grose is illogical, theoretically indefensible, and here absurd since Mrs Grose accepts the ghosts wholly and finally for an illogical reason: Flora's language, which can just as easily be explained by the very 'facts' from the past, told by Mrs Grose herself, which the child would have forgotten but which would have returned to her under the shock of the governess's behaviour in naming Miss Jessel to Flora for the first time, in the second and last lakeside scene. This same illogical reason is however a proof for Reed since he himself identifies with Mrs Grose ('These broken phrases show that Mrs Grose, although she has not seen the ghosts, agrees with the governess as to their corrupting influence' [1949: W197].) This is true in itself, but according to the preceding argument the reader must agree also. He goes on:

Such corroborating testimony is not all. The governess has been so shaken by the events of the story that she demands positive proof that her deductions are sound. When, in the tension of the final scene, Miles utters the corrupting servant's name, which he has so long withheld [already commented], the governess has *her conclusive proof* that demons did exist for the boy – either visually or mentally [?] – *since otherwise* he certainly would not have had the slightest inkling of the meaning of her pressing insinuations. (Reed 1949: W198)

This final scene is interpretable and has been interpreted differently (Goddard 1957: 265; Jones 1959: 316), and remains inexorably ambiguous. Moreover nothing in it tells us that the governess 'has her conclusive proof' – for one thing she hardly needs it. My point is, however, that the argument slides from the 'corroborative testimony' of Mrs Grose to the implication of a similar 'corroborative testimony' of Miles (for the governess, whose conviction the reader has long been aware of, but not necessarily shared); but the opening statement about corroborative testimony is so categorical, together with the previous argument about reader identification with Mrs Grose, that the reader is implicitly assumed to take over the governess's conviction as well. Evans also uses Mrs Grose as proof, but in a different though equally insidious way:

One could not, incidentally, wish for stronger evidence of the stability of the governess's personality than the fact that, although the housekeeper herself has seen nothing, she does not doubt that her friend has – a point which James, who certainly sees the necessity for it, drives home again and again. (Evans 1949: W206)

The critic calls the author in aid of his own argument, which does not hold water. At a more abstract level: X (say a psychoanalyst) admits that Y (say a patient) 'sees' Z, therefore Z exists. Hoffmann repeats the same argument even more insidiously: 'Her belief in the *existence* of [i.e., no longer the mere fact that the governess sees] the ghosts is important corroborative evidence for both the governess and the reader' (1953: W217).

Another illogical argument from the 'horrors' uttered by Flora is applied to the governess's influence, together with Miles's final (ambiguous) address:

It is Mrs Grose ... who ... embroiders ... it is the governess who gobbles every morsel ... That she carries her insinuations to the children themselves (despite what she says to the contrary) *is indicated by* Mrs Grose's declaration, after she had taken over Flora, that she has heard 'horrors' from the child. Miles also betrays that the governess has implied an evil relationship between him and Quint, *for* when in the last scene she calls his direct attention to her specter (Miles 'glaring vainly over the place and missing wholly'), the boy guesses at what she means him to see and *names her as a fiend*: 'Peter Quint – you devil!' (Cargill 1956: W229–30)

Mrs Grose's declaration *could* but does not necessarily indicate this, and the last scene is interpretable in at least two ways as well as this one. The influence of the governess on the children is much more ambiguous than a simple corruption by insinuation of corruption: until the last lakeside scene, when she names Miss Jessel and frightens Flora so much that the child falls ill (two possible interpretations), the governess's whole behaviour could have been seen by the children as eccentricity, nervousness and possessiveness, and by Miles in particular as an excessive curiosity about his school and excessive possessiveness about his person.

3.3. Extratextual arguments

These are of the type: 'How Many Children Had Lady Macbeth?' They have been chiefly invoked in connection with the identification of Quint by Mrs Grose, but also for various other interpretations, and they raise an important theoretical principle.

Wilson (1934: 117–18) explains the identification with the possibility of a resemblance between Quint and the master (extratextual), but withdrew this very inadequate argument later to accept that of Silver (1957: 242, the governess has inquired in the village). But other critics have sought elsewhere:

The details that the governess supplied the housekeeper after the second occasion *must have come from another source – from the prattle of her youngest charge and from her own seemingly artless prompting to the children.* (Cargill 1956: W229)

Flora had indeed shown her the house 'secret by secret' (which Cargill italicises for emphasis) at the end of the first chapter (her arrival), but the narrator tells Mrs Grose explicitly that the children have never mentioned the previous servants. Her 'artless prompting' is so artful as to be incomprehensible to them if they are innocent (as Cargill supposes).

Of course, she may be lying, but on that level the entire story can be a lie (which has also been suggested). In reading a fiction, and especially an ambiguous fiction, the theoretical principle is that we may take into account only the lies encoded in the text.

In particular, Silver tries to demolish the two chief objections to the hallucination theory: that the governess gives a detailed description of Peter Quint, and that she has never previously heard of him. First, he cites the governess' remark concerning the stranger on the tower – how she had 'made sure' he was 'nobody from the village.' Silver considers this evidence [sic, = as evidence] that she has been asking questions in the village, and thereby presumably learning about Quint. *Actually it probably means that she has been making inquiries among other servants at Bly.* (Jones 1959: W305)

Why? Silver's explanation is encoded in the text, as well as the information that the village is only twenty minutes away (James 1966: 20, just before the second apparition). The information that she has *not* made inquiries among the servants is also explicitly stated (James 1966: 18, just before the second apparition, when her explanation to herself is as yet purely social). An imprecise time has passed, rendered by a description of her classes with her charges, before the second apparition, and the 'I made sure' to Mrs Grose would refer to this period, as a partial and internal analepsis (see chapter 2, p. 36, and also below).

It is true that Silver's explanation is insufficient in the sense (which no one has picked up) that if she had learnt so much about Quint's physical appearance she would also have learnt that he was dead, and would therefore not have expressed so much fright, after her description, in learning that fact from Mrs Grose: 'Died! I almost shrieked.' But here we touch on the whole question of the narrator's *énonciation* and time of narration (*instance narrative*) which I shall analyse in chapter 8.

It is also important to make a distinction between the extratextual which can be inferred from elements encoded in the text (like Silver's argument), and the extratextual which cannot, or which are inferred from elements specifically denied (as in Cargill and Jones above). Jones continues:

Second, Silver considers it significant that the governess can discuss Quint's death although we never witness Mrs Grose supplying her with these facts; *he feels James would not 'suppress' a scene of such importance.* But that is absurd –

Mrs Grose undoubtedly held many 'off-stage' talks with the governess, and Quint's death may well have been discussed during the conversation mentioned at the beginning of Chapter VI. Moreover, although *Silver suggests that Mrs Grose might not have known the facts of Quint's death,* such ignorance is almost inconceivable under the circumstances. Therefore, we can only conclude that he has neither proven his case against the governess nor demonstrated that the ghosts are unreal. (1959: W305)

The conclusion does not follow but that is beside the point here. At first sight this argument seems to be of the second extratextual type, and inadmissible, like his earlier argument about the inquiry at Bly, and certainly the first part of the second italicised sentence about 'off-stage' talks in general is of that type. The whole argument is confused, and typical of the way traditional critics will talk of characters in fiction as if they really existed, had a life of their own outside the text, at the same time sliding back to the author's technique and or intentions. When one looks at it more closely and refers back to the text, however, one can see that in the second part of that sentence Jones is right (and of course Silver's argument in the third italicised sentence is also a non-inferable extratextual argument, and inadmissible).

What is in question here under the vague phrase 'Quint's death' are the detailed circumstances of Quint's death, pondered over by the governess in her room (chapter 6). A conversation with Mrs Grose has just taken place (in dialogue, not just 'mentioned' as Jones says), about Quint, and ends (in the text) with Mrs Grose bursting into tears. The next paragraph speaks of the control necessary the next day and the following week when the two women frequently re-discussed the subject. Then the narrator returns in time to that night, after the conversation, when she couldn't sleep and suspected Mrs Grose of having kept things back [James's italics]:

It seems to me indeed, in raking it all over, that by the time the morrow's sun was high I had restlessly read into the facts before us almost all the meaning they were to receive from subsequent and more cruel occurrences. What they gave me above all was just the sinister figure of the living man – the dead one would keep a while! – and of the months he had continuously passed at Bly, which, added up, made a formidable stretch. The limit of this evil time had arrived only when, on the dawn of a winter's morning, Peter Quint was found, by a labourer going to early work, stone dead on the road from the village: a catastrophe explained – superficially at least – by a visible wound to his head; such a wound as might have been produced (and as, on the final evidence, *had* been) by a fatal slip, in the dark and after leaving the public-house, on the steepish icy slope, a wrong path altogether, at the bottom of which he lay. The icy slope, the turn mistaken at night and in liquor, accounted for much – practically, in the end and after the inquest and boundless chatter, for everything; but there had been matters in his life, strange passages and perils, secret disorders, vices more than suspected, that would have accounted for a good deal more. (James 1966: 27–8)

Such an abundance of detail can have only two sources: the village (i.e., before the second apparition and the ensuing conversation with Mrs Grose, which would resolve the problem of the identification but poses the problem of her shriek of terror on learning that Quint is dead); or Mrs Grose, with whom she has just talked, in which case she is mulling it over in free indirect discourse, a perfectly legitimate technique.

Also perfectly legitimate is the omission of one or more parts of a conversation (or even of narration), the ellipsis being filled in later by analepsis. Here the analepsis as *information* is complete, but as fact of a conversation more detailed than what is given having taken place, it is only implicit, though the phrase that introduces the conversation makes it clear enough ('We had gone over and over every feature of what I had seen', p. 25), and the passage of time is minimal. The conversation is given, but not terminated by an exit of Mrs Grose, just as, for that matter, the conversation that ends the preceding chapter is not 'terminated': the narrator does not give us her final or continued reaction to Mrs Grose's statement 'Yes, Mr Quint is dead.'

The source of the details, then, is an inferable extratextual conversation, inferable not only from the circumstances and the small time elapsed, but from the free indirect discourse in which the facts are given.

Extratextual arguments which are inadmissible are the theory of Knight Aldrich (1967: 375), according to which Mrs Grose is the mother of the children and therefore the villain of the piece, and the following paragraph by Katan:

Flora does not stop at simply removing herself from the influence of the governess. In the subsequent hysterical outburst *she accuses the governess of everything that Miss Jessel had done in reality*, thus identifying her present governess, not without reason, with the dead governess. *In this way Flora makes it clear* that the governess has, at least in fantasy, the same sexual desires as Miss Jessel had. (1962: W332)

The conclusions may well be acceptable psychoanalytically and in a sense so general that they are obvious, but nothing in the text justifies the italicised premises. The same applies to the supposedly hereditary madness of the governess's father, extrapolated from the word 'eccentric' (Cargill 1956: 230; Goddard 1957: 248).

Another equally unjustified statement by Cargill, about the extent of the governess's relationship with Douglas as explanation for the existence of the narrative, raises an interesting problem:

> But she herself *had realized the danger of a recurrence of her madness, and when Douglas had urged marriage upon her and she had repeatedly refused,* she had resolved upon writing out the history *of her aberration* in order that *he* might understand [*he* italicized by author]. Is not this the most plausible explanation to account for his possession of the narrative? [From which he further argues that her honesty makes her a heroine not a villain.] (1963: K159)

Nothing in the Introduction of course justifies the lines I have italicised, but this type of extratextual argument is linked to that of Rubin (1964: 350ff), according to which Miles is Douglas (and therefore did not die, the whole story being concocted, or at least 'altered' as to its ending, by the governess to tell Douglas how much she loved him, both as child and adult). Such arguments, though strictly inadmissible, could be said to be *partially* encoded in the very presence of the elaborate frame provided by the author. The whole question of the frame, as developed by Lotman and Uspensky, will be discussed in chapter 7.

4. The significance of the narrative

From these quotations it is clear that the interpretations are multiple, nor have I distinguished them, or even the main two theories, since the same faults of paraphrase and argument are found on both sides and my main purpose here is methodological. I shall therefore end this chapter with a brief summary of the two main groups (ghosts/hallucinations) and a consideration of the theoretical principles involved.

4.1. The ghosts are 'real'

Here the interpretations are moral, theological, allegorical, poetic (otherwise it's a 'mere' ghost-story). It is a tale of horror, of corrupted innocence, an allegory of good and evil, of the fall (pride and the desire for knowledge versus Edenic innocence). Only the nuances change. Either Quint is the devil (evil pre-exists), or evil (though represented by Quint and Miss Jessel) is brought about by the pride, curiosity, possessiveness and incompetence of the governess. For Dorothea Krook (1962) the story is a Faustian allegory: the governess is Faust in her pride and desire for knowledge but also, in her efforts to protect the children from evil, the angel who tries to save Faust.

For Heilman (1948: 174ff) the narrative is a poem. Unfortunately he demonstrates this mainly in symbolic terms (the children are 'symbols' of the human condition), and by listing the metaphors and comparisons, which are not particularly original since they are part of the governess's *énonciation*, e.g., adjectives like 'divine' etc. (cp. chapter 3, p. 68 and note 5, for Todorov's constraint on a poetic reading of the pure fantastic).

4.2. *The hallucinations*

Here one is mainly in the 'Freudian' interpretation, that is to say, psychoanalysis of the governess, though few critics seem to have read Freud (even those against, e.g., Porter *et al.* 1942: 167: 'quite beyond the Freudian explanation . . . Here is one place where I find Freud completely defeated').

Wilson was the first to vulgarise the governess as 'a neurotic case of sex repression' and to assume that falling in love and 'repressing' it (which the governess does not) could be a cause of hallucination, and many critics followed suit, in terms so naive that I forbear to quote them.

As for the few critics who are more knowledgeable, they fall into other errors, from the point of view of literary theory. Cargill (1956: 223ff) relies on author-intention but argues persuasively that James had good reasons to wrap his history in ambiguity, namely the hysterical case of his sister Alice, to whom he was very close and whose journal he must have read after her death in 1892. Certainly James was in touch with the psychiatric circles of his time, both through the doctors treating her and through his brother William, and Cargill tries to show that he may have had at least indirect access (through a review by his friend F. W. F. Myers) to *Studien über Hysterie* by Freud and Breuer (1895), in which the case of Miss Lucy R. is described, a governess who was victim of (olfactory) hallucinations and in love with her employer.

Alexander Jones refutes this, discussing the differences between the two cases and Freud's whole description of conversion hysteria, for the development of which two conditions were necessary (to

Freud then): 'first, a memory too painful to be retained in the consciousness; second, an actual traumatic moment', at which the suddenly emergent incompatibility is repressed back into the subconscious. He shows that neither of these conditions is met in TS:

James's governess had no painful memory of her employer; to the contrary, she thought him charming. Moreover, she made no attempt to repress her infatuation but poured out her feelings freely to Mrs Grose. Finally, she thoroughly enjoyed her life at Bly until her encounters with Peter Quint and Miss Jessel. Lest it be thought that these encounters might qualify as traumatic moments, let us remember that traumatic moments must *precede* [Jones's italics] any related hallucinations; the latter are symptoms or effects – they cannot be their own causes. Since Freud explained his theory clearly and fully, it seems unlikely that James would compose a study of hysteria in which none of the basic requirements for hysteria are present. (1959: W304ff)

In the revised version of his 1956 essay, Cargill (1963: K145ff) has strengthened his case. He regards the letter from the headmaster, forwarded unopened by the Master, as the traumatic moment which reveals to the governess his indifference not only to the children but to herself, thus paralleling Miss Lucy R.'s similar realisation. I doubt whether this, as expressed in the text, can on its own qualify as a traumatic moment, but Cargill does make the point that an author is not a scientist. He also gives more convincing evidence for the possibility that James was aware of the Freud–Breuer work.

In spite of the appeal to James's (unknown) intentions, both these critics have at least read Freud, but each derives from him a different diagnosis. Jones asks: 'Why are Freudian critics content to depict the governess as hysterical?' and answers, not without irony: 'Using their present methods one could "prove" that she is afflicted with pedophilia erotica and is therefore attempting to seduce little Miles' (which is often suggested). He then goes on to show that very possibility and concludes that his evidence is 'as solid as much of the data presented by Wilson, Cargill, Silver and Goddard. Yet it does not constitute unassailable proof [of course]; rather, it demonstrates the shortcomings of excessive ingenuity.' Whereupon he falls back into the (real) intentional fallacy:

The odds are astronomical that James was *not* writing a tale of sexual abnormality. What, then, was he attempting to do? Goddard has asserted that James's conscious intention is unimportant ... Nevertheless, before we examine the tale, it is interesting to note James's own comments. (1959: W308)

The very notion of 'unassailable proof' in psychoanalysing a character who does not exist except as marks on paper (who has no past, no dreams, no transfer to an analyst) is absurd, but I shall return to this in a moment.

John Lydenberg (1957: W273ff) who holds a median position between ghosts and hallucinations (the ghosts exist but the real evil comes from the governess), uses the word 'hysterical' many times but comes up with a Frommian diagnosis:

she appears as an almost classic case of what Erich Fromm calls the authoritarian character: masochistic in that she delights in receiving the tortures as an 'expatiatory victim' . . . and at the same time sadistic in her insistence on dominating the children and Mrs Grose. (1957: W278)

Naturally this does not account for hallucinations but it doesn't try. He concludes (without attempting to explain the co-presence of compulsive neurosis and hysteria, two opposing though in *some* cases not incompatible types of neuroses) that the governess is 'hysterical, compulsive, sado-masochistic' (1957: W290).

As for M. Katan, M. D. (1962: W319ff), his 'causerie' is so naively and ramblingly expressed (though printed in *The psychoanalytic study of the child*), that I forbear to quote him extensively. In spite of the colossal error cited earlier and his absurd remarks about 'little Henry', he does make some interesting points about the primal scene as supposedly witnessed by the children (extratextually of course, but the text is certainly ambiguous enough to allow such an 'interpretation'). He is confusing, however, in his terminology, using the word 'psychotic feature' with reference to the delusion of being watched, and applying it to the fact that 'the man on top of the tower does not take his eyes off the governess' (1962: W326).[8] Similarly he talks about a delusion shared by two as *'une folie à deux'*, which changes (in this case) to *'une hallucination à trois'* and later to *'une fantaisie à trois'* (meaningless in French, the correct term being *fantasme*). 'The ghosts are the result not only of the guilty conscience of the governess but also the guilty conscience of the children!' (1962: W329). He finally arrives, by an extratextual argument which takes the prize, at *'une fantaisie à quatre'*:

In the past, when the ghosts were still living persons, the bachelor had visited the children many times. Now that these persons are dead and the children need the bachelor's guidance more than ever, he does not want to have anything to do with them. What other conclusion can we draw than that these dramatic events have frightened him and that as a result he withdraws from the situation, that he shies away from the ideas which are already shared by the governess and the children [the governess whom he hasn't met yet and who hasn't yet seen any ghost]? Thus the bachelor is – and this causes us no small surprise – the fourth participant in what then becomes 'une fantaisie à quatre'. He runs away from the obscure stirrings of the oedipal feelings which have so strongly aroused the other three. Clearly, the bachelor is modeled after the illustrious example of the author himself (1962: W330).

Caught between being God the Father and the illustrious author, the gay and irresponsible bachelor doesn't seem to please the critics much. They are nevertheless right, but in a sense of which they are unaware, as we shall see in chapter 7 (p. 181).

There is also a later article by Mark Spilka (1963), which is disappointing despite its seductive title: 'Turning the Freudian screw: how not to do it'. Spilka accuses the Freudians chiefly of not being sufficiently Freudian, which is true enough, but he has little to contribute himself. The Freudian critics, he says, 'seem oddly Rousseauistic: they believe in Original Innocence ... Hence they minimize or rationalize Miles's dismissal from school, Flora's verbal horrors, and the reports of earlier evils, as childish peccadilloes' (1963: 248). Or again:

A second Rousseauistic notion, that the governess exacerbates quiescent evils, seems equally untenable. So far as one can see, neither the ghosts nor the children need incitement. What the governess does, out of egoistic righteousness, is to force rather than ease two drastic confrontations. Her flaw is one of character, not compulsion. (1963: K249)

But the Freudian theory would be precisely (or ought to be) that she exacerbates quiescent evils or, in Freudian terms, provokes the return of the repressed (in herself, in the children), and the statement that the children need no incitement is irrelevant (and unwarranted by the text). As for the ghosts, well, yes, Spilka returns to the ghost theory, insisting on the social aspect already evoked by Wilson and treated by Lydenberg, and above all blaming the Freudian critics for their lack of rigour:

In their fidelity to a system crudely applied and narrowly conceived, they have themselves failed to 'throw light upon imaginative truth'. More specifically, they have failed to allow for secondary elaboration, for infantile sexuality, for civilization and its discontents – for those Freudian principles, in short, which can be made to subserve imagination in appraising James's story. As I hope this paper attests, such principles can be of enormous service to criticism, especially with the literature of the last two centuries. (1963: K253, italics author's own.)

Unfortunately the paper attests nothing of the sort, apart from these quotations and the undeveloped, unused phrase, thrown in there as if by chance, about secondary elaboration. But the conclusion is admirable, and will serve to precipitate my own, which is this:

Without going here into the present controversy as to what precisely constitutes a literary text, I assume as empirically evident that a literary text, and more especially an ambiguous one, does inevitably produce many interpretations, whereas a non-literary text does not. This particular text, however, has for its brevity produced a veritable 'case' which is particularly revealing in its confusions.

Allowing for the passage of time since some of the more traditional pieces, a text which can generate, not only different interpretations but so many erroneous readings can indeed be regarded, on the one hand as an author's 'intended' test of his reader's inattention, a text composed on the very principle of ambiguity; but on the other, also as a text structured (intentionally or not) on the same principle that a neurosis is structured. I am not opting here for or against the ghosts, the governess's narrative is neurotic in both hypotheses. And the structure of a neurosis involves the attempt (often irresistible) to drag the 'other' down into itself, into the neurosis, the other being here the reader. This structure is successful, as we have seen, which is why I called the governess's state (her language) 'contagious'.

Whether the success is due to conscious (intended) or unconscious skill it is not my purpose here to argue, and if I have quoted so fully from so many critics, it was primarily as a study in non-methodology, but also to clear a path through the tangled bush of traditional criticism, to free the text from these many layers of misreadings (not the readings, some of which I shall accept 'as read'), to dispose of them as it were, so as to be able once again to look at it as a text, and above all to bring out a few theoretical principles without which no text can be analysed in a clear perspective, and which can be reduced here to three broad principles:

(1) a respect for the genre to which a text ostensibly belongs, even if that genre is in any one instance transgressed;

(2) a rigorous distinction between the metalanguage (the language of the critic) and the language of the linguistic object examined. This means not only avoiding traditional paraphrase, but understanding the elementary and not so elementary techniques of a literary text and the terms that poetics (as one type of metalanguage) has elaborated for these, employing

those terms and not the language of the object, except in quotation (if possible correct);

(3) a respect for the textuality of the text.

It is in the light of these three principles that I shall now analyse *The Turn of the Screw* (chapters 7, 8).

7

The Turn of the Screw: mirror structures as basic structures

Since it is my purpose to preserve the total ambiguity of the TS text, I shall not argue for the ghosts or for the hallucinations, but try to show that the text is structured on poetic principles that function in both hypotheses.[1]

Nevertheless, because of the confusions and naïveté of the 'psychological' interpretations, it will be necessary to place the hallucination theory on a sounder basis, which is also a structural one. The ghost theory as such presents no difficulties (the onus of proof is on the natural explanation, for the supernatural cannot be 'proved'), but it should emerge strengthened by the poetic structure as brought out. Indeed there is a general level on which both hypotheses rejoin each other: the ghosts tend to be called emanations of (a) the evil within the governess, or (b) a pre-existent, evil, she acting as transmitter; likewise hysteria is both a personal and a socially produced illness.[2]

1. The crack (Spaltung)

I have already said in chapter 6 (p. 154) that one cannot, strictly, psychoanalyse a fictional character, one can only give a psychoanalytical interpretation of a text. This includes us, the reader. But insofar as we can, in a limited way, psychoanalyse a fictional character, we might as well get certain things straight. Much has been said on the cause of the governess's state. In the simplest of the ghost hypotheses, the mere appearance of the ghosts and the evil they represent could make her 'hysterical' in the popular sense, but not hysterical in the psychoanalytical sense since, as Alexander Jones has pointed out (1959: 305), the hallucinations are the symptoms and cannot be their own causes (see chapter 6, p. 153 above).

It is clear that her falling in love and surmounting this love because unattainable is not in itself a sufficient cause for hallucinations of this order, although it is at the base, as is all desire, of the triggering elements (*Wiederspaltung*).[3]

Jones quotes Freud and Breuer (1920 [1895]) *Studies on hysteria* on the two necessary conditions for conversion hysteria, and says that neither is fulfilled (see chapter 6, p. 153 above): 'first a memory too painful to be retained in the consciousness; second, an actual traumatic moment' (Jones 1959: 304ff) at which the suddenly emergent incompatibility is repressed back into the subconscious.

Jones bases his remarks solely on *Studies on hysteria* (on the supposition, demonstrated by Cargill [1963: 161ff] that James could have been acquainted with it). More to the point is Freud's linguistic work on the mechanism of jokes *Witz und seine Beziehung zum Unbewussten* (1960 [1905]), *Das Unheimlich* (1933 [1919]) and above all the *Project for a scientific psychology* (1895, published posthumously in 1950).[4] In this last, as Mehlmann (1975) has shown recently, Freud practically destroys the commonly held notion of the traumatic event, splitting, in effect, that event in two: the first (in the example of the *Project*), a sexual aggression, the second an insignificant event linked to the first by apparently marginal but in fact metonymic elements. The traumatic event in fact consists of a metonymic relation between the two, a displacement through which the elements shared by both cause the second to symbolise the first and reactivate it. The symptoms (in this case a fear of entering shops alone) are constituted by these metonymic relations and occur in a third instance.

Obviously a fictional text that does not explicitly deal with the first moment cannot give us the material to reconstruct it, nor, *a fortiori*, the metonymic relation between it and the second moment – hence the absurdity of 'psychoanalysing' a fictional character in the usual sense. We do, however, have the symptoms, which are structured into both a psychic and an artistic whole. We also have two possible second moments or triggering elements (*Wiederspaltung*), one of which has been picked up by Cargill. The other has gone unnoticed. Yet both form an integral part of the symptomatic structure, around which is organised the artistic structure.

Cargill (1963: 145ff) suggests that the governess's receipt of her employer's letter (chapter 2), which is only a covering note to the headmaster's letter forwarded unopened, qualifies as 'the traumatic moment' because it reveals his indifference, not only to the children but to herself. Certainly the text brings out an element of disappointment, even of shock (my italics):

The postbag that evening – it came late – contained a letter for me which, however, in the hand of my employer, I found to be composed *but of a few words* enclosing another, addressed to himself, with a seal still unbroken. 'This, I recognise, is from the head-master, and the head-master's an awful bore. Read him, please: deal with him; but mind you don't report. Not a word. I'm off!' *I broke the seal with a great effort – so great a one that I was a long time coming to it; took the unopened missive at last up to my room and only attacked it just before going to bed.* I had better have let it wait till morning, for it gave me a second sleepless night. (p. 10)

Since, however, this is only a brutal confirmation of the in-junction already given and accepted in London, the most we can say is that it puts an end to any fluttering hope of a reversal she might have entertained on receiving the letter. It is thus not exactly on a par with the hopes entertained by Miss Lucy R. (*Studies on hysteria*) as Cargill states. The metonymic repetition of the injunction (general→particular), however, suggests that the injunction is itself in metonymic relation with a 'first' moment and is of immense structural importance. I shall return to it.[5]

The other possible triggering element for the crack or rather the recrack (*Spaltung, Wiederspaltung*) comes before this, in chapter 1 The governess is impressed, on arrival, with the sheer size of Bly, which contrasts with her expectations:

I had received in Harley Street a narrower notion of the place, and that, as I recalled it, made me think the proprietor still more of a gentleman, suggested that what I was to enjoy might be a matter beyond his promise. (p. 7)

She makes a similar relation about Flora's beauty:

She was the most beautiful child I had ever seen, and I afterwards wondered why my employer hadn't made more of a point to me of this. I slept little that night – I was much too excited; and this astonished me too, I recollect, remained with me, adding to my sense of the liberality with which I was treated. (p. 7)

This movement of expansion, expressed in terms of pleasure, related to her employer and contrasting with the dim expectations as given by Douglas in the Introduction, creates the psychological setting for the desire of 'a matter beyond his promise'. But there is more:

The large impressive room, one of the best in the house, *the great state bed*, as I almost felt it, the *figured full* draperies, *the long glasses in which, for the first time, I could see myself from head to foot*, all struck me – like the wonderful appeal of my small charge – as *so many things thrown in*. *It was thrown in as well*, from the first moment, that I should get on with Mrs Grose in a relation over which, on my way, in the coach, I fear I had rather brooded. The one appearance indeed that in this early outlook might have made me *shrink again* was that of her being so inordinately glad to see me ... so glad ... as to be positively on her guard against showing it too much. (p. 7)

There are several elements here, which will all structure the text. Among the things 'thrown in', the *suppléments*, later to be projected out in displacement or inversion, are: power, sexual pleasure (the great state bed, as in a master bedroom), the figured full draperies, the long glasses, the extraordinary charm of the child, the relationship with Mrs Grose, ambiguous from the start with pleasure and fear; and a secret suggested, another, *outer* secret, not ostensibly connected with whatever her own private secret might be.[6]

The most important element is that of the long glasses. It may seem bizarre to us that a young girl of twenty should never have seen herself whole in a mirror.' The realistic touch is unerring: one can imagine the vicarage with its small hall mirror for adjusting a hat before going to church – the hat so important by its absence in the text, first for the identification of Quint and then, at the end, for both the governess and Flora as a reflection of Miss Jessel always being without one. But, far more important, these 'long glasses' could be said to set in motion the entire crisis (psychic) and artistic structure (literary).

In his famous essay 'Le stade du miroir' (1966 [1936]) and elsewhere in his writings (1966, 1973a), Lacan has shown the primordial role played by the mirror in the formation of identity (*la constitution du sujet*). Unless the child correctly goes through the three stages (to simplify: recognition of the other, recognition of the other as self, recognition of the other as self but other), he remains in the state of partial identification related to what Lacan calls '*le corps morcelé*, an awareness only of separate parts of the body and never of its totality. And *le corps morcelé* is of course related to the castration anxiety and through this to life and death (see also Laplanche 1970).

I shall not go into Lacan's theory in detail, nor psychoanalyse the governess in the light of it – indeed I have absurdly simplified it. Nor am I suggesting that James had read Lacan.[7] What I do propose to do is to show that the mirror, *le corps morcelé*, together with the sudden expansion of a previously restricted consciousness with which it is here juxtaposed, and which it implicitly also provokes, forms the principle on which the text is structured.

2. The mirror-structure

Critics have already remarked on the governess's ability 'to project Quint and Miss Jessel to great distances, across lakes; to the tops of towers and so on' (Van Doren in Porter *et al.* 1942: W165). Van Doren also mentions the fact, without drawing any significance from it (he is for the ghosts), that the first two apparitions of Quint 'do not reveal anything except the upper half of him. Once he is standing behind a sort of balustrade on top of the tower; another time he is merely looking in a window, but the lower half of him is not there – it is as if he were in some ghastly way truncated' (1942: W164).

In fact Quint is never seen whole, but always truncated, since the fourth and last apparition is also at the window and the third, on the stairs, is curiously foreshortened, the narrator–governess being higher than he and describing only the hideous 'long gaze' and then 'the villainous back that no hunch could have more disfigured', as 'the low wretch [in life] to which it [the figure, i.e., in death] had once belonged' turns and passes down the staircase 'into the darkness in which the next bend was lost' (James 1966: 41).

In other words, only one piece of him, and this with a disfigurement negatively added. There is also a split and chiasmus, for it is, grammatically, the 'low wretch' (life) who is made to turn, not the 'figure' seen (death).

Miss Jessel, however, is seen both whole and foreshortened, but less explicitly truncated than Quint: first at a distance across the lake (whole), secondly also on the stairs but at the bottom, 'seated on one of the lower steps with *her back* presented to me, *her body half-bowed* and *her head*, in an attitude of woe, *in her hands*' (chapter 10: 43); she then vanishes without looking round, and it is not stated whether she *rises* to do so. Thirdly, in the schoolroom, but sitting at the table, hence implicitly cut off, and she does rise, still presumably behind the table, before vanishing. And lastly on the other side of the lake again, 'as big as a blazing fire'.[8]

There is also an expansion and compression of space, for the distances are not always 'great', as Van Doren says, indeed only the first of Quint is at a distance and the first and last of Miss Jessel. All the others are explicitly or implicitly close (the window, the stairs, the schoolroom).

A third variation is that of height. Quint appears first on a tower (up), then at a ground-floor window (level), then on the stairs (down) and finally at the same window (level).[9] Miss Jessel first

appears on the other side of the lake (level), on the stairs (down), in
the schoolroom (upstairs but level with the governess, and of course
at her present social level), and finally by the lake again (level).
This variation could be said to be generated by the opening
metaphor:

I remember the whole beginning as a succession of flights and drops, a little
see-saw of the right throbs and the wrong. After rising, in town, to meet his
appeal (p. 6)

A see-saw implies another person at the opposite end, a person
who must necessarily be up, level or down.

Both apparitions, moreover, first appear outside (on the tower, by
the lake), but even here there is a disjunction: Quint is seen from the
grounds but on the tower (horizontal frontier between out and in),
Miss Jessel completely outside. Quint will appear inside the house
only once (on the stairs), but twice at the window (vertical frontier
between out and in). Miss Jessel, who is closer to the governess's
own identity, will appear first outside, twice inside (the stairs, the
schoolroom), and lastly outside again.

There is a fifth type of contrast: Quint is seen, as to the top half,
in a detail which verges on the absurd and which, of course has been
the main obstacle to the hallucination theory (explicable however),
a type of detail which reminds us of Nathaniel's obsessive description of Coppelius in E.T.A. Hoffmann's 'The Sandman', also
much concerned with seeing (from a cupboard, through a window,
from the top of a tower). Whereas Miss Jessel, despite the
governess's claim to Mrs Grose that she has described both 'to the
last detail, their special marks – a portrait on the exhibition of
which she [Mrs Grose] had instantly recognized and named them',
is not only in fact first identified by the governess as 'my predecessor' (p. 31), and only then named by Mrs Grose (exactly as if the
governess had not until then known the name), but described only
in the vaguest terms, convenient to the situation, conventional in
any ghost story: 'a figure of quite as unmistakable horror and evil: a
woman in black, pale and dreadful – with such an air also, and such
a face!' (p. 31). '"In mourning – rather poor, almost shabby. But –
yes – with extraordinary beauty ... Oh handsome – very, very," I
insisted, "wonderfully handsome. But infamous"' (p. 32). Since the
governess already knows that Miss Jessel was pretty (p. 12), was
particular but not about all things (p. 12), died in mysterious
circumstances (p. 13), that Quint 'liked them young and pretty' (p.

12), was 'too free with everyone' (p. 26) and is moreover dead (p. 24), this can hardly be called an inexplicably detailed description, and later ones are equally vague.

What do we see in a mirror? Idealised or ugly reflections, according to our emotional needs and physical states, according to the light, the quality of the mirror; parts of ourselves or ourselves whole (but never in the round), from different angles and at different distances according to the position of the mirror, and in any case always reversed, never as others see us. Just as, 'in language, our message comes to us from the Other ... in inverted form' (Lacan 1966: 9). I need not reiterate here James's obsession, so frequently attested in the *Notebooks* (1947) and in his practice as a writer, with the consciousness as mirror, more or less polished according to the subtlety of the character (an image also found in Hoffmann), or with the word and concept of 'picture', which sends him, every time it occurs, into a positive orgy of pleasure.

The picture, and *a fortiori* the mirror-image, is thus particularly useful (in both hypotheses) for a case of projected evil or sickness. As a structure both external (physical) and internal (psychic) it positively forms the text as we have it.

For a mirror is not only a reflected instance, it is also a frame, as is a picture, as is any work of art (Lotman 1970; Uspensky 1974), which concentrates, and so intensifies, all that is explicitly within it, and leaves implicit all that is without. Or to quote Lacan in relation to the 'screen' (to which I shall return): 'dans son rapport au désir, la réalité n'apparaît que marginale' (1973a: 99).

The whole TS text is not only itself elaborately framed in this sense, it is also structured on mini-framings of scenes that open out on or frame other scenes. I shall return to these structural frames later. But there is also another kind of framing, not dealt with by Lotman or Uspensky; at the semantic level, that is, the signified is itself framed (or not) by other signifiers, and this semantic framing forms the sixth and last of the contrasts I have been dealing with. For within these structurally framed scenes, the very apparitions of Quint are also *described* as if framed – with variations: by the crenellated wall, by the dining-room window (twice, and very explicitly), by the staircase (a sort of frame but more implicit) and at the same time by 'the tall window that presided over the great turn of the staircase' (p 40). Miss Jessel however is free of such explicit framing: she appears twice by the lake (itself an implicit mirror-image, but unframed), once at the foot of the stairs (implicit frame), once in the schoolroom (an implicit frame both physical and social).

There are thus six axes of variation: far/near, up/level/down, out/frontier/in, whole/cut, detailed/vague, framed/unframed.

These contrasts modulate the narrative both psychoanalytically and poetically. It is clear that if there has been a division of the gay bachelor, object of desire (Wilson 1934; Katan 1962), into the unattainable employer and his highly sexualised and over-accessible (though dead) valet, then the latter may himself be split – far/near etc., partly wearing his master's clothes (but the waistcoat only), invisible from the waist down but detailed, and always intensified by a frame – whereas Miss Jessel, who is not only the governess's actual predecessor and sexual/social equal but who gave in to her desires, is seen first whole (like the governess in the mirror), then cut, free of explicit frame-intensification, and blurred, conventional, as with a refusal to see. The whole system of repetition and reversal is the very language of the unconscious.

It is also the language of poetry. For the poetic structure, that of the mirror, with all the play of vision-variation it affords, functions around this same system of repetition and reversal at work in the projection of these images. In table 7.1, first separating male and female apparitions, we have (Q = Quint, J = Jessel, four apparitions each).

Table 7.1

	far near	up level down	out frontier in	whole cut	detail non	frame non
Q1	+	+	+	+	+	+
Q2	+	+	+	+	+	+
Q3	+	+	+	+	+	+
Q4	+	+	+	+	+	+
J1	+	+	+	+	+	+
J2	+	+	+	+	+	+
J3	+	+	+	+	+	+
J4	+	+	+	+	+	+

The conjunctions and disjunctions are clear: for *far/near*, a parallel movement with a final disjunction as Miss Jessel removes at a distance; for *height*, a parallel between Q2-Q4 and J1-J3 (J1 occurring after Q2), with a disjunction at Q1 (up) and J4 (repetition of level, Miss Jessel appearing level three times); for *out/in*, disjunction after the first appearance outside of each, Quint moving in via the frontier and back to the frontier, Miss Jessel moving in twice then out again, and not appearing at a frontier; for *whole/cut*, semi-disjunction, Quint being always truncated, Miss Jessel first whole, then twice not, then whole; for *detail*, almost complete disjunction, Miss Jessel being wholly vague, Quint vague only once; for *framing*, almost complete disjunction, Quint being wholly and explicitly framed, Miss Jessel framed only once, and implicitly.

Table 7.2

	far	near	up	level	down	out	frontier	in	whole	cut	detail	non	frame	non
Q1	+		+			+				+	+		+	
Q2		+		+			+			+	+		+	
J1	+			+		+			+			+		+
Q3		+		+				+		+	+		+	
J2		+			+			+		+		+	+	
J3		+		+				+		+		+	+	
J4	+			+		+			+			+		+
Q4		+		+				+		+		+	+	

Secondly, the same movements can be observed in the story's progression (see table 7.2). The table shows the progression, on each axis, from variation early in the story, via a tendency to repetition in the centre and back to variation, except for the up/down and the detail/non-detail axes, where the repetition comes towards the end. Most of the apparitions are level except for Quint's startling first (up), and one each in the centre of the story (down, after which her eyes are 'sealed' and she sees nothing for about a month). Quint is described in some detail for his first three apparitions and Miss Jessel never, Quint rejoining her in this at his last appearance when the emphasis is not on him but on Miles.

This carefully varied effect of a distorting mirror also affects the 'communication' between the governess and the apparitions. There is a deep exchange of looks, for the apparitions, like mirror reflections, are silent. And silence is horror: 'It was the dead silence of our long gaze at such close quarters that gave the whole horror, huge as it was, its only note of the unnatural' (p. 41). Since each apparition is called a horror ('He's a horror', p. 22, 'the woman's a horror of horrors', p. 32), and since Miles's dismissal from school 'was really but the question of the horrors gathered behind' (p. 57), Felman suggests that 'in the governess's eyes the word "horror" defines both what the ghosts *are* and what the letters [sent/unsent] *suppress*, leave out ... act as a kind of pendant to the missing *content* of the letters'; cp. Miles's 'nothing' and the governess on Quint: 'he's like nobody' (Felman 1977: 23).' Could it not be said that the ghosts are in reality nothing other than the letters' *content* and that the letters' content could thus itself be nothing other than a *ghost-effect?*' (Felman: 150). She adds in footnote that the signifying chain of letters would be by the same token a chain of ghosts, the erased letter being like the return of the dead, and both like the story of the unconscious, the return of the repressed through the insistence of the signifier. And she points out that the link with *writing* is made by the governess herself: 'So I saw him as I see the letters I form on this page' (p. 17) i.e., the letters in the 'story-letter' written to Douglas. Thus to see ghosts = to see letters. 'But what is "seeing letters" if not, precisely, *reading?*' (Felman: 151 – the governess's story is also that of her own reading of her story – whereas Mrs Grose can't 'read', being illiterate.) The story-letter 'is structured around a sort of necessity short-circuited by an impossibility, or an impossibility contradicted by a necessity, of *recounting an ellipsis* ... of writing *a letter about what was missing in the initial, original letter*' (Felman: 144).

Certainly the governess reads what she wants into these silent letters. From Quint's searching look at her (second apparition) she reads that 'he also saw and recognised' and later as he looks beyond her that 'he had come for someone else'; in the third that he knew her terror had dropped from her, and the last apparition is carefully organised so that Quint appears each time she has a moment of triumph or presses her advantage too far with Miles. Similarly she reads a vast amount of information in Miss Jessel's appearances.[10]

The mirror-effect is not only used for the apparitions, however. It is particularly projected onto Mrs Grose, not of course with variations on the same axes since Mrs Grose is necessarily close and level (physically if not socially), nor is she physically described except in her movements, and all but three of the conversations with her occur indoors, usually in the schoolroom at night.[11]

The mirror effect is achieved here through description of movement and in dialogue. The scene of Quint's second apparition (chapter 4) and the subsequent elaboration with Mrs Grose (chap-

ter 5) are quite astonishing in this respect, and set the perpetual to-
and-fro motion going with force. The governess sees the unknown
man she had seen on the tower, framed in the ground-floor window.
Her reaction is exactly that of a monkey in front of a mirror: to go
behind the mirror (a child does not do this). She rushes out, sees
nothing. Further, she places herself in *his* position and peers in, as if
to see what he saw, herself where she no longer is.

There is then a complete repetition, Mrs Grose comes into the
dining-room, sees the governess peering in, looks terrified, rushes out
and, after a partial explanation, places herself in the governess's
exposition and peers in. The dialogue emphasises this double
movement:

Just what you saw from the dining-room a minute ago was the effect of that.
What *I* saw [J] – just before – was much worse. (p. 22)

What the governess had seen was a man, as yet unidentified but
to be described in detail to Mrs Grose, and who turns out to be
dead. What Mrs Grose saw was the governess 'white as a sheet . . .
awful'. A ghost.

And later, Mrs Grose having 'turned away a little':[12]

Slowly she faced me again. 'Do you fear for them?'
We met in another long look. 'Don't *you?*' [J]. Instead of answering she
came nearer to the window and, for a minute, applied her face to the glass.
'You see how he could see', I meanwhile went on. (p. 23)[13]

This mirror-structure will recur throughout. The governess and
Mrs Grose will always be exchanging long looks, reading into each
other's faces (in the governess's narrative of course, i.e., what she
thinks Mrs Grose thinks she thinks), and this too is constantly
emphasised in dialogue:

'I don't wonder you looked queer,' I persisted, 'when I mentioned to you
the letter from his school!'
'I doubt if I looked as queer as you!' she retorted with homely force.
(p. 37)

Mrs Grose is even momentarily identified with Miss Jessel in one
of these mirror-movements:

'And without coming nearer?'
'Oh for the effect and the feeling she might have been as close as you!'
My friend, with an odd impulse, fell back a step. (p. 31)

Miss Jessel, as a projection (in the hallucination theory) or a
double (in the ghost theory), is here suddenly mirrored in Mrs

Grose, and not surprisingly. For Mrs Grose is not merely the commonsense foil to the governess that she is always presented as, she is also the governess's mirror, her transfer even, in the psychoanalytical sense that every event is elaborated with her, and that the governess absolutely needs to convince her.[14] Even the first apparition is prefiguratively followed by a meeting with an anxious and motherly Mrs Grose in the hall, although at this stage the governess imparts nothing, as in the beginning of a transfer. From then on the governess as character will need her after every major apparition and after the children's pranks/sinister conduct; the governess as narrator needs her for the artistic framing of her narrative.

For apart from the two brief apparitions on the stairs (followed by a spell of non-seeing), no apparition is narrated *whole*: something, and often a great deal, is kept back from the reader, to be given only later, in elaboration with Mrs Grose. Mrs Grose is the governess's necessary mirror, who must be made to believe, made to accept the governess's image of herself. And she is also the literary device through which the narrator distributes her information to her reader (Douglas) and indirectly to us: the information is itself *morcelée*, as in Barthes's semic and hermeneutic codes (1970, see chapter 2 above). I shall return to this aspect in more detail in the next chapter, on the surface structure of narrative and dialogue. Here these elements are part of the mirror-structure and that of frames within frames, frames expanding into wider frames: the elaborations.

The mirror-structure is also projected onto the children, particularly Miles. Both the children are constantly watched for reflected signs of what she thinks they see, and what she thinks they think of her. The latter is made very specific in the scene with Miles on the way to church:

I remember that, to gain time, I tried to laugh, and I seemed to see in the beautiful face with which he watched me how ugly and queer I looked [reversal of beauty and ugliness]. (p. 55)

Flora too, is searchingly gazed at for a reaction (or for a reflection of a greater evil) after her small escapade behind the window-blind in chapter 10, the elements of vision and light particularly brought out in the vocabulary ('with the flame of the candle full in the wonderful little face ... something beautiful that shone out of the blue of her own ... Flora luminously considered' etc.). And of course Flora has herself been framed in the window, but invisibly, hidden behind the *blind* as opposed to the framing of the *visible* apparitions in the governess's *sight*. The dialogue also emphasises the mirror-structure:

> 'You were looking for me out of the window?' I said. 'You thought I might be walking in the grounds?'
> 'Well, you know, I thought some one was' – she never blanched as she smiled out that at me.
> Oh how I looked at her now! 'And did you see anyone?'
> 'Ah, *no!*' [J] she returned. (p. 42)

And when the governess asks her why she had pulled the curtain of her bed to conceal her absence and Flora replies 'Because I don't like to frighten you!' the governess insists: 'But if I had, by your idea, gone out –?' Flora turns the argument neatly, mirror-like (like Miles later), back onto the governess's own behaviour: "Oh but you know," she quite adequately answered, "that you might come back, you dear, and that you *have!*"' [J].

In other words the governess has watched Flora watch out of the window, for Miss Jessel as she supposes, but Flora (wittingly or unwittingly) replaces the supposed Miss Jessel with the governess herself (supposedly out there and in fact not, and in any case to return): on the other side of the mirror there is (or is not) nothing.

Another reversal of positions, simpler and clearer, occurs with the actual apparitions by the lake: the first time, the governess and Flora are on the near side and the governess sees Miss Jessel on the opposite bank, behind Flora who faces the governess; the last time, the governess and Mrs Grose do not find Flora on this spot (where the governess expected her to be) and go round the lake to the other side where they find Flora; when the governess sees Miss Jessel, it is on the opposite bank, i.e. where they had been the first time. The image is exactly reversed, with Flora facing the supposed apparition but looking only at the governess. Only now there is a third element, Mrs Grose, and the verbalisation she has unwittingly aroused in the governess.

But there is an even more interesting reversal of positions after Flora's second nocturnal rising to the window, when the governess goes to an empty room in the tower to see what Flora is looking at and sees, not Miss Jessel as she expects, nor even Quint, but a figure gazing up at the tower 'as at something that was apparently above me', and is at once convinced there is someone on the tower. The 'presence on the lawn' turns out to be Miles, who is thus distanced

and foreshortened into the very position of the governess herself as
the unknown man on the tower (if he was there) must have seen her
when she first looked up from the grounds and saw him looking
down at her. The see-saw image is implicit: the governess is up
(though not on *top* of the tower), Miles is down, whereas before she
was down and Quint was up (and higher); there is not only reversal
and substitution (Miles for governess, governess for Quint), but in
effect suppression of the governess who is *de trop* in the second
instance, a mere voyeur, hence the completely logical supposition
that Miles can't be gazing at her and that Quint must be in his
initial position, i.e., on the tower above her. In Lacan's terms, she is
both in the picture and out of it.[15]

The governess's image of herself as 'screen' between the ghosts
and the children, although a morally motivated image, is in itself
sufficiently startling in the 'light' of Lacan's remarks on light and
the eye upon and in a picture. In our text, the constant play of
positional exchange is also 'reflected' in all the dialogues between
the governess and Miles, all structured as a see-sawing power game
between the governess's authority as governess and adult, and the
personality of the child who throws back her words at her, often
altered or reversed.

Just as there are four apparitions of each sex, each child is given
four 'scenes'.[16] These scenes are all, naturally, with the narrating
governess. One of the scenes with Miles is out of doors, on the way
to church, Miles very much the little gentleman and winning out
over her – a pivotal scene in the narrative syntax as we shall see; the
other three are indoors, two in his room with Miles in bed (chapters
14, 17), i.e., down but winning nevertheless; and the long final scene
in the dining-room where Miles both wins and loses.

Two of the scenes with Flora are out of doors: the first by the lake,
and the last by the lake; and two indoors (chapter 10, cited above p.
170, the second prank, same chapter). In all of them Flora also
wins, flooring the governess either by her silence (the first and third)
or in dialogue; or in outburst (second lake scene). I do not count her
final outburst of foul language as 'scene' since this is only reported
by Mrs Grose.

3. The figure four

Four apparitions of each sex, four scenes with a child of each sex,
this may well appear fortuitous. But a mirror not only reflects and

distorts, it frames, and a frame is normally four-sided. And the figure four literally frames the text.

The story itself is elaborately framed in a quadripartite structure of mathematical precision. There are:

(1) *Four main living characters at Bly* (the 'spectators'): the governess, Mrs Grose, Miles, Flora. Cross-linked:

    (a) the governess and Mrs Grose; Miles and Flora
    (b) the governess and Miles; Mrs Grose and Flora (at the end)
    (c) the governess and Flora; Mrs Grose and Miles (she gives information about him).

(2) *Four ex-guardians* (all failing in some way): the uncle, Mrs Grose, Quint, Miss Jessel. Cross-linked:

    (a) the uncle and Mrs Grose (alive; also linked at the end since she is to take Flora to him); Quint and Miss Jessel (dead)
    (b) the uncle and Quint (male, master/valet); Mrs Grose and Miss Jessel (female, housekeeper/governess)
    (c) the uncle and Miss Jessel (he gives information about her in the Prologue); Quint and Mrs Grose (information, identification).

(3) *Four presently concerned with the children*: the governess, Mrs Grose, Quint, Miss Jessel. Cross-linked:

    (a) the governess and Mrs Grose; Quint and Miss Jessel
    (b) the governess and Quint; Mrs Grose and Miss Jessel
    (c) the governess and Miss Jessel; Mrs Grose and Quint.

(4) *Four in a supposed evil relationship*: Quint, Miss Jessel, Miles, Flora. Cross-linked:

    (a) Quint and Miss Jessel; Miles and Flora
    (b) Quint and Miles; Miss Jessel and Flora
    (c) Miles and Miss Jessel (last scene, the 'error'); Quint and Flora (only through the supposed collusion with Miles and supposed witnessing of primal scene).

Cargill (1963: 157) notes that the story is presented 'within a frame, for unlike most of James's stories, *The Turn of the Screw* is a tale with an elaborate portico'. This portico, the Introduction, contains *four narrators*: Griffith (narrator of the first, extratextual, ghost-story), the I–narrator, Douglas, the governess (whose manuscript is discussed in advance and listened to by those present). These are also cross-linked, though less completely since Griffith does not link up with the governess except in that he reiterates the information that she was ten years older than Douglas:

(a) Griffith and Douglas (tellers of ghost-stories about children; one turn of the screw and two); the I–narrator and the governess: as transmitter of her manuscript, which he copies out for 'us', present readers, after Douglas's death, i.e., we do not have the 'original'; this apparently gratuitous recopying of the text by the I–narrator (for there is no plausible reason why he should not have given us the original as given to Douglas) is on the one hand another aspect of James's joke or 'trap' (we have no guarantee that he copied it accurately), but, on the other, further emphasises the loss of origin, the curiously Derridean *trace* of lost origin and the curiously Lacanian 'rehandling of the signifier' in a complex chain of transmission, each transmittor or addressor having first been a receiver or addressee, a reader who turns narrator (cp. Felman 1977: 124).

(b) Douglas and the governess; Griffith and the I–narrator (instigators of Douglas's tale, commentators and questioners);

(c) the I–narrator and Douglas; Griffith and the governess.

There are also *four readers* or receptors of the story: Douglas, the I–narrator, the other listeners staged, and us. These are also cross-linked:

(a) Douglas and the I–narrator; the others and us (we are in a way also the others);

(b) Douglas and his listeners; the I–narrator and us;

(c) Douglas and us; the I–narrator and the others (discussion in the absence of Douglas).

There is also, in another, more metaphoric sense, the governess as 'reader' of her own story (Felman 1977: 151, see p. 167 here), but here she is also 'us', since we are unavoidably drawn, through identification (a mirror-structure, a transfer), into reading with her, reading 'all the meanings' she reads 'into the facts' (James 1966: 27). Thus it could be said that the 'original' narrator (reader of her story) rejoins the final readers of her story who also, in their critical activity, become in their turn transmitters. The 'turn' of the screw indeed, is an endless spiral.

Felman (pp. 121–2) also points out the several narrators of the Prologue, but gives only three, that is, she omits Griffith, correctly from her point of view since Griffith is not in any sense a narrator of TS, and Felman is concerned here with the weird chain of transmission given for TS in the Prologue, the frame as she also calls it, echoed inside the story by the chain of letters (and ghosts, see p. 167 here).

The story's origin is therefore not assigned to any one voice which would assume responsibility for the tale, but to the deferred action of a sort of *echoing effect* ... It is as though the frame itself could only multiply *itself*, repeat itself ... be its own self-framing ... If ... the story is preceded and anticipated by a repetition of the story, then the frame, far from situating, as it first appeared, the story's *origin*, actually situates its *loss*, constitutes its infinite deferral.

And again she compares this to *psychoanalysis as a story*. However, Griffith's story (un*told* in the text but summed up), is not only the instigator of TS, but of its title (one child = one turn of the screw, two = two, which as she points out later in her analysis of that metaphor, is idiomatically and physically impossible: one gives *another* turn, and another, thus apparently but in fact deepening the hole, in a spiral, not a circle (Felman 1977: 170–3), just as *turn* means also *change, displacement, direction, choice of sense, re-turn* (pp. 178–9). The *original* story (Griffith's), that of the 'one turn', is thus also an origin which is lost, and I feel that even for her own argument Griffith plays a role.

The governess's narrative is as we have seen constituted in fours. Moreover it consists of twenty-four chapters, which fall naturally into four sections of six chapters each:

1–6 *The initial situation and its preliminary alteration*: arrival, letter from the school with covering note from the Master, exchange of information with Mrs Grose, the first two apparitions of Quint and first elaboration with Mrs Grose, more extraction of information, the first apparition of Miss Jessel (i.e., all the *données*).

7–12 *Development towards the central pivot*: further elaboration with Mrs Grose, the two apparitions on the stairs, the children's escapades, Mrs Grose's appeal that the uncle be sent for, the governess's threat to leave if Mrs Grose should send for him.

13–18 *Precipitation towards the fundamental alteration*: the governess's eyes are sealed, Miles's challenge about his school and threat to make his uncle come down, third apparition of Miss Jessel, in the schoolroom.

19–24 *Alteration effected*: showdown with Flora and last apparition of Miss Jessel, result and reversal of result, showdown with Miles and last apparition of Quint.

This may seem a rather bare summary, but it does bring out the narrative structure of the text as an integral part of its 'portico', the text within its frame. For the portico has several obvious functions:

(1) that of suspense build-up (Douglas is an expert at it)
(2) that of setting the circumstances for the telling of the tale

(a) in mood (ghost-stories round the fire)[17]
(b) in generic expectation (conditioned to expect ghosts, we expect the supernatural, even at the first appearance of a man on the tower)
(3) that of giving information not contained in the governess's narrative
(a) about her character and background
(b) about her employer
(c) about the previous governess, about the housekeeper
(d) elements in time before her narrative starts and after it ends.

Now (3) (d) is by far the most important of these functions structurally, for it not only enables the governess's narrative to start with her arrival at Bly and end with Miles's death, entrusting the before and after to Douglas's viewpoint, but it also contains the beginning and end of the bare structure, which is the most abstract structure in that it is the structure of all folk-tales and most myths: an injunction is given, accepted, and transgressed, with a certain result.

4. The bare structure

It is in the Introduction that Douglas tells of the employer's main condition that the governess should on no account trouble him. Yet by the end of the governess's narrative she has not only *decided* to trouble him (though the letter is stolen by Miles), she has also behaved in such a way as to involve him anyway (a sick child, then a dead child).

We are not of course told the sequel, except, in the Introduction, that 'she never saw him again'. We are left to infer some sort of involvement on his part, if not with her directly (something she could not foresee), at least via Mrs Grose, and since the Prologue also tells us that ten years later she was governess to Douglas's sister, presumably she was not in any way blamed, or not sufficiently, to prevent her from further practising her profession. And of course she was 'cured', in the hallucination theory, though still impelled to write her narrative in the form its real author presents it to us. The real result then, is not so much 'punishment' as the text we read.[18]

The injunction however is repeated in her narrative (chapter 2, the Master's letter), though its force is modified (see section 1), and here it splits into two injunctions:

(1) deal with him (the headmaster)
(2) mind you don't report.

And the governess disobeys (1) but obeys (2), at least for the time being. It could be said that she disobeys (1) in order to obey (2), since a mere sister's governess could probably not really deal with a headmaster, and even finding a new school would presumably have to pass through the Master (the critics' accusations that she does nothing ignore these social features in relation to this specific unreasonable demand by the employer). The split of the two masters emphasises the split injunction: 'the Master' (in Mrs Grose's terminology, which the governess accepts when in conversation with her) and the headmaster; to tackle the second she must bother the first. So she doesn't. But she produces a servant.

By the dead centre of the narrative, however (chapter 12), she has experienced such things and imparted them to Mrs Grose in such a way that it is Mrs Grose who begs her to make the Master come down. The governess's reaction is revealing, for she has a sudden attack of 'reality' (the 'natural' explanation), inevitably accompanied by the realisation of what he may think:

'And who's to make him?' [come down]
She had been scanning the distance, but she now dropped on me a foolish face. 'You Miss.'
'By writing to him that his house is poisoned and his little nephew and niece mad?'
'But if they *are*, Miss?' [J]
'And if I am myself, you mean? That's charming news to be sent him by a person enjoying his confidence and whose prime undertaking was to give him no worry.' (pp. 49–50)[19]

We may note the inverted mirror effect (they are mad/she is mad, which is in fact an alternative). And when Mrs Grose insists:

I quickly rose and I think I must have shown her a queerer face than ever yet [mirror]. 'You see me asking him for a visit?' No, with her eyes on my face [mirror] she evidently couldn't. Instead of it even – as a woman reads another – she could see what I myself saw [mirror]: his derision, his amusement, his contempt for the breakdown of my resignation at being left alone and for *the fine machinery I had set in motion to attract his attention to my slighted charms*. She didn't know – no one knew – how proud I had been to serve him and to stick to our terms; yet she none the less took the measure, I think, of the warning I now gave her. 'If you should so lose your head as to appeal to him for me –'
She was really frightened. 'Yes, Miss?'
'I would leave, on the spot, both him and you.' (p. 50)[20]

This curiously empty blackmail is characteristic of the contradictory wish: the pride in obeying him as her only point of contact with him, and the desire to disobey. Interestingly, this attack of reality, produced by fear of the employer's reaction, is followed by a longish period (a month) during which she stops seeing the ghosts, though she is convinced that therefore the children see all the more now that she can no longer act as 'screen'. Whereas the consequence of the second threat (by Miles) to bring the uncle down, is reversed: she starts seeing again. But now the apparitions will have a much more direct and dire result. In chapter 14 Miles challenges her about his school and threatens to get his uncle to come down (note the repetition of the governess's question to Mrs Grose 'Who's to make him?'):

'But who'll get him to come down?'
'*I* will!!' [J], the boy said with extraordinary brightness and emphasis. He gave me another look charged with that expression and then marched off alone into church. (p. 57)

Her first impulse at this threat, as before, is to leave. Collapsed on a tombstone, she decides to escape while they are at church, walks home, sinks down at the foot of the stairs, on the very spot and in the same position as Miss Jessel [mirror], suddenly remembers that this is where she had last seen 'the spectre of the most horrible of women', and goes up to the schoolroom to collect some things. There, of course, she sees Miss Jessel (chapter 15). The scene is considerably elaborated in chapter 16 with Mrs Grose, when she imparts a very different decision, exactly opposite in fact to that of her previous conversation with her:

'As I've told you, however, it doesn't matter.' [that Miss J. wants Flora]
'Because you've made up your mind? But to what?'
'To everything.'
'And what do you call "everything"?'
'Why to sending for their uncle.'
'Oh Miss, in pity do,' my friend broke out.
'Ah, but I will, I *will* ! [J] I see it's the only way.' (p. 61)

She goes on to say it's their uncle's fault for leaving such people in charge. Mrs Grose replies that he didn't really know them, that the fault is hers, and she turns quite pale. The question of the uncle's reaction returns between them and once again makes the governess quite crude in her fear that her employer will get the wrong idea of her (from Miles, from Mrs Grose or the bailiff):

'Well, you shan't suffer,' I answered.

'The children shan't,' she emphatically returned.

I was silent for a while; we looked at each other. 'Then what am I to tell him?'

'You needn't tell him anything, *I'll* tell him' [J].

I measured this. 'Do you mean you'll write – ?' Remembering she couldn't, I caught myself up. 'How do you communicate?'

'I tell the bailiff. *He* writes' [J].

'And should you like him to write our story?'

My question had a sarcastic force that I had not fully intended, and it made her after a moment inconsequently break down. The tears were again in her eyes. 'Ah Miss, *you* write!' [J] (pp. 61–2)

Gone is the notion of 'saving the children'. She thinks only of saving herself. Similarly after the scene on the way to church she had thought of Miles only in terms of a power struggle and precipitated a much more dangerous apparition before Miles could put his threat into action. Then, here, Flora's supposed danger is explicitly indifferent to her in the light of her real fear, indeed the renewed apparition, together with the elaboration, is a dramatic way of introducing her complete change of mind, otherwise inexplicable, to Mrs Grose (who had not witnessed the scene with Miles). She also manages to turn this decision of hers into a plea from Mrs Grose, with a show of hesitation on her side, and even asks Mrs Grose, with an apparent wilting of authority, what she should say, but when this turns against her with Mrs Grose's kind offer to 'tell him' for her, she is quite brutal in reaction, for this is the last thing she wants: she doesn't quite trust Mrs Grose yet to give 'her' version.

In the next chapter (17) she starts the letter but can't write it and goes listening at Miles's door.[21] There follows the ambiguous scene with him about his behaviour and what she/he will have to tell the uncle. She says she has begun a letter and Miles retorts 'Well then, finish it!' This indirect information that Miles has no intention of himself writing (as might have appeared from his 'I will' to the question 'who'll get him to come down'), but merely of 'getting him' to come down by forcing her to act, seems to produce an upsurge of gratitude and relief that first brings back her curiosity, for she starts questioning him about 'what happened before', the scene ending with her passionate exclamation and the candle incident; and secondly it relaxes her, for in the following chapter (18), she tells Mrs Grose that she has written but does not tell her that the letter is still in her pocket, and we later learn (after Miles has stolen the letter) that it contained only 'the bare demand for an interview', a demand unlikely, given the employer's strict injunction, to have much effect on him. This constant fluctuation in the transgression is symptomatic: something more dramatic still is needed.

And so there comes the showdown after Flora's disappearance, which causes her at last to place the letter in the hall before taking Mrs Grose to the lake (chapters 19–20). The result of the scene by the lake is contrary to all her expectations: Flora, who hasn't even glanced at the apparition, but only at her and with loathing, has fallen ill; Mrs Grose hasn't seen anything and believes there was nothing. This result-chapter (21) is also immensely revealing. The governess cares nothing about Flora's condition and is positively vulgar about her ('the chit', etc.) in her fear of the probable effect on her employer:

'Flora has now her grievance, and she'll work it to the end.'
'Yes, Miss: but to *what* end?' [J]
'Why that of dealing with me to her uncle. She'll make me out to him the lowest creature–!'
I winced at the fair show of the scene in Mrs Grose's face [mirror]; she looked for a minute as if she sharply saw them together. 'And him who thinks so well of you!'
'He has an odd way – it comes over me now,' I laughed, '–of proving it! But that doesn't matter. What Flora wants of course is to get rid of me.' (p. 75)

Mrs Grose concurs, but the governess suddenly turns the tables on her and tells her that *she* must go, and take Flora 'straight to her uncle'. Mrs Grose, who has acutely followed the previous argument, asks: 'Only to tell on you?' The governess replies:

'No, not 'only'! To leave me, in addition, with my remedy.'
She was still vague. 'And what *is* your remedy?' [J]
'Your loyalty, to begin with. And then Miles's.' (76)

After a brief talk about Miles having tried to tell her something she adds very clearly:

'I can't, if her uncle sees her [Flora], consent to his seeing her brother without my having given the boy – and most of all because things have got so bad – a little more time.'
My friend appeared on this ground more reluctant than I could quite understand. 'What do you mean by more time?'
'Well, a day or two – really to bring it out. He'll then be on *my* [J] side – of which you see the importance. If nothing comes, I shall only fail, and you will at the worst have helped me by doing on your arrival in town whatever you may have found possible.' So I put it before her, but she

continued for a little so lost in other reasons that I came again to her aid. 'Unless indeed,' I wound up, 'you really want *not* to go.' [J] (p. 76)

Mrs Grose then of course agrees at once, and says she couldn't have stayed anyway (because of Flora's terrible language, to which the governess's reaction is 'thank God', surprising Mrs Grose, 'it so justifies me'). Mrs Grose now believes, but for the wrong reasons, and the whole chapter ends on a curious reversal of the governess's earlier determination to 'save' the children:

'I'll get it out of him. He'll meet me. He'll confess. If he confesses he's saved. And if he's saved –'
'Then *you* are?' [J]. The dear woman kissed me on this, and I took her farewell. 'I'll save you without him!' she cried as she went. (p. 79)

Exit Mrs Grose, and the last three chapters lead to the final showdown with Miles and Miles's death, which necessarily must involve the uncle, though hardly in the way the governess had planned.

What we have then is an injunction (Prologue, repeated but split in chapter 2), which is obeyed until exactly halfway in the story, but by means of a disobedience that in effect creates a great deal of the trouble, since a direct confrontation with either the headmaster or the Master would have avoided all the extraction of the other, 'outer' secret from the housekeeper and in the end from Miles. Then, halfway, the events cause Mrs Grose to suggest (though not in those terms) transgressing that injunction. This produces a violent reaction but nevertheless precipitates transgression, not only with a letter but through more violent behaviour, the result of which, *vis à vis* the uncle, the governess cannot then face, so that she neatly reverses it, not without abasing herself to the housekeeper who is 'so lost in other reasons that I came again to her aid' (p. 76), and with what she manages to express as an order but is in fact a humble plea that Mrs Grose present her version before Flora's while she deals with Miles so that he too will be on her side. In this grammar of narrative it is Mrs Grose and Miles who are to do the saving, who are to save the governess from the ill effects, on the man she loves, of having transgressed his injunction in a much more violent way than if she had bothered him in the first place (which would have been a different story). All the rest (the ghosts, the possessive love for Miles, the supposed witnessing of the primal scene, etc.) forms the means, the symptoms, or in grammatical terms, the disposition, the ordering of events (*agencement, sjužet*) in the text we actually read.

This disposition or *agencement* is so infinitely complex that it has masked the bare structure and led the critics into the very elaboration of the symptoms for which they most blame the governess. I have already shown in chapter 6 how the governess's state and discourse is contagious, and Felman picks out other examples of this, notably in lexical items (the *danger* of the psychoanalytic method; which *does violence*; Wilson's theory *attacked* point by point, Freud completely *defeated*, Wilson's reading called *hysterical blindness*, 1934: 98–100). 'Through its very reading, the text, so to speak, acts itself out' (p. 101). Felman herself analyses the complexity of the *agencement* in a way that throws an enriching light on my own analysis, not only through the chain of signifiers (letters, ghosts) that metaphorise each other as well as the return of the repressed, but through the notion of the Master, lawful proprietor, as embodying the supreme instance of power, an aporia, a relation of non-relation (the unconscious), law as a form of censorship, which paradoxically makes possible the story of the impossibility of writing to the censor about what was initially missing (1977: 145–6). And later Felman associates this Master of flight with James himself, who in his subsequent letters and Preface constantly evades the issue, 'refuses to read our letters, sending them back to us unopened', so that his 'very mastery consists in the denial and in the deconstruction of his own mastery', assuming the role of Master 'only through the art of claiming his literary "property"' (p. 205).[22]

This 'mastery', however, is appropriated (as one appropriates features of a person loved) by the governess, whose 'reading' of her own story is a perpetual quest (like that of the critics), for a *definitive* meaning, that is, a meaning which excludes all the ambiguities perceived (in the ghosts, in Mrs Grose's spoken word, in that of the children) by '*reducing* and *eliminating* them' (see chapter 8 here, pp. 210ff). There is a constant equivalence made between 'knowing' and 'seeing' ('*Know?* by *seeing* her' p. 32). But,

'knowing' is to 'seeing' as the signified is to the signifier: the signifier is the *seen*, whereas the signified is the *known*. The signifier, by its very nature, is ambiguous and obscure, while the signified is certain, clear, and unequivocal. Ambiguity is thus inherent in the very essence of the act of seeing ... By the same token, ambiguity is fundamentally excluded from the act and the domain of 'knowing' ... The reading strategy employed by the governess entails, thereby, a dynamic relation between *seeing* and *knowing*, a conversion of the art of seeing into the fact of knowing. (Felman 1977: 156–7)

However, reading begins with an awareness of ambiguous signifiers, implying 'a *knowledge* from which the governess is barred'. The source of reading is lack of knowledge, but the act of reading 'implies at the same time the assumption that knowledge *is*, exists, but is *located in the Other*' (Felman: 157). It is this knowledge in/of the other which 'must be *read* . . . , appropriated, taken from the Other . . . "If the unconscious has taught us anything," writes Lacan, "it is first of all this: that somewhere, in the Other, 'it' knows . . . The very status of knowledge implies that some sort of knowledge already exists, in the Other, waiting to be taken, seized." (Lacan 1975: 81, 89)' (Felman: 157–8). But 'the subject presumed to know' is precisely what sustains the transfer in the psychoanalytical situation. Thus the governess's quest for knowledge, from Mrs Grose, from the children, 'paradoxically places her in the role not of analyst but of analysed and, of *patient* with respect to the children presumed to know, who hence themselves occupy unwittingly the very place, the very structural position of the *analyst*' (p. 159).

This of course, as I showed before Felman's essay appeared, also applies to Mrs Grose (here, and chapter 8). Naturally this is not how the governess sees herself, but rather as a 'screen', with the children as 'patients' (Felman: 159–60), Miles 'as appealing as some wistful patient in a children's hospital' (James 1966: 63), but at the same time, Miles as her 'remedy'. The confession of the whole 'truth' of what he 'knows' will be the cure (for him, for her). But as Felman points out, and as I pointed out in chapter 6, the 'confession' ends in a question: 'In considering that question as an answer, the governess in effect stifles its nonetheless ongoing questioning power' (Felman: 161). Moreover, her triumph

both as a reader and as a therapist, both as an interpreter and as an exorcist, is rendered highly suspicious by the death of what she had set out at once to *understand* and to *cure* . . . It therefore behoves the reader to discover the meaning of this murderous effect of meaning; to understand how a child can be killed by the very act of understanding'. (p. 161)

This Felman does by analysing (pp. 162–6), through the 'fierce split' in [the governess's] attention 'which makes her not only miss the child's reaction to her question (about the letter) but "grasp" him to keep him with his back to the window' (James 1966: 84), 'to keep the boy himself unaware' (p. 85), how 'the very act of *reading* the child's knowledge turns out to be an act of suppressing, or *repressing*, part of that knowledge' (Felman: 166), how to grasp is to understand, but also 'to close one's arms, to stifle', how to '"master" to understand and "*see it all*" [implied], is in this text, ironically enough, to occupy the very place of *blindness* ... to be blind with victory ["I was blind with victory", James 1966: 87], but also, and quite literally, to be triumphant *out* of blindness' (Felman: 167–8). And Felman later goes on to remind us that the attempt to *master* meaning, which ought to lead to unification, to the elimination of its contradictions, can occur only at the cost:

of an added split or distance, or an irreversible 'separation'. The seizure of the signifier creates an unrecoverable *loss*, a fundamental and irreparable *castration*: the tightening screw, the governed helm, bring about 'the supreme surrender of the name', *surrender* meaning only by *cleaving* the very power of their holder. Meaning's *possession* is itself ironically transformed into the radical *dispossession* of its possessor ... the attempt at *grasping* meaning and at *closing* the reading process with a *definitive* interpretation in effect discovers – and comprehends – only death (Felman: 175).

And she calls TS 'the story of meaning as such (or of consciousness) [which] turns out to be the uncanny story of the crime of its own detection' (p. 176). The implications of all this 'madness of interpretation' for critical (and psychoanalytical) readings are both comical ('James's 'trap', not for the naive but for the sophisticated reader, 'the jaded, the disillusioned, the fastidious', Preface p. 120) and alarming (see Felman 1977: 185–207).

5. The bare structure and the mirror-structure

Certainly it is this madness of interpretation (that of the governess, and ours) which has most effectively masked the bare structure I have discussed in the previous section: that of a basic injunction (in Felman's terms the law, the censor) and its transgression, for it has not really been noticed as basic structure but only as incident, although it underlies the text and links it, not only with the frame, but with the mirror-structure (the text being also mirror of the frame and vice versa). And this in both hypotheses: 'the elaborate machinery' she sets in motion to 'attract his attention' applies equally to hallucinations and to ghosts as evil pre-existent but not normally visible except to the predisposed. For it is never mentioned that from the ghosts' viewpoint in the governess's notion of their intentions, her ability to see them is a nuisance except, if this were a banal story, to frighten her away; indeed, in her own notion of their capacity, there is a time when her eyes are sealed to their supposedly continued visitations. A less complex story would provide a different motivation in which the ghosts would want to be seen by the main character. In this one *they* ought not to want this, but *she* needs to be in the picture, not only as saviour in the drama produced, but also to be looked at, outside the picture as voyeur of the communication between the ghosts and the children, inside the picture as screen between them.

The bare structure is also intimately linked with the projection of *le corps morcelé*, itself evident in all the splits and suppressions analysed by Felman as both causes and results of any attempt to master meaning as unimpaired totality. For Mrs Grose, who as we have seen functions as the governess's chief mirror, is the superficial instigator of the transgression. But the *initial* injunction, the really weighty one on which the job depends, and the *final* result of its transgression (implicit punishment), are not in the governess's narrative. She leaves them out, that is, she has entrusted them verbally and much later to Douglas – the final result only indirectly (but the real final result is the narrative). What she does give us is the second, more specific injunction, more specific in the sense that it concerns only one incident and would not, without the information about the absolute general command of the Introduction, in itself seem so dire and untransgressible in the circumstances. This second injunction is split in such a way that she can only disobey the first in order to obey the second (instead of vice versa, which would be another story).

Similarly she gives us the immediate, specific result of the 'fine machinery' she has set in motion towards transgression, a result which she neatly reverses by a split: not she but her mirror-image, Mrs Grose, will deal with it. This can be formulated as follows:

Frame		*Narrative*		*Frame*
general	specific	'machinery' via	immediate	final
absolute	injunction	mirror-images	specific	result
injunction	(split)	to transgression	result	
			(split)	
		transgression		

Her own text, in other words, is itself truncated, at both ends. Within this text, what we have is a very fine development of the simplest grammar of narrative. Using Todorov's terms:[23]

Frame	ā	injunction or initial situation
Narrative		
1–6	a	alteration of initial situation implicitly towards *b*
7–12	a'	elaboration of *a* towards explicit suggestion of *b*
13–18	a"	precipitation towards *b*
19–24	b + c	transgression and implicit immediate punishment (fear of greater punishment + psychic and emotional shock)
Frame	¢	no overt social punishment (elided: a presumed emotional punishment)

Within the governess's narrative the events are themselves framed by scenes of elaboration which far outweigh the actual events in length and detail. Table 7.3 summarises the narrative in the light of what has been discussed in this essay.

From the table we can see just how the expansion functions in relation to the events: four apparitions of each sex, four scenes with a child of each sex, three of which (two for Flora and one for Miles) coincide with an apparition: Miles is only 'shown' together with an apparition in the last scene, Flora in the first and last – he is older and therefore more directly questionable – but only in the final showdown, and Flora's first lets all hell loose by 'confirming' the governess in her suspicion that the children also see. The framework of elaboration makes up an equal number to the events (eight apparitions, eight scenes/twelve elaborations or scenes with Mrs Grose, four self-elaborations), but their content and length far exceed the amount of text given to the events, extremely brief for the apparitions, relatively brief for the scenes with the children (those with Miles longer than those with Flora). The overweight of elaboration is compensated by the interweaving of the underlying event, the preparation towards transgression (twice in elaboration with Mrs Grose, twice in scenes with Miles). This preparation is in four stages, two of female instigation, two of male. The transgression itself is split into two: the letter written by the governess, and the event that is bound to involve the uncle; each of these is again split into two: the letter written but not posted, then posted; the event leading to Flora's illness, the event leading to Miles's death. That is, four stages as well for the transgression.

Thus a relatively complex disposition (*agencement*) in what James called a pot-boiler is generated by a drastically bare structure. And this reflects the very structure of desire, which is at the basis of all narrative (the desire to know), but more particularly at the basis of

Table 7.3*

Elaboration frame (masc.)	*Masculine events*	*Feminine events*	Elaboration frame (*fem.*)
1.		Arrival g, mirror. F's beauty	→ G1
2. G2 im/ex ← (stairs)	Letters U and H		←
3.	→ Q1 (out/up) ←		
4. G3 ∅ (hall)	→ Q2 (frontier/level)		
5. G4 im/ex (id.Q) (out)	←		
6. G5 im/ex (schlroom?) →		J1 + F1 (out/level)	→ hint J ←
7.			→ G6 im/ex → (unstated)
8. G7 ex ← (schlroom?)			→ G7
9. g1	→ Q3 (in/down)		→ g1
		F2 (g bedroom) J3 (in/down)	← ∅
10.	(M on lawn) ←	F3 (at window)	← g2
11.	M1 (in) ←		
12. G8 im →			→ G8 im
		pT1 (G sugg/g reaction)	←
13. g2 ←			→ g2 (eyes sealed)
14.	M2 (out) pT 2(M)		← → g3 (churchyard,
15.		J3 (in/level)	← stairs)
16.	→	pT 3 (g decis. +	→ G9 in (G room)
17.	pT 4 (can't write) M3 (in)	threat)	←
18.	→	T1 (written but not posted) F disappears T2 (posted)	
19.		⎰ F4	→ G10 (pre-elab) ←
20.		⎱ F4/J4 = real T(a) or T3	→ G11 (neg reaction)
21.			G12 ex (g room)
22.	M4		← g4
23.	M4		
24.	M4/Q4 = T(b) or T4		

Abbreviations:

Q and J numbered = apparitions, M and F numbered = scenes with Miles or Flora,
G numbered = scene with Mrs Grose, placed to left or right according to whether the conversation concerns chiefly a masculine event (Quint/Miles) or a feminine one (Jessel/Flora), or on both sides if both.
im/ex after G indicates the governess imparting information (about the apparition or the children's present behaviour) or extracting it (about the past)
g numbered = self-elaboration by the governess, also placed on masculine or feminine side or both

U = Uncle
H = Headmaster
pT = preparation for transgression

T = transgression (masculine or feminine side according to instigator).
∅ = no elaboration.

both the ghost-story (in all its interpretations both simple and complex) and the story of hallucinations (in all its interpretations both simple and complex, even that in which the governess could be said to provoke 'the return of the repressed' in the children, who do then share her hallucinations). Both hypotheses can be read into the see-saw of the power game, the bits and pieces of information, of body images and identifications projected up and down, out and in, far and near, in detail and in dust before her/our eyes, she and ourselves like Mrs Grose 'a receptacle of lurid things', but with a desperate need for both intensification (which a frame provides) and systematisation into a desired coherence (which a frame provides). But the frame is constantly being expanded and shrunk, like the narrator's consciousness at the beginning, and it positively bursts, expanded to metaphysical heights and shrunk to sordid suppositions and trivial though passionate questioning as the figure of Quint, in the last chapter, appears and disappears at the window, 'like a sentinel before a prison' (the prison of her consciousness too), the window which is the frontier between in and out, between here and the beyond, between the 'where' of Miles and the 'there' of the governess; and vanishes as Miles jerks round and sees 'but the quiet day' and dies as the frontier shatters. Which is why the 'sequel', such of it as we are given, could only occur in the outer frame, the portico, the end in the beginning.

8

The surface structures in
The Turn of the Screw

1. What are surface structures?

In the good old days of the New Criticism, people often spoke of 'structure' as opposed to 'texture', and all seemed beautifully clear. Structure simply meant how a text was constructed, i.e., thematically interwoven, balanced, climaxed and resolved, in short its general surface form, and movement or rhythm. Texture was the detail, i.e., the 'style', the 'images', the vocabulary, the rhythm of sentences, the irony, the paradox, sometimes (especially for poetry) the syntax and the grammar.

Thematics, however, including certain particular aspects of it such as irony, could clearly partake of both structure and texture, as could various notions of form such as rhythm and repetition. Conversely the notion that grammar and syntax could apply equally to structure and to texture did not exist, nor did that of any formal (explicit) link between structure and texture. The distinction between the two seems in fact to have corresponded to what Genette (1972) now calls macrotext and microtext.

Since then much work has been done on 'narrative grammar', indeed there are so many 'grammars' that it would be confusing and irrelevant to discuss them in this kind of book. Many are what the generative grammarians would call 'weak hypotheses', as Jonathan Culler discovered (1975), and some are abstract models equivalent to structural description in generative grammar but incapable of generating all the grammatical sentences [or, for narrative, texts] of a language and none of the ungrammatical ones which is the basic requirement of a valid grammar. And even if they did claim to do so it would involve calling a text 'grammatical' (acceptable to a native speaker) or 'ungrammatical', and this again would be based on an imperfect analogy between 'linguistic competence' (the grammar we have in our heads, which enables even an illiterate native speaker or a small child to understand and to form sentences he has never

188

heard before), and 'literary competence', in which the word 'competence' verges on its more usual, non-technical meaning of special ability. The very notion of an 'unacceptable' text is absurd, and undefinable. (See however Van Dijk 1976, for some interesting attempts.)

Personally I have come to believe that the very notion of narrative 'grammar' is erroneous, based on a false analogy with sentence grammar, and I shall therefore not pursue this further. I shall however retain the notion of levels of structure, for they seem indispensable, but, despite my use of 'surface structures' (from generative grammar), I shall avoid the opposite term 'deep structure' as (a) too specific to generative grammar (i.e., not open to individual vagaries, see below, but implying rules that transform the deep into surface structure), and (b) a mere analogical fad of some contemporary criticism ('deep' somehow implying more profound in an evaluative sense).[1]

The distinction between 'story' and 'discourse' (Barthes 1966; Todorov 1970b; Genette 1972) is now well established, *histoire* being the skeleton, or events as they are supposed to have occurred, *discours* being the flesh and blood or the way these events are presented, in time, speed, point of view, distancing etc., or what Genette (1972) reorganises as time, mood and voice. This distinction is the same as that made by the Russian Formalists between *fabula (histoire)* and *sjužet (discours* or *agencement,* treatment).

But *histoire,* or the bare bones, could be (for any one text):

(1) a brief synopsis (which can vary from person to person);
(2) the abstract formulae resulting from this or that type of analysis (Propp, Bremond, Greimas, Todorov, Kristeva, to cite only a few), of which there might be several within one type of analysis, according to the number of axes chosen; these may vary in degree of abstraction from pure signs and semiotic systems (Todorov, Greimas, Kristeva) to semantic investments (Propp, Bremond). For instance, what I have called the 'bare structure' of TS (in chapter 7) is such an abstract formula, with semantic investment;
(3) the 'narrative sentence', which can also vary with each reader: e.g. for Genette (1972) the narrative sentence of *A la recherche du temps perdu* is 'Marcel becomes a writer'; all the rest is what enabled him to do so.[2]

Nevertheless, the problem of diversity remains: someone else could find another 'bare structure': mine, provokingly for a ghost-story, contains no mention of either ghosts or hallucinations, this in order that it might function in both hypotheses, and for theoretical reasons I shall deal with later.

Similarly, what exactly is meant by 'surface structure?'

(1) The very distinction *histoire-discours* suggests that *discours* in the sense of exposition, ordering of events (*agencement* or *sjužet*), is surface structure, and so it is, although it requires a degree of abstraction to be perceived, however unconscious this becomes with 'literary competence'. To give an easy example, most readers slide easily into the past with a flashback but may also be conscious that it is a flashback; an analyst like Genette goes further and calls it an analepsis and subdivides it into different types. The reader's recognition of the flashback is equivalent to the native speaker's recognition of a sentence's acceptability, since both recognitions are acquired by the practice of deciphering narratives/sentences. Other techniques of *discours* may be less easily perceived.

(2) 'Surface structure' could, however, and in a sense should be the surface of the text we actually read. And this seems more difficult to distance oneself from, witness the fact that work on these micro-textual aspects is relatively recent in the history of rhetoric or even of criticism – roughly from the Russian Formalists on. It is this aspect of surface structure that I shall be dealing with in this chapter, rather than that described above (*agencement*), which together with the 'bare structure', I discussed in chapter 7 (i.e. the frame and the mirror-structure).

(3) There would thus be two surface structures: A, the presentation of events and B, the sequences of words we read; macrotext and microtext. In other words, what used to be called 'structure' and 'texture' would be two different levels of the surface structure. The 'abstract structure' or abstract formula would then be what some would call the 'deep structure', and what I prefer to call the underlying or bare structure.

I shall describe the surface structure B (SS.B) in *The Turn of the Screw*, and try to discover how it might be explicitly linked to surface structure A (SS.A) and to the bare structure (BS) as analysed in chapter 7. There I dealt with presentation of events, inversions, delays, fragmentation of information into description and subsequent elaboration, showing that it was a mirror-structure and a framed one; and with the abstract or bare structure, which was stated in the following formula:

Frame		*Narrative*		*Frame*
1st injunction	2nd injunction	transgression mechanism and transgression	1st result	final result

2. The surface structure B

The narrator of TS, after the Introduction (frame), that is, from chapter 1 to the end of the text (chapter 24), is the governess. Consequently all the elements of the surface structure, whether A or B, occur under her (fictitious) responsibility.

SS.B, however, has its own type of frame, which Uspensky (1974: 137) has described as 'compositional'. Discussing the importance of the frame in different semiotic spheres, he emphasises the way in which, in any work of art, a special world is presented to us, with its own space and time, ideological system and systems of behaviour, to which we are, in our first perception of it, in the position of an external spectator, but into which we enter, accustoming ourselves to it, and gradually perceiving it from within, assuming a point of view internal to the work:

The transition from the real world to the representation is particularly significant as one of the phenomena in the creation of the 'frame' of the artistic representation. Compositionally it is expressed in a definite alternation between description structured from within and description structured from without and the transitions between them.

Bearing in mind this important aspect of the frame, which reflects at SS.B, all I had to say about the frame for the BS and SS.A in chapter 7, I prefer here to treat the problem in terms of metatext.

For although the surface structure is the narrator's (fictional) responsibility, there will naturally be an author's metatext (AM), which indirectly tells the reader things the narrator does not state directly. And, in the case of a dramatised and self-conscious narrator like the governess, there will also be a narrator's metatext (NM) upon her own narrative. Since the two metatexts share, on the whole, the same elements, there will be instances when it is not easy to decide whether the metatext is AM or NM. I shall therefore deal with them first separately under a heading *General features*, where the distinction is usually obvious (and will be discussed when not), then together under a second heading *Specific features*, by which time the distinction should be clear.

2.1. AM and NM: General features

In a general sense everything said by anyone characterises the speaker, whether he is the author in person, an invisible narrator, a dramatised but non-participating narrator–observer, or a participating narrator–character. Insofar as it characterises him indirectly it is a metatext, and will occur in various forms in any narrative where the author does not assume direct responsibility for a statement. When he does, the metatext occurs only when a character speaks without direct comment from the author.

2.1.1. Author's metatext (AM). The very first sentence of TS is highly metatextualised by the author, except for the first two words which are both AM and NM:

I remember the whole beginning as a succession of flights and drops, a little see-saw of the right throbs and the wrong. (p. 6)

I remember denotes what it says, the fact that she remembers. It connotes (as NM) that what the receiver (Douglas) is about to read took place some time before the fact denoted, a time clear to the receiver, but not clear to us without the information (AM) we already have from the Prologue (frame). Thus (because of the Prologue) we know already what both metatexts tell us, but it is important to be reminded of it straightaway (as we shall be again many times), since the whole truth of the narrative depends (fictionally) on the narrator's memory. *The whole beginning* connotes (AM) a tendency to dramatise ('the beginning' would have been enough for denotation), and, by the same token, the narrator's type of talent, for the fact that any narrator must have at least the talent to keep us interested (a talent lent by the author) is of great importance, as I have already partly shown in chapter 7. Direct (conscious) references to the narrator's art belongs to narrator's metatext; this is indirect (AM). *As a succession of little flights and drops* denotes her alternating impressions, connotes the above *plus* a certain instability of the narrator (AM). *A little see-saw of the right throbs and the wrong* (adding to the talent-metatext with a telling metaphor) connotes (AM) all the above *plus* a tendency to see things in Manichean and moralistic terms (up/down; right/wrong).

Thus the first sentence tells us more, and cumulatively, about the narrator than she appears to, and the first chapter is strongly metatextualised in this way, chiefly as author's metatext, so that the reader can indirectly as well as directly get to know the narrator–character. Several sentences for instance betray a tendency to exteriorise inner feelings (a tendency obviously important in both hypotheses – ghosts or hallucinations – but especially in the latter):

I ... found all my doubts *bristle again* (p. 7). [first edition: found myself doubtful again – see below for this formula] – denotation: doubts; connotation: doubts are autonomous, animate and animal (AM).

a country the summer sweetness of which *served as a* friendly welcome (p. 7). [first edition: seemed to offer me] – autonomous and personified (AM).

my fortitude *revived* and, as we turned into the avenue, *took a flight* that was probably but a proof of the point to which *it had sunk* (p. 7) – autonomous and part-bird, part object or animal, duality up/down (AM).

what *greeted me* was a good surprise (p. 7) – autonomous and personified.

Similarly she projects her own impressions:

She was the most beautiful child I had ever seen, and I afterwards wondered why my employer hadn't made more of a point to me of this (p. 7). [Why should he? first edition: 'had not told me more of her' – which he might well have done].

I have already commented in chapter 7 on her sudden expansion of consciousness, on the way she feels flattered by the welcome and on her hidden desires, all indirectly communicated (AM) in her description of Bly and of her room. Her possessiveness, too, is already betrayed (AM) with a curious use of the possessive adjective: 'the crunch of *my* wheels on the gravel' (p. 7) for the carriage sent to fetch her; so '*my* little girl' (p. 8). And naturally her vocabulary is that of her rank and class ('convenience' as well as 'vehicle', unspecified, 'a civil person' for the housekeeper Mrs Grose), as well as that of her age and character ('beatific', 'radiant image of my little girl', 'angelic beauty', 'with the deep sweet serenity of one of Raphael's holy infants' – all on p. 8; 'becoming tremendous [first edition: immense] friends' (p. 9). This last feature is true of any reasonably competent author and also belongs to the more specific category of utterance (*énonciation*) which I shall discuss below.

Thus the first chapter gives us, over and above what the narrator consciously tells us, information about her: she is impressionable, highly strung, dualistic, has a tendency to dramatise and to exteriorise, has a narrator's talent, hidden desires of love, power and possession, she is imaginative or at least fanciful (which she tells us more directly later).

Most of these features will continue to be metatextualised in varied syntactic ways. The tendency to exteriorisation, for instance, is revealed in impersonal constructions for notions, perceptions, and feelings: '*There came to me thus* a bewilderment of vision' [Q1] (p.

16); '*it was intense to me*' [first edition: 'I had the sharpest sense'] 'that
... he never took his eyes from me' [Q1] (p. 17); '*It came to me*
straightway ... that she knew nothing' (p. 18); '*It had been promptly
given me* ... to face that mystery [school] without a pang' (p. 19);
'*Something or other had brought nearer home to me* that I had all but pinned
the boy to my shawl' (p. 54); '*My perambulations had given me* meanwhile
no glimpse of him [Miles]' (p. 79); '*But an extraordinary impression
dropped on me* ... that I was not barred now' [before Q4] (p. 82).

Inversely, external phenomena are given active, half-personifying
verbs: 'an incident that, *presenting itself* the second evening, had
deeply disconcerted me' (p. 10) – the incident is first exteriorised
and made autonomous, then made to affect her, which accurately
reflects the mirror-structure of event, inversion and elaboration
noted in chapter 7. Or vice versa just after: 'The first day ... I was to
see *it wind up* to a change of note' (p. 10). So with the more ghostly
events: 'the remarkable things that presently *gave their first sign*' (p.
15); 'Then it was – with the very act of *it announcing itself* – that her
identity *flared up* in a change of posture' [J3] (p. 59).

So noun and verb phrases emphasise a split personality: '*Agitation
... had held me and driven me*' (p. 17); 'My conclusion *bloomed there*
with the real rose-flush of his innocence' (p. 19); '*something within me
said*' (p. 26); '*The way this knowledge gathered in me*' [J1] (p. 29). Or,
more interestingly, a split between a feeling and its metaphorical
projection: '*No hour of my stay ... was so assailed* with apprehensions' (p.
79). And the many reflexives like '*I found myself*', '*to ask myself*', '*I
heard myself* break into a sound' [J3], '*I heard myself* say' [J4] etc. (pp.
11, 16, 59, 70).

Her possessiveness is betrayed again by an occasional possessive
slightly out of place: '*my* document' (p. 10) for the letter from the
headmaster to her employer, '*my* children' (p. 20), '*my* [J] boy' [pp.
26, 44). And by the use of *give, offer, take, have, bring out, put before*, for
'tell' (pp. 11, 25, 26, 27, 32, 61, 70, 78), which suggests that she
regards information as a possession, an object: 'the truth as I *gave* it
to her' (p. 25).

New features are also added metatextually, for instance a tendency to fuse the other with herself in an occasional odd use of *we* or
our for *I–my* or even *the*: '*our* distance' [between Quint and herself –
Q1] (p. 16): 'in *our* prodigious experience' [hers and Mrs Grose's,
but in fact hers, see chapter 7 on the mirror-relation, and below, p.
218]; 'for recurrence [of ghosts] *we* took for granted' (p. 34); 'what it
was least possible to get rid of was the cruel idea that, whatever I

had seen, Miles and Flora saw *more* [J] . . . Such things naturally left
on the surface . . . a chill that *we* vociferously denied that *we* felt, and
we had *all three*, with repetition, got into such splendid training that
we went, each time, to mark the close of the incident, almost
automatically through the very same movements' [it is her assumption that they see, or feel, anything, or indirectly deny it with 'loud
demonstrations'] (p. 53); 'I seized, stupefied, his supposition – some
sequel to what *we* had done to Flora' [Q4; = I, but she here fuses
with Mrs Grose] (p. 88).

Another is a certain prudishness in her use of euphemisms: 'While
I took in *what I did take in*' (p. 16); '*Whatever it was that I knew*' (p. 18)
– though these are also instances of narrator-delay (NM, see p. 204
n. 8 above); '*my new lights*' (p. 38); '*the business*' (pp. 40–57); '*the
sources of my trouble*' (p. 45); '*my predicament*' (pp. 50–1); 'I had seen
nothing . . . *that one had better not have seen*' (p. 51); '*the whole thing*' (pp.
55, 71) '*the question between us*' (p. 56); 'I had read into what our [for
'my'] young *friend had said to me* the fullness of its meaning' [= threat
to make uncle come down] (p. 57); '*the question of the horrors gathered
behind*' [his dismissal from school] (p. 57); 'the wide window through
which, that other day, I had seen *what pulled me up*' [before Q4] (p.
81).

There are also specific uses of vocabulary, but as these are usually
either doubly metatextual (AM or NM) I shall deal with them
under NM.

In first-person narrative this type of AM is usually rich at the
beginning in order to build up our image of the narrator despite
him or herself, but diminishes considerably as the narrator becomes
more conscious and tells us many of the same features himself. And
the governess, who, like most of James's characters, is superconscious
(but with a flawed consciousness), does naturally tell us a great deal
about herself, thus taking over the author's task.

2.1.2. Narrator's metatext (NM). This is where the narrator's metatext
(NM) comes in (almost all the previous examples were of AM), and
if it is not always as subtle as AM, it has more facets. I have found
three main types among these 'general' features alone. Two of them
are denotative, as opposed to the third which is connotative:

Direct comment ⎤	denotation	
The narrative instance ⎦		
Indirect comment	connotation	(metatext proper)

The reason why denotation enters into NM is that the denotative types can have two levels, one of which is connotative and metatextual, so I prefer to keep to the general term metatext.

2.1.2.1. Direct comment. Direct comment occurs whenever the narrator tells us something about himself/herself which, in a third-person narrative, would be said by the author or another narrator. This is not metatext in the connotative sense so far described, but in the sense of a metalanguage, as when we use critical terms to speak of a poem. In narrative this metalanguage is usually an ideological or at any rate moral judgment, made by the narrator upon him/herself as character: in doing so I was selfish, brave, mad, etc. It is, of course, denotated, and as such part of the narrative which tells of a selfish/brave/mad person, but inevitably also implies a certain distance, not merely of the character with regard to him/herself at the time (synchronic) but of the narrator later in time (retrospective), who 'knows' (fictionally) how it all developed and whose judgment is in theory (and fictionally) more objective but who also, and this is important, rehandles his or her material in the light of that judgment, just as an author does. Thus, there are two levels: internal to the fiction (at the time) and external (later).

In chapter 1, for instance, there is the night sound 'I *fancied* I heard . . . But these *fancies* were not marked enough to be thrown off, and it is only in the light, or the gloom, I should rather say, of other and subsequent matters that they now come back to me' (p. 8). This *tells* us, on the first level, that she was fancying sounds, and on the second (still NM), what the AM had already implied, that she is fanciful. The additional fact that it is immediately followed by narrative instance (the narrator speaking in the present tense, as she narrates, see 2.1.2.2. below) further marks the distinction. The chapter also ends with her fancy of Bly as a castle of romance and then as a great drifting ship (p. 10). Even when a narrator adds an adverb to his way of acting or speaking (as an author would), we have the two levels: 'offering it, on the spot, *sarcastically*' (p. 11). She is being sarcastic/she can be sarcastic; cp. '*My question had a sarcastic force I had not fully intended*' (in the key chapter 12, p. 61, cp. chapter 7 above) where the second level is also in direct comment, and so less metatextual. Or when she says '*I cropped up in another place*' (p. 12), this tells us that she cornered Mrs Grose elsewhere (or on another tack), which is internal to the fiction, and it also tells us that she is driven by curiosity and giving way to a tendency to push Mrs Grose 'fairly to the wall' (as she says directly later, p. 35).

Similarly the direct statement, when she realizes that Mrs Grose does not see Miss Jessel in chapter 20 ('I felt my own situation horribly crumble' [J4] (p. 72) tells us of her shock and disappointment at lack of proof, but also announces the fundamental selfishness which becomes more explicit in the next chapter (see chapter 7 above). Or when Miles finally confesses that he 'said things' at school, in the last chapter, she says 'There was somehow less of it than I had expected' (p. 87), this tells her disappointment but also readmits the tremendous build-up of morbid curiosity earlier described, and the let-down. There are also a few examples of the narrator speaking of herself in the third person, that is, adopting briefly the point of view of another: 'She herself [Mrs Grose] had seen nothing . . . , and nobody in the house but *the governess was in the governess's plight*' (p. 25); 'They had never, I think, wanted to do so many things for *their poor protectress*' (p. 38); 'He was too clever for a *bad governess, for a parson's daughter*, to spoil' (p. 39); she [Mrs Grose] addressed her greatest solicitude to *the sad case presented by their deputy-guardian*' (p. 45). This denotes what it says (she is a sad case) but also says 'look how objective I am being'. And we may also see an AM on split personality.[3]

This type of double-level NM, sometimes mingled with AM, is partly what makes Jamesian discourse so complex, and in fact there are relatively few examples of 'pure' double-level direct comment, for most are intertwined with other elements to be examined. But there is a definite rhythm to them, for most occur, naturally enough, in the passages of self-elaboration (see chapter 7 above). Such examples, however, tell us little more than the indirect message that the narrating I is being objective, as in the frequent direct comments about being 'under a charm', 'a great wave of infatuation and pity', her ignorance, confusion, vanity, etc. (there is a spate of them on p. 14). The more interesting examples of such double-level direct comment, though they are few, occur during 'scenes' (slowed-down action, with or without dialogue, as opposed to self-elaboration of these) and reveal her technique with Mrs Grose, and her consciousness of it, e.g. during the famous scene when she 'leads' her to identify Quint: '*I quickly added stroke to stroke* (p. 23)'; '"But he *is* [J] handsome?" *I saw the way to help her.* "Remarkably!"' (p. 24) [after Q2]; and again after J1: '*Then to show I had thought it all out:* "My predecessor – the one who died"'' (p. 31); '*I now recognized to what I had at last, stroke by stroke, brought the victim of my confidence*' (p. 32); and after J3: '*I had by this time formed the habit of having Mrs Grose literally well in hand in advance of my sounding that note*' (p. 60, after 'I came home . . . for a talk with Miss Jessel'). It is difficult not to feel that the narrator (as opposed to the author) is not conscious of a double interpretation (ghosts/awareness of possible madness and its technique). The same double awareness occurs with Quint's lowness of class, which she shifts, so as not to insist 'in such company, on the place of a servant in the scale' to lowness of behaviour: '*There was a way to deal with that, and I dealt*' (p. 33); this, together with the quoted comment, denotes her tact, connotes her snobbery. Or, with Miles after his escape, her 'thrill of triumph over his real embarrassment' (p. 46), then her loss of it, and the whole passage about how he 'had' her as long as she continued to 'defer to the old tradition of the criminality of those caretakers of the young who minister to superstitions and fears' (p. 47); all these denote her ups and downs and difficult situation, but connote her sense of power and class-consciousness.

Similarly in the crucial chapter 12, the governess *leads* Mrs Grose to the suggestion that the uncle must be sent for (transgression, see chapter 7 above), and the direct comment accompanying this is odd enough in the context (why 'scrupulously'?) to give off an additional NM that tells us indirectly that she is aware of doing so:

'. . . They've [ghosts] only to keep to their suggestions of danger.'
'For the children to come?'
'And perish in the attempt?' Mrs Grose slowly got up, *and I scrupulously added*: 'Unless, of course, we can prevent!'
Standing there before me while I kept my seat she visibly turned things over. 'Their uncle must do the preventing.' (p. 49)

On the whole, however, there are few 'pure' examples during 'scenes', none, except this one, if it is one, in the pivotal chapter 12 (transgression suggested by Mrs Grose – led up to with other elements), nor in chapter 14 (transgression threatened by Miles). They occur mostly in self-elaboration, except for the climax in the last scene (chapter 24) where for the first time self-consciousness in double-level direct comment interweaves with the action as she observes her own courage, elation, infatuation, blindness of victory, sternness and pity.

2.1.2.2. Narrative instance (n.i.). As NM, narrative instance is more clearly metatextual in the special sense described under direct comment, since the time element is clearly denoted. The very first words I *remember* place the narrator firmly in the narrator's writing time (narrative instance), and recur twice more in the first chapter, as well as: '*I fear* [I had rather brooded]', '*I can still see* [Mrs Grose's broad face]', '*I have not seen* Bly since the day I left it, and *I dare say* that *to my present older and more informed eyes* it would show a very reduced importance' (p. 9).

Features in n.i. can but do not necessarily concern the character of the narrator, which as we have seen is at first chiefly conveyed through AM. In chapter 1 we have the lawn, an impulse, a brooding, a face, a question of size in n.i. But the last quotation perfectly expresses the function of n.i.: *to my present older and more informed eyes* this is how the story went (implication double: more objective/ rehandled).

Nor is n.i. only indicated by the present tense, though that is its most frequent form in this text. It can use adverbials of time: 'The one appearance, indeed, *in this early outlook*, that might have made me shrink again' (p. 7); 'I wondered *even then* a little why she [Mrs Grose] should wish *not* [J] to show it' (p. 7); 'so monstrous was I *then* ready to pronounce it that such a child ... should be under an interdict' (p. 13); '*I afterwards wondered why my* employer ...' (p. 7); 'and nothing else perhaps, when I thought of such occasions *afterwards*, gave me so the suspicion ...' (p. 51).

In such cases the time is not that of n.i. but implies a retroactive knowledge. The time denoted is internal to the narrative but connotes a future known in the n.i. (*even then* as opposed to later suspicions, *early outlook* as opposed to later ones). Indeed this future can be directly expressed as such: 'But I was to be *later on* so much more overwhelmed' (p. 17); '*I may as well say at once that I on no other occasion* saw him [after Q3] in the house' (p. 43). The first example is part of suspense, or what Genette (1972) calls an *amorce* (hint about the future) as opposed to a *prolepsis* or flash-forward, information given in advance, as in the second example.

There are many examples of n.i. in TS, and they are frequently used to bring out (with more 'objectivity') the same character features dealt with under direct comment. Their rhythm, however, is much more even, since the narrator is constantly present, and the function of n.i. is more varied.

It can be used merely to introduce a manner ('I *recollect* throwing off', p. 2), an impression ('in the clear twilight, I *remember*', p. 16), a personal feature: 'I *say* courage because I was beyond all doubt already far gone' (p. 21 – an ambiguous comment in the context of the courage she suddenly feels during the second apparition of

Quint). Or to ironise: 'I *dare say* I fancied myself in short a remark-able young woman' (p. 15). Or to bring out retroactive knowledge *and* overdramatization inside the fiction: '*I remember how* on this occasion . . . I felt the importance of giving the last jerk to the curtain' (p. 35). Or even n.i. dramatisation '*I call it a revolution* [Miles's] because *I now see how* . . . the curtain rose on the last act of my dreadful drama' (p. 55). Or to admit: 'One of the thoughts that, *as I don't in the least shrink now from now noting*, used to be with me in these wanderings was that it would be as charming as a charming story suddenly to meet someone' [before Q1] (p. 15). Or to correct: 'as the light faded – *or rather, I should say*, the day lingered' (p. 15, cf. p. 23, after Q2: '"At this same hour." ["Almost at dark," said Mrs Grose.] "Oh no, not nearly. I saw him as I see you."') But above all to emphasise: 'I thought of more things than one. But there's only one *I take space to mention*. I wondered why *she* [J] should be scared' [after Q2] (p. 21).

This type of emphasis, which recurs throughout, often expresses her consciousness in the writing act of re-creation, that is, her consciousness as narrator:

To me at least, *making my statement here with a deliberation with which I have never made it*, the whole feeling of the moment returns [. . .] *I can hear again, as I write*, the intense hush. [Q1] (p. 16)

Hence also the difficulty of remembering correctly, even of under-standing: '*I am unable even to remember at this day* what proposal I framed for the end of his holidays and the resumption of his studies' (p. 14); '*I can say now* neither what determined nor what guided me' [before Q3] (p. 40); '*I should never get to the bottom – were I to let myself go even now*' [of her 'prodigious private commentary' on the children] (p. 39); '*How can I retrace to-day* the strange steps of my obsession?' (p. 52). The act of rememoration is even devalued: 'It seems to me indeed, *in raking it all over* . . .' (p. 27, first edition 'in retrospect').

As narrator she is conscious, more especially, of the art needed to make clear: '*as I recall the way it went it reminds me of all the art I now need to make it a little distinct. What I look back at with amazement* is the situation I accepted' [Miles's education] (p. 14); '*I scarce know how to put my story into words that shall be a credible picture* of my state of mind' (p. 28); '*I can't express* what followed *save by saying that* the silence itself . . . became the element into which I saw the figure disappear' [Q3] (p. 41).

This difficulty is compared with the same difficulty inside the narrative: 'No, no: it was useless to attempt to convey to Mrs Grose, *just as it is scarcely less so to attempt to suggest it here*, how ... he [Miles] fairly shook me with admiration.' (p. 47)[4]

She is not only conscious of her duty as narrator: 'There was a Sunday – to *get on*' [before Q2] (p. 20); '*I find that I really hang back; but I must take my horrid plunge*' ... [before Q3] (p. 40); '*But I so far succeeded in checking the expression of this view that I will throw, just here, no further light on it than may be offered by the mention* of my final observation to Mrs Grose' (p. 37). She is also conscious of contrasts in many things: 'He was ... a living detestable dangerous presence. But that was not the wonder of wonders; *I reserve that distinction for quite another circumstance: the circumstance* that dread had unmistakably quitted me' [Q3] (p. 41). She indulges in rhetorical repetition within n.i. itself: '*I remember* that the book I had in my hand ... *I recall further* ... *I figure finally* ... *I recollect in short* ...' [before Q3] (p. 40).[5]

I showed in chapter 7 how the governess's elaborations with Mrs Grose have a dual function: she needs them as character, for psychoanalytic reasons, and she needs them as narrator, for artistic reasons (suspense, delayed information, interpretation that must not overload the actual scenes of the apparitions or the scenes with the children). They are in themselves a kind of metatext. So it is with narrative instance. The text is fairly punctuated with such n.i., which reminds us constantly of the time elapsed, and therefore of the narrator's fallibility. Of course, n.i. is a fiction, a convention; all the detail she gives us in her re-creation of every moment, every look exchanged, every thought that flashes through her mind, is there (impossibly, after maybe thirty years) to contradict this fallibility and the difficulty of remembering. But the convention is also there, as a conflicting metatext.[6]

But in all this art, this duty as narrator to convince, to keep up the suspense, to lead and mislead, does she not (in the fiction of character as narrator) 'arrange things?' Alternatively, with the fictional time elapsed, does she not, in 'arranging things', make the odd slip, or contradict herself? But here we enter into our third category, that of indirect comment, where NM can become more difficult to distinguish from AM.

2.1.2.3. Indirect comment. Indirect comment is more properly a narrator's metatext, since it is purely connotative, thus paralleling the purely connotative AM. Although it is hard at times to distinguish the two, they are theoretically quite distinct. NM occurs whenever the narrator describes his or her behaviour but without comment (the reader then judges).[7]

The most obvious examples are straight descriptions of her own behaviour, such as over-reaction, especially with regard to the children, who are not only described in extravagant terms (*beatific, angelic, revelation*, etc., at first, *ugly, old old woman, the chit* later), but who also cause her to behave extravagantly, even at first, when, after receipt of the letter and her questions to Mrs Grose, Flora appears just as Mrs Grose says: 'You might as well believe it of the little lady. Bless her ... *look* [J] at her!' The governess turns and looks (description), feels the force of the comparison and, 'catching my pupil in my arms, covered her with kisses in which there was a sob of atonement' (p. 11). We only have to put ourselves in Flora's position to know (if we were in doubt) that it is over-reaction. There is no direct comment, yet the phrases 'covered her with kisses' and 'a sob of atonement' show that the narrator is conscious of over-reaction for the circumstances. In a third-person narrative it would be AM (or NM with another narrator). Later this consciousness is expressed in direct comment: 'moments when I knew myself to catch them up by an irresistible impulse and press them to my heart. *As soon as I had done so I used to wonder – "What will they think of that? Doesn't it betray too much?"* ... *children perpetually bowed down over and hugged*' (p. 38).

Of course, by then, all is more contextualised and one could argue that in the light of her beliefs she does not over-react, or that if the children are guilty she doesn't, if they are innocent she does, from their viewpoint, e.g., after Miles's question about his school: 'I stopped as short as if one of the trees of the park had fallen across the road' (p. 55); and later: 'It literally made me bound forward (p. 56).' Again here there is no direct comment (NM: over-reaction) but elsewhere there is, which shows explicitly that she is conscious of it: 'oh I brought it out now even if I *should* [J] go too far ... But I knew in a moment after this that I had gone too far' (p. 65, bedroom scene, direct comment). And her reaction to Flora's first escapade hovers between indirect and direct comment: 'I must have [n.i..] gripped my little girl with a spasm that, *wonderfully, she submitted to without a cry or a sign of fright*' (p. 42).

What the early instance (p. 11) indirectly tells us is of a tendency anyway to over-react, before anything really terrible has happened. Her reaction to the first appearance of a man on the tower (chapter

3) is, in the circumstances, over-reaction, though, of course, in the light of later convictions her concern as narrator is here to build up a ghostly atmosphere. Her decision to protect the children from the by-then 'ghosts' by offering herself as screen (chapter 6) is also expressed, without comment, in extravagant terms (she sees herself as expiatory victim), and her retrospective imagining of Quint's death, as presumably (see chapter 6, p. 149) described by Mrs Grose, is highly coloured by her conviction that he is sinister, was a monster, etc., even if by then this conviction is contextualised by her beliefs (he is a ghost) and by her interpretation (itself over-reaction) of what Mrs Grose has told her.

Other examples of behavioural NM are: 'The presence on the lawn – *I felt sick as I made it out* – was poor little Miles himself' (p. 45). The reader is left to judge whether she feels sick from shame at all her suspicions or from fear for Miles in the grip of Quint. Similarly when she describes Flora's expression, in the showdown scene by the lake [J4] 'that appeared to read and accuse and judge me' (p. 71) and 'a countenance of deeper and deeper, of indeed suddenly quite fixed reprobation' (p. 72) there is a clear metatextual displacement of her own guilt into external accusation.

Then there is the famous sentence [after Q2] about her checking in the village after Q1, which is metatextual in that it is expressed negatively: '"Nobody from the village?"/"Nobody – nobody. I didn't tell you, but I made sure"' (p. 22) – and indeed it wasn't noticed for many years (Silver 1957). But here it is difficult to decide whether it is AM or NM, though either way the narrator describes herself as leading Mrs Grose towards the identification. Both A and N are telling us that she checked and therefore *could* have learnt about Quint and his appearance. Since, however, there would then be, as I pointed out in chapter 6, a contradiction in her shriek of surprise on learning that he is dead (which she could hardly have avoided also learning in the village, in view of the inquest and scandal mentioned in her reconstructing analysis), there is here a question of consciousness: if the narrator is unconscious of her process (as character) of pre-identification, it is AM telling us so, and the shriek is part of that unconsciousness; if the narrator is conscious of this process as character, she is either telling us (NM) that she as character was unconscious (and would therefore have forgotten the information that the valet was dead), or telling us that she is cheating as narrator. This third possibility seems un- likely in the general tone of honesty, and would pose grave problems since the whole narrative could be a lie, unless we regard the whole narrative as an indirect message (to Douglas) that she was hallucinated, or at least reserves her judgment (cp. pp. 205, 213 here). Not that the narrator doesn't cheat, but this occurs as artistic privilege, that is, as part of the normal technique of suspense and delay.[8] There are, however, some examples which are more difficult to place in the category of artistic privilege, either because the technique is flawed, or because the example really *is* NM.

When, for instance, she tells us that her first night 'I believed I recognized, faint and far, the cry of a child' and that, at another moment, she was 'starting as at the passage, before my door, of a light footstep' (p. 8), these are part of suspense, forewarning, hints or *amorces* of the ghostly events to come. But there is no justification for the first: Miles isn't there yet and Flora is with Mrs Grose, nor do the children ever later cry out in their supposed silent communication with the ghosts. Either the author has slipped up (or telling us the narrator has), or the NM is telling us that she as character was prone to imagine things. In favour of the latter it must be noted that both sentences are given as suppositions (see 2.2.1. below).

Such *amorces* can also take the form of false previsions, or of judgments that turn out to be false (which the narrator must know). These vary a good deal. There is the early judgment ('it came to me'), on her return from the first apparition, that Mrs Grose 'knew nothing whatever that could bear upon the incident I had there ready for her' (p. 18)[9] – which turns out to be untrue, but without specification by the narrator, who merely becomes convinced of the opposite. There are, of course, false previsions which are recognised as false, as when she has 'the acute prevision' that the children will make a huge fuss at her desertion (chapter 15, p. 58) and is then surprised when they don't (chapter 16), or when she says to Mrs Grose 'you shall see' [Miss Jessel] on the way to the lake (chapter 19, p. 68) and is then astounded by 'the proof that her eyes were hopelessly sealed' (chapter 20 [J4], p. 72). The NM in both cases tells us that despite her language of conviction she can make mistakes, for as narrator she is pretty careful with her past instincts: 'I felt, in a fierce rigour of confidence, that if I stood my ground a minute, *I should cease – for the time at least – to have him* [Quint] *to reckon with*' [Q3] (p. 41). The forecast is a prolepsis and true, with the qualifying phrase, since he doesn't appear again till the very end. She is right, too, about the place where the boat would be in chapter 19 [before J4], and says so.

Naturally such forecasts are narrator's hindsight. And she can cheat a little, as when she says, after the incident of the letter: 'I felt forthwith a new impatience to see him; it was the beginning of a curiosity that, *all the next hours, was to deepen almost to pain*' (p. 11, true as narrator statement unverifiable within the text, but for much longer than this specific limitation, which, in the circumstances, is also an example of over-reaction). And she cheats a lot when she gives us a false prolepsis in chapter 22: 'He [Miles] had at any rate his freedom now; *I was never to touch it again*' (p. 80). She touches it again with such formidable pressure in the long scene which follows that he dies of it. This can hardly be NM since she is lying in narrative instance; it can only be AM on narrator-unconsciousness (or the narrator's conscious lie, but cp. p. 204, and below).

Apart from false previsions, the narrator also lies in straight narrative, for example during the crucial scene of Mrs Grose's identification of Quint [after Q2]:

Mrs Grose's large face showed me, at this, for the first time, the far-away faint glimmer of a consciousness more acute: I somehow made out in it the delayed dawn of an idea *I myself had not given her* and that was as yet quite obscure to me. (p. 23).

Since she has already replied that the man was not a gentleman, then hinted at the uncanny with the 'what' and the 'horror' of 'What *is* [J] he? He's a horror ... God help me if I know *what* [J] he is!' and finally firmly planted in Mrs Grose's mind the notion of harm to the children (which produces 'the delayed dawn of an idea'), this is either the narrator's unconscious lie (AM telling us she is lying or misremembering – and that she is doing the planting), or the narrator's conscious lie (NM telling us, if we notice, that she is lying, but this produces the same difficulty as the checking in the village, mentioned on p. 204, if regarded as NM; cp. also p. 213, and above here).

Other examples, if not of lies, at least of contradiction, are less serious. She tells us, several times, that Mrs Grose is unimaginative, whereas she had made Mrs Grose say: 'And afterwards I imagined – and I still imagine. And what I imagine is dreadful' (p. 33).[10] When in chapter 21 she secures Mrs Grose's support with regard to her employer and says: 'if I might continue sure of that I should care but little what else happened' (p. 78), she is either lying as narrator (AM), against herself as character, since she has just undertaken to save Miles, or, on the contrary, telling us (NM) the truth we have already seen (chapter 7), that she cares only about herself. She goes on: 'and if my friend would answer for my honesty I would answer for all the rest' (p. 78). Yet she has always known Mrs Grose's belief in her honesty, and has just, on the contrary, made sure that Mrs Grose would answer for a good deal more than that (see chapter 7). In the last scene with Miles [Q4] she says: 'My sternness was all for his judge, his executioner [the headmaster]' (p. 87), which is patently untrue in the context of the pressure she puts on him in order to find out what he had done at school.

As we can see, most of these contradictions between what she says and the context are ambiguously NM or AN. As NM these last examples would not be lies but indications of the type of self-convincing she was liable to indulge in as character. As AM they suppose narrator-unconsciousness of this.

Lies by the character are unambiguously NM. They are uncommented by the narrator but so obvious they might almost be followed by 'I lied' in direct statement. These are less frequent than critics have stated. But there are a few, notably the lie in chapter 8, often picked up, about how if she had 'made it up', Mrs Grose could have identified *both* the apparitions from her detailed descriptions, whereas she herself had identified the second as 'my predecessor', leaving only the naming to Mrs Grose. And there is the series of hysterical exaggerations to Mrs Grose in chapter 16, after J3: 'I only went with you [to church] for the walk ... I had then to come back to meet a friend ... I came home, my dear ... for a talk with Miss Jessel' (p. 60). The lie here is not that she communicated with Miss Jessel since that would be possible in both hypotheses (see chapter 7, p. 167, n. 10 above).[11] But that she came home with that intention, which is patently untrue, though, of course, part of her technique with Mrs Grose, of which she is conscious (see p. 197 here).

Other lies are to Miles, and they, too, are tactical lies but uncommented: '"Why when I went down – went out of the house."/"Oh yes. *But I forget what you did it for*"' (p. 55). Or her complicated version, more or less true, of Flora's illness (p. 81). Or her flattering lie:

'Though I've renounced all claim to your company – you're so beyond me – I at least greatly enjoy it. *What else should I stay on for?*'
    ... 'You stay on just for *that* [J]?'
    '*Certainly. I stay on as your friend and from the tremendous interest I take in you till something can be done for you that may be more worth your while. That needn't surprise you.*' (p. 83)

This is soon unmasked by Miles when she asks him to tell her '"Out, straight out. What you have on your mind, you know."/"Ah then is *that* [J] what you've stayed over for?"' and she has to "'make a clean breast of it. It was precisely for that"' (p. 83). A later one is not unmasked by Miles but might just as well have been, it's so illogical: '*I know everything.*"/He gave me at this his longest and strangest look. "Everything?"/"Everything. Therefore *did* [J] you –?" I couldn't say it again. Miles could, very simply. "No. I didn't steal."/ ... "What then did you do?"' (p. 86). These lies of the last scene produce another NM when Miles, playing for time, pretends he has to go out 'to see Luke', and she comments: 'I had not yet reduced him to quite so vulgar a lie, and I felt proportionately ashamed' (p. 84). In view of her own, the shame may be double-edged even as NM. Or else she is wholly unconscious, and it is AM.

Finally, there can be metatext (ambiguously NM or AM) through a specific use of vocabulary, slightly unexpected in the context, indicating a shift or even implying the opposite:

> Then it was that the others, the outsiders, were there ... causing me ... to tremble with the fear of their addressing to their younger victims some yet more infernal message or more vivid image than they had thought *good* enough for myself. (p. 53)

This is NM as irony (= *bad*), but AM as comment on the inner meaning of the irony (a perverse form of jealousy).

> Say that, by the dark prodigy I knew, the imagination of all evil *had* [J] been opened up to him; all the *justice* within me ached for the proof that it could ever have flowered into an act [shift: justice = also obsessive curiosity, AM and/or NM]. (p. 66)

> 'And where's Master Miles?'
> 'Oh *he's* [J] with Quint. They'll be in the schoolroom.'
> 'Lord, Miss!' My view, I was myself aware – and therefore I suppose my tone – had never yet reached so calm *an assurance* [= hysterical calm before climax, AM and/or NM]. (p. 67)

> He had picked up his hat, ... and stood twirling it in a way that gave me, even as I was just nearly reaching port, a *perverse* horror of what I was doing [shift: perverse goes with what she is doing, not with her horror of it – probably AM]. (p. 84)

As we can see, NM through indirect comment often turns on contradictions within the narrative or event apparent slips, and in some cases one could say it is simply author's carelessness. But rarely, I do not feel that contradictions in a text of this kind are merely careless.[12] When the narrator tells us in chapter 13 of hugging the children and wondering if it doesn't betray too much, and that she 'could have sworn that one of them had, with a small invisible nudge, said to the other: "She thinks she'll do it this time [come out with it] – but she *won't* [JJ]"' (p. 51), and then in chapter 18 tells of her efforts not to betray herself (p. 65), the contradiction is a clear NM about fluctuation. And when in chapter 19 she is convinced that Flora took the boat over despite her size because 'at such times, she's not a child' (p. 69 – in fact Flora *could* have walked round, as is made clear when they do so themselves in 'ten minutes', for them, and the boat *could* have been hidden earlier, with Miles), and then later when she finds the boat gone, after Mrs Grose has taken Flora away (which *could* be by boat), expresses surprise at 'Flora's extraordinary command of the situation', the contradiction says the same.

Metatext in indirect comment in fact turns on the question of consciousness, and it isn't always easy to determine whether it is the author or the narrator who shows consciousness of the extra information we glean. In the cases of character-behaviour and character-lies it is NM, in others it mostly is, but sometimes not. Nor does this matter in practice. For metatext is always essentially the reader's text; it depends on the reader's attention (about which James cared so much), and can therefore vary a good deal, not only in degree, but in specific judgments as to whether the information implied comes direct from the author or is filtered through the narrator's consciousness.

When, for example, the narrator tells us in chapter 22 that her ordeal demanded 'only another turn of the screw of ordinary human virtue' (p. 80) she cannot know, as fictional narrator and character, that her story will be given that phrase as title, in a different sense, actually by the author and fictionally by the I–narrator of the prologue, out of the conversation. This is AM, a large wink from author to reader. But when, on coming in from the first apparition, she says she 'achieved an inward revolution' (p. 18) and says nothing to Mrs Grose, whereas Miles's decision to speak out in chapter 14 is called a revolution (p. 55), we have a not immediately visible NM or AM, according to the reader's judgment (revolution = silence/speech). Similarly, when she insists, in n.i. during the first two apparitions (Quint), on the difficulty of knowing how long they lasted (pp. 17, 21), yet obsessively denotes time not only for everything else (*moment, instant, minutes, seconds*, etc.), but during *all* the apparitions, there is a metatext on the impossibility/possibility of narration (NM) and/or on her confusion as narrator (AM).

Indirect comment in NM parallels indirect comment in AM. It is the area where they sometimes fuse, either as double metatext or as alternatives, in the same example. It is also an area where features more specific than the *general features* so far examined can fuse AM and NM.

2.2. *Specific features*

These are simply metatextual features which are more specific to this text, or at least highly developed here, though they could of course occur elsewhere.

The governess's problem evolves, on the one hand, around her state of mind – her doubts and certainties, her search for information and 'proof'; and, on the other, around her relationship with Mrs Grose as 'mirror' and 'transfer', whom she needs to convince and with whom she elaborates her experiences (see chapter 7). The surface structure of her narrative reflects these two phenomena on two main axes: that of the distinction between *énoncé* (statement) and *énonciation* (utterance); and that of syntactic complementarity.[13]

2.2.1. Statement and utterance. In a sense, of course, a first-person narrative is by definition wholly in the utterance mode, since all depends on the narrator's perception and talent. But as we shall see there is bound to be a distinct difference between sentences that state and sentences that qualify. Nor do the two categories divide simply into third-person and first-person sentences: a third-person sentence can be qualified by adverbial shifters: *probably, perhaps, perceptibly, clearly, doubtless, somehow,* etc.; or by verbal shifters: *she felt that, he was sure,* or the impersonal constructions already noted – *it came to him that,* etc., which can also be in narrative instance (*it comes to me, I suppose,* etc.), and subjunctives like *might*; or by adjectives and nouns of judgment specific to the character, already noted; and, of course, by questions. While a first-person sentence, though the presence of 'I' makes it strictly speaking utterance, can be an objective statement about oneself, such as 'I went into the house'.

In the first chapter, for example, the narrator uses the categories clearly and correctly. Her journey, her arrival, and things observed are told as feeling and perception when it is so (the ups and downs, the see-saw image, etc.) and as statement when no feeling is involved: '*as we turned into the avenue*', '*the pair of maids looking out*', '*there immediately appeared at the door, with a little girl in her hand, a* civil *person*' ['civil', as class term and judgment, is utterance] (p. 7).

Nevertheless the utterance mode thoroughly predominates, from the first n.i., *I remember* to the phrases of judgment, e.g., the above sentence continues: 'who dropped me as *decent* a courtesy *as if I had been the mistress or a distinguished visitor*' – with James's much favoured use of *as if*. All is impression, supposition, fear and wonder: '*made me think . . . suggested that* what I was to enjoy *might be . . .* The little girl *. . . affected me* [first edition, *appeared to me*]; I afterwards *wondered, astonished me, remained with me, my sense of*; the large, *impressive* room, the great state bed, *as I felt it . . .* the long glasses . . . *all struck me*, the one *appearance . . . that . . . might* have made me shrink again . . . and that, *with reflexion, with suspicion, might of course* have made me uneasy *. . . I felt quite sure* she would presently like me' (pp. 7–8).

The mingling of supposition or feeling with certainty in *might of course* and *felt quite sure* will become a recurrent feature.[14] All this on the first page. And it continues. The sounds she hears at night are given honestly in the utterance mode ('*I believed I recognised*, quoted p. 204). So is her reaction the next day: '*What I felt . . . I suppose* [n.i.] *. . . could fairly be called* [n.i.] *. . .* it was *probably at the most*' (p. 99). Similarly, all the imagined dialogues between the children or herself and the children are clearly introduced as imaginary (chapters 10, 13, 15).

The whole text is so thoroughly impregnated with utterance that I need give no further examples as such. Many already given under *General features* are interwoven with utterance, and once noticed it springs to the eye, and, is, of course, the main cause of the famously complex Jamesian sentence. It constitutes a perpetual AM on the complicated consciousness of his characters and, here, on the narrator's desperate attempt at honesty.

There are, however, two specific features of utterance and statement I should like to discuss. First, the terms of certitude, including pseudo-logic, and second, the use of statement for utterance.

2.2.1.1. Utterance: terms of certitude. Terms of certitude, when expressed personally, tend to metatextualise their opposite, as when we say 'I'm *sure* I put the keys on the table' [but I may be wrong]' or even 'a *certain* tone' [kind of], 'A *certain* age' [uncertain], just as the denial of certainty can imply a fair degree of certainty, as when the narrator says: 'and *I was not even sure* that in spite of her exemption it was she who had the best of the burden' [= I was pretty sure she had not] (p. 25). Terms of certitude in fact tend to be used for the uncertain, for what can *not* be said as statement. They belong to utterance, but a form of utterance that tries to pass off as a strong form of statement what should be said as utterance – unlike utterance proper which expresses perception, feeling, doubt, supposition, questioning.

Consequently, when the narrator uses such terms, we have a general AM on her tendency to assert what should be said as supposition, and a specific NM implying that what she asserts could be otherwise. She does this less frequently than might appear from the force of each instance, but it is always for suppositions (which may or may not be true): 'able to *asseverate* to my friend that I was *certain* ... that *I* [J] at least had not betrayed myself' (p. 35); 'I felt an instant *certainty* that Flora had extinguished it' (p. 43); 'It was not, I *am sure to-day as I was sure then*, my mere infernal imagination: it was *absolutely* traceable that they were aware of my predicament' (p. 50); '*I could have sworn* ... I *would have been ready to swear* that, *literally* ... *this conviction* of the secret of my pupils' (pp. 51, 52); 'my *absolute conviction* of his secret precocity' (p. 63); 'I at once *felt sure* she had just come out of the copse' (p. 70); 'It was the very confidence that I might now defy him [Quint], as well as the *positive certitude* ... of the child's unconsciousness' [Q4] (p. 85). Or, more clearly metatextual, a mixture of certitude with qualification: 'At that moment, *in the state of my nerves, I absolutely believed* she lied' (p. 42).

Equally metatextual (AM) are the instances of pseudo-logic and her curious use of the word 'proof', which are more frequent and more insidious than the more obviously hysterical terms of certitude, e.g., on Miles's beauty and serenity:

I took this as a *direct disproof* of his having really been chastised. *If* he has been wicked *he would have* 'caught' it, *and I should have* caught it by the rebound – *I should have* found the trace, *should have* felt the wound and the dishonour. [This 'proof' of innocence by beauty will be used to 'prove' the opposite later, see below.] (p. 19)

'The man. He wants to appear to *them* [J].' That he might was an awful conception, and yet somehow I could keep it at bay; which moreover [keeping it at bay], as we lingered there, was what I succeeded in practically [qualification] *proving*. I had an absolute certainty that I should see again what I had already seen [certitude, NM on liability, and correct prevision], but something within me said [impersonal construction] that by offering myself bravely as the sole subject of such experience ... I should serve as an expiatory victim ... The children in special I should thus fence about and absolutely [certainty] save [curious 'proof']. (p. 26)

This peculiar process will continue. In chapter 6 she says the suspense didn't last as suspense: 'it was superseded by horrible *proofs* [i.e., J1 and her belief that Flora sees]. *Proofs*, I say, yes – from the moment I really took hold [a kind of subjective qualification, characteristically ambiguous]' (p. 28). In chapter 8, after the rhetorical outburst about her processes, mentioned in note 5 ('It was a pity ...'), she continues: 'Yet if I had not indulged, to *prove* there was nothing in it, in this review' (p. 35). In chapter 10 (Flora's second escapade): 'That she now saw ... was *proved* to me by the fact that she was disturbed neither by my re-illumination nor by the haste I made to get into slippers and a wrap' (p. 44)

In chapter 12, she admits this process as character (in dialogue):

'Lord, you do change!' cried my friend./'I don't change, I simply *make it out* [= work it out] [... wild statements about the children and the ghosts ...] I go on, I know, as if I were crazy; and it's a wonder I'm not. What I've seen would have made *you* [J] so; but it has simply made me more lucid, made me get hold of still other things.' My lucidity must have seemed awful ... 'Of what other things have you got hold of?' [the irony is NM] (p. 48).

Then, after more wild statements and the argument that the children's 'more than earthly' beauty and 'absolutely unnatural goodness' shows them (cp. proof by beauty above) to have been not good but only 'absent', and to belong to Quint and Miss Jessel, who 'want to get them' (itself a contradiction if 'they're his and they're hers', cp. p. 221), Mrs Grose mutters 'Laws!' and the narrator says: 'The exclamation was homely, but it revealed [?] a real acceptance of *my further proof* of what, in the bad time ... must have occured' [i.e., her interpretation of all that Mrs Grose has in fact told her] (p. 49). In chapter 13 she admits (despite earlier assertions) that 'it was not yet definitely proved' that the children saw. But this is followed by a double false syllogism. She hasn't seen anything since the apparition on the stairs.

What I then had an ugly glimpse of was that my eyes might be sealed just while theirs were most opened. Well, my eyes *were* [J] sealed, it appeared, [utterance] at present – a consummation for which it seemed blasphemous not to thank God ... I would have thanked him with all my soul had I not had in a proportionate measure this conviction [term of certitude] of the secret of my pupils. [She sees no ghosts, therefore her eyes are sealed; if her eyes are sealed those of the children might not be; therefore the children see the ghosts.] (p. 52)

In chapter 16 she says Miles was expelled

'For wickedness. For what else – when he's so clever and beautiful and perfect? Is he stupid? Is he untidy? Is he infirm? Is he ill-natured? He's exquisite – so it can be only *that* [J]'. [She had used the same argument as 'direct disproof' of his guilt earlier [p. 19], see above.] (p. 61).

In chapter 19 she says that their not seeing the boat '"is the strongest of *proofs*. She has used it to go over . . ."' (p. 69). And when Miss Jessel appears [J4]: 'my thrill of joy at having brought on a *proof*. She was there, so I was justified; she was there, so I was neither cruel nor mad . . .' (p. 71). In other words, a ghost appearing to her is a proof that ghosts appear to others. It never seems to occur to her that ghosts (in the ghost interpretation) can be invisible to others by choice, and not just because the others' eyes are 'sealed'. And the fact that Mrs Grose does not see Miss Jessel is called (as with herself earlier) 'this hard blow of *the proof* that her eyes were hopelessly sealed' (p. 72), just as Miles is 'barred' in the last scene (p. 82), and 'by my success, his sense was sealed and his communication stopped' (p. 85). I have already mentioned the illogical lie to Miles in chapter 24 ('I know everything'), and the climax comes when she wants Miles to name Quint as 'proof' in the highly ambiguous last scene when Miles first supposes she is seeing Miss Jessel (after the incident with Flora), then, when she insists that 'it's' not Miss Jessel, asks '"It's *he* [J]?" I was so determined to have *all my proof* that I flashed into ice to challenge him. "Whom do you mean by 'he'?"' (p. 88). That she accepts his 'surrender of the name' after these leading questions, and his final 'where?' as her proof is the final culmination in a long series of misuses (see also chapter 7 above, p. 182).

One can't help smiling at her complaint, when Mrs Grose says 'the master' thinks so well of her, that 'He has an odd way . . . of proving it!' (p. 75). But it is difficult to decide whether all this anti-logic is AM or AN. As AM (narrator unconscious) it is clear enough. As AN it is the narrator misleading (*leurre*, a justified technique) the reader, but also, if the reader is not misled, an indirect message (to Douglas in the fiction, to us outside) that she was hallucinated, or at any rate that she reserves her judgment (cp. pp. 204, 205 above).

2.2.1.2. The use of statement for utterance. Statement (a declarative sentence) is naturally less assertive than terms of certitude, and when correctly used passes unremarked, which is perhaps why the governess's sliding into statement for suppositions that should be said as utterance has not, as such, been noticed. And yet this, too, springs to the eye. She does this in three main ways: as narrator when she drops 'estrangement' words, as narrator during the apparitions, and as character in direct speech.

2.2.1.2.1. The dropping of 'estrangement' words. This happens for the first time in chapter 1, when, after all the tortuously suppositious phrases about Mrs Grose's relief at her arrival, and after the first dialogue with her she exclaims: 'Oh *she was glad I was there!*' (p. 9).

The first dialogue is given almost pure, with little narrator-interpretation. Uspensky (1974) has termed such interpretation of another's inner thoughts, when the narrator is limited to an outside view, as expressed through 'words of estrangement', that is, of appearance at guessing (*seemed to, visibly, discernibly, as if, her face expressed, I read into her expression,* etc.) The 'estrangement' stresses the narrator's outside position, and these terms, which are also utterance, positively stud every dialogue with Mrs Grose.[15] This is natural enough since she is the governess's 'mirror' (see chapter 7).

It is therefore the exceptions that are marked, and interestingly enough they are extremely few, but increase towards the end as the narrator becomes more involved and less careful. After the first example in chapter 1 there is nothing till chapter 9, the only example there being with one of the ghosts in the silent communication she has with them ('as hideous as a real interview' she says during this fourth apparition, Q3, p. 41) and thus equivalent to dialogue: '*He knew me* as well as I knew him; . . . but I had, thank God, no terror. *And he knew* I hadn't' (p. 41). The latter sentence however is immediately qualified by utterance: 'I found myself at the end of an instant magnificently aware of this.'

Other examples are in chapter 14 (Miles's revolution): 'There was something new, on the spot, between us, and *he was perfectly aware* I recognized it' (p. 55), which is double non-estrangement, hers of his: he is said to be aware, not of 'something new' but of her awareness. In chapter 16, with Mrs Grose: 'It was this, of a truth, that made her, *as she filled out my picture,* gape' (p. 60) – the qualification 'of a truth' applies only to the main sentence. In chapter 21 (the final 'result' scene with Mrs Grose), we suddenly get three: 'My visitor's trouble *was truly great*' (p. 74, after a question); 'I put it before her, but she continued for a little *so lost in other reasons* that I came again to her aid' (p. 76); '*She couldn't know my reasons* for a calmness after all pretty shallow' (p. 78, at Mrs Grose's conclusion that Miles 'stole *letters* [J]' at school – the statement is likely, of course, but an assumption nevertheless). Then in the last two chapters we suddenly have ten, two in chapter 23: 'laughing out through his gravity, *he could pretend* we were pleasantly jesting' (p. 83); and later: '*But it was for each other we feared!*' (p. 84, a narrator half-lie for herself, a guess for Miles); then eight in chapter 24: '*he knew* that he was in presence, but *knew not* of what, and *knew still less that* I also was and *that* I did know [double estrangement]' (p. 85); 'The only thing *he felt* was rather a dreary little surprise' (p. 86); 'he was at me in a white rage, *bewildered*, gazing *vainly* over the place and *missing wholly*, though it now, to my sense, filled the room like the taste of poison ... But he had already jerked straight round, stared, glared again, and *seen but the quiet day*.' (p. 88). The narrator has forgotten her usual care in qualifying and over-qualifying with estrangement words her perceptions of what others see and feel and think. This is AM on the narrator, unless, as with the terms of certitude, we take it as NM on herself as narrator.

2.2.1.2.2. Mingling of statement with utterance for the apparitions. The descriptions of these are extraordinarily skilful. We have already seen how estrangement is dropped for communication with Quint, but this is exceptional. All other instances of such communication are qualified by utterance. Q1: '*seemed* to fix me, from his position, with just the question, just the scrutiny through the fading light, that his own presence provoked' (p. 17); Q2: 'He remained but a few seconds – long enough *to convince* me he also saw and recognized ... On the spot *there came to me the added shock of a certitude that* it was not for me he had come. He had come for some one else' (pp. 20–1 – the last statement–sentence comes under the heavy qualification of the first); J1 is not described as such, only what precedes; Q3 has been quoted (p. 214); J2 is but a glimpse; J3: 'she had looked at me long enough *to appear* to say that her right to sit at my table was as good as mine to sit at hers' (p. 59); J4: 'I consciously threw out to her – with *the sense* that, pale and ravenous demon as she was, she would catch and understand it – an inarticulate message of gratitude' (p. 71); 'the figure that, on the opposite bank, without a movement, as rigidly still *as if* catching, beyond the interval, our voices' (p. 73). In the last scene (Q4) Quint merely appears and disappears to the rhythm of her pride, but the implication is by then that he understands, and even here it is qualified: 'For there again, against the glass, *as if* to blight his [Miles's] confession and stay his answer, was the hideous author of our woe' (p. 88).

This is for the supposed 'communication', given, with consistent honesty, in the utterance mode. The actual descriptions however are a cunning mixture of utterance and statement: utterance, a great deal of it, for the facts of her perception, reactions, and for all the atmosphere before, during and after, the impressions of hush and unnatural stillness, and for *some* of the surrounding physical circumstances, but statement for others ('The rooks stopped cawing ... The gold was still in the sky, the clearness in the air'), and, above all a preponderance of statement for the positions, the looks, gestures or acts of the figures themselves, e.g., Q1 (exceptions designated thus: ⟨ ⟩ with utterance italicised):

> the man who met my eyes ... the man who looked at me over the battlements ... We were confronted ... ⟨*this visitant ... and there was a touch of the strange freedom, as I remember, in the sign of familiarity of his wearing no hat – seemed* to fix me ... with just the question ...⟩ We were too far apart to call to each other ... He was in one of the angles, the one away from the house ⟨very erect, *as it struck me*⟩, and with both hands on the ledge. ⟨*So I saw him as I see the letters I form on this page*⟩; then, exactly, after a minute, ⟨*as if* to add to the spectacle⟩, he slowly changed his place – passed, looking at me hard all the while, to the opposite corner of the platform. ⟨Yes, *it was intense to me* that during this transit he never took his eyes from me, and *I can see at this moment* the way his hand, as he went, moved from one of the crenellations to the next.⟩ He stopped at the other corner, but less long, and even as he turned away still markedly fixed me. He turned away; ⟨*that was all I knew*⟩. (16–17)

This skilful blending of statement with utterance for the physical aspects of the apparitions (surrounding circumstances and gesture or position) will recur in all the descriptions. It is, of course, the essence of the fantastic: to anchor the supernatural in the natural, and yet to build up subjective horror and fear. The shift from utterance to statement is perfectly exemplified in the incident when she spies from the tower window and sees Miles on the lawn looking up at '⟨something that was *apparently* above me. There was *clearly* another person above me⟩ – there was a person on the tower' (p. 45). This is not an apparition since she is not in a position to see, but it has the same atmosphere. Similarly just before, with Flora at the window: 'Hidden, protected, absorbed, ⟨she *evidently* rested on the sill – the casement opened forward⟩ – and gave herself up' (p. 44). The qualification 'evidently' is attached to a verifiable fact, the suppositions (absorbed, gave herself up) have none.

As such, this kind of shift from utterance to statement is AM on the narrator's deceiving and self-deceiving use of language and indirectly on the character's. As skill it is NM that says: 'I'm using art to convince you.'

2.2.1.2.3. Statement for utterance in direct discourse. Every critic has noticed the governess's 'lies', without usually distinguishing narrator-lie from character-lie, nor between different types of character lies. I have already dealt with most of them under narrator's metatext. What we have here, however, is the straight use of statement, by the character, usually under pressure of emotion, for what should be said as utterance. They are not lies, they express conviction. The first example, like the narrator's Free indirect discourse about Mrs Grose being glad (see p. 214 above), occurs early, in chapter 2, and is about Miles, after receipt of the letter. It is *first* introduced, however, by a form of supposition (can have) though categorically expressed (*but one*), and there's a long sentence of utterance in between:

'That can have but one meaning.' Mrs Grose listened . . . she forebore . . . so that, presently, to put the thing with some coherence . . . I went on: 'That he's an injury to the others'. (p. 11)

This is relatively qualified, but it is interesting that the first shift of this kind (Mrs Grose's relief in chapter 1) occurs about the possibility of a secret to be discovered (the 'outer', *unheimlich* secret as opposed to the inner, *heimlich* one, see chapter 7, p. 161, note 6 above, and Cixous [1975: 51]); here the *unheimlich* propels the whole story. There are no further examples for some time (I don't count instances such as her report that she saw 'An extraordinary man looking in', etc. or her description, since I assume she does see the figures, whether ghosts or hallucinations). But once the identification made, and the knowledge acquired that Quint is dead (i.e., a ghost), the process begins (chapter 6), still, however, mingled with utterance, but separately:

'He was looking for little Miles.' ⟨A portentous clearness now possessed me [utterance]⟩. '*That's* [J] whom he was looking for.'
'But how do you know?'
'I know, I know, I know!' ⟨My exaltation grew. [utterance]⟩ 'And *you* [J] know, my dear!'
She didn't deny this, but I required, ⟨I felt [utterance]⟩, not even so much telling as that. She took it up again. 'What if *he* [J] should see him?'
'Little Miles? That's what he wants!'

She looked immensely scared again. 'The child?'
'Heaven forbid! The man. He wants to appear to *them*' [J]. (pp. 25–6)

From then on the process will accelerate: ' "They *know* [J] – it's too monstrous: they know, they know!" ... "Why all that *we* [J] know ... Two hours ago, in the garden" – ⟨could scarce articulate⟩ – "Flora *saw*! [J]" ' [after J3] (chapter 6, p. 30); Mrs Grose asks 'She has told you?' and the governess replies: 'Not a word – that's the horror. She kept it to herself!' ... [illogic], followed by an utterance reply in answer to Mrs Grose's 'Then how do you know?'/'I was there – ⟨I saw with my eyes: saw that⟩ she was perfectly aware'; ' "... and in the midst of it she came."/"Came how – from where?"/ "From where they come from!" ' (p. 31) 'Flora doesn't want me to know' (p. 31) 'She only fixed the child ... With a determination – ⟨indescribable [utterance]⟩ With a kind of fury of intention' ... 'Intention?'/'To get hold of her ... *That's* [J] what Flora knows' (p. 32).

This shift into statement for utterance occurs whenever the governess discusses the supposed relationship between the ghosts and the children with Mrs Grose. When she is *narrating* her self-elaborations she is more circumspect and wraps them up in terms of supposition or of certitude. But she needs to convince Mrs Grose. And these are not suppositions to her, or lies, they are convictions. They become particularly strong in the crucial scene of elaboration with Mrs Grose, after Miles's escapade in chapter 10 and her analeptic continuation of it in chapter 11, that is, in chapter 12, the pivot chapter in which Mrs Grose suggests sending for their uncle; and again in chapter 16, after the third apparition of Miss Jessel (itself after Miles's threat to send for his uncle) which precipitates the final action. Similarly in chapter 19, on the way to the lake and the showdown with Flora [J4], and again in chapter 21 (the 'result' chapter where she manipulates Mrs Grose into 'saving' her with her employer), though here it is Flora's attitude and intentions with regard to herself she is categoric about. They disappear in the last three chapters where the dialogue is much too ambiguous and staccato, and thoroughly interwoven with narrative utterance.

Everything said by the governess as character, in direct speech, is in theory NM, but perhaps, in such cases, AM, too: the author fuses with his narrator to reveal the character.

2.2.2. Syntactic complementarity.[16] The last feature I shall deal with, specific to this text (and to James generally) is syntactic complementarity. I say 'specific' though it can, of course, occur elsewhere, but is particularly developed here.

It is in fact a special version of what every author does: distribute the information to be divulged among his characters. And here we are aware of the author lending a technique to the narrator–governess, since it occurs not only elsewhere in James but in the TS 'frame', the Prologue. Douglas says (of his story):

> 'It's beyond everything. Nothing at all that I know touches it.'
> 'For sheer terror?' I remember asking.
> He seemed to say it wasn't so simple as that ... He ... made a ... grimace.
> 'For dreadful–dreadfulness'. (pp. 1–2)

> 'In her successor's place,' I suggested, 'I should have wished to learn if the office brought with it –'
> 'Necessary danger to life?' Douglas completed my thought. 'She did wish to learn ...' (p. 5)

> ' ... all the more so because of his main condition.'
> 'Which was –?'
> 'That she should never trouble him – but never, never ...' (p. 6)

In the first example the I–narrator prolongs the syntax of Douglas's sentence to add a further question, and Douglas replies, using the same syntax (which could have completed his own sentence). In the second Douglas 'completes his thoughts', i.e., the I–narrator's question, which was left in abeyance, then answers it. The third is like the first, but more 'normal' in the sense that Douglas's statement, which is part of his act of suspense, requires the question, but that question could have been stated whole (what was it?) instead of continuing the syntax *as if Douglas had said it*. And that is the point: the syntax of one sentence is shared out, instead of being said by Douglas alone.

This technique of sending back the ball is highly developed in all the conversations between the governess and Mrs Grose, and plays an important part in the governess's prompting of Mrs Grose. The question to determine, however, is who has the initiative (as Douglas has it). And it is not always the governess. When she asks if the boy is as remarkable as Flora, Mrs Grose replies:

> 'Oh Miss, *most* [J] remarkable. *If you think well of this one!*' – and she stood there with a plate in her hand, beaming ... –
> 'Yes; if I do – ?'
> 'You *will* [J] be carried away by the little gentleman'. (pp. 8–9)

Here the governess merely repeats the syntax, does not prolong it, though Mrs Grose does in her reply. Or in chapter 2, after 'the child's dismissed from his school,' Mrs Grose gives her the look which she 'seemed to try' to take back (see note 15 above), then asks '"But aren't they all – ?"/"Sent home – yes. But only for the holidays. Miles may never go back at all"' (p. 10). This is presented as a wilful misunderstanding, but the technique can also be used for real ones, e.g., the dialogue quoted pp. 217–8, with the co-reference mistake on 'he' – Miles or Quint.[17]

Mrs Grose certainly takes the initiative of non-completion at times, but it is out of innocence, or apparent innocence, and at any rate from good will and simple emotions: 'Would you mind, Miss, if I used the freedom – ?' 'To kiss me? No!' (p. 14). And the governess usually completes by finishing the question in such a way as either to delay: '"What in the name of goodness is the matter –" . . . "With me? . . . Do I show it?"' – p. 21) or to go a good deal further: '"But if he isn't a gentleman – ?"/"What is [J] he? He's a horror."/"A horror?" [repetition]/"He's – God help me if I know what [J] he is!"' (p. 22). The last reply syntactically completes the question, but there has been another suggestive question and repetition in between.

When it is the governess who has the initiative of the incomplete question, which is more frequent, she is usually getting information out of Mrs Grose (about the children and the past) rather than imparting it to her (about the apparitions):

'I take what you said to me at noon as a declaration that you've [J] never known him to be bad.' [Question disguised as a statement, a frequent tactic of hers.]
[. . .] 'Oh never known him – I don't pretent that [J]!'
I was upset again. 'Then you have [J] known him –?'
'Yes indeed, Miss, thank God!'
On reflexion I accepted this. 'You mean that a boy who never is –?'
'Is no boy for me [J]!' (11–12)
'Did she [J] [her predecessor] see anything in the boy –?'
'That wasn't right? She never told me.'
I had a scruple, but I overcame it. 'Was she careful – particular?'
Mrs Grose appeared to try to be conscientious. 'About some things – yes.'
'But not about all?'
Again she considered. 'Well, Miss – she's gone. I won't tell tales.' (p. 12)

She becomes very good at it, picking, for instance, on Mrs Grose's 'for one thing' to go on, syntactically, so as to make sure not to forget the 'other' thing (returning later to the first):

'You reminded him that Quint was only a base menial?'
'As you might say! And it was his answer, for one thing, that was bad.'

'And for another thing?' I waited. 'He repeated your words to Quint?'
'No, not that. It's just what he *wouldn't* [J] ...' (p. 36).

This process continues, especially in the early dialogues, and it must be said that Mrs Grose also plays the game extraordinarily well, completing not only the unfinished questions, but the questions disguised as statements, sometimes also unfinished:

'It does strike me that my pupils have never mentioned –!'
She looked at me hard as I musingly pulled up. '*His having been here and the time they were with him?*'
'The time they were with him [repetition], and his name, his presence, his history, in any way. They've never alluded to it.'
'Oh the little lady doesn't remember. She never heard or knew.'
'The circumstances of his death?' [governess] I thought with some intensity. 'Perhaps not. But Miles would remember – Miles would know.'
'Ah don't try him!' broke from Mrs Grose.
I returned her the look she had given me. 'Don't be afraid.' I continued to think. 'It *is* [J] rather odd.'
'*That he has never spoken of him?*'
'Never by the least reference. And you tell me they were "great friends"'.
(p. 26).

As the extracting of information about the past becomes less and less necessary, because successful, and the giving of information about apparitions more and more successful, because necessary, a second kind of complementarity creeps in, not shared but merely interrupted, by repetition on the part of Mrs Grose, in the form of either questions or interjections, with the governess simply continuing her own sentence (her *own* syntactic complementarity): '"and in the midst of it *she came.*"/"Came how – from where?"/"*From where they come from!* ..."' (p. 31); '"*She only fixed the child.*"/... "Fixed her?"/ "Ah *with such awful eyes!*"/... "Do you mean of dislike?"/"God help us, no ['normal' reply]. Of something much worse." [shared complementarity]/"Worse than dislike?" [shared] .../"*With a determination* – indescribable. *With a kind of fury of intention.*"/ ... "Intention?"/"*To get hold of her*"' (p. 32).

She is imparting all the information, and the sentences italicised could be one sentence. But as we reach the first 'transgression' chapter (12) the shared complementarity returns, Mrs Grose partaking again in the process, contributing, though prompted, and still also questioning:

'They're [the children] not mine – they're not ours. *They're his and they're hers!*'
'*Quint's and that woman's?*' [contribution]

'*Quint's and that woman's.* [governess's repetition, in affirmation] *They want to get hold of them.*'
[. . .] 'But for what?' [question]
'*For the love of all the evil that,* in those dreadful days, the pair put into them' (p. 49).[18]

And when Mrs Grose does rise to the bait and suggests sending for the uncle:

'By writing to him that his house is poisoned and his little nephew and niece mad?'
'But if they *are* [J], Miss?' [contribution]
'*And if I am myself, you mean?*' [completion of question] (pp. 49–50)

When, however, the governess is afraid Mrs Grose might send for him herself, we get a mere interjected question again:

'*If you should so lose your head as to appeal to him for me –*'
She was really frightened. 'Yes, Miss –?'
'*I would leave, on the spot, both him and you.*' (p. 50)

In the second 'transgression' chapter (16) the mixed process of interjected question and prompted contribution recurs:

'And what did she say?' I can hear the good woman still, and the candour of her stupefaction.
'*That she suffers the torments –!*'
It was this, of a truth, that made her, as she filled out my picture, gape. 'Do you mean,' she faltered, '– *of the lost?*' [contribution]
'*Of the lost. Of the damned. And that's why, to share them –*' I faltered myself with the horror of it.
But my companion, with less imagination, kept me up. 'To share them –?' [repetition as question]
'*She wants Flora.*' . . . As I've told you, however, *it doesn't matter.*'
'*Because you've made up your mind?* [contribution] But to what?'
'*To everything.*'
'And what do you mean by "everything"?' ['normal' question]
'Why *to sending for their uncle.*'
'Oh, Miss, in pity do,' my friend broke out.' (pp. 60–1)

Syntactic complementarity as well as repetition returns in the pre-elaboration before the final showdown with Flora by the lake (chapters 18–19), and in the last chapter with Mrs Grose (the 'result' chapter, when the governess inverts the consequences, see chapter 7 above), about Flora's reactions, which the governess guesses, and Mrs Grose's, which she prompts. Mrs Grose's last sentence, that shows the governess as the one who will be 'saved', is in syntactic complementarity: '"If he confesses he's saved. And if he's saved —"/"*Then you are?*" The dear woman kissed me on this, and I took her farewell. "I'll save you without him!" she cried as she went' (p. 79).

Repetition, which I have mentioned, is a more 'normal' way of conducting a strange or strained dialogue, and this also occurs as we have seen, but is not syntactically complementary. It is often combined with inversion, especially in the governess's more startling effects on Mrs Grose: '"I ... saw she was perfectly aware."/"Do you mean of *him* [J]?"/"No—of *her* [J]."' (p. 31),[19] and other examples at the beginning, e.g., '"how did he get in?"/"And how did he get out?"' (p. 23). But Mrs Grose is also capable of this, in her own particular kind of irony:

'But not to the degree to contaminate —'
'To contaminate?' — my big word left her at a loss.
I explained it. 'To corrupt.'
She stared, taking my meaning in; but it produced in her an odd laugh.
'Are you afraid he'll corrupt *you* [J]?' (p. 12) [repetition and inversion].
'... but it has only made me more lucid, made me get hold of other things.' ...
'Of what other things have you got hold?' (p. 48) [repetition only].

The technique of repetition and inversion is the one used in dialogues with the children, which are indeed a kind of game. With Miles, however, who does seem to have a 'shared' or at least a guessed knowledge, if only of 'the question between them' (that of his school), this technique is mingled with syntactic complementarity, but of the second kind described above (his own syntactic complementarity), that is, he has the initiative and continues his own sentence (though in the first example he completes her question), the governess merely interjecting a question, i.e., acting like Mrs Grose, but in order to prompt him and out of fear of betraying herself: '"Well," he said at last, "just exactly in order that you might do this."/"Do what?"/"Think me — for a change — *bad* [J]"' (47); '"Does my uncle think what *you* [J] think?" ... "How do you know what I think?"/"Ah well, of course I don't; for it strikes me you never tell me. But I mean does *he* [J] know?"/"Know what, Miles?"/"Why the way I'm going on."/ ... "I don't think your uncle much cares."/ ... "Then don't you think he can be made to?"/"In what way?"/"Why by his coming down"' (p. 57). In the last scene, however, the strained ambiguity of the dialogue is entirely carried out with repetition and inversion.

Syntactic complementarity, then, implies a knowledge or half-knowledge shared by two characters, so that they are constantly completing each other's half-uttered thoughts. It is AM in the double sense that the information is distributed bit by bit by the narrator (see chapter 7, p. 169, *le corps morcelé*), and as indirect comment on the narrator as unconsciously showing how she as character prompted Mrs Grose (if this is conscious NM then the whole narrative is a lie, cf. pp. 204, 205, 213 above). Above all it reflects the mirror-structure discussed in chapter 7 above. Mrs Grose is her constant mirror and transfer whom she has to convince but whom she manipulates into throwing back her own image, her own convictions, and evil shared, though each at first has a different piece of it, past and present, which fuse in the governess's projecting type of perception, her own inner secret, whatever it is, needing the alien, other, unfamiliar, non personal or family secret in order to project itself. And this shared knowledge becomes, inevitably, a shared language, a shared sentence.

3. Theoretical considerations

Ambiguity is at the core of the pure fantastic. And yet, because my purpose was to preserve the ambiguity of the text and therefore not to enter into the ghosts/hallucinations polemic, but to find structures that function in both hypotheses, I have in effect evacuated ambiguity from my purposely neutral 'abstract structure', implying thereby that ambiguity occurs somewhere or other at the surface, either in SS.A or in SS.B or both. In chapter 5 I analysed the ambiguity of Poe's 'The Black Cat' through the unresolved enigmas of the hermeneutic code, and in an obvious sense ambiguity is apprehended at the surface, but that applies to everything in a text. Clearly ambiguity is not at the surface. In sentence grammar for instance an ambiguous sentence has two different deep structures, one for each sense: e.g., Chomsky's famous example, *Flying planes can be dangerous* (to fly planes/planes that fly). Before considering this problem however, I shall first summarise my findings, then try to link them together in an overall model.

The abstract on 'bare structure' of TS, in the sense of the narrative sentence for this text only, was in chapter 7 found to include the 'frame' (the Prologue), although the frame in this sense does not occur in every text. The whole story of transgression and its mechanism (the events) is framed by external and internal injunctuon and by immediate and final result.

SS.A (*sjužet*, i.e. disposition, presentation, or *agencement*) was then shown to be itself thoroughly framed, in various ways but in particular through a mirror-structure and a system of inversion and variation that corresponded to the psychic structure of projection (hypersensitivity to and identification with external phenomena for the supernatural hypothesis, hallucination for the natural hypothesis). Even in chapter 7 this aspect was already and inevitably illustrated with SS.B quotations.

SS.B (the sentences we read), examined here, reveals a further framing by means of author's metatext and narrator's metatext (i.e., a double frame, NM within AM). Both function at the phraseological level; the very sentences of the first-person narrator denote what is said but connote either AM, or NM, or both, and sometimes it is undecidable which. Framing here is then a question of sentences with two meanings, not necessarily ambiguous as to ghosts/hallucinations, but double-level as to denotation (which usually does represent the ghost-story) and connotation (which contains all the elements for the hallucination theory but also other elements about the character, relevant to both interpretations).

AM functions through the narrator's text, in her grammar, her syntax and vocabulary (statement/utterance) and other rhetorical elements such as the contradictions and distantly inverted parallelisms examined here; it also functions in the dispositional (SS.A) elements such as event/elaboration and the inversion examined in chapter 7. NM functions through more specifically narrative techniques (which would be assumed by the author or an invisible narrator in a non first-person narrative), such as double-level (phraseological) direct comment, narrative instance, and indirect comment (description of behaviour, contradictions, uncommented lies, etc.). Specific aspects of all these features (AM or AN) were treated separately for emphasis, under first, statement and utterance, and second, syntactic complementarity, the latter being particularly relevant to the mirror-structure of SS.A, 'reflecting' it as SS.B. What we have then is the schema:

| Abstract structure of transgression | → surface structure A | → surface structure B |

The transgression structure has already been represented in more detail as:

Frame		*Narrative*		*Frame*
Exterior injunction	interior injunction	transgression mechanism transgression	immediate result	final result

SS.A would include (apart from the more familiar features of time, mood and voice), for this text, the organisation into event and the elaboration that mirrors and frames the event:

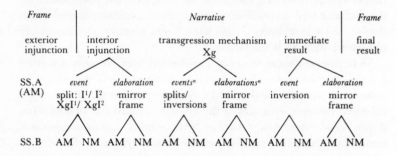

SS.B would be all that we read but with the author's metatext and the narrator's metatext at the most abstract level, made more manifest in (for AM) *indirect comment*, and (for NM), in *narrative instance, direct comment* and *indirect comment*. These in turn are then each expressed in either statement or utterance (S/U), and both these can each be further manifested in the indirect discourse of the narrator (i.d.) or in the direct discourse (d.d.) of the characters (except for narrative instance where there can be no direct discourse of characters). Direct discourse itself can be further subdivided into syntactic complementarity, repetition and inversion, which can only express themselves through direct discourse.

All these structures could thus be represented vertically by continuing the tree-structure below AM and NM, but it would be fastidious to do so since the subsidiary structures would mostly be repeated under each node. Such a tree-structure, which can more easily be imagined from the above description than actually written out, would not of course be a generative grammar but merely an abstract model for this one text.[20]

However, as I say, this model does not account for ambiguity, since, having postulated an abstract structure that functions in both hypotheses, I have been obliged (otherwise the complex tree would be merely duplicated), to leave it out provisionally. Where then does it occur?

In an excellent book (*The concept of ambiguity – the example of James*, 1977), Shlomith Rimmon deals with disjunction as the source of ambiguity. But disjunction itself is of two types: inclusive (a ∨ b) and exclusive (a ∧ b), often confused. This can also be expressed as the difference between contraries, which cannot both be true but could both be false, and contradictories, which cannot both be true *and* cannot both be false (cp. chapter 3, p. 56, note 1 on the logical rectangle). Rimmon adds a sign of her own to denote ambiguity: $\wedge$. That is, ambiguity combines co-presence (.) with exclusive disjunction ($\wedge$), it is: a *and* b (.) + a *or* b ($\wedge$). This in order to distinguish the absolute ambiguity she is dealing with from looser uses of the term to cover anything from polysemy (several meanings) to mere vagueness.

The narrative ambiguity that concerns her results, she tells us, from the existence of two mutually exclusive *fabulas* (stories) in one *sjužet* (treatment), or in Genette's terms two *histoires* in one *discours*. For instance, in *The Figure in the Carpet*: there is a secret clue in Vereker's work/there is not (i.e. Vereker was joking, paranoiac, etc.). Or, in TS: the governess and the children see ghosts at Bly/the governess has hallucinations. (And similarly for *The Lesson of the Master* and *The Sacred Fount*.)

The way this actually operates is through what James called 'the glory of the gap' ('The new novel', 1914, discussing Conrad's *Chance*. See also chapter 2, p. 34 above). All narratives have information gaps since none can render every detail of the corresponding 'reality', and these can range, *in centrality* from the most trivial, automatically and even unconsciously filled in by the reader (e.g. the governess must have been born), to a gap so crucial that it becomes the very subject of the narrative. Gaps also differ in *duration* (usually in proportion to their centrality), from a briefly suspended item of information (e.g. a name) to the permanent gap that is not filled in at all.

A gap can also be situated at *different levels*, in the *fabula* (story) or only in the *sjužet* (discourse, treatment). For instance in the classic detective-story there is no gap in the *fabula* but only in the *sjužet*, and the late filling in is 'merely an element of the composition, not of the narrated world'. This is perhaps misleading since the 'narrated world' is surely both the murder and the quest for the murderer, the structure of the detective story being in fact story 2 (*sjužet*, i.e., here, quest) in search of story 1 (*fabula*, i.e. murder), which is then actually incorporated into story 2 in summary, as the 'solution'. But this does not affect the gap argument: in an ambiguous text, the gap is *central, permanent*, and situated in *both the fabula and the sjužet*. In other words, a gap in the *fabula* necessarily entails a gap in the *sjužet*, while a gap in the *sjužet* need not entail a corresponding gap in the *fabula* (e.g. the detective story). This is why permanent gaps in the *fabula* are the most radical type of gap. Finally, there is the *manner in which the gap is filled*, mainly of two kinds: *external probabilities* (from the more or less automatic to the highly problematic if the cultural background is unfamiliar), and *internal indicators* within the text, which can range from explicit telling near the gap to distant telling or no telling at all. In the latter case the text deliberately frustrates our attempts to fill in the gap, either by providing no clues or by providing contradictory clues which, in totally ambiguous narratives, yield two mutually exclusive *fabulas* in the same *sjužet*. This is basically what Barthes was analysing, in his own way, through his hermeneutic code, with its false clues, partial answers, delayed answers (etc.) to enigmas, and as we saw with 'The Black Cat', two enigmas remain unanswered, as 'gaps'. Gaps can also be perceived linearly (as in *The Figure in the Carpet, The Sacred Fount*, or 'The Black Cat'), or retrospectively (as in *The Lesson of the Master*, or *Sarrasine*), or both, as in *The Turn of the Screw*, where the central gap occurs early, but becomes itself divided into 'local gaps', so that there is a double relation of the action and hermeneutic material and we are forced to go back on our tracks, rereading the action material hermeneutically.

Thus the gaps which Rimmon deals with concern the wholly ambiguous text. They are central, permanent, situated in both *fabula* and *sjužet*, and are prevented from being filled in by two mutually exclusive systems of gap-filling clues. It is these clues which she then analyses in the four James texts, according to two main systems: *an equilibrium of single-directed clues* (clues which support one or other of the two hypotheses are distributed through the narrative but perfectly balanced); and *the double-directed clues* (scenes, conversations, verbal expressions, which are themselves ambiguous and thus support the two hypotheses simultaneously. Both of course can be present. In TS the process is complex, for the conflictual *single-directed* clues follow each other within sequences, with the result that a whole scene containing them becomes *double-directed*. In other words, the double-directedness of the unit is often stronger than the recognition of sequential single-directed clues within the unit. Inversely, so many double-directed clues derive their double-directedness from this interaction that they resemble a sequence of single-directed clues. Hence the critics' endless and fruitless polemic.

Now it is obviously true that the ambiguity of TS, while present in the *sjužet*, i.e. in both my SS.A and SS.B, results from two mutually exclusive *fabulas* in that *sjužet*, and that my 'abstract structure' does not account for this, purposely since the transgression mechanism functions in both hypotheses. In other words my abstract structure is not a *fabula*, but simply describes the particular mechanism *through which* the two *fabulas* are organised into one *sjužet*.

The process can thus be reformulated (cp. diagram p. 225).

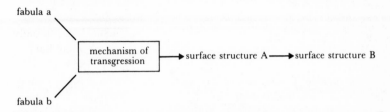

Naturally the ambiguity of the mutually exclusive *fabulas* also comes out in SS.A, at the level of events/elaboration (see p. 226 and at SS.B, in the author's metatext and the narrator's metatext, expressed, through indirect and direct comment and, for NM, in narrative instance, and in statement and utterance which can each occur in both indirect and direct discourse, the latter further showing the features of syntactic complementarity, repetition and inversion which would seem to belong wholly to AM (unless we can determine that the narrator is conscious of these and their tactical or other significance, and hence imparting it to us).

Whether or not we are interested in this or any other theoretical model, one main feature of the pure fantastic that should have emerged from these last three chapters, and especially from the analyses of TS in chapters 6 and 7, is its great complexity and sublety, as compared to the uncanny and the marvellous, if not to realism. The complexity and sublety of the latter, however tends to be thematic and ideological, with the result that its *fabula* is diffuse and its *sjužet*, though complex and superficially dense, replete, is in fact transparent, both as ideal aimed at (language as window on the world), and as technical motivation. The complexity and sublety of the pure fantastic lies in its absolute ambiguity, so that instead of one diffuse *fabula* we have two clear, simple, but mutually exclusive fabulas, and consequently a superficially transparent, non-replete (economical) *sjužet*, which is in fact dense and utterly baffling. That is no doubt why pure fantastic texts are usually short, relatively: it would be impossible to keep it up over a trilogy.

PART IV

The unreal as real: the modern marvellous

9

The evil ring: realism and the marvellous

In 1937, J. R. R. Tolkien published *The Hobbit* (H), one of those charming stories for children and adults which the English are so good at. He then began to work on a sequel, and during the fifties he produced *The Lord of the Rings* (LR), a vast trilogy – or hexalogy since each volume contains two books – that takes up the story of the magic ring of invisibility found by the hobbit Bilbo Baggins during his adventures (H).[1] LR starts in much the same homely and humorous vein as that of H, with Bilbo, now a hundred and eleven but mysteriously preserved by the ring, giving a farewell birthday party. He wants to end his days among the Elves of Rivendell and is leaving his luxury burrow to his nephew Frodo, aged thirty-three. In mid-speech he slips the ring on his finger and vanishes in a bang and flash, his old friend Gandalf the Wizard having secretly attended and added a bit of magic of his own, to make it look like a party trick and so preserve the secret of the ring's ownership, as he later explains to Bilbo in the back room. Indeed, throughout, Gandalf is the great explainer.

But LR is, or slowly becomes, a very different book, weighed down, not only by mechanisms inherent to the marvellous, but also by the mechanisms of the realistic novel. It is this machinery of realism, and the way it affects that of the marvellous, that I propose to examine here.

I shall first briefly recall the main properties of the marvellous, and then show how the marvellous in LR is altered by the mechanisms of the realistic novel examined in chapter 4.

1. The marvellous

Let us recollect the basic division made by Todorov (1970b; 1975) of the fantastic into (1) the uncanny (the supernatural events explained), (2) the pure fantastic (ambiguity as to whether the events have a supernatural or a natural explanation), (3) the marvellous (supernatural accepted). The explanation however, can come at various points, and is often withheld till the end, or alternatively, in the pure fantastic, not given at all, thus preserving the ambiguity beyond the text (as in *The Turn of the Screw*). Todorov therefore posits two further categories, on either side of a median line representing the pure fantastic:

Uncanny | fantastic–uncanny | fantastic–marvellous | marvellous

There seems to be no explicit 'opening-out' to the right, that would correspond to the opening out on to realistic fiction to the left, although Todorov says that his scheme is open at both ends, but one can suppose an opening out towards cosmological myths such as those of the Greek Titans, sun-myths, angelic orders and so forth. This imbalance is not important and Todorov insists throughout on the principle of dominance in any one text, the model being purely theoretical and the frontiers flexible.

I should say at once that all types of fantastic, whether uncanny, pure fantastic or marvellous (or merged), need to be solidly anchored in some kind of fictionally mimed 'reality', not only to be as plausible as possible within the implausible, but to emphasise the contrast between the natural and the supernatural elements. This 'reality' may be reduced in the pure marvellous but is still necessary. Thus even in a myth gods may eat, drink, mate and hold councils, and in a fairy-tale the hero will live in a hut in the forest, or in the outskirts of Baghdad, and have concrete adventures among streams, woods, streets, palaces, people wearing clothes that may be described, and so on. Indeed such elements are necessary to all narrative. It is only the transfer into the marvellous of elements said to be specific to the realistic novel that I shall be examining.

There are also certain features inherent to the marvellous itself, though possibly not specific to it as marvellous but as popular narrative: one of these elements is reduplication. Adventures often come in triplicate for instance (three brothers, only one of whom succeeds, or three tasks, only the third of which is successful), just as adjuvants and opposants can be reduplicated at the surface but are simply different semantic investments of the adjuvant/opposant opposition in the basic structure, as analysed by Propp (1928; 1968) and later more especially by Greimas (1966, 1970). Bremond (1966) has also shown an element of arbitrariness in the structure of such narrative, as when he says, after each example of possible 'degradation' or 'amelioration': 'the narrative may stop here, but if the narrator should choose to go on, one form is particularly privileged in this case'. Since he claims to be giving a pure theory applicable to all narrative and gives no textual examples, it is difficult to judge whether this is a feature of the marvellous: intuitively I would say it is a feature of unsophisticated narrative, including folk-tales and popular modern fiction.

2. 'Lord of the Rings'

The dominance in LR is clearly that of the pure marvellous, since no surprise is created by the magical elements. Its form is that of the quest, not merely in the general sense that the basic form of all narrative is a quest (for success, for a secret, for the conquering of evil or chaos either external or internal, for the understanding of oneself, of the world, of a situation, or even of narrative itself), but in the more transparent sense that it is a heroic quest, and thus akin to both the heroic period (*Odyssey*) and to the fairy-tale in which the hero goes off on an explicit adventure (to kill a dragon, rescue a princess, bring back a treasure or a rare or impossible object), and encounters incarnated adjuvants and opposants.

LR actually reverses the usual quest formula: Frodo must get rid of the evil ring, and since it is indestructible and unlosable, the only way is to reach Mount Doom, at the heart of the Evil Power's vast sphere of influence, and drop it into the fire that originally forged it. As Frodo himself says (for all is explicit in LR): 'What is to be my quest? Bilbo went to find a treasure, there and back again; but I go to lose one, and not return, as far as I can see' (p. 100). Frodo's quest is an anti-quest. Yet this final aim, which is on the thematic level, does not affect the quest-structure. In most quests, adventures pile up on the way, the return journey being rapid, easy, and accompanied by a treasure. Here too the adventures pile up on the way and the return journey is swift, minus the treasure (except for peace), although there is then a bathetic repetition of the quest in the mini-war that is continued in Hobbit-land (the Shire) after the destruction of the central evil power, so that 'peace' is further postponed. The main difference, however, between quest and anti-quest here is the nature of the physical goal (gain/loss of treasure); whereas for example the *Odyssey* is an anti-quest both structurally and thematically: all the adventures occur on the return journey, in fact the return *is* the quest, its physical goal or treasure being 'home' (*i.e.* return). The differences may be formulated as shown in the diagram below:

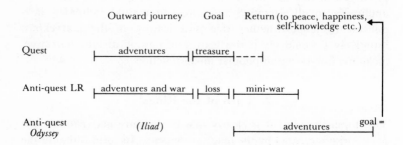

The first book of LR has a fairly lively pace, despite much padding in the form of delay in starting off, a good deal of travelogue, bathetic incident (great physical danger followed by nothing or by purely magical aid, the forgetting of warnings followed by no consequences), and adventures that seem (and turn out to be) irrelevant to the main quest: the murdering trees, the Barrow Downs, from which the hobbits are saved by Tom Bombadil, neither the trees nor the barrows being clearly linked with the rise of the Evil Power, nor is Tom more than an incidental adjuvant, to be forgotten later. The real quest starts at Bree (chapter 10!) with the introduction of the second chief adjuvant Strider, alias Aragorn (Gandalf being the first but having temporarily disappeared), and of sinister characters (spies of Saruman, himself a wizard turned spy for Sauron, the Evil Power). Aragorn accompanies the hobbits to Rivendell, which they reach after various adventures. The second book, however, is extremely static: rest at the Elf kingdom of Rivendell, the interminable Council of Elrond, the forming of the Grey Company, enormous delay in departure. By the end of this second book the Grey Company is split and we have to follow the adventures of its different members.

The fact of having separate adventures is not in itself a destructuring element. In the thirteenth century prose romance *La Queste del Saint Graal*, for instance, we follow the separate adventures of all the knights in quest of the Holy Grail, and similarly in Malory's fifteenth-century version of it (*The Tale of the Sankgreal*), which is only a small part of his huge cycle of Arthurian romances. But they are all on the same quest, it is like a race, a competition, so that the different spiritual flaws of each knight structure the text. In

LR only Frodo as Ring-Bearer is on the quest, and it is in my opinion the reduplication of adjuvants that seriously weakens the structure, in other words one of its weaknesses is due to exaggerating and making explicit an element inherent to or at least often found in the marvellous, but more symbolically (e.g. triplication), and often not even evident at the surface.

Apart from minor adjuvants, who are very numerous (eighteen), Frodo will have no less than eight chief adjuvants (the Grey Company), three of which are other hobbits: Sam Gamjee, his loyal servant and chosen by Gandalf, will be a true adjuvant, without whom Frodo could not have succeeded in his quest. Merry and Pippin merely accompany them, and their nuisance role (which they feel as such) is in fact to split the Company, *so that* separate adventures can be followed. It is true that they are incidentally responsible, through a chance meeting, for the destruction of Saruman by the Ents, and Gandalf is careful to emphasise that this has been their role (book III/chapter 5, p. 127 and p. 131), in answer to Aragorn who complains of the wild-goose chase they have led him on. And Pippin's curiosity when he steals Saruman's crystal ball from Gandalf, gazes into it, screams and faints from the power of the Evil Eye, is again stressed by Gandalf as having revealed to him the communication-system between Saruman and Sauron (book III, chapter 11, p. 255). Indeed Gandalf the great explainer often seems to be explaining the author's intentions by justifying his digressions *a posteriori*, in other words to make explicit the 'motivation' in Genette's sense (see p. 86, note 7). These are the only two incidents in which Merry and Pippin are in any way functional, the second more economically since its function is merely to reveal information, whereas the first (their chance meeting with the Ents), starts long before, with their capture by the Orcs, which causes Aragorn, Legolas and Gimli to trail them (the goose chase Aragorn complains of) and abandon Frodo and Sam, *so that* Frodo and Sam should achieve the quest alone. The later further split of Merry and Pippin does not even receive this kind of over-transparent structural motivation or any motivation at all.

The warrior Boromir's role (apart from simply representing warrior-men in the Grey Company), is more structural, but even more transparent: his function is wholly to introduce dissension in the Company (book II/chapter 10), *so that* it can split, *so that* Frodo and Sam should be alone in the quest, *so that* the adventures may be separated. When that is achieved Boromir is got rid of (dies). The dwarf Gimli and the elf Legolas seem to have no functional role at all except to represent dwarf and elf in the Grey Company.

As for the wizard Gandalf, and Aragorn the man and future king, they curiously duplicate each other. Both lead the Grey Company (often in disagreement). Both are extraordinary fallible, *so that* more adventures are created by their mistakes (see p. 245 below). Both disappear underground for a large chunk of narrative, Gandalf when presumed dead in Moria Mountain (ii/chapter 5, return iii/chapter 5), Aragorn when he follows the Paths of the Dead (v/chapter 2) to reach the coast faster and save the battle of the Pellenor Fields outside Gondor (v/chapter 6). There are also two Elf kingdoms, Rivendell and Lothlorien, each giving rest, food, advice and protective gifts, each creating much delay.

But many more reduplications concern the war subplot, not the main quest, and this war subplot is expanded out of all proportion to the quest (in size, but not in interest, it seems to be the main plot). This expansion produces further reduplications. To mention only a few, Faramir, himself a duplicate of his brother Boromir (but 'good') duplicates, with his riders, Eomer and the Riders of Rohan; two kings have quarrelled with their sons, Theoden and Eomer, Denethor with Faramir, and two hobbits swear an oath of fealty to these kings, Pippin to Denethor, Merry to Theoden. The only difference between the kings is that Theoden recovers from the evil power he was under while Denethor does not. Such parallels can of course poetically structure a narrative, but here they have no functional purpose but delay, and eventually pointless death. Nor are the oaths of fealty functional: it is not Theoden whom Merry saves in battle but his niece Eowyn, and Pippin has to betray Denethor, gone mad, to save his son Faramir. These kings are mere relative illustrations of the evil influence, and they are got rid of. A vast amount of time is wasted in talk, delay, explanation, quarrels and doubts about the route, as in 'real' life, but not, normally and to that extent, in the marvellous. In other words, the mechanisms of duplication and digression inherent to the marvellous are used by Tolkien for expansion in the direction of 'realism', particularly in the war subplot rather than in Frodo's quest, but also in the sections preceding the solitary part of Frodo's quest. And it is the way this is done which I now propose to examine through Hamon's fifteen procedures of realism described in chapter 4, which, it may be remembered, I decided to redistribute under two main heads, the (pedagogic) plethora of information, and the (pedagogic) need for readability, which form the basic contradiction of realistic discourse, so that each affects the other all the time. This redistribution is repeated here for convenience, with the Hamon number in brackets, and I shall also briefly recapitulate the relevant points as I deal with each procedure.

2.1. Plethora of information

(1) *The appeal to memory* (1): ostensibly assuring the coherence and readability of the text but in practice requiring a constant circulation of information about the fiction's past and future, often through a character specific to that purpose.

(2) *Knowledge of the author circulated through substitutes* (6): slices of knowledge, 'index-cards' that create specialist characters and pretext functions.

(3) *Description* (15): exhaustiveness in re-presenting the real within the fiction, and pretext syntagmas and characters as description-openers.

(4) *Redundancy and foreseeability* (7): the programmed act (a character's social sphere and ritualised activities).

(5) *Cyclothymic rhythm of good/bad* (14): a result of 3 (15) and 4 (7), the realistic desire for exhaustiveness producing a need to review each term of any logical opposition.

(6) *Defocalisation of hero* (10): hero important element of readability, but defocalisation to avoid *le romanesque* leads to plethora of information (several heroes, many viewpoints, description-openers, discontinuity, repetition etc.)

2.2. Readability

(1) *Semiological compensation* (5): to make the plethora of information more accessible extra codes (illustrations, diagrams, genealogical trees etc.).

(2) *Psychological motivation of characters (2): the justification for a narrative sequence (post hoc ergo propter hoc).*

(3) *Demodalisation* (9): the neutral, 'transparent' style, window on the world, detonalised and simply assertive. Avoidance of subjective locutions (utterance), emphases, italics, quotations.

(4) *Disambiguation* (11, 12, 13): reduction of ambiguity, effacement of being/seeming opposition, refusal of false clues (the text in a hurry).

(5) *The parallel story* (3): history, geography, etc., references to which function like quotations in a pedagogic discourse, insures the effect of the real while allowing an economy of description (3 (15)). As we shall see however, this 'readability' level will be used for plethora of information in LR.

3. 'Lord of the Rings' and realistic procedures

3.1. The plethora of information

3.1.1.   The appeal to memory (1) requires a constant circulation of information (ancestry, tradition, the family, a childhood traumatism–), flashback, summary, returning obsessions and other means, the text referring to its *déjà-dit* or, inversely, to its own future via prediction, presentiment, project, contract, injunction, warning, desire, a lack to be remedied. There is usually a character who knows the antecedents, warns, and infers, such as the family doctor, the childhood friend. In LR, Bilbo ostensibly performs this role in that he passes on the ring to his nephew Frodo – a device typical of sequels (I/chapter 1). But he is equivalent to a dying father, and rapidly vanishes from the scene, to reappear only in Rivendell as a doddering old hobbit who makes up songs about the past and is writing a history (II/chapter 1), then again on the return journey, when he relegates his task as historian to Frodo (V/chapter 6). The real knower is Gandalf, and I shall return to the manner of his role later (see section 3.1.6. *The parallel story*).

3.1.2. Knowledge of the author circulated through substitutes (6). This as I pointed out is really the same as (1), except for the type of knowledge circulated. Like (1) its ostensible function is readability, since the pedagogic act disguises its utterance for the sake of 'objectivity', so that the author's information is often given to a specialist character (guide, engineer, doctor, painter), who informs a non-specialist. We thus get three pretext-functions: the attentive look, the explanatory word, the technical act. They are pretext-functions in that they rarely play a role in the logical correlation of sequences; they are not part of a vital quest for knowledge, as in the fantastic. Their role is simply to convey information about the world. To this we may bracket:

3.1.3. Description (15), which comes from the same belief that the world is accessible to denomination, a belief that generates a desire for exhaustiveness, while the assumption of the world's discreteness leads to an aesthetic of the discontinuous, a composition in *tableaux*, slices of life, descriptions, details, a sort of synecdochic fragmentation, an impression of mosaic. Description is not of course specific to realistic discourse, but its distribution and function are (see chapter 4 for description-openers and syntagmas). Thus gratuitousness, length and repetition in both information-giving and description seem to be a recurrent feature of realistic discourse rather than of the marvellous.

In Hamon's rigid formulations these ways of circulating information are not all constant features of LR, since Tolkien has invented his world, which is not particularly technological or intellectual: *e.g.* when Aragorn's sword is forged anew there is no 'technical act' or detailed description of the process, which is magical and secret (II/chapter 3, p. 362). There is a kind of 'technical act' when Gandalf tests the ring of Frodo's fire at the beginning of the story (I/chapter 2, p. 80), or when he reads the runes to open up Moria (II/chapter 4, p. 416). But these are brief and wholly functional.

Nevertheless there is such 'knowledge' to be circulated, including magical knowledge, and the means employed are those of realistic discourse. Much of it passes through Gandalf, often by way of explanation to ignorant hobbits (Pippin is curious, Sam is suspicious, Frodo is anxious). Similarly every reappearance of a vanished character is followed by his story, irrelevant to the main quest except to give information about a different part of that invented world. Other information comes directly from the omniscient narrator, either as ostensibly through the eyes of characters, every arrival being followed by a description however urgent the action is (*e.g.*, the description of Minas Tirith when Gandalf arrives with Pippin in V/chapter 1), or frankly as narrator information (*e.g.* historical and other information on Minas Tirith, V/1, or information about the horrible Shelob in Cirith Ungol, her connection with Gollum and with the Evil Power (IV/chapter 8), which has to be followed naively, with 'But nothing of this evil ... did poor Sam know ...' (p. 424). Descriptions of course abound, seen, usually, through a character's eyes (and mood), especially Frodo's.

3.1.4. Redundancy and foreseeability (7), *i.e.*, description of the character's social sphere and of ritualised daily activities, is normally rare in the marvellous (see above), but does occur in LR, though it merges with general circulation of knowledge. Whenever we leave Frodo for the innumerable parallel actions, or even before the split of the Company, when Frodo's task is immediately in question but statically so (in Rivendell), this and other informative procedures of realism bog down the narrative. This occurs, precisely, in the rest-periods, so I shall consider it together with:

3.1.5. Rhythm of cyclothymia (14), each 'bad' phase being succeeded by a 'good' phase. In an adventure-story, this tends to take the form of rest-periods after each terrible adventure: the idyllic rest in Rivendell after the adventures before, at, and after Bree (book II/chapters 1–3, pp. 289–368), the repetitively idyllic rest in Lothlorien after Moria (II/chapters 6–8, pp. 443–91). And it is often in these rest-periods that gratuitous information is given, even when the situation is urgent and dangerous.

The long rest in Rivendell (book II) occupies three chapters (eighty pages) and includes: Frodo's recovery and explanations, the banquet (description), much talk, songs, historical information, nature (description, idyllic), the interminable Council of Elrond, preparations for departure including the sending out of scouts who return with no information, and gifts, counsels, long farewells. At Elrond's Council, the whole history of the ring is given all over again, each member adding his mite and Elrond recapitulating, all this to conclude that Frodo is the one to take the ring to Mount Doom, which we knew from the start. The whole period is a delay (a) for the reader, (b) for the characters: but they feel (magically) that they have been in Rivendell only a few days, though it turns out to have been a much longer period (during which of course the enemy has grown stronger and more informed). Thus we get a curious use of the marvellous (magic time-reduction) for a disjunction of reader and characters: they are spared the boredom experienced by the reader. In fact the function of the feast, the Council, the preparations, the farewells, apart from delay, is ritualistic (7) and cyclothymic (14) on the one hand, and 'realistic' on the other (6, circulation of knowledge, 15, description), with possibly a 'saving' touch of irony as to long councils of war and official behaviour in general (but cp. Barthes on irony, chapter 2, and chapter 14 here for further discussion). Part of the Council's function may also be genuinely recapitulative, for readers who had not understood or forgotten the point of the quest and its background as explained by Gandalf to Frodo at the beginning (see below, over-coding, in *semiological compensation*, under *readability*). The entire Rivendell episode, however, is also part of the mechanism of:

3.1.6. The parallel story (3) which normally belongs not here but under readability (see p. 239): the realistic narrative is hitched to a megastory (history, geography), itself valorised, which doubles and illuminates it, creating expectations on the line of least resistance through a text already known, usually as close as possible to the reader's experience. Exoticism is reduced to the familiar. This gives points of anchorage, allows an economy of description and insures a general effect of the real that transcends any actual decoding since the references are not so much understood as simply recognised as proper names.

In the marvellous, there is usually no such megatext, at most a vague setting (Baghdad, a city, a village), in no specified time. SF usually creates a fictional historico-geographico-sociological megatext but leaves it relatively vague, concentrating on technical marvels.

LR, however, like SF but more so, is particularly interesting in that there is such a megatext, not pre-existent but entirely invented, yet treated with the utmost seriousness and in great detail, thus destroying the element of recognition and hence readability which this feature provides in the realistic novel, and causing on the contrary a plethora of information and the collapse of the referential code (cp. p. 42 and p. 101 above).

That is to say, it is treated *as if* it existed, except that instead of allowing an economy of description and ensuring a general effect of the real, it needs on the contrary to be constantly explained (since it is unfamiliar), either by the omniscient narrator, or by his substitute Gandalf, or other substitutes. Whole societies are created: warrior-men, kings and rulers good and bad, dwarves, elves, wizards, trolls, orcs. Only the hobbits are a point of anchorage in the familiar, and in two directions: that of 'real' village life in England, and that of a genre familiar to English readers of *Winnie the Pooh, Puck of Pook's Hill* etc. (*e.g.*, Bilbo is very Pooh-like, and also makes up songs). The history of these societies is given, in narrator pauses, in songs, or by Gandalf or others, to explain their characteristics as well as the whole world that lies behind the history of the ring. And what cannot somehow be put into the text by these means is collected in long appendices (see *Semiological compensation*, p. 247).

The megatext also creates the ambiguity of Gandalf's role as chief adjuvant and information-giver. When he persuades Frodo to go on his antiquest, he tells him the history and significance of the ring. This information is necessary, not only (1) for the reader (2) to persuade Frodo, but also (3) to reintroduce in advance the evil character Gollum (from whom Bilbo 'won' the ring in H), whose final role in the disposal of the ring Gandalf dimly foresees (naturally), and (4) to establish the theme of pity for Gollum, which will recur often, thus enabling Gollum on each occasion to escape and so fulfill his role. The information is thus quadruply functional. And in several instances Gandalf's information is economically functional in this way, well-timed but mysterious and incomplete enough to keep up the interest, as it should be in any story, whether marvellous or realistic.

But Gandalf is also foolishly fallible in a transparently motivated way, that is, when his adjuvant role is forgotten for that of author-substitute and information-giver. For example, when he leads the Grey Company through the depths of Moria and, already attacked by the horrible Orcs, finds the tomb of Belin and a big book in a hall and starts poring over it, telling his friends the history of Moria and of the dwarves who dug into it (book I/chapter 5, pp. 417–19). This megatextual information is irrelevant to the quest. It does however have the functional purpose of delaying the Company, *so that* the Troll attack can take place, *so that* Gandalf can disappear under the bridge of fire and out of the narrative – temporarily as it turns out – *so that* Aragorn can take over (and be equally fallible), *so that* that Company may eventually split and separate adventures start, *so that* the hero Frodo and his faithful Sam can be isolated. Gandalf's reappearance, much later (II/chapter 5), is the occasion not only for him to hear and comment on the adventures of the Grey Company since he left them (although Aragorn says it would take long, p. 125), but also to relate his adventures (although saying that there is no time to do so, pp. 133ff), also at a moment when action is urgent. Indeed Gandalf's obsession with information and talk often seems to have this sole function of delay and error, in order to provoke further adventures. He is always exclaiming 'why did I delay?' or 'we have already tarried too long', and the reader can but agree. Aragorn is an even more ambiguous adjuvant in that he duplicates Gandalf's tendency to delay and error but without the ostensible motivation of knowledge about the megatext. Indeed Aragorn is perpetually losing his way or choosing the wrong way, and does almost nothing right until his transfigured reappearance to win the battle of Gondor, apparently single-handed, after also disappearing from the narrative to pass through the Paths of the Dead.

Of course, such fallibility is not only the essence of story-telling (although in the marvellous it is the hero, not the adjuvant, who is fallible), but a realistic feature here imported into the marvellous: Aragorn, future king and a kind of Christ-figure, often described after some decision as growing 'tall', is nevertheless 'human'. Gandalf, though a wizard, can only perform minor magic, often with the help of his friends Gwaihir the eagle or Shadowfax the swift horse, and remains limitedly 'human' too, though also growing 'tall' at solemn moments. But in LR, Gandalf's fallibility incarnates the author's, in the form of (a) catastrophic delay through pointless information about the megatext, and (b) endless repetition of the same devices. This seems a serious flaw, showing up the purely reduplicating motivation and combining the weakest features of both realistic discourse (excessive circulation of information) and of the marvellous (accumulation of adventures).

However, it is not only Gandalf's delays that are provoked by the need to convey information about the megatext, but delays in general, either incarnated in the minor characters or unincarnated and straight from the narrator as long chunks of description of this or that world, about which the information given is basically irrelevant to the main quest, over-visibly fulfilling the mere role of *l'effet du réel* and, on the whole, for those reasons, failing to make this or that world 'real'.

3.1.7. Defocalisation of the hero (10). The identity of the hero is an important element of readability and disambiguation. But if the author over-differentiates the hero he risks a deflation of the realistic illusion, thus reintroducing the heroic, the marvellous, the *romanesque*. He therefore uses several *counter-procedures* to level down the text, the chief of which is defocalisation, by constant variation of viewpoint, or by not giving the actantial position and the valued qualities to the same character. Unlike the hero of the marvellous, that of realistic narrative will not cumulate the roles of subject and beneficiary: he may become an object, or a virtual subject, never acceding to the status of real (and glorified) subject, or a beneficiary of negative values (illnesses, false information, bad luck). He can even be 'forgotten' (or can 'forget himself', be lost in thought, in description), hence the discontinuity of his emotional life, made up of euphoric and dysphoric moments.

LR, although belonging to the marvellous, amply illustrates this tendency of realistic discourse. Frodo as Ring-Bearer and quester is 'clearly' the hero, and yet the narrative constantly reduces him, even annihilates him through absence while we follow the tedious adventures of Aragorn, Gandalf, Merry and Pippin (then Merry *or* Pippin), Theoden and all the innumerable others. The point of view is constantly varied after book II (and in a briefer, less drastic way in the first two books), actantial positions and valorised qualities being over-liberally distributed among all these others. Such variations entail more information-giving at every shift, if only to remind the reader where he is.

This defocalisation is partly to render, 'realistically', the full extent and complexity of the war and its diverse fronts, treacherous protagonists and so forth. But it is Aragorn who is 'glorified' at the end of this war (he kneels before Frodo for a moment but Frodo crowns him). Frodo is fifty when he goes on the quest, is wounded early, falls ill when back in the Shire. And it is only much later, after the bathetic post-quest repetition of the war on a miniature scale in the Shire, that Frodo, old and sick, leaves to rejoin Bilbo, Gandalf and the Elf-people (whose end is inevitable after the destruction of the Evil Power, which brings about the passing of the Elf age and the coming of the king, Aragorn). Frodo vanishes with them over the sea, in a poetically described Norse ship-funeral – a kind of anti-glorification. The 'motivation' of the war as military diversion of the enemy away from Frodo is also motivation in Genette's sense (see chapter 4, p. 86, note 7): the realistically necessary defocalisation and actantial reduction of the hero (not found in H) brings about the diversion of the war subplot and the resulting qualitative reduction of the hero. The mechanism of treating the hero prominently but not too prominently belongs to realistic discourse, and its inappropriateness to the marvellous is all the more patent in that narrative interest is sustained only when we rejoin Frodo and his faithful Sam. Yet even they are split by Frodo's apparent death and capture at the end of book IV, so that when (after ten whole chapters of book V), we thankfully return to them, it is Sam we follow until he finds and rescues Frodo. The hero, in fact, is remarkably absent, and the beneficiary of many negative values. Even so, Frodo's and Sam's qualities of homely doggedness, loyalty, human fear, weakness, and courage are far more 'real' to us (in the sense that the realistic novel is made 'real' to us) than the magic powers and supernatural courage, wisdom (etc.) of Gandalf and Aragorn, despite all their 'human' but unconvincing (because transparently motivated) errors and delays. Gandalf and the others are devices, Frodo and Sam are characters ('realistic' ones in that the marvellous must always be anchored in the familiar), who in this sense win out against the magical adjuvants ostensibly belonging to the marvellous but weighed down with mechanisms of realistic discourse, since they are over-transparently used for excessive circulation of information. A paradoxical situation indeed, but not held in the artistic tension that true paradox requires, and this precisely because of the over-realistic over-defocalisation of the hero.

3.2. Readability

In realistic discourse, readability is not only an end in itself (entertainment), not only one of the ways of rendering the textual support of information 'transparent' and of effacing narrative utterance (pedagogic), but also a particular and contradictory aspect of the information-circulation. The sheer amount of information calls for clarity, and various counter-procedures are used to achieve this.

3:2.1. Semiological compensation (5) or *redundancy and over-coding*: if the reader has no access to the cultural code A of the setting, he will have access to a complementary code B, even, in extreme cases, to illustrations (Jules Verne, Crichton), photographs, drawings, diagrams, genealogical trees.

Clearly LR is overcoded in this way, since the megatext, being wholly invented and unfamiliar, has to be constantly explained. Apart from the 'hypertrophic' redundancy in the text itself, the recapitulations and repetitions, there are long appendices, not only on the history and genealogy but on the languages of elves, dwarves, wizards and other powers, together with their philological development, appendices which, though ostensibly given to create belief in the 'reality' of these societies, in fact and even frankly, playfully reflect the author's private professional interest in this particular slice of knowledge, rather than narrative necessity, since all the examples of runic and other messages inside the narrative are both given in the 'original' and 'translated'. Nor are the histories and genealogies in the least necessary to the narrative, but they have given much infantile happiness to the Tolkien clubs and societies, whose members apparently write to each other in Elvish.[2]

Apart from history, a whole megatextual geography is created, so complex and necessarily unknown to the reader that maps are provided, without which he could hardly follow (should he really want to) the numerous references to the points of the compass (especially in the many quarrels or dilemmas about which direction to take), or the numerous references to Bree, Rivendell, Lothlorien, Anduin the Great River, Edora, Minas Tirith, Gondor, Minas Mogul, Mordor, Fangorn, and many other place-names. The scale of the maps, like that of the plot, gets larger in each volume. Indeed the very maps are over-saturated, with ranges, rivers, regions and sites not mentioned in the narrative, though oddly enough they omit some that are, such as Isengard, the stronghold of Saruman and title-subject of a whole chapter (though the river Isen is marked), or the Pellenor battlefield outside Minas Tirith, also figuring as a chapter title.

Since the megatext is not 'already known', it cannot fulfil the readability requirement, but on the contrary, produces a pseudo-exoticism, much of which can be savoured simply as such, rather than tactically understood, except when understanding is vital to the narrative (for instance in the dilemmas about direction). Hence the maps, and of course a great deal of repetition: when we have read Minas Mogul and Mordor many times in the evil context, and Minas Tirith and Gondor many times in the good, as a city and kingdom in danger, to be saved from the enemy and as one possible goal for the Grey Company, we gradually cease to confuse them: as in pedagogic discourse.

3.2.2. The psychological motivation of characters (2) functions as an *a posteriori* justification for the narrative sequences, the *post hoc ergo propter hoc* of narrative. This is certainly more strongly developed in LR than in most tales of the marvellous, including SF, where traditionally at least the psychology of characters is superficial, sufficient only to produce the traitor, the weakling, the tyrant necessary to the plot. In LR it is more developed, not in the sense of profundity or subtlety (as in realistic narrative), but in the sense that it is more dwelt upon than is usual in the marvellous. But its role is much more transparent than in realistic narrative, which goes to considerable lengths to mask the *a posteriori* aspect. Thus the pride and envy of Boromir are necessary to his attempt to get the ring from Frodo and to Frodo's consequent decision to go it alone (and hence to the split of the Grey Company), but is so emphasised as to make the attempt foreseeable. Frodo's non-heroic yet proud and tenacious nature is necessary to the type of struggles he has. Sam's homely wisdom, loyalty and commonsense are necessary to his final role in accompanying and saving Frodo (he is the typical English NCO or otherwise loyal servant). The obviousness belongs to the marvellous, but the insistence to realism. The arbitrariness of character is more evident when features are inconsistent e.g. the fallibility of Gandalf and Aragorn (realism) serves to create the errors and delays that provoke more adventures (marvellous), but is all the more unconvincing in Gandalf in that he so readily uses magic in battles and similar occasions, and unconvincing even in Aragorn who, after all his errors, appears to win the battle of Gondor by his mere presence, transfigured as it were by his passage through the Paths of the Dead.

Other characters belong wholly to the marvellous, that is, they are barely motivated psychologically, if at all. This normally does not weaken the marvellous, which has few and transparently actantial characters. But in a story which borrows from realism the notion of a portrait of society on a large canvas, with many characters, this arbitrariness seriously weakens the interest. The characterial features of Merry and Pippin, though hobbitish, are vaguer than those of Frodo and Sam exactly inasmuch as their role is much less clear and merely part of the enormous machinery of reduplication. Pippin's curiosity, however, is brought in (a) to reveal inadvertently the way the crystal ball of Saruman was used as a communication system with Sauron (functional: belonging to both marvellous and realism, indeed to all narrative); (b) later (on the ride to Minas Tirith) to circulate non-functional mega-textual information through Gandalf's replies to his questions (realism).

The dwarf and elf characteristics of Gimli and Legolas are wholly gratuitous, serving only, in their quarrels and 'impossible' friendship, to illustrate dwarf and elf characteristics. They thus belong (as they should) to the marvellous in their reduplicative role and their lack of psychological motivation, but to realism in their non-function: they are there exactly as a butcher or a clerk or a miner might be there in a realistic novel, as butcher/clerk/miner stereotypes. Indeed their roles are even more merely reduplicative than those of Merry and Pippin – a sword-thrust here, an arrow-shot there, even long sight (all of which could have been given to Gandalf or Aragorn, and even the hobbits have dwarf-made swords). So with other reduplicating characters: Theoden, king of

Rohan, ageing and helpless at Edora because under the evil power, then galvanised into action by Gandalf and henceforth loyal and brave, or Denethor, steward king of Gondor, even more under the evil power and hence useless and even harmful in his folly during the siege of Gondor (so that Faramir can be in mortal peril, so that Pippin can be instrumental in saving him), the whole episode a pointless diversion and delay. Paradoxically, the attempts at the psychology of minor characters such as Faramir, Eomer, Eowyn, Beregond, appear as naive and gratuitous intrusions from the realistic novel, precisely insofar as their roles are part of the reduplicative machinery (see also p. 251).

As for the innumerable elf-adjuvants, they have no 'psychology' beyond infinite goodness and a certain magic power. The only attempt at 'psychology' is the scene of the elven Lady Galadriel's temptation by Frodo's offer of the ring (II/chapter 7, p. 473), but since she is bound by the quest-story and the genre to resist, the scene is gratuitous, indeed the 'temptation' is put into the past in her speech of refusal. We are in the marvellous, where only the hero may carry out the quest and each actant has his assigned role. My objection is that here so many of them have not, or that too many are clustered upon one small role. The elves' role is to send messages, offer rest, cure, magical gifts, solemn welcomes, farewells and counsels (often empty). As so often in tales of good and evil, the good are dull, and the evil, insofar as they are individually incarnated, are the most convincing and even original. Gollum as ambiguous villain/adjuvant is in his creepy-crawly way the most 'naturally' motivated character of the entire trilogy. Indeed it could be said that the three ring-bearers (Gollum who had it, Frodo, and Sam who takes over Frodo's burden when he thinks that Frodo is dead) are the only unmechanically motivated characters in the book. Gollum, however, is what E. M. Forster called a character 'in the flat' (as opposed to 'in the round'), recognised, like Mrs Micawber, by a trick of speech.

Here again then, these three apart, we have the weakest feature of both the realistic and the marvellous combined: in realism, psychology motivates the action and the circulation of information, but often also in itself constitutes the information. Here we also have psychology (though of a simple kind) that motivates the action and the information-circulation (realism), and the gratuitousness of which is in proportion to the reduplicativeness of the roles, i.e. the transparence of the motivations (marvellous).

3.2.3. Demodalisation (9) or *transparent writing*, a strongly detonalised and assertive discourse: no locutions like *seems, as it were, perhaps*, etc., no emphases, italics, quotations, which are the privileged marks of narrator utterance in the fantastic. This also leads to a refusal of euphoric or dysphoric themes such as idyllic places, love-scenes, ecstasies, tear-jerker scenes, spectacular deaths, which belong to the *romanesque*.

Tolkien's discourse is not demodalised in this way, and in this sense belongs to the marvellous. Indeed it is even occasionally embarrassingly modalised, in a way more akin to Victorian melodrama or popular fiction than to the equivalent *romanesque* today, especially in its biblico-epic style for solemn moments, and in its often execrable verse. In addition, there are idyllic scenes (Rivendell, Lothlorien, and others), and sinister ones (Moria, Cirith Ungol, Mount Doom), as well as spectacular deaths (Gandalf's pseudo-death, Boromir's death and boat-burial, Faramir's near-death on the funeral pyre, Denethor's suicide on it, Eowyn's pseudo-death, Frodo's pseudo-death, the final crumbling of Sauron and his evil power, Saruman's death). But since these deaths are mostly those of wholly minor characters of the vast war subplot, or of the totally unincarnated evil power, the reader remains uninvolved. The only exceptions are Gandalf's and Frodo's apparent deaths, which are certainly a kind of shock, though much attenuated by the genre-expectation that neither the chief adjuvant nor the hero can die before the end.

Similarly there are love-scenes, though few, and only among minor characters (Eowyn's love for Aragorn, Faramir's love for Eowyn), which is just as well, for they are a curious mixture: although written in a modalised style (as in the marvellous, when they occur), they are so genteel (puritanical and idealised) that the effect seems muted, as if demodalised (realism). But realism is not usually puritanical and idealised in its love-scenes, and these belong rather to the *romanesque* (e.g. Dickens) or to popular love fiction (sub-romantic pseudo-realism), which adds to the impression they give of being naive intrusions from realistic fiction (see psychological motivation, p. 250). As for Aragorn's final marriage into the elf-line (book VI/chapter 5, p. 310), it is given two lines, and seems to belong wholly to the marvellous, as a mere 'reward' for successful adventures. That is, its demodalisation is beyond that of realism and belongs to the folk-tale aspect of the marvellous in its treatment of love. It is however given a politico-genealogical wrapping (explained of course by Gandalf who counsels this marriage), and in this sense belongs to realism. But it is so completely unmotivated (marvellous), except by these *a posteriori* politico-genealogical considerations, that the reader again is uninvolved, all the more so because it is sprung on him without any hint of an idyll (the lady Arwen merely appeared briefly by her brother Elrond's side at the feast in Rivendell, in ii/chapter 1, so long ago and among so many other elves that the reader has forgotten her existence).

In other words, *romanesque* conventions and slight elements of realism are evident, but the pure marvellous flattens them out, both with its stronger features (modalisation, here misused), and with its weaker features (lack of psychological motivation). What we have then is an unconvincing intrusion of elements belonging to realism in general (true depiction of passions), but rejected by the naturalistic school as *romanesque*. These elements are juxtaposed with and neutralised by the weakest elements of the pure marvellous (accumulation of adventures, transparence of motivation).

3.2.4. Disambiguation (11,12,13). This includes *the reduction of ambiguity* (11), *the effacement of all play with the being/seeming opposition* (12), and *the refusal of false clues (leurres)* or what Hamon also calls *the text in a hurry* (13), that is, the swift explanation of false clues or mystery which may have been introduced for suspense, despite realistic tenets. These are all aspects of the same need for clarity (no guessing games), but the last creates a tension between the slowness and fullness of the information-circulation and the swift explaining away of mystery.

The marvellous does not have the basic ambiguity (natural/supernatural) of the fantastic, and seems to differ also from even the fantastic – marvellous in its degrees of hermeneutic gaps to be filled as we read, and in the swiftness with which these are filled. On the whole the marvellous does not exploit mystery, only narrative suspense, but this is a generalisation. There are even differences within one author. A writer such as Lovecraft, for instance, can present an entire book as a dream from the start (*The Dream-Quest of Unknown Kadath*), although the implication is always that these adventures in time and space represent some lost truth, more real than our reality, mysterious certainly but unquestioned by the reader who bathes as it were in a poetic haze, and is not given a sensation of having to guess or resolve anything. Some of Lovecraft's tales however make a great deal of play with false clues, and the being/seeming opposition. In *The Shuttered Room*, for example, the narrator inherits his grandfather's house and slowly, rationally fighting against the evidence, resolves the mystery that grips it, which in the end must be accepted as one of supernatural horror. It thus belongs to the fantastic–marvellous, but its structure is that of a detective-story (uncanny): story 2 as quest for story 1. A writer such as Vonnegut also varies (indeed some of his stories contain little or no marvellous): *The Sirens of Titan* is a quest by the hero for his own personality, via catastrophic experiences on other planets, and makes considerable play with hermeneutic gaps and the seeming/being opposition, but as we shall see in the next chapter, this play is ironic. A folk-tale may seem to have less mystery and suspense, but it is hard to say how much of this may be due to generic expectation, the listener in fact knowing the tale by heart and taking pleasure, as children do, in the repetition. It is thus difficult to generalise, given the enormous variety.

A long adventure story like LR, however, needs to introduce suspense and mystery and false clues, as well as play with seeming/being – at least during the course of the story since by definition the hero of the marvellous succeeds in his quest.

Yet such mysteries as occur in LR are quickly resolved by explanation, or, when not resolved at once, the resolution is so clearly hinted at that we expect and patiently wait for it, and sure enough it comes. Thus Aragorn is first introduced as the ambiguous Strider, but is ambiguous for no more than a few pages, and his final destiny as king is clearly hinted at throughout. Frodo hears the patter of feet in Moria, soon after identified by Aragorn as Gollum's; Sam sees a log with eyes following them down the river, at once identified as Gollum. Gollum himself retains his ambiguous role to the end, but this was forecast in a general way by Gandalf at the start. Theoden is ambiguous but quickly clarified (toward the 'good'), Denethor is ambiguous but quickly clarified (towards the 'bad'). Boromir's behaviour is foreseeable; and so on. Only the 'death' of Gandalf and the 'death' of Frodo seem genuine false clues but here the rule of the genre commands that neither should die so soon, and when Gandalf reappears all is (unnecessarily) explained, just as Sam learns within twelve pages that Frodo is not dead (II/chapter 10, pp. 432–44). That is to say, in the first case, the delay is due to a change of focus, 'abandoning' the 'dead' person, and not to textual play with the seems/being opposition, while in the second case there is little or no delay.

Thus we have a combination of the *romanesque* and the realistic, but with the swift disambiguation procedures of the realistic, the only exception being due to defocalisation, also a realistic technique.

4. Conclusions

The techniques of realism, when invading the marvellous, have a very curious effect. For they not only weigh down and flatten out the narrative like an iron, they actually change its genre, or come very near to doing so. They do not of course change it into realistic narrative: the presence of the marvellous is too pervasive. Above all, the presence of a wholly invented and wholly unfamiliar (and magical) megatext makes a realistic narrative impossible.

This invented megatext, however, combined with all the realistic techniques described, pushes the narrative into allegory, or very nearly. The realistic text refuses allegory, as it does the *romanesque*, but sometimes, though for different reasons, comes perilously close to it, via symbolism. Tolkien himself has denied any allegorical intention.[3] But whatever his intention, the fictional megatext, technically modelled as it is on the 'real' megatext of realistic fiction, produces allegory, precisely because it can only give 'the effect of the real' by analogy, and the realistic mechanisms encourage the reader to project his megatextual habits onto the fictional megatext, which is in fact pretty close to mid twentieth-century history: an evil power that spreads its evil over neighbouring powers, some of which submit, some of which try to resist. There is a Fifth Column in the shape of Saruman the White (Wizard turned traitor), and a network of Allies (each represented in the Grey Company). There are air attacks and air reconnaissance raids by the huge black Nazguls – singularly ineffective, however, and serving only the rhythm of terror that more often than not turns into bathetic non-event, in the form of an elven-arrow or other easy magic, or a mere flying away after a ghastly shriek. There are spies, and radio-communication in the form of the magic crystal balls, as well as the radar of the Red Evil Eye seeking out the ring as it approaches (again, most ineffectively, otherwise the story would be different, and much shorter). There is a vast war on several fronts, with decoy action to the West, great battles (in which, however, only the heroes do heroic deeds single-handed and Gandalf or Aragorn by their mere appearance terrify the foe away). And so forth.

The megatext in fact, far from allowing an economy of

description, so weighs down the narrative that the reader can even experience the elements of the marvellous as actually interfering with the war-story, cheating as it were. Even at the beginning of the adventures, just before Rivendell (end of book II), when Frodo, already wounded, is carried across the ford on Glorfindel's horse to attack the black Riders, it is a narrative disappointment for the reader, who has just basked in the more realistic and even boy-scoutish adventures at Bree and after, to find that all is solved by a sudden magic waterfall. And so it is with the earlier adventure of the trees and the Barrow Downs, resolved by Tom Bombadil's magic, and with many later adventures. The marvellous and the realistic are not so much blended as bathetically juxtaposed.

As the story advances, or rather ambles in travelogue, stumbles in delays and spreads out in reduplications, it is as if the evil power of the ring that weighs down Frodo with its intolerable burden were paralleled by the (evil?) power of realistic discourse as it weighs down the marvellous. But alas, this power does not make the textual support 'transparent', or its motivations invisible.

10

Titan Plus: the new science fiction (Vonnegut and McElroy)

I should perhaps say at once that in my view there is no 'new' science fiction in the sense of a new wave, a genuine renewal in different ways by many writers. From the fifties onwards, some writers became more 'serious', that is, wrote better, used science more intelligently (adding the human 'sciences'), tried to develop what it had been most accused of lacking: the psychology of character; in other words, moved away from the (degenerated) wonder stories towards the realistic novel. But, with a few exceptions, two of which I shall examine here, there has been little or no formal regeneration, and the resurgence of the pure marvellous, such as we get in Tolkien or, on other planets, in Ursula Le Guin and others, is a sign that the type of 'cognitive' SF described by Suvin has run, if not into a rut, certainly into specific difficulties.

The chief of these, as I have suggested (ch.4, ch. 9), is that of the referential code (Barthes), or the megatext, the parallel story (Hamon), in other words the circulation of information about the world invented, which is unlike the world we already know in the realistic novel where the referential code is one of recognition, a code much inflated in the classic realist novel of the nineteenth century (Barthes, Hamon). We have seen how clumsily it operates in Tolkien, and I have mentioned similar problems for SF in chapter 4. This problem does not seem to have been resolved. We continue to get clumsily juxtaposed narrator-intervention, or knowledgeable characters giving long explanations to innocent visitors, or even two knowledgeable visitors explaining things to each other, or innocent visitors looking up the whole history of a planet or of the universe in the planetary library (see ch. 4, p. 101).

An interesting example is Stanislaw Lem, a fairly recent writer and one of the best, who has steadily moved from SF to the philosophic essay in SF form. In *The Star Diaries* (1971, trans. 1976, but see below), there is a hilarious story, ('The Twentieth Voyage')

256

of Ichon Tichy (the hero) as time-traveller from the twenty-seventh century, who comes to send the 'contemporary' (twenty-third century) Tichy to another planet to direct their earth-history remodelling programme. Incredible mistakes are made, and each time Tichy exiles the bungling engineer to a century on earth, thus accounting for Plato, Aristotle, da Vinci, Spinoza, Napoleon and other geniuses. The knowledge, the wit, the sheer invention, are immensely entertaining, but the narrative is an episodic accumulation of one experiment after another. Alternative history crushes out 'story', the 'cognitive' aspect (Suvin) demolishes, not the 'fiction' of the pseudo-history, but the fiction of the adventure (Tichy's), except for the amusing double-identity at the beginning and end.

More telling is 'The Twenty-First Voyage', where Tichy is sequestered underground among courteous robot-monks, and spends his entire time, only concessionally interrupted by an incident, either reading or listening to a whole history of alternative theology, which had to adapt to newer and newer conditions as creatures could create or alter themselves at will, as differences between machines and natural creatures vanished, as conversions and anti-conversions could be induced by button-pushing 'instant disputation', and so forth. It is another alternative history, of theology, and naturally benefits immensely from the distancing afforded by SF. It is as amusing, as satirical, as thoughtful and at times as profound as Swift. But there is no story. It is basically an essay, which could have been written *as* an essay with hypothetical examples from the future. No real use is made of the fiction form. It is what Amis has called 'the idea as hero', taken to its extreme.

Lem varies a good deal in respect to this problem, which is not a problem for him: according to a translator's note to *The Star Diaries* (pp. 320–3), Lem wrote the journeys from 1964 to 1971, and their numbering conceals their true chronology. The twentieth and twenty-first came last, and he has moved purposefully 'from playful anecdote to pointed satire to outright philosophy ... gradually the boundary between fiction and non-fiction blurred, so that by the '70s Lem was – and still is – producing works which cannot easily be classified as either ... Much to the discomfort of his critics, and to the disappointment of many of his fans, who have pleaded "Write us more things like *Solaris*", Lem is not content to repeat his previous successes.'

That of course is his choice. But as we shall see the philosophical point about the whole history of mankind being pointlessly manipulated from outer space is made much more lightly and economically by Vonnegut, and as part of the story. And Lem himself is extremely varied. *Memoirs Found in a Bathtub* (1971a) is the Kafkaesque quest of a man lost in a future pentagon, and there is no circulation of information about the world, since on the contrary the utter bafflement has to be preserved.

But, more generally, the problem has existed ever since Olaf Stapledon's *Last and First Men* (1931), which is an alternative history of mankind from the First World War to about two million years hence, written *as* history, in the tone and terminology of the historian (cp. ch. 4 n. 2). Of course we all know by now that the writing of history cannot be objective, but when we read history the referential code is very powerful. When all that basic reference disappears, the fun of alternative history disappears, unless it can be integrated into a fiction, as in Philip K. Dick's *The Man in the High Castle* (1962).

I shall now discuss two novels which seem to me not only to avoid this problem but to reinvigorate SF.

1. Kurt Vonnegut: 'The Sirens of Titan'

Vonnegut's *The Sirens of Titan* (1959), like Tolkien's *Lord of the Rings*, but not in the same way, is an anti-quest. The hero, Constant Malachi, has everything he wants, a fabulous fortune and business empire (inherited), good looks, health, and no desire to be sent into space. He is tricked into it, his fortune lost. On Mars he has his memory effaced, and therefore his old personality and even his name, but slowly reacquires a certain minimal independence of mind. His quest is not sought for, but forced upon him, and, thus denuded, all he will seek for, on Mars and later, is his friend Stony Stevenson and the love of the family he is told he has founded. He will only get a semblance of the latter, and a final illusion of the former, at the moment of death.

The Sirens of Titan is also an anti-folktale, for instead of the false hero being exposed and punished and the hero being rewarded, Malachi Constant is his own false hero: as Unk, the mindless soldier on Mars who mindlessly murders his best friend Stony Stevenson on orders from the antennae in his brain, and as the weary Space Traveller who returns to Earth and to a hero's welcome, only to be revealed to himself and to the crowd, by Winston Niles Rumfoord who is the brain behind the entire enterprise, as in fact Constant

Malachi, a symbol of all that the new post-Martian-war society abhors. He is asked if he has one good thing he can say for himself, and when he answers at last that yes, he had a friend, Stony Stevenson, Rumfoord tells him that Stony is dead, and that he, Unk, murdered him. He is thus punished, in both identities, officially as Malachi, personally as Unk.

Tolkien's Frodo is also a reluctant hero, who has a treasure, the ring, but his quest is to get rid of it, whereas Malachi loses his fortune as a way of getting him off on his quest. Frodo eventually returns to peace and home-comforts, Malachi ends up solitary on Titan, a satellite of Saturn, in the semblance of family life with Bee, his wife, and Chrono, his son, who refuses to have anything to do with them and lives wildly in the hills. Frodo gains 'wisdom' (of an easy kind), and is eventually transfigured in a mystical death-journey. Malachi's death journey is towards Earth, with Salo, the robot-messenger from Tralfamadore, who like so many robots, is the only character with human feeling, and in the end replaces Stony Stevenson, the 'friend' Malachi had unwittingly murdered on Mars. But Malachi does not even known that Salo is such a friend, for Salo hypnotises him into believing he is with Stony Stevenson. Frodo's anti-quest is simply a mere thematic inversion, Malachi's is somewhat more complex. But how heavily serious and cumbersome is the realistic machinery Tolkien puts in motion to create this simple anti-quest, compared to Vonnegut's brevity and light touch.

For *The Sirens of Titan* is a science fiction story which turns upside down, by using them ironically, all the conventions not only of science fiction but of the realistic novel. That is, it turns upside down the thematic conventions of science fiction and the technical conventions of the realistic novel shared by science fiction.

The thematic conventions of science fiction are inverted from the start, in an introductory page postdating the narrative instance to a mere century or so after our own time. ('Everyone now knows how to find the meaning of life within himself/But mankind wasn't always so lucky' – first two sentences, p. 7); and dating the events to 'less than a century ago' (p. 7), which turns out to be: 'The following is a true story from the Nightmare Ages ... between the Second World War and the Third Great Depression' (last sentence of introduction, p. 8), i.e. almost contemporary to the reader's time, when 'Gimcrack religions were big business' (p. 7). This distancing, so brief and economical, whereby our own time or soon after is seen by an alien eye, is more typical of the eighteenth-century *roman philosophique* than it is of much traditional science fiction, which tends either proudly to avoid all moral satire or on the contrary to lean heavily on continuous indirect allegory. Utopia ('Everyone now knows how to find the meaning of life within himself') is thus dismissed as if it were a mere technical discovery, another gadget, and placed a mere century hence. The real subject is now (or soon after).

Similarly space travel is treated as an ignorant fad, implicitly opposed, as unconscious projection, to 'the meaning of life within oneself'.

Mankind flung its advance agents ever outward, ever outward. Eventually it flung them out into space, into the colorless, tasteless, weightless sea of outwardness without end.
It flung them like stones. (p. 7)

For within the story space exploration has been suspended by the governments of the earth after the discovery of 'the chrono-synclastic infundibula' (p. 13) into one of which Winston Niles Rumfoord, 'a member of the one true American class' (p. 26) had run his private spaceship and thus become dematerialised, existing (with his dog Kazak) only as wave-phenomena and materialising only every fifty-nine days on his large estate in Newport, Rhode Island.

Rumfoord thus lives out of time and knows the future. But his powers are actually limited for although he appears to organise the entire plot, he turns out to be in fact used by the machine-inhabitants of the distant planet Tralfamadore. He is only 'locally' (i.e. for Earth, Mars, Mercury, Titan) right in his prophecies: Malachi does, as he foretells, go to Mars, then to Mercury, then back to Earth, then to Titan (where Rumfoord says at the beginning that he 'has met' him, though Malachi has never been there or heard of it), he does 'mate' with Rumfoord's wife Beatrice and does have a son called Chrono, who does own a 'good luck piece' (found by chance), which does turn out to be extremely important. Rumfoord knows the future both because he organises the events and because he lives out of time (he cannot for instance 'organise' Chrono's finding of the good luck piece), but of course chiefly the latter, since he organises the events in the sure knowledge that they have happened that way. But the real power belongs to Tralfamadore, and Rumfoord turns out, but only towards the end, to have been both aware and not aware of his instrumentality. For Rumfoord, when he is not a wave-phenomenon or a brief materialisation on Earth, is permanently materialised on Titan ('For reasons as yet mysterious, the spirals of Rumfoord, Kazak, and Titan, coincided exactly', in a Taj Mahal palace 'built by Martian labor' (p. 267) and with the help of Salo, the machine-messenger from Tralfamadore. As Rumfoord says to Malachi, Beatrice and Salo on Titan, when he is about to be 'taking [his] leave of the Solar System':

'There is something you should know about life in the Solar System', he said. 'Being chrono-synclastic infundibulated, I've known about it all along. It is, none the less, such a sickening thing that I've thought about it as little as possible.

'The sickening thing is this:

'*Everything that every Earthling has ever done has been warped by creatures on a planet one-hundred-and-fifty thousand light years away.* The name of the planet is Tralfamadore.

'How the Tralfamadorians controlled us, I don't know. But I know to what end they controlled us. *They controlled us in such a way as to make us deliver a replacement part to a Tralfamadorian messenger who was grounded right here on Titan.*' (pp. 296–7, author's italics.)

Rumfoord knows and does not know: he knows the fact but prefers to forget it; and he knows the end but not the means. Tralfamadore, perhaps too obviously, represents pointless Providence, that is, both God and Satan, both the addresser and the opposant in a Greimas scheme, or, in Propp's, both the king who (through Rumfoord) or Destiny who (through the king, Rumfoord), dispatches the hero; and, as Destiny also, the opposant. Tralfamadore is absent, and uses everyone, even Salo, its messenger, whose spaceship energy is UWTB or the Universal Will to Become, with which he has helped Rumfoord organise the Martian invasion of Earth. Salo has been stuck on Titan for millions of years, waiting for the spare part. Meanwhile (and this information is given towards the end by the omniscient narrator, not via Rumfoord) Tralfamadore sends him many messages to say that the spare part is on the way, these messages being in the form of earthly monuments such as Stonehenge, the Wall of China or the Golden House of Nero. Thus all the achievements of man are merely part of Tralfamadore's plan to rescue its messenger. But what is the message that Salo bears from Tralfamadore to the far end of the Universe? He must on no account open it. Taunted by Rumfoord to do so, in the name of the friendship Salo begs from him (the machine having acquired feelings), he does so, but after Rumfoord has been expelled from the Solar System. The message is one dot, which in Tralfamadorian means 'Greetings'. Or, in Rosset's terms, reality is meaningless, 'idiotic': *id iota*.

The invasion from Mars, unlike that of Wells, is made by men, recruited from Earth by Rumfoord and his agents, and trained into a vast army of soldiers, who learn to live on oxygen 'goofballs', swallowed, and whose memories are wiped out. Electrodes placed in their brains cause unbearable pain whenever an independent thought or memory occurs. The invasion is intended and planned to be a fiasco, so that Rumfoord can create his new religion of 'God the Utterly Indifferent', in which Constant Malachi (his name means 'faithful messenger'), at last brought back from Mars via Mercury, unwittingly plays his planned messianic role of The Lonely Space Wanderer, only to be reviled and revealed as in fact Constant Malachi, the original of the Malachi dolls sold as evil fetiches, and to be sent off into exile on Titan, with his unloving and now unloved and ugly wife Beatrice and his unloving delinquent son Chrono, who has the spare part in the form of his good-luck piece.

Thus the entire space-and-power-structure of science fiction, and all its idealistic utopian/anti-utopian futurology, are negated and turned into meaningless absurdity. The absurd as such is not of course particularly new, and Vonnegut's work is often marred by sentimentality and a certain facility, but his incorporation of the absurd into science fiction (which often takes itself very seriously), creates a happy blend of 'space-opera' comics (which do not) and of the Kafkaesque tradition which has evolved, through Beckett, Borges and others, into a kind of resolute humour in the face of despair, as the dominant expression of our time.

The conventions of realistic fiction are also treated ironically. As in the later work of Gass, Brautigan, and other 'Postmodernists', but on the whole more obviously, there is a type of stylisation which consists in taking the clichés of various models and using them humorously as a kind of wink to the reader.[1] Models can be of many kinds – the idyllic, the heroicomic, etc., but here the model is chiefly types of narration that have become petrified formulae. These are not always the exact formulae examined by Hamon in relation to late nineteenth-century realism, but the formulae of all realistic fiction. For instance the author's voice, which for Hamon is passed through substitutes, is here frankly an omniscient narrator, as in Balzac and other earlier realistic writers. It will therefore be useful to run through Hamon's procedures but with other, more general references (e.g. Genette, Barthes), and see what happens to them in Vonnegut.

There is, first of all, no 'plethora' of information, only the information strictly necessary to the plot: with a few jocular exceptions, all is done in favour of 'readability'.

The appeal to memory for instance (about the past and future) is, in realistic discourse, ostensibly for coherence and readability, but in practice clogs the text, through flashback, warning and prophecy etc., usually by means of a specific character created for the purpose. Obviously Rumfoord fulfils this role, as does Gandalf in Tolkien, but unlike Gandalf the obsessive explainer, Rumfoord is excessively brief, mysterious even, and unlike the doctor, childhood friend (etc.) of realistic fiction, Rumfoord is the very organiser of the plot. The flashback and forward information is also, and mostly, taken over by the omniscient narrator, who can shift his viewpoint freely.

This omniscient voice is heard from the start, not only in the introductory page, but in the first words of the narrative: 'There was a crowd' (p. 8). The viewpoint is external and we are told why the crowd gathered: for the materialisation, said to be about to occur. We are told that 'the crowd wasn't going to get to see the materialization', and why: 'The materialization was strictly a private affair on private property', followed by narrator-comment: 'The materialization was going to take place, like a modern, civilized hanging, within high, blank, guarded walls' (p. 8). The viewpoint then shifts momentarily to the crowd: 'The crowd knew it wasn't going to see anything, yet its members found pleasure in being near, in staring at the blank walls and imagining what was happening inside' (pp. 8–9). The materialisation in fact is de-mystified, presented as an unusual but by now routine phenomenon, just like a hanging. The viewpoint then widens, as in realistic fiction (or 'metonymic' films with close-up/panoramic shots), to a much wider perspective, but this too is treated jocularly, as a child's inscription on a schoolbook: 'The town was Newport, Rhode Island, U.S.A., Earth, Solar System, Milky Way. The walls were those of the Rumfoord estate' (p. 9). The crowd scene ends (*foreseeability*) with the description of two people in the crowd, (the pointless detail, for *l'effet du réel*, since the two people are irrelevant to the plot and never return), absurdly detailed, but also absurdly brief enough to function like a wink to the reader.

Later we get the classic pretence of ignorance which so often introduces a new character in the classical realistic novel (see Genette 1972, external focalisation, p. 208) and of course in films: 'A slender man in the clothes of an Edwardian dandy got out of the limousine and showed a paper to the policeman guarding the door' (p. 11). This ignorance is immediately contradicted: 'He was disguised by dark glasses and a false beard.' And a few sentences later:

The man who had let himself in was the first person ever invited by Mrs Rumfoord to a materialization. He was not a great scientist. He was not even well-educated. He had been thrown out of the University of Virginia in the middle of his freshman year. He was Malachi Constant of Hollywood, California, the richest American – and a notorious rakehell. (p. 11)

And a few pages later: 'His name meant *faithful messenger*' (p. 17). Or again, about a pointless detail (Barthes's *L'effet du réel*): 'Constant was following a damp green path the width of a lawn mower – what was in fact the swath of a lawn mower' (p. 16). And another flagrant contradiction of omniscience: 'He climbed from bowl to bowl [of a fountain], *intending* .... What Constant had in mind, *presumably*, was a first-class message from God or someone equally distinguished' (p. 17, my italics).

The conventions of omniscience are thus treated ironically, either through contradiction or through the classic pluperfect flashback, but giving pointless information (e.g. Malachi's expulsion from the University of Virginia is irrelevant both to the plot and to characterisation, he could have become a rich playboy without it). Similarly we are given zany details about Beatrice Rumfoord's title for the book of poems she 'had' published, when all that matters (if at all) later is that she wrote a poem on Mars; whereas Malachi, as Unk, finds, much more dramatically and thanks to the dying words of Stony Stevenson, a long letter, apparently from Stony, in which all apprehended facts and doubts were secretly recorded in an attempt to regain memory, and the letter turns out to be signed Unk. Beatrice's poetic gift is thus a pure 'technical' motivation, which enables Rumfoord to say: 'And it is perhaps food for thought ... that this supremely frustrated man was the only Martian to write a philosophy, and that this supremely self-frustrating woman was the only Martian to write a poem' (p. 163).

Omniscience is also thoroughly underlined by narrator interference, so long considered, by the post-Jamesian critics, as unacceptable (though Booth and later Genette have shown that this criterion is not and cannot be absolute), e.g.:

It is worth stopping the narrative at this point to say that this cock-and-bull story told to Beatrice is one of the few known instances of Winston Niles Rumfoord's having told a lie. (p. 58)

'Known' by whom? By the omniscient narrator. But he adopts the tone of the historian ('one of the few known instances'), which ridicules the detail, and he does so as a means of giving information about the plot direct to the reader.

The first chapters are constant shifts, as soon as a scene gets interesting, between the viewpoint omnisciently given in indirect style, of Constant, Rumfoord and Beatrice (*defocalisation of hero*), as well as omnisciently given extracts from or accounts of pseudo-documents: *A Child's Encyclopaedia of Wonders and Things to Do* for the description of chrono-synclastic infundibula (*the parallel story*, but of course, here imaginary); a book called *The American Philosopher Kings*, by a certain Waltham Kittredge; for an analysis of Rumfoord's class (*author's knowledge circulated through substitutes*): here the 'index-card' of author's knowledge is disguised, not by a character-filter, but by an article, i.e. it *is* the index-card, and the author of the article, though fictive, plays no other role in the fiction. Knowledge of the world is later given more traditionally through dramatised scenes (the revivalist meeting against space travel, ch. 1; the President's speech, ch. 2), but these are of course comical not 'serious' treatments, and again, extremely brief. Similarly in chapter 3 knowledge of the world is given through, first a highly stylised treatment of the big business boss visiting his manager in the office (*redundancy and foreseeability*, but in fact unforeseeable because zany, besides, Constant is wholly ignorant of business, and ruined); and secondly through an equally stylised flashback ('A history of Magnum Opus, Inc., is perhaps in order at this point' (p. 71) about Constant's father and the origin of the fortune (zany), for it was acquired 'without genius and without spies':

This was Noel Constant's system:
He took the Gideon Bible that was in his room [he lived permanently in Room 223 of Wilburhampton Hotel], and he started with the first sentence in Genesis.
The first sentence in Genesis, as some people may know, is: 'In the beginning God created the heaven and the earth.' Noel Constant wrote the sentence in capital letters, put periods between the letters, divided the letters in pairs ... then he looked for corporations with those initials, and bought shares in them ... His very first investment was International Nitrate. After that came Trowbridge Helicopter, Electra Bakeries [etc.] (pp. 73–4)

Chapter 4 shifts to Mars and a character called Unk, Soldier in the Martian army (apparent *defocalisation of hero*). But the reader is almost at once given a wink, through a brief take-off of the classical portrait (*description/semic code*): 'Unk was forty years old. Unk was a well-made man – a light heavy-weight, dark-skinned, with poet's lips, with soft brown eyes in the shaded caves of a Cro-Magnon brow-ridge. Incipient baldness had isolated a dramatic scalplock' (p. 98), which repeats word for word (with the 'Cro-Magnon brow-ridge' as unmissable signal in case we miss it), the earlier description of Constant (p. 17), except that there the age was thirty-one and came at the end of the description. Similarly Rumfoord on Mars tells Unk his own story as Constant Malachi, in an anonymous but transparent allegory that only Unk does not grasp, and even this fact is told: 'he hadn't caught on that the woman on Earth in Rumfoord's story was Bee, was his own mate' (p. 164), just as later the pretended ignorance of the omniscient narrator when Unk returns to Earth as the Lonely Space Wanderer ('A seeming wild man stood in the churchyard [description ...]') is at once contradicted: 'The man was Unk' (p. 217).

This play with narrative models continues throughout. The Martian invasion (the imagined *parallel story*) is elided and given afterwards in flashback summary, not directly from the omniscient narrator's knowledge but by the narrator through Rumfoord's (Wellsian) *Pocket History of Mars*, itself absurdly telegraphic, and introduced thus, and with the same fusion of historical and fictional figures (treated on the same level), that we find in realistic fiction (*the parallel story* and the *referential code*):

It has been said that Earthling civilization, so far, has created ten thousand wars, but only three intelligent commentaries on war – the commentaries of Thucydides, of Julius Caesar and of Winston Niles Rumfoord.

Winston Niles Rumfoord chose 75,000 words so well for his *Pocket History of Mars* that nothing remains to be said, or to be said better, about the war between Earth and Mars ...

The usual course for such a discomfited historian is to describe the war in the barest, flattest, most telegraphic terms, and to recommend that the reader go at once to Rumfoord's masterpiece.

Such a course is followed here. (pp. 165–6)

All Vonnegut's chapters are subheaded with exergual quotations from fictitious works, often by Rumfoord or by minor characters such as the Reverend C. Horner Redwine (who expects and finds the Lonely Space Wanderer), or by fictitious authors who play no role in the narrative. Both the parallel story and the author's moral comments are thus given through a transgression of narrative levels, characters and author changing places (See ch. 12, p. 333 above). For the role of exergues (from Greek ez-ergon, or *hors d'oeuvre* in its literal sense, i.e. extratextual) is the author's appeal to authorities outside the text, not inside the fiction. Certainly there is not the plethora of *semiological compensation* ('readability') we find in Tolkien's maps and appendices and long Gandalfian explanations, and the author's comments (referential code), though they also occur in the text, but brief and comical, are here given the feel of transgressed levels, the author filtering them through a character but in a place usually reserved to the author (chapter headings and subheading quotations), in intertextuality, here self-reflected back into the fictional text. This functions *also* as semiological compensation, but comically. Similarly the whole story of Salo is given directly by the narrator, in a brief summary that ludicrously contrasts with the millions of years invoked. No mystery is allowed to subsist (*disambiguation*) without swift and even arch but brief narrator explanation, and the psychological motivation of characters is similarly transparent, sometimes even in italics (e.g. p. 247). Only occasionally is information filtered through the characters, as in Rumfoord's (unnecessary) allegory of Constant's life, or in his brief dying explanations, or when, just as we are wondering how Unk manages to escape the pain in his antennae, which comes from Boaz's control-box, Unk tells him post-factum that he had emptied it of its contents and filled it with toilet-paper (p. 178).

The narrative model in fact hovers between the realistic novel and the children's story. Nothing remains of Hamon's fifteen procedures (that is, they are all there, but shrunk in the service of readability, all turned upside down by ironic treatment), except the *cyclothymic rhythm* with its fragmentation, but this too is, on the one hand and at a more general level part of any story and, on the other, also fundamentally transformed since Malachi's fate goes from good (outwardly fortunate) to bad to worse, and the peace he finds in the end is illusory.

There remains *demodalisation*. In a sense the writing is demodalised in that all 'grand style' is avoided (as it is not in Tolkien), the syntax and vocabulary are childishly easy to read. But of course, technically, as I have shown, there is a high degree of stylisation in the parody of and play with narrative models. The effect of this stylisation is to draw the attention to the signifiers over and above the signifieds, to the text over and above the supposed referent. I say 'over and above', not 'rather than', for its transparency does not, as in in 'modernist' experiments (Joyce, Woolf, etc.) obscure or ambiguate the signified. On the contrary, there is a clear plot, easily followed, clearer than in many science fiction stories with their scientific paraphernalia. Four genres are thus blended in light-touch irony: science fiction, the realistic novel, the children's story, the marvellous (but as anti-quest).

Vonnegut's book is by no means his most original, nor is his work in general as subtle as that of other 'Postmodernists'. But I have chosen it here, partly because it is one of the earliest (1959), apart from Barth, so that it forms a useful transition, with McElroy, to the next chapter; partly because it is science fiction, which is my topic here; and partly because it makes such a startling contrast with McElroy's *Plus* (1976).

2. Joseph McElroy: *Plus*

2.1. *Cognition*

Plus starts much more mysteriously with two exophoric pronouns, *i.e.* pronouns without preceding co-referents (*he/it*):

He found it all around. It opened and was close. He felt it was himself, but felt it was more.

It nipped open from outside in and from inside out. Imp Plus found it all around. He was Imp Plus, and this was not the start. (p. 3)

The first pronoun *he* is thus soon identified by equivalence (He found it all around/Imp Plus found it all around), and then by equation (He was Imp Plus), though we do not know 'who speaks', the narrator or Imp Plus. And later 'he' questions the identification: 'He had many aims. He?' (p. 6). But *it* remains mysterious, except that 'it was more', and 'this [it?] was not the start'.

This 'more' will recur throughout, representing both the title (*Plus*) and the story of growth. The 'it' *is* the growth, the 'more', though this is never said explicitly, but implied more and more clearly. The first chapter ends with the same sentence: 'And what there was more of was not only glucose./ There was more all round' (p. 12). The second chapter opens: 'More where?/In the light. In the units of it which found their place in Imp Plus' (p. 13).

From that opening syntactic equivalence and that equation there *appears* to be an outside narrator commenting on Imp Plus, but we soon realise that the narrative is told throughout (except for dialogue with Earth, which is given in capitals) in both indirect and free indirect discourse from inside Imp Plus's mind (and mind is the word, since Imp Plus is a human brain in a capsule on orbit in space), as he painfully tries to observe, to think, to recollect. The reason, in fact, for the reader's feeling of narrator-presence is the constant use of the name, *Imp Plus*, as in indirect discourse, but avoided on the whole in free indirect discourse, except initially and for occasional reminders if the free indirect discourse goes on for a long time, or on the contrary is interrupted then taken up again. Free indirect discourse, we may remember, is a *mixed* discourse, the narrator's voice still felt in the character's speech or thought, chiefly through tense and the third person. Here it is felt in the same sense, but more so for the repetition of the name. The repetition however, is precisely part of Imp Plus's constant struggle for identity. But what a highly original use of free indirect discourse, compared to the usual and now stereotyped use of it for information-giving through the character's thoughts, doubts and dilemmas about other characters, the world, and his own emotions and judgments of that world.

The entire first chapter is a variation on types of apprehension, although we do not know as yet what Imp Plus is trying to apprehend (or what Imp Plus is), at first in ultra simple forms (my italics): finding and feeling (he *found*/he *felt*); cognition and memory: 'Imp Plus *knew* there was no skull' (p. 3). 'Imp Plus *remembered* there was no skull. Yet *knew* there was no need to be *thinking* this' (p. 3). 'Imp Plus *remembered* having *prepared to remember*' (p. 4). 'Some of what he had *meant* to *remember* he *did not* for a while. He *recalled* stalks' (p. 5). 'A sharp drop. And through this Imp Plus *thought*: or was suddenly *looking back at having thought*' (p. 6). 'The impulses asked for a galvanometer reading – quantum yield of light radiation – which Imp Plus knew but also now for the first time did not' (p. 6). Seeing: 'Imp Plus knew he had no eyes. Yet Imp Plus *saw*. Or *persisted in seeing*' (p. 3). 'He recalled stalks. They were long and he *did not see* any around' (p. 5). 'Yet as for sockets, Imp Plus knew there were no sockets, for there *happened into the head* of Imp Plus *the picture* of a man' (p. 4). Wanting: 'There had been another lifting and he had *wanted* it ... He *did not want* to go back to it' (p. 3). Observation, identification and judgment, though in the form of existential statements, not of verbs linked to Imp Plus: '*There was* a lifting all around ... This lifting *was good* ... that lifting *had not been good* . . . But this new lifting *was good*' (p. 3). '*There was* a brightness. *It was* more outside than inside. *It was* also everywhere' (p. 3). 'There were birds around, and they were still as shadows' (p. 3).

Very soon, but more slowly, comes the ability to question, to deny, to make logical links, to question questions: 'Imp Plus did not have sockets, for if there were sockets where would they have been? There was no skull' (p. 3). 'Now what were the shadows if not the figures of birds?' (p. 5). 'If it was by sprouts that Imp Plus persisted in seeing without eyes, then there were optic stalks. Imp Plus must have those – If not optic stalks, what?/Were such questions travelling in answer to the impulses? /Negative, negative' (p. 5). 'From the message pulses through this change he knew his loss was real. His loss of all but a fraction./All but a fraction of what?/Imp Plus had lost the knowledge of what had been lost' (pp. 5–6).

All these occurrences, as we can see, are constantly transformed not only by denial and doubt, but by awareness of identity of the 'it', the 'all around', with himself: 'But there was a brightness, and it folded. Or Imp Plus folded it' (p. 4). 'The brightness packed around him. A part of the brightness became him./ The brightness of the Sun.' (p. 5). 'What came to Imp Plus amid the brightness was that some of him was left./So some of the gradients were Imp Plus./Which was why he could fall into himself' (p. 6). 'Then to Imp Plus came his own answer. From himself but also from the Sun. But also from Earth which seemed equally far away' (p. 19). 'Imp Plus knew that the more that was all around and was from him was growing from his brain' (p. 79).

The words pour on, since no thinking can exist without formulation, yet throughout there is a parallel convention that Imp Plus is not using words but impulses (and the play on Imp Plus/Impulse is constantly stressed by close contiguity in the first chapter, though the word *impulse* becomes less and less frequent later, reduced to *pulse* then disappearing almost entirely). From the start Imp Plus is aware of words as words, but seems to know them only as he captures them through impulses, sometimes without their meaning (author's italics): 'Sockets was a word' (p. 3) 'Imp Plus remembered having prepared to remember. And the word *vegetable*. It was not a man' (p. 4). 'Imp Plus knew the word *word* and the word *idea*, but not what one was' (4). 'Imp Plus had the word *operation*' (p. 6). 'He heard the word *hear*. It was direct from the impulses, or it was by his coming between' (p. 6), 'and he recalled arriving here, and thought that soon here for the first time sleep

would occur, which meant waking too. He repeated *here*, for there
was something in it./Here' (p. 7). 'Imp Plus recalled years but not
what one was. Or when' (p. 8). 'Holes of motion, holes of light in a
lattice he knew on sight but had not seen before. He did not know
lattice' (p. 13). '*Imp* was a word. So was *Plus* [this after an exchange
in capital letters with Earth, IMP PLUS CHECK GLUCOSE LEVEL etc., to
which he partially answers]. On the Concentration Loop Imp Plus
had answered messages from Earth that used the words *Imp Plus*.
Imp Plus could talk./IMP PLUS TO GROUND: ARE SPROUTS FROM OPTIC
STALKS?/But from inside somewhere and not from Earth came an
answer he had not requested in so many words: IMP was
International Monitoring Platform. The answer came from inside.
From Imp Plus. Not from Earth' (pp. 10–11).

Sometimes Earth does not understand a word used by Imp Plus
in a direct message: 'IMP PLUS DO YOU READ? DO YOU READ? REPEAT
WHAT IS SPROUTS?' (p. 11). More often however Earth picks up a
word when not in direct communication, a word used by Imp Plus
in his thoughts, but Imp Plus either does not understand or ignores
the question: 'Until the wings near three times the body became
again *shearwater*; and a new transmission said, CAP COM TO IMP PLUS
SAY AGAIN IMP PLUS SAY AGAIN WATER WHAT WATER?' (p. 14).

The shadows on the walls were more. Not larger, not exactly smaller. But
more. Like a tree grown out of birds ... and a bird with wingspread three
times the rest of it seen once on Earth one late spring, seen by someone who
stood outside a car.
Imp Plus had not prepared to remember these.
And now desired only to obey his Operation TL frequency and answer
Earth's transmissions.
SAY AGAIN IMP PLUS. WHAT SHADOWS? CHECK DUAL ATTITUDE
STABILIZER. WE READ NO CHANGE. CHECK ATTITUDE STABILIZER. IF YOU
HAVE CHANGED ATTITUDE YOU MAY BE GETTING SHADOWS. But Imp Plus
had not said *shadows* to Ground.
The answer was that Imp Plus was able to think in transmission. (p. 11)

This game continues throughout, creating a double consciousness
of signifieds and signifiers. Words themselves are played upon, *e.g.*
impulse, or ATTITUDE, above, in a context suggesting altitude, and yet
definitely attitude in both senses, just as 'persisted in seeing' (p. 3) is
both psychological and durative, and as *inclined* is both psychological ('he inclined to think', p. 4) and, more usually, physical (or
both): 'They were messages, and Imp Plus had *inclined* to receive
them' (p. 3); 'Imp Plus had been told *gradient* and the pulses down

along it, and he *inclined to* receive them' (p. 5); 'A difference leaned between./It was a change that *inclined* to and from the green thing' (p. 5); 'Through the brightness the messages *inclined* along a gradient. Imp Plus *inclined* to receive them. He *inclined* through the brightness.' (p. 5); 'Everywhere he went there was a part just missing. A particle of difference. And in its place an *inclination*. A sharp drop./And through this Imp Plus thought' (p. 6); 'So some of the gradients were Imp Plus' (p. 6).

That is to say, through these double meanings the physical gradients (attitudes, inclinations) are transformed, they *are* Imp Plus. The same occurs with the word *raised*: 'Impulses on a frequency from Earth raised questions but not that question. Earth had raised Imp Plus and could be rid of him' (p. 9). The stock phrase 'Travel light' (used by a woman in Imp Plus's memory) is also Travelling on Light, or Operation TL. The very words *head, mind, figures*, are there and not there, in stock phrases, that is, dead, denied, but already regalvanised by the context: 'Impulses piled up in the head. Imp Plus had no skull. Imp Plus had no head. Imp Plus had always had a head for figures. Now what were the shadows if not the figures of birds?' (p. 5). 'And falling into himself but then being put in mind of the impulses by means of the impulses' (p. 7). And much later, when the brain becomes aware of having grown strange wings or starfish limbs (for the birds, which are not shadows, turn out to be limbs): 'Imp Plus gave light, though he was no *star* ... And the earlier shadows of his body on the capsule bulkheads – he knew *body* – had looked like *starlings*. The wings and tails, not the motion' (p. 14). And later still, the anagram: '(Central body? Brain bairn)' (p. 209).

For that is what the 'story' is. The brain of Imp Plus, sent out into space for experiments with solar energy storing, stores so much that it grows a body, and more and more memory, and more and more independent capacity to think for itself, not to answer Earth, to give Earth wrong information. Imp Plus remembers, too, in fragments, his life as a man on earth (probably dying of lung cancer), scenes with a woman by the sea, with another by a Mexican fire, and bits of conversations with 'the Acrid Voice' about his future state, about his planning, precisely, to use the sun to save himself. Words become more technical, though few (which seem but are not invented cytoplasts, chloroplasts, cytochromes, lumens, chlorella, Langerhans, morphogens), but never in the sense that these block our understanding; they are clear in the context. Similarly the simple sentences of the beginning become more complex, 'grow', and the anaphoric re-petitions also grow limbs, acquire new meanings and transformations.

The narrative technique in fact, is that of poetry, and that of the creative process itself. It is as if McElroy had wanted to fictionalise the words of William Gass, themselves about the poetic reading process:

Yet the new self with which fine fiction and good poetry should provide you is as wide as the mind is, and musicked deep with feeling. While listening to such symbols sounding, the blind perceive; thought seems to grow a body; and the will is at rest amid that moving like a gull asleep on the sea. (*Fiction and the Figures of Life*, 1970, p. 33.)

2.2. The hidden sentence

The most startling feature of this technique however is the apparent 'generation' of the text from the famous Chomsky sentence (1957). *Colourless green ideas sleep furiously*, which is said to be 'nonsensical' but 'grammatical', and its variation *Furiously sleep ideas green colour-less*, which is said to be both 'meaningless' and 'ungrammatical'. Leaving aside their grammaticality (recognisable as sentence by a native speaker), and remembering that Chomsky's context was a statistically probable occurrence, the sentences are nonsensical pre-sumably because they do not obey semantic restrictions: *green* cannot be *colourless*, *ideas* cannot be *green*, nor can they *sleep*, nor can anyone or thing *sleep furiously*. But, as many people have pointed out, both sentences would be 'grammatical' and 'meaningful' in poetry (which is, ultimately, about grammar, or all the things one can do to language, extending its possibilities beyond grammar). I believe someone wrote a poem out of them. Indeed, both could have been written by Dylan Thomas (in fact both, by chance no doubt, make up the same iambic pentametre with inverted first foot and rein-forced fourth, which is what may have given rise to this obvious but basically irrelevant objection from literary people). One can't help wondering why Chomsky hit upon such poetic sentences, each of which, once uttered, has such a poetic inevitability about it, when so many others would have proved his point better.

For what is colour but a reflection in the human eye? An idea. A word. On the second page it comes, and again and again: 'Imp Plus remembered having prepared to remember. And the word *vegetable*. And a green thing like an idea. Imp Plus remembered words he did not know' (p. 4); 'The green thing was not to eat. Imp Plus knew *eat*. Imp Plus made the grade. The green thing was not to eat. It had eyes and they ate' (p. 4); 'Imp Plus inclined to think the green thing ate light. Imp Plus had prepared to remember that eyes develop from a need for nourishment. That was the way, but the word for it did not come' (p. 4); 'It was a change that inclined to and from the green thing' (p. 5); 'The impulses asked for a galvanometer reading ... And the green thing was being named. But the names slid down a gradient that opened and inclined to many gradients' (p. 6); [the name or names, *chlorella, chlorophyll, algae* and others come later]; 'And the shadows were too slow to be the shadow of the frequency; and having thought this Imp Plus saw that as with the eyes of the green thing before him so with the frequency propagating waves, Imp Plus made acts of observation' (p. 7).

The word *green* (etymologically cognate with *grow*, cf. *grünen* in German), occurs 127 times in the text, and thirteen times with the word *idea*:[2]

Ch. 1:	a green thing like an idea. (p. 4)
Ch. 3:	had felt the green thing an idea and called it *chlorella*. (p. 25)
Ch. 4:	and with it the green thing was now like an idea. (p. 55)
Ch. 5:	Still, in the green and golden sunlight of the algae beds and their glassy cover, he found an idea that he was becoming some place else. (p. 60)
	an idea that was not green came to him. (p. 75)
[twice]	But, with its cast shadow, it was an idea. Yet not like the green thing, the algae./Though, like the green thing, someone else's idea. (p. 76)
[twice]	It was like an idea, other ideas besides resilience ... The chlorella bed had seemed to him an idea long ago. But then he had tried to stop himself, for he did not know *idea*. He had recalled it; but he did not know it. He knew the green chlorella, knew that it gave him part of his air. (p. 77)
Ch. 10:	For they were the idea of green that he had thought to himself so long ago that he had almost lost the power to forget the name of

these bodies which he saw now were really
blue-black as if before the Sun had gone
away. (p. 161).

the rings of each blue-black molecule that
held the idea of green. (p. 163)

the blue-black idea of green. (p. 163)

the blue-black bodies of green idea. (p. 167)

[blue-black then occurs several times alone,
with 'tail', or 'tail of the blue-black inner
molecule'.]

Ch. 12:   So nearly crossing the lives of brain and
algae that in the shadow of the idea of green
Imp Plus could seem to the Acrid Voice to
be photosynthetic. (p. 195)

From these quotations we can see several things:

(1) The rhythm suddenly increases in chapter 5, and again,
though less, in chapter 10. Thus over the twelve chapters the
incidence is: 1, 0, 1, 1, 5, − − − −4, 0, 1.

(2) Words are introduced with the word *green* which will then, by
themselves (or do anyway like *algae*), suggest green: chlorella, algae,
photosynthesis.

(3) Other colours are introduced, which blur or cancel the idea of
green (green and golden sunlight, blue-black idea of green, three
times in varied form).

As to (1), there is also a distinct rhythm to the occurrence of *green*
without the word *idea*. Chapter by chapter: 7, 6, 30, 33, 10, 5, 8, 2,
4, 8, 3, 14. The large increase here is in chapters 3 and 4, then a
drop in chapter 5, a dwindling, and a rise again in the last chapter,
where however the green is chiefly that of the 'large pale green room
on earth' and 'the smaller pale green room', frequently mentioned
before but concentrated on now as Earth takes control and Imp
Plus slowly ceases to exist. The rhythm for *idea* alone is: 2, 0, 2, 1,
10, 0, 2, 1, 0, 4, 0, 7. Thus altogether:

green + idea:	1	−	1	1	5	−	−	−	−	4	−	1
green:	7	6	30	33	10	5	8	2	4	8	3	14
idea:	2	−	2	1	10	−	2	1	−	4	−	7

I shall return to this question of rhythm later.

(2) There are over 200 words which suggest green (215, but as we
are here in an area of possibly subjective interpretation, from
unambiguous 'palest olive' to 'plants', which in some contexts could
mean electricity, I leave the figure vague, for a mere general idea),

and the word Acrid occurs 145 times: the Acrid Voice (occasionally hand, particles etc.) on earth, connected sometimes with green and sometimes with smoke (the Acrid Voice person smoked heavily, to the discomfort of the dying man that was Imp Plus). The Acrid Voice is even remembered to have said: '*Maybe* . . ., *maybe* you'll turn *green*' (p. 54).

(3) More important, there are very many instances of other colours (p. 348) and some 700 instances of other colours clearly suggested, either in the word itself or by previous association with a colour (foam, milk, chalk, snow, sand, dune, pollen, parts of the body etc.). This high number would seem to cancel the importance of green, but no, it merely cancels the greenness of green, by co-presence, just as 'the green and golden sunlight' and 'the blue-black idea of green' above cancel it, or, elsewhere, the frequent blue-green of the algae and anabaena beds (in the capsule), or of the sea (in his memory), and the often mentioned green blackboard on earth. The rhythm shows this too.

For in the first chapter, *green* occurs seven times (once with *idea*), and is clearly suggested seventeen times. All other things mentioned are *colourless*, that is, evoke no colour, but light or dark (more particularly: brightness, dark shearwater, shadows, light) or absence ('like an absence of obstacles') or both: 'a particle of difference', 'the absence where particles were missing', 'a light with absence', 'blazing like a trace', etc.), or invisible processes (particles, X-rayed, impulses, quantum yield of light radiation, etc.), and technical terms which either mean invisible processes but strongly suggest colour (e.g. *photosynthesis*, which suggests *green*) or, inversely, strongly suggest colour but in fact have none (e.g. *salmonella*, suggesting 'salmon' pink, but in fact colourless bacteria, or rather bacteria whose colour cannot be determined). Both of course require a degree of knowledge. The chapter as we saw is chiefly about thought, apprehension, words, movement, impulses. Only towards the end are four other colours slipped in, all relating to memories: 'The last Apollos had left the Moon. They had raised their faceplates, lifted off their helmets with the *golden* sunshades' (p. 9); 'Small *white* birds with *pink* sides and *black* scissor-tails' (p. 9).

Chapter 2 (*green* six times) introduces *white*caps and laughter that had been '*gray*ing or dampening or decaying a graph' (p. 19), '*gray*ed the graph' (p. 20), and the word *camouflage*, which refers to radio camouflage (colourless) but may evoke for us either the green/brown camouflage of military equipment or an animal's ability to adopt the colour of its surroundings (usually also green brown). And there are twenty-five instances of words suggesting other colours (sea, seabird, spray, crest, arms, wings), as opposed to only a few in the first chapter.

In chapter 3 *red* is introduced for the first time (reddening skin, p. 28). Red is the opposite of green in the spectrum, and will occur more and more, either as red or as crimson (107 times, and 104 clear suggestions like blood, flame, fire, often also accompanied by the colour). Red is chiefly connected with a crimson flash or a flaming red gland which worries Imp Plus, which may be the pituitary gland according to a much later explanation by Ground: 'In some memory of the Acrid particles he was nonetheless receiving Cap Com's admission that even with the tightest security he might have learned of a pituitory tumor – and that a tumor of the pituitary gland results in discoloration of the optic chiasma' (p. 211) which is medically correct, and the phrase 'discoloration of the optic chiasma' has previously occurred many times. At the end there is also the 'crimson process', which could refer to the same gland tumour (a process inside Imp Plus's brain) or to something more technological like the red shift (or both).

But red is also the last colour in the spectrum, and *infra-red* (p. 149) is colourless. So is *ultra-violet* (four times, p. 140) at the opposite end, and red and violet are three times mentioned together: 'the red and violet double distance ... the red and violet down there with their alien promise of green' (p. 45); 'Ground could not see the radiating red and violet below the fiber plugs' (127). But violet is the least frequent colour in the text apart from orange. Red and green are the most frequent.

Blue is next to violet in the prism, and is the second most frequent after red (fifty-eight, + forty-three clear suggestions). It is connected at first only with the sea (in his memory) but from chapter 4 also with the algae, the 'chlorella' beds (*e.g.* 'glistening green and blue green of the algae beds', p. 46; 'a blur of green and blue less here than in his own chlorella beds', p. 57). And from chapter 5 we have 'Dark blue and pale brown were on the spoke or wing adjacent', (p. 76), and a blue dart ('he saw there in the brain a blue dart' p. 63) or 'blue line', which will recur frequently, paralleling the crimson gland of flame. But blue is also often vague (as blue-green) or 'red and near blue' (p. 173) or 'cloudy blue'. Earth appears as 'a solid curve of dusky, blue-mottled pearl' (p. 92) and as 'the blue-mottled pearl of the hemisphere' (p. 123) or a 'cloudy blue thing' (several times, ch. 11). And blue gets cancelled into both green and red: 'More blue but more distant than green. More green than the long wavelengths of blood Imp Plus saw were red' (p. 38).

Thus if red cancels green, and red and violet end up colourless or have an 'alien-promise of green' (p. 45) and blue is constantly amalgamated to green, or to gray (pearl, cloudy) or to black (the blue-black idea of green) we get, despite the vivid and constant mention and evocation of colours, an implied colourlessness. The *word* 'colourless' does not occur in the text, only 'discolor' and 'discoloration', but colourlessness is constantly implied:

(1) in notions of transparence (frequent), e.g. water, watery, acquous humour, etc. and the word 'transparent' and others. Also the word *albedo* (from *albus*, white, but meaning in astronomy the ratio between the light reflected from the surface and the total light reflecting on this surface). *Albedo* is once linked to 'ultra-violet' (p. 140), to 'saffron salts' (p. 165), and defined as sun radiation come back from earth (p. 168).

(2) the rainbow, or iris, or spectrum (all colours)

(3) the word *color* itself, unspecified, e.g.: 'the waves of color were the pulsing of the rainbow' (p. 39), 'Serum mulled of sweet color' (p. 41); 'She laughed and the blue-green water tipped into her mouth and was her color' (p. 75, i.e. became pink), 'colors of thickness' (p. 75), 'the colored and discolored and loose and also absent teeth' (p. 76); 'the woman's other-colored eyes' (p. 91), 'the staggering spectrum of countless whole new colors were like many arcs' (p. 97), 'changing shades' (p. 120), 'color-coded', twice (p. 126), 'the pulse of its color' (p. 135), 'the strange words *radii of color* were true' (p. 137); 'the thought of this colored its cause' (p. 146); 'past motion and past color' (p. 166); 'raining light and color down the dark sides' (p. 186) etc.

(4) other, more technical words, containing a root that suggests colour *or* colourlessness (*chloro*plasts, *chloro*phyll, cyto*chromes*). *Chloros* is pale green in Greek but suggests colourlessness in certain derivatives such as chloral (a thin, oily, colourless liquid), chloral hydrate, chloromine etc., and yellow and greenish yellow in others (chloranil, chlorine). *Chroma* of course suggests colour, and now means the purity of colour, but also suggests yellow or green in chrome yellow, chrome green. And many technical words connected with light processes (particles, ultramicrons, photosynthesis etc.).

(5) the innumerable words for light (p. 456) and dark (p. 152) and clear suggestions of them (p. 69).

The other colour words in the text are: black, gray, white, silver (including platinum, once) gold, amber, blond, cream, yellow, saffron, orange, coral, salmon, brown, tan, maroon. Orange is several times assimilated to red, and yellow to orange, and red to pink, in fact all the colours are frequently merged or altered by juxtaposition or accumulation (the blood-blanched locks of enzyme, p. 61; singed pink, amber-gold, amber-red, gray-amber, amber-gray, gray-glinting crystal, gray crystal, blue-brown, chalky-brown, gold-pink, gold-shadow, gold and many-coloured, gold-shadowed pink flows, etc.). Good examples of change by accumulation are:

The discs and eggs were just green till Imp Plus looked at the still more packs of light flown in to hit the discs and eggs, and then the discs and eggs were also as orange as the inner flesh of raw carrot slice and as yellow as what he did not recall but at once all green, and he could see the orange and yellow or not see it. (p. 44)

Maybe he didn't mind his [the newsvendor's] gapped teeth, brown, yellow, black, blue, gray, green, hard enamel cream, because he could not see them. (p. 53)

below and in front of the once discolored, now shadowed crossing of the eye tracts was the unfurling and more banked gland of flame which still warmed into brown, maroon and amber boundaries four bodies which were one and were where the blue dart had once brightly cut. (p. 83)

Imp Plus recalled that the blond and ash-red, green-gilded or silvered yellow did not belong to the planes and chambers: (p. 84)

And the color here or down the planes or swelling the drops might show orange, or blue-green from a point beneath, but then be chalky brown or singed pink from higher off – say ten o'clock. *Ten o'clock* came to him. (p. 84)

As I write, I am watching two powerful sprays revolving over orchards on a green mountain-side. At every slow turn each differently catches the morning sunlight, the one expanding its white line into 'cream', 'blond', 'singed pink', 'tan', and brown; the other into cream, light green, green, blue, mauve. A stronger and evening light would have revealed deeper colours, and as the slanted morning sun moves to noon the colours will vanish. But does one ever see clearly in a rainbow all and only the seven colours given in the prism (violet, indigo, blue, green, yellow, orange, red)? These however are all represented in Plus (except *indigo* as a word, expressed as *dark blue*), as are all the in-between paler others, and as are *black* and *white*, strictly speaking not 'colours' but the colour of darkness and total light. *Gray* is but pale black. *Gold* and *amber* shiny versions of yellow, *silver* a shiny version of white.

It would be fastidious to analyse or even to quote all the occurrences, but see p. 280 for a table (manually compiled): figures

Table 10.1

Total	Ch.	Nominal prism colours						Black	Gray	White
		Violet	Blue	Green	Red	Orange	Yellow			
7	1	—	—	⑦	—	—	—	1	—	1
6	2	—	—	6	—	—	—	—	2	2
32	3	—	1	[30]	1	—	—	1	2	4
56	4	2	⑧	[33]	5	3	5	1	1	4
34	5	—	[13]	⑩	⑨	—	2	2	4	3
15	6	—	6	5	2	1	1	1	3	3
17	7	—	1	⑧	4	—	4	2	5	—
31	8	2	⑦	2	[20]	—	—	1	3	2
36	9	5*	⑦	4	[19*]	1	—	—	—	—
26	10	—	⑧	⑧	⑨	—	1	6	1	1
23	11	—	6	3	[14]	—	—	2	—	—
46	12	—	1	[14]	[24]	—	⑦	2	1	3
329		9	58	130	107	5	20	19	22	23
					(see coral)					
					(see saffron)					

*Ultra-violet 4 times, infra-red once.

above ten are in square blocks, figures from seven to ten in a circle (below seven occurrences of one colour in one chapter I regard as probably below the level of conscious notice, except of course once one has become aware of the play of colours). We can see that *green* is introduced visibly, but quietly, in chapter 1, with only four other colours. Chapter 2 drops slightly to six/four. Chapters 3 and 4 leap up on *green*, and *blue* becomes noticeable (eight). Chapter 5 drops on *green* (ten) but five of these are with the word *idea*, and the *blue* rises to thirteen, and *red* becomes noticeable (nine), as well as *silver* (eight). Chapter 6 (the centre) drops below the threshold but every colour except *violet* (and *saffron, coral, tan*) is mentioned (plus one solitary *maroon*), *blue* and *green* the most (six, five). With chapter 7 we rise again above the threshold with *green* (eight) and *gold* (thirteen), cp. chapter 5 with green, blue, red and *silver*. In chapters 8 and 9 there is the leap of *red* (twenty, nineteen, the gland), and *blue* becomes noticeable again (seven, seven), while *green* drops very low, and other colours are few (but chiefly *silver* and *gold* in chapter 9). In chapter 10 *blue, green* and *red* are roughly equal (eight, eight, nine), other colours are few (but chiefly *black* with six). In chapter 11 *red* goes up again (fourteen), *blue* drops to six and *green* to three. And in the last chapter *red* leaps to its maximum (the gland, the

				Other colours						Total
Silver	Gold	Amber	Blond/ Cream	Saffron	Coral/ Salmon	Pink	Brown	Tan	Maroon	
—	1	—	—	—	—	1	—	—	—	4
—	—	—	—	—	—	—	—	—	—	4
—	1	—	—	—	—	—	—	—	—	8
1	4	—	1	—	—	—	1	—	—	13
⑧	4	1	—	1	1	—	4	—	—	28
1	—	3	1	—	—	2	5	—	1	20
—	[13]	1	—	—	—	1	—	2	—	24
—	—	1	1	—	—	—	1	—	—	9
5	5	4	—	—	—	—	3	—	—	17
—	—	1	—	2	—	—	1	—	—	12
—	—	2	—	—	1	—	—	—	—	5
—	1	1	—	—	1	—	1	—	—	10
15	29	14	3	3	3	4	16	2	1	154

crimson process), *green* goes up to fourteen (doubling its occurrence in chapter 1) and towards the end *yellow* comes into notice (seven) with 'the yellow of the flaming gland's power' (p. 210), also called the 'yellow-soak', as the 'discoloration of the optic chiasma' comes into effect.

Green is thus more omnipresent than any other colour, its opposite *red* coming next. The prism colours double the others (329/154). But all colours are there, and all colours merge and change into one another. Colours are in the eye of the beholder, and here the beholder has no eyes, but 'persists in seeing'. Colour is an idea. But his sight is also an idea. A progression in chapter 5 makes this clear:

Forgot the Mexican thorn that had cut his feet (near the silver-leaf flower that sprang up under the flash-light – . . . the winter newsstand in which the hooded vendor with always open half-laughing mouth and rotten teeth had a bandage so loose you could see in one socket a pale red purse like a body hole. All came together loosely arrayed by a force. It was there and touched Imp Plus who could feel it but not reach it.

It was like an idea, other ideas besides resilience . . . But then he had to stop himself for he did not know *idea*. He had recalled it; but he did not know it. He knew the green chlorella, knew that it gave him part of his air. Wasn't that all? And now also knew that the spokes had membranes with sight. But he persisted in feeling that the spread and the poles and the open chances of this sight were more than sight and more than what they'd felt like.

Here on Earth orbit he leaned out in all the axes of his spines to this force that had him but that he had not learned to touch. The force was dispersed in the outlying parts. It was like an idea if Imp Plus only knew *idea*. It was the idea of his sight. (p. 77)

Colourless green ideas. What about sleep then? Yes, it occurs too, many times, and also already in the first chapter, soon after the first juxtaposition of *green* with *idea* (p. 3) and the many references to *the green thing* (pp. 3–6). For Imp Plus needs sleep as he needs green (the oxygen from the chlorophyll of the algae) and ideas, to survive and to grow. A whole paragraph is devoted to it. But sleep too is somehow annulled as a phenomenon, in a context of brightness and in that it never occurs wholly, only on one side of the brain. It seems even to be a mere word, an order, and a puzzling one:

The brightness that was the Sun or from the Sun passed him many times between what he knew and what he nearly knew. Sleep was on one side, then on the other, never on both. The *word* for sleep was on only one side but now had come to be an audible line along the middle between the two sides. Audible because impulses from Ground said the word. But audible now along some middle because Imp Plus had the word. And when Ground said SLEEP, the word occurred also as that line along the middle so that only one side sank into sleep and not both. But this was new, and for a time Imp Plus did not need to know why Ground ran Gs – ran EEGs – thinking both sides of him were asleep when in truth during any given EEG – which Imp Plus now· made into *electroencephalogram* – only one side had responded to Earth's transmission SLEEP. Or both had, but only one side slept. But then he did not have just two sides, or so he thought – which meant he was in error. The Sun passed many times between sleep and not-sleep, and the impulses in Imp Plus were outside of him, and he recalled arriving here, and thought that soon now here for the first time sleep would occur, which meant waking too. (p. 7)

Such a lot of *sleep*, after such a lot of *green* and the first conjunction of *green* and *idea* ('a green thing like an idea', p. 4), certainly brings the Chomsky sentence to mind. And in the Chomsky sentence sleep is also annulled, by its subject (can ideas sleep?) and by the adverb *furiously*. *Colourless* and *furiously* are the only two words (first and last or last and first of each sentence) which do not occur in the text, but as we have seen, 'discolor/discolored/discoloration' do and colour-lessness is permanently suggested. As to *furiously* the entire text is a furious attempt at survival, and anger, anguish, ill-will and despair occur frequently together towards the end. *Sleep* is continually annulled and negated, questioned, split and scattered, it is not a normal, restful sleep, it is a furious sleep.

Already in chapter 1 it is mysteriously linked with the 'more' of growth but also with the less of lack: 'Imp Plus knew more. Knew it through what he could have called *sleep*, which was sleep with something missing, sleep itself' (p. 8). Sleep is denied: 'if he had been sleeping (which he had not)' (p. 17, ch. 2).

Sleep is an order disobeyed, or half disobeyed: 'Darkness . . . had been steady and as familiar as Ground's order SLEEP' (13, ch. 2); 'and against the order SLEEP Imp Plus had stayed awake on one side or other or both' (22, ch. 2); 'He had not slept when told to sleep. Was there part that slept and he didn't know?' (55, ch. 4); 'He heard Ground speak of sleep, and he was of two minds but did not know *mind*' (89, ch. 6). 'And the Dim Echo very close by was saying to Ground, OK./ For Ground had ordered Imp Plus to sleep' (89, ch. 6).

So ends chapter 6. But chapter 7, in which there is a positive orgy of sleep/non-sleep (thirty-seven occurrences, to one, two or three in other chapters, eleven in chapter 1 and none in chapters 3, 5, 8 and 9), starts:

But Imp Plus did not sleep. He let the Dim Echo do the sleeping for him, was that it? Yet also Imp Plus did not know sleep. The word for it from Ground felt like a line along a middle between two sides (p. 90).

The Dim Echo (which later turns out to be himself, the other part of his brain) is doing the sleeping: 'the part which the Dim Echo sleeping nearby might give a name to' (p. 91). But that sleep is contradicted by brightness: 'The Dim Echo was asleep. With lights on. Asleep lighted by the glove of feelers the Sun's departed hand had left. Did the wings sleep? What light disturbed their membranes?' (p. 92).

Yet it is also the Dim Echo who seems to be uttering the *words*: 'and not by the Dim Echo's slow words (which Imp Plus kept to himself) SLEEP. SLEEP. LIGHT PRECEDES DEEP SLEEP. COLD WILL COME WITH DARK CYCLE' (p. 94). (Here there is also much about 'rapid eye movements', later REM, which are the movements made by the eyes when one dreams.) 'Imp Plus had the words of the Dim Echo asleep or half awake' (p. 95). The words were: 'O.K., optimum warmth. Solar flow holds. Glucose stable. Glucose beautiful. Cold will come when dark cycle comes. Sleep. Imp Plus had not let the words go to

Earth.' (p. 95). 'Yet the Dim Echo who when dark cycle had come had O.K.'d the order SLEEP, now did not seem to know the dark cycle had come ... because the Dim Echo slept' (p. 95).

The words were evidently from Ground, though Imp Plus thought they were from the Dim Echo and hadn't let them 'go to Earth'. Ground in fact takes over:

IMP PLUS ... WE READ HIGH CORTICAL ACTIVITY, LOOKING LIKE R.E.M. SLEEP IN ALL AREAS WE MONITOR. BUT THIS IS LIGHT SLEEP PERIOD IMP PLUS TOO EARLY FOR R.E.M. SLEEP.
Imp Plus held on to the slow answering words of the Dim Echo and did not let them go, cold will come with dark cycle. Light sleep precedes R.E.M. sleep. Sleep. ARE YOU ASLEEP OR NOT, IMP PLUS. DO NOT BREAK SLEEP CYCLE BUT ANSWER IF YOU CAN. (p. 96)

As Imp Plus later comments to himself: 'For Ground asked if Imp Plus was asleep, and asked again, like a child aiming to wake a grown up' (p. 100). And of course Imp Plus has 'grown'. But in another sense he is the child of Earth, the brain-child or 'brain bairn'.

Right through chapter 7 the 'split' sleep of Imp Plus/Dim Echo will continue: 'How long had it [Dim Echo] been asleep? It had been asleep when it said "Cold will come"' (p. 97). 'Imp Plus thought the Dim Echo knew. But the Dim Echo slept' (p. 100). 'So that splitting he thought himself in two, thought of how Ground's word SLEEP was like a line along a middle and tried to see if the Dim Echo was on one side' (p. 101). 'He would tell better where the Dim Echo was when the Dim Echo stopped sleeping. He thought when the time came Ground would draw the word SLEEP back, for Imp Plus had once felt it as a line along a middle and saw he had not stopped feeling this. But did not want to do things by halves' (109, another word-play).

Sleep is contradicted: 'Ground said waking and deep sleep were not possible at the same time yet Ground read rapid low-voltage waves which were waking, at the same time that it read volleys of high-voltage spikes and R.E.M. equivalents, which meant deep sleep' (p. 103).

Sleep is used in the one sense where it means something else, and it is annulled by memory-failure:

Yet through another night saw that once there had been no Dim Echo.

The night with the woman by the Mexican fire.

Not the woman at the California sea.

The pale one on the night plateau.

Slept with her. He had said SLEEP. What he had meant, he could ask the Dim Echo, but the Dim Echo had not been around the fire and it was Imp Plus who had said to the woman ... The words he had said were 'Sleep with me.'

But he could not remember what this had meant, if it had meant SLEEP. (p. 110)

Throughout chapter 7 sleep is overpoweringly present, yet for ever cancelled, half-cancelled, pushed over to the Dim Echo, who *is* Imp Plus. There is then a long gap till chapter 10 (where also occurs the blue-black idea of green, and variants), which mentions sleep once: 'the larger and the smaller green rooms, the place where he lay down and let go his controls. To sleep with a Voice not Acrid, not Good' (160, ch. 10). Sleep is here the death of Imp Plus as man, before the experiment, when the brown woman with a gold ring uses a silver syringe. The same sleep recurs in chapter 11: 'and of words given not in the small or the large green room but between the two, in sleep, a statement learnt: "Spin-stabilizer rocket orients spin axis at right angles to plane of Sun's apparent path." / So maybe Imp Plus could do a thing or two to halt or unspin the jump ...' (174, ch. 11). Imp Plus is now being jolted down from orbit to orbit, and the remembered sleep of death is linked with hope of survival. And sleep returns again three times in the last chapter, when Imp Plus is dying at last in his descent, and remembers the sleep he had (but was convinced he hadn't had) as brain in orbit:

Imp Plus dreamed of a sleep in which he had known photosynthesis. / A divided sleep long ago in an orbit in phase with Earth's Go-system, when he knew photosynthesis and used such words – a time when glucose was decreasing and he had been a Dim Echo of himself. (p. 186)

The next instance is linked with *idea*, and thoroughly cancelled in a series of oxymora about existence:

He heard the lattice like a sleep he was part of all around and in him say, No water needed.
   Imp Plus came to be aware of not having existed. To be a gap. Not like the elsewhere that pain could wish for. Imp Plus was part of a foresight which was that he would again not exist but did exist now and would again. He was in other arcs of the oval and believed correctly that there were elsewhere other simultaneities like himself. It was an idea of them.
   And he thought then that they were ideas or like ideas. And then he became aware of having just then not existed. (p. 201)

The last occurrence is in indirect speech, about something said by the 'Acrid Voice' from Ground, in the long 'private conversation' it has (unheard by Ground) with what is left of Imp Plus's consciousness. And it cancels the whole notion that Imp Plus had not slept, but cancels it dubiously with the word 'apparent' (apparent to Imp Plus, and perhaps to Ground as well): 'for the Acrid Voice was saying that if the yellow-soak had appeared on the join of what had been the brain's halves ... then this location indicated that this yellow was the hormonoid serotinin which if increased might account for Imp Plus's apparent sleeplessness' (p. 210).

The yellow, so frequent in the last chapter, is, like the red, explained away as an internal brain-phenomenon. The effect of Ground's explanations about red and yellow, each of which has so often been merged and juxtaposed with orange, pink, brown, green, blue, gold, and the general cancellation of all colours by each other, by the overall emphasis on light and dark (especially light), and by the innumerable suggestions of colourlessness, is to blur the whole notion of all the colours so frequently mentioned, which themselves merge with and blur the green idea, the green idea which slept. Slept a sleep constantly cancelled in a fury of words, of desperate effort, rapture, light, division, split colours, absence of obstacles, of particles, of colours, of green ideas.

Plus is on the face of it a 'mimetic' or 'realistic' novel, in the sense that its words mime an imagined 'reality'. It does not, like some metafiction, attempt to destroy its own fiction by transgressing narrative levels or by any other means. Yet the poetic function far outweighs the referential function, and (like much poetry) it deconstructs in paradox and self-cancellation the very words it uses. Fundamentally, *Plus* is about cognition, and cognition is a paradox, whereas *The Sirens of Titan* (like most science fiction) is about the world and its purpose, and turns narrative conventions inside out to show that the world has no purpose. If we apply Frye's modes, briefly, to these two novels, we find that the hero's power of action is, for Malachi, equal (neither superior nor inferior) in kind and in degree to man but not to nature, and this places him in low mimetic (like the realistic novel); or, if we regard him as inferior in degree (as Unk, with his memory effaced), then he is inferior not in kind but in degree to man but not to nature, and this places him in ironic; as for Rumfoord (also a sort of hero), he is superior not in kind but in degree to man and to nature, and this places him in romance. This mixture is what we would expect of science fiction (see chapters

Table 10.2

	Superior				Inferior				
	in		to		in		to		
	kind	degree	man	nature	kind	degree	man	nature	
Myth	+	+	+	+	+	+	+	+	Ø (*Imp Plus*)
Romance (*Rumfoord*)	–	+	+	+	–	+	+	+	Ø (*Imp Plus*)
High mimetic	–	+	+	–	–	+	+	–	Ironic (*Unk*)
Low mimetic	–	–	+	–	= –	–	+	–	Low Mimetic (*Malachi*)

3 and 4 above). Imp Plus, however, is inferior in kind (if we regard an isolated human brain as not wholly human), in degree, to man and to nature; or (if we regard the brain as the same kind), inferior not in kind but in degree to man and nature. The first puts him in the non-existent category opposite Myth in the inferior column of my diagram (see chapter 3, p. 58), the second in the non-existent category opposite romance. See table 10.2 for part of that diagram.

From this alone *Plus* is not the usual kind of science fiction. It is closer to poetry, and uses all poetry's techniques of word-play and repetition, inversion, paradox, or language to point to and to go beyond language. It is as if (as if because *Plus* was published the same year) McElroy had wanted to fictionalise, as well as a green idea, certain passages in William Gass's *On Being Blue* (1976):

So sentences are copied, constructed, or created . . . ; each titillates, invites, conceals, suggests . . . ; nevertheless, the lines in Stevens or the sentences of Joyce and James, pressed by one another into being as though the words before and the words after were those reverent hands both Rilke and Rodin have celebrated, clay calling to clay like mating birds, concept responding to concept the way passionate flesh congests, every note a ripple on the breast, at once a triumphant pinnacle and perfect conclusion, like pelted water, I think I said, yet at the same time only another anonymous cell, and selfless in its service to the shaping skin as lost forgotten matter is in all walls; . . . for Rabelais was wrong, blue is the color of the mind in borrow of the body; it is the color consciousness becomes when caressed; it is the dark inside of sentences, sentences which follow their own turnings inward out of sight like the whorls of a shell. (pp. 56–8)

Blue? Or blue-green? Or colourless green ideas? Why the
Chomsky sentence? Because Chomsky, although he led linguistics
away from the arbitrary grammars of language (la langue) to the
grammar of actually spoken sentences (la parole), is nevertheless
only interested in the deep structures of sentences, in the operations
we effectuate to transform these deep structures into the sentences
we utter, and, ultimately, in the abstract universals of human
thought. Zavarzadeh has called the language of *Plus* 'computer
language' (in an MLA paper, MLA conference 1978). Nothing
could be further from the truth, even if a computer is 'represented'
in the fiction by Ground's control of Imp Plus. McElroy has in fact
used the Chomsky sentence to generate a narrative poem, it is a
'narrative sentence' in a much more interesting sense than Genette's
'narrative sentence' (see chapter 8, p. 189, note 2 above). For the
poet, in general, or McElroy, in particular, is interested in the
sentence less for its abstract structure than for its contradictions, its
ambiguities, its qualities of density and clarity, of obstacle and
absence of obstacle, or, in more conventional terms, its aesthetic
quality. Which sleeps, but furiously.

PART V

The real as unreal: some modern texts

11

The real as unreal: Robbe-Grillet

1. Baroque strains

'Certainement la Quêteuse étoit belle ...' wrote Furetière in the opening pages of *Le Roman bourgeois*. 'N'attendez pas pourtant que je vous la décrive ici, comme on a coûtume de faire en ces occasions.' Or again, earlier: 'je ne veux pas même vous dire comme est faite cette Eglise, quoi qu'assez célèbre: car ceu qui ne l'ont point vûe, la peuvent aller voir, si bon leur semble; ou la bâtir dans leur imagination comme il leur plaira'.[1]

It may seem a little perverse to open a chapter on Robbe-Grillet the obsessive describer with a quotation from a seventeenth-century novelist who facetiously refuses to describe. But the connection is not so remote: Furetière made Sterne possible, and one aspect of Sterne contains the germ of the anti-novel, for Sterne in *Tristram Shandy* compared his book to Locke's *Essay concerning the Human Understanding*, which he called 'a history-book ... of what passes in a man's own mind',[2] basing his construction not on plot but on memory and association, which enable him to be anywhere at any time. And Sterne, and the seventeenth-century rhetoric of anti-rhetoric that preceded him, are highly relevant today.

Rejection is always interesting. Even early rhetoricians, and Hamlet, knew that protesting much could mean the opposite. And just as Chaucer's protestations that he knows nothing of rhetoric are in themselves rhetoric, in the best sense, presaging the use of a particular skill, so when Robbe-Grillet tells us, repeatedly, that what he has just described is 'un entrecroisement de lignes sans signification'; 'et cela ne signifie rien non plus'; 'mais cette scène ne mène à rien'; 'décor qui ne conduit à rien', we may assume the contrary.[3]

When Furetière refuses to describe his beautiful alms-collector, he manages to get a fairly detailed impression, if not of this woman, certainly of *a* woman, into the reasons he gives for refusing to

describe. And he has preceded his remarks on the Eglise des
Carmes with two pages about how other writers would have given it
porches, balconies, columns and generally turned it into something
as magnificent as the Temple of Diana at Ephesus. This serves to
produce in our minds the idea of a church, not of this church
necessarily but of porches, balconies and columns, so that the refusal
to describe, far from leaving us in an imageless vacuum, acts rather
as a sudden pin-pointing from the general idea of a church to the
particular, simpler and less grand church in question which, however, he need not describe. The technique is like making a ring on
a map. Or like a framed and enlarged inset. Or like a type of
camera close-up after a panoramic view. As a technique it contains
a paradox in the very way of passing from general to particular: of
all possible churches, it says, this is the one I mean; on the other
hand it could be any church; it has no significance in its specific
features, other than the fact that it is the one I mean; its selection by me is
its whole significance.

Occupatio or the refusal to describe is of course very old. In the
vernacular we find it already in the twelfth century (e.g. in *Cligés*,
by Chrétien de Troyes, lines 2534 ff). There, however, the device is
comparatively simple. By the seventeenth century the whole paradox of anti-rhetoric as in itself rhetoric, anti-style as in itself a style,
had burst out all over Europe into a vast and complex movement
broadly called Baroque – a term I shall not go into here since its use
and subdivisions have occasioned more words from scholarly pens
than almost any other term. So far, with the brief exception of
Flann O'Brien's *At Swim-Two-Birds* (which more properly belongs
to metafiction) and the even briefer but incidental exception of La
Rochelle's *Gilles* (realism) in chapter 5, made in order to illustrate
types of encoded reader, I have analysed narratives which would all
be placed, in Todorov's classification, under either the pure fantastic
or the marvellous, and I have tried to show the relationships, formal
and historical, which such narratives might have, on the one hand,
with older and other forms such as allegory, myth, marvellous
journeys, heroic or lyric poetry, and, on the other, with the long
tradition of realistic fiction, from the Menippean satire to the
picaresque, from the *roman philosophique* and utopias/anti-utopias to
nineteenth-century realism and after.

The '*nouveau réalisme*' of the fifties, as it was then called, seems to
me to mark a partial return to the seventeenth-century 'baroque'
tradition, rediscovered in England during the twenties and thirties,

and in France not until the forties, the French 'Baroque' poets having been more thoroughly over-shadowed than in England, indeed eliminated, by seventeenth and eighteenth-century French classicism and its long cultural aftermath. I say 'partial' because naturally such 'returns' are never total, too many other developments having occurred in between, notably, for the novel, that of realism.

It is interesting nevertheless that one modern study has defined the Baroque vision as having at its core 'a systematic doubt in the validity of appearance, a doubt which expresses itself as an obsessive concern for appearance. Baroque poetry cannot 'imitate nature' as literally as either Renaissance or neoclassical poetry; in it the multiple realities of earthly experience are always melting together to emerge in new combination as the hard unity of art' (Warnke 1961: 2).

Doubt in the validity of appearance has of course become endemic, indeed, epidemic, in our time, and Robbe-Grillet, by denying only the significance, tragic or absurd, with which we have endowed the universe ('the universe is neither meaningful nor absurd. It quite simply *is*', 1962; 1965, p. 53), would seem on the contrary to be reasserting the validity of appearance simply as appearance, were it not for his obsessive concern.

It is also interesting that apart from what is too often, and too loosely, called 'imagery' the most intrinsic quality of Baroque art, including poetry, is the new complex awareness it shows in its exploitation of time and space relations and in the elaborate precision with which these are established. Poetry, by a bizarre use of tenses and other means, produces slide-rule leaps in time together with a new effect of instantaneousness.[4] Perhaps M. Gaëtan Picon had these qualities in mind at the time when he suggested of Robbe-Grillet's art: 'Nous vivons peut-être le moment d'un préclassicisme.'[5]

Now I have no intention of playing hunt-the-label or of proving that Robbe-Grillet is really a Baroque poet in disguise. Apart from the fact that he writes prose, he is best known, even by those who do not read him, as having abjured the one feature for which Baroque poetry is best known, even by those who do not read it, namely metaphor. I would like, however, to make two points about this.

First, it is only the pathetic fallacy which Robbe-Grillet has abjured in metaphor, that is, the endowing of nature and inanimate objects, with our human needs or emotions. Ruskin battled against it long ago, but it has obstinately survived, some might say rightly so, and even symbolism and the use, by writers of the twenties, thirties and forties, of what T. S. Eliot called objective correlatives (objects or elements in nature that stand for, or become points of convergence for human emotions), are strictly speaking a form of pathetic fallacy. Robbe-Grillet's cleansing operation is thus a recurrent and healthy one.[6] However, he is by no means against metaphors or comparisons which liken object to object, or which bring a physical situation, as Aristotle would say, 'before the eye in action'; e.g., when he calls the chequered red and white oilcloth in *Dans le labyrinthe* (my italics) 'le *damier* de petits carreaux rouges et blancs' (p. 40); and 'l'enfant ... une *tache* noire' (p. 41), 'le filament ... enfermé dans sa *cage* de verre' (p. 16, bordering on the pathetic fallacy) or more originally, when he says of the boy's voice, which had broken the silence: 'et la phrase, sans personne pour l'avoir prononcée, semblait être une *légende au bas d'un dessin*' (p. 147, a very Baroque idea).[7] Admittedly these are infrequent, and presented, when unusual, as somebody's impression (semblait, on dirait): but they show that the author does not reject the analogical way of thinking as such. Indeed, analogy in its non-metaphoric sense is so intricately exploited that it could be called a means of structure, as I hope to demonstrate.

The second point is that metaphor in the best Baroque poetry is neither just decorative nor anthropomorphic but functional, one of the many means developed by those poets for the purpose of resolving the contradictory aspects of emotional experience in relation to the changing validities of time and the physical world. When Donne turns a flea into 'our marriage bed, and marriage temple' or says to the sun 'This bed thy centre is, these walls, thy sphere', or of his lady-love 'She is all States, and all Princes, I',[8] he is shifting the perspective quite as suddenly as Robbe-Grillet does with a swift verbal close-up or a camera-swerve away from, say, the eyes of A, the 'narrator's' wife in *La Jalousie* (1957: 77–80) to the parapet of the terrace and then to the banana-segment in the distance. In Donne the shift is part of a complex argument, but the argument itself is a way out of an emotionally untenable position stated as an intellectual dilemma. Today, and in prose, the process is necessarily much less overt, reflecting unconscious or semi-conscious fears, and Robbe-Grillet's pronoun-less narrator averts his eyes from a visual image because it may, and eventually does, lead to other visual images which are too painful.[9] Paradoxically he nevertheless has to live out, if not act out, these other images. But the sudden swerve away, like the refusal to describe, has served to isolate the first image, to frame it.

The words 'frame' (cp. chapter 7) or here, 'enlarged inset' which I have been using in relation to the world of emblematic art, is peculiarly apposite to Robbe-Grillet's technique. But 'enlarged inset' is more apposite than 'frame', for it is not the narrative form which is framed (as *The Turn of the Screw* is framed by its Prologue), but the signifieds within the narrative (as Quint is framed by the crenellated wall). And Robbe-Grillet goes further, by transgressing narrative levels (see below). I am often reminded of documentary television, in which a commentator sits beside a vast blow-up of a politician, a place, or other topic: there are two pictures, the picture of the topic and the picture in the television set (the narrator). Robbe-Grillet has himself declared that in a photograph or film, the angle, the black-and-whiteness, the two dimensions, and above all the frame, give significance to any sight which in 'reality' seems insignificant. I would add that the significance may be illusory (indeed, many film-directors rely too heavily on it) but that the significance given by the frame is the strongest, because it is the significance of selection, this perspective of reality being framed rather than any other; and that it implies, like any picture, at least a minimal degree of composition.

'L'homme "Baroque" construit en soi ou autour de soi un monde imaginaire', wrote Jean Rousset (1961: Introduction), 'dans lequel il s'installe comme en un monde plus réel, non sans garder par devers soi une certaine conscience de vivre en un mirage'. Or again: 'le Baroque se définit essentiellement par l'union du mouvement et du décor'. And on mirrors and water:

plaisir pris à douter, à se tromper sur des identités changeantes, qui se prolonge en un plaisir supérieur, celui de prendre la figure pour la réalité, l'apparence pour l'être, le théâtre pour la vie; ivresse toute proche de celle qu'on demandait alors aux voûtes peintes de Pierre de Cortone et du Père Pozzo, aux décors en trompe-l'oeil, aux Sosies, à la pièce insérée dans la pièce.[10]

Robbe-Grillet himself makes a quite unprecedented use of pictures within pictures. One need only remember the framed engraving of the gardens in *Marienbad*, where the camera closed-up and either swerved off or seemed to go right through the engraving into the 'real' gardens. This is a 'transgressive' use, analogous to the transgression of narrative levels (see chapter 12, p. 333 above), since one is passing from a fiction within the fiction (the picture) to the reality represented in the fiction. Similarly but non-transgressively, the photograph of A in *La Jalousie* always leads to A on the terrace, the link being the café-table in the photograph and the coffee-table on the terrace, but with no change at all in the tone of the description.

In *Dans le labyrinthe* the device has become extremely complex: the framed café-scene above the chest of drawers in the room is described to us, like all else, not by a dramatised narrator but (or so it seems) by a sort of omniscient narrator who may or may not be the sudden 'I' at the end of the novel. The final 'I' is at that point clearly the doctor who looked after the dying soldier at the end, and possibly but not necessarily the 'bourgeois' (with similar clothes and umbrella) who spoke to the soldier in the street and was earlier in the café. As for the soldier, he is never described as himself seeing the picture, but each time the picture is described (perhaps as seen *throughout* by the soldier in the room where he is *in the end* revealed to be dying), it comes to life as the real café, and the soldier is there; at other times the soldier looks into the café from outside, over the chin-level curtain on the glass of the door, as if looking at a picture, with three soldiers, each of whom looks like him. There is a similarly self-identifying complexity in the soldier's fantasies about the photograph in the room of the ground-floor flat where he sits drinking wine after asking his way: the soldier in the photograph, wearing a recruit's uniform, is the woman's husband, unheard of since a certain Battle of Reichenfels (from which this soldier has just returned). At one point he imagines the scene when the woman now speaking to him took this photograph, before the soldier's departure. The transition from this reconstruction to the reality of the room is achieved by a mere change of determiner from *sa femme* to *la femme* (p. 69), almost imperceptibly because already at *sa femme* the description of the soldier going in again (after the taking of the photograph), into the dark corridor and into the flat, could apply to this soldier also. By framing a soldier under a street-lamp in the sun at the beginning of a war, the author also reframes in our minds (since the soldier is indoors now) and in the perspective of contrast, the soldier we have got to know so well, under many street-lamps, in the snow and bitter cold, at the end of a war.

Robbe-Grillet's technique, with its elaborate formalism, might well be said to give artistic significance, as the frame does (and as does the technique of defamiliarisation or distancing–*ostranenie*, see chapter 2 p. 19 above), to what he has stated and continues

throughout both to imply and to state is in itself without significance. This is a paradox with which Beckett is also much concerned:
'Yes, Watt could not accept . . . that nothing had happened, with all
the clarity and solidity of something . . . for the only way one can
speak of nothing is to speak of it as though it were something' (*Watt*
(1945) 1953; 1958: 83–4). A paradox, moreover, worthy of the best
Baroque imaginations. The next section will be an attempt to
examine it by means of a detailed analysis of *Dans le labyrinthe*, in the
light also of another and related paradox, namely that nothwith-
standing the age-old distinction between formalism and realism,
formalism *is* realism.

By this I mean rather more than what Nathalie Sarraute (1956b;
1963: 121–36) seems to mean when she says that the so-called
formalists are the true realists whereas the so-called realists are the
formalists because essentially imitators of forms invented by the
'true' realists. I agree with this, just as I agree with Bruce Morissette
(1959) that Robbe-Grillet's every obsessive dwelling, every cut,
swerve and merging by association re-create a psychological reality
which is far more convincing, for our time, than that re-created by
description of psychology or other means in the realistic novel. I
shall certainly take it for granted here that Robbe-Grillet does
create for us, so that we are experiencing it rather than merely
observing it, the psychological reality inside the lost soldier of *Dans
le labyrinthe*. But this is as it were, almost by the way, and he does
considerably more, in that he *also* does the opposite. Or rather,
Morissette's is one possible (realistic) reading. But one can also
argue that the very insistence on accurate detail (declared to be
insignificant), while leaving us with a very clear idea of something
(a street, a room), obliterates, as refusal to describe does with
Furetière's church, the very specificity it so insists on; and that the
constant shifts of perspective produce only uncertainty. As Lodge
(1977a: 10) says:

No amount of patient study could establish, for instance, the identity of the
man with the heavy coat and hat and stick encountered by Moran in
Beckett's *Molloy*. We shall never be able to unravel the plots of John Fowles'
The Magus or Alain Robbe-Grillet's *Le Voyeur* or Thomas Pynchon's *The
Crying of Lot 49* because these novels are labyrinths without exits.

And where form is as highly developed as in Robbe-Grillet, and as
highly charged with passion, form is in itself the reality, while the
represented reality is made to seem unreal.

2. Reality as trompe l'oeil

The first sentence of *Dans le labyrinthe* (p. 9) is ostensibly by an I–narrator: 'Je suis seul ici, maintenant, bien à l'abri.' (I am alone here now, safe and sheltered.) We do not know who 'je' is. The final nine-page section, after the soldier's delirium dream, begins (p. 211): 'A ma dernière visite, la troisième piqûre a été inutile. Le soldat blessé était mort.' (At my last visit there was no need for the third injection. The wounded soldier was dead.) But even in these last nine pages, told (as we now know from that sentence) by the doctor, the pronoun is again avoided until the very last phrase, 'et toute la ville derrière moi', (and the whole town behind me). Between the first sentence and 'A ma dernière visite' the first-person singular is not used except in dialogue. But, like the pronoun-less narrator in *La Jalousie* (which can be read either as an objectivist narration or as the interior monologue of a jealous man, see chapter 12 p. 331 below), this pronoun-less narrator is in a sense two people at once, the (now withdrawn) I–narrator possibly reconstructing it all afterwards, and the soldier, in the third person, whose sight, hearing, thought, confusion, hunger, fatigue and pain we are made to share as if we were he, although we are also frequently made to see him from the outside, or from a distance, and even from someone else's viewpoint (e.g. the boy's). The narrator is thus closer to the omniscient author of the old conventions, without, of course, the butting in, but as we shall see he is not really the omniscient narrator, he is the soldier in a timeless vacuum, framed by the I-narrator and constantly counterpointed by an implied outside observer who could be the I-narrator or the soldier himself.

After 'Je suis seul ici' (p. 9) the second sentence is: 'Dehors il pleut, dehors on marche sous la pluie en courbant la tête, s'abritant les yeux d'une main tout en regardant quand même devant soi, à quelques mètres devant soi, quelques mètres d'asphalte mouillé.' In the next sentence it is cold, and there is wind in the leaves that moves the shade of branches on the white walls, and by the end of the paragraph time has again changed to: 'Dehors il y a du soleil, il n'y a pas un arbre, ni un arbuste, pour donner de l'ombre, et l'on marche en plein soleil, s'abritant les yeux d'une main tout en regardant devant soi, à quelques mètres seulement devant soi, quelques mètres d'asphalte poussiéreux où le vent dessine des parallèles, des fourches, des spirales.'[11]

This opening paragraph epitomises the mood of the whole novel, as it were out of time. It is like an opening theme in a symphony, closely related to the main theme but not in itself the main theme. For of course the action of the book is in bitter snow, and the recurrent phrase soon becomes 'Dehors il neige.' People, as well as the soldier, do walk at various times with their hand up to protect their eyes, but from the snow blizzards, not from the rain or sun, nor is the street later either wet or dusty but a clean or a trampled white. Not till the very end, when the first person comes in again, do we get the phrase 'Dehors il pleut.' Yet the present tense is used throughout the first paragraph, and throughout the book (except in a few flashbacks for the *soldier*'s attempts to understand what happened a moment ago, on the previous occasion, *etc.* made unambiguous by the use of the imperfect). Thus the play with time, normally marked in a narrative with tenses (e.g. the pluperfect) or with shifters (*yesterday, later, a moment ago etc.*) is totally unmarked by the narrator.[12] This instantaneousness is at a different moment from the instantaneousness to come. The place, a small town, is the same, though the streets may or may not be the same throughout. But the time in terms of the weather, though described particularly, is here made general by the triple change. The particularisation into winter, and all further spatial and temporal developments, are yet to come.

At the end of that first paragraph, however, a subsidiary theme (visual) is stated: 'le vent dessine des parallèles, des fourches, des spirales'.

This is by no means as subsidiary as it looks, for it is to receive a very full treatment, as full as that of the snow, though less immediately obvious because part of it; yet the snowscape would be nothing without it. Furthermore, it is also given its balancing independent importance, beyond the reach of the snow, indoors, where we are at once taken: 'Ici le soleil n'entre pas, ni le vent, ni la pluie, ni la poussière' (p. 9) (here the sun does not enter, nor the wind, nor the rain, nor the dust).

We are still, then, with the I–narrator who can see or conceive the street in its various seasonal aspects, but he is indoors. From then on, however, we may or may not be still with him as objectivity takes over.

The dust, in that list, at once becomes a less negative link than the wind, rain or sun which do not enter, for there is after all dust inside, a fine dust on all horizontal surfaces, on the varnished table, on the polished floorboards, on the veined marble of the chest of drawers. And in this dust patterns occur, the round or square or rectangular traces of objects once there but since displaced, identifiable by the shape left behind, notably that of a round glass ashtray. This roundness is linked with the circle of light projected by the lamp onto the ceiling, but the circle is imperfect, cut by one of the walls which, unlike the other three, is covered from top to bottom and over most of its width by heavy red curtains. The curtains lead back to what is beyond them. 'Dehors il neige. Le vent chasse sur l'asphalte sombre du trottoir les fins cristaux secs, qui se déposent après chaque rafale en lignes blanches, parallèles, fourches, spirales ... recomposant de nouvelles spirales, volutes, ondulations four-chues, arabesques mouvantes aussitôt disloquées' (p. 11).[13]

So the in/out play of shapes begins, like an abstract painting in motion, except that the analogies are occasionally non-visual: here the noise of heels on the pavement acts as the next link, again negatively, for it is then said that they cannot be heard inside: 'La rue est trop longue, les rideaux trop épais, la maison trop haute' (p. 12). ('The street is too long, the curtains too thick, the house too high.') The height of the house, so casually mentioned here, is important (see below). We are back indoors. On the polished floor, felt slippers have traced shining paths from the bed to the chest of drawers, from the chest of drawers to the chimney-piece, from the chimney to the table. A sort of cross, or knife, or dagger, lies to the right ... On the edge of the lamp a small fly walks, projecting a deformed shadow on the ceiling ... 'Dehors il neige. Dehors il a neigé, il neigeait, dehors il neige' (p. 14).

With this sudden mixture of tenses the first theme, which amounts to 'we are watching this out of time', recurs briefly, but plunges us straight back into instantaneousness. Time, however, has already passed: 'Les flocons serrés descendent doucement, dans une chute uniforme, ininterrompue, verticale – car il n'y a pas un souffle d'air – devant les hautes façades grises' (pp. 14–15).[14] Before, the wind was blowing the snow in twists and spirals over a still dark pavement; heels could be heard. Now the snow is vertical, there is no breath of wind. Imperceptibly the visual pattern of shapes becomes a pattern of time as the shapes take us indoors and out by a process built on analogy.

But already the anti-rhetoric warns us off. After a description of the rectilinear street and the cross-roads and the converted gas lamp on the corner, lit though in full daylight (the street-lamp echoing the indoor lamp) we are told: 'Mais c'est un jour sans éclat, qui rend toutes choses plates et ternes. Au lieu des perspectives spectaculaires auxquelles ces enfilades de maisons devraient donner naissance, il n'y a qu'un entrecroisement de lignes sans signification' (p. 15).[15]

These very lines, however, lead us back to the room: 'A la limite du mur et du plafond, l'ombre de la mouche, image grossie du filament de l'ampoule électrique' (p. 15). Then, quietly, the next paragraph begins: 'C'est encore le même filament, celui d'une lampe identique ou à peine plus grosse, qui brille pour rien au carrefour des deux rues, enfermé dans sa cage de verre en haut d'un pied de fonte, ancien bec de gaz aux ornements démodés devenu lampadaire électrique' (p. 16).[16] After which comes the first description of the soldier standing in the circle of light, in the snow. One naturally remembers the fly on the ceiling.

The parallelism is clear, and carried out with an almost mathematical consistency, the linguistic transition being either an expression of similarity like *même, un autre, aussi, un motif analogue* etc., or more often, mere contiguity, the next scene being described without any linguistic indication that it is not the same scene.

For example, the portrait of the soldier is a detailed close-up of both the ornate lamp-base and the man leaning against it – tired, cold and grey-looking with a one-day old beard. The pavement is now white without traces and snow has accumulated a little on the lower edge of the lamp-base:

Mais le bas de la capote a balayé quelques-uns de ces menus amas, de même que les chaussures en changeant plusieurs fois de position, ont tassé la neige dans leurs alentours immédiats, laissant par endroit des taches plus jaunes, des morceaux durcis à demi soulevés, et les marques profondes des têtes de clous rangées en quinconces. Devant la commode, les chaussons de feutre ont dessiné dans la poussière une large zone brillante ... De l'une à l'autre est tracé un étroit chemin de parquet luisant; un second chemin va de la table jusqu'au lit. Parallèlement au mur des maisons ... un chemin rectiligne marque aussi le trottoir enneigé. D'un gris jaunâtre, produit par le piétinement de personnages maintenant disparus, il passe entre le lampadaire allumé et la porte du dernier immeuble, puis tourne à angle droit et s'éloigne dans la rue perpendiculaire, toujours longeant le pied des façades, au tiers environ de la largeur du trottoir, d'un bout à l'autre de sa longeur.
Un autre chemin repart, ensuite, du lit vers la commode (p. 18).[17]

During this very description, in and out of doors, time has passed again, for the virgin pavement is now marked by a yellow path 'produit par le piétinement de personnages maintenant disparus', echoing the traces left in the dust by objects displaced in the room

(p. 10). The visual counterpointing continues, from the patterns in the dust to the dagger-like cross, to the striped wallpaper with its dagger-handle-or-flame-or-clove motif ('un motif analogue orne encore le papier peint des murs' [p. 19], *encore* suggesting either that the I–narrator is seeing this much later or that the paper is old at the time, or both); and from the flame motif to the lamp, to the fly and back again to the soldier under the lamp, this time with the famous oblong box under his arm:

Dehors, le ciel est toujours de la même blancheur sans éclat. Il fait jour encore. La rue est déserte: ni voitures sur la chaussée, ni piétons sur les trottoirs. Il a neigé; et la neige n'a pas encore fondu ... La platitude de tout ce décor ferait croire, d'ailleurs, qu'il n'y a rien derrière ces carreaux, derrière ces portes, derrière ces façades. Et toute la scène demeure vide: sans un homme, ni une femme, ni même un enfant. (pp. 23–4)[18]

The first statement of theme is now over. We are given a sudden camera-swerve back to the interior. But the purpose now is to lead us to another interior, that of the café. Consequently the switch is not by visual analogy – whether positive or negative – but by violent contrast, from (dead) 'life' to represented life, from absence of anyone to a crowd, but a crowd in an engraving:

Le tableau, dans son cadre de bois verni, représente une scène de cabaret. C'est une gravure en noir et blanc datant de l'autre siècle, ou·une bonne reproduction. Un grand nombre de personnages emplit toute la scène. (p. 24)[19]

The people are then described in detail, including the proprietor, the group of bourgeois gentlemen, the boy, and the three soldiers, who make a contrast of stillness with the crowd around them. The calligraphic legend below the engraving 'datant de l'autre siècle' is 'La défaite de Reichenfels' (p. 26). Once again we are snatched for a second into the timeless continuum. But now the soldiers are further described and imperceptibly we slip into the fiction's 'reality'. The boy (who was also on the picture, starting out of its proscenium frame or, in the 'real' café, at the door) talks to the tired soldier (pp. 30–1), at semi cross-purposes. (All the dialogue in the book, whether or not taking place at cross-roads, is at cross-purposes.) The soldier looks out. 'Dehors il neige' (p. 31). Now the snowflakes are being chased horizontally by the newly risen wind. He looks for the street names, but the night (so it is now night) is too black, and in any case a street name would hardly help him in a town he does not know (p. 31). He goes down a perpendicular street with similar lamps more widely spaced, 'dont la clarté maigre illumine au passage la chute oblique des flocons' (p. 32) ('their meagre light catching the snowflakes in their slanting fall'). The snowflakes change direction, are quicker, are horizontal again, are vertical, horizontal, hit him in the face when he turns back, fall slowly now. The streets are perpendicular, parallel, the path he has just trod is 'jalonné par l'alignement des lampadaires électriques' (pp. 31–3, 'punctuated by the row of electric lamps'). The boy he meets (and later keeps meeting at various times) vanishes down the road, reappearing like a moth in the light of each lamp as he swings around it and runs on, his cape echoing the soldier's coat. 'Il fait jour de nouveau, le même jour terne et pâle. Mais le réverbère est éteint' (p. 41, 'It is daylight again, the same dull and pallid daylight. But the street-lamp is extinguished.')

The composition in motion is one of lines, circles and crosses, fairly simply at first, linking the street, the room with (probably) its picture, and the café, until the rhythm suddenly quickens at what may be termed the end of the first movement, with the dramatic scene in the ground-floor corridor into which the boy has led the soldier and then vanished through a door on the other side of the block (if it is the same boy); a woman comes out of a flat, screams and slams the door, another rushes upstairs, four or more storeys (pp. 55–6); a third woman appears from a third door in the same corridor, they talk, he asks about a street, she tells him to wait, and before shutting her door says: ' "Fermez donc sur la rue ... il vient du froid dans toute la maison" ' (p. 58, 'Close the street-door ... It makes the whole house cold.'). The soldier walks back to the front door, shuts it and finds himself in the dark (clearly the woman's flat is on the ground-floor, see below). He closes his eyes and sees the cross-roads, the lamps, the snow, the boy. For the first time we are definitely told that the soldier is visualising in memory, rather than (presumably) seeing what is being described. Here this acts as resolution of the main theme. But by the end of the book it has become part of a complicated pattern of data as experienced and/or re-experienced through fatigue and then through delirium.

For the moment, however, the pattern continues over a more complex field of experience which now includes the woman, her one-legged lodger or lover, the boy, who seems to be her son, the barracks, as well as the room, the street and the café. At the opening of the 'second movement', we are first back in the room ('De la commode à la table il y a six pas', p. 59, 'From the chest of drawers to the table it is six steps'), then back in the corridor with the soldier and a quickening rhythm of patterns:

Noir. Déclic. Clarté jaune. Déclic. Noir. Déclic. Clarté grise. Déclic. Noir. Et les pas qui résonnent sur le plancher du couloir. Et les pas qui résonnent sur l'asphalte, dans la rue figée par le gel. Et la neige qui commence à tomber. Et la silhouette intermittante du gamin qui s'amenuise, là-bas, de lampadaire en lampadaire (p. 61).[20]

Sometimes the pattern of lines, circles and crosses is in minute close-up (e.g. 'hachurée', 'of a man's hand', a metaphor which also occurs in *La Jalousie*; or the circle and cross imprint of the boy's shoes in the snow). Sometimes it is in longshot. Sometimes it is slow, sometimes quick, like the snow, sometimes vertical sometimes horizontal, sometimes oblique. But always as part of a pattern of time passing within a timeless eye.

3. Ambiguity as distancing

I have analysed these early pages in some detail in order to show how carefully Robbe-Grillet constructs his interrelations of space and time, turning them also to account as a means of creating the ambiguous and confusing atmosphere which the soldier is experiencing. Indeed the complexity of these interrelations increases as more and more data crowd into his experience of what turns out to be the last two conscious days of his life. The continual denial of significance, moreover, is part of that same experience, since rectilinear streets as such would tend not to have significance to him.

But where there is analogy there is significance, even if limited to the fact of analogy, just as one of two parallel lines has the added significance of being parallel to the other, which it would not have by itself. Robbe-Grillet is not just playing a complex moving game of noughts and crosses with his circles, curves, squares and inter-crossing lines that are 'without significance'. Significance is a matter of context. The soldier does not, at the time he is in the street, see the inside of the room; indeed, at this stage in the novel we do not know that he will be/has been dying/will die/has died inside that room. The slow dawning of a context is achieved by the extra-temporal, apparently omniscient, but constantly doubt-instilling narrator. Yet the narrative is not, or probably not, despite its top-and-tailing in the first person, really reconstructed by the I–narrator, nor is it told by the soldier. It is more like an objective depersonalised recreation of the soldier's mental contents as he waits and walks in the street and sits in the café, sits in the woman's flat, sleeps at the barracks, walks the street, is shot from a motorbike, lies in (another?) woman's flat. It is presented instantaneously, yet out of time, experienced and re-experienced through the dying soldier's delirium, when all the data of the preceding days have acquired a dream-like intensity that nevertheless confuses time, accuracy and even subjective identity, so that the soldier could be seeing himself from outside himself as well as reliving incidents and collocations of data with omissions, shifts, or added detail as if through the expanding and contracting lens of memory and imagination; but instantaneously, merging with direct experience. The I–narrator at the end is simply a further telescopic removal, which rounds off (or frames) our sensation of having *also* experienced the data as reconstructed by him, or anyone else, outside.

The point is important because it explains a certain ambiguity of perspective which is in effect a double ambiguity.

First, there is the play on the paradox of narrative time and narrated time (Müller 1948, Weinrich 1964, Genette 1972), in the best Baroque tradition.[21] For example, the shoebox shaped parcel. After the first café-scene (stemming from the picture) and the conversation with the boy, the soldier is back in the street, and meets the boy, who takes him to the café, after which he is back in the street, meets the boy (again?) who asks him were he slept ('Par là – A la caserne? – Oui, si tu veux, à la caserne' – this long before the scene at the barracks), and also what he has in the box. When the boy has gone, the soldier looks at the windows in the grey façades, and suddenly the red curtains are being described, and the chest of drawers, and the picture. And on the picture the boy is sitting on the floor, staring at the foreground, holding the shoebox shaped parcel in his arms. There follows a speculation on what the artist intended the boy to be staring at, presumably the door, though he is looking too low, etc. But now the real soldier comes in.

The picture (called 'The Battle of Reichenfels') dates from 'the other century' (p. 24), and the boy on it is holding the shoebox shaped parcel. Earlier still, immediately after the first introduction of the parcel under the soldier's arm, the box itself had become the link, as the dust had been, back to the room with the chest of drawers: 'La boîte enveloppée de papier brun se trouve maintenant sur la commode. Elle n'a plus sa ficelle blanche, et le papier d'emballage, soigneusement replié sur le côté du parallélépipède, bâille légèrement en un bec aux lignes précises ... Juste au-dessus est accroché le tableau' (p. 22).[22]

This is the very first mention of the picture and at the same time a flash-forward to a time at the end of the novel, after the soldier's death, when the doctor–narrator finally opens the parcel, which turns out to be a biscuit-tin containing letters from a girl to a soldier called Henri Martin, now dead, on whose behalf our soldier had been trying to deliver the box at an address he could not find or remember. But even the room, with its chest of drawers, red curtains, etc. is ambiguous. At first it seems to be high up (see p. 300). The room in which the soldier has his bread and wine and talks to the woman (and later dies?) is however on the ground-floor (see p. 303 above). It also has a chest of drawers, red curtains, a crack on the ceiling etc. and its paths in the dust are made by the boy's felt slippers. Only the table is sometimes covered with a red and white check oilcloth (itself a link with the similar table in the café, as the woman is a link to the woman serving drinks in the café or in the picture). At one point the soldier notices that the red curtains are not made of heavy velour, but of a light material. There could thus be two almost identical rooms, one high up (in which the soldier is dying? Or after the soldier's death in the ground-floor room?) with the picture, and belonging to the I–narrator (the doctor), the box being on his chest of drawers; or the box is on the chest of drawers in the woman's flat, the ground-floor room of which the soldier is getting to know in intense but increasingly confused detail during his final agony. The latter is more likely, but the point is it doesn't matter. The high room could be the narrator's or it could be a confusion of the dying soldier who thinks, with the curtains drawn, that he is in a high room, merging it perhaps with the high room he later (i.e. earlier) is taken up to at the barracks, where he looks out of the window and sees himself knocking at the front door a moment before (and this too could be a memory fusion). Similarly he may be staring at the picture from the bed, thinking that it represents the café-scene through the glass-door and also fusing that with another crowded café or canteen scene nearer to the battlefield; and reading the inscription as The Battle of Reichenfels.

We are made to see, creator-like, the same objects in different time-scales, yet as instantaneously as language, which takes time, can make it. This is a very Baroque (as well as Cubist and post-Cubist) situation, in which the same object can be several things at once, or seen in two or three different perspectives simultaneously. Here it is achieved by analogy, and by apposition within the present tense (together with time and place shifters like *maintenant, dehors, etc.*), rather than by metaphor, explicit paradox or other specifically Baroque methods. But it operates throughout as a means of structure which forces us to experience from inside the author's narrative time – itself identified with the strange processes inside the protagonist's mind – and not in narrated time, vicariously from our own time-scale.

This first aspect of the double ambiguity is considerably enforced by the second aspect, namely the choice of a confused person as central figure or experience who because of his condition is likely to get things out of the routine focus (another form of estrangement or distancing): here a lost and exhausted soldier, elsewhere a morbidly jealous husband, a delayed adolescent, a puzzled detective, or, in *Marienbad*, a woman disorientated by a hyperbolic extension of the 'haven't-we-met-before' seduction line. The soldier's fatigue blurs the time-scale further. He does not know which day it is, only which part of the day. At one moment he has the number 12345 on his cape, which he tells the boy is not his number (because the cape is not his); at another the boy accuses him of having unsewn his number; later (i.e. earlier), in the barracks dormitory, his wet cape is taken from him and he is given another, with no number, with which he walks out in the middle of the night, in a high fever; in the café he has his number or he has not, he is taken for a deserter or he himself goes looking for a deserter in another room (a fusion with the barracks, itself a fusion with his previous barracks and the dying owner of the box); in the barracks dormitory there is no shelf behind the bed, and he puts the box under his pillow but suddenly there is a shelf and the box is on it (a memory of the other barracks). He sees objects with intense clarity but as he lies dying he feels the urge to make an inventory of everything in the room, the implication being that his obsessive concern for phenomena, indeed the entire book, is the desperate inventory of a dying man.[23] He is not sure about anything, even whether it is the same boy he keeps meeting.

4. Language versus camera

I have used terms like close-up and links, but Robbe-Grillet's effects are essentially literary, despite his obvious affinity with the cinema.

They could not be achieved by a camera without ominous close-ups which would of course enable us, the 'normal' viewer, to remember and therefore *not* to be confused, *not* to be like the soldier; to be, that is, outside. Even without close-ups, one would remember the boy's face. One would certainly remember a sentence just uttered, and indeed in most books one would see it. Here, when the soldier is particularly confused, we are not given the actual sentence, only a description of its movement: 'Il s'arrête aussitôt, sur une phrase incertaine, bouclée à la hâte dans une direction que le début n'annonçait guère, et dont le caractère interrogatif est si peu net que la femme conserve la possibilité de s'abstenir d'y répondre' (p. 72), followed later by his attempt to reconstruct it: 'Le soldat essaye maintenant de se rappeler les termes exacts qu'il vient d'employer. Il y avait le mot 'caserne', mais il ne parvient pas à se souvenir de la phrase bizarre qu'il a prononcée' (p. 72).[24] And in the phrase I quote on (p. 294 above) the author achieves a similar effect by means of a very Baroque (and, as we now know, integral) comparison of a sentence to a legend at the foot of a picture (p. 147).

Or again there is the scene (pp. 43–4) in which the boy in the snow under the lamp suddenly seems closer without apparently having moved. In a film this would merely seem like a closer close-up. Nor could a camera reproduce (except by other means, such as swift juxtapositions of contrary images) the speculative tone which from the very beginning makes one thing possibly something else (*sans doute, si toutefois, peut-être, cette solution semble douteuse*, etc.). As in Beckett's novels (cp. *Watt*: 'Other possibilities occurred to Watt, in this connexion … etc.'), alternative suppositions are given about the most trivial objects, even the source of the dust or the dagger in the room, as if the observer were a detective *ad absurdum*, and paradoxically this makes phenomena not absurd but more quintessential, seen in all their possible beings. Things are not only perhaps something else but can even be something quite other than what they have just been described as, especially towards the end:

'C'était ça que tu voulais me dire?
– Non, répond le gamin, c'était pas ça.'
Alors ils ont entendu le bruit, très lointain, de la motocyclette.
Non. C'était autre chose. Il fait noir. De nouveau c'est l'attaque, le bruit sec et saccadé des armes automatiques. (p. 160)[25]

And on p. 182:

Le soldat est couché sur le dos, tout habillé …

Non. C'est en réalité un autre blessé qui occupe la scène, à la sortie de la salle de café pleine de monde. Le soldat vient à peine d'en refermer la porte qu'il voit s'approcher de lui un jeune collègue, conscrit de l'année précédente ... [There follows a brief confusion with another soldier, a hero of Reichenfels, then the young man tells him that his friend is dying and calling for him].[26]

Such denial is perhaps the nearest we come to the Baroque technique of particularising by taking the opposite into account, but in general the constant doubt is built up through analogy, unmarked time-shifts and expressed suppositions.

The stream of consciousness did achieve something like this effect, but as a purely naturalistic reproduction of disorganised chaos and self-intrusions, and without the clear formal paradox of precision in space with a blurring of time which itself shifts the precision in space (see chapter 12, p. 323 below). Here we share the mental content of the confused soldier, but with such a high degree of formal patterning, selecting, and framing that another narrator is constantly implied both ever-present and non-present at the same time, and always denying the very implication.

5. The Baroque and the uncanny

Robbe-Grillet's refusal to find or to grant significance to phenomena has much the same opposite effect as *occupatio* or the refusal to describe, for it serves to emphasise that he has already given them and is continually giving them the significance of a complex and ever moving formal relationship to each other, as well as to the time-scale they inevitably move under. He may repeat 'et cela ne signifie rien non plus' (p. 76), but his careful artistry belies the statement. And other statements are laid across that one, and others again, parallel, perpendicular, segmented and circular, by an analogical process based on the formal relationship of things but never announced by a change of tone or style, and only barely supported by almost imperceptible verbal devices, sometimes as simple as the 'and' of Biblical narrative. Yet, by the end of the novel, the snow (so dear to Baroque poets as emblem of evanescence) has become inextricably bound with the time sequence and with the blurred process of the soldier's experience towards oblivion and death. So that, despite the author, yet through his art, it has acquired a fleeting significance other than itself (p. 196):

Et la couche nouvelle qui se dépose ainsi peu à peu sur les traces de la journée, arrondissant les angles, comblant les dépressions, nivelant les surfaces, a vite fait d'effacer les chemins jaunâtres laissés par les passants le long des maisons, les empreintes isolées du gamin, les deux sillons parallèles que le side-car a creusés au milieu de la chaussée. Mais il faudrait s'assurer, d'abord, que la neige tombe toujours.[27]

I have brought out certain 'baroque' aspects of Robbe-Grillet's art, not to claim a wholesale 'return to baroque', but to show that the bizarre leaps in time and perspective, together with an effect of instantaneousness and a transgression of narrative levels, fundamentally disturb familiar values by distancing and producing a disquieting – some would say subversive – uncertainty.

But these effects, by different means, are also those of the uncanny. In Todorov's theory, the fantastic–uncanny is a type of text where the ambiguity of supernatural/natural is eventually resolved with a natural explanation. In the 'pure' uncanny there is little or no supernatural, but only the bizarre or horrific, and this opens out onto all narratives with strange or unusual events, and ultimately onto all realistic fiction. Between the fantastic–uncanny and the pure uncanny hovers the murder-mystery or detective-story, with its natural explanation of a perfectly natural but often chilling murder, and which does or did sometimes include strong hints of the supernatural (in Poe, in John Dickson Carr's *The Burning Court*, in Agatha Christie's *Ten Little Niggers*).

Robbe-Grillet's novels do not, of course, contain supernatural elements, but some are distinctly linked with the detective-story (*e.g. Les Gommes, Le Voyeur*) and with horror (*Le Voyeur, Projet pour une révolution à New York*). These elements, however, are not treated as mysteries to be solved (there is, of course, no 'explanation'), and not even as horror, but in a calm, assertive, realistic tone, which nevertheless, through constant doubt, supposition of alternatives, and bizarre shifts in perspective, produce *an* effect of the uncanny if not the same effect.

12

Transgressions

Robbe-Grillet and Nathalie Sarraute were perhaps the best-known exponents of the French *nounveau roman*, which became a force in the fifties, although Sarraute had published *Tropismes* in 1939 and *Martereau* in 1948. Robbe-Grillet's first novel *Les Gommes* was published in 1953, and Robert Pinget's first novel, *Graal Filibuste* dates from 1956 (Paris). Barthes's first attempt to theorise this new kind of writing, *Le Degrè zéro de l'écriture*, appeared in 1953. Both Sarraute and Robbe-Grillet early expressed their astonishment that the only narrative discourse recognised by the majority of readers should be that of the nineteenth century, based on the truth of representation, and each tried in very different ways to alter this discourse.

It is true that the novel seems to have lagged some fifty years behind the other arts, which all underwent their equivalent crises early in the century; lagged behind, even, other language forms such as poetry and drama. But changes in the novel had been occurring elsewhere. Borges published his *Ficciones* in 1956, but most of these texts had appeared in print during the early forties and even in the thirties, though not in wide circulation. Beckett published *Murphy* in 1938, but was ignored, and apparently the proofs or typescript of *Watt* were bombed during the war: it did not finally appear till 1953, after the success of *Waiting for Godot*, and it was printed in Paris, by the Olympia Press, not by the firm who published his plays. The resistance was great, in France but especially in England, where traditionalist critics and realistic novelists organised strong campaigns, which they no doubt feel they have won.

Meanwhile, the movement continued to develop, into the '*Nouveau nouveau roman*' and, now in America, 'Postmodernism'. How sadly devoid of content these critical labels are, compared to the deep changes that have occurred. I shall try to describe 'postmodernism' in the next chapter, but now, after analysing in detail one novel by Robbe-Grillet, I would like to deal with what has been

311

happening since the fifties, in the light of one concept only, that of transgression – which, since the 'rules' fluctuate and evolve, is often a matter of degree. I shall base my investigation on Gérard Genette's 'Discours du récit' in *Figures III* (1972, but see also 'Les frontières du récit', in *Figures II*, 1969). That is, instead of studying one author, I shall examine the classical structures analysed by Genette, insofar as they are transgressed. Genette himself has already pointed out certain authors who transgress the 'limits' of any single structure, though his primary task is to define these limits. My three main texts will be *Compact* by Maurice Roche (1966), *Nombres* by Philippe Sollers (1968), and *Projet pour une révolution à New York* (shortened here to *Projet*) by Alain Robbe-Grillet (1970), but I shall refer to others by these authors and to other authors, including later Beckett, and Sarraute whose individual experiment sets her quite apart from the others. She is not, if we must use such labels, '*nouveau nouveau*' but just '*nouveau*'. Robbe-Grillet, too, is always associated with the *nouveau roman*, not the *nouveau nouveau roman*, but his later texts are every bit as interesting as, though different from, the *nouveau nouveau roman* and also form a useful contrast. Almost everything I shall be saying about *Projet* also applies to *Topologie d'une cité fantôme* (1976). I chose the former because I happen to prefer it.[1]

Genette's basic distinction between *story* and *discourse* (*fabula-*

Table 12.1

Time	Mood	Voice
Order	*Distance*	*Time of narration*
analepsis	narration of events	ulterior
prolepsis	(diegesis/mimesis)	anterior
(exterior/interior/	narration of speech	simultaneous
mixed; repetitive/	(narrativised discourse	interwoven
completive; partial	transposed discourse	
/complete)	reported discourse)	
Duration	*Perspective*	*Narrative levels*
pause	nonfocalisation	extradiegetic
scene	internal focalisation	intradiegetic
summary	external focalisation	metadiegetic
ellipsis		
Frequence	alterations:	*Person*
singulative (2 types)	paralipsis	heterodiegetic
repetitive	paralepsis	homodiegetic
iterative		

Functions of the narrator: narrative, metanarrative, communicative, testimonial, ideological.

sjužet) seems to be yet another manifestation of the content/form division, but here at least there is no evaluation of the one at the expense of the other. Genette constantly reminds us that the many categories and subcategories he has to treat separately for analytical purposes are elements that often appear simultaneously in the text. Indeed, the very distinction *histoire/discours* is precisely one of the notions that writers of the *nouveau nouveau roman* have wished to explode. But Genette's emphasis is, like theirs on creativity, on discourse, story being simply what has to be reconstructed by the reader through the discourse.

His three main categories are time, mood, and voice, which he has thoroughly disentangled from earlier confusions. Table 12.1 for clarity summarises the categories:

1. Time (order, duration, frequence)

1.1. Order

Writers have always changed the narrative order of the events they recount, from the epic beginning *in medias res* to the present day, but the transitions are clearly marked, if not by narrator comment, at least by adverbial shifters and by tense (e.g., the pluperfect for the analepsis, the future for the prolepsis).[2]

The use of the present tense throughout, first by Dujardin, then by Gertrude Stein, then by Joyce in *Finnegans Wake*, and later by Robbe-Grillet and others, clearly flattens out all such clear markings in a perpetual present. 'A continuous present is a continuous present', wrote Gertrude Stein as if it were a rose. 'I made almost a thousand pages of a continuous present. Continuous present is one thing and beginning again is another thing' (*Look at Me Now*, p. 25). In fact Stein does not use the present tense in her long novels, not even in *The Making of Americans* of which she speaks here. She seems to be referring to the lack of movement, to the elimination of story through a static style with many continuous forms (was saying), which plays on minute variations of vocabulary or syntax within repetitions, re-stating, to insist on its uniqueness, the same episode, even a trivial one, where normal narrative would go on to another. But she certainly helped to launch the idea: 'And a great deal of the Making of Americans was a struggle to do this thing, to make a whole present of something that it had taken a great deal of time to find out, but it was a whole there then within me and as such it had to be said.' ('The Gradual Making of "The Making of the Americans"', p. 147). Conversely, in *Molloy* Beckett plays with the very marking off, by the present tense, of general comments from event in traditional narrative.

> I went. I had forgotten where I was going. I stopped to think. It is difficult to think riding, for me. When I try and think riding I lose my balance and fall. I speak in the present tense, it is so easy to speak in the present tense, when speaking of the past. It is the mythological present, don't mind it. (*Molloy*, pp. 33–4).

When there is no 'story' in the usual sense (as in Roche and Sollers, or, earlier, in some Stein), or when the discourse follows the order of events in such story as there is (as in most imitators of the *nouveau roman*), the use of the present has no other effect than simultaneity (see section 3. Voice). But Robbe-Grillet exploits this fusion of time in his novels by using the present whatever the order of events, so that, as we have seen, we never quite know when (and whether) something is occurring, or recurring (or being recalled), the only time markers being contingent ones, such as slight differences in the retelling, in the position of objects, or in the climate (the rain, the snow, no snow, thick snow, slanting snow, etc. in *Dans le labyrinthe*). Thus it is never clear whether events are lived or re-lived, an ambiguity used by these novelists to challenge the traditional notion of representation in fiction, where nothing is 'lived' except by the author in his writing experience and the reader in his reading experience.[3]

Genette notes the areas in a classic text where there is danger of interference (redundancy or collision); first, in an internal analepsis that is homodiegetic.[4] This is naturally the area most exploited by the *nouveau roman* (Sarraute, Beckett, Robbe-Grillet), precisely in order to create this interference with little or no marking of the analepsis (Sarraute and Robbe-Grillet in particular), because the notion of the fictional character and his 'background' is challenged – indeed the heterodiegetic analepsis is a mark of the traditional novel, inconceivable here. Similarly the marked prolepsis, which gives story-information in advance (the canonic 'we shall see later that' or 'I never saw/was never to see him again', as for example in *The Turn of the Screw*: 'she never saw him again' in the framing Prologue), is barely conceivable in this type of novel since the concept of the narrator as by definition knowing more than character or reader has also gone. Tense is either used to blur order (Robbe-Grillet, Sarraute), or it becomes wholly a category of voice (see section 3.1), and in later novels the whole question of order becomes irrelevant, since the very notion of 'event' is transgressed.

1.2. Duration (narrative pace)

I must comment here on a curious theoretical dilemma in Genette, who distinguishes four main categories (ST = story time, NT = narrative time):

Descriptive pause:	NT = n, ST = 0 (story stops,	NT∞ > ST
	NT infinitely greater than ST)	
Scene:	NT at same pace as ST	NT = ST
Summary:	NT is less than ST	NT < ST
Ellipsis:	NT = 0 (elided), ST = n	NT∞ < ST
	(NT infinitely less than ST)	

Genette notes the asymmetry (anathema to a structuralist): there is no movement corresponding to NT < ST (summary), but he himself almost gives the solution. Having said that the descriptive pause should not be confused with all pauses (which can include author intrusions) or with all descriptions (which can advance the story, as often happens in Proust), he also adds that NT > ST 'serait' a sort of slowed down scene, lengthened by extra-narrative elements or description and, further, that pure dialogue cannot be slowed down.

I would say that only pure dialogue can be represented as NT = ST (within the narrative convention, for there can be no theoretical guarantee that dialogue 'really' = ST since, if really 'pure', it will note no gestures, looks, or hesitations except through typography and punctuation, and such gestures if noted take longer to say in language than to perform). There is no theoretical difference (in this context of pace) between narrator-comment on gestures or sighs or sinking hearts and narrator-comments on thoughts, memories, emotions, or observations that so often breaks up dialogue in the traditional novel, expanding it to a much 'slowed down scene'. Thus it seems to me that any scene other than pure dialogue is the missing NT > ST, while NT = ST should be reserved for pure dialogue, or at most for dialogue with only the briefest stage directions ('he said', etc.)

This distinction is important since NT > ST and NT∞ > ST are precisely the areas exploited by the *nouveau roman* and by the *nouveau nouveau roman*. On the one hand, both early Beckett and Sarraute expand, as through a microscope, subthreshold inner dialogue and monologue. On the other, Robbe-Grillet, who on the contrary externalises his central consciousnesses into all that they perceive, uses little dialogue, and when he does, merely to punctuate the slowed-down description, thus inverting the earlier modern novel's use of much dialogue punctuated by brief description. Sollers in *Nombres* uses none, and in *H* is closer to Beckett, or to Molly Bloom's 'internal monologue' (see section 2. Mode).

Genette himself notes that there remains the narration detailed with actions, gestures, and events told more slowly than they can be accomplished. An extreme example is Claude Mauriac's *L'Agrandissement* (1963), which spends 200 pages on two minutes, though here the lengthening is not really an expansion of duration but consists of insertions such as rememorated analepses.

In general then, what we get is a type of narrative that concentrates almost wholly on the 'missing category' NT > ST (the slowed-down scene) and NT∞ > ST, but not through the use of the traditional descriptive pause since there is no 'story' to 'stop' for static description. There is, however, always action of some kind, if only a soldier waiting, a woman ironing; or a man watching, entering, leaving, climbing; or crawling (*Labyrinthe, Projet, Nombres,* Beckett's *Comment c'est*). We have seen how NT > ST functions in Robbe-Grillet's *Dans le labyrinthe*. In Sarraute (all her novels, see bibliography), there is no narrator-voice, and what expands is a multitude of voices, unspecified, reconstructed by the reader gradually, recognisable only from what is uttered. But what is uttered is an expansion, as under a microscope, of all that goes on at the threshold of consciousness, below dialogue (which also occurs, also unspecified as to the identity of the speaker), often undistinguished from the rest, in the sense that we do not always know whether it is spoken or inwardly rehearsed, or imagined. And there are ellipses (NT∞ < ST) to be reconstructed from these semiconscious utterances.

Robbe-Grillet also plays with the ellipsis (NT∞ < TS). His characters often appear and disappear without explanation or transition, so that we have to reconstruct (or the narrator reconstructs with explicit suppositions in the conditional, or with alternatives, *soit, à moins que* – e.g., *Projet,* p. 28), a (possible) previous appearance or event, however minor, even a mere gesture, given in the pluperfect: 'J'étais alors arrivé à la hauteur de l'escalier, et j'avais posé une main sur la rampe [... act itself elided]. Elle était presque parvenue ainsi devant la porte de sa chambre ... Laura a murmuré, tout bas, qu'elle avait peur ... Je n'avais plus la main sur la rampe, à présent, ni sur quoi que ce fût. Et il m'était difficile d'inventer autre chose du même genre' (*Projet,* p. 45).[5]

Such narrative either rejects or considerably reduces NT = ST

(Genette's scene, my 'pure dialogue'), as well as NT < ST (summary), which are the mark of the traditional novel. Robbe-Grillet does have dialogue in his narratives but it is rare, and although a post-elliptic statement in the pluperfect such as that quoted above is a kind of summary, it does not summarise plot elements in the sense meant by Genette – nor are the many suppositions in *Labyrinthe* (about the boy's disappearance, which door, etc.) summaries in that sense.

None of these categories apply to Roche, whose 'story', insofar as there is any, is altogether subsumed in discourse: I suppose NT = T($T → N).

1.3. Frequence

Genette's four categories are:

(1) to tell once what happens once: the singulative
(2) to tell n times what happens n times: also singulative
(3) to tell n times what happens once: the repetitive
(4) to tell once what happens n times: the iterative.

The first two obviously belong to the 'norm', and the third to special effects of repetition, particularly developed in Robbe-Grillet (for example, the caterpillar incident in *La Jalousie* (1957), retold obsessively and each time with further exaggeration of the neighbour's virility and the wife's femininity). This also occurs in Sarraute, but through the 'utterances' of the voices (for instance the aunt's fuss about her new arched door and velvet curtain in *Le Planétarium*, 1959).

The fourth, the iterative, 'normally' occurs at the opening of a classical narrative (scene laid, family introduced, with habits and background), and sometimes later for similar new introductions or in pauses. For a narrative in the past tense, the iterative in French is the imperfect and, in English, a grammatical equivalent (*would, could, used to, often + past*, etc.). Genette shows how the iterative was exploited to an unusual extent by Proust to describe social activities, one *soirée* coming to represent many. For a narrative in the present, there is no grammatical distinction between the punctual and the continuous, so that the frequence indicated by the present tense is more ambiguous and depends on the context.

The iterative is clearly non-narrative, as its use in classical narratives indicates: the actual story starts with a clearly marked singulative (One day/On just such a day, X got up . . . etc.), and, in French, with the *passé simple*, clearest mark of the traditional novel (cp chapter 4, p. 94 above). Theoretically, then, a narrative wholly in the iterative is impossible, since nothing specific and punctual happens, but only the usual, habitual things which by definition cannot make a story. And naturally this is one of the transgressions we find, most clearly in later Beckett. *The Lost Ones (Le Dépeupleur*, 1970) is written wholly in the iterative present. It describes the perpetual milling around of people in a vast cylinder and the exact rules they follow, such as when and how and in what order they can climb the ladders, or how long they can stay on the ledges. It presents a busy universe, yet nothing 'happens' other than this perpetual motion. Both the English and the French versions are written in the present tense, that is, the continuous or universal present used for describing a generalised, permanent state of affairs as opposed to punctual actions which have a beginning and an end:

Vus sous un certain angle ces corps sont de quatre sortes. Premièrement ceux qui circulent sans arrêt. Deuxièmement ceux qui s'arrêtent quelquefois. Troisièmement ceux qui à moins d'être chassés ne quittent jamais la place qu'ils ont conquise et chassés se jettent sur la première de libre pour s'y immobiliser à nouveau . . . Mais cette rémission ne dure jamais qu'une seconde . . . De tous temps le bruit court ou encore mieux l'idée a cours qu'il existe une issue. Ceux qui n'y croient plus ne sont pas à l'abri d'y croire de nouveau pp. 12, 15 and 16).[6]

How It Is (Comment c'est, 1961), which also describes a perpetual motion of crawling in the mud, catching up with Pim and being caught up by Bom, likewise uses the continuous present in both English and French, as does *Imagination Dead Imagine (Imagination morte imaginez*, 1967b).

The French present tense is also exploited by Sollers in *Nombres*, but in opposition to the imperfect (see Section 3. Voice), and, like the imperfect, for both punctual and continuous actions, e.g. (punctual): 'Vous ouvrez les yeux, vous énumérez ce qui passe devant vos yeux ... [continuous] Il y a toujours pour vous quelque chose à voir (4.28, p. 42),[7] the second use making the preceding use ambiguous. The imperfect tense sequences are often combined with the infinitive, non-finite participles (the present participle already exploited by Claude Simon), or the subjunctive (non-finite); in other words, with punctual time extracted from the verbs: '... "moi" cependant de plus en plus égaré dans le texte, posé, arrêté

dans un coin du texte et ne faisant plus réellement que passer [. . .]
dehors inscrit de tous côtés, étalé de façon permanente ou plus
profondément dissocié ou rêvé n'étant jamais ce qui échappait ou
restait, changeait et revenait avec d'autres, ne bougeant pas et
n'existant pas . . . milieu oû il suffisait de mettre deux termes en
présence pour que les opérations aient lieu' (3.47, pp. 62–3).[8]
It is not, then, tense alone that distinguishes singulative from
iterative, but also context and meaning. Thus the imperfect can be
iterative: 'Il lui arrivait de s'arrêter sans rien dire [. . .] Je
m'inclinais comme d'habitude' (Beckett, *Assez*, 1966: 19). Or singulative but continuous: 'Nous n'étions pas à la montagne cependant.
Je devinais par instants à l'horizon une mer dont le niveau me
paraissait supérieur au nôtre' (*Assez*, p. 22).[9] 'Je marchais donc à
travers les rues, et le soleil était revenu' (*Nombres*, 3.15, p. 29); 'Je
voyais mon histoire et une dernière fois dans cette histoire ce qui
avait pris [pluperfect] la forme du système imposé, ordonné . . .'
(*Nombres*, 2.22, p. 36).[10] In English, which distinguishes the iterative
from the singulative continúous, the latter examples would be
rendered either by the past (we were not in the mountains) or by
the past + present participle (I was walking). The present tense is
ambiguous in both languages since it can express, according to the
context, both the iterative (as in *Le dépeupleur*) and the singulative, as
more usually in Robbe-Grillet: 'Laura laisse retomber le rideau de
tulle, jette un coup d'oeil au magnétophone et constate' (*Projet*, p.
68).[11]

Beckett tends to use the two aspects of present or imperfect
naturally, as the need arises, once the initial choice of past or
present is made. Robbe-Grillet, in *Projet*, shifts his tenses continually.
Roche was, to my knowledge, the first to use different tenses in
formal opposition to each other, with a different typography to
mark the opposing fragments (*Compact*, 1966). In 1968 Sollers took
this up in *Nombres* with opposing sections. But as these shifts and
formalisations are combined with others, I shall return to them in
section 3.1. Voice. My main point here is to emphasise that it is the
iterative category of Frequence which, further developed from
Proust, is particularly exploited by these writers, the punctual aspect
of time being suspended; and that even the singulative use of the
present or imperfect is inevitably continuous or imprecise as to time,
implying that the action could be a repetition (*Projet*).

Thus we can see, by referring to Genette's schematic treatment of
time (NT/ST), that the writers of both the *nouveau* and the *nouveau*

nouveau roman are deliberately blurring ST:

Order: anachrony unmarked, through the use of the present tense
            (Sarraute, Robbe-Grillet, Sollers, Roche).

Duration: NT privileged over ST, which tends to disappear in NT > ST
            and NT ∞ > ST or, the other extreme, NT ∞ < ST as in ellipsis
            (Robbe-Grillet, Sarraute). Or, in Roche, a new form by
            poetic juxtaposition: NT = T($-N).

Frequence: ST suspended by a vast exploitation of the iterative, both
            present and imperfect, as well as present and past
            participles.[12]

2. Mood (distance, perspective)

Since mood touches on so many intertwined problems, it will be
necessary first to summarise Genette's beautiful classification and
then to show how the various transgressions operate. One can tell
much or a little, more or less directly (distance), and one can tell it
from this or that point of view (perspective).

2.1. Distance

The Platonic distinction between mimesis and diegesis reappeared
in post-Jamesian criticism as 'showing' and 'telling'. Aristotle had
neutralised it in favour of two versions of mimesis. But the very
notion of mimesis is an illusion: unlike dramatic representation,
narrative cannot imitate the story it is telling; it can only tell it, and
give an illusion of mimesis, unless the object imitated is language (as
in dialogue). Genette therefore distinguishes between narrative of
events and narrative of speech.

Narrative of events is always a transcription of the non-verbal
into the verbal, and its textual mimetic factors can be summed up as
two elements in inverse ratio: the quantity of information and the
presence of the narrator. To show is to give as much information as
possible with the least attention to the informant. To tell is on the
contrary to reveal the act of telling more than what is told. Thus
mimesis is defined as a maximum of information and a minimum of
narrator, diegesis as a minimum of information and a maximum of
narrator.

Since to show takes longer than to tell, these factors are also
related to time (duration – e.g., scene vs. pause or summary), and to
voice (narrator presence). Mood is in fact the combined result of
features that do not belong to it.

Proust, according to Genette, is a paradox who cannot be assimilated to this 'norm': his work consists of vast scenes (mimesis) and
also of constant narrator presence (diegesis), with an intensity that
runs counter to the Flaubertian 'rule' of a minimum of narrator
presence, for the 'transparence' of the text. Proust would then be
(like Balzac, Dickens, Dostoevsky but more so) at the extreme of
showing and telling. I am not at all sure of this 'paradox', this non-
assimilation to a 'norm' created theoretically by Genette. The
Flaubertian 'rule', like the post-Jamesian preferences for telling, was
a fashion, a theory not even observed by its authors. Genette's
distinction is a theoretical one, useful for determining the dominance of showing or telling (not mutually exclusive) in any one
author or period. The 'paradox' seems to me rather that the full-
fledged 'realistic' novel produced at periods which believed in the
truth of representation, exploits both mimesis and diegesis to a
maximum.

If verbal imitation of events is only an illusion, narrative of speech
seems on the contrary condemned to absolute mimesis, which, as
Socrates demonstrated to Cratylus, would amount to a duplication
of the world. Genette distinguishes three main forms, familiar in
traditional stylistics, and gives a type sentence for each.

(1) narrativised discourse – the most distant (I informed my mother of
my decision to marry Albertine)
(2) transposed discourse – two styles:
    (a) indirect (I told my mother that I absolutely had to marry
Albertine)
    (b) free indirect (I went to find my mother: it was absolutely
necessary that I marry Albertine)
(3) reported discourse (= direct discourse) 'I said to my mother (or: I
thought): it is absolutely necessary that I marry Albertine."' (Proust's
actual sentence, Pléiade III, 1131).

According to Genette, Plato favoured the most distant, but had
less influence in this than Aristotle, who maintained the superiority
of pure mimesis – hence the canonisation of drama and its influence
on the narrative genre. Oddly enough, as Genette points out, it was
by emphasising this mimesis of speech (subdramatic model) that the
twentieth-century novelist tried to emancipate himself, effacing the
last traces of narrative presence. This I think is the real 'paradox':
that in trying to emancipate himself from the heavy machinery of
the nineteenth-century realistic novel, the modern novelist turned

towards the theatre (an extreme example is the work of Ivy Compton-Burnett, almost entirely in dialogue), to which, as Sarraute pointed out long ago (1956), it can but be inferior, without the advantages of actors and production. Interesting and even fascinating though Compton-Burnett's work may be, it did not regenerate the novel (nor did it make good plays when adapted to the 'theatre'). The novel, like any art form, must have its own strength, and concentrate on the elements which the novel can exploit better than other arts, or which only the novel can exploit. (Cp. my remarks on language and the camera, with regard to Robbe-Grillet, p. 308 above.)

Another extreme in the use of direct discourse is found in the 'interior monologue', in which direct discourse is prolonged to the last sentence. Genette remarks that, as Joyce saw, this should be called 'immediate discourse', its essence being not that it is interior but that it is freed from all narrative presence. He also makes three important points, often ignored:

First, there is a close link between this immediate discourse and reported (direct) discourse, the only formal distinction being the absence of a declarative introduction 'He said'. (And, of course, the expansion.)

Second, that there is on the contrary an important difference between immediate discourse and the free indirect style of transposed discourse: in free indirect discourse the two instances are fused as the narrator takes over the character's speech or thought and assimilates it to his own (this applies even if they are the same person); whereas in immediate discourse the character is substituted for the narrator. (See chapter 2, n. 9 for more recent work).

Third, there is a frequent confusion of intimacy ('stream of consciousness') with lack of logic: the use of immediate discourse is supposed to show rambling thoughts. This is true only if the discourse happens to be rambling (Molly Bloom). See below, section 2.3, for Beckett's use.

I should like to add two points: First, that what Genette calls 'immediate discourse' seems remarkably close to what Voloshinov (1929, = Bakhtin) calls 'free direct discourse', which seems to me to make for a clearer typology (direct/indirect, free direct/free indirect). The narrative voice speaks, untrammelled by space, time or comment. When it is filtered through a character (Molly Bloom, Malone), it may well be called 'interior monologue' or 'immediate discourse', but when it is literally a disembodied voice, representing neither a character nor a narrator (nor the author *per se*), but rather the discourse itself (*H*), the term 'free direct discourse' seems more appropriate, as it may be also in *Malone Dies*, with Malone as the only narrative voice for the whole novel.

The second point is that free indirect discourse (FID), first developed in the nineteenth century for closer realism, was particularly exploited by the 'Moderns' (Joyce, Woolf, Faulkner and others including Mansfield and Lawrence) to create an ambiguity as to whose voice we are in fact hearing. In Lawrence this seems unconscious, haphazard, almost a stereotype, but in the others it often suggests metatextual subtleties of a kind similar to those analysed as AM and NM in chapter 8 above. All these writers, however, believed in representation, and their extreme exploitation of FID seems to me to have tired out the device, which, as Ann Banfield has shown, is a wholly literary invention (the sentences in FID being 'ungrammatical' in the direct and indirect discourse of 'normal' speech). As I suggested in chapter 4 (p. 94), FID (especially in the third person) is now a stereotype of the realistic novel, and is not found in these modern texts, whereas immediate discourse has been highly developed, from Beckett and Sarraute on.

The only representative of the *nouveau roman* to exploit and develop the immediate discourse of characters is Nathalie Sarraute, and in this alone she is absolutely distinct from the others. Her first text (hardly a novel) was *Tropismes* (1939), and tropism is a term from biology, meaning the response of an organism to outside stimuli. It has been defined as a dynamic gradient: in an organism A, the stimulus at point b will spread to the furthest portions of A, not instantaneously but in a diminishing gradient. We cannot deal with either the stimulus or the organism in a non-existing isolation.

Nathalie Sarraute explores this aspect of external stimuli such as objects, events, words, as they affect, in a dynamic gradient, the subconversations on the threshold of consciousness. Like the neurologist who records and amplifies impulses of pain, she creates the necessary outside stimuli, however slight, then records and amplifies the complicated interplay of approaches and withdrawals, instincts and calculations, the rare moments of sincerity ('those states of grace'), the pain caused by absent-minded rebuffs or by the way words lose their usual efficacy in the face of the opaque.

In her third novel *The Planetarium*, the subconversation carefully prepares the dialogue on the surface of a situation, and the dialogue in turn affects the subconversation. The situation, usually domestic and trivial but emotionally charged, is treated as a whole organism.

But subconversation and dialogue are unmarked by *he said, she thought* etc., which for Sarraute mean narrator-interference, turning the situation into a watched tennis-match (*L'Ere du soupçon*, 1956b). We are *in* the subconversation and dialogue, as immediate discourse. The whole novel is a kind of colloidal chemistry of fluctuating self-images, almost irrespective of who is experiencing what stimuli. By which I mean that although it is always clear, from what is said or thought, whose dialogue or subdialogue we are in, this is not of such primary importance as in a conventional realistic novel. The intensely subjective is treated, not so much with 'ironic detachment' – that critical cliché bestowed on the most esteemed 'lady-novelists' – as with total scientific objectivity and humility, qualities not prominent in Virginia Woolf with whom Sarraute is so often ineptly compared. These half-conscious movements and murderous impulses are viewed like organisms caught and enlarged in an electron microscope. But the metaphoric title swoops the perspective from submicroscopic to giant-telescopic, our psychic energies being implicitly seen also in terms of planets revolving round stars, galaxies receding from one another or colliding through the forces of gravitation, electromagnetism and nuclear reactions. This is a poet's rather than a novelist's concept, for poets often see the trite, the personal and the mundane in cosmic terms. And Sarraute has single-mindedly pursued her exploration of this cosmo-psychic space, from *Tropismes* to '*Disent les imbéciles*' (1976), further refining her very individual use of immediate discourse, to such an extent that it is impossible to class her either as or with the *nouveau* or the *nouveau nouveau roman*.

2.2. *Perspective*

Here Genette clarifies earlier confusions between mood (who sees) and voice (who speaks): they may be the same person but need not be, and are therefore theoretically distinct. The presence/absence of narrator (N) belongs to Voice, the point of view to mood (see his table, Genette 1972: 204). Genette prefers to avoid visual terms and uses 'focalisation', but takes up Pouillon's classification (*Temps et roman*, 1946, denoted as P below), as did Todorov in *Communications* 8 (1966):

(1) *Nonfocalisation or focalisation zero*
      (P: view from behind: N knows more than character)   N > C
(2) *Internal focalisation*

(P: view with: N knows same as character) $N = C$
  (a) fixed [e.g. Strether, *Bartleby's* narrator]
  (b) variable [*Mme Bovary*; Stendhal]
  (c) multiple [epistolary; Huxley's *Point Counterpoint*;
      Faulkner's *As I Lay Dying*
(3) *External focalisation*
  (P: view outside: N knows less than character)

Genette points out that internal focalisation is rarely used rigorously since the focalised character's appearance, behaviour, and thoughts can never be described objectively (though there are ways, such as mirror scenes and dialogue), particularly if the narrator is the character. I should like to add that external focalisation is even more difficult to use rigorously, since all information about a character's past, for instance, is excluded.[13]

Genette reminds us that focalisation can be varied (polymodality: restriction + omniscience) and that the post-Jamesian rule against such variations (not always observed by James) is arbitrary, a fashion in the name of greater realism.[14] But then so was external focalisation (Hemingway, Hammett) a fashion in the name of realism.

2.3. Transgressions in mood

The first impulse, in the *nouveau roman*, was to push the earlier reduction of narrator presence to the absolute limit of elimination,that is, to continue in the previous direction of mimesis. Thus Beckett, whose early novels (*Murphy, Watt*) tell the 'story'[15] of Murphy and Watt in the third person, later adopts immediate discourse and internal focalisation in the first person (*Malone Dies*): not, however, for 'rambling thoughts', but with a rigorous, if neurotic, logic. And Nathalie Sarraute consciously rejects all narrator interference when presenting, through internal (multiple or variable) focalisation, her characters' subthreshold sensibilities – fragmented and contradictory, transmuted by each other. It is only through the sensibilities themselves (thus foregrounded) that we can know whose they are – hence her annoyance when she is compared to Virginia, Woolf or even (more ignorantly, for despite the elimination of the narrator, she exploits immediate discourse, not dramatic dialogue) to Ivy Compton-Burnett. Here too we have the 'intimacy' of immediate discourse, representing both the spoken and the unspoken, and either way neurotic, but used very rigorously.

And the whole of *H* by Philippe Sollers (1973) is an unpunctuated immediate discourse of the same formal type as Molly Bloom's, but again, not 'rambling'.

Robbe-Grillet took a different direction. While ostensibly ruthlessly eliminating narrator presence, he in fact plays with it by paradoxically combining external focalisation (externalising all phenomena) and internal focalisation (as seen by a central consciousness, but wholly unpersonalised and even sometimes unidentifiable). In *Dans le labyrinthe*, the soldier is described externally and sometimes at a distance, and yet all else that we see seems to be seen through his eyes, with so many weird confusions and slightly altered repetitions that the focalisation, despite the meticulous precision, is blurred. We cannot know whether it is that of the soldier reliving his experience in delirium, or that of an undramatised narrator, or that of the doctor who suddenly appears in the first person at the end. In *La Jalousie* (1957) we have the extreme case, cited by Genette, of a central character, unpronouned, who can be deduced only from his focal position. In *Projet* there is an 'I' whose viewpoint is constantly shifted to that of his victim or others, in a transgressive way to be considered under Voice (section 3.3. Person).

More recent novelists, having rejected the very notion of mimesis, of story (which subsists, though undermined, in Robbe-Grillet), and of fictional character, have in effect returned to narrator presence, but in a manner so different from the traditional that it can hardly be called the same thing. Fictional character is abolished in favour of pronouns (see section 3.3. below), and once story is abolished in favour of *écriture* (discourse in Genette's optic), the *je* is neither the undramatised narrator (omniscient or restricted) of the traditional novel nor a dramatised narrator, but the *je-écrivant*, closer to the dramatised 'I' of the dramatic lyric best analysed by Robert Langbaum (1957), or, according to a recent further distinction by Ralph Rader (1976) that of the 'mask lyric' familiarised by Pound and Eliot. Yet in fact this *je* is closer to the author, but neutralised as mere emitter, even though, as in Roche and Sollers, things (often events belonging to the narrative act) may happen to him.

Roche's obsessive image, in all his texts, is that of the human skull or 'Mnémopolis' and all that is inside it. Most of his titles mean this: *Compact* (1966), *Circus* (1972), *Codex* (1974), and his latest, simply *Mémoire* (1976). Fictional mimesis is reduced to non-existence, except as juxtaposed joke fragments, like the 'story' of the Japanese doctor in *Compact* who bargains for the blind protagonist's tatooed skin: the *je* is blind because he looks inward, as the poet does. Indeed, Roche has brought the novel right back to its original source in poetry: not, however, as the 'poetic novel' tried to do, with richly decorative vocabulary, breathless sensibilities, and biblical rhythms, but as if turning to a contemporary 'original source', a *poésie concrète*, hard and rigorous.

Sollers's *Nombres* is very different, discursive rather than fragmented, and much more calculated, as its title implies.[16] Each fourth section is a reflection on the 'narrative' of the previous three, but this 'narrative' concerns the act of narration, in a precisely described physical space (ultimately a three-sided square or proscenium stage), which even borders on allegory:

Cependant j'arrivais du côté de ma propre histoire. Cela m'était signalé par la tentative de me situer à la périphérie d'un cercle qui serait passé par 'nous tous'. (2.6, p. 19)

Le récit avait beau être interdit, il n'était donc pas impossible de se glisser sous cette interdiction – sous sa ligne – de suivre les deux directions à la fois. (3.35, p. 51)

(et pourtant le récit continue: trajet double, montée d'une force sans garantie, et la question qui se pose alors plus loin que votre mémoire demande comment noter à la fois la forme et le son [...]) (4.40, p. 56)

(et ainsi, vous êtes comme devant le portique de l'histoire elle-même, sur sa scène brusquement redressée et illuminée [...]) (4.48, p. 63)[17]

What has happened in both Roche and Sollers is not only, as in Robbe-Grillet, a return to distance by rejecting narrative of speech (wholly in *Nombres*) for narrative of events (diegesis, maximum of narrator), combined with slowed-down scenes (mimesis, maximum of information), but also a reduction or total undermining of 'story', so that the 'information' does not apply to a story about people (as it still does in Robbe-Grillet, though undermined by subtle transgression), but to textual production. This story is constantly abolished and regenerated out of textuality, and the narrator is emptied of all features save those of textual production and the experience it implies. The technique of mimesis is not only combined with that of diegesis, but also used for non-mimesis. The focalisation is internal and fixed, despite the shifts of pronouns (see Voice, 3.3.), but since no 'information' is given about this 'narrator', other than his spatio-temporal narrative experience, externalized as it were, Genette's terms become more or less irrelevant, transgressed, fused.

3. Voice

Voice concerns narrative instance, often confused with point of view (mood) or with the (real) authorial moment of writing. Such a fusion is legitimate only in genuine autobiography, not in fiction where the narrator is himself a fiction, however close he may be to the author; and often he is dramatised as quite other.[18]

Thus the narrator situation is never the same as the author's writing situation. It is the narrator situation that Genette considers under Voice, according to the traces it (fictionally) leaves in the narrative discourse it is (fictionally) supposed to have produced.[19] Analysis of this situation can only proceed by tearing apart the tissue of close links between the narrative act, its protagonists, its spatio-temporal reductions, and its relations with other narrative situations implied in the same narrative. Elements which often function simultaneously must be dealt with separately. These elements are: (1) Time of narration, (2) Level of narration, (3) Person.

3.1. Time of narration

Owing to a lack of symmetry in the structure of language, one can tell a story without specifying the place, but not without specifying the time in relation to the narrative act, since one has to use tenses. Most narrative is in the past tense, as seems 'normal' (narrative after story), but predictive narrative has always existed (prophetic, oracular, apocalyptic, astrological), and since Dujardin's *Les Lauriers sont coupés* (1887, in *'monologue intérieur'* or immediate discourse), and of course Joyce's *Finnegans Wake*, we have narrative in the present tense. Genette distinguishes four types of narration:

(1) ulterior (past tense)
(2) anterior (theoretically in future tense, though a prophetic dream might be in the present or past)
(3) simultaneous (present tense)
(4) interwoven.

3.1.1. Ulterior time is used in the vast majority of narratives. Although Genette makes interesting points, notably about the fictitious zero-duration of the narrative act, it is not relevant to the novelists discussed here, who all consider the (punctual) past tense as a 'mark' of the traditional novel.

3.1.2. Anterior time is rare in narrative tradition, and usually occurs only at the second narrative level, a prophecy or dream occurring within a narrative, though Genette does not say why. The reason is, I feel, the need to believe that the event recounted actually took place, or is taking place: no one believes a prophet, and even a prediction needs to be realised within the narrative for sense and interest. Science fiction, although about the future, commonly post-dates its narration. The Apocalypse, too, uses the past tense.

Thus the use of the future tense by Maurice Roche for all the sequences in italics in *Compact* is a fundamental undermining of the reader's need to believe in fictional events. This transgression opens the text, with the second person singular of a voice in effect addressing itself (author's italics);

> *Tu perdras le sommeil au fur que tu perdras la vue. Tandis que tu pénétreras la nuit, tu pénétreras dans la nuit de plus en plus profonde; ta mémoire, labile déjà, s'amenuisant à mesure que – au sortir d'une longue léthargie – tu prendras conscience de ton état. (Comment désormais faire le départ du jour et de la nuit?)*
>
> *Tu seras là, sur un lit – dans une chambre sans doute. Les yeux écarquillés tu scruteras ce désert sombre→et l'espace s'élargissant te permettra-t-il d'aller si loin encore que tu ne puisses jamais revenir à toi?*
>
> *Mnémopolis que tu pourras hanter sous ton crâne sera une ville seule et obscure. Pas de rues pas de canaux nul labour alentour (ça? – les circonvolutions de ta cervelle), mais des vestiges auxquels tu tenteras de te raccrocher.* (pp. 15–16)[20]

This use of the future in effect contradicts what I have said about predictive narrative. Predictions are usually of a general nature, often vague, cryptic, even symbolic, unless they are orders – but there is a limit to detail even in orders.[21] Here, as with the 'intense' use of the iterative, the detail and intensity are such that we do believe that what is predicted not only will occur but is occurring/has occurred, while at the same time not occuring, abolished, a mere fiction of words.

Similarly, in *Sans* (1969) Beckett combines the future tense with a pronounless impersonal *passé simple* which then becomes a verbless *jamais*. The result is less precise:

> Jamais ne fut qu'air gris sans temps chimère lumière qui passe. Gris cendre ciel reflet de la terre reflet du ciel. Jamais ne fut que cet inchangeant rêve l'heure qui passe [a sort of absolute iterative].
>
> Il maudira Dieu comme au temps béni au ciel ouvert l'averse passagère . . . Il bougera dans les sables ça bougera au ciel dans l'air des sables. Jamais qu'en rêve le beau rêve n'avoir qu'un temps à faire . . . Il revivra le temps d'un pas il refera jour et nuit sur lui les lointains (pp. 7–10).[22]

Or with the fusion more obvious, in *H* (1973):

ça doit venir d'assez profond dans les masses pour que le truc éclate comme ça en plein jour un enterrement petit-bourgeois voilà faudrait la classe ouvrière peut-être peut-être mais quand même ils sont là et bien là pas ailleurs donc quelque chose demande demandait redemandera à être représenté de façon correcte quoi attention oui attention mais quand même ah voilà je vous attendais là mot d'ordre anticommuniste mais enfin merde. (p. 13)[23]

Or as supposition of inevitability in *Projet* (1975):

Et tout à l'heure, quand il fera son entrée au 'Vieux Joë,' pour rendre compte à Frank de sa mission et réparer ses forces avec une double rasade de bourbon sec, l'orchestre d'un seul coup s'arrêtera de jouer, le trompettiste soudain muet, sans penser dans sa stupeur à laisser retomber son instrument privé de sens, le détachera seulement de sa bouche, avec lenteur, pour l'immobiliser en l'air à dix centimètres des lèvres qui conservent encore la crispation du soliste en plein fortissimo, tandis que toutes les têtes dans la salle se tournent d'un même mouvement vers la porte donnant sur la rue, afin d'apercevoir à leur tour ce que les musiciens ont vu les premiers, du haut de l'estrade: la figure ensanglantée qui vient de faire son apparition dans le cadre rectangulaire déterminé par l'ouverture béante, sur le fond noir de la nuit. (pp. 61–2)[24]

In this last quotation the future forecast slips into the event itself, in a transgressive manner typical of Robbe-Grillet (see section 3.2. Levels).

The future in a sense emphasises the 'authority' of the narrator's voice, here no longer eliminated, but neutralised, undramatised, hàving become almost a computer prediction, a renovated return to the 'omniscient' voice but so fused with time-extracting devices and/or simultaneity, so emptied of 'narrator comment' (since there is no 'story' to comment on), that the effect is, paradoxically, of non-presence: 'seul le texte parle'.

3.1.3. With *simultaneous time* we get simpler effects. Genette says that in principle this is less complex than the others since a rigorous coincidence of S/N eliminates all interference and all play with time. This is not so. As I have said under Time (order), the use of the present tense merely removes the *marking* of anachronies, just as the cinema has eliminated its equivalents to the pluperfect for flashbacks (announced in dialogue, superimposition, fade, melt, etc.). Scenes are often shuffled like a pack of cards (e.g. Renais). So it is in Robbe-Grillet, as we have seen in chapter 11, (and implicitly in Sarraute). Moreover, Robbe-Grillet also plays with narrator interference in the form of level transgression and person (see sections 3.2. and 3.3. below).

The confusion of instances (S/N), as Genette points out, can here function in two different directions, according to whether the emphasis is laid on S or N. If on story, we get a 'behaviourist' type of novel in the present tense, pure events, as in many apparent imitations of the *nouveau roman*. This can seem like the essence of objectivity since the narrative utterance disappears in favour of total transparence (in other words, belief in mimesis); if on narrative, as in 'interior monologue', the coincidence S/N favours the discourse, and the action seems reduced to a mere pretext (already in Dujardin, stronger in Beckett, Claude Simon, and further developed in the *nouveau nouveau roman*). The present tense joins the two instances (S/N) and breaks the delicate balance, allowing the text, with a slight displacement, to shift over either to S or N, and the *nouveau roman* has exploited this ambivalence. Thus *La Jalousie* can be read either in the objectivist way (complete absence of jealous man) or as the interior monologue of a husband obsessively spying on his wife. *Nombres*, though less so because of the *je*, can also be read as the objective spatio-atemporalised intellectual adventures of a depersonalised, almost absent *je*, or as a disincarnated authorial discourse of a non-existent narrative. *H* opts less ambivalently for the latter.

3.1.4. Interwoven time, the most complex in principle since it must have several interacting instances of narrative, is also the most difficult to analyse for narrative instance: for example, a journal form may loosen up into a long monologue with a non-determined time position, as in Camus's *L'Etranger*. Moreover, the close proximity of S and N can produce the effect of friction (this is what happened today and this is what I think of it this evening), an effect already exploited by Gide in *La Symphonie pastorale* (1919), and much more highly developed in Butor's *L'Emploi du temps* (1956), where the narration can never keep time with the living. But this, combined with transgressive levels, is, as Genette reminds us, already fully realised in *Tristram Shandy*, where the basic rule that the duration of the narration must not exceed that of the story is constantly transgressed by Tristram: he is 364 days late in his narration, and since he lives 364 times faster than he writes, it follows that the more he writes, the more there is to write.

Curiously, Genette does not deal here with the *passé composé*, used by Camus and typical of the diary form since it contains both past and present to express that closeness of S/N. It is in. that diary context impossible in English, where it usually implies on the

contrary (unless accompanied by 'just') greater distance and gene-
rality: for example, 'I have been to Paris'; 'I have eaten caviar'
(sometimes, many times) vs. 'I went to Paris'; 'I ate caviar' (today,
this summer). Robbe-Grillet uses it to confuse narrative instance,
particularly in *Projet* where it is interwoven with present, pluperfect,
and imperfect:

Je fais un pas dans sa direction. Elle fait aussitôt un pas en arrière . . . C'est à
ce moment que, au-dessus de nos têtes, quelque chose s'est fait entendre . . .
Mais, à mi-voix, Laura a dit . . . J'étais alors arrivé à la hauteur de
l'escalier, et j'avais posé une main sur la rampe. Pour la rassurer, j'ai, sans
bouger la paume ni les autres doigts, donné trois coups secs du bout d'un
ongle sur le bois rond. Laura a sursauté, et elle a regardé ma main. J'ai
refait mon geste. (pp. 44–5)[25]

The effect is sometimes curious: 'Quand elle a semblé morte, j'ai
relâché mon étreinte' (p. 19).[26] But such an effect is also due to a
shift of narrative level (see section 3.2.)

In *Compact*, Roche uses a different typography for sequences in
different tenses. These sequences are truly 'interwoven', sometimes
breaking into each other in mid-sentence (Roche says the structure
is that of serial music), and each sequence has a different pronoun.
In his Preface Sollers gives a table of the text's 'musical score'. See
table 12.2 below.

Table 12.2

Récit	Personne	Temps
hypothétique	tu	futur
	vous	conditionnel
parlé	il ('japonais')	présent
narratif	je/on/nous	présent
		imparfait
descriptif	impersonnel	imparfait
(modulation de		présent
la narration)		

In later novels Roche uses the non-finite infinitive a great deal, thus
placing his 'story' in a hypothetical future of desire.

Sollers himself who had already exploited pronouns in *Drame*
(1965), also exploits tenses in *Nombres*, where the first three in each
series of four sections are in the imperfect (both punctual and
iterative), and the fourth (reflection on the 'narrative'), in brackets, is
in the present tense, non-finite participles, and infinitives. Already
in *bing* (1966), Beckett had dispensed with finite verbs altogether:

'Corps nu blanc fixe invisible blanc sur blanc. Seuls les yeux à peine bleu pâle presque blanc. Tête boule bien haute yeux bleu pâle presque blanc fixe face silence dedans. Brefs murmures à peine presque jamais tous sus. Trace fouillis signes sans sens gris pâle presque blanc sur blanc. Jambes collées comme cousues talons joints angle droit' (p. 10).[27]

3.2. Levels of narration

This is a distance not in time or space but in the relations various people have with the narrative: some are inside, some outside. For example, in *Manon Lescaut*, Renoncourt is writing his (fictitious) memoirs (extradiegetic, i.e. outside the story of Manon) in which he meets des Grieux (diegetic or intradiegetic), who tells his story (metadiegetic). *The Arabian Nights* is similarly structured (story of sultan, Scheherezade's stories, in which characters often tell stories). I must admit these prefixes are confusing, and do not express exactly what Genette is demonstrating: *meta*diegetic does not give the idea of the levels going *down* (since *meta* means *over*), and I would prefer *infra* (which also sticks to Latin). In the case of *Manon* moreover, the main story *is* that of Manon (i.e. this level is *diegetic*, and he should not have used it as alternative to *intradiegetic* for the level above. For *The Arabian Nights*, the story of the Sultan executing his wives would be extradiegetic, Scheherezade's stories diegetic, and stories told by characters inside the stories meta(infra)diegetic. I hope this makes things clearer.

The relations between the levels can be:

(1) directly causal (this is why I'm here: des Grieux; Ulysses in Phaeacia)
(2) purely thematic (analogical, contrastive), implying no spatio-temporal continuity: an illustration (and I suppose a simile or allusion in poetry)
(3) 'no explicit relation': the act of narration itself fulfills the diegetic function – entertainment, obstruction, independent of content (*The Arabian Nights*).

These levels interest us here only insofar as they are transgressed. Genette calls such transgressions metalepses, and cites several examples, from Sterne's bold effects to Cortazar's story 'Continuidad de los Parques' (in *Final del Juego*), in which a man is murdered by a character in the novel he is reading, to Pirandello, Genet, and Borges who all exploit the metalepsis.[28]

Naturally metalepsis is most felt where a story is being told, and so occurs less (in the form described by Genette) in the *nouveau nouveau roman* than in, say, Borges (his strange stories of a country and a universe existing only in one or two copies of an encyclopedia, of the imaginary work of an imaginary author, etc.), or in Robbe-Grillet, whose camera eye focuses on a picture (a book, a press-cutting, a fantasy, or a prediction), then slides into the scene and makes it actual. This is very highly developed in *Dans le labyrinthe*, and in *Projet* the very dialogue becomes the equivalent of the framing picture, or vice versa, the narrative every now and again appearing to be part of an interrogation by the 'revolutionary' plotters of the murders. Thus after a description ('Son coeur bat si fort qu'elle a l'impression ... Elle a renoncé à la lutte," (p. 18)[29] we get:

'Et ensuite?
Ensuite elle s'est calmée peu à peu. Elle a de nouveau remué faiblement ... Quand elle a semblé morte, j'ai relâché mon étreinte. Je me suis déshabillé très vite et je suis revenu près d'elle ... J'ai eu de nouveau cette impression de grand fatigue, déjà ressentie en montant l'escalier, un moment auparavant. Laura s'est endormie tout de suite dans mes bras.'
– Pourquoi est-elle si nerveuse? Vous comprenez que cela représente un danger supplémentaire, inutilement.' (pp. 18–19)[30]

The novel slides in and out of this 'report', which itself becomes more and more confused as the reporter seems to be lying or misremembering (e.g., pp. 76–8), and in any case we can never be sure whether the images of violence are actually 'happening' or are part of mere crazy dossiers.

When there is no 'story' in the usual sense, and no narrator in the usual sense, the only form of metalepsis possible (though it may not be considered such by Genette) is intertextuality. Certainly it is not the same kind, yet it is another text, with exactly the same relation as Genette's second thematic relation (for what is simile, quotation, or allusion, developed or not, but another story brought into a story?). Of course the intertextuality is not usually assumed by a character (though it could be); it is brought in by the dramatised 'I', the quasi-author I spoke of earlier. Genette makes it clear that as long as a shift of level is assumed by the narrator there is not metalepsis. Thus the narrator's responsibility in the thematic relation would be marked either by verbal transition (from 'I will tell the story of' to the 'as when' of simile) or by typography (e.g., quotation marks). Thus Sollers's *prélèvements* (as Kristeva calls them) in *Nombres* are all in quotation marks, assumed by his 'I', and his ideograms (also thematic) are set aside at the end of sections.[31]

This kind of intertextuality, only recently made much of by the

French, goes back to Pound (in whom both Sollers and Maurice Roche, as well as Denis Roche who has translated him, are very interested), and as such is more familiar to us. Pound, however, went much further than Sollers, juxtaposing idioms of all periods, regions, and domains, veritable metalepses in the jumbling of narrative levels in that named characters may tell their story or someone else's, either in their own idiom or in Pound's version of it. Similarly in Maurice Roche, innumerable levels are integrated into the text, especially in *Circus* (1972): bars of music, phrases and sections in other languages, mirror text, rebuses, anagrams, runes, hieroglyphs, signs from the *Guide Michelin*, from an electroencephalogram, from Arabic, forming not only texts within texts but metalepses in much the same sense as his author-interfering and punning proof corrections: 'se͜ṽṁage, fou ⌐ tu, passer à l'̸s [with /o in margin], camar̖de [with ̖a in margin] etc., and his typographic extensions such as:

$$F^{olie}_{iole} \qquad ecou \diagdown^{r} ter \qquad inimagina^{bl}_{ir}es$$

$$\text{(p. 9)} \qquad\qquad \text{(p. 25)} \qquad\qquad \text{(p. 72)}$$

or anagrams (Ecrit/Récit) or acrostics:

Enseignement lumineux. S'instruire
en s'amusant

:

                                    r   r
                                    e   e
                                    p   p
        culture confort loisirs drague *drogue*
                                    s   s

$$\text{(p. 29)}^{32}$$

In *Mémoire* there is a dream (the author's) translated into Brazilian by Haroldo de Campos.

3.3. Person

The last category of Voice is that of person: a narrative is heterodiegetic (absent narrator telling the story of others) or homodiegetic (narrator present as participating character). As Genette points out, absence is absolute, but there are degrees of presence: the narrator can be the hero (autodiegetic) or the narrator can have a secondary role as observer.[33]

The movement from one to another is felt as an infraction, though it occurs frequently in the classical novel (e.g., the disappearance of the early witness in *Madame Bovary*). The most flagrant example comes halfway through *Moby Dick*, where we pass from the narrator Ishmael's consciousness to the consciousness of Captain Ahab. The twentieth century has pressed further with changes of pronoun for the same character (*je – il* for Balzac's Bianchon in *Autre étude de femme*, *il→je* in Proust's *Jean Santeuil*) and, as Genette says, the recent novel goes beyond even this limit with 'un vertige pronominal'.

The most daring forms of this emancipation [his note: see for example J. L. Baudry's *Personnes*, Seuil, 1957] are not perhaps the most perceptible, owing to the disappearance of the 'character's' classical attributes – proper name, physical and moral features – and with them the landmarks of grammatical circulation. The most spectacular example of this transgression can be found in Borges's story 'The Form of the Sword' [*Ficciones*], precisely because it occurs in a wholly traditional narrative system that emphasises the contrast, and in which the hero begins his infamous story by identifying with his victim, to reveal in the end that he is in fact the *other*, the cowardly denouncer, treated, until that point, with the scorn he deserves, and in the third person. (p. 254, my translation.)

Spectacular perhaps, but marked, explained, too 'perceptible' and unmysterious. In *Projet*, Robbe-Grillet goes much further than this, for the actions of the *je* are the same actions later or previously (or both) given to another: the passage quoted on page 334 above is preceded by a description in the third person (*l'homme, l'agresseur*), and later his escape is again assumed by the *je*, and this throughout, combined with the constant metalepses in and out of reports and imaginings, produces an eerie effect, close to the fantastic, or, in Todorov's terms, to the uncanny.

As for Roche, and later Sollers, they use only pronouns, each attached to a tense. In my copy of *Compact* the author has inscribed: 'une loterie de pronoms,

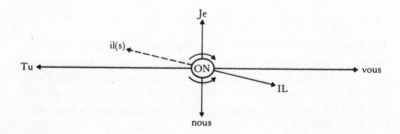

en attendant de perdre le verbe être'.[34]

In *Nombres* the first person sometimes becomes *il* and splits into two:

Ainsi, je commençais à faire sortir dans les rêves l'existence à qui je racontais ce rêve au moment où il était moi ... Il y avait donc maintenant: le dormeur dans son propre corps et vivant avec d'autres ceci ou cela/la fonction qui le racontait en expliquant parfois faussement ses choix/la scène qui, pendant ce temps, continuait dans le vide [...] (2.34, pp. 49–50)

Sometimes it becomes *nous*:

et je tourne en me répétant, nous tournons en nous transformant [...] (4.24, p. 38)[35]

There is a mysterious *elle*, headless, which sometimes refers to a sentence. And, in the fourth (present tense) sections, a *vous* (= *vous* and *je*).[36]

Thus in both Roche and Sollers even the narrator/author is abolished in a choreography (it is too orderly to be called a vertigo, or even, for that matter, a 'lottery') of mere pronouns.

4. The functions of the narrator

Genette describes five different functions, according to different aspects of narrative. They do not quite correspond to Jakobson's six functions of communication (e.g., there is curiously no real equivalent to the poetic function except at best the first), and although I don't find this final coda to Genette's work particularly revealing, I will use it by way of conclusion to show (roughly) which are the most exploited by the three main authors studied here:

1. Narrative f.	– all that concerns the story	R–G	
2. Metanarrative f.	– all that refers to the text		
3. Communicative f.	– the narrative situation (*narrateur*/*narrataire*)	Roche	Sollers
4. Testimonial f.	– orientation of n. towards himself		
5. Ideological f.	– authorised commentary		

5. Conclusion

I have concentrated on these apparently 'merely technical' transgressions because they are the most relevant to these authors. The 'ideas' behind them are, I hope, implicitly clear. Many imitators have taken over this or that technique (especially the present tense) as a mere trick, without in any way altering their fundamental attitude towards fictional representation. I am not concerned with them. However, it is generally true that the same mimetic crisis has on the whole found different solutions in England and especially America, that is, through a change of 'content' only. At the lowest level, any 'realistic' novel about a hitherto unfamiliar domain (football, mining, Timbuctoo) or with a zany plot, is regarded as a revelation. At a much more interesting level, the turning away from realistic representation has taken the way of the fantastic, the absurd, the carnivalesque (Barth, Vonnegut, Barthelme, Brautigan, and others), with corresponding formal mutations. Certainly the French experiments seem very dry to many Anglo-American readers.

I do not know myself where the novel will go. One quality is scarce in the French experiments, that of humor: slight in Robbe-Grillet and almost non-existent in Simon, Butor, Sollers, Ricardou, and others, stronger in Pinget and Sarraute (I discount Beckett as in fact Irish). The *nouveau nouveau roman* takes itself very seriously, and humour in the hilarious, explosive sense we know and I like seems to occur (to my knowledge) only in Maurice Roche. This reservation apart, there are other explosions, which I find exciting and in their own serious way humorous, the explosions of almost every notion traditionally associated with narrative. The intellectual stimulus is undeniable.

13

Eximplosions

1. Silence and the limits of consciousness

Towards the end of a landmark essay, 'The Aesthetics of Silence' (1967, reprinted 1969), Susan Sontag wrote:

art, in the modern conception, is always connected with systematic transgressions of a formal sort. The systematic violation of older formal conventions practiced by modern artists gives their work a certain aura of the unspeakable – for instance, as the audience uneasily senses the negative presence of what else could be, but isn't being, said; and as any 'statement' made in an aggressively new or difficult form tends to seem equivocal or merely vacant. (p. 31)[1]

These features, however, 'must not be acknowledged at the expense of one's awareness of the positivity of the work of art', and she ends the section with this crucial paragraph:

For instance, each work of art gives us a form or paradigm or model of *knowing* something, an epistemology. But viewed as a spiritual project ..., what any work of art supplies is a specific model for meta-social or meta-ethical *tact*, a standard of decorum. Each artwork indicates the unity of certain preferences about what can and cannot be said (or represented). At the same time that it may make a tacit proposal for upsetting previously consecrated rulings on what can be said (or represented), it issues its own set of limits. (pp. 31–2)

It may seem odd to speak of 'decorum' – that ultra-classical concept – in a context of an art that most critics describe in more explosive terms. But Sontag is right, not only in emphasising the limits of any new art form, but also in distinguishing, as she does a moment later, between two styles, loud and soft, in which contemporary artists advocate silence.

The loud style, which tends to be frenetic and over-generalising, is a function of the unstable antithesis of plenum and void. It is often apocalyptic and must endure the indignity of all apocalyptic thinking, that of outliving the prophesied end and setting 'a new date for the incineration of consciousness and the definitive pollution of language and exhaustion of the possibilities of art-discourse' (p. 32). The soft style is more cautious, and basically 'an extension of traditional classicism: the concern with modes of propriety, with standards of seemliness. Silence is only "reticence" stepped up to the nth degree', though of course 'in the translation of this concern from the matrix of traditional classical art, the tone has changed – from didactic seriousness to ironic open-mindedness' (p. 31). But its advocates (such as John Cage, Jasper Johns) are reacting

> to the same idea of art's absolute aspirations (by programmatic disavowals of art); they share the same disdain for 'meanings' established by bourgeois-rationalist culture, indeed for culture itself in the familiar sense. What is voiced by the Futurists, some of the Dada artists, and Burroughs as a harsh despair and perverse vision of apocalypse is no less serious for being proclaimed in a polite voice and as a sequence of playful affirmations. (pp. 32–3)

One might say in fact that the 'unstable antithesis of plenum and void' is itself at the basis of that other antithesis of loud and soft, which Sontag expresses more frequently as paradox: 'The art of our time is noisy with appeals for silence' (p. 12): 'The tendency is toward less and less. But never has "less" so ostentatiously advanced itself as "more"' (p. 14); 'in the era of the widespread advocacy of art's silence, an increasing number of works of art babble. Verbosity and repetitiveness are particularly noticeable in the temporal arts of prose fiction, music, film and dance' (pp. 26–7).

It is true that art is suffering from an acute consciousness of plenum and void, that is 'foundering in the debilitating tide of what once seemed the crowning achievement of European thought: secular historical consciousness. In little more than two centuries, the consciousness of history had transformed itself from a liberation ... into an almost insupportable burden of self-consciousness. It's scarcely possible for the artist to write a word (or render an image or make a gesture) that doesn't remind him of something already achieved' (p. 14). Language is experienced as fallen, corrupt, weighed down by historical accumulation (p. 15).

Hence the dream of a wholly ahistorical and therefore un-alienated art, and silence (not literal of course, except in artistic or real suicides like Rimbaud's, Lautréamont's, Maiakovsky's, etc.), as a metaphor for a cleansed, non-interfering vision. Traditional art invites the *look* – mobile, voluntary, varying in intensity. Modern art invites the *stare* – steady, unmodulated, fixed, with its character of compulsion, unsolicited but allowing no release from attention (p. 15). Art should be approached like a landscape, which demands no understanding, no imputations of significance, no investment of anxieties or sympathies but, rather, the spectator's absence, 'it asks that he not add anything to *it*'. A contemplation, which means self-forgetfulness:

Toward such an ideal plenitude to which the audience can add nothing, analogous to the aesthetic relation to nature, a great deal of contemporary art aspires – through various strategies of blandness, of reduction, of deindividuation, of alogicality. In principle, the audience may not even add its thought. All objects, rightly perceived, are already full. This is what Cage must mean when, after explaining that there is no such thing as silence because something is always happening that makes a sound, he adds, 'No one can have an idea once he starts really listening.' (p. 16)

This, we may note, is in absolute contradiction with Barthes's now more fashionable notion of 'writerly' text, in which the reader participates actively, as well as with all the more recent critical activity on the reader (see chapter 2 above), the latter however chiefly concerned with more traditional texts. For Barthes though, it is precisely the modern text which is *scriptible*. Similarly 'plenitude', in the sense of obsessive information-giving, is regarded by Barthes as a mark of the classic text, the 'readerly', which the reader passively absorbs. And Sontag appears to contradict herself in the very next paragraph when she says that 'plenitude – experiencing all the space as filled, so that ideas cannot enter – means impenetrability. A person who becomes silent becomes opaque for the other; somebody's silence opens up an array of possibilities for interpreting that silence, for imputing speech to it' (1969: 16). And again later when, considering the various uses of silence, one of them is said to be to 'keep things open', for 'speech closes off thought. (An example: the enterprise of criticism, in which there seems no way for a critic not to assert that a given artist is *this*, he's *that*, etc.)' (pp. 19–20).

We may perhaps fruitfully contrast this possible contradiction (or paradox) with Julia Kristeva's view of modern literature as that which (more or less) consciously sets out to enlarge the limits of the human signifiable, as opposed to the media whose function is to collectivise the systems of signs and even the unconscious.[2] Modern 'experience-of-limits' writing singularises, and goes very far into the mechanisms that constitute human consciousness, even to the obscure mechanism of so-called primary narcissism, where the subject constitutes himself – and insofar as he opposes – into another (psychosis). In this sense it take over from psychoanalysis and is its strangest rival, psychoanalysis having itself taken the place of a certain kind of literary fantasy. This was incidentally one of the reasons for which Todorov placed the fantastic in a limited period, its 'themes' having become the privileged domain of psychoanalysis.

According to Kristeva then, modern literature of the 'experience of limits' would have recaptured this domain. With Artaud, Bataille, Burroughs, she says, writing seems to have a more direct access to the asymbolic proper, to psychosis, through the logical and phonetic drift which pulverises and multiplies meaning, pretending to play with it or to flee it in order the better to endure it, or the cut-up of Burroughs unfolding and leaving in suspense the logic of the narrative and of the speaking subject. And she compares this exploration of the imaginative area to the relation with the mother, to the pre-sign, as for example in the theatre of gesture, sound, colour, rhythm (Cage, Bob Wilson). Writing is a technique of the imaginary, of the *fantasme* (fantasy in the psychological sense), but has always simulated, mimed, what is communal in this fantasy. With the experience of limits, that imaginary is led to a point where it leaves the community. 'It fixes in signs what, in the imagination, is irreducible to the experience of others, what is most singular, even if no one escapes that singularity.' In fact 'we confront idiolects, which proliferate, uncontrollable, and the only risk (huge) is that they will remain solitary, invisible monuments in a society that tends on the contrary to uniformisation'.[3] The one-time fantasmatic *camera obscura* (such as the characters of nineteenth-century fiction) has become a brilliant television screen, and writing has now ventured out as reconnaissance-scout to the limits of the unnamable, 'distrusting the unconscious as best-seller, fantasy for all, warned by the experience of the twentieth century that by generalising fantasy one reaches the most massive, that of the extermination camp ... Never before has this exploration of the limits of meaning been attempted in such an unprotected manner, that is, without religious, mystical or other justification.'

These are large claims, though Susan Sontag is perhaps more cautious, more aware of contradictions and of limitations (I shall return to this point later). And other large claims have been made for 'postmodernism', notably by Ihab Hassan. But first, we should perhaps clarify the notion: what exactly is 'postmodernism', if we must use that term, and who represents it?

2. 'Postmodernism' – what is it?

Susan Sontag mentions few novelists, though when she talks of the emptying out of consciousness as prerequisite to the ability to perceive what one is 'full of', what words and mechanised gestures one is stuffed with, she contrasts Rilke's and Ponge's 'benign nominalism' with the more brutal nominalism found in the aesthetics of the inventory, of dehumanisation and impersonalisation (Roussel, early Warhol films, early Robbe-Grillet), and when she discusses the ambivalent attitude to language (a high estimate of its powers and past health/an awareness of its current dangers), she notes that this leads to an impulse towards a discourse that 'appears both irrepressible (and in principle interminable), and strangely inarticulate, painfully reduced', giving Gertrude Stein, Burroughs and Beckett as examples of 'the subliminal idea that it might be possible to out-talk language, or to talk oneself into silence' (pp. 24–5; 27). She comments that this, though not a very promising strategy, is not so odd since the aesthetics of silence is often accompanied by 'a barely controlled abhorrence of the void', and that

accommodating these two contrary impulses may produce the need to fill up all the spaces with objects of slight emotional weight or with large areas of barely modulated color or evenly detailed objects, or to spin a discourse with as few as possible inflections, emotive variations, and risings and fallings of emphasis. These procedures seem analogous to the behaviour of an obsessional neurotic warding off a danger (p. 27).

She adds that the emotional fires feeding such a discourse may be turned down so low as to make it become a 'steady hum or drone. What's left to the eye is the neat filling of a space with things, or, more accurately, the patient transcription of the surface detail of things' (pp. 27–8), and seems here to have Robbe-Grillet in mind (for objects, and, possibly, for emotive impulses, Nathalie Sarraute), although, as I hope I have shown, there is much more to their work than that and, moreover, this 'abhorrence of the void' and uninflected discourse are precisely, as I mentioned above, what Barthes and Hamon after him attribute to the nineteenth-century realist novel, but for ideological reasons and with consequent effects quite the opposite to those of Robbe-Grillet.

But Sontag is concerned with the general aesthetics of modern art, not with the detail of specific works, and the term 'postmodernism' had not gained currency at the time of her still remarkable, elegant essay, in many ways a proleptic summary of much that has been said since. 'Postmodernism' is now opposed to 'modernism' (Joyce, Pound, Eliot, Woolf, Stein etc.) as not so much a falling off (Levin), but as something 'new', more 'Modern'. But there seems to be a certain confusion as to just what it involves.[4]

I find both terms peculiarly unimaginative for a criticism that purports to deal with phenomena of which the most striking feature is imagination, and I shall use them only when discussing critics who use them. For one thing, they are purely historical, period words, and in that sense traditional. In his stimulating but mimetically chaotic *Paracriticisms* (1975), Ihab Hassan at one point quotes eight critics (Ter Braak, Barthes, Blanchot, Starobinski, Poulet, Walter Benjamin, Morse Peckham and Frye) to show that their statements form a mosaic in which a certain movement can be discerned 'away from the literalities of critics and away from its previous formal and historical definition ..., a movement beyond the control of the art object, toward the openness, and even the gratuitousness ... of existence' (p. 27).

But what does he mean by 'previous formal and historical definitions'? The very terms 'modern' and 'postmodern' (which he adopts) are historical, and as to formal definitions, surely any attempt, including his own, to discuss this particular explosion in art is bound to use some formal definitions, if only in the gathering together of the typical features of 'modern' and 'postmodern' art.

Secondly, they are self-cancelling terms, and this may be particularly apt for an art continually described as self-cancelling. But although criticism can thus be imbued with its objects, as Hassan brilliantly demonstrates with his constant counterpoints, revisions, queries, digressions, other visions, and juxtaposing typography, I don't think that the labels should to that extent contain such built-in obsolescence. As C.S. Lewis said in quite another context: 'Surely the analysis of water should not itself be wet?' (1967). For the labels are self-cancelling in an uncreative way. The Romantics used the term 'modern art' until Schlegel popularised the term 'romantic' as opposed to 'antique' or 'classical'. Henry James used the term 'the new novel'. Our New criticism, whatever its other qualities, hardly seems new today, nor does the *Nouvelle critique* of the fifties. The French were obliged to use *nouveau nouveau roman* after the *nouveau roman*. I always preferred the term *anti-roman* for that particular phenomenon, which at least meant something (and in fact dates back to the sixteenth century with Sorel's *Le Berger extravagant*, subtitled *anti-roman*). Claude Mauriac spoke at the time of *alittérature*

(1958), but neither of these caught on. 'Postmodernism' is a sort of English equivalent to *nouveau nouveau*, for it merely means moderner modern (most-modernism?), although it could in itself (and sometimes does) imply a reaction against 'modernism'.

These terms seem to me to be completely lacking in content, and the danger is that anyone may (and does) tend to put any content he likes into them, whereas traditional terms like – at random – symbolism, imagism, futurism, surrealism, did give some sort of orientation as to what was at stake.

Thirdly, and by way of corollary, the terms are simply lazy, inadequate. For fifty years or so we were content to call anything difficult of access modern art. In retrospect, much of it seems less or not at all difficult of access, so that the term 'modern' is *now* used to cover any of the 'great names' which have survived. But if we are going to put D. H. Lawrence (for eroticism and apocalyptism) and Hemingway and Proust and Kafka and Pound and Yeats and Eliot and Faulkner and Mann and Gide and Musil and Stevens and Virginia Woolf and Joyce etc. into the same modernist ragbag, the term becomes meaningless except as a purely period term, itself obsolescent since modern by definition means now. Hassan admits privately that the term 'postmodernism' is unsatisfactory, and in his book rightly insists on fluctuating frontiers, regarding Kafka as more postmodern than modern, and naturally points to antecedents such as Rabelais and Sterne; and in his MLA paper he says that:

we continually discover 'antecedents' of postmodernism – in Sterne, Sade, Blake, Lautréamont, Rimbaud, Jarry, Tzara, Hoffmannsthal, Gertrude Stein, the later Joyce, the later Pound, Duchamp, Artaud, Roussel, Broch, Queneau and Kafka. What this really means is that we have created in our mind a model of postmodernism, a particular typology of culture and imagination, and have proceeded to 'rediscover' the affinities of various authors and different moments with that model. We have, that is, reinvented our ancestors – and always shall.

This is aptly playful, but, as he himself implies in his 'always shall', not very illuminating (the 'moderns' rediscovered the Metaphysical poets, the Romantics rediscovered the Middle Ages, the Classics rediscovered the Greeks and Romans, as did the Renaissance in other ways, etc.). And what is that model of 'postmodernism'? How can one talk of a 'model' if one rejects both historical and formal definitions? Hassan approvingly quotes Murray Krieger who asks, in *The tragic vision* (1960): 'how, if we limit ourselves to technical literary definitions, can we find for the tragic any meaning beyond that of Aristotle? The answer is, by moving from formalist aesthetics to what I would term "thematics"' (Hassan 1975: 7). The irony of that statement lies in the fact that 'thematics', thus presented as a new idea, has long been considered (from the Russian Formalists right through to Post-Structuralist deconstructionism) as the heavy death-mask of traditional criticism, to which, apparently, we are now urged to return.

In fact of course, nothing is ever so ruthlessly to be rejected as *dépassé*, except in its manner and method. Both formal and thematic definitions are necessary, as are both subjective and objective approaches. But the dangers of all these and any others should be kept in mind, as well as the confusing effect of mixing them up without appearing to. Art can and does have that freedom, indeed the difficulty is precisely, as I said in chapter 3, that art is continually exploding genre-theory and even, as now, the very notion of genre. But criticism to my mind cannot imitate art all the way unless it claims to be itself an art (which may occur, but very rarely), in which case it ceases to be just criticism and becomes itself subject to criticism, thus producing yet more objects for our aesthetic attention in a general whirling of words, when one of the main features of the new art is supposed to be the precipitation, through expression of course, towards exhaustion and silence.

The dangers of excessive formalism are well-known. The dangers of excessive thematics are also well-known, but seem to have been forgotten, and are less obvious, because from long tradition we respond well to the synthesis of thematics, whereas formalist analysis is more off-putting. The dangers of mixing them up seem perhaps not dangerous at all to Anglo-American critics, who have never submitted kindly to the rigid categorising of the European mind. Here are some examples from *Paracriticisms*, in which we are given various lists of features.

Postmodernism, Hassan first tells us, is characterised by the following:

Art cancels itself
Art deprecates itself
Art becomes a self-reflexive game
Art orders itself loosely, at random
Art refuses interpretations, fancy pretends to be fact and vice versa. (1975: 21)

Four of these five categories are ostensibly thematic and ideological (but would involve formal transgressions if analysed), nor are they in any way evaluated (e.g. in 'real life', self-deprecation merely causes everyone to take it at face-value and not as 'modesty': would that be so in art?). And the last but one (art orders itself loosely) is formal, though, as such, aptly loose, since the reason for it is naturally also' ideological. Later Hassan names seven main features of modernism, which he projects onto postmodernism to show the differences and developments (pp. 49–51). These are:

(1) *Urbanism* which in postmodernism [Pm] becomes not only the city but also the global village [McLuhan's term], the spaceship earth, the city as cosmos; and a contrary theme of fragmentation, anarchy, diversity.

(2) *Technologism* which in Pm, becomes run-away technology, futurism, a split between Technophiles and 'Arcadians'; as well as the change in the actual physical materials of art and a boundless dispersal by the media, matter dissolving into concept, and the computer as substitute for consciousness.

(3) *Dehumanisation* (in the Ortega y Gasset sense of elitism, style takes over), which in Pm becomes anti-elitism, participation, diffusion of the ego, art as optional; but also irony as self-consuming, an entropy of meaning, insane parody, negation, Camp, abstraction taken to its limits and turning to a new concreteness, humanism yielding to infra-humanism.

(4) *Primitivism* which in Pm leads away from the mythic to the existential, then to the post-existential ethos of psychedelics and madness, or else to a new Rousseauism or the primitive Jesus.

(5) *Eroticism* which in Pm goes beyond the Lawrence trial to a new sexuality, a polymorphous perversity, a new androgyny and solipsist play.

(6) *Antinomianism* which in Pm becomes counter-cultures, beyond alienation, acceptance of discontinuity, a cult of apocalyptism as renovation or annihilation.

(7) *Experimentalism* which in Pm leads to open, discontinuous, improvised, indeterminate or aleatory structures, to simultaneism and the impermanence of art, fantasy, play, humour, happenings, parody, intermedia, fusion of forms, confusion of realms, art viewed as anything else in life.

Now all these categories are thematic except the last (experimentalism), which in a sense applies to all new art forms of any period. The thematic categories, moreover, seem wild generalisations: do we not find urbanism (his modernist examples: Baudelaire's *Cité fourmil-lante*, Proust's Paris, Joyce's Dublin, Eliot's London, Dos Passos's New York, Döblin's Berlin) in Dickens, in Defoe, in Pope, for that matter in Horace, and Technologism in Zola? Primitivism in, precisely Rousseau (or Blake), eroticism in *Fanny Hill*, and anti-nomianism in most periods? The city (or technology, or whatever) has changed, and the ideology behind the use, but not the theme as theme. That leaves dehumanisation, which does seem a specifically modernist feature, but if it is defined purely in the Ortega y Gasset sense, then elitism and style have existed since the mediaeval and the Renaissance court poets, and, inversely, anti-elitism is an ex-tremely dubious generalisation for many postmoderns, who are no more read by the masses than their predecessors, and are just as proud of and angry about it.

Some of the supposed changes, in postmodernism, too, seem doubtful. For instance 'a new androgyny' is surely already present in Virginia Woolf's *Orlando* and even, in a special sense as Barthes has shown, in Balzac's *Sarrasine* – not to mention Plato. And many of the subcategories are in fact formal: under *urbanism*, the postmoder-nist contrary 'theme' of fragmentation, anarchy, diversity is hardly a 'theme' but a technique (reflecting the theme or rather the fact), and found already in Eliot and especially Pound. Under *Dehumanisation*, 'insane parody' has always existed, though perhaps 'insane' is a question of degree and individual judgment, while parody is a formal category and reappears under *experimentalism*. Under *anti-nomianism*, the 'acceptance' of discontinuity, stated thus as an idea, a will, must surely take concrete form, and indeed reappears under *experimentalism*. We may note, however, that discontinuity is re-garded as a feature of realistic discourse by Hamon, a result of various needs (to circulate information, to describe the world, to defocalise the hero), though admittedly it forms part of the con-tradictions inherent in realism (see chapter 4 above).

The categories under *experimentalism* seem equally imprecise and unspecific. Romantic poetry must surely have seemed discontinuous, improvised, indeterminate and aleatory to the classics (as did metaphysical poetry in retrospect), with a fusion of forms and a confusion of realms. So did modernism appear to its predecessors. Nor are fantasy, play, humour and parody the prerogatives of the postmoderns. This leaves us with simultaneism, intermedia, the impermanence of art, happenings, and art viewed as anything else in life. But the last two are thematic and ideological, though obviously agents of formal change (like all the thematic categories), besides, even the eighteenth century was concerned with the imper- manence of art ('We write in sand' said Waller). We are then left with simultaneism, intermedia and happenings as specific to the experimentalism of the postmoderns. Happenings in the strict sense are surely impossible in written work (even poetry readings as happenings rely on a previously concocted text, written or learnt by heart), unless he means a once-only improvisation, in which case it ceases to be literature (even jazz-sessions are either recorded or lost). Thus, for literature, we have only intermedia and simultaneism as specific features, the first only exploited by few (as intrusions of poetry, or of the iconographic, sometimes of cinematographic, techniques, and the latter more exploited by the French than by the American postmodern writers). Clearly this does not get us very far, and the category *experimentalism*, though true, is much too vague. For the fact is that all the previous, thematic categories are made manifest through the last, but the tremendous overweight of privi- lege given to thematics does not really allow Hassan to show this fusion, and the separation of thematic and formal features confuses without fusing them.

Later Hassan does give us some more specific 'modern forms' arising, directly or indirectly, out of Joyce's *Finnegans Wake*, the structure of which is 'both structurally over-determined and sem- antically under-determined', but with coincidence as structural principle (identity and accident, recurrence and divergence), as well as the gratuitousness of every creative act. This leads to:

– *parodic reflexiveness* – not of course new (Sterne, Gide, Gombrowicz) but particularly current after the war (Nabokov's *Pale Fire*, Cortazar's *Hopscotch*, Borges' *Ficciones* [the latter in fact mostly published before the war], Genet's *Journal du voleur*, Beckett's *How It Is*, Barth's *Lost in the Funhouse*). These are so extraordinarily different however that only the label unites them, in a fragile way, for the term is not defined.

– *recreation of reality*: – time, place, character, plot are shattered. In Modernist fiction this was sometimes achieved by 'a quasi-objective, quasi-cubist' breakdown of surfaces (Gertrude Stein, Alfred Döblin), or by dissolving surfaces into language (Proust, Faulkner). Joyce is said to do both. This cleared the way for 'neo-realist' fictions (Robbe-Grillet, Butor's *Mobile*) and 'surrealist' fictions (Hawkes' *The Cannibal*, Wurlitzer's *Nog*). Both mean dissolving the distinction between subjective and objec- tive categories in the pervasive fantasy of the work. Fact and fiction acquire the same aspect, get blurred [as in *Pale Fire*, and some other works mentioned under parodic reflexiveness]. In Post-modernism this also leads to the nonfiction novel, where reality is objectively reported but is more fantastic than fiction [see p. 351].

- *non-linear form*: – circular, simultaneous, coincident. A mosaic, a montage. Chance as principle of aesthetics (the shuffle-novel, e.g. Marc Saporta's *Composition 1* [and, in another sense, Cortazar's *Hopscotch*, Sanguineti's *Il Giuoco dell' Oca*, see p. 359].

- *the problematics of the book*:– typography, marginalia, notes, sketches etc., which defy sequential reading. Mixed media (visual and auditory, poetic and narrative), discontinuity (Dos Passos, Döblin's *Berlin-Alexanderplatz*, Mallarmé's *Un coup de dés*, or earlier, Sterne, Rabelais, The Book of Kells!). In Postmodernism, John Cage, Ronald Sukenick [only in *The Death of the Novel and Other Stories*], Donald Barthelme, Ray Federman, Eugene Wildman.

(Hassan 1975: 85–7)

These are still fragile generalisations, with lists of names, but much more helpful than the earlier categories and subcategories, few of which are new or specific to postmodernism. What would seem to be new is their combination, and if we take any one criterion or even several we can find them earlier: e.g. on the last three above, Pound is a postmodern, yet clearly he is not in other ways. But how many of these writers do combine them all, and how well? Later, Hassan's 'Map of vanishing fiction' (1975: 104–6) is pleasantly fanciful, for he imagines two lines meeting in the future, the left one for the literature of 'exhaustion' (Barth's term) or novel of silence, the right one for the fantastic novel and science fiction. Some people are at the centre, some to the left (towards silence), some to the right (towards the fantastic).

Paracriticisms is essentially a summary book rather than a critical one, and my further summarising of it has been partly to give the newcomer a general idea of 'postmodernism', partly to show that there is still, as always in criticism of contemporary literature, a certain amount of confusion, and partly to show the advantages and disadvantages of this new form of criticism, though I have perhaps dwelt more on the disadvantages: for *Paracriticisms*, like the works it deals with, must be read, with its 'dialogical' manner and its immense but lightly carried learning. It is a book full of 'exits', rather like Barthes's codes, and reading it is in fact a little like reading later Barthes, *Le Plaisir du texte* for instance, in which one feels as if one were replunging into the intuitive and personal richness of the best New criticism but after having been through the rigours of structuralism, left behind by Barthes but somehow there in his tone and terminology. Hassan is more carefree (more slapdash at times), but the stimulus from both the learning and the provocative manner is felt.

3. Towards more precision

Before turning to the few authors I have chosen to discuss, I would like to narrow down Hassan's wide sweep by briefly describing two other critics, already mentioned, Mas'ud Zavarzadeh and David Lodge, for both are much more usefully precise.

Zavarzadeh's book (1976) deals, I have said, wholly with the non-fiction novel as a modern phenomenon, though this too has certain antecedents such as Defoe's *Journal of the Plague Year* or Twain's *Life on the Mississippi*, both 'generically ambiguous' (p. 51). It gives an extremely thoughtful and acute typology of prose narrative, and an equally thoughtful and acute analysis of the non-fiction novel, whose practitioners,

through a neutral registration of experiential situations, have captured the fictive nature of technetronic culture. They reject the notion of art as the creation of order out of chaos and the writer as seer. In their works the mythic underside of the surrealistic facts of post-industrial society is revealed and the indeterminacy of truth in extreme situations where fact and fiction converge is enacted. (p. 4)[5]

Perhaps I should have included some non-fiction in this study, for it is certainly part of the inversion of real and unreal that I am dealing with, but one can't do everything, and Zavarzadeh has done it much better than I would. Here I am only concerned with what he calls *transfiction*, and will merely recapitulate his terminology for 'postmodernism', which seems to me far more precise than that tiresome word.

He makes a preliminary point about what he calls the 'non-totalizing sensibility which has emerged since the late 1950s and whose literary manifestations can be seen in such works as Barth's *Giles Goat-Boy*, Pynchon's *Gravity's Rainbow*, Mailer's *Armies of the Night*, Barthelme's *City Life*, Warhol's *a* and Wildman's *Montezuma Ball* (Zavarzadeh 1976: 3 n. 2). By 'non-totalizing sensibility' he means the resistance to interpretation, and to all the widely differing examples of it mentioned above he gives the widely generic term of *supramodernist* narrative (which I don't like any better than 'post' modernist):

The contemporary writer's approach to the world-as-it-is, free from any imposed scheme of meaning or extracted pattern of significance, and the emergence of such noninterpretive narrative forms as 'transfiction' and the 'nonfiction novel' – two radical narrative reactions to the current epistemological crisis – are telling indications of the deep changes which have taken place in the postwar consciousness and which caused a new distribution of narrative energy ... In transfiction, by means of a baroque overinterpretation of the human situation, writers like John Barth, Thomas Pynchon, Donald Barthelme, and Steve Katz have repudiated the claims of the totalizing novel to an integrated view of existing realities. Nonfiction novelists moved in the opposite direction. (p. 4)

Transfiction, then, is narrative which uses what the Russian Formalists called 'baring literary devices'. It unmasks literary conventions and turns them into counterconventions to 'shatter the illusion of reality which is the aesthetic foundation of the totalizing novel' (p. 38). The narrative tension thus created varies in degree according to the different modes of transfiction, which he calls (a) *metafiction*, (b) *surfiction*, (c) *science fiction*.

(a)   *metafiction* 'is ultimately a narrational metatheorem whose subject matter is fictional systems themselves'. It 'exults over its own fictitiousness ... The informing matrix of metafiction is, in Roland Barthes's words, "that asymptomatic zone where literature appears to destroy itself as a language object without destroying itself as a metalanguage".[6] The only certain reality for the metafiction writer is that of his own discourse, so that 'the credibility of fiction ... is re-established not as an illuminating commentary on life but as a meta-commentary on fiction itself'. Main counter-techniques: flat characterisation, contrived plots, untilinear sequences of events, all foregrounded as part of an extravagant over-totalisation, a parody of interpretation which shows up the multiplicity of the real and the naivety of trying 'to reach a total synthesis of life within narrative'. Over-totalisation 'creates a work with low-message value at the zero-degree of interpretation, thus freeing the narrative from an anthropomorphic order-hunting and insuring that, as Barthelme says, there is nothing between the lines but white spaces, [an attitude which] echoes Witold Gombrowicz's concept of the mocking of meaning and his advice to readers (in *Ferdydurke*) to "start dancing with the book instead of asking for a meaning".' (pp. 39–40).

(b)   *surfiction* (Ray Federman's term but Zavarzadeh's definition) also lays bare the conventions of narrative, 'but the tension between technique and counter-technique is reduced in the work of the surfictionists, who prefer to move out of the aesthetically incestuous world of metafiction and directly engage the reality outside (rather than inside) the fictional discourse'. E.g. Steve Katz, Gilbert Sorrentino, Ronald Sukenick, Ray Federman, Ishmael Reed. They 'refuse to make any

claim to interpreting reality and instead regard what Sukenick in his
98.6 calls "the law of mosaics, a way of dealing with parts in the
absence of wholes" to be the only valid approach to contemporary
experience.' (p. 40)

(c) *science-fiction*, whose main literary device laid bare is the narrative
theme itself, 'turned into a pararealistic countertheme based on an
implied "as if", thus creating an entirely subjunctive field of narration.
Extrapolation is substituted . . . for the conventional interpretation of
the totalizing novel. Even in "social science fiction", a conspicuously
fictitious and hypothetical posthuman situation is projected, rather
than a simulacrum of the experiential world . . . creating a world
discontinuous with the world in which the readers conduct their lives
and thereby undermines the possibility of totalizing the present
human situation.' (pp. 40–1)

Zavarzadeh has a great deal more to say in this chapter on
'supra-modernist' narrative, but this summary will I hope have
narrowed down the stimulating but over-wide perspectives I have
been dealing with so far. His comments on science fiction add
considerably to Suvin's more dogmatic approach (see chapter 4
above), although of course the danger of simple allegorisation is ever
present, either in SF itself or in the reader's 'interpretation'. The
subjunctive mood is often ignored by critics, particularly in 'politic-
fiction', which can range from parochially over-specific journalistic
imaginings (such as pre-election French novels supposing that the
'Union de la gauche' would win the 1974 elections), to much more
fundamentally distanced novels such as Philip K. Dick's *The Man in
the High Castle*, in which the Germans and the Japanese have won
the Second World War and an 'as if' novel supposing the opposite is
discussed, one man saying that things would have been much worse,
everything overrun by communism (I simplify). This kind of SF is
not supposed to be prophetic (nor is any other, as Suvin points out),
and to judge it as such is irrelevant (see chapter 4, note 2 above).
Similarly Anthony Burgess's *1984/1985*, whatever its possible weaknesses, cannot be discussed (as it was at a round table in Paris in
1979) at the low level of the 1985 UK elections undoubtedly
disproving his thesis, the argument being, incredibly, that Orwell
had written his *1984* much longer ago, which somehow made it more
valid (no doubt it is, but not for that reason).

I have already analysed two 'postmodern' or 'supramodern' SF
novels in chapter 10, and here will only look at 'metafiction' and
'surfiction', but will first narrow down the critical possibilities
further.

In *The modes of modern writing* (1977a), David Lodge takes the famous Jakobson distinction between the axis of combination (contiguity) and the axis of selection (substitution), or rather, he takes the rhetorical aspects of this distinction, that between metonymy and metaphor (see chapter 2, p. 23 above) and applies it to twentieth-century literature, to show that there is a continuous pendulum movement between the metonymic and the metaphoric modes. Thus,

what looks like innovation – a new mode of writing foregrounding itself against the background of the received mode when the latter becomes stale and exhausted – is therefore also in some sense a reversion to the principles and procedures of an earlier phase ... The metaphor/metonymy distinction explains why at the deepest level there is a cyclical rhythm to literary history, for there is nowhere else for discourse to go except between these two poles. (p. 220)

Lodge traces this pendulum movement with great sensibility from the beginning of the twentieth century (the 'modernist' reaction against the metonymic realism of James, Bennett, and others, the 'antimodernist' reaction of the thirties against that). But 'postmodernist' fiction is 'a certain kind of avant-garde which is said to be neither modernist nor antimodernist ... It tries to go beyond modernism, or around it, or underneath it, and is often as critical of modernism as it is of antimodernism ... [and] obviously offers an interesting challenge to the explanatory powers of the literary typology expounded above' (p. 221).

Thus Beckett's early work (*More Pricks than Kicks*, 1934) 'shows him just beginning to detach himself from the modernist tradition, especially from the technique of Joyce, with whom, of all modernist writers, Beckett has the closest affinity' (Lodge 1977a:221). And after analysing the story 'Dante and the Lobster', which still alludes to a prior myth that is a key to its meanings [as in Joyce, Pound, Eliot], Lodge says that there is nevertheless a good deal in that text that is not accountable in these terms, notably the last line which scuttles the story. So in *Murphy* (1938) and *Watt* (1953; 1958 – composed 1942-5), we get disconcerting narrator interventions and metafictional comments, together with a general uncertainty, especially in *Watt*. This uncertainty becomes endemic in postmodernist writing and, unlike obscurity (which can be cleared up), occurs.

at the level of narrative rather than style. No amount of patient study could establish, for instance, whether the man with the heavy coat and hat and stick encountered by Moran in *Molloy* is the man Molloy designated as C, or Molloy himself, or someone else . . . We shall never be able to unravel the plots of John Fowles's *The Magus* (1966) or Alain Robbe-Grillet's *Le Voyeur* (1955) or Thomas Pynchon's *The Crying of Lot 49* (1966) for they are labyrinths without exits' (Lodge 1977a: 226).

And Lodge compares this with other 'exits', that is the endings of many modern novels, which are not merely open-ended, as in the modernist novel (cp. Eco 1962, Kermode 1968), but often have multiple endings, false endings, mock endings or parody endings (Muriel Spark's *The Driver's Seat*, 1970, *Not to Disturb*, 1971, John Fowles's *The French Lieutenant's Woman*, 1969, the title story of Barth's *Lost in the Funhouse*, 1968, the five endings of Brautigan's *A Confederate General from Big Sur*, 1964, the joke 'mayonnaise' ending of his *Trout Fishing in America*, 1967) (p. 227).

If Jakobson is right, Lodge says, 'it should be possible to categorise postmodernist writing under one heading or the other' (metonymic/metaphoric), for the theory implies that 'if you attempt to group topics according to some other principle, or absence of principle, the human mind will nevertheless persist in trying to make sense of the text thus produced by looking in it for relationships of similarity and/or contiguity; and insofar as a text succeeds in defeating such interpretation, it defeats itself' (p. 228). At any rate Lodge decides, wisely I think, but for the wrong reasons, that such categorisation would not be profitable, for 'if we extend the term "postmodernist" to cover all writers to whom it seems applicable [a curiously circular process], we might identify them individually as either metaphoric or metonymic, but it would be difficult to show that their work, considered *collectively*, has any bias towards one pole or the other' (p. 228). But surely Jakobson never suggested that one or other pole should ever apply *collectively*. His examples are either specific (e.g. Griffith vs. Chaplin in film, and only with regard to specific effects), or else generic but as a tendency (epic and the novel vs. lyric etc.), and of course his very definition of the poetic function (see p. 24 above) implies the presence of both, as would in fact any utterance using any kind of substitution (slang, learned synonym etc.).

Be that as it may, Lodge decides to 'define the formal character of postmodernist writing by examining its efforts to deploy both metaphoric and metonymic devices in radically new ways, and to defy (even if such defiance is ultimately vain) the obligation to choose between these two principles of connecting one topic with another. What other alternatives might there be?' (p. 228).

His 'other alternatives', however, are not, strictly speaking, alternatives to these two poles (which Lodge has said is impossible, 'if Jakobson is right'), but exacerbated forms of one or the other, that is, they are alternatives to earlier metonymic and metaphoric modes of connecting one topic with another, and Lodge is more interested in that chronological alternative than in linking these supposed alternatives back to either of the two poles (he does sometimes, but not systematically). Thus we have (I summarise):

(1) *Contradiction* (p. 229): the self-cancelling discourse of Beckett, or paradoxes such as Leonard Michaels's 'It is impossible to live with or without fictions' (1975) or Vonnegut's Bokonist religion in *Cat's Cradle* (1963) which is based on 'the heartbreaking necessity of lying about reality and the heartbreaking impossibility of lying about it'.

But self-cancelling discourse is an exacerbated form of paradox, and literary discourse has always exploited paradox (indeed Michaels's paradox is a simple substitution of 'fictions' for 'woman' in a perfectly current cliché). Or again:

'one of the most emotively powerful emblems of contradiction, one that affronts the most fundamental binary system of all, is the hermaphrodite'. [Actually the fundamental binary system is $+/-$, positive or negative, and Lodge is 'investing' it, biologically, besides, biology and grammar both recognise a neuter]. Examples: Gore Vidal's sex-changing Myra/Myron Breckinridge [in two separate novels however, 1968, 1975, so very much contiguous]; Brigid Brophy's *In Transit* (1968) in which the central character can't remember his/her sex; Julian Mitchell's *The Undiscovered Country* (1968) where the hero changes sex, then becomes a hermaphrodite; a passage in *Giles Goat-Boy* (Barth, 1966), where the caprine hero [and surely *that's* more interesting?], locked in copulation with Anastasia, answers the computer question ARE YOU MALE OR FEMALE? with YES and NO simultaneously.

This too is an exacerbated form of what has always existed, since Plato, and in the more playful form of travesty, in Shakespeare (see also p. 348 above for *Orlando* and *Sarrasine*).

Contradiction then, is not an 'alternative' to the metonymic/metaphoric modes but a combination. Paradox, though apparently contiguous, is a substitution of *and* for *or* ($\bullet$ for $\wedge$, just as ambiguity, in Rimmon's term, is $\wedge$, see chapter 8). The hermaphrodite is similarly, in Barthes's terms, the transgression of antithesis, that is, a metaphoric reversal of a rhetorical (contiguous) figure.

(2) *Permutation* (p. 230): instead of trying to evade selection by giving (for instance) alternative endings (a form of contradiction), the postmodernist writer may try to exhaust all the possible combinations of a given field, as in some stories of Borges and certain passages in Beckett (Watt's socks, stockings, shoes, slippers etc., combined on one foot and the other, or the famous distribution of sucking stones in *Molloy*).

It should perhaps be noted here that Borges, with characteristic economy and distance, never dramatises permutation (nor is he exhaustive but selective, even ending with an etc. or equivalent); rather he describes narrative possibilities in invented fictional works which he describes briefly from the outside, whereas Beckett incorporates the permutations into his fiction.

Despite the word 'selection' which may give the impression that we are in the metaphoric mode, this is in one sense an exacerbated form of contiguity (e.g. for Beckett, realistic description, of which it is a kind of parody, or, for Borges, critical description). But in another more general sense given by Lodge, that both modes involve selection and selection means leaving something out (as do all works of art), it is a substitution of exhaustiveness for selection, though an exacerbated form of the exhaustiveness of description of the 'real' world in the classical novel. However, basically it is an exacerbated form of contiguity (the socks, shoes, etc.)

(3) *Discontinuity* (p. 231): metonymic writing exploits 'a readily intelligible kind of continuity based on spatio-temporal contiguities; the continuity of metaphoric writing is more difficult, but not impossible, to identify.' Continuity enables a work of fiction to impose 'its vision of the world upon the reader, displaces the "real world" with an imagined world in which the reader (especially in the case of realistic fiction) lives vicariously.' And naturally postmodernist writers evade this [many examples].

However, since so much has been made of discontinuity in postmodernist writing, I must again insist that this is entirely a question of degree. Only the simplest fairy-tale or the most elementary narrative forms are wholly continuous, and the novel has been playing with time and space shifts and discontinuous moments for a long time, as does the cinema, indeed these are the marks of the realistic novel as opposed to myth, romance, the uncanny, the fantastic, the marvellous. Postmodernism, and in most cases modernism, have simply taken the process to its logical conclusion. Instead of and, more often, as well as, chapters, long sections, analepses and shifters marking the discontinuities, we get brief sections (a page, a paragraph, a sentence) and typographic devices; and, more important, instead of a basic 'story' we can reconstruct through the discontinuities, we get (but not as often as is claimed) a flouting of this possibility and, in some extreme forms a wilful exploitation of the non-sequitur (Barthelme, Michaels, Federman, to some extent Brautigan), which, when the statements are mere bald notations of the narrator's life, as in Michaels's story 'In the Fifties' quoted as a simple example by Lodge, can be far more tedious than the most tediously gap-filling realism, once the joke is established – though Michaels is usually more exhilarating.

Discontinuity obviously belongs to the metonymic pole, in exactly the same way as the syntactic 'figures' of rhetoric, as opposed to the 'tropes', belong to it, playing with contiguity through inversions, chiasmus, anaphora, ellipses except that in narrative the units are larger so that what is omitted can be correspondingly enormous. For in theory discourse can link anything to anything, however apparently disconnected, and inversely even the fullest description leaves out something.

(4) *Randomness* (p. 235): the only distinction between this and the complete non-sequitur discontinuity above is that 'true randomness can only be introduced into a literary text by mechanical means', since, as Burroughs says, 'you cannot will spontaneity'. Hence the scissors and cut-ups. 'A similar method of introducing an element of genuine randomness', Lodge says, is B. S. Johnson's *The Unfortunates* (1969), which was issued 'in loose-leaf form' (in a box), for the reader to shuffle himself.

Actually they were loose *sections*, an important difference, and the method is not so similar since Burroughs' random element is introduced at source, as part of the creative process, the reader having one set result, whereas in Johnson it is left to the reader. However, in whatever order one reads *The Unfortunates*, it is still a realistic and dreary novel of a football player returning to his Midlands hometown, though the principle can be used more originally (as in Saporta's *Composition 1*). In no case does it affect the syntax, as it might but does not with the cut-up technique, since the chunks are in themselves continuous, and merely juxtaposed. Lodge feels that such experiments are 'the least interesting, because most mechanical way of trying to break out of the metaphor/metonymy system'. Of course one does not break out of it (see below), but surely it is not the 'mechanical' aspect which makes it uninteresting, merely the results in the specific cases. Elements of mechanical randomness have been used in the visual and musical arts to great effect (but of course they are freer from 'meaning' and grammar), and if the postmodernist driving notion is the non-interpretability of the world, mechanical elements are in principle perfectly acceptable; but 'elements' only, as far as language art is concerned, since a total 'true' randomness would lead to asyntactical, agrammatical, and even, phonetically, alexical strings of jibberish.

The reader-randomness in Johnson and Saporta should of course be distinguished from the 'guided' order of reading one finds in Cortazar's *Hopscotch* or Sanguineti's *Il Giuoco dell'Oca*, where no element of randomness is present, only one of choice. In *Hopscotch* each chapter ends with the number of another chapter the reader could proceed to (with a summary of the alternative order at the beginning), and in Sanguineti the alternative order is similarly based on a game.

Randomness of course belongs to the contiguity axis: out of a potential series you allow chance to select this segment rather than that. All that has happened is that the artist's will voluntarily gives way to outside chance as opposed to the obscure but nevertheless determined waywardness of 'inspiration', the unconscious etc. In that sense there is substitution (of chance for will), but only at the productive level. As the other end (in the text), the effect belongs to contiguity. So here too we have the metonymy mode exacerbated, but the possibilities are limited by the sequential nature of language itself.

(5) *Excess* (pp. 235–9): The very word shows that this too is exacerbation of one or the other pole, and here Lodge is quite specific. Both the metaphoric or metonymic are parodied and burlesqued and tested, 'as it were to destruction ... Pynchon's *Gravity's Rainbow* (1973) for instance takes the commonplace analogy between rocket and phallus and pursues its ramifications relentlessly and grotesquely through the novel's enormous length' [indeed, to detumescence]. We get 'metaphoric overkill' more locally in Barthelme's 'absurd cadenza of comparisons for the collection of moonrocks' ('A film', *Sadness*, 1972) and Brautigan's bizarre comparisons in *Trout Fishing in America* (1967). They all strain, as Lodge says, the principle of similarity to breaking point. But pure substitution (metaphor) is also taken to excess (e.g. 'Trout Fishing in America' can be a person, a corpse, a hotel, a pennib, an adjective).

In other words, the extremes of poetry come into the novel,

though in a less concentrated way: 'Trout Fishing in America' as a noun phrase breaks the subcategorisation rules (Chomsky 1965: 95) and even becomes an adjective. But Cummings did this years ago, more systematically and more subtly (he is never mentioned in the various lists of 'moderns'). And what Chomsky (1965) calls selectional rules are broken when the narrator buys a 'used' trout stream in a wrecking yard, stacked in various lengths or in boxes of scrap. For some reason Lodge puts this last example in *short circuit* (his next category), to illustrate the reality/fantasy short circuit, but both stream and junk can be bought in 'reality', there is no confusion of fiction and reality (except on a general level which applies to all metaphor), simply a fusion of semantic categories in the fiction.[7] Another example would be the narrator's name in Brautigan's *In Watermelon Sugar* (1970) which is said to be 'anything that comes into your mind', the possibilities given being not other names but random incidents, while watermelon sugar is a substance everything is made of (windows, burning oil, lives).

We get 'metonymic overkill' when the discourse is overloaded with specificity and presents the reader 'with more detail than he can synthesize into a whole'.

The example here is Robbe-Grillet (from *Le Voyeur*), and although I don't agree that it is impossible to 'make a sketch or diagram of the harbour' from the description (the translation given is particularly inaccurate in more ways than Lodge notes, as extra difficulty), or that such a synthesis is necessary, I agree with his general proposition of overkill. This is early Robbe-Grillet, and a particularly over-loaded passage. From *La Jalousie* on the metonymic overkill is used much more purposefully, more lightly and more elegantly.

(6) *Short-circuit* (pp. 239–45): this is simply the much discussed transgressions of the dividing line between fiction and reality, which can take the form of (a) 'combining in one work violently contrasting modes – the obviously fictive and the apparently factual; (b) introducing the author and the question of authorship into the text; (c) exposing the conventions in the act of using them', or 'laying bare the device', in Russian Formalist terms. 'These ploys are not in themselves discoveries of the postmodernist writers – they are to be found as far back as *Don Quixote* and *Tristram Shandy* – but they appear so. frequently in postmodernist writings, and are pursued to such lengths as to constitute, in combination with the other devices we have surveyed, a definitely new development.'

I am not sure that pursuing an old device to 'such lengths' constitutes a new development, but combining it with others clearly does. Lodge gives some of the best examples (from Nabokov, Vonnegut, Coover), but it is fast becoming a cliché (e.g. in Sukenick's *Up*, and again in *98.6*, but see pp. 380–4 below). Obviously much depends on how it is done. There is a world of difference between the brief description Lodge gives from Sukenick, which ends 'I sit at my desk, making this up', and Coover's opening 'I wander the island, inventing it' ('The Magic Poker', 1973), which is itself intriguing, with its poetic use of 'wander' as a transitive verb. Similarly the narrator-intrusions into Barth's 'stories' in *Lost in the Funhouse* (1968) vary from extreme sublety to downright crudeness, as do his device-baring devices, and the crudeness is irritating, however much one may enjoy the book as a whole, which in-cidentally is a novel, not a collection of stories as often thought: it begins at the utmost beginning with 'Night-Sea Journey' and goes on with the boy Ambrose, who often sees himself proleptically as famous author, then reaches that author.

'Night-Sea Journey' is an example of Barth's curious mixture of subtlety and crudeness: according to 'Seven Additional Author's Notes' in the Penguin (1972) edition, 'The narrator of "Night-Sea Journey" ... is not, as many reviewers took him to be, a fish. If he were, their complaint that his eschatological and other speculations are trite would be entirely justified; given his actual nature, they are merely correct.' We are not in fact 'given' his actual nature, and the obvious metaphor of swim = life and sink = death is so over-exploited that one tends at first to read the whole thing as a transparent allegory (the swimmer as man), and in a sense it is. But (and this is where the subtlety comes in), the narrator–swimmer is a sperma-tozoon, all his companions 'sinking', and the tailless God he has heard of makes this clear, as does the 'She' (as shore) towards the end. Whether this alters the 'triteness' of his eschatological specu-lations is a moot point, and I may say that the sperm-race was much more delightfully and economically treated in a French pop-song (*Spermatozoïdes*, by Ricet Barrier). But this is only by way of illustrating the point that triteness is not made less trite by being put in the mouth (?) of a spermatozoon if he is the narrator, and that similarly narrator-intrusions such as 'Is this supposed to be amusing?' and 'I hope this will be a short story' do not have enough ironic subtlety to conjure the possible boredom the narrator seems afraid of. Or again: '"Why do you suppose it is," she asked, long parti-

cipial phrase of the breathless variety characteristic of dialogue
attributions in nineteenth-century fiction, that literature people such
as we talk like characters in a story?' ('Title'). This is both subtle
and crude, crude as observation (this late in the day), subtle as
syntactic substitution (outside the dialogue) and as transgression
(inside the dialogue) of fiction and reality. There are many such
examples, and many also of just crudeness. But as Lodge says,
'postmodernist writing tends to be very much a hit-or-miss affair',
though 'many of these books and stories are imaginatively liberating
to a high degree, and have done much to keep the possibility of
writing in the very process of asserting that the most familiar ones
are closed' (p. 245).

As he points out, this kind of transgression (of text as metaphor
and metonymy of life) is by no means new, and even its 'postmodernist' exploitation is very much present in 'modernist' writing
(Pirandello, Thornton Wilder, Perez de Ayala, Cela, Flann O'Brien
are never mentioned in the reiterated lists, nor, for other elements,
Alphonse Allais or Thurber, or Calvino and rarely Queneau or
Gombrowicz). Muriel Spark's first novel, *The Comforters* (1957) uses
short circuit much more originally (though even then it seemed to
me an amusing variation on a familiar gambit): Caroline hears a
ghost typewriter and voices, and becomes convinced that someone is
writing a novel about her and her friends. Towards the end she has
gone away to 'rest' and writes a letter to her boy-friend, who reads it
and tears it up in small pieces, scattering them on Hampstead
Heath, then wonders how the letter got into the book. The 'self-
reflexive' transgression of levels American postmodernists make so
much about not only has quite a long history but is often relatively
clumsy.

Lodge's 'alternatives', then, are not alternatives to the
metaphoric/metonymic poles (and perhaps merely his terminology
or syntax were unclear, for he seems in practice to agree), but
exacerbations. Yuri Lotman (1970; translation 1977) has said that
the freer the paradigmatic axis, the more rigid the syntagmatic, and
vice versa. This seems to me obviously true. Burroughs for instance,
is free to the point of 'true' randomness (but only sometimes) with
the syntagmatic axis (contiguity), so the paradigmatic axis (selection) is correspondingly rigid, for ever the same drug world and
apocalyptic account of goodies and baddies. Vonnegut, Brautigan
and Reed are free on the paradigmatic axis, and the syntagmatic
axis is correspondingly rigid (for I do not count the length or brevity

of sections as a form of unrigidity): the syntax is ultra-simple,
sequence is obeyed apart from shifts normal to the novel. The novels
of Pynchon are positively and even heavily rigid on the syntagmatic
axis, and only the obscurity of the symbolic search gives them a sort
of paradigmatic freedom. The ideal would seem to be equilibrium,
for instance in Barthelme (where there is excess, it is in different
places).

Lodge also says, ending his book:

if postmodernism really succeeded in expelling the idea of order (whether
expressed in metonymic or metaphoric form) from modern writing, then it
would truly abolish itself, by destroying the norms against which we
perceive its deviations. A foreground without a background inevitably
becomes the background of something else. Postmodernism cannot rely
upon the historical memory of modernist and antimodernist writing for its
background, because it is essentially a rule-breaking kind of art, and unless
people are still trying to keep the rules there is no point in breaking them
and no interest in seeing them broken. (p. 245).

14

Metafiction and surfiction:
a simpler formal approach

1. Parody and stylisation

I have several times remarked that these critics seem to make high claims for the 'postmodernist' phenomenon, though both Sontag and Lodge are more cautious, each ending on a qualifying note. However, one must allow for and even welcome the hope and excitement that any new experiment creates, there is little enough of it in 'establishment' circles. I would now like briefly to examine a few of these writers, in the light of another broad but formal division which, by cutting across all the philosophic, semiotic, psychoanalytical, thematic and formal considerations we have had so far, may perhaps clarify the picture: that between parody and stylisation.

1.1. Parody

Many of the 'postmodernist' novels, mentioned under various labels but all part of Zavarzadeh's *metafiction* (over-totalisation, parody of interpretation) are implausible but (technically) realistic representations of the modern human situation which I discussed in chapter 1, namely the inversion of real/unreal or, in other terms, they dramatise the *theme* of the world's non-interpretability. Barth's long novels, *The Sot-Weed Factor* (1960) and *Giles Goat-Boy* (1966) would be the first manifestations of this, though perhaps only retrospectively, for at the time they were appreciated as uproarious satires, closer to the Menippean tradition. And of course *The Sot-Weed Factor* also stylises, in the sense that it parodies seventeenth-century English, but I shall define stylisation more precisely later.

Thus John Fowles's *The Magus* (1966) is 'about' the individual's construction of reality. Nicholas is lured into the rich magnate Conchis's property on a Greek island, and at first does not know that his experiences are artificially concocted. Slowly he loses all his certainties, but each time he thinks he has understood what is real and what is illusion, the real is revealed as another illusion. This is Conchis's 'godgame', so named because it is not 'really a game and there is no God' (except Conchis). Lodge has called this a maze without exit, the plot of which we cannot unravel, but this is not so: there are explanations throughout and a final explanation, when Nicholas is told that *all* was organised, and how, and his resulting rage, self-pity and despair are not so much at having been tricked as at realising that the godgame has ended, that Conchis and his 'assistants' have loaded the dice and quit the game, that he is back where he started but now lost, unwatched by them, stripped of significance, of spectators, that life is not a performance, as Ernst von Glaserfeld puts it in a thoughtful article (1979).

Von Glaserfeld points out that as long as man acts for spectators he is neither free nor human (well, I would say only that he is not free, since man is by definition a social animal). Further, that it is not the Magus who has loaded the dice that drove Nicholas nearly out of his mind but the way he himself interpreted the events: he had loaded the dice long ago, by accepting a commonplace and naive view of the world, thinking he knew what the world was like.

Fowles comes to the core of constructivist epistemology when he lets Conchis explain the idea of coincidence [when he tells the two stories, of the rich collector in Paris and the farmer in Norway]: 'There was no connection between the events. No connection is possible. Or rather, I am the connection, I am whatever meaning the coincidence has.'

As Glaserfeld notes, this is an everyday paraphrase of Einstein's revolutionary insight that in the physical world there is no simultaneity without an observer who creates it. In the modern constructivist theory of knowledge,

not only coincidences are seen as arising out of the experiencer's own activity, but also the events that are coinciding, the notions of space and time, of motion and causality, and even those experiential compounds that we call objects – they all come about through the experiencer who relates, who institutes differences, similarities and identities, and thus creates for himself a stable world of sorts.

(Cf. Piaget, *La construction du réel chez l'enfant*, 1967, or, in physics, Heisenberg, *Physics and philosophy*, 1958.) Fowles is concerned with the pragmatic and ethical aspect of this.

Von Glaserfeld admits that it is 'in many ways an old-fashioned novel', and compares it to Fournier's *Le Grand Meaulnes* or to

Pirandello, but insists that 'seen in the framework of the history of ideas, it belongs to the front of constructivist thought'.

So there we have it, the old split between form and content. The 'theme' is new (though a *de*constructionist 'theme' would be 'newer'), the form is old-fashioned. There is indeed not a line, not a formal device (or represented speech, thought, action or scene) in the book that does not belong to the most traditional realistic novel – which is why of course, it is so 'readable' despite its plot's complexities. And many of the 'postmodernist' novels or, to use Zavarzadeh's more precise term, metafictions, are of this type. Robert Coover's *The Origin of the Brunists* (1966) is an ironic investigation of mystical sects in America, with typical viewpoint shifts and a local newspaper editor providing the ironic authorial eye, with all the paraphernalia of detailed description, description-openers, narrator explanation in pluperfect analepsis, lengthy, free indirect discourse of the most fatigued kind, narrator comment to dialogue of the 'participial phrase' variety parodied by Barth, and so forth, though some passages are given in the present tense, here only a historic present. *The Universal Baseball Association Inc* (1968) has a lighter, more slangy modern tone, but technically differs in no way from the mainstream novels of the thirties, forties, fifties (etc.). *The Public Burning* (1977) is more 'outrageous' in subject matter, because it imaginatively dramatises a well-known contemporary political figure, Vice-President Nixon, during one week just before the execution of the Rosenbergs, and has him meet Uncle Sam (who protects, scolds and guides him) in odd visionary moments. But it is also dead-pan realistic, and that is of course the point: all Nixon's thoughts, worries, ambitions and ludicrous moments are imaginary, but set forth in what reviewers call 'utterly convincing', 'forcefully realised' (etc.) terms. Only the 'intermedia' *intermezzo*, in dramatic form ('The Clemency Appeals – A Dramatic Dialogue by Ethel Rosenberg and Dwight Eisenhower') between President and Prisoner (Pres/Pris) is given the full parodic treatment of scene-description and stage-directions.

Coover is concerned with history and our constant reinterpretation of it (though of course his over-interpretation is yet another interpretation), just as Fowles is concerned with man's interpretation of the world. One can see him moving from both traditional and parodic representation of contemporary problems to stylisation, and in his short stories (*Pricksongs and Descants*, 1969, i.e. between *Baseball* and *Public Burning*) he moved over entirely to stylisation.

But in *The Public Burning*, the parody is intermittent, that is to say although it pervades the whole, there is no manifest difference between what I call 'dead-pan' realism and realism, except where the topic (e.g. the meetings with Uncle Sam) makes it clear. In a sense of course, parodic representation is one long stylisation of realism, but the balance is delicate. I shall return to this problem in a moment.

Similarly Pynchon's *V.* (1963) and *Gravity's Rainbow* (GR) (1973) are vast quests for meaning in a man-centered world where the multiplicity of interpretive systems make it impossible to envisage a whole form of which the fragments would be parts (cp. Melvyn New, 1979). They draw on SF motifs (anti-utopia, the talking computer, radio-controlled characters, loss of identity and dehumanisation generally).[1] *V.* rather heavily parodies the spy-story in all the sections of the past as 'recovered' by the main quester Stencil, which dramatise the decadence of diplomatic and colonial old Europe before and after the First World War. GR cancels all provisional realities by making all the characters paranoiac, drugged, hallucination-prone, and although each fantasy may be filtered through Pirate Prentice's talent for entering the fantasies of others (see McHale 1979: 91), on a sort of Chinese box principle, this naturally does not function like a 'principle' at all, so that the madness device becomes repetitive as we pass from one to another. Thus, unlike *The Magus* and Coover's books or Barth's, and despite many stylistic felicities, they are not (and presumably not meant to be) 'readable' in the book industry's sense of 'entertaining', chiefly because the 'theme' is considerably more blurred than in Barth's social satire or Fowles's 'constructivist' theme or Coover's non-interpretability of history. It is blurred, first in itself – the object of the quest or anti-quest is couched in old-fashioned symbolic terms such as the phallus/rocket business in GR and the 'scratching the surface' notion that pervades *V.*, for instance in the Vheissu motif which is a sort of paradigm for the whole work (Vheissu as a lost civilisation but also a constantly changing surface, an aesthetic pleasure, a luxury, this very much explained and over-determined, pp. 155, 220), and symbolism of this kind is notoriously over-exploited in modern realistic fiction; it is blurred in the very over-interpretation Zavarzadeh speaks of, which 'creates a work of low-message value at the zero-degree of interpretation'; and it is blurred in the clogging traditional mechanisms of the realistic novel that inevitably go with interpretation, and, *a fortiori*, with over-interpretation.

One such blurring would have been enough, but the heaviest is the third. Even the present tense and present participles used in GR seem a mere pointless substitution for the past and pluperfects of other sections, the present is a historic present (as in the nineteenth-century novel), and the past would do just as well; despite the time-shifts (clearly marked), it does not have the eerie effect we get from its atemporal use by Robbe-Grillet. Apart from the occasional present tense (occasional only in *V.*, and used in a traditional way for generalisation), and some 'intermedia' bad verse and songs (but one finds songs in realistic fiction, even in Tolkien), we get the whole realistic machinery, including the defocalised heroes and the constant shifts of viewpoint, parodied (within the parody of the novelist writing a novel) by Barth in 'Life-Story' (*Lost in the Funhouse*), with his letter-characters:

D comes to suspect that the world is a novel, himself a fictional personage ... Moreover E, hero of D's account ... B called upon a literary acquaintance ... To write merely C comes to suspect that the world is a novel ... If I'm going to be a fictional character G declared to himself ... How revolutionary J appears to be ... If he can only get K through his story I reflected grimly [I being both a letter and pronoun] etc.

Of course here the letter represents the author's various versions (versions of himself and versions torn up), but it also accurately reflects the formula of modern realistic fiction, whereby A is introduced, then B in the next section, then C, then back to A, then D and so forth in infinite permutations. In *V.* for instance this technique apparently amounts to parody (new place/new person + explanatory description, or vice versa):

As the afternoon progressed, yellow clouds began to gather over Place Mohammed Ali, from the direction of the Libyan desert. A wind with no sound at all swept up rue Ibrahim and across the square, bringing a desert chill into the city.
    For one P. Aïeul, café waiter and amateur libertine, the clouds signalled rain. (p. 52)
The bierhalle north of Ezbekiyich Garden had been created by North European tourists in their own image ... But so German as to be ultimately a parody of home.
    Hanne had held on to the job only because she was stout and blond. A smaller brunette from the south had stayed for a time but. (p. 76)
Dudley Eigenvalue, D.D.S., browsed among treasures in his Park Avenue office/residence. Mounted on black velvet in a locked mahogany case, showpiece of the office, was a set of false dentures, each tooth of a different precious metal. (p. 138)

In April of 1899 young Evan Godolphin, daft with the spring and sporting a costume too Esthetic for such a fat boy, pranced into Florence. (p. 141) Miss Victoria Wren, late of Lardwick-in-the-Fen, Yorks., recently self-proclaimed a citizen of the world, knelt devoutly in the front pew of a church just off Via dello Studio. (p. 151)

But when parody of such a clumsy method is repeated throughout, almost as a tick, one starts taking it at face-value, which is particularly unfortunate when one of the 'counter-techniques' (Zavarzadeh) is flat characterisation. The defocalisation is pushed to extremes to prevent us from identifying with any of the characters by staying too long with them, so that when we return to them and their supposedly absurd but flatly, realistically told activities (hunting alligators in New York sewers, having a nose altered by a plastic surgeon, getting drunk, having sex, stealing supplies from ship, etc.), we hardly care, as we hardly care in 'real life', with its 'meaningless' millions and their 'meaningless' activities, indeed we would, as in real life, have trouble remembering them were it not for their often highly motivated names (Profane the 'schlemihl', Stencil, McClintic Sphere, Schoenmaker the plastic surgeon, Eigenvalue, Pig, The Whole Sick Crew, etc.) and those with ordinary names we have forgotten. The same a fortiori applies to GR. This in theory does not happen with the model parodied, which tries (and sometimes fails) to make us identify and care, and it is a moot point whether parody of a model for its failures, in dead earnest and at such length, is true parody or simply the model in its fatigued aspect. For if we roughly summarise (as per chapter 5) the determination of the Barthes codes in Pynchon, we find that the action and the hermeneutic codes are underdetermined (as in realistic fiction), the referential and the symbolic over-determined (as in realistic fiction) and only the semic (character) supposedly underdetermined (flat characters) yet in fact using the same techniques, parodied. Thus the one element of realistic fiction generally regarded as its crowning achievement (though essentially fantasmatic) is the only one supposedly parodied (but in a way which borders on equally fantasmatic) imitation.

Sukenick also plays with defocalisation but much more lightly, in Out (1973), in which the hero changes names in each chapter (and the chapters are numbered backwards, starting with 1%, and from 9 down consist of paragraphs of 9, then 8 then 7 (etc.) lines. It is possible also that Sukenick may be parodying the mystery of V. in 98.6 (1975: 53) when the central character vomits in the bathroom and feels jerked up by the neck:

> something is holding him by the neck shaking him like a doll something
> huge but invisible. It has long v-striped fingernails many parallel stripes red
> white and blue surprisingly Hallmark with horizontal continuations out
> from the top to the v. ... V why v what is it is the question. What does it
> want he wants it to leave him alone he can't take any more of this.

And later in Israel a specific character has v-striped fingernails. If
this does refer to Pynchon then the whole parody business is
becoming ultra-incestous.

Metafiction in the sense Zavarzadeh defines (parody of interpretation) raises the same problems as that raised by the self-
reflexiveness of 'Is this supposed to be funny?' in Barth's 'Title' in
Lost in the Funhouse, and self-reflexiveness is a form of stylisation (see
below). If only the topic distinguishes Coover's dead-pan realism
from realism, and if in Pynchon the very topic is drowned in parody
of realism that fuses with realism, just where or how does the reader
feel the difference between totalisation and non-totalisation,
between interpretation and over-interpretation (or parody of interpretation), between realistic techniques and parody (if it is parody) of
realistic techniques? If the parody (or the stylisation) so fuses with
the model parodied as to become the model, the parody ceases. Or
at any rate the reader starts running back to Booth (who, in *The
rhetoric of irony* has exquisitely tried to formalise the problem of
deciding whether to read a passage as ironic or not) and to want to
know 'where the author stands'.

For Bakhtin (1929a; 1973), who has done so much to clarify the
various types of dialogical utterance (the degree to which the other
discourse is heard in the first), parody appropriates, as object, an
existing discourse, but introduces into it an orientation diametrically
opposed to its own, whereas imitation takes seriously and appropriates another discourse. Between the two he places stylisation, that
'slight shadow of objectivization' (p. 157) thrown upon the series of
procedures used by the other's discourse. The styliser is careful not
to confuse the other's voice with his own (as does the imitator), nor
does he set off a clash between the two voices (as does the parodist).
He simply lets the presence of another voice (another style) be heard
beneath his own. Stylisation however can tip over into imitation 'if
the stylizer's enthusiasm for his model breaks down the distance
between them and weakens the deliberate sensation that the repro-
duced style is indeed that of *another person.* For it was precisely that

distance that created the conditionality [i.e. the convention] in the first place' (p. 157). The danger is thus closer than for the parodist, with his 'opposite orientation'.

Why then do we experience this tipping over into realism in these parodic representations of a modern theme? I believe that this is because there is *parody* of interpretation and totalisation but *stylisation* of the realistic techniques of interpretation, which verges on imitation, thus destroying the distance, and infecting the parody, itself precariously balanced on a form/content opposition: for 'over-interpretation' is not, as *technique*, sufficiently opposed to 'interpretation' to stop the discourse from tipping over into imitation, although the basic *thematic* orientation (the non-interpretability of the world) is in diametrical opposition to that of the model.

It is all very well to talk of the 'zero-degree of interpretation ... freeing the narrative from an anthropomorphic order-hunting and insuring that, as Barthelme says, there is nothing between the lines but white spaces' (Zavarzadeh). But this hardly differs, as view, from the New criticism notion that, in Macleish's words, 'a poem should not mean, but be' (chapter 2, p. 25). A huge novel is unfortunately not a poem, and the concrete result, with its sheer weight of realistic techniques and over-interpretation in Pynchon's case, is that one cannot, in fact, follow Gombrowicz's advice and 'start dancing with the book instead of asking for meaning' (as one can with *Ferdydurke*): the book is too clumsy, it keeps treading on one's toes.

There is of course no reason why we should not appreciate these novels 'straight', that is, not as metafiction but as realistic and/or satirical dramatisations of serious contemporary problems. But in that case there is no essential difference (except, precisely, the 'counter-techniques: flat characterisation, contrived plots', see p. 352 above) between them and earlier such novels (and the best): Musil and Mann also dramatised problems that were highly contemporary, so did Lawrence, or for that matter Tolstoy, or Balzac (*The Magus* is then a modern version of *A la recherche de l'absolu* or *Les illusions perdues* and its sequel, *Splendeurs et misères des courtisanes*). And there is only the power of the controlling intelligence, the abiding interest of the central idea, to distinguish *these* from more popular versions (Galsworthy down). To take the difference between dramatisation of a theme and stylisation further back, it is like the difference between Langland and Chaucer, or between the second part of *Le roman de la rose* (by Jean de Meung, who didacticised and philosophised it) and the first part (by Guillaume de Lorris, who used the allegorical 'style'); or, more extreme both ways, between Bunyan, who used the by then moribund allegorical form to dramatise the Christian ideal, and Lyly, who in *Euphues* stylised *à outrance*; or, to raise the level again both ways and to show that this is not an issue of 'realism' vs. 'fantasy', between Swift or the philosophical novel generally, and Defoe, who 'stylised' documentary style for fictional purposes and thus laid the basis for the rise of the realistic novel.

Lodge calls *The Magus* (wrongly as I said, for all is explained) and Pynchon's *The Crying of Lot 49* and Robbe-Grillet's *Le Voyeur* 'labyrinths without exits', and certainly the labyrinth is a powerful image in modern writing (Borges' library in 'The Tower of Babel', Robbe-Grillet's *Dans le labyrinthe*, Butor's mysterious itineraries, Lacan's Moebius bands and other puzzles, see Rosset *Le réel*, 1977: 17). But the important qualification is 'without exits'. As Rosset points out (pp. 17–18), the labyrinth as such is not at all a place of non-significance but a place of one significance, one exit, however hidden and hard to find. To this he opposes, as paradigm of the modern situation, the confusion of paths in line 360 of Sophocles' *Antigone* (*Pantoporos aporos ep'ouden erchetai*) which, although it *means* 'having all paths he is never without one', can be translated literally as 'having all paths, pathless he walks towards nothing', a situation which is not only that of Oedipus (that enigma on two feet, that deluded man, that self-styled detective who uncovers the true murderer, himself, that double man whose double vanishes progressively, as first certain, then probable, then improbable but still possible, then impossible), but also that of modern man (p. 18). Thus one can hardly 'dance' through or with a labyrinth, but one must get out of it or die. But pathless at the forking of many paths one can but 'stand and stare' (in Sontag's sense, not in W. H. Davies's). But Oedipus is blind. And Pynchon's reader is blinded, by his own attempt to play detective.

Both Pynchon and Coover (like Barth) have a foot in both camps, but whereas Coover's stories are more overt stylisations, *The Crying of Lot 49*, though much (much) shorter than *V.* or *Gravity's Rainbow*, and closer to stylisation (of a quest) than parody, is still a dramatised quest of the unattainable, and as such less rich than Barthelme's stylisation of a quest in *The Dead Father* (see below). The stylisation however is in a sense double, for the other model is the very process of reading: Oedipa Mass 'reads' the 'reality' around her as a difficult book (as does Nicholas in *The Magus* though he gets glosses), but this is *also* the 'theme' dramatised. However, so much has been written about *Lot 49* that I shall merely use it as a transition to:

1.2. Stylisation

Interestingly enough, modern attempts at stylisation are all remarkably short (often short stories), while the parodies or parodic representations are all remarkably long. This may be a coincidence of my reading, but I think that the type of stylisation I have in mind is difficult to sustain (Pynchon's, for instance, is simply repetitive). As I said, the novels which take the theme of the world's noninterpretability and dramatise it are in a sense long stylisations of the realistic novels which interpreted the world, but there is a fragile frontier between that stylisation and the literary model. Parodic dramatisations of a theme work on the principle of expansion. Stylisation, on that of reduction. Inversely it may be that the very length required for parodically dramatising (as opposed to stylising) such an important theme as well as the realistic techniques supposedly stylised but in fact imitated, make this stylisation tip over into the (lengthy) models.

This may happen *in fact* with stylisation, when it verges on imitation, but *in theory* it cannot happen with pure stylisation, for although it may vary in subtely, when successful *as* stylisation it is always clear as stylisation of a model. I have already spoken of Barth's *Lost in the Funhouse* and its variations of tone, and Coover's stories are similarly varied, rather like experiments in the true sense, which may or may not come off. 'The Magic Poker' is perhaps the most obvious (and so the most discussed and quoted) stylisation of the writer's creative act, and also visibly influenced by Robbe-Grillet in its present tense time-shifts and incidents repeated but changed (here explicitly by the writer's creative act), and has the same uncanny poetry. Others are more concerned with the illusion/reality shift and the games people play, with themselves, with each other, but 'The Gingerbread House' and 'Seven Exemplary Fictions' are clear stylisations of literary models.

Olga Scherer, who has most closely studied the Bakhtinian 'voices', (1974, 1976), notably in Faulkner, has recently turned her attention to William Gass in a remarkable essay ('La stylization', 1979: 65–85). Without taking up her detailed typology (qualitative and quantitative stylisation, the latter further subdivided, p. 69), I shall merely recall a few points, the first being that there are of course innumerable models, 'prototexts' being infinite; secondly that the semantic value of the reiterable sign in the chosen model must be infallible, that is, limited and coherent, not containing another value, from another model (though there can be several models), nor contain just any old value, which would weaken the distance either by introducing a potential contradiction or by reducing the value to irrelevance (p. 67).

In Gass's *Omensetter's Luck* (1966), we find the idyllic model, 'one of the most tenacious in American literary tradition' (p. 70, my translations throughout) for instance in the descriptive introduction of Omensetter: 'Brackett Omensetter was a wide and happy man. He could whistle like a cardinal ... He knew the earth ... He listened to the bees ...' (and all that follows, with stylistic repetition of formulas), and, later: 'A bee flew by his face. Omensetter was a wide and happy man. Fact' (Scherer 1979: 71). Similarly the minister Furber's 'secret polemic' (Bakhtin's term) is itself very Dostoevskian, but also contains an imaginary interlocutor called Horatio. This does not, as Scherer points out, refer back to any actual dialogue between Hamlet and Horatio, 'but to a more abstract notion of Hamletism', or a literary model of hesitation and tragic conflict, 'of which Horatio is one of the infallible and reiterable signs' (p. 67).

Another model in Gass is that of the narrator. In 'The Pederson Kid' (*In the Heart of the Heart of the Country*, 1958) the stylisation of the 'naive' or 'unconscious' narrator tends to fuse into imitation of the model, whereas in 'Mrs Mean' the opposite happens, the omniscient narrator is stylised almost to the point of parody. Thus, although clearly only an outside observer of Mrs Mean (he knows what towels and doylies she has only because he has seen them on the line or through the windows, etc.), he is an over-informed *voyeur*, sure of his conclusions as to the mentality of his neighbours ('I rest my stories on their backs. They cannot feel them') and boasts of his superiority. He even intensifies his authority by giving himself an assistant-narrator, his wife ('My wife and I find it strange that they should ...') – 'an impossible procedure for a serious omniscient narrator who, even if he burdened himself with a wife, could hardly invoke her to affirm himself as true interpreter of the world' (Scherer 1979: 73). I should like to add, however that the wife does not merely affirm or duplicate him, for, insofar as she is given any role, she is the one who has the 'nice', the 'charitable' interpretations, she is as it were the 'ordinary' man in him, not the transcendant omniscient one:

My wife maintains that Mrs Mean is an immaculate housekeeper and that her home is always cool and dry and airy. She's very likely correct as far as mere appearance goes but my description is emotionally right, metaphysically appropriate. My wife would strike up friendship, too, and so, as she says, find out: but that must be blocked. It would destroy my transcendance. It would entangle me mortally in illusion. (p. 105).

Gass fluctuates between parody and a stylisation so undistanced that it fuses with the model. In the long central part of *Omensetter's Luck*, entitled 'The Reverend Jethro Furber's Change of Heart', the model is the stream of consciousness, and through this the 'secret polemic', but ultimately both refer back to an original single and total model, that of 'puritan hypocrisy' (Scherer 1979: 78), and the familiarity of these models, together with the serious tone, tend to make the entire section (the main part of the book) tip over into a secret discourse taken seriously, i.e. the same problem we found in parody. As Scherer observes, Gass, in his war against genres (see interview in the same number of *Delta*), is aware that all forms, and even the polyphonic discourse discovered by Dostoevsky, however revolutionary at the time, degenerate. The remedy, according to Scherer, would be 'either to inject the model with new strength by abandoning ... the more or less deterministic philosophical positions [subsequent ones] and rediscover the original inspiration of polyphonic discourse; or ... to avoid the infallible and reiterable marks of the model that are most tired, by reducing them to the conventional. Gass has opted for this second solution, with unequal success' (p. 77). And obviously the second solution is more liable to the danger of tipping over into imitation, since the marks are 'reduced to the conventional'. But at its best it is particularly subtle.

This can be seen in 'Icicles', the hero of which, Fender, is a real-estate salesman, from the start crossed by two primary models: the first a contemporary, socio-economic one (publicity discourse), where the relation between being (a man) and having (a property) is reversed into possession of man by the property; the second, a literary model, goes all the way back to the early nineteenth century and subsequent treatments of the inefficient office-clerk whose living is nevertheless his job (see Scherer 1979: 79 for examples). The fusion of these two models is particularly rich, and well demonstrated by her. But personally I feel that the 'narrator' model is *also* lurking in the boss Pearson's admonitions to Fender: 'Keep your ears to the ground, Fender. Listen. Listen with all you've got, with the whole business – hard – with your eyes, with your nose – with the soul, Fender ... That's how we get on in this business' (p. 123), and later: 'People pass on ... but property, property endures ... That's why it's called real, see? ... People are property. Does that seem like a hard saying, people are property? Not even real?' (p. 130). Pearson (a person), the boss (a narrator) runs a 'business' which involves listening hard, with all one's being (itself a business, 'the whole business', as the narrator's being, which is listening, is his business), but being is having, possessing (being possessed by), and his 'business' is 'real' property (reality/represented reality), which will survive (a literary work), unlike people who are unreal, mere Fenders, who fend off reality or defend themselves badly in the system but get owned by the 'real' property, or rather by the melting aspect of it, the icicles that 'go with the house', and who become characters in a work that survives. The paradoxical complexity is much richer than that of 'Mrs Mean' ('to see, to feel, to know, to possess', p. 119), but it would take too long to demonstrate here. In any case, if this third model is also present, it is subtly, almost surreptitiously introduced, and would add to the already subtle crossing of the other two.

Brautigan and Barthelme are much more overt stylisers. Brautigan's *The Hawkline Monster* is subtitled *A Gothic Western*, thus declaring its two models, *The Abortion* is subtitled *A historical romance 1966*, and *Willard and his Bowling Trophies* is a hilarious take-off of pointless Mafia murder. The Gothic, the Western, the Gangster film have of course often been parodied, even by the same medium as the model, but Brautigan's take-offs are not parodies in the usual sense of *exaggerating* the features of the model for an opposite purpose. On the contrary, instead of chilling tension and stereotyped gestures there is bare reduction, in simple, factual sentences (statement for utterance/*énoncé* for *énonciation*, contrary to the governess's main discourse in *The Turn of the Screw*), and coming from a dead-pan, omniscient narrator (who has made a big come-back in both metafiction and surfiction), who 'dips' into every character's mind in a way that would shock the post-Jamesian school, but briefly, with a throw-away mechanism, the minds being almost empty:

During supper Greer and Cameron casually watched the Hawkline Monster about the throats and in the hair of the Hawkline sisters.
  The monster was very informal during the meal. Its light diminished in

METAFICTION AND SURFICTION

the necklaces and the shadowy moving color in the sisters' hair was motionless, fading almost into the natural color of their hair.

The meal was steaks and potatoes and biscuits and gravy. It was a typical Eastern Oregon meal and eaten with a lot of gusto by Greer and Cameron.

Greer sat thinking about the monster and thinking how this was still the same day they had awakened in a barn in Billy . . .

Cameron counted random things in the room. He counted the things on the table: dishes, silverware, plates, etc . . . 28, 29, 30, etc.

It was something to do.

Then he counted the pearls that the Hawkline Monster was hiding in: . . . 5, 6, etc. (p. 140).

The chapter (28 lines) is called 'Counting the Hawkline Monster'. The tone throughout is casual, inconsequential. Similarly in *Willard and his Bowling Trophies* we follow the sex-life of two separate couples in two separate apartments of the same house in San Francisco, one couple playing (badly) at sadism, the other having a room full of bowling trophies under the watchful eye of a huge papier-mâché bird, Willard. Elsewhere, the Logan brothers have had their bowling trophies stolen. They set out to find them, for three years, from one state to another, living on filling-station hold-ups and in dingy hotel rooms, one drinking beer, one reading comics, the other waiting for a phone-call with information about the bowling trophies, the arbitrary roles later permutated. Eventually, the Logan brothers locate the house and kill the wrong couple, shouting 'BOWLING TROPHY THIEVES DIE!' We never know how the trophies got to that room or whether the Logans find out their mistake or get the trophies back. The stylisation is one of tone (the dead-pan Bogart style) and reversal: the unreal world of the cinema, which has spread to and is being overtaken by 'real life', is treated, not with the whipped up and quickly forgotten sensationalism of the media, but like buying cornflakes or opening a can of peas. As in *Trout Fishing in America*, *In Watermelon Sugar* (idyllic models), and *A Confederate General from Big Sur* (idyllic drop-out model), the extravagant is stylised into the norm.

Barthelme also uses reduction to bare, factual sentences, statement for utterance, but his stylisation is much more mysterious. *The Dead Father* (1975) for instance is a mythic, heroic quest, but treated ironically, the giant quester being 'dead' (Joycean model) and eventually buried in a quarry-sized hole dug by bulldozers, that is, as R. Davis has pointed out (1979), he is psychoanalytically dead but in fact, during the mythic journey, alternately comatose and frenetic, and his fits of slaying (e.g. 'in a grove of music and musicians', p. 18) are both biblical in tone and wildly implausible:

First he slew a harpist and then a performer upon the serpent and also a banger upon the rattle and also a blower of the Persian trumpet ... the Dead Father slew a cittern plucker and five lyresmiters [long list of more and more absurd instruments]. The Dead Father resting with his two hands on the hilt of his sword, which was planted in the red and steaming earth.

My anger, he said proudly.

Then the Dead Father sheathing his sword pulled from his trousers his ancient prick and pissed upon the dead artists, severally and together, to the best of his ability – four minutes, one pint. (pp. 18–19).

Moreover, the Dead Father is drawn by a cable (chained, like Prometheus) and his assistant–quester–son is highly suspect in his attitude. The son's story of his 'initiation' is also treated with irony, and of course the 'father' is itself both a literary and a psychoanalytical model (see especially R. Davis, 1979). The point is, however, that the mythic quest and the mythical elements are not the 'key' to the meaning (as in 'modernist' writing and as R. Davis appears to think), but are stylised as in themselves meaningless, or rather as meaning no more than what the text literally says, nothing 'in between the lines'.

Another model is the fairy-tale glass mountain ('The Glass Mountain', in *City Life*, 1970), which 'stands at the corner of Thirteenth Street and Eighth Avenue', climbed by the I–narrator as crowds watch. The climb is told in one hundred numbered paragraphs, ranging from one word ('11. "Shithead"./12. "Asshole".') to eighteen lines (p. 80), but more often one simple sentence, and ends: '100. Nor are eagles plausible, not at all, not for a moment.' *City Life* also plays with visual models in a most intriguing way (e.g. 'At the Tolstoy Museum', see especially Maurice Couturier, 1979, on the collapse of discourse, the contamination of the figurative, and the 'problem' of focalisation of the subject, with all the filtering techniques invented to deal with it, being simply abolished [by free direct discourse, see p. 322]. Jamesian complexities are stripped bare: 'Where is the figure in the carpet? Or is it just ... carpet?' (*Snow White*, 1967: 129). Meaning is itself one of our many fictions.

Barthelme's stylisation is not only more mysterious than Brautigan's or Gass's, but also more varied, and so, inevitably, a hit-or-miss affair, to use Lodge's term about postmodernism in general. Some of his pieces have a certain *New Yorker* smartness that leaves one with the emptiness, not of the 'stare' but of disappointment (relative to his other texts), but this of course is a subjective reaction.

Finally I have chosen two books by writers whom Zavarzadeh mentions under *surfiction*, Ishmael Reed and Ronald Sukenick. They are utterly different from each other. Zavarzadeh, we may recall, says that surfiction also lays bare the conventions of narrative but less incestuously than metafiction, and prefers to 'engage' the reality outside (rather than inside) the fictional 'discourse' and refuses 'to make any claim to interpreting reality' [i.e. not even in the parody of 'over-interpretation']. But since surfiction also stylises (as opposed to parodically and hugely dramatising the theme of non-interpretability in basically realistic form), I prefer my broad division, for surfiction is not essentially very different from the stylisation considered here: Reed is as whacky as Barth and as zany as Brautigan, while Sukenick is as directly engaged with 'the reality outside' as Gass, and only the stylisation in each is individual.

Reed's *Yellow Back Radio Broke-Down* (1969) is a strongly stylised send-up of the Wild West, to the point of parody in Bakhtin's sense of an orientation diametrically opposed to that of the model. The hero, for one thing, the Loop Garoo Kid, is the baddy, and he is black, a black cowboy being inconceivable in the racist model. The only Indian is one solitary left-over, Chief Showcase, who flies in his private plane to and from Paris to pick up the latest Cardin 'jacket with fur in the hood', dropping off in mid-desert to save the Loop Garoo at one point, or in Washington to talk to Field Marshall Theda Doompussy Blackwell, an elderly queer in a wig, and Pete the Peke, Congressman. There is complete anachrony since the President (Frenchy) is Thomas Jefferson, who 'likes niggers a whole lot' (p. 145) and appropriates twenty-five hundred dollars to add to his collection of mammoth's bones at Monticello. Loop's enemy is Drag Gibson, who has close-circuit television in his room to spy on his own gang, and who is more and more defeated by Loop's voodoo, although a last minute visit from the Pope slightly restores his prestige. The Pope (dropping his American–Italian accent) tells Drag how to catch the Loop Garoo, by bribing his stray artist supporters to steal the mad-dog's tooth around his neck, which Loop, pretending to sleep, allows them to do. The Pope visits Loop in jail and has a very funny pope-to-devil dialogue with him ("You're his Son too, Loop', p. 196), Loop refusing to 'end this foolishness and come on home', for 'even martyrdom can be an art form, don't you think?' And when the Pope says, 'So you think by allowing

yourself to be humiliated by mortals he'll respect you too, huh?'
Loop answers, 'No I just wanted to show the world what they were
really up to. I'm always with the avant-garde' (p. 197). Loop's
execution is inevitably stopped at the last minute by the Field
Marshall, 'dressed like a Dresden doll', Drag falls into the swinepit
he used for punishing others (the pigs later discuss this unexpected
dessert) and almost everyone is massacred by sudden spears from
the children who had survived an earlier massacre and formed their
own community ('We decided to create our own fiction', p. 18).
'They all ignored the Loop Garoo Kid left standing on the scaffold and
cheated out of his own martyrdom.' He rides off on his green horse after
the Pope, reaching the coast to see the ship on the horizon and plunging
in after it. 'Well I'll be damned, and hallelujah, here comes the Loop,
the Pontiff smiled. Thomas Jefferson was out of a job but that was O.K.
too' (last sentence, p. 213).

The story is told in a racy 'western' vernacular and brief paragraphs with spaces in between (even in dialogue) like separate film-
shots. Almost every page is a stylisation of cultural archetypes,
European, African and American, but chiefly the latter, and as we
have seen above there are also 'art' models. When Loop wakes to
find himself surrounded by 'a shabby crew' of horsemen: 'It was Bo
Shmo and the neo-realist gang' (p. 38). 'So sympathetic Americans
sent funds to Bo Shmo which he used to build one huge neo-realist in-
stitution in the Mountains. Wagon trains of neo-social realist com-
posers writers and painters could be seen winding up its path' (p. 39).

Ronald Sukenick seems almost neo-realist in contrast, but again,
in such a stylised way that the effect can be unreal, though this
varies a good deal. *Up* (1968), despite a couple of tales within the
tale (Strop Banally) and a mock review of 'The Adventures of Strop
Banally, by Ronald Sukenick' (pp. 38–41 – a self-indulgently and
implausibly long review), and the author appearing as Ron or
Ronnie or 'our hero later called Suchanitch Subanitch Sookenack
Bookenack Sackanook and so on' (p. 97), is straight-faced narrative
of scenes and dialogue between people, with a lot of sex, mildly
funny but no more interesting than many reportage-of-daily-life
novels. *Out* (1973) has diminishing paragraphs and changing names
(see p. 369 above), but ultimately the dead-pan stylisation of
reportage in simple sentences and the present tense for vivid but not
(as in Robbe-Grillet) paradoxical use is in constant danger of fusing
with the model, and unless one is particularly fascinated with sex
and violence, the model is uninteresting.

In *98.6* however (1975), Sukenick seems to find the more subtle balance between realism and its stylisation that the 'slight shadow' requires. The first part, 'Frankenstein' (a place, which could be San Francisco but later acquires the sense of America during 'the Dynasty of the Million Lies' and 'the Slaughter' and, on another level, modern civilisation, monster-builder), is told in the third person, present tense and unpunctuated sentences, as a reportage-collage of sex scenes, dialogues, poetic moments and frank narrator comment which, in the present tense, tends to fuse with free indirect discourse (see below). Each chapter starts with a double figure (times or American-style dates, it doesn't matter which, the precise but arbitrary notation being itself a stylisation of diary writing): '12/25 the blond comes in two parts. One part comes in a red Triumph 500 ... 1/17 the blond comes in two parts here comes the second part she falls in love with him' (pp. 30, 32). Or:

10/23 he has a thing and that is that he's only interested in the extraordinary. He thinks that the extraordinary is the answer to The Problem. For example he'd rather sit at home and watch the hummingbird at the feeder outside his window than go through the motions of a common seduction with nothing special about it. ... He believes in powers meaning the extension of the ordinary to the point of the incredible and he believes that these powers are real though they can't be willed and they belong to everyone who isn't blinded by the negative hallucination of our culture. A negative hallucination is when you don't see something that's really there. (p. 11).

And there is a very funny 'chapter' in which his car, first called a canoe, then a boat, 'sailing down 7th Avenue', having lost its brakes, metamorphoses itself sentence by sentence, as does the place:

the car hurtles down the street ... turning off the ignition he finds he can slow the careening motorcycle in fact he manages to stop the Harley pretty fast for such a heavy machine. He gets off tinkers with the mechanism isn't able to fix it luckily a motorbike like that is just light enough to carry though it's no bag of feathers especially when you're not even sure which direction to take in a city like this. It's discouraging but still he can think of worse situations than carrying a broken ten speed bike through the streets of Paris. In fact he feels it's a good thing that all he has to lug around with him is his pogo stick even though it's sadly wilted and he feels terribly deserted being so completely lost in a city whose name he even forgets. (pp. 28–9)

But these are occasional moments, and mostly we're in the reportage style of *Up*. In the second and longest part, 'The Children of Frankenstein', the 'he' at first seems to have become Paul, one of many in a settlement, who try to reinvent life, to become 'mutants', among whom is Ron, the original 'he', a writer, and the third person shifts to anyone of them: 'Ron is writing a book. He has a novel idea as a matter of fact it's an idea for a novel. His idea is to write a novel by recording whatever happens to their group so that they're all characters in his book including himself' (p. 68). But later: 'Hi Ron. How's the novel about us going says Paul./I'm not writing it'. And later still: 'What chaos. Cloud [as Ron has become] clutches his head. Cloud no longer believes any of this is happening. This is not real life. What was happening is now all over. It lacks credibility. Cloud is writing a novel again. It's almost finished' (p. 147). That is, when things lack credibility he can start writing again. Or, more self-reflexively still, and as rather an in-joke: 'Cloud has tried up and he has tried out. Neither of them works. Maybe nothing works' (p. 131), which refers within the fiction to one of his many philosophies ('all the horizontal things are interchangeable, the vertical ones unique', p. 104) and outside the fiction to his previous fictions.

The narrative voice in fact moves fast from one character to another. The present tense and unpunctuated sentences appear to resolve the 'narrator–filter' problem (in Barthelme, it disappears, see pp. 322, 378); even the much exhausted free indirect discourse is refreshed, since only the third-person part of the narrator's voice is retained (and, as in *Plus*, more often the name than 'he', which reinforces the narrator's voice), but not the tense modifications (see chapter 4, p. 94 above). Sometimes this produces comic effects: 'As he was saying Eucalyptus has a dark side as well as a bright like the moon' (p. 122); 'The Fakers believed that beyond the bogus there is nothing the emptiness of the cosmos. Ralph can't agree more' (p. 150). While frequently narrator discourse and direct discourse (and even indirect discourse, as in the passage preceding the above), fuse: 'The Antifrankenstein is going to be the salvation of Frankenstein that's the only way to do it it's the last chance they've thought about it' (p. 140). The whole style in fact is partly an imitation partly a stylisation and further extension of Gertrude Stein's.

The characters as we can see decide to change their names after a potlatch or other sexual or ritual experiences. Ron becomes Cloud, Evelyn his girlfriend becomes Eucalyptus (and when she leaves him for a rival community, Eve), Joan becomes Valley, Paul becomes Wind, Ralph (after resisting) becomes Quasar (but it doesn't stick), etc. The settlement is Earth, a neighbouring one is Krypton (the

Superman planet), its spaced out inhabitants, behaving like space visitors, called Altair, Betelgeuse (later Beetle Juice), Cassiopeia (who escapes to Earth but keeps her name), until they go primitive Jesus and are called Joseph or Mary and their settlement Golgotha. Ron's settlement, like all utopias, disintegrates, and not the least interest is precisely the 'unusual-slice-of-life' interest of realistic novels (which Sukenick is somewhat ironic about in a fascinating essay on the politics of language, 1979). Cloud eventually 'bursts' and becomes 'he again, and even 'I', and even (once) 'Someone'.[2] The poetic idyll is interrupted brutally by the third part, 'Palestine', where 'I' takes over, in a curiously shifting way, in unreal conversation with Bobby Kennedy, who is both assassinated and still alive, at the White House and apparently at the same time on a beach, or with a rabbinic figure of a sage. In fact all the figures in the novel, but particularly Ron, 'filter' a general commentary on life, so that the 'narrator–filter' problem, apparently resolved by the style, is as much present as in the realistic novel.

Cloud for instance has invented 'psychosynthesis', as opposed to psychoanalysis, and psychosynthesis is based on the Mosaic Law (parts in the absence of wholes), an absurd contradiction since synthesis means making a whole out of parts. But the contradiction seems not to be a joke, for the context continues apparently in earnest. Eucalyptus has 'dropped psychoanalysis not because it did no good but because she didn't want to spend the rest of her life preparing for the rest of her life' (p. 122). 'Cloud feels that life is a lot like a novel you have to make it up' (122), while Blossom

no longer has to filter events through the particular distortions of her psychology psychology was the mark of a previous era. What we have instead of psychology is imagination. In any case psychology was always the science of the imagination but as a medical science was obliged to treat it like a sickness. For Bud and Branch imagination is a cure what does it cure why itself of course. It cures psychology. Which is to say it cures nothing it's just a beginning but a beginning has one great advantage it allows us to proceed. (p. 123)

This somewhat Beckettian last sentence inverts (more simply than Kristeva's authors, see p. 342) the notion expressed in Todorov that the themes of the fantastic left literature because they were taken over by psychoanalysis, and Sukenick is obviously serious here, filtering his own ideas through the characters, as indeed the narrator-voice does throughout. But unfortunately his ideas are often more naive. The imagination is much less rich than in

Brautigan, Barthelme or Reed, closer to fancy in the Wordsworthian
distinction.

Yet the book is much more than 'slice-of-life'. For despite the
basic realism, Sukenick seems to be the only writer to whom all of
Hassan's seven categories (see p. 347 above), if we accept their
vagueness, apply, including 'experimentalism'. His text has all the
shifting poetry of, precisely, parts in the absence of wholes, even if
the wholes keep returning in filtered narrator-comment. There are
word-play and dual-function sentences that effect sudden transitions
by applying to both the preceding and the subsequent event (e.g. p.
149, the dying seal and Valley's miscarriage and back again, or even
a mere exclamation mark conferring dual function: 'Jesus Christ!
comes skidding down the logging road with Joseph and Cassiopeia
. . . Come on Mary says Joseph he steers her back to Jesus Christ!' (p.
157). Cloud keeps seeing or hearing 'The Missing Lunk': 'if they
don't understand it [his nonsense language] the Lunk can hide
there. As soon as they understand it they hunt it down and then
The Lunk is Missing again' (p. 161). The Missing Lunk is also
Cloud himself after he has 'burst': 'Because he cries a lot . . . The
Missing Lunk cries a lot' (p. 161). And author-thoughts filtered
through Cloud are also treated with a certain self irony, for his
nonsense language is 'a vertical language all others are horizontal.
Bjorsq is a deep language all others are flat. Bjorsq is a window
language all others are mirrors . . . He thinks all this is very clever.
He thinks he has figured it out . . . He's so smart' (pp. 161–2). There
is a poem:

Reflection on the mirror
The mirror.
The mirror is double.
The mirror is ee/or
The mirror is separation.
The mirror is painful.
The mirror is self-conscious.
No more self no more conscious.
End of reflection. (p. 163)

For what Sukenick is ultimately concerned with is the uniqueness
of the real, even if it has to be its 'idiocy' in Rosset's sense, its non-
doubleness, the uniqueness of the 'ordinary made extraordinary', of
the real made unreal. And if he doesn't always succeed, that is part
of the 'hit-or-miss' character of the task, which is quite unusually
difficult, and is being tackled in many ways.

If we imagine a circle, the upper half representing parodic dramatisation, the lower half stylisation, with a fluctuating dividing line and the content of the circle representing the 'task', then the writers I have discussed could be noted round the circumference, representing various segments or slices of the circle: at the top of the upper half (parody of realism), Fowles (almost straight representation); to the left, Barth (pure parody, towards stylisation, but satirical, light of touch); to the right, Pynchon (ostensibly parody, towards stylisation, but still heavily realistic in manner), then Coover (further towards stylisation). Beneath Coover, in the lower half (stylisation), Gass (still tipping back into realism), then Brautigan (stylisation), then Barthelme (pure stylisation); moving up to the left, back towards parody, Reed; then, almost realistic dramatisation again but in a highly individual style, bordering on imitation rather than stylisation of a specific (Steinian) model, Sukenick. But such imaginings are 'schemas', anathema to these writers, which is why I don't dare draw it, but give it discursively, that it might get lost.

2. Where do we go from here?

Towards silence, exhaustion? Or a new beginning? A good 'theory' (model), I said in chapter 3, should be able to 'predict', not in the futurological sense, but in accounting for all the theoretical possibilities. As I also said, I am not a pure theorist, and even less a prophet, and critical prophecies have a way of being undone by artists. Apocalyptic prophets can be pessimistic (total destruction) or optimistic (death and renewal).

One absurd fallacy should perhaps be got out of the way: the 'death of the novel' has been announced for half a century or more, and journalistic critics always mock this and point out that thousands of novels go on getting published and read, because people will always want 'stories'. That is entirely beside the point. Stories of one kind or another (even stories about stories) will indeed always continue, but they have always found and will continue to find their home in different forms. When the mediaeval verse romance got exhausted it became prose romance, and when that got exhausted, roughly in the fourteenth century, romances went on being written for at least a hundred years, and even well (Malory), just as Chaucer wrote an excellent verse romance (but in stanza form) a century after its heyday. But stories eventually found a more vivid form in the theatre, which regalvanised story-telling later into epic, then satire and the novel. The great nineteenth-century novel has continued, in both diluted and revivified forms, right through the twentieth, but it has for a long time shown signs of exhaustion in its turn, so that stories have escaped into the new media, film and its younger, as yet babbling offspring television. Hence the 'elitist' wave of experiment and iconoclastic deconstructionism and stylisation of various kinds. The wave itself, in its concern about non-interpretation and its self-reflexive ways of dealing with it, is a sign of decadence and apocalyptic premonitions, like the multiplication of rhetorics and their concern for systems of meaning.

It is true however that iconoclasm as such cannot last (I mean the individual works may last but not the deconstruction). As Lodge says in a more specific context, 'it would truly abolish itself, by destroying the norms against which we perceive its deviations'. Similarly Susan Sontag:

The present prospect is that artists will go on abolishing art, only to resurrect it in a more retracted version. As long as art bears up under the pressure of chronic interrogation, it would seem desirable that some of the questions have a certain playful quality.

But this prospect depends, perhaps, on the viability of irony itself. (p. 33)

I have postponed the problem of irony, and clearly I shall not solve it here, it would require a book in itself, and has had, from others. Barthes, we may remember, dismisses it as just another code that merely shows the superiority of one voice over another, which closes off the plurality of codes, and he insists that it has disappeared from modern writing, thanks to the degree zero of tone, already nascent (as uncertainty of irony) in Flaubert – for the idol must be disculpated (S/Z, 1970: 44–5, 98, 139–40, 206). Sontag also casts doubt on irony, for although it has been valued from Socrates on as a serious method of seeking and holding one's truth and saving one's sanity, 'as it becomes the good taste of what is, after all, an essentially collective activity – the making of art – it may prove less serviceable' (p. 34). She adds that we need not judge it as categorically as Nietzsche, who equated the spread of irony throughout a culture with decadence and the approaching end of that culture's vitality, but 'there still remains a question as to how far the resources of irony can be stretched. It seems unlikely that the possibilities of continually undermining one's assumptions can go on unfolding indefinitely into the future, without being checked by despair or by a laughter that leaves one without any breath at all' (p. 34).

Similarly Hassan talks of a self-consuming irony (under dehumanisation, see p. 347 above).

As we have seen, the writers I have surveyed here depend a great
deal on irony, on more than a humdrum collusion with the reader
(for collusion there must be). Some of the irony is naive, curiously
mingled with earnestness and sometimes (if it is irony) astonishingly
regressive in character, for instance in the treatment of sex, which is
often ludicrously, limitedly and it seems unconsciously phallocratic
in most of the writers examined here, with the exception of
Barthelme and Brautigan. But the healthy signs are surely the very
elements of naivety I have here and there commented on, not by way
of carping but to bring them out as such. If Frye is right, an
exhausted literature turns to more popular forms, either directly, in
the sense that these forms are themselves taken more seriously by the
'central' tradition, or indirectly, in the sense of parody and
stylisation by the 'serious' artists of that 'central' tradition. The fact
that this is happening so late, so long after the forms have become
stereotypes, oft-parodied and even declared moribund, is one of the
paradoxes of American literature: its naivety, its vigour, as well as
the undeniable fact that it is now sometimes overrated simply
because it is American, and the culture of a great power always has
more sway (for itself, for others) than that of minor countries,
especially if its language becomes quasi-universal. But perhaps
European experiments against realistic fiction in the early part of
the century (Gide, Pirandello, Surrealism on) were themselves part
of an exhausted tradition. Sukenick (1979) has pleaded for an even
more radical breakaway of American literature from its European
roots, since America, with its many and enriching non-European
elements, is culturally far wider than Europe, and certainly all dead
and dying models are grist to its parody-mill: Westerns are no
longer made, the Gothic is over a century old, the gangster film long
overtaken by life, science fiction weighed down by clichés and only
here and there renewed, the realistic novel, by now a popular form,
long declared dead, and only its most tired and nineteenth-century
features parodied or stylised, etc. Similarly the notion that nothing
visible is real or unique but a spectacle, a duplication which is the
mark of the unreal was the basic philosophy of surrealism (see
Rosset 1979:14), of which American 'postmodernism' often seems a
late and diluted imitation. The lateness then is itself a naivety
(hence the frequent fusions of stylisation and model), which should
regalvanise procedures, more vigorously perhaps than their more

sophisticated European antecedents. Just as Don Quixote, a mock-romance long after the romance had died, was the beginning of modern fiction, or Tristram Shandy the end and the beginning of the modern novel in one, so the result now should be a new strength, new forms, even realistic ones, stripped of their tired formulas and interpretive mania, merely showing the real, in its unique 'idiocy', as the fantastic which it is. For ultimately all fiction is realistic, whether it mimes a mythic idea of heroic deeds or a progressive idea of society, or inner psychology or, as now. the non-interpretability of the world, which is our reality as its interpretability once was (and may return). A fantastic realism. A new classicism perhaps: 'nous vivons peut-être un pré-classicisme', as Gaëtan Picon said of Robbe-Grillet.

But not, I think, the romantic 'new gnosticism' Hassan rhapsodises, whereby, according to McLuhan, Buckminster Fuller and others including of course Teilhard de Chardin who sparked it all off, the old gnostic dream and the new technological dream, after the present period of transition or disjunction, would converge toward a universal consciousness, the consciousness of God in Susan Sontag's terms, or the noossphere in Chardin's (or perhaps, though I doubt that this is her meaning, beyond the 'limits of the signifiable' in Kristeva's), the planet being as it were wrapped in telepathic or electronic thought of more and more brains working away. Hassan admits that the radical insufficiency of the human condition still offers intractable resistance to the old gnostic dream, and this resistance, he says, whether we call it evil (ananke) or The System, must be acknowledged, without assent.

At the risk of siding with ananke or The System, I am less optimistic about the gnostic dream. This consciousness that is to wrap the planet seems to me dangerously like the pollution that may stifle it. For every work of incomparable genius in all fields there are millions of tons of paper wasted in garbage, in exactly the same way as every benefit of civilisation is paid for not only in entropy but in pollution and extremely ugly politics to get hold of raw materials – what's left of them, not to mention the thousands of children's brains atrophied from lack of protein. The gnostic dream of the best scientific, technological and artistic brainstuff enveloping the earth seems to me essentially an elitist dream, akin to J. D. Bernal's (ironic, SF) suggestion that mankind may eventually divide into two species, the scientists and the others, the scientists colonising the heavens but reverencing the earth as a sort of zoo (*The World, the*

Flesh and the Devil, 1929), or else not far removed from Wells's collective mind or world-wide information service (*World Brain*, 1938), which presupposes an unprecedented harmony of minds: a mad and perhaps naive fusion of oblivion and utopia one could call oblitopia. Let the artists dream their gnostic or other dreams and produce verbal or other structures of them, but why if art is to be regarded as 'no more nor less than anything else in life' (Hassan's words, see summary p. 347 here), should these dreams at the same time be given the supreme power of enveloping the planet (conquering the world), when neither those dreams nor man have shown the slightest capacity for solving the world's real problems, only a brilliant capacity for displacing them? At any rate, that envelope of brainstuff, more and more words and formulas and forms, continuous or discontinuous, theoretical or intuitive, not only seems to me yet another displacement, but also has me dead scared, even if like everyone else and in my infinitesimal way I am contributing to it, or to the garbage. I prefer to struggle more humbly inside that paradox, which to me is nevertheless the fundamental one today and the true symptom of mutation: the paradox of the liar who says he is a liar, the paradox of using words to say meaninglessness, the paradox of letting everyone *prendre là parole* when everyone knows that real power, whether political, economic, social, psychological or even mystical, functions silently and has no need of the semblance of speech, even though it never ceases to use that semblance to persuade that we participate. If art can cope with that kind of terror and humour, it has a long future yet.

Notes

2. The rhetoric

1. 'What is *semiotic* pertains to the signs "out there", in the texts and in the world ... just as *rhetoric* is the objective structure of any discourse, *history* is a sequence of actions and events, *grammar* is the mechanism we have in our brain even if we cannot read and write. On the other hand: *semiotics* is metalanguage used to analyze semiotic structures, just as *rhetorics* is metalanguage employed to analyze rhetorical structures (which are ultimately, in my opinion, the same as semiotic structures), *history* in the second sense (or *historiography*) is the account of these actions and events, and *grammar* in the second sense is the formalized analysis of the grammar we have in our heads.' (Valesio, 'The practice of literary semiotics: a theoretical proposal', 1978: 16.)
2. Cp. the various Greek words on the same root: *kritikos* (one able to discern, especially in language, a grammarian, a scholar); *krites* (judge, umpire, especially in poetic contests); *kriteon* (interpreter of dreams); *kriterion* ((a) the means; (b) the place or tribunal).
3. Theory (*theoria*), a systematic statement of the principles involved, a speculation.
4. Cp. Valesio (1978:1): 'That general theory in the human sciences is virtually non-existent, and what there is is little use – this much I will not try to demonstrate, but beg leave to take for granted. That there can ever be a general theory of the human sciences in the sense in which this concept is used in the other sciences – this is a moot point which would require a detailed analysis ... I will confine myself to noting that, if it turns out that no such general theory is possible, this would not be a limitation or a weakness of the human sciences, but rather a reflection of their peculiar nature.'
5. Cp. R. Jakobson (1962), V. Erlich (1965), T. Todorov ed. (1965), L. Matejka and K. Pomorska eds. (1971) for accounts or anthologised translations of the Russian Formalists, and A. Shukman (1977) for complete bibliography of translations of Formalist texts.
6. See also Bremond's (1972) account and criticism of Greimas in *Semiotica* v:4, 362–83.
7. I am indebted to my colleague Olga Scherer for helping me to clarify this point. See especially Ingarden 1931:296: 'It is undoubtedly correct

that metaphysical qualities appear on the basis of represented objective situations and objects and do not constitute a special stratum of the literary work of art'

8. See Scherer (1977b) for a more sympathetic account of Ingarden.

9. A great deal of closer analysis of types of discourse has been done, notably by V. N. Voloshinov (*Marxism and the philosophy of language*, 1929; trans. 1973 – a censorship-evading title), who adds 'free direct discourse'. And Ann Banfield has done a considerable job of analysing free indirect discourse, which she calls 'represented speech and thought', through the strict methods of transformational grammar (1973: 1–39, 1978a: 415–54, 1978b: 281–314). Cp. also Brian McHale's survey of recent accounts of free indirect discourse in the same journal as Banfield 1978b (McHale 1978: 249–87). See also modification made by Mieke Bal (1977) to Genette's account of focalisation. Bal points out that internal focalisation bears upon him who sees, whereas external focalisation bears upon him who is seen, and proposes a separation between the focaliser and the focalised, which enables her considerably to refine the latter category.

10. For deconstructionism in action see *Deconstruction and criticism* essays by Harold Bloom, Paul de Man, Jacques Derrida, Geoffrey Hartman, J. Hillis Miller, London 1979. For a long, thoughtful but basically adverse review of this, see 'The deconstruction gang', by S. L. Goldberg, *London Review of Books* (22 May – 4 June 1980).

3. Historic genres/theoretical genres: Todorov on the fantastic

1. In the logical rectangle (used by Greimas for the deepest level of his narrative 'grammar', 1970: 135–55 and 1976, and called *les structures élémentaires de la signification*), a significance S_1 (say *white*) has its contrary S_2 (say *black*, though on a different semantic axis it could be *red* for instance); each also has its contradictory (non-S_1 or $\bar{S}_1$; non-S_2 or $\bar{S}_2$) which, unlike black/white, is *always* its mere negation: non-white, non-black. Thus the two vertical (and downward) relations are relations of implication (black implies non-white but not vice versa):

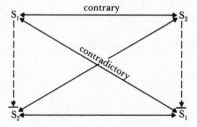

See also Greimas (1976) for practical application to Maupassant's story *Deux amis*.

2. *The fantastic*, pp. 17–18. The quotation from Lévi-Strauss (in Richard Howard's version, presumably translated straight from Todorov) comes from *Structural anthropology*, tr. Claire Jacobson and Brooke Grundfest Schoepf (Garden City, NY, 1967), p. 271: 'The term "social structure" has nothing to do with empirical reality but with models which are built up after it.'

3. Stanislas Lem, 'Tzvetana Todorova fantastyczna teoria literatury' (Tzvetan Todorov's fantastic theory of literature), *Teksty* 5: 11(1973). I am here much indebted to my colleague, Olga Scherer, who gave a critical account of this essay in the seminar which we run jointly at the University of Paris VIII.

4. Cp. Todorov, 'The origin of genres' in *New Literary History* 8:1. (Autumn 1976) and, in French, in *Les Genres du discours*. (Paris, 1978).

5. Cp. my 'poetic' reading of *The Turn of the Screw* in chapter 7, a study of structural rhetorical devices which function in both hypotheses (ghosts or hallucinations) and therefore sustain the hesitation. This type of poetic reading does not kill the fantastic, nor does it represent what Todorov means by a poetic reading. Cp. my remarks on Heilman's reading (1948) of '*The Turn of the Screw* as poem' (ch. 6, p. 52), which however is not strictly a poetic reading in the sense meant by Todorov, since any fiction can use rhetorical devices. But by reading so much 'symbolism' (of a vague kind) into the narrative he does tend to destroy it as fiction, and therefore as fantastic. The same would apply to Krook's reading of it as a Faustian allegory (1962).

4. Science fiction and realistic fiction

1. According to Rabkin (1976:121), there is a prescription whereby a good work of SF may make only one assumption about its narrative world which violates what is known about our world and then extrapolate the whole narrative world from that difference. See also Ketterer 1974 (in Rose 1976:149) for categories based on the extrapolation involved: future consequences of present circumstances; consequences of a modification in an existent condition; a startling *donnée* or rationale that puts humanity in a radically new perspective. For Rabkin this startling donnée is achieved by a 180° reversal (or less) from the 'ground rules' of the text, but his precise working out of this supposition seems to me theoretically unsatisfactory, for although his book makes fascinating reading, in the end almost anything is fantastic, even a character-error. See also Toloyan's review (1980).

2. Cp. Rose (1976: 2): 'Science fiction, contrary perhaps to popular opinion, is rather poor as an instrument of scientific prediction, but it is an excellent medium for the exploration of the taste, the feel, the human meaning of scientific discoveries.' Similarly Robert Conquest (1963, in Rose: 34) suggests that 'possibility fiction' might have been a better name than science fiction, and Raymond Williams, in a thoughtful essay on 'Utopia and science fiction' (in Parrinder ed 1979:62) reminds

us that the utopian mode has to be read in history's changing context, 'which itself determines whether its defining subjunctive tense is part of a grammar which includes a true indicative and a true future, or whether it has seized every paradigm and become exclusive in assent and dissent alike'. So with SF, it is written in a subjunctive mood, not a future but an 'as if', a 'what if'. Cp. J. B. S. Haldane's non-fiction *Possible Worlds* (1927), which C. S. Lewis suggests should be included, with Geoffrey Dennis's *The End of the World* (1930), in his eschatological sub-species, where SF tends to separate from the novel, e.g. Stapledon's *Last and First Men* is not novelistic at all. It is indeed in a new form – the 'pseudo-history' (1967, in Rose 1976). The term 'possible worlds', like 'alternative world' has now become accepted for a certain type of SF which postulates a different version of history (if Napoleon had won Waterloo etc.)

3. These have been translated, for Todorov's book, as 'utterance' (*énoncé*) and 'uttering' (*énonciation*) which is not very satisfactory, and I shall adopt different terms myself in chapter 8. To avoid confusion here I shall stick to the French terms, since the distinction is not crucial to my argument. See chapter 2, p. 26) for distinction.

4. Hamon's article also gives in footnote a brief but well-documented survey of previous work on the problem of realism.

5. Cp. also Genette (1972) who says that in narrative the only absolute mimesis is in dialogue, i.e. language imitating language (see chapter 12 here, p. 321). Cp. also, more complexly, Bakhtin (1929a; 1973) on parody and pastiche as dialogical.

6. Cp. Genette (1969), 'Vraisemblance et motivation', who argues that plausibility (*le vraisemblable*) is (a) the general common sense of the time, and (b) conformity to the genre.

7. Cp. Genette (1969), on motivation in this technical sense. His example is from *La Princesse de Clèves*, by Mme de Lafayette: the Prince de Clèves does not die (as it appears) because his *gentilhomme* has behaved like an idiot; his *gentilhomme* behaves like an idiot *so that* (technically) the Prince de Clèves may die.

8. Thus, in Maupassant's *Deux amis* (a story about two men who go fishing outside Paris during the Prussian encirclement), the following would be 'ungrammatical' (unacceptable) sequences: *the two friends laid an ambush and killed Bismarck; * the two friends, heading their battalion, delivered Paris from the Prussian encirclement (426, n.31).

9. Hamon cites Riffaterre (1971b) who rewrote a page of Zola, changing all the geographical names from the Ardennes to South West France, and concluded that the alteration of the reference to the real had not threatened the mimesis of the real.

10. In the *nouveau roman* however, this visual element is mostly used transgressively (see chapter 11, p. 302).

11. A particularly interesting example is Proust's etymologist Brichot (*Sodome et Gomorrhe*, Pléiade edn, pp. 888–90), who by commenting on

the etymology (the language) of place names fulfils a double role as 'linguistic mosaic' (learned language) and as megatext (geography).

12. Hamon cites Jakobson's article 'Notes marginales sur la prose du poète Pasternak' (1935: 1970) in which he comments on the difficulty of discovering the hero, who is decomposed into a series of elements and accessories, and replaced by a chain of his own states, objectivised, or of objects, animate or inanimate, that surround him. It could be added that any narrative that purports to give a portrait of society on a large canvas will divide its attention among several main characters (cp. *War and Peace*). In *Middlemarch*, for instance, the central character appears at first to be Dorothea Brooke, but we then shift to Lydgate, and return to Dorothea only intermittently.

13. Strictly speaking anaphora is repetition in the same syntactic or metrical position, but Hamon seems to use it as synonym for any repetition, as do many structuralists and semioticians.

14. Cp. Henri Mitterand (1973) who shows that certain heroic and even some mythic features underlie the narrative functions in Zola.

15. This paragraph is entirely based on an unpublished work-in-progress paper, '*Ce mal d'être deux*', in a seminar at the University of Paris VIII, and it contained many more complex varieties than the simple scheme can show here.

16. The right-hand column is a subjective estimate, based not on detailed analysis but on general impression from fairly wide reading. However, its value as general impression should give a rough guideline.

5. The encoded reader

1. For over-determination cf. Michael Riffaterre's definition: 'The effect of over-determination is to transfer the meaning of one word to several, as it were saturating the sentence with that meaning, so that the reader feels the sentence keeps on confirming overtly what he gathered from a single word.' ('Semantic over-determination in poetry'. *PTL*, 2:1 (1977), 1–19).

2. I shall use Roland Barthes's codes as a kind of shorthand for types of information, but clearly any other procedure would do in this particular context, nor does this represent a full use of Barthes's method. (See *S/Z*, Paris: Seuil, 1970; Eng. trans. by Richard Miller, New York: Farrar, Strauss and Giroux, 1974, and ch. 2 here, pp. 38–42 for brief account.)

3. In *Great American Short Stories*, edited by Wallace and Mary Stegner, New York: Dell Books, 1957, from Washington Irving's *Sketchbook* (1820).

4. Penguin Modern Classics, London, 1967.

5. In *Great Short Works of Edgar Allan Poe* (Perennial Classics, New York, 1970).

6. At the University of Paris VIII, in collaboration with my colleague Olga Scherer, to whom I owe this observation.

7. The clearest example is Dostoevsky's *Notes from the Underground*, which has strongly influenced modern fiction (notably Faulkner and Sarraute and, explicitly, Ellison's *Invisible Man*). See also Scherer, 'Absalon et Absalon', *Letters Modernes*, 1 (Paris: Minard, 1974, pp. 1–24) and 'La contestation du jugement sur pièces chez Dostoievski et Faulkner', *Delta*, 1976, 47–62 (Université de Montpellier).

8. See, for example, Wolf Schmid, *Der Textaufbau in den Erzählungen Dostoevskijs* (Munich: Fink, 1973). Schmid not only disagrees that Dostoevsky is dialogical, but argues that such a structure (of autonomous voices emancipated from the creative author) is ontologically inconceivable, and prefers to characterise Dostoevsky's technique as text-interference. This in my view is to fall into the very trap that Bakhtin analyses in his first chapter, namely his predecessors' and contemporaries' 'monological' reading of Dostoevsky. Bakhtin of course admits that there are large monological chunks in Dostoevsky, but his purpose is to bring out the extraordinary nature of the technique in its incipient stage. And even if he were wrong about Dostoevsky, this would not alter the validity of his theory as theory, so original and requiring such a change (an Ingardenean, and even, almost a Derridean change) in our view of a work of art, that many are bound, as Schmid does, to fall back on more traditional concepts.

9. An extreme example of the code under-determined, though not relevant here, would be anagrammatical poetry, which also depends on a balance between the over-determined (the sort of places where anagrams are most likely to occur or to begin, such as the first line, or word, or letter; and sufficient recurrence for the anagrams to be perceived at all) and the under-determined ('hidden' anagrams). For theories of anagrammation, see Saussure, 'Anagrammes', partially published by Starobinski in *Mercure de France*, Feb. 1964; Kristeva, 'Pour une sémiologie des paragrammes' in *Semeiotike* (Paris, Seuil 1968: 174–206; originally in *Tel Quel* 1966); Jean Starobinski, *Les mots sous les mots* (Paris: Gallimard, 1971) and Anthony L. Johnson, 'Anagrammatism in poetry: theoretical preliminaries', *PTL* 2:1 (1977), 89–118.

10. Unfortunately this unrigorous kind of reading is so easy and so popular that it is all too frequently used on texts belonging to the first two categories, often missing much of their structure or hitting it by chance or through parasitical criticism.

11. Susan Suleiman, 'Ideological dissent from works of fiction: toward a rhetoric of the *roman à thèse*', *Neophilologus* 60:2 (April 1976), 162–77.

6. 'The Turn of the Screw' and its critics: an essay in non-methodology

1. I shall limit my study to two collections of essays: *A Casebook on Henry James's 'The Turn of the Screw'* (Willen 1971, ref. W); and the essays

accompanying the Norton Critical edition of the text (Kimbrough 1966, ref. K) (some of which overlap with the former). Quotations from James's text will be from the Norton edition (James, 1966 plus reference). The text itself will be referred to as TS.

2. Many critics remind us of the ambiguity but keep forgetting it themselves, just as many reiterate Wilson's point that the governess narrates the whole story, but keep forgetting it, although it is crucial. The first point has already been taken up by Perry and Steinberg (1974, dealing chiefly with the story of David and Bathsheba), who suggest that the co-existence of incompatible systems be called 'multiple systems of gap-filling', but also take up *The Turn of the Screw* to show that the attempt to establish a correct and single hypothesis is absurd. (See also Rimmon (1977), discussed in chapter 8.) I shall not therefore return to this point here. As to the second, I shall make a detailed analysis of the governess's narration in chapter 8.

3. See chapter 2, pp. 27–8, for the discrediting of the 'intentional fallacy' as not in fact fallacious, either as a return to a consideration of the author (or implied author), or simply as addresser of the words we read.

4. See chapter 2 (p. 26) for definition, and chapter 8 for analysis of the governess's *énonciation*.

5. Barthes (1970), see chapter 2. Barthes separates the semic code (or voice of the person which creates character) from the action code (voice of experience), quite rightly for his purpose, but it is clear that the semes which (whether scattered or gathered together in a 'portrait') make up a character must also include their actions (e.g., for Miles or the uncle below, though in these statements the actions are read into the text by the critics).

6. In his revised version (1963: 155), Cargill suggests that the allusion to *Jane Eyre* and to *The Mysteries of Udolpho* ('Was there a "secret" at Bly – a mystery of Udolpho or an insane, an unmentionable relative kept in unsuspected confinement?' 1963: 17), should be read as 'the dilemma which confronts the reader as well as the governess – he must choose between a supernatural explanation, such as confronts the reader of *The Mysteries of Udolpho* or a natural one such as is given him in *Jane Eyre*: a mad woman?'

7. Casebook edition (Willen 1971): 'most impossible'. Not included in the Norton textual notes on the changes made by James (there are also other omissions of this kind).

8. Even on the level of psychoanalysing a non-existent fictional character this is confusing: hysteria is the only neurosis that can become a psychosis, and hallucinations can occur in both conversion hysteria and psychosis, but if the governess were psychotic she would be wholly unable to work, or relate to reality in any way, and would certainly not have found a job later, or told Douglas so calmly and charmingly about her experience. Psychosis was, and maybe still is, incurable.

7. 'The Turn of the Screw': mirror structures as basic structures

1. This chapter is a revised version of an essay published as 'The squirm of the true' in *Poetics and Theory of Literature* 1:2 (1976). Since then, an excellent essay by Shoshana Felman has appeared 'Turning the screw of interpretation', *Yale French Studies* nos. 55–6 (Summer 1977), which also makes use of Lacan, different from mine but with which I wholly concur. In order to distinguish mine from hers, I shall refer to hers as Felman, in brackets or in footnote. TS = *The Turn of the Screw*. All quotations from the text are from the Norton Critical Edition (James 1966), with only the page number. All italics are mine unless followed by [J] for James.

2. I use 'illness' rather than evil to obviate the curious puritanism of some Anglo-American critics, for whom 'hysteria' and other psychoanalytic terms seem merely to have replaced 'sin'. I can only insist that Freud only spoke of an original lack. With regard to 'pre-existent evil' cf. Lacan: 'La béance de l'inconscient, nous pourrions la dire *pré-ontologique*. J'ai insisté sur ce caractère trop oublié – oublié d'une façon qui n'est pas sans signification – de la première émergence de l'inconscient, qui est de ne pas prêter à l'ontologie' (1973b:31).

3. I use '*surmounting* this love', as opposed to 'repressing', so often used by the critics. Repression is an unconscious process. As has often been pointed out, the governess is perfectly conscious of her feelings and expresses them freely to Mrs Grose (though only in terms of being 'carried away in London'). It has not however been noticed that this conversation even takes place in front of Flora (chapter 1). See Lacan (1973b: 33): 'Ce qui est ontique, dans la fonction de l'inconscient, c'est la fente par où ce quelque chose dont l'aventure dans notre champ semble si courte est un instant amené au jour – un instant, car le second temps, qui est fermeture, donne à cette saisie un aspect évanouissant.'

4. See J. Mehlmann (1975), who in the steps of Lacan gives us a brilliant reading of Freud's *Jokes* on Freud's own principles as expounded in the *Project*.

5. Felman (1977: 138–48, 'The scene of reading: the purloined letters') also notes the importance of this letter, but as an element in the 'chain' of letters: that of the headmaster to the Master, the letters the governess intercepts, from the children to their uncle, the letter Mrs Grose wants sent to the Master about the goings on at Bly (and one might add, can't write herself, since she is illiterate, and can't entrust, as she normally does, to the bailiff, see p. 178, here), the governess's letter to the Master which is intercepted by Miles and destroyed. All these letters have the same addressee: the Master [except, in fact, this one, the Master's cover-note to the governess, which repeats the injunction]. All the letters to the Master have an empty content (no reason given for Miles's dismissal; children's letters not given; governess's letter 'a bare request for an interview' in which Miles found 'nothing', five times repeated – 86). All require a seal to be broken (violation). And

Felman points out that TS is itself a letter (to Douglas), 'a story about letters' (p. 139). The letters in fact 'become a crucial dramatic element in the narrative plot precisely because of their unreadability [...] it is precisely *because* the letters *fail* to narrate that there is a story at all: there is a story *because* there is an unreadable, an unconscious. Narrative, paradoxically, becomes possible to the precise extent that a story becomes *impossible* – that a story, precisely "won't tell" [Prologue, p. 3]' (p. 143). 'The letters in the story are thus not simply *metonymic* to the manuscript which contains them; they are also *metaphorical* to it: they are the reflection *en abyme* of the narrative itself. To read the story is thus to undertake a *reading of the letters*, to follow the circuitous paths of their changes of address' (p. 141). However, 'it is not what the letters *say* which gets the story started, but what they *don't say*: the letters as such are *unreadable* ... in precisely the same way the unconscious is unreadable' (p. 141–2).

6. See Hélène Cixous (1975:51), who in her revealing analysis of Freud's 'Das Unheimliche' suggests that in *unheimlich* there are always at least two secrets: the 'family' secret (*heimlich*, familiar), which I maintain that in this text we cannot know or analyse, and the alien secret (*le secret étranger*), the *Un-* which bars the first secret, without suppressing it, by taking it out of itself towards 'un dehors qui l'éloigne du repli familial'.

7. James, however, must have been perfectly aware that mirrors and their adjuncts (windows, spectacles, telescopes, etc.) are a constant motif in the supernatural, notably in E. T. A. Hoffmann. Nor is it so by chance. In this text, this odd detail about the governess's upbringing, and the castration shock it ought in theory to provoke, is a fine example of the writer's intuition having little need of specific reading in contemporary or (of course) later scientific discoveries.

8. The children are also, though to a lesser extent, truncated, Flora behind a curtain yet seen by the governess, Miles foreshortened on the lawn, or in the extraordinary comparison early on: 'They were like those cherubs of the anecdote who had – morally at any rate – nothing to whack!' (p. 19).

9. I do not count as an apparition the governess's certainty that 'someone' is on the tower above her when she spies from the empty tower room to find out who Flora is looking at from her window, and sees Miles on the lawn gazing up to a point above her. She cannot 'see' anyone. This scene however does effect an interesting reversal (see the end of section 2. pp. 170–1).

10. In this respect it is worth noting that the governess's elaborations with Mrs Grose, which can so easily be read and have been read as lies, could be interpreted as true in both hypotheses. If the apparitions are hallucinations (emanations of herself), she can as naturally imagine what they say; if they are ghosts, there is nothing in ghost-lore that forbids thought-transference. The third apparition of Quint is specifically dramatised as such: 'the thing was as human and hideous as a real

interview' (p. 41). After the third apparition of Miss Jessel, when Mrs Grose asks if Miss Jessel spoke, the governess does not in fact lie but answers 'It came to that' (p. 60). During the fourth apparition of Miss Jessel the governess even 'consciously threw out to her [...] an inarticulate message of gratitude' [for appearing in front of Flora and Mrs Grose] (p. 71), and after the collapse of the demonstration: 'I had nothing to do but communicate again with the figure that, on the opposite bank ... as rigidly still as if catching, beyond the interval, our voices' (p. 73).

11. Flora slept in the governess's room (chapters 1, 9, 10, 20), a fact which James seems to have remembered when correcting the first Periodical version of TS (1898, referred to as P. in: Kimbrough 1966) in chapter 6: the conversations at night with Mrs Grose take place in the schoolroom (15/10–11, P. has 'Mrs Grose's room', corrected to 'school-room', 27/3, P. has 'the kitchen', corrected to 'schoolroom'). They meet only once in Mrs Grose's room (chapter 16, the governess seeks her out), and once in the governess's room (chapter 21, after Flora has been moved out). In chapter 8, however, James seems to have slipped up on his corrections: 'Late that night, while the house slept, we had another talk in my room' (24/8–9). Most of the conversation is summarised, but in view of the topic and the governess's scrupulous care never to speak to the children about the ghosts, it seems highly unlikely that she would risk Flora overhearing. Unless, of course, this is part of James's little game of clue-planting (which would reinforce the 'natural' explanation of Miles's identification in the last chapter, first of Miss Jessel and then, by association, of Quint; it would also provide a build-up for Flora's sudden loathing at the end, but weaken the shock element that makes her ill).

12. She twice turns away and back, and does this frequently in subsequent dialogues, just as Douglas keeps turning towards the fire with his back to his audience in the Introduction, and turning back to face them again; just as Flora turns her back to the apparition of Miss Jessel, and just as Miles, in the last scene, turns several times to face the window and back. Cp. E. Wilson (1934: 130ff) on the Jamesian character so frequently turning his back on experience, and H. Cixous (1970: paragraph 2, 'Le dos de James'), who takes up this idea as a constant threat of death, disguised, metaphorised.

13. The whole scene can be analysed as a mirror-dialogue which largely accounts for Mrs Grose's identification of Quint. Goddard (1957: 253–7) went a long way in this direction, showing how step by step the governess plants the seed in Mrs Grose's mind. I do not wholly accept his notion that she was not listening to the actual description, but Silver's (1957: 243) explanation (the inquiry in the village) makes it unnecessary.

14. See Lacan: '... s'il y a un domaine où dans le discours, la tromperie a quelque part chance de réussir, c'est assurément l'amour qui en donne le modèle. Quelle meilleure manière de s'assurer, sur le point où on se

trompe, que de persuader l'autre de la vérité de ce qu'on avance! N'est-ce pas là une structure fondamentale de la dimension de l'amour que le transfert nous donne l'occasion d'imaginer? A persuader l'autre qu'il a ce qui peut nous compléter, nous nous assurons de pouvoir continuer à méconnaître précisément ce qui nous manque' (1973a: 121).

15. See Lacan: 'dans le champ scopique, le regard est au dehors, je suis regardé, c'est-à-dire je suis tableau ... il y a quelque chose qui instaure une fracture, une bipartition, une schize de l'être à quoi celui-ci s'accommode, dès la nature ... C'est ce qui entre en jeu, manifeste-ment, aussi bien dans l'union sexuelle que dans la lutte à mort. L'être s'y décompose, d'une façon sensationnelle, entre son être et son sem-blant ... Le leurre joue donc ici une fonction essentielle' (1973a: 98). He goes on to say that if a lighting effect so dominates us as to appear like a milky cone that prevents us from seeing what it illuminates, the mere introduction of a small screen shades, as it were, that milky light and reveals the object hidden. This screen is in effect a central field *in* the picture, an absence, a hole, reflecting the pupil behind the eye and hence the subject always elided as subject of the geometrical plane. Man, as opposed to the animal (who in its mimetic function writes itself into the picture) can isolate the function of the screen, 'et en joue. L'homme, en effet, sait jouer du masque comme étant ce au-delà de quoi il a le regard. L'écran est ici le lieu de la médiation' (p. 99). And of course, because of this screen, 'la réalité n'apparaît que marginale' (p. 99).

16. 'Scene' does not here necessarily imply dialogue, but is used in the sense defined by Booth (1961) and Genette (1972), as a slowing-down of the action to roughly the time it would take in 'reality' or more (allowing for descriptions, thoughts, etc.), as opposed to 'summary', which is faster. See chapter 12 here.

17. Felman (120–33) also emphasises the spatial aspect of this part of the frame: 'Since the narrative space of the prologue organises both a *frame around the story* and a *circle around the fire*, since the fire and the story are both placed at the very *center* of the *narration*, the question could arise as to whether they could be, in any way, considered *metaphors of each other* in the rhetorical constellation of the text' (p. 120). 'Including not only the content of the story but also the figure of the reader within the fireside circle, the frame indeed leaves no one *out*: it pulls the outside of the story into its inside by enclosing in it what is usually outside it: its own readers. But the frame at the same time does the very opposite, pulling the inside outside: for in passing through the echoing chain of the multiple, repetitive, narrative voices, it is the very *content*, the *interior* of the story which becomes somehow *exterior to itself*, reported as it is by a voice inherently alien to it and which can render of it but "The shadow of a shadow," a voice whose intrusion compromises the tale's secret intimacy and whose otherness violates the story's presence to itself' (p. 123). Later she points out that the last letter internal to the fiction (from the Governess to the Master) is intercepted by Miles and

burnt: 'the *fire inside the story* turns out to be, precisely, *what annihilates the inside of the letter*; what materially destroys the very "nothing" which constitutes its *content*. And since the letters in the story are metaphorical to the manuscript of the story as a whole . . . we can see that what the fire indeed consumes, in burning up the letter, is nothing other than the very *content* of the story . . . in every sense of the expression, *letters burn* . . . the fire is the story's center only insofar as it *eliminates the center*: it is analogous to the story's *content* only insofar as it consumes, incinerates at once the content of the story and the inside of the letter, making both indeed impossible to read, *unreadable*, but unreadable in such a way as to hold all the more "breathless" the readers' circle round it.' (pp. 147–8).

18. In chapter 6 I dealt with 'extratextual arguments' as unacceptable because not encoded in the text, but made a possible exception of Rubin's theory that Miles is Douglas (in which case he does not die), on the grounds that this theory could be said to be partially encoded in the very presence of the elaborate frame. In view of the extraordinary repetition of the figure four and other parallels it can hardly be a coincidence that the governess finds a job ten years later with a young girl who has a brother of university age (Miles/Flora, Douglas/sister; also, on the level of the fictional cause for the narrative: governess/ sister; Douglas/Miles = Douglas as a boy in the story she tells him). This would then be James's little joke, the whole story being concocted by the governess, or at least altered as to its ending, to convey to Douglas the extent of her love both past and present. But then, of course, it is a different story.

19. She had, strictly speaking, had another attack of 'reality' in the previous chapter (chapter 11) when, after fetching Miles from the lawn and when about to question him in his bedroom she says: 'He could do what he liked, with all his cleverness to help him, so long as I should continue to defer to the old tradition of the criminality of those caretakers of the young who minister to superstitions and fears. He "had" me indeed, in a cleft stick; for who would ever absolve me, who would consent that I should go unhung, if, by the faintest tremor of an overture, I were the first to introduce into our perfect intercourse an element so dire?' (pp. 46–7). But here the 'natural' explanation is regarded as a nuisance in the particular situation, an old tradition to be deferred to and which has been carefully deferred to, though the uncle's possible opinion of her hovers in the 'who', preparing the ground for chapter 12. From Mrs Grose's suggestion on, and every time the possible direct involvement of the uncle is in question, she will have an attack of reality, and in more and more brutal terms.

20. In the original periodical (see n. 9 above), the chapter (or instalment) continues:

'Then what's your remedy?' she asked as I watched the children.

I continued, without answering, to watch them. 'I would leave *them*,' and went on. [J]

'But what *is* your remedy?' she persisted. [J]

It seemed, after all, to have come to me then and there. 'To speak to them.' And I joined them.

This makes more sense of chapter 13's opening ('It was all very well to join them') since all the chapters except, with the cut, this one, are thus syntactically or semantically linked; and it also makes more sense of 'my remedy' and 'what *is* your remedy?' in chapter 21 (see end of section 4). But the repetitiveness does weaken the threat with which the chapter now ends, and one can see why James cut.

21. Felman (138ff) links the governess's difficulty in starting her letter with the general difficulty for the narrator to begin, in the Prologue: 'I can't begin. I shall have to send to town .... The story's written', says Douglas. Secondly, the TS is in a locked drawer, thirdly, it has to be sent to him in order for there to be a narrative at all. These three features are immediate consequences of double implication in the fact that 'the story's written': (1) the story is a *text* and not just a series of events: it has its own *place*; it exists as a material object. (2) As a material object, the manuscript is independent of the narrator, who is, rather, himself dependent on *it*: the narrator is dependent on the place and materiality of the written word. However, she later refers to the governess's letter as 'the unfinished letter of the governess to the Master which Miles intercepts and destroys' (p. 144) to show how all the letters are structured around the impossibility of recounting an ellipsis. This is misleading, for the governess does not send 'an unfinished' letter, but only 'the bare demand for an interview' (p. 78), though this of course does not alter but equally expresses 'the impossibility of recounting an ellipsis'. The 'unfinished' state of the letter occurs here, in chapter 17, when Miles says 'Well then, finish it!'

22. Cp. my remarks on the gay bachelor as 'God the Father' and 'the illustrious author' in chapter 6, p. 155.

23. Todorov (1969): action *a* (which alters a given situation); action *b* (transgression); action *c* (punishment). As Boccaccio's transgressions are chiefly against injunctions merely encoded in general custom, Todorov does not need a notation for the injunction (usually encoded in folk-tales and to which Propp gives a place among his pre-misdeed functions, noted with Greek letters). For present purposes I prefer Todorov's ultra-simple formulation and will merely use a negative *a* for injunction (prohibition).

8. The surface structures in 'The Turn of the Screw'

1. See Bloomfield (1976) especially parts IV, V, and VI for a survey and discussion of some of these problems, and a full bibliography.
2. This 'narrative sentence' seems to me another false analogy with linguistics, where the deep structure of a sentence has a clear re-lationship with the surface structure, 'recoverable' through a set of

operations which can be made explicit as 'rules' in the Chomsky sense (1965: 9); whereas the 'narrative sentence' represents the barest of bare bones, whose relationship with the surface cannot be made explicit in the same way, even by positing 'expansion rules', which would in effect be so vast (particularly, as we have seen, in realistic discourse), so varied and so *ad hoc* that they would cease to be rules. Genette's 'narrative sentence' is not only the ultimate in reductionism, it is trivial, and gives no insight. As Ms Anita Kermode said to me, one might as well say that the narrative sentences of *Moby Dick* [or *Huck Finn*, or *Portrait of the Artist* or *Ulysses*] are 'Ishmael [Huck/Stephen] becomes a writer'. For even if Huck and Ishmael are not what Booth calls 'conscious narrators' (conscious of the act of writing), there is, in the theoretical sense described here, little difference. Or, to take an example fresh in the reader's mind, with all its emphasis on *writing*: 'the governess becomes a writer' would be the narrative sentence of TS. I hope that my 'bare structure' is more revealing, however bare (reductive).

3. This type of double-level comment by the narrator is quite distinct from direct comment by the character *in dialogue* (direct discourse), which is internal to the fiction, as when the governess says to Mrs Grose: '"I'm rather easily carried away. I was carried away in London ... Oh I've no pretentions," I could laugh, "to being the only one"'' (p. 9). I shall not be considering such examples unless they produce a NM (see 2.1.2.3., lies by the character; 2.2.1.5. *Direct discourse*, and 2.2.2. *Syntactic complementarity*). The *narrative* direct comment 'I could laugh,' however, is double-level (she laughed/she is capable of laughing at something painful, even if it is a *rire jaune*).

4. This same difficulty has been previously expressed, in the same scene, but without n.i., in direct comment: 'had left her meanwhile in little doubt of my small hope of representing with success even to her actual sympathy my sense of the real splendor of the little inspiration with which, after I had got him into the house, the boy had met my final articulate challenge' (p. 46).

5. Just as she indulges in rhetorical repetition in ironic *direct comment*: In answer to the letter?" *I had made up my mind.* "Nothing at all."/"And to his uncle?"/*I was incisive.* "Nothing at all."/"And to the boy himself?"/*I was wonderful.* "Nothing at all"' (p. 14). Similarly (p. 35), the repetition of '*It was a pity*' about her obsessive recapitulations, 'in my delusion' of signs and suspicions. Both these examples are double NM: I am being rhetorical (as above)/I am being objective and ironical.

6. The manuscript was (fictitiously) written, or at least *sent*, to Douglas just before she died, twenty years before Douglas's reading of it to his friends (Prologue, p. 2). Douglas had met her forty years before the reading (p. 3), and the events had taken place some ten years before they met, since Douglas was in his second year at University, she was ten years older (p. 3) and had been twenty at the time of Bly (p. 4). Thus there is a lapse of fifty years between the events and Douglas's reading, and thirty

years between the events and the *sending* of the manuscript (though of course it could have been written earlier, soon after the verbal telling of the story to Douglas).

7. This and direct comment are chiefly what critics notice in traditional character-analysis, without always realising that, in first-person narrative, there *is* a NM, but rather judging these actions as though the narrator were unaware of them. I shall give only a few examples, since the governess's behaviour has had so much critical attention, and return to the question of consciousness later.

8. Some of the governess's so-called lies have been attributed to her out of a misunderstanding of these techniques. E.g., the analysis about the circumstances of Quint's death, mentioned above, or another one about Flora's game: the stillness *during* the apparition [J1] (p. 30), *followed*, but in *later recollection*, by Flora's supposed attempts to divert her attention, 'the portentous little activities . . . the perceptible increase of movement . . . the gabbling of nonsense and the invitation to romp' (p. 35). Both these are *narrator*-recollection (or self-elaboration, see chapter 6) but not *character*-lies. For analepsis, see Genette (1972) and chapter 1 here. Her euphemisms, too (see here, p. 195), are sometimes part of narrator-technique (delay).

9. 'I had ready for her' is AM as the language of the hysteric.

10. The several critics who have argued (chapter 6) that plain, unimaginative Mrs Grose represents the commonsense reaction, so that when she finally believes, we should too, because we identify with her, are in fact identifying with the governess's view of her.

11. The later 'lie', often cited, about Miss Jessel speaking, is not one, since she qualifies it: 'It came to that' (p. 60). Similarly during the apparition [J3] (p. 59). See section 2.2.1.2.

12. This despite James's claim to have written a pot-boiler and other extratextual information that he dictated it. Later editions show that he revised carefully.

13. The terms *énoncé-énonciation* are difficult to render since 'utterance' has different meanings in philosophy and in linguistics. The American translation of Todorov's book on the fantastic (1973) chooses 'utterance' for *énoncé* and 'uttering' (the act) for *énonciation*, but again these terms connote other things in English ('enunciation' is used chiefly in contexts of elocution, e.g., 'a clear enunciation'). I prefer the clearer term 'statement' for *énoncé*: the 'objective' statement, like 'the coffee-pot is on the table'; and 'utterance' for *énonciation*: the sentence (which may also be an 'objective' statement) subjectivised with shifters such as, of course, the first-person pronoun, but, more important, terms of perception, belief, feeling, doubt, certitude, judgment, questioning, etc., e.g. verb shifters: I saw, I felt, I think, I am sure, I wondered whether, etc. the pot was on the table. See Todorov (ed. 1970) for special number on *L'énonciation*.

14. See below for terms of certitude.

15. Sometimes to the point of absurdity: 'She gave me a look that I remarked at the moment; then, *visibly*, with a quick blankness, *seemed* to

try to take it back' (p. 10) – Can one take back a look? She even uses estrangement words of herself, which strictly is not possible (see Barthes (1966: 19) and Genette (1972: 210), on the misuse of *sembler* for inner view), but interesting for a supposed split personality, and obviously useful in the pure fantastic: 'I *seemed* at any rate for an instant *to trace* their [Mrs Grose's eyes] evocation of her [Jessel] as distinctly as I had seen her by the pond' (p. 33); I *seemed to see* in the beautiful face with which he [Miles] watched me how ugly and queer I looked' [mirror] (p. 55). Possibly *seem* is less startling in this misuse than *sembler* in French. Genette gives an example picked by Proust out of Balzac's *Le Lys dans la vallée*: 'Je descendis dans la prairie afin d'aller revoir l'Indre et ses îles, la vallée et ses coteaux, *dont je parus un admirateur passionné*' (*Contre Sainte-Beuve*, Pléiade edition: 270–1). But the procedure is that of a split (impersonal mode or 'estrangement' for personal mode) and as Barthes points out, the procedure is even grosser in *The Murder of Roger Ackroyd* (see chapter 5, p. 117 above), since the murderer says 'I', as if he were not the murderer.

16. I owe this notion and the term to my colleague Olga Scherer, who works with me in a seminar on theory at the University of Paris VIII.

17. The other and notorious mistake on 'he' in chapter 2 ('He' [employer] seems to like us young and pretty'/'Oh he [valet, for Mrs Grose] did') is achieved through repetition, not complementarity.

18. See dialogue on p. 198 for the narrator comment 'I scrupulously added', from the same conversation, which leads Mrs Grose to say 'their uncle must do the preventing'.

19. We may note that the similar inversion, but the other way round, in the last scene with Miles ('Is she *here* [JJ?' p. 88) could also be an effect of distant inversion (him/her p. 31, she/he p. 88) by the author (AM), like the 'revolution' (= silence/speech) mentioned on p. 208.

20. Note for experts: although it may have more general implications as model, as 'grammar' it would be equivalent to a sentence grammar that generated only one form of sentence. Moreover, even to 'generate' this text the phrase-structure rules would be extremely uneconomical (I worked them out, in *PTL* 2:3, 1977, and came to that conclusion), nor are there any transformational rules. Lastly, there is a degree of arbitrariness in the node levels near the surface (at bottom of tree): it would be equally possible to invert the positions of indirect/direct *discourse*, indirect/direct *comment* + narrative instance, though the order I chose seems a more correct sequence of abstraction. I shall not further pursue this false analogy with linguistics.

9. The evil ring: realism and the marvellous

1. J. R. R. Tolkien, *The Hobbit* (1937), *The Fellowship of the Ring* (1951), *The Two Towers* (1953), *The Return of the King* (1955). (London, George Allen & Unwin). The edition used is *The Authorized Edition of the Works of J. R. R. Tolkien – The Lord of the Rings* (Ballantine Books, New York, seventh printing, 1969).

2. A certain type of Tolkien criticism relies heavily on source-finding in Old Norse and other materials, apparently under the impression that the documentary attestation of names increases the ultimate 'truth' of the book – a common fallacy of criticism founded on the premises of realism, even when applied to the marvellous.
3. In the Foreword to LR, Ballantine edition.

10. Titan Plus: the new science fiction (Vonnegut and McElroy)

1. I am aware of the danger in calling clichés 'ironical', that is, of attributing to the author's skill what could simply *be* clichés. I shall return to the problem of irony in chapter 14 and for the moment merely present such a reading, with, I hope, convincing evidence, as one possible reading, namely mine.
2. All the statistics that follow have been collected manually, so that there may be a slight margin of error. Their purpose here is not statistical but rhythmical.

11. The real as unreal: Robbe-Grillet

1. Furetière, *Le Roman Bourgeois*, 1666 (in original spelling): 'Certainly the alms-collector was beautiful ... Do not however expect me to describe her here, as is customary on such occasions.' 'I do not even want to tell you what this church looks like, although it is fairly famous: for those who have not seen it, can go and visit it if they should wish; or build it in their imagination, as they please' (my translation).
2. *Tristram Shandy*, bk. II, ch. 2 (ed. T. C. Livingstone, Everyman's Library, London, 1955, p. 62).
3. *Dans le labyrinthe* (éditions de Minuit, Paris, 1959), pp. 15, 76, 179, 185. All quotations will refer to this edition. All translations are from *In the Labyrinth*, trans. Christine Brooke-Rose (Calder & Boyars, London 1967): 'there is only a meaningless criss-crossing of lines'; 'nor does this signify anything either'; 'but the scene leads to nothing'; 'another scene that leads to nothing'.
4. See, especially, analyses by Lowry Nelson Jr., in *Baroque lyric poetry* (Yale University Press, 1961).
5. G. Picon, *Mercure de France*, June 1957: 303. 'We are perhaps living through a pre-classicism.' Cp. chapter 2 on Frye's cyclic theory, according to which the ironic mode went back to the mythic mode, is now being followed by the romance mode and therefore should (in theory) lead on to high mimetic.
6. Even here he is not absolutely ruthless: there is the famous passage about the heart of the ice-cube in *La Jalousie*. It is a dead metaphor in French, and Robbe-Grillet admitted to me when I pedantically taxed him with it that he was simply not vigilant enough. So in *Dans le labyrinthe*: surface ... *vierge* (p. 17), *têtes* de clous (p. 18, a dead metaphor), le papier d'emballage ... *baille* (p. 22), clarté *maigre* (p. 32), neige *vierge* (p. 51).

7. 'On the red and white chequerboard of the oilcloth'; 'the child ... an irregular black smudge'; 'the filament ... enclosed in its glass cage'; 'and the sentence, without anyone appearing to have uttered it, seemed to be a caption under an engraving'.

8. John Donne, 'The Flea', line 13, 'The Sunne Rising', lines 30, 21, in *Songs and Sonets* (*Complete Verse and Prose*, ed. John Hayward, Nonesuch Press, London and New York, 1945).

9. See Bruce Morissette, 'En relisant Robbe-Grillet', analysis of *La Jalousie* in *Critique*, July 1959. I do not, however, agree with his use of the term 'corrélation objective' for 'le support de ses [man's] passions'. It seems too close to Eliot's objective correlative (a form of pathetic fallacy) for comfort, and indeed is probably a translation of it.

10. '"Baroque" man builds within and around himself, an imaginary world in which he settles as in a more real world, not without retaining a certain consciousness of living in a mirage ... The essence of the Baroque can be defined as the union of movement and décor'; 'pleasure in doubting, in mistaking changing indentities, which is prolonged in a more refined pleasure, that of taking the figure for the reality, the appearing for the being, the theatre for life; a dizziness close to that which was then enjoyed in the painted vaults of Pierre de Cortone and of Father Pozzo, in the *trompe l'oeuil*, in Sosias, or in the play within the play.'

11. 'Outside it is raining, outside in the rain one has to walk with head bent, hand shielding eyes that peer ahead nevertheless, a few yards ahead, a few yards of wet asphalt ... Outside the sun is shining, there is not a tree, not a bush to give shade, one has to walk in the full sunlight, hand shielding eyes that look ahead, a few yards ahead only, a few yards of dusty asphalt where the wind traces parallels, curves and spirals.'

12. This is why I prefer to use the old term *flash*back here, and later *flash*forward, rather than *analepsis*, which is normally marked.

13. 'Outside it is snowing. The wind drives the fine dry crystals over the dark asphalt of the pavement, and with each gust the crystals fall in white lines, parallels, curves, spirals ... forming renewed spirals, scrolls, forked undulations, arabesques in motion and then again disrupted.'

14. 'Outside it is snowing. Outside it has snowed, it was snowing, outside it is snowing. The massed flakes descend gently, their fall steady, uninterrupted, vertical – for there is not a breath of wind – in front of the high grey houses.'

15. 'But the daylight is without brightness, making everything look flat and dull. Instead of the spectacular perspectives which these rows of houses ought to display, there is only a meaningless criss-crossing of lines.'

16. 'In the angle of the wall and ceiling the shadow of the fly, a blown-up image of the filament in the electric bulb ... It is again the same filament, that of an identical lamp, or one hardly larger, which is shining uselessly at the crossing of the two streets, enclosed in its glass cage at the top of its cast-iron column, an old-fashioned ornate gaslamp converted to electricity.'

17. 'But the bottom of the coat has swept away a few of these small deposits, just as the boots in their several changes of position have produced small piles of snow around them, leaving some yellower spaces here and there, half-lifted harder pieces and the deep marks of nailheads in quincunx patterns. By the chest of drawers the felt slippers have traced a large bright zone in the dust ... Between the two they have traced a narrow path of gleaming parquet; another path goes from the table to the bed. Parallel with the houses ... a rectilinear path also defines the snow-covered pavement. Yellow-grey in colour, from the trampling feet of people now gone, it passes between the lighted street-lamps and the door of the last building, then turns at right-angles and continues up the perpendicular street, still alongside the houses, about a third of the way across the width of the pavement, along its whole length.
    Then another path begins, going from the bed to the chest of drawers.'

18. 'Outside the sky has the same heavy whiteness. It is still day. The street is deserted: no traffic on the road, no pedestrians on the pavements. It has been snowing; and the snow has not yet melted ... In any case it would appear from the flatness of this whole décor that there is nothing behind these window-panes, behind these doors, behind these walls. And the whole scene remains empty: not a man, not a woman, not even a child.'

19. 'The picture, in its frame of varnished wood, is of a café scene. It is a black and white engraving, dating from the last century, or a good reproduction. A large number of characters fills the whole scene.'

20. Darkness. Click. Yellow light. Click. Darkness. Click. Grey light. Click. Darkness. And the footsteps resounding on the wooden floor of the corridor. And the footsteps resounding on the asphalt, in the street that is stiff with frost. And the snow beginning to fall. And the boy's recurring silhouette diminishing in size, over there, from lamp-post to lamp-post.'

21. See also Lowry Nelson Jr., 'The uses of time in poetry', in *Baroque lyric poetry* (1961: 29).

22. 'The box wrapped in brown paper is now lying on the chest of drawers. The white string has gone, and the wrapping paper, tidily folded back on the short side of the oblong box, is gaping slightly like a beak of precise lines ... Immediately above hangs the picture.'

23. Cp. Beckett's *Malone Dies*, where Malone keeps saying he must make an inventory of his possessions. Similarly in *Molloy*: 'When the time comes to draw up an inventory of my goods and possessions. Unless I lose them between now and then. But even lost they will have their place, in the inventory of my possessions.'

24. 'He stops at once, on an uncertain phrase that swerves hastily in a direction unheralded by its beginning, and so vaguely interrogative that the woman can reserve the right to abstain from answering ...
    'The soldier now tries to recall the exact terms he has just used. There

was the word "barracks", but he cannot manage to recall the strange phrase he has uttered.'

25. '"Was that what you wanted to tell me?"
"No", the boy answers "It wasn't."
Then they heard the sound, very far away, of the motorbike.
No. It was something else. It is dark. It is another attack: the sharp, staccato sound of the automatic rifles.'

26. 'The soldier is lying on his back, fully dressed .... No. It is in fact another wounded man who occupies the scene, at the exit of the crowded café room. The soldier has hardly closed the door when he sees a young fellow-soldier come up to him, a conscript of the previous year.'

27. 'And the fresh layer thus gradually covering over the day's traces, rounding off the angles, filling in the dips, levelling the surfaces, has quickly effaced the yellowish paths left along the houses by the passers-by, the boy's isolated tracks, the two parallel furrows made by the sidecare motorbike in the middle of the road.
But it should first be ascertained whether the snow is still falling.'

12. Transgressions

1. See bibliography for editions and translations. Page numbers will be given after the quotations in French, which will be translated in footnote, with the page-number of the translation. Quotations from texts which have not appeared in translation were translated, in the original essay of which this chapter is a revised version (*Contemporary Literature* XIX:3, 1978, University of Wisconsin) by Carl Lovitt, so brilliantly (especially for Roche) that I am keeping them, marked Lovitt in brackets after the quotation.

2. To take an example at random: in Poe's *The Fall of the House of Usher* there are ten different time positions in analepsis, from a few minutes before the narrator's arrival at the house to several centuries earlier, and seven of these occur in the first three paragraphs. All are clearly marked grammatically.

3. The present tense does, of course, also occur in the classical novel, as a kind of historical present to bring the scene actively before the reader (e.g., in Dickens's *David Copperfield*, in George Eliot's *Scenes of Clerical Life*), or in description of a real or fictitious place presented as still existing, and it is quite frequent in these functions in later fiction (e.g. in Carson McCullers's *The Ballad of the Sad Café*).

4. An internal analepsis is a flashback to a point *after* the beginning of the story, as opposed to external analepse, which gives information about a time *before* the beginning of the story. A homodiegetic piece of narrative is one about the same person who is in question, as opposed to heterodiegetic, about a different person, e.g., a character newly introduced, whose past would be given in heterodiegetic analepsis.

5. 'I had then reached the stairs, and rested one hand on the banister ...

She had almost reached the door of her room ... Laura murmured in a very low voice that she was frightened ... I no longer had my hand on the railing, now, nor on anything at all. And it was difficult for me to invent something else of the same kind' *Projet* (pp. 33–4).

6. 'Seen from a certain angle these bodies are of four kinds. Firstly those perpetually in motion. Secondly those who sometimes pause. Thirdly those who short of being driven off never stir from the coign they have won and when driven off pounce on the first free one that offers and freeze again ... But this remission never lasts more than a little less than a second ... From time immemorial rumour has it or better still the notion is abroad that there exists a way out. Those who no longer believe so are not immune from believing so again' *The Lost Ones*, (pp. 13, 17 and 18).

7. 'You open your eyes, you enumerate what passes before your eyes ... There is always something for you to see' (Lovitt). Ellipses in quotations from Lovitt's translations, as here, indicate their presence in the original text; square-bracket ellipses indicate an omitted section.

8. '... "me" meanwhile more and more astray in the text, set, arrested in a corner of the text and really doing no more than pass [...] outside inscribed on all sides, permanently laid out or more profoundly dissociated or dreamt; outside never being what escaped or remained, changed and returned with others, neither moving nor existing ... midst where faces flowed and spoke, enjoyed and undid their traits, midst where putting two terms in the presence of one another was enough for operations to take place' (Lovitt).

9. 'Sometimes he stopped without saying anything [...] I bowed as usual' (Lovitt). 'We were not in the mountains, however. Occasionally I glimpsed at the horizon a sea whose level appeared higher than our own' (Lovitt).

10. 'I walked along the street, the sun having reappeared'; 'I saw my story and, one last time, that in my story which had taken the shape of an imposed, ordered system ...' (Lovitt).

11. 'Laura lets the tulle curtain fall back, glances at the cassette and notices' (*Projet*, p. 53). The ambiguity of the present tense used singulatively is particularly useful also for the repetitive as practised by Robbe-Grillet: the same sentence, or a sentence with contingent differences, recurs, suspended as it were between the iterative and the punctual, singulative.

12. As with the present tense, the use of present and past participles as such is not new, having occurred in classical description, e.g., in the remarkable opening of *Bleak House*, where main verbs are omitted entirely. What is new is its extension beyond brief effect in a description.

13. Cp. the lapse in Hemingway's *The Killers* (a stock example, with Dashiel Hammett, of external narration): 'Nick had never had a towel in his mouth before' – a fact which an external narrator cannot know. The only way (pedantically speaking) he can give such information

and remain external is to make another character (who knows Nick's past) say it, or to put it in Nick's mouth, already, however, full of towel.

14. Both E. M. Forster (1949) and Wayne C. Booth (1961) showed the pointlessness of this rule. Moreover, most new movements and 'rules' tend to be made in the name of a greater realism, whether outer or inner; the *nouveau roman* was first attached to a more general concept, *nouveau réalisme*, influenced by phenomenology. The current rejection of all realism is itself a form of realism, that of *écriture*. The 'real' merely gets displaced whenever an earlier exploitation becomes exhausted.

15. I use 'story' in quotes to emphasise the fact that the first challenge to 'realistic' mimesis occurred through content, e.g., various kinds of 'absurdity' of the story (Kafka, Borges, Beckett).

16. *Nombres*, however, not in the sense of 'chiffre' (which represents and signifies), but in the more mysterious ways of mathematics, with its infinite numbers, negative, imaginary, irrational, and ideal numbers, etc.; or, as Kristeva puts it ('L'Engendrement de la formule', *Semeiotike*, 1968), a signifying complex as geno-textual unit, that 'engenders' the 'phenotext' or actual text. We may note a similar preference in recent American fiction for short sections, numbered (Barthelme, Coover), or chapter-headed in capitals (Brautigan), or otherwise typographed (Vonnegut), but these are not so 'mathematical' or rigorously presented.

17. 'Meanwhile I was coming from the direction of my own history. This was indicated to me by the attempt to situate me on the periphery of a circle that would have passed through "us all"'; 'The narrative might well be prohibited; it was not therefore impossible to slip under this prohibition – under its line – to take both directions at the same time'; '(and yet the narrative continues, double course bearing an unguaranteed force, and the question that is then raised beyond your memory asks how to note form and sound at the same time [. . .])'; '(and thus, you are, as it were, before the porticoes of history itself, on its scene brusquely erected and illuminated [. . .])' (Lovitt).

18. To make the distinction clear, Genette cites the omniscient narrator in *Le Père Goriot*: he *knows* the Pension Vauquer and its inhabitants, Balzac *imagines* them.

19. Narrative instance isn't necessarily identical and invariable in the same work, as Genette points out: the adventures of Ulysses are told by two narrators, Homer and Ulysses, while the adventures of Swann and of Marcel are told by one narrator, Marcel, and theory must take this (and other more complex possibilities) into account.

20. 'You will lose sleep as you lose sight. As you penetrate the night, you will penetrate a deeper and deeper night; your memory, already failing, wearing away to the extent that – emerging from a long lethargy – you will lose consciousness of your state (Henceforth how are day and night to be told apart?).

You will be there, on a bed – in a room no doubt. Eyes wide, you will scrutinize this somber desert, and will expanding space allow you to go so far you won't be able to return to yourself?

Mnémopolis that you will be able to haunt beneath your skull will be a city lone and obscure. No streets no furrows no ploughing about (it? – the convolutions of your brain), but traces of which you will attempt to catch hold' (Lovitt).

21. In Vonnegut's *The Sirens of Titan*, the character who appears to be organising, and to a large extent does organise, the earthly and interplanetary events, Winston Niles Rumfoord, lives out of time, and can therefore tell the hero, Constant Malachi, that he will go to Mars, then to Mercury, then return to Earth, and end up on Titan, and that he will mate with Rumfoord's own wife Bee and have a son. All of which occurs. But he goes into no details, either because he does not wish to, or, as it also turns out, because he cannot order everything, some details being left to chance and to Constant's efforts at free will. Moreover, as he later discovers and apparently did not foresee, he is himself being used by the Trafalmadorians (see chapter 10).

22. 'Never was but grey air timeless no sound figment the passing light. No sound no stir ash grey sky mirrored earth mirrored sky. Never but this changelessness dream the passing hour.

He will curse God again as in the blessed days face to the open sky the passing deluge ... He will stir in the sand there will be stir in the sky the air and sand. Never but in dream the happy dream only one time to serve ... He will live again the space of a step it will be day and night again over him the endlessness.' (*Sans* 1969; trans. *Lessness*, 1970, pp. 7–10).

23. 'it must come from fairly deep in the masses for the thing to burst like that in broad daylight a petty bourgeois burial there it'd take the working class perhaps but all the same they're there and definitely there not elsewhere thus something asks, asked, will ask again to be represented correctly what careful yes careful but all the same I was waiting for you there anticommunist password but well shit' (Lovitt).

24. 'And in a little while, when he appears in "Old Joe's" to report to Frank on his mission and to recoup his strength with a double shot of bourbon, the band will suddenly stop playing, the trumpet-player mute, without thinking in his astonishment of putting down his mean-ingless instrument, will merely take it away from his mouth, holding it motionless in the air about three inches from his lips which still keep the tense position of a soloist in the middle of a fortissimo, while all the heads in the room turn with a single movement toward the street door, in order to see in their turn what the musicians have seen first from the bandstand: the bloody face which has just appeared in the rectangular frame formed by the open door against the black background of the night.' (*Projet*, p. 48).

25. 'I take a step in her direction. She immediately steps back ... At that very moment, over our heads, we could hear something ... But Laura, half-whispering, said ...

I had then reached the stairs, and rested one hand on the banister.

To reassure her, I tapped three times with the tip of one fingernail on the wooden rail without moving my palm or the other fingers. Laura gave a start and looked at my hand. I repeated my gesture.' (*Projet*, p. 33).

26. 'When she seemed dead, I released my grip.' (*Projet*, p. 11).

27. 'Fixed white bare body invisible white on white. Only the eyes barely pale blue nearly white. Head bulb quite high eyes pale blue nearly fixed white front silence inside. Curt murmurs barely nearly never all known. Trace clutter signs senseless pale gray nearly white on white. Legs stuck like sewn heels joined right angle' (Lovitt).

28. This kind of transgression also occurs in Nabokov and is much practised by contemporary American writers (Vonnegut, Barth, Coover, see chapter 14 below).

29. 'Her heart is pounding so loud that she has the sense . . . She has given up the struggle' (*Projet*, p. 10).

30.   'And then?'
      'Then she gradually calmed down. She stirred a little once again . . . When she seemed dead, I released my grip. I undressed very fast and came back to her . . . Again I had that impression of tremendous fatigue which I had already experienced on my way upstairs a moment before. Laura fell asleep at once in my arms.'
      'Why is she so nervous? You know that means an extra danger – for no reason' (*Projet*, pp. 10–11).

31. Sollers has said somewhere that Pound's ideograms are merely decorative, unlike his, but this of course is untrue, as any book on Pound, including my own (1971), frequently demonstrates.

32.

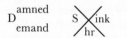

'luminous instruction.
Teach yourself for fun

            :

        culture   comfort   leisure   r   r
                                      seduce   sedate'
                                      p   p
                                      a   o
                                      s   s
                                      t   e

(Lovitt).

33. I am always surprised when Genette, the great namer of categories, suddenly gives no name, and feel like giving one. Since he uses the Latin prefix *auto*-here, I suggest *alter*diegetic, (an observer tells the story, mainly of someone else), to distinguish it from the Greek *hetero*- of the wider 'narrator absent' category.

34. The last sentence courteously refers to my novel *Between*, in which the verb *to be* is never used (for reasons inherent to the novel).

35. 'Thus, I was beginning to bring forth in my dreams the existence to which I was telling this dream at the moment when it was me [...] There were now: the sleeper in his own body living this or that with others/the function who told it, at times falsely explaining his choices/ the scene that, meanwhile, continued in the void [...]'; 'and I turn as I repeat myself, we turn as we transform ourselves' (Lovitt).

36. Butor was the first to write a whole novel in the second person plural *vous*, which can imply you/one/I (*vous/on/je*) (*La Modification*, 1957). English imitations clearly cannot achieve the extraordinary distancing of *vous*.

13. Eximplosions

1. The pagination refers to the English edition, London, Secker & Warburg, 1969.

2. In an opening address to a forum on 'Postmodernism' at the Modern Language Association Conference, New York, 1978. The paper was read in a translated version, but for various reasons I have preferred to summarise and translate directly from the French original.

3. *Idiolect* is here used metaphorically, as often in modern criticism of poetry that borrows linguistic terms (e.g. J. P. Thorne, 1965, on the poetry of Cummings, each poem producing its own 'grammar' and being its own 'idiolect'). Strictly speaking *idiolect* is a language only its speaker understands (a contradiction in terms since language by definition communicates), for instance a language one person has invented, for himself alone.

4. In 'The question of postmodernism' (forthcoming *Bucknell Review*), Ihab Hassan gives a brief history of the term. It was first used by Federico de Onis in his *Antología de la poesía española e hispano-americana 1882–1932* (Madrid 1934), and taken up by Dudley Fitts in the *Anthology of Contemporary Latin-American Poetry* (Norfolk, Conn., 1947), but both meant a minor reaction against modernism, and later both Irving Howe (1959) and Harry Levin (1960) 'wrote of postmodernism rather disconsolately as a falling off from the great modernist movement. It remained for Leslie Fiedler and myself, among others, to employ the term during the sixties with premature approbation, and even with a touch of bravado. Fiedler had it in mind to challenge the elitism of the high modernist tradition in the name of Pop. I wanted to explore that impulse of self-unmaking which is part of the literary tradition of silence.' Since then a vast critical bibliography has accumulated, notably, and more recently: Kermode (1968), Tanner (1971), Szabolsci (1971), Hassan (1971, 1975), Fiedler (1975), Zavarzadeh (1976), Lodge (1977a), Calinescu (1977). Other highly relevent books: Trilling's *Beyond culture* (1965), John Cage's *Silence* (1961), George Steiner's *Language and silence* (1967), *In Bluebeard's Castle* (1971b), Susan Sontag's *Styles of radical will* (1969).

5. Zavarzadeh analyses the non-fiction novel in several modes: (1) 'Exegetical (the stubborn fact)', John Hersey's *Hiroshima*, 'a literali-

sation of Thoreau's belief that "if men would steàdily observe realities only" they would realize that "reality is fabulous"' (Zavarzadeh 1976: 95), and William Styron's *The Confessions of Nat Turner*, Truman Capote's *In Cold Blood*; (2) 'Testimonial (the contingent donnée)', Norman Mailer's *The Armies of the Night* and Tom Wolfe's *The Electric Kool-Aid Acid Test*; (3) 'Notational (the austere actuality)', Oscar Lewis's *Five Families, The Children of Sanchez, La Vida*, and, in its extreme form, Andy Warhol's *a*, which is an immense transcript of a tape-recorded orgiastic weekend in Warhol's apartment, 'a surrealism of daily life lived by Warhol and his friends' (p. 185), in which one of the 'actants' says: 'We're pushing realism to its fullest extent. Fiction is dead. What people are interested in is autobiography. Confession. Andy's novel does the same thing the films do: record reality all the way' (quoted Zavarzadeh 1976: 186). Whether people are in fact interested in this particular reality is perhaps another point: in *L'Ère du soupçon* (1956b), Nathalie Sarraute complained that the media had created just such a mentality, whereby people were only interested in 'le petit fait vrai', reflected at a higher level by the spate of books on biography, travel and non-fiction generally, which get far more attention, whatever their quality, than fiction does, and the 'actant's' comment would seem to go further in the direction of 'the system', though clearly the non-fiction novel at its best is an important phenomenon.

6. 'Littérature et méta-langage', *Essais critique* (1964: 106; transl. 1972: 98). In this brief essay, Barthes argues that for centuries literature did not reflect upon itself (its being, as opposed to its figures), nor did writers imagine that literature could be submitted to the logical distinction of object-language and meta-language. With the first stirrings of 'la bonne conscience bourgeoise', literature began to feel itself as double. The phases are roughly: a craftman's consciousness of literary fabrication, pushed to painful scruple and the torment of the impossible (Flaubert); the heroic will to fuse literature and the thought of literature into one written substance (Mallarmé); the hope of evading literary tautology by for ever promising to write, and writing this (Proust); the voluntary and infinite multiplication of meaning, in literary good faith (surrealists); inversely, the rarifying of meaning, in the hope of obtaining a mere presence of literary language, a sort of white (but not innocent) writing (Robbe-Grillet).

7. The semantic restrictions given by Chomsky ($\pm$ abstract, $\pm$ animate, $\pm$ human etc.) would not in fact account for this metaphor, since *stream* and *junk* are both (in his sense) inanimate, but clearly the metaphor is a fusion of the nature/culture polarity.

14. Metafiction and surfiction: a simpler formal approach

1. There is in fact remarkably little thematic or formal difference between Pynchon and Samuel R. Delaney (*Triton, Dahlgren*), a Science Fiction

writer turned 'experimental' and treated seriously as 'New' SF by postmodernist critics (but not by SF critics who find these self-indulgent, in sex and violence as well as in prolixity and preciousness).

2. Despite my occasional criticism of some aspects of Sukenick's writing, I seem to be very much on his wave-length: I published a novel called *Out* in 1964, and in *Such* (1965) my main characters are called Someone and Something. The novel I have been intermittently working on, still in draft form and before reading *98.6*, has characters that create themselves out of constellation names (Orion, Andromeda, and a Cassandra-Cassiopea word-play). *Tant pis*. At least I have managed to make my last footnote about my own work.

Bibliography

Abbreviations
NLH: *New Literary History* (University of Virginia, Charlottesville).
PTL: *Poetics and Theory of Literature* (University of Tel-Aviv) North-Holland Publishing Co., Amsterdam. Stopped in 1979 in favour of *Poetics Today*.

Abrams, Meyer, 1976. 'Rationality and imagination in cultural history: a reply to Wayne C. Booth', *Critical Inquiry* 2:3, 447–64.

    1977a. 'The deconstructive angel', *Critical Inquiry* 3:3, 425–38.

    1977b. 'Behaviorism and deconstruction: a comment on Morse Peckham's "The infinitude of pluralism"', *Critical Inquiry* 4:1, 181–93.

Amis, Kingsley, 1960. *New maps of hell*, London.

Anderson, Poul, 1979. *A stone in heaven*, New York.

Auerbach, Erich (1946). *Mimesis – the representation of reality in Western Literature*; trans. 1953, Willard R. Trask, Princeton.

Austin, J. L., 1962. *How to do things with words*, Oxford and New York. (The William James Lectures delivered at Harvard University in 1955.) Oxford University Press paperback 1971.

Bakhtin, Mikhail, 1929a. *Problemy Kvorchestva Dostoïevskogo*, Leningrad; 2nd edn 1963, *Problemy poetiki Dostojevskogo*, Moscow; trans. 1973, R. W. Rotsel, *Problems of Dostoevsky's poetics*, Ann Arbor.

    1929b. *See* Voloshinov 1929; 1973.

Bal, Mieke, 1977. 'Narration et focalisation', *Poétique* 29 (Feb.), Paris.

Banfield, Ann, 1973. 'Narrative style and the grammar of direct and indirect speech', *Foundations of Language* 10:1, 1–39.

    1978a. 'Where epistemology, style and grammar meet', *NLH* 9:3, 415–54.

    1978b. 'The formal coherence of represented speech and thought', *PTL* 3:2, 281–314.

Barth, John, 1956. *The Floating Opera*, Appleton; revised version 1967, New York.

    1960. *The Sot-Weed Factor*, New York; 1965, paperback.

    1966. *Giles Goat-Boy*, New York; 1967, paperback.

    1967. 'The literature of exhaustion', *Atlantic*, (August), 29–34. Also in Klein, Marcus (ed. 1969).

1968. *Lost in the Funhouse*, New York; 1969, paperback; 1972 Penguin.

Barthelme, Donald, 1967. *Snow White*, New York.

1970. *City Life*, New York; 1976, paperback.

1975. *The Dead Father*, New York; 1976, paperback.

Barthes, Roland, 1953. *Le degré zéro de l'écriture*, Paris; trans. 1974, Annette Lavers, *Writing degree zero*, London.

1964. *Essais critiques*, Paris; trans. 1972, Richard Howard, *Critical essays*. Evanston, Ill.

1966. 'Introduction à l'analyse structurale des récits', *Communications* 8, 1–27; trans. 1975, 'Introduction to the structural analysis of narrative', *NLH* 6:2 (Winter), 237–72. Also in 1979.

1968. 'L'effet du réel', *Communications* 11, 84–9.

1970. *S/Z*, Paris; trans. 1974, Richard Miller, *S/Z*, New York.

1972. *Le plaisir du texte*, Paris; trans. 1976, Richard Miller, *The pleasure of the text*, London.

1979. *Image, music and text* (essays); trans. Richard Howard, New York.

Beckett, Samuel, 1934. *More Pricks than Kicks*, London; 1972, New York.

1938. *Murphy*, London; republished 1958; 1970, New York.

(1945) *Watt* (MS. lost); first published 1953, Paris; 1958, republished.

1951. *Molloy*, Paris; trans. 1955, Patrick Bowles and author, New York.

1952. *Malone meurt*, Paris; trans. 1958, author, *Malone Dies*, London.

1953. *L'innommable*, Paris; trans. 1958, author, *The Unnamable*, London.

1961. *Comment c'est*, Paris; trans. 1963, author, *How It Is*, London.

1966. *Assez*, Paris; trans. author, in 1967a, *No's Knife*.

1967a. *No's Knife – collected shorter prose 1945–1966* [includes *bing* and *Imagination dead imagine*], London.

1967b. *Têtes-Mortes*, trans. from English by Ludovic and Agnes Janvier [*D'un ouvrage abandonné, Imagination morte imaginez, bing, sans*] Paris.

1969. *Sans*, Paris; trans. 1970, author, *Lessness*, London.

1970. *Le dépeupleur*, Paris; trans. 1972, author, *The Lost Ones*, New York.

Benveniste, Emile, 1966. *Problèmes de linguistique générale*, Paris; trans. 1970, *Problems in general linguistics*, Miami.

Bergonzi, Bernard, 1961. *The early H. G. Wells – a study of scientific romances*, Manchester.

Bergonzi, Bernard (ed.), 1976. *H. G. Wells: a collection of essays*, Englewood Cliffs, N.J.

Bleich, David, 1976. 'The subjective paradigm', *NLH* 7:2.

Bloom, Harold (with Paul de Man, Jacques Derrida, Geoffrey Hartman and J. Hillis Miller), 1979. *Deconstruction and criticism*, London.

Bloomfield, Morton, 1976. 'Stylistics and the theory of literature', *NLH* 7:2, 271–311.

Booth, Wayne C., 1961. *The rhetoric of fiction*, Chicago.

1974. *A rhetoric of irony*, Chicago.

1976. 'M. H. Abrams: historian as critic, critic as pluralist', *Critical Inquiry* 2:3, 441–5.

Borges, José Luis, 1956, *Ficciones*, Buenos Aires. Trans. 1962, together with stories from other collections, as *Labyriths*, New York.

Borkin, Ann (ed.), 1972, *Where the rules fail: a student's guide: an unauthorized appendix to M. K. Burt's 'From deep to surface structure'*, with a foreword by George Lakoff, by students of the University of Michigan. Mimeograph, Indiana University Linguistics Club, July.

Bradbury, Malcolm, and McFarlane, James (eds.), 1976. *Modernism, 1890–1930*, Harmondsworth.

Brautigan, Richard, 1964. *A Confederate General from Big Sur*, New York; 1973, paperback.

1967. *Trout Fishing in America*, New York; 1972, paperback.

1970. *In Watermelon Sugar*, New York; 1973, paperback.

1971. *The Abortion – a historical romance 1966*, New York.

1974. *The Hawkline Monster: A Gothic Western*, New York; 1976, paperback.

1976. *Willard and his Bowling Trophies*, New York; 1977, paperback.

Bremond, Claude, 1964. 'Le message narratif', *Communications* 4, 4–32, Paris.

1966. 'La logique des possibles narratifs', *Communications* 8, 60–78.

1972. 'Le "Modèle Constitutionnel" de A. J. Greimas', *Semiotica* V:4, 362–83, The Hague.

1973. *La logique du récit*, Paris.

Brooke-Rose, Christine, 1971. *A ZBC of Ezra Pound*, London and California.

1976a. 'The squirm of the true – an essay in non-methodology', *PTL* 1:2, 265–94.

1976b. 'The long glasses – a structural analysis', *PTL* 1:3, 513–46.

1977. 'Surface structures in narrative', *PTL* 2:3, 517–62.

Brophy, Brigid, 1968. *In Transit*, London.

Burgess, Anthony, 1978. *1984/1985*, London.

Butor, Michel, 1957. *La modification*, Paris.

Cage, John, 1961, *Silence* (essays and lectures), Middleton.

1964, *A Year from Monday* (lectures and miscellaneous writings), Middleton.

Calinescu, Matei, 1977. *Faces of modernity: avant-garde, decadence, kitsch*, Bloomington, Ind.

Capote, Truman, 1966. *In Cold Blood*, New York.

Cargill, Oscar, 1956. 'Henry James as Freudian Pioneer', reprinted in Willen (ed.) 1971, pp. 223–38.

1963. '*The Turn of the Screw* and Alice James', reprinted in Kimbrough (ed.) 1966, pp. 145–65 (revised version of Cargill 1956).

Chklovski, Victor, 1919. 'Iskusstvo kak priem' in *Poetika*, Petrograd; and in *O theorii prozy*, Moscow–Leningrad 1925; trans. T. Todorov, 'L'art comme procédé, in Todorov (ed.) 1965.

Chomsky, Noam, 1957. *Syntactic structures*, The Hague.

1965 *Aspects of the theory of syntax*, Cambridge, Mass.; 1970, paperback.

Cixous, Hélène, 1970. 'L'écriture comme placement', *Poétique* 1, 35–50, Paris.

·1975. 'Fiction and its phantoms: a reading of Freud's *Das Unheimliche* (the "Uncanny")', *NLH* 7:3.

Coghill, Nevill, 1944. 'The Pardon of Piers Plowman', *The British Academy Lecture*, Proceedings of the British Academy.

Conquest, Robert, 1963. 'Science fiction and literature'. *The Critical Quarterly* V, 355–67, London, reprinted in Rose (ed.) 1976.

Coover, Robert, 1966. *The Origin of the Brunists*, New York; 1978, paperback.

  1968. *The Universal Baseball Association Inc. J. Henry Waugh, Prop*, New York; 1971, paperback.

  1969. *Pricksongs and Descants – fictions*, New York; 1970, paperback.

  1977 *The Public Burning*, New York.

Cortazar, Julio, 1963. *Rayuela*, Buenos Aires; trans. 1966, Gregory Rabassa, as *Hopscotch*, New York; 1975, paperback.

Couturier, Maurice, 1979. 'Barthelme ou la contamination', *Delta* 8, Montpellier.

Culler, Jonathan, 1975. *Structuralist poetics: structuralism, linguistics and the study of literature*, London.

  (1976) 'Prolegomena to a Theory of Reading', Lecture at English Institute, Cambridge, Mass. (In Suleiman 1980.)

Davis, R., 1979. 'Barthelme: Post-Modern Paternity', *Delta* 8, Montpellier.

Delaney, Samuel R. 1974. *Dahlgren*, New York. 1976. *Triton*, New York.

Dick, Philip K., 1962. *The Man in the High Castle*; 1965, Harmondsworth.

Dujardin, Edouard, 1887. *Les lauriers sont coupés*, in *La Revue Independante*; republished 1925, with Preface by Valéry Larbaud, Paris.

Eco, Umberto, 1962, *Opera aperta*, Milano.

  1978 'Possible worlds and text pragmatics in "Un drame bien parisien"', in *The role of the reader: explorations in semiotics of texts*, Bloomington, Ind.

Enck, John J. 1966. '*The Turn of the Screw* and the Turn of the Century', in Kimbrough (ed.) 1966, pp. 259–69.

Erlich, Victor, 1965. *Russian Formalism: history – doctrine*, The Hague.

Evans, Oliver, 1949. 'James' air of evil: *The Turn of the Screw*', reprinted in Willen (ed.) 1971, pp. 200–11.

Fagin, Nathan B., 1941. 'Another Reading of *The Turn of the Screw*', reprinted in Willen (ed.) 1971, pp. 154–9.

Felman, Shoshana, 1977. 'Turning the screw of interpretation', *Yale French Studies* nos. 55–6. (*Literature and psychoanalysis: the question of reading – otherwise*). Also in 1978 as 'Piège pour la psychanalyse: le tour de vis de la lecture'.

  1978. *La folie et la chose littéraire*, Paris.

Fiedler, Leslie, 1956. 'The new mutants', *Partisan Review* (Autumn).

  1975. 'Cross the border – close that gap; postmodernism', in *American Literature Since 1900*, ed. Marcus Cunliffe, New York.

Firebaugh, Joseph J., 1957. 'Inadequacy in Eden: knowledge and *The Turn of the Screw*', reprinted in Willen (ed.), 1971, pp. 291–7.

Fish, Stanley,

  1970. 'Literature in the reader: affective stylistics; *NLH* 2:1, 123–62.

  1976a. 'Interpreting the *Variorum*', *Critical Inquiry* 2:3, 465–85.

1976b. 'Interpreting "Interpreting the *Variorum*"', *Critical Inquiry* 3:1, 191–6.

Forster, E. M., 1949. *Aspects of the novel* (1927) London.

Foucault, Michel, 1961. *Folie et déraison, histoire de la folie à l'âge classique*, Paris; revised edn, Paris 1972.

1966. *Les mots et les choses*, Paris; trans. 1970, Alan Sheridan-Smith, *The order of things*, Tavistock Publications.

Fowler, Roger, 1977. 'Cohesive, Progressive, and Localizing Aspects of Text Structure', in *Grammars and Descriptions*, ed. Van Dijk and Petöfi, New York, and Berlin.

1979. 'Linguistics and, and versus, Poetics', *Journal of Literary Semantics* 8, 3–21.

Fowles, John, 1966. *The Magus*, Boston; 1978, revised version.

1969. *The French Lieutenant's Woman*, London.

Freud, Sigmund, (1895). *Entwurf einer Psychologie*; trans. 1950, E. Mosbacher and J. Strachey, *Project for a scientific psychology*, standard edn, vol. I, pp. 283–397, London.

(1895). *Studien über Hysterien* (with J. Breuer); trans. 1920, J. Strachey, *Studies on hysteria*, standard edn, vol. II, London.

(1905). *Witz und seine Beziehung zum Unbewussten*, trans. 1960, J. Strachey; *Jokes and their Relation to the Unconscious*, standard edn, vol. VIII; pp.9–238, London.

(1910). '"Wild" psychoanalysis', standard edn. vol. XI, pp. 221–2.

(1919). *Das Unheimliche*; trans. 1955, J. Strachey, *The 'Uncanny'*, standard edn, vol. XVII, pp. 219–56, London.

Frye, Northrop, 1957. *Anatomy of criticism*, Princeton; 1969, paperback, New York.

1976. *The secular scripture – a study of the structure of romance*, Cambridge, Mass.

Furetière, Antoine, 1666. *Le Roman Bourgeois*, Paris.

Gass, William, 1958. *In the Heart of the Heart of the Country*, New York; 1969, paperback. With Preface by Gass 1977.

1966. *Omensetter's Luck*, New York; 1972, paperback.

1970. *Fiction and the figures of life*, New York.

1976. *On Being Blue*, Boston.

(1979). 'An Interview with William Gass' (Régis Durand), *Delta* 8, Montpellier.

Genette, Gérard, 1969. 'Frontières du récit, *Figures II*, Paris.

1972. 'Discours du récit', *Figures III*, Paris; trans. 1979, Jane E. Lewin, *Narrative discourse*, Cornell.

Glaserfeld, Ernst von, 1979. 'Reflections on John Fowles' *The Magus* and the construction of reality', *Georgia Review* (Summer), 444–8.

Goddard, Harold C., 1957. 'A Pre-Freudian reading of *The Turn of the Screw*', reprinted in Willen (ed.) 1971, pp. 244–72.

Goldberg, S. L., 1980. 'The deconstruction gang', *London Review of Books*, 22 May – 4 June.

Goldmann, Lucien, 1955. *Le dieu caché*, Paris; trans. 1964, Philip Thody, *The hidden god: a study of tragic vision in the 'pensées' of Pascal and the tragedies of Racine*, London.

1964. *Pour une sociologie du roman*, Paris.

1970. *Marxisme et sciences humaines*, Paris.

Gombrowicz, Witold, 1937. *Ferdydurke*, Warsaw; trans. 1961, Eric Mosbacher, London.

Greimas, A. J., 1966. *Sémantique structurale*, Paris.

1970. *Du sens*, Paris.

1976. *Maupassant – la sémiotique du texte: exercices pratiques*, Paris.

Grice, H. P., 1975. 'Logic and conversation', in P. Cole and J. L. Morgan (eds.), *Syntax and semantics 3, Speech acts*, pp. 41–58, New York.

Guéron, Jacqueline, 1975. 'Langue et poésie: mètre et phonologie', *Change de forme*, Paris.

Halliday, M. A. K., 1970. 'Language structure and language function', in J. Lyons (ed.), *New horizons in linguistics*, pp. 140–65, Harmondsworth, Penguin.

1973 *Explorations in the functions of language*, London.

Hamon, Philippe, 1972. 'Qu'est-ce qu'une description?' in *Poétique* 12, 465–85.

1973. 'Un discours contraint', *Poétique* 16 (*Le discours réaliste*), 411–45.

Hartman, Geoffrey, 1976. 'Literary criticism and its discontents', *Critical Inquiry* 3:2, 203–20.

Hassan, Ihab, 1971. *The dismemberment of Orpheus: toward a postmodern literature*, New York.

1975. *Paracriticisms – seven speculations of the times*, Urbana, Chicago and London.

1981. 'The question of postmodernism' (forthcoming, *Book Review*).

Heilman, Robert, 1948. '*The Turn of the Screw* as peom'; reprinted in Willen (ed.) 1971, pp. 174–88.

Heinlein, Robert, 1961. *Stranger in a Strange Land*, New York.

Heisenberg, Werner, (1958). *Physics and philosophy – the revolution in modern science*, London; 1959 and 1963.

Hillis Miller, J. 1977. 'The critic as host', *Critical Inquiry* 3:3, 439–47.

Hirsch, E. D., 1967. *Validity in interpretation*, New Haven, Conn.

Hoffman, Charles, G., 1953. 'Innocence and evil in James's *The Turn of the Screw*' reprinted in Willen (ed.), 1971, pp. 244–72.

Holland, Norman, 1968. *The dynamics of literary response*, New York.

1976. 'The new paradigm: subjective or transactive?', *NLH* 7:2, 335–46.

Holquist, Michael, 1968. 'How to play Utopia: some brief notes on the distinctiveness of Utopian fiction', *Yale French Studies* XLI, 106–25; reprinted in Rose (ed.) 1976.

Howe, Irving, 1959. 'Mass society and postmodern fiction', *Partisan Review* 26, 420–36.

Huntington, John, 1975. 'Science fiction and the future', *College English* XXXVII, 345–52; reprinted in Rose (ed.) 1976.

Ingarden, Roman, 1931. *O dziele literackim*, Warsaw; trans. 1960, *Das*

Literarische Kunstwerk, Tübingen, 2nd edn; 1973, *The literary work of art*, Evanstan, Ill.

Irving, Washington, (1819–1920). *The Sketchbook of Geoffrey Crayon, Gent* (incl. *Rip Van Winkle*). Edition used, in *Great American Short Stories*, ed. Wallace and Mary Stegner, 1957, New York; 1961, paperback.

Iser, Wolfgang, 1974. *The implied reader – patterns of communication in prose fiction from Bunyan to Beckett*, Baltimore.

Jakobson, Roman, 1935. 'Randbemerkung zur Prosa des Dichters Pasternak'. *Slavische Rundschau* VII, 359–74; trans. 1970: 'Notes marginales sur la prose du poète Pasternak', in *Questions de poétique*, Paris.

   1956. 'Two aspects of language and two types of linguistic disturbances', in *Fundamentals of language*, ed. Roman Jakobson and Morris Halle, The Hague.

   1957. *Shifters, verbal categories and the Russian verb*, Russian Language Project, Dept. of Slavic Languages and Literatures, Cambridge, Mass.

   1960. 'Linguistics and poetics', in Thomas A. Sebeok (ed.), *Language and style*, Cambridge, Mass.

   1962. *Readings in Russian Poetics*, Ann Arbor.

James, Henry, 1934. *The Art of the novel*, ed. R. P. Blackmur, New York.

   1947. *The Notebooks of Henry James*, ed. F. O. Mathiesson and Kenneth Murdock, New York.

   1966. *The Turn of the Screw*, ed. R. Kimbrough, Norton Critical edn., New York. Originally published in *Collier's Weekly* XX: 17, XXI: 2, 27 Jan. – 16 Apr. 1898.

   1968. 'The new novel' (1914), in *Selected Literary Criticism*, ed. Morris Shapiro, London.

Jauss, Hans-Robert, 1970. *Literaturgeschichte als Provokation der Literaturwissenschaft*, Frankfurt; English version: 'Literary history as a challenge to literary theory', *NLH* 2:1, 7–37.

   1975. 'The idealist embarrassment – observations on Marxist aesthetics', *NLH* 7:1, 191–208.

Johnson, Anthony L., 1977. 'Anagrammatism in poetry: theoretical preliminaries', *PTL* 2:1, 89–118.

Johnson, B. S., 1969. *The Unfortunates*.

Jones, Alexander E., 1959. 'Point of view in *The Turn of the Screw*', reprinted in Willen (ed.), 1971 pp. 304ff.

Katan, M. (M.D.), 1962. 'A causerie on Henry James's *The Turn of the Screw*', reprinted in Willen (ed.) 1971:319–37.

Keenan, E. L., 1971. 'Two kinds of presupposition in natural language', in C. J. Fillmore and D. T. Langendoen (eds.), *Studies in linguistics and semantics*, pp. 45–52, New York.

Kenner, Hugh, 1968. *The Counterfeiters*, Bloomington, Ind.

Kenton, Edna, 1924. 'James to the Ruminant Reader: *The Turn of the Screw*'; reprinted in Willen (ed.) 1971, pp. 367–78.

Kermode, Frank, 1966. *The Sense of an ending*, London and New York.

   1968. 'Objects, jokes and art', in *Continuities*, London and New York.

Ketterer, David, 1974. *New worlds for old: the apocalyptic imagination, science fiction and American literature*, Bloomington, Ind.

Klein, Gerard, 1977. 'Discontent in American Science Fiction', *Science Fiction Studies* 4, part 1 (March), 3–13.

Klein, Marcus, 1969. *The American novel since World War II*, New York.

Kimbrough, Robert (ed.), 1966. *see* James 1966.

Kincaid, J. R., 1977. 'Coherent readers, incoherent texts', *Critical Inquiry* 3:4, 781–802.

Knight Aldrich C. (M.D.), 1967. 'Another Twist to *The Turn of the Screw*'; reprinted in Willen (ed.) 1971, pp. 367–8.

Krieger, Murray, 1960. *The tragic vision – variations on a theme in literary interpretation*, New York.

Kristeva, Julia, 1968. *Semeiotike: recherche pour une sémanalyse*, Paris.

1970. *Le texte du roman (Approaches to Semiotics 6)*, The Hague.

Krook, Dorothea, 1962. *The ordeal of consciousness in Henry James*, Cambridge.

Lacan, Jacques, 1966. *Ecrits*, Paris; trans. 1977, Alan Schneider, *A selection*, Tavistock.

1973a. *La séminaire 1964*, livre XI, *Les quatre concepts fondamentaux de la psychanalyse*, Paris; trans. 1977, *Four fundamental concepts of psychoanalysis*, London.

1973b. *Le séminaire 1972–73*, livre XX, *Encore*, Paris.

Laing, R. D., 1967. *The politics of experience*, New York.

Langbaum, Robert, 1957. *The poetry of experience*, New York.

Laplanche, Jean, 1970. *Vie et mort en psychanalyse*, Paris; trans. 1976, Jeffrey Mehlmann, *Life and death in psychoanalysis*, Baltimore.

Le Guin, Ursula, 1969. *The left hand of darkness*, New York.

Lem, Stanislaw, 1961. *Solaris*, Cracow; trans. 1970, from French by Joanna Kilmartin and Steve Cox, London and New York.

1967. *The Cyberiad (Cyberiada*, Cracow); trans. 1974, from Polish by Michael Kandal, New York.

1971a. *Panietnik znaleziony w wannie*, Warsaw; trans. 1973, Michael Kandel and Christine Rose, *Memoirs Found in a Bathtub*, New York.

1971b. *Dzienniki Gwiazdowe* (written from 1964 to 1971), Warsaw; trans. 1976, Michael Kandel, *The Star Diaries*, New York.

1973. 'Tzvetana Todorova fantastyczna teoria literatury', *Teksty* 5:11, Warsaw.

1974. 'The time-travel story and related matters of SF structuring', trans. by Hoisington and Suvin, *Science Fiction Studies* I, 143–54, reprinted in Rose (ed.) 1976.

Levin, Harry, 1960. 'What was modernism?', *Massachusetts Review* 1, Cambridge, Mass.

Lewis, C. S., 1967. *Of other worlds: essays and stories*, ed. Walter Hooper, New York.

Lips, Marguerite, 1926. *Le style indirect libre*, Paris.

Lodge, David, 1966. *The language of fiction*, London, New York.

1971. *The novelist at the crossroads*, London, New York.

1977a. *The modes of modern writing – metaphor, metonymy and the typology of modern literature*, London, New York.

1977b. 'Modernism, antimodernism and postmodernism', Inaugural Lecture 1976, University of Birmingham (abridged version of main thesis in 1977a).

1979. 'Historicism and literary history: mapping the modern period', *NLH* 10:3, 547–55.

Lotman, Yuri, 1970. *Struktura khudezestvenogo teksta*, Moscow; trans. 1977, R. Vroom, *The structure of the artistic text*, Ann Arbor.

Lubbock, Percy, 1921. *The craft of fiction*, London.

Lukács, Georg, 1920. *Theorie des romanes*, Berlin 1963; trans. 1970, Jean Clairvoie, *La théorie du roman*, Paris; trans., 1971, Anna Bostock, *Theory of the novel*, Boston and London.

Lydenberg, John, 1957. 'The governess turns the screw', reprinted in Willen (ed.) 1971; pp. 273–90.

McElroy, Joseph, 1976. *Plus*, New York.

McHale, Brian, 1978. 'Free indirect discourse: a survey of recent accounts'. *PTL* 3:2, 249–87.

1979. 'Modernist reading, post-modern text: the case of *Gravity's Rainbow*', *Poetics To-Day* 1:1–2, 84–110, Tel-Aviv.

Mailer, Norman, 1968. *The Armies of the Night*, New York.

de Man, Paul, 1971. *Blindness and insight – essays in the rhetoric of contemporary criticism*, New York.

1973. 'Semiology and rhetoric', *Diacritics* 3.

Matejka, L. (and K. Pomorska) (eds.), 1971. *Readings in Russian Poetics: Formalist and Structuralist views*, Cambridge, Mass. •

Mauriac, Claude, 1958. *L'alittérature contemporaine*, Paris.

Mehlmann, Jeffrey, 1975. 'How to read Freud on jokes: the critic as Schädchen', *NLH* 6:2, 439–61.

Michaels, Leonard, 1975. *I would have saved them if I could*, New York.

Miner, Earl, 1976. 'The objective fallacy and the real existence of literature', *PTL* 1:1, 11–31.

Mitchell, Julian, 1968. *The Undiscovered Country*, London.

Mitterand, Henri, 1973. 'Fonction narrative et fonction mimétique', *Poétique* 16, Paris.

More, Thomas, (1516). *Utopia*, ed. 1975, Robert M. Adams, New York.

Morissette, Bruce, 1959. 'En relisant Robbe-Grillet', *Critique* (July), Paris.

Müller, Günther, 1948. 'Erzählzeit und Erzählte Zeit', *Festschrift Paul Kluckhohn und Hermann Schneider gewidnet*, Tübingen.

Nabokov, Vladimir, 1962. *Pale Fire*, New York.

Nelson, Lowry, Jr, 1961. *Baroque lyric poetry*, New Haven, Conn.

New, Melvyn, 1979. 'Profaned and Stenciled texts: in search of Pynchon's *V*', *Georgia Review* (Summer), 395–412.

Nietzsche, Friedrich Engels, 1969. *On the genealogy of morals*; trans. Walter Kaufmann and R. P. Hollingdale, New York.

O'Brien, Flann, 1939. *At Swim-Two-Birds*, London. 1967, Penguin Modern Classics.

Ortega y Gasset, José, (1925). *The Dehumanization of Art* (including 'Notes on the novel'), trans. 1968, Werf *et al.*, Princeton.

Palmer, R. D., 1969. *Hermeneutics: interpretation theory in Schleiermacher, Dilthey, Heidegger and Gadamer*, Evanston, Ill.

Parrinder, Patrick, 1979a. 'Science fiction and the scientific world view', in Parrinder (ed.) 1979.

1979b. 'Characterization in science fiction: the alien encounter, or Ms Brown and Mrs Le Guin', in Parrinder (ed.), 1979, pp. 148–61.

Parrinder, Patrick (ed.), 1979. *Science fiction – a critical guide*, London.

Peckham, Morse, 1977. 'The infinitude of pluralism', *Critical Inquiry* 3:4, 803–16.

Peirce, Charles S., 1955. 'Logic as semiotic: the theory of signs', in *Philosophical writings of Peirce*, New York.

1960. *Collected Papers*, ed. Charles Hartshorne and Paul Weiss, vols. 1–2, Cambridge, Mass.

Perry, Menakhem, 1974. (With Meir Steinberg): 'The King through ironic eyes: the narrator's devices in the story of David and Bathsheba and two excurses on the theory of narrative text'. *Ha-Sifrut* 1, 256–92; in English summary in Ziva Ben-Porat and Benjamin Hrushovski 1974, 'Structuralist Poetics in Israel', *Papers on Poetics and Semiotics* 1, Tel-Aviv University.

1979a. 'Literary dynamics', in *Poetics Today* 1:1–2.

1979b. 'The combined discourse – several remarks about the definition of the phenomenon'. (Paper read at Symposium no. 2, Tel-Aviv, July 1979, to be published in *Poetics Today*.)

Piaget, E., 1967. *La construction du réel chez l'enfant*, Neuchâtel.

Picon, Gaëtan, 1957. 'Lettre: du roman expérimental', in *Mercure de France* (June), 300–4.

Popper, Karl, 1959. *The logic of scientific discovery*, London.

1963. *Conjectures and refutations – the growth of scientific knowledge*, London.

Porter, Katherine Ann (with Allen Tate and Mark Van Doren), 1942. 'James: *The Turn of the Screw*. A radio symposium', reprinted in Willen (ed.) 1971, pp. 160–70.

Pouillon, Jean, 1946. *Temps et roman*, Paris.

Preminger, A., *et al.*, 1975. *The Princeton Encyclopedia of Poetry and Poetics* (revised and enlarged edition) Princeton.

Priest, Christopher, 1978. 'New wave science fiction', *The Encyclopaedia of Science Fiction*, London.

Prince, F. T., 1973. 'Introduction à l'étude du narrataire', *Poétique* 14, 178–96.

Propp, Vladimir, 1928. '*Morfologia Skazki*, Moscow; trans. Laurence Scott, *The morphology of the folk-tale*; revised 1968, Louis A. Wagner, Austin, Texas.

Pynchon, Thomas, 1963. *V.*, New York; 1964, paperback.

1966. *The Crying of Lot 49*, New York; 1967, paperback.

1973. *Gravity's Rainbow*, New York; 1974, paperback.

Rabkin, Eric S., 1976. *The fantastic in literature*, Princeton.

Rader, Ralph W., 1976. 'The dramatic monologue and related lyric forms', *Critical Inquiry* 3:1, 131–52.

Reed, Glenn A., 1949. 'Another Turn on James' *The Turn of the Screw*', reprinted in Willen (ed.) 1971, pp. 189–99.

Reed, Ishmael, 1969. *Yellow Back Radio Broke-Down*, New York; 1977, paperback.

Richards, I. A., 1924. *Principles of literary criticism*, London; 1960, paperback.

1929. *Practical criticism*, London; 1964, paperback.

Riffaterre, Michael, 1966. 'Describing poetic structures', *Yale French Studies*, nos. 36–7; reprinted in French in 1971a.

1971a. *Essais de stylistique structurale*, Paris.

1971b. 'L'explication des faits littéraires', *L'enseignement de la littérature*, ed. Serge Doubrovsky and Tzvetan Todorov, pp. 353–5, Paris.

1977. 'Semantic over-determination in poetry', *PTL* 2:1, 1–19.

Rimmon, Shlomith, 1977. *The concept of ambiguity – the example of James*, Chicago.

Robbe-Grillet, Alain, 1953. *Les gommes*, Paris.

1955. *Le Voyeur*, Paris; trans. 1958, Richard Howard, *The Voyeur*, New York.

1957. *La Jalousie*, Paris; trans. 1959, Richard Howard, *Jealousy*, New York.

1959. *Dans le labyrinthe*; trans. 1967, C. Brooke-Rose, *In the labyrinth*, London.

1962. *Pour un nouveau roman*, Paris; trans. 1965 (with *Instantanés*) see below.

1963. *Instantanés*, Paris; trans. 1965, Barbara Wright, *Snapshots – towards a new novel*, London.

1970. *Projet pour une révolution à New York*, Paris; trans. 1972, Richard Howard, *Project for a revolution in New York*, New York.

1976. *Topologie d'une cité fantôme*, Paris.

Roche, Maurice, 1966. *Compact*, Paris.

1972. *Circus*, Paris.

1974. *Codex*, Paris.

1976. *Mémoire*, Paris.

Rose, Mark (ed.), 1976. *Science fiction: a collection of critical essays*, Englewood.

Rosset, Clément, 1977. *Le réel – traité de l'idiotie*, Paris.

1979. *L'objet singulier*, Paris.

Rousset, Jean (ed.), 1961. *Anthologie de la poésie baroque française*, vol. 1, Paris.

Rubin, Louis D. Jr, 1964. 'One more Turn of the Screw', reprinted in Willen (ed.) 1971, pp. 350–66.

Sanders, Scott, 1979. 'Characterization in science fiction: the disappearance of character', in Parrinder (ed.) 1979.

Sanguineti, Edoardo, 1967. *Il Giuoco dell'Oca*, Milano.

Saporta, Marc, 1962. *Composition no. 1*, Paris.

Sarraute, Nathalie, 1939. *Tropismes*, Paris; republished 1957; trans. *see* 1956b.

1948. *Martereau*, Paris; trans. 1959, Maria Jolas, *Martereau*, New York

1956a. 'Ce que voient les oiseaux', *Nouvelle Nouvelle Revue Française* (Jan.) reprinted in 1956b.

1956b. *L'Ere du soupçon*, Paris; trans. 1963, Barbara Wright, *Tropisms and the age of suspicion*, London.

1959. *Le Planétarium*, Paris; trans. Maria Jolas, *The Planetarium*, London.

1963. *Les fruits d'or*, Paris; trans. 1964, Maria Jolas, *The golden fruits*, New York.

1968. *Entre la vie et la mort*, Paris.

1972. *Vous les entendez?* Paris.

1976. *Disent les imbéciles*, Paris.

Sartre, Jean-Paul, 1947. *Qu'est-ce que la littérature?*, Paris; trans. 1950, Bernard Frechtman, *What is literature?*, London.

Saussure, Ferdinand de (1915). *Cours de linguistique générale*; 1969, 3rd edn, Paris; trans. 1960, Wade Baskin, *Course in general linguistics*, London; 1974, Fontana paperback.

1964. 'Anagrammes', ed. J. Starobinski, Mercure de France (Feb.), Paris. *See also* Starobinski, 1971.

Scherer, Olga, 1974. 'Absalon et Absalon', *Lettres Modernes* 1, 1–24 Paris.

1976. 'La contestation du jugement sur pièces chez Dostoievski et Faulkner', *Delta* 3, 47–62, Montpellier.

1977a. 'Texte – contexte – prototexte – métatexte', *Trema* 2, 35–44.

1977b. 'Ontologie de l'oeuvre littéraire d'après Roman Ingarden', *Actes du colloque 'La France devant les Slaves: Histoire et théorie littéraire'*, U.E.R. de littérature générale et comparée, Univ. de Paris III.

1979. 'La stylization', *Delta* 8, 65–85, Montpellier.

Schmid, Wolf, 1973. *Der Textaufbau in den Erzählungen Dostoevskijs*, Munich.

Scholes, Robert, 1967. *The Fabulators*, New York.

1970. 'Metafiction', *Iowa Review* 1, 100–15.

1974. *Structuralism in literature*, New Haven, Conn.

1975. *Structural fabulation*, Notre Dame, Ind.

Scholes, Robert, and Rabkin, Eric S. (eds.) 1977. *Science fiction: history, science, vision*, New York.

Searle, John R., 1975. 'The logical status of fictional discourse', *NLH* 6:2, 319–32.

Shukman, Ann 1975–8. *A bibliography of translations of Formalist writings*, vol. 4 of *Russian Poetics in translation*, ed. A. Shukman and L. M. O'Toole, 1975–8, University of Essex.

Silver, John, 1957. 'A note on the Freudian reading of *The Turn of the Screw*', reprinted in Willen (ed.) 1971, pp. 350–66.

Sollers, Philippe, 1961. *Le parc*, Paris.

1965. *Drame*, Paris.

1968. *Nombres*, Paris.

1973. *H*, Paris.

Sontag, Susan, 1966. *Against interpretations*, New York.

1969. *Styles of radical will*, New York. The essay 'The aesthetics of silence' originally appeared in *Aspen*, nos. 5 and 6, 1967.

Spark, Muriel, 1957. *The Comforters*, London.
1970. *The Driver's Seat*, London.
1971. *Not To Disturb*, London.
Spilka, Mark, 1963. 'Turning the Freudian screw: how not to do it', reprinted in Kimbrough (ed.) 1966, pp. 245–53.
Stapledon, Olaf, 1931. *Last and First Men*, London; reprinted 1968, with *Star Maker* (1937), Dower Publications, paperback.
Starobinski, Jean, 1971. *Les mots sous les mots*, Paris.
Stein, Gertrude, 1934. *The Making of Americans*, New York; reprinted 1968.
1971. *Look at me now and Here I am: writings and lectures, 1911–45*, ed. Patrizia Meyerowitz, Harmondsworth.
Steinberg, Meir, *see* Perry 1974.
Steiner, George, 1967. *Language and Silence*, New York.
1971a. *Extraterritorial*, New York.
1971b. *In Bluebeard's Castle*, New Haven, Conn.
Sukenick, Ronald, 1968. *Up*, New York.
1969. *The death of the novel and other stories*, New York.
1973. *Out*, Chicago.
1975. *98.6*, New York.
1979. 'Eight digressions on the politics of language', *NLH* 10:3, 467–77.
Suleiman, Susan, 1976a. 'Ideological dissent from works of fiction: toward a rhetoric of the *roman à thèse*', *Neophilologus* 60:2 (April), 162–77.
1976b. 'Interpreting ironies', *Diacritics* 6:2, 16–17.
Suleiman, Susan (ed.), 1980. *The reader in the text*, Princeton.
Suvin, Darko, 1979. *Metamorphosis of science fiction*, New Haven and London. This is an English, revised and expanded version of his *Pour une poétique de la science fiction*, Presses Universitaires de Québec 1977, of which the most important chapters had already appeared in different versions in various reviews: the *Modern Language Review*, no. 1 (1971), *College English*, no. 3 (1972), *Foundation*, no. 2 (1972), *Genre*, no. 3 (1973), *Studies in the Literary Imagination*, no. 2 (1973), *Science-Fiction Studies* 4 (1974), 10 (1976), *Clio* 1 (1974), the *Minnesota Review*, no. 4 (1975), *Comparative Literature Studies*, no. 4 (1973). All quotations will be from the 1979 book.
Szabolsci, Miklos, 1971. 'Neo avant-garde modernism – some questions and suggestions', *NLH* 1:3, 49–70.
Tanner, Tony, 1971. *City of Words: American fiction 1950–1970*, London.
Thorne, J. P., 1965. 'Stylistics and generative grammers'. *Journal of Linguistics* 1:1, 49–59.
Todorov, Tzvetan, 1966. 'Les catégories du récit littéraire', *Communications* 8, 125–51.
1968. 'Poétique', in *Qu'est-ce que le structuralisme?*, ed. F. Wahl, Paris.
1969. *Grammaire du Décameron (Approaches to Semiotics 3)*, The Hague.
1970a. 'Problèmes de l'énonciation' in Todorov (ed.) 1970.
1970b. *Introduction à la littérature fantastique*, Paris; trans. 1973, Richard Howard, *The fantastic – a structural approach to a literary genre*, Press of the Case Western Reserve University; 1975, Cornell Paperback.

1970c. 'Les transformations narratives', *Poétique* 3, 322–33; also in *Poétique de la prose*, Paris 1971; trans. 1977, Richard Howard, *Poetics of prose*, Cornell.

1975. 'La lecture comme construction', *Poétique* 24, 417–25; added in translation to *Poetics of prose*, see above.

1976. 'The origin of genres', *NLH* 8:1, 159–69; in French in 1978.

1978. *Les genres du discours*, Paris.

Todorov, Tzvetan (ed.), 1965. *Théorie de la littérature: textes des formalistes russes*, (ed. and trans.), Paris.

1970. *Langages* 17, *L'énonciation*, Paris.

Toloyan, Kachig, 1980. Review of Eric S. Rabkin's 'The fantastic in literature', in *Comparative Literature* 32 (Summer), 291–5.

Trilling, Lionel, 1965. *Beyond culture – essays on literature and learning*. New York.

Uspensky, Boris, 1970. *Poetika kompzicii*, Moscow; trans. 1974, V. Zavarin and S. Wittig, *The poetics of composition*, Berkeley.

Valesio, Paolo, 1978. 'The practice of literary semiotics: a theoretical proposal', *Centro Internazionale di Semiotica e di Linguistica, Working Papers*, no. 71, series D, (Feb.), Università de Urbino.

Van Dijk, Teun A., 1972. *Some aspects of text grammars*, The Hague.

1975a. 'Action, action description, narrative', *NLH* 6:2, 273–94.

1975b. (Van Dijk *et al.*). 'Recalling and summarising complex discourse', University of Amsterdam mimeograph.

1976. 'Narrative macrostructures – logical and cognitive foundations', *PTL* 1:3, 547–68.

Vidal, Gore, 1968. *Myra Breckinridge*, New York.

1975. *Myron*, New York.

Voloshinov, V. N., 1929. (probably by Bakhtin under Voloshinov's name) *Marxizm i filozofia jazyka*, Moscow; trans. 1973, L. L. Matejka and I. R. Tibunik, *Marxism and the philosophy of language*. New York and London.

Vonnegut, Kurt, Jr, 1959. *The Sirens of Titan*, New York.

1969. *Slaughterhouse Five*, New York.

Warhol, Andy, 1968. *a*, New York.

Warnke, Franck J., 1961. *European metaphysical poetry*, New Haven, Conn.

Watt, Ian, 1957. *The rise of the novel*, London.

Weinrich, Harald, 1964. *Tempus*, Stuttgart; trans. 1973, Michele Lacoste, *Le temps: le récit et le commentaire*, Paris.

Wellek, René (with Austin Warren), 1949. *Theory of literature*, New York.

West, Muriel, 1964. 'The death of Miles in *The Turn of the Screw*', reprinted in Willen (ed.), 1971, pp. 338–49.

Wildman, Eugene, 1970. *Montezuma Ball*, Swallow Press, Chicago.

Willen, Gerald (ed.), 1971. *A casebook on Henry James's 'The Turn of the Screw'*, New York.

Wimsatt, W. K., Jr, 1954. (with Monroe C. Beardsley). 'The intentional fallacy', 'The affective fallacy', in Wimsatt, *The Verbal Icon*, Louisville.

1968. 'Genesis: an argument resumed' in Wimsatt, *Day of the Leopards*, New Haven, Conn. 1976.

Wolff, Robert Lee, 1941. 'The genesis of *The Turn of the Screw*', reprinted in Kimbrough (ed.) 1966, pp. 125–32.

Woolf, Virginia, 1928. *Orlando*, London.

Zavarzadeh, Mas'ud, 1976. *The mythopoeic reality – the postwar American nonfiction novel*, Urbana.

Zumthor, Paul, 1971. 'Style and register in mediaeval poetry', in S. Chapman (ed.), *Literary style: a symposium*, pp. 263–77, New York.

1972. *Essai de poétique médiévale*, Paris.

Index

433